NATIONAL GOVERNMENTS
AND THE WORLD WAR

THE MACMILLAN COMPANY
NEW YORK · BOSTON · CHICAGO · DALLAS
ATLANTA · SAN FRANCISCO

MACMILLAN & CO., LIMITED
LONDON · BOMBAY · CALCUTTA
MELBOURNE

THE MACMILLAN CO. OF CANADA, LTD.
TORONTO

NATIONAL GOVERNMENTS

AND THE

WORLD WAR

BY

FREDERIC A. OGG
PROFESSOR OF POLITICAL SCIENCE IN THE
UNIVERSITY OF WISCONSIN

AND

CHARLES A. BEARD
DIRECTOR OF THE BUREAU OF MUNICIPAL RESEARCH
NEW YORK CITY

New York
THE MACMILLAN COMPANY
1919

All rights reserved

320.94
O34n

COPYRIGHT, 1919,
By THE MACMILLAN COMPANY.

Set up and electrotyped. Published January, 1919.

145504

Norwood Press
J. S. Cushing Co. — Berwick & Smith Co.
Norwood, Mass., U.S.A.

PREFACE

IF the World War has demonstrated one thing above another, it is the power of political institutions, ideals, and practices — national and international — to contribute to or detract from human welfare. The late conflict arrayed state against state, people against people; yet it was, at bottom, a struggle between two great schemes of human government, — autocracy and democracy. On the field of battle, democracy has triumphed. The victory can, however, be regarded as complete and final only in the measure in which democracy is prepared to bring intelligence and sanity to the new and great tasks which it has assumed. Even Americans and Englishmen need a fuller realization of the bearings of governmental organization and practice upon public well-being, a better knowledge of the political experience and problems of other peoples, and a new enthusiasm for national and international reconstruction on lines such as will conserve the dearly-bought gains of the recent conflict.

The present volume is offered as an aid to the diffusion of this sort of knowledge and spirit. It deals mainly with comparative government and undertakes to show what the heritage and genius of the principal peoples lately engaged in the World War have meant in the shaping of contemporary political institutions and ideas. It seeks also to describe the great changes wrought in governmental organization and procedure during the war, and to point out the major political problems that remain for settlement during the early years of peace.

The first of the authors named on the title page is responsible for Chapters IX–XXVI inclusive, and for Chapter XXVIII; the second, for Chapters I–VIII inclusive, and for Chapter XXVII.

F. A. O.
C. A. B.

DECEMBER 12, 1918.

CONTENTS

CHAPTER		PAGE
I.	INTRODUCTION: NATIONAL IDEALS AND GOVERNMENT	1

PART I. GOVERNMENT IN THE UNITED STATES

II.	BUILDING THE AMERICAN SYSTEM OF GOVERNMENT	15
III.	THE FEDERAL SYSTEM	41
IV.	THE CONGRESS: HOW LAWS ARE MADE	62
V.	THE PRESIDENT	86
VI.	THE NATIONAL ADMINISTRATION	110
VII.	OUR DEMOCRACY: PRIVILEGES AND DUTIES OF CITIZENSHIP	128
VIII.	GOVERNMENT IN WAR TIME	145

PART II. GOVERNMENTS OF THE ALLIED NATIONS

IX.	THE RISE OF FREE GOVERNMENT IN ENGLAND	165
X.	THE ENGLISH CONSTITUTION	181
XI.	THE MINISTRY AND THE CABINET	196
XII.	PARLIAMENT AND THE GROWTH OF DEMOCRACY	220
XIII.	PARLIAMENT AT WORK	247
XIV.	POLITICAL PARTIES: CONSTITUTIONAL ISSUES	272
XV.	POLITICAL PARTIES: ECONOMIC AND SOCIAL ISSUES	291
XVI.	GREATER BRITAIN: THE SELF-GOVERNING COLONIES	304
XVII.	THE FRENCH CONSTITUTION: PRESIDENT AND MINISTRY	325
XVIII.	PARLIAMENT AND PARTIES IN FRANCE	346
XIX.	JUSTICE AND LOCAL GOVERNMENT IN ENGLAND AND FRANCE	373
XX.	DEMOCRACY IN ITALY	405
XXI.	THE GOVERNMENT OF BELGIUM	421

CONTENTS

PART III. GOVERNMENT IN THE TEUTONIC STATES

CHAPTER		PAGE
XXII.	THE GERMAN EMPIRE AND ITS CONSTITUTION	435
XXIII.	THE IMPERIAL GERMAN GOVERNMENT	456
XXIV.	THE GOVERNMENT OF PRUSSIA	483
XXV.	CROSS CURRENTS IN GERMAN POLITICS	504
XXVI.	AUSTRIA-HUNGARY AND ITS GOVERNMENT	531

PART IV. THE WAR AND POLITICAL RECONSTRUCTION

XXVII.	AMERICAN WAR AIMS IN RELATION TO GOVERNMENT	556
XXVIII.	THE PROBLEM OF INTERNATIONAL GOVERNMENT	572

INDEX 593

NATIONAL GOVERNMENTS
AND THE WORLD WAR

NATIONAL GOVERNMENTS AND THE WORLD WAR

CHAPTER I

INTRODUCTION: NATIONAL IDEALS AND GOVERNMENT

The Democratic Ideal. — For more than two hundred years a great political ideal has been taking form and spreading throughout the earth: governments must derive their powers from the consent of the governed. This ideal inspired Cromwell, Hampden, Pym, and Milton in their struggle against the tyranny of the Stuarts and in its name Charles I was sent to the scaffold. A new and bolder interpretation of it animated Thomas Jefferson, Patrick Henry, James Otis, Samuel Adams, George Washington, Alexander Hamilton and their revolutionary followers in waging war against the dominion of George III and establishing on this continent a republic. In renouncing allegiance to the British king the founders of the American nation wrote their enduring article of faith in the Declaration of Independence:

"We hold these truths to be self-evident, that all men are created equal, that they are endowed by their Creator with certain unalienable Rights, that among these are Life, Liberty, and the pursuit of Happiness. That to secure these rights, Governments are instituted among Men, deriving their just powers from the consent of the governed, That whenever any Form of Government becomes destructive of these ends, it is the Right of the People to alter or abolish it, and to institute new Government, laying its foundation on such principles and organising its powers in such form, as to them shall seem most likely to effect their Safety and Happiness."

Long afterward, Thomas Jefferson, whose pen drafted the Declaration of Independence, set forth in a letter to a friend the grounds of the essential confidence in mankind which gave firm assurance to those who ventured upon the great American experiment. "We believed," he said, "that man was a rational animal, endowed by nature with rights and with an innate sense of justice; and that he could be restrained from wrong and protected in right by moderate powers confided to persons of his own choice and held to their duties by dependence on his own will. We believed that the complicated organization of kings, nobles, and priests was not the wisest nor best to effect the happiness of associated man; that wisdom and virtue were not hereditary; that the trappings of such a machinery consumed by their expense those earnings of industry they were meant to protect, and by the inequalities they produced exposed liberty to sufferance. We believed that men, enjoying in ease and security the full fruits of their own industry, enlisted by all their interests on the side of law and order, habituated to think for themselves, and to follow reason as their guide, would be more easily and safely governed than with minds nourished in error and vitiated and debased, as in Europe, by ignorance, indigence and oppression."

The Autocratic Ideal of Government. — The democratic principle has been compelled to battle every step of the long way from despotism to liberty against the ancient doctrine that government belongs by divine right to kings whom it is the duty of the people to obey in all things. Nowhere has this old doctrine been more clearly stated than in the language of the German Emperor, William II: " My grandfather, by his own right, set the Prussian crown upon his head, once more distinctly emphasizing the fact that it was accorded him by the will of God alone . . . and that he looked upon himself as the chosen instrument of heaven. . . . Looking upon myself as the instrument of the Lord, without regard to the opinions and intentions of the day, I go my way. . . . I welcome with all my heart those who wish to assist me in my work, no matter who they may be, but those who oppose me in this work I will crush. . . . The only pillar on which the realm rested was the army. So it is to-day. . . . The Spirit of the Lord has descended upon me because I am the Emperor of the Germans. I am the instrument of the Almighty. I am his sword, his agent. Woe and death to all those who shall oppose my will! Woe and death to those who do not believe in my mission! Woe and death to

NATIONAL IDEALS AND GOVERNMENT 3

the cowards! God demands their destruction, God who, by my mouth, bids you (the Army) to do His will."

This is the theory of despotism with which the principles of the Declaration of Independence will no more mix than oil and water. Despots may be benevolent; they may be willing to do many things for the people; but government of the people and by the people is hateful in their sight, because it undermines their power and belies their slander upon mankind that it is incapable of self-government. As a modern author, Mr. Ramsay Muir, in writing of William II's ancestors, the old Kings of Prussia, puts it: "The Benevolent Despots labored, indeed, untiringly to improve their dominions; they fostered agriculture and industry, they created academies of science, they revised and codified the laws, they carried out great public works. But they were laboring — or at any rate Frederick was laboring — not so much for the welfare of his own subjects as for the creation of a powerful State. He was the architect of the future Great State, his subjects only the bricks and mortar. It was necessary that they should be numerous, so as to fill the ranks of a conquering army, and prosperous, so as to support its burden; it was important that the Great State should be fully equipped with all the resources of modern knowledge, both for practical purposes and for prestige. But the State did not exist for the sake of the people; the people existed for the sake of the State. They must not presume to form opinions and preferences of their own; it was theirs to be used by the King-Architect for such purposes and according to such plans as he might desire. Let them be educated; they will be more useful so; but let their education impress upon them the duty of obedience and the privilege of being a Great King's implements in the building of a Great State. For the State is omnipotent; the people only the clay out of which it is formed. Such was the real conception of Enlightened Despotism and its aims at the moment when it reached its highest development, on the eve of the French Revolution. It was nowhere more clearly grasped or more efficiently put into operation than by Frederick of Prussia (1740-1786)."

Practical Application of the Ideal of Self-Government — in England. — In this brief introductory chapter no complete record of the progress of government by the consent of the governed can be entered, but a word must be said of its significance in the history of England, the United States, and France. In the first of these countries, the development of government by the people has taken place slowly as liberty has broadened down from precedent to precedent, and at no time has the abstract principle underlying it been stated so fully as in the Declaration of Independence. Nevertheless, the Bill of Rights enacted by the English Parliament in 1689 laid the democratic basis of government for all time:

" 1. That the pretended power of suspending of laws, or the execution of laws, by regal authority, without consent of Parliament, is illegal.

" 2. That the pretended power of dispensing with laws, or the execution of laws by regal authority, as it hath been assumed and exercised of late, is illegal. . . .

" 4. That levying money for or to the use of the Crown, by pretence of prerogative, without grant of Parliament, for longer time or in other manner than the same is or shall be granted, is illegal.

" 5. That it is the right of the subjects to petition the king, and all commitments and prosecutions for such petitioning are illegal.

" 6. That the raising or keeping a standing army within the kingdom in time of peace, unless it be with consent of Parliament, is against law. . . .

" 8. That election of members of Parliament ought to be free.

" 9. That the freedom of speech and debates or proceedings in Parliament, ought not to be impeached or questioned in any court or place out of Parliament.

" 10. That excessive bail ought not to be required, nor excessive fines imposed; nor cruel and unusual punishments inflicted.

" 11. That jurors ought to be duly impaneled and returned, and jurors which pass upon men in trials for high treason ought to be freeholders. . . .

" 13. And that for the redress of all grievances and for the amending, strengthening and preserving of the laws, Parliament ought to be held frequently."

The nineteenth century saw in England steady progress in the democratic principles enunciated in the Bill of Rights in 1689. The Reform Bill of 1832 distributed representatives in the House of Commons more equitably throughout the nation, and forty-three new boroughs were created with one or two members each, according to their respective populations; the counties were divided into election districts and assigned a representation more in harmony with the number of their inhabitants; the suffrage was given in the towns to all citizens who owned or rented houses worth ten pounds (about fifty dollars) a year and to renters as well as owners of land of a certain value in the country.

Scarcely had this Reform Bill been signed when more radical measures were demanded. Doctrines of democracy were spread among the people, and in 1867 a law was passed extending the suffrage to every adult male in the larger towns who occupied for twelve months, either as owner or tenant, a dwelling within the borough and paid the local poor tax; also to lodgers who paid ten pounds or more a year for furnished rooms. In the country it permitted those to vote who owned property which produced an income of at least five pounds net a year and all renters paying at least twelve pounds annually. Thus the number of voters was doubled.

About twenty years later, namely, in 1884, the suffrage was again widened, some two million men, mostly agricultural workers, being admitted to the franchise. This measure of reform, great as it was, did not complete the establishment of manhood suffrage, and from time to time the subject of "still more democracy" was vigorously agitated. In order to make more effective the power of the democratic branch of the government, the House of Commons, the House of Lords in 1911 was deprived of its hereditary power of absolute veto on measures passed by the lower chamber. At last in February, 1918, in the midst of the World War, Great Britain enfranchised all the men who were voteless under the old laws and enlarged political freedom by bestowing the suffrage upon about six million women.

Practical Application of the Ideal of Self-Government — in France. — In the course of democratic progress one nation has influenced another, the pendulum swinging back and forth. The Revolution of 1688 in England, which gave to the world the declaration of principles cited above, had a profound influence in France, where at the time the government was in the hands of an absolute monarch — Louis XIV. Before the middle of the eighteenth century there had sprung up in France a group of powerful writers who advocated self-government for the French people. Perhaps the most influential of these was Jean Jacques Rousseau, whose book on " The Social Contract " startled the world with the slogan that man was born free but is everywhere in chains and that for the sovereignty of kings should be established the sovereignty of the people. Thirteen years after the American Declaration of Independence a French national assembly overthrew the absolute monarchy, founded a popular government, and issued the famous Declaration of the Rights of Man embodying the following principles: " Men are born and remain equal in rights. Social distinctions can only be founded upon the general good. Law is the expression of the general will. Every citizen has a right to participate, personally or through his representative, in its formation. It must be the same for all. No person shall be accused, arrested or imprisoned except in the cases and according to the forms prescribed by law. No one shall be disquieted on account of his opinions, including his religious views, provided that their manifestation does not disturb the public order established by law. The free communication of ideas and opinions is one of the most precious of the rights of man. Every citizen may, accordingly, speak, write and print with freedom, being responsible, however, for such abuses of this freedom as shall be defined by law. . . . All citizens have a right to decide, either personally or by their representatives, as to the necessity of the contribution to the public treasury, to grant this freely, to know to what uses it is put, and to fix the proportion, the mode of assessment and collection, and the duration of the taxes. Society has the right to inquire of every public agent an account of his administration."

The Assembly which drew up the French statement claimed, in its address to the people, that " the rights of man had been misconceived and insulted for centuries " and that it was their intention to " reëstablish them for all humanity in this declaration which shall serve as an everlasting war-cry against oppressors."

Shortly after the enunciation of the Declaration of the Rights of Man, France followed the example of the United States and established a republic, proclaiming ideals of liberty, equality, and fraternity to all the nations of the earth. Unhappily the new republic was short-lived, for in the wars that followed it was overthrown by Napoleon I, who in turn was supplanted by a king, Louis XVIII, in 1815. Thirty-three years later, the French again set up a republic and published the Declaration of the Rights of Man once more. At that time, 1848, French principles were accepted by the liberal parties which had come into existence in every state of Europe and were actively engaged in promoting the cause of popular government, a free press, equality of all before the law, and the abolition of the vestiges of the feudal system. Moreover the national spirit which had awakened during the Napoleonic era was at work and served more than anything else to excite opposition to autocracy. The Industrial Revolution was also beginning to quicken the thought and arouse the aspirations of the great mass of the population. Those who lived by the labor of their hands and were employed in the new industries which were rapidly developing, now had their spokesmen, especially in France and in England, and claimed the right to vote and to mold laws to meet their particular interests. So in 1848 the rights of nations and of the laborer were added to the rights of man, which had been the main issue in the first French Revolution.

The second Republic, like the first, was short-lived, for it was swept away by the Louis Napoleon whom France had put at the head of her Republic as a professed democrat. He, too, like his more famous uncle, the first Napoleon, had his day. In the Franco-Prussian war of 1870 the Emperor was overthrown. France was defeated at the hands of Germany, and emerged finally from the struggle a republic for the third time. After four years of discussion, France framed in 1875 a new plan of government which students of politics regard as one of the most democratic in existence. The French parliament is more powerful than the Congress of the United States. It not only elects the president, who is under the control of a ministry representing the majority in the chambers, but it may by meeting in joint session amend the constitution without the necessity of submitting the changes to the people for their ratification. There is no supreme court in France to declare the measures of parliament unconstitutional, and the president cannot veto them. Like the members of the English cabinet, the French ministers resign when they find their policy is no longer supported by a majority in the Chamber of Deputies.

Practical Application of the Ideal of Self-Government — in the United States. — Almost immediately after the American Revolution attacks were made upon all the old practices of government that seemed contrary to the lofty doctrines of the Declaration of Independence. The first state constitutions had imposed property and religious qualifications on the right to vote and hold office. In a few years there appeared advocates of a wider democracy: the opening of all offices to all freemen and the vesting of the right to vote in all freemen. These new advocates based their pleas on the simple principle of the Declaration of Independence: governments derive their just powers from the consent of the governed. In time the ideal conquered, and during the first half of the nineteenth century property and religious qualifications on the right to vote were abolished. About the same time the idea took root that human slavery was incompatible with the principle of self-government and human worth upon which the founders of the republic had based their revolt against George III. Jefferson and Washington were of that opinion; and when Lincoln stood upon the battle-field of Gettysburg to justify in the eyes of the world the great war for the preservation of the Union he turned once more to the nation's old article of faith, saying:

" Fourscore and seven years ago our fathers brought forth upon this continent a new nation conceived in liberty and dedicated to the proposition that all men are created equal.

" Now we are engaged in a great civil war testing whether that nation, or any nation so conceived and so dedicated, can long endure. We are met on a great battle-field of that war. We have come to dedicate a portion of that field as a final resting-place of those who here gave their lives that that nation might live. It is altogether fitting and proper that we should do this.

" But in a larger sense we cannot dedicate — we cannot consecrate — we cannot hallow this ground. The brave men, living and dead, who struggled here, have consecrated it, far above our poor power to add or detract. The world will little note nor long remember what we say here, but it can never forget what they did here. It is for us the living, rather, to be dedicated here to the unfinished work which they who fought here have thus far so nobly advanced. It is rather for us to be here dedicated to the great task remaining before us — that from these honored dead we take increased devotion to that cause for which they gave the last full measure of devotion — that we here highly resolve that these dead shall not have died in vain — that this nation, under God, shall have a new birth of freedom — and that government of the people, by the people, for the people, shall not perish from the earth."

It was in the spirit of the Declaration of Independence that the people of the United States wrote into their constitution the thirteenth amendment abolishing slavery, and the fifteenth amendment forbidding any state to disfranchise citizens on account of race, color, or previous condition of servitude. At the same time a new agitation was under way applying the old principle to the women of the nation; and at the opening of the twentieth century state after state, including such great commonwealths as California and New York, admitted women to the franchise on the same terms as men. National leaders, like President Wilson, Mr. Roosevelt, and Mr. Hughes, declared their approval of the new application of the old doctrine, and on September 30, 1918, President Wilson went before the Senate to urge as a war measure and a measure of justice the passage of a national amendment enfranchising women throughout the United States. On that occasion he recurred once more to the ideal of government by the people:

" This is a people's war, and the people's thinking constitutes its atmosphere and morals, not the predilections of the drawing-room or the political considerations of the caucus. If we be democrats indeed and wish to lead the world to democracy, we can ask other peoples to accept in proof of our sincerity and our ability to lead them whither they wish to be led nothing less persuasive and convincing than our actions. Our professions will not suffice. Verification must be forthcoming when verification is asked for. And in this case verification is asked for — asked for in this particular matter. You ask by whom? Not through diplomatic channels, not by foreign ministers, not by the intimations of parliaments. It is asked for by the anxious, expectant, suffering peoples with whom we are dealing, and who are willing to put their destinies in some measure in our hands, if they are sure we wish the same things that they do. . . .

"Through many, many channels I have been made aware what the plain, struggling work-a-day folk are thinking, upon whom the chief terror and suffering of this tragic war falls. They are looking to the great, powerful, famous democracy of the West to lead them to the new day for which they have so long waited; and they think, in their logical simplicity, that democracy means that women shall play their part in affairs, alongside men and upon an equal footing with them. If we reject measures like these in ignorant defiance of what a new age has brought forth, of what they have seen but we have not, they will cease to believe in us, they will cease to follow us or to trust us.

"They have seen their own governments accept this interpretation of democracy — seen old governments like that of Great Britain . . . promise readily and as of course, this justice to women, though they had before refused it, the strange revelations of this war having made things new and plain to governments as well as to peoples."

Realizing that government by the consent and in accordance with the purposes of the governed depends for its permanence and success upon the wisdom of the citizens, the people of the United States, as well as those of France and England, have spent huge sums of money on popular education, universal, free, and non-sectarian. In 1916 over three-fourths of the American children of school age were enrolled in the common schools and three-fourths of those enrolled were in attendance; there were over eleven thousand public high schools, with more than a million students; and in the West and South free colleges and universities opened the gateways of the highest learning to the people. Every decade has seen some new and important extension of the principle of universal education. Even amid the very crisis of the Great War England reorganized her system of popular schools, adding heavy drafts upon her already burdened treasury. The people are not only to govern themselves; they are to live worthily, and mold the forms and functions of government to noble public ends.

The Forms of Government by the People. — Although national history and national tradition may produce even in democratic countries wide divergencies in the outward trapping of government, nevertheless certain fundamental convictions are common to all those nations based upon the consent of the governed principle. They are as follows:

All political power must be derived from the people.

All public functionaries who make laws or execute them must be chosen directly or indirectly by the people.

To the people must belong the right to alter the forms of government and to determine the nature and kinds of work undertaken by it.

Each nation can choose freely its ways of living subject to the equal rights of other nations.

From these principles it follows that the military power — the army and the navy — is subject to the civil power. An eminent German professor has touched the vital spot when he says: " The question by which to decide the essential character of a state is the question, Whom does the army obey? " Throughout the Central Empires, — Germany, Austria-Hungary, Turkey, — the army has belonged to the Emperor or Sultan as the case may be. In the democracies that have opposed the Central Empires the army obeys the representatives chosen by the people. This is an ancient principle in England. Early in the reign of William and Mary a mutiny occurred in the English army. Parliament did not want to give the new king unlimited control over the troops in putting down this mutiny, lest he might put himself at the head of a standing army and renew a danger that had shown itself under the Stuarts. So Parliament gave the king control over the army for the following six months only. Later, Parliament got in the habit of extending the king's control over the army for a year at a time; each year it must still be renewed by passing a new law called the Army Bill.

In the United States, Congress has the right to declare war, to raise and support armies, but no appropriation of money to that use is permitted for a longer term than two years, in order that there may be expressions of popular will in the matter. Congress has power to provide and maintain a navy; to make rules for the government and regulation of the land and naval forces; to provide for calling forth the militia to execute the laws of the Union, suppress insurrection and repel invasion; to provide for organizing, arming, and disciplining the militia, and for governing such part of them as may be employed in the service of the United States. The President of the United States, it is true, is Commander-in-chief of the Army and Navy, but he is elected as a representative of the voters and his tenure is four years.

The Application of the Autocratic Principle — in Germany. — Many examples of absolute and tyrannical government can be selected from the long course of oppression in the earth, but it is not necessary to look beyond the German Empire as it existed when the United States declared war against it. That empire was a federation of twenty-two kingdoms, duchies, and principalities, and three " free cities." The King of Prussia was the German Emperor in virtue of his right as king. There was an imperial parliament consisting of the imperial council composed of agents of the several kings, princes, and dukes and the three free cities, and also a lower house or *Reichstag* composed of representatives elected by universal manhood suffrage. There was a high minister, the chancellor, chosen by the Emperor and responsible to him alone, not to the representatives of the voters as in England and France. Laws could not be made without the consent of the Reichstag, but that was about as far as its power extended. War was made by the Emperor, who possessed absolute command of the army and navy. It is true that an " offensive " war required the approval of the imperial council, but that was a matter of form. The popular branch of the government had no control over the declaration of war under any circumstances. It has been correctly called a " talking machine." The Emperor appointed officers and ministers without consulting it, and found it ready to yield when he called upon it for grants of money.

Prussia Practically an Absolute Monarchy. — It must be remembered also that the German Emperor possessed great powers as King of Prussia, which contained more than one-half the population and territory of the Empire and sent seventeen of the sixty-one members of the imperial council. It had a " constitution " which was " graciously " granted by the King to the people in 1850. Under this constitution the government of Prussia was in the hands of the King and a few great landlords ("Junkers") and rich men. There was, it is true, a "popular branch" composed of deputies elected by the voters, but the election system was so arranged that two-thirds of the "popular" representatives were chosen by a small group of wealthy men, while the great mass of the voters could select only one-third of the members. In Prussia the King ruled by divine right. There he was "King, by the Grace of God." The people were his "subjects" in name and in fact. The inhabitants of Prussia had protested against this system for many years before the war, but without effect. The Kaiser and the Prussian ruling class were determined to keep their power and to beat down the democratic aspirations of their subjects.

The Iron Rule of the Hohenzollerns in Prussia. — The history of Prussia and this system of government is mainly the history of one ruling family, the House of Hohenzollern, which began more than three hundred years ago to build the little district of Brandenburg into a great kingdom. By devoting enormous sums to the army and treating the people as mere taxpayers and "food for cannon," the Hohenzollerns succeeded in establishing a strong military power. They seized the territory of their neighbors without qualms and without apologies. They made war first upon one country and then upon another, always in the hope of gaining more territory.

By this method they and their barons were able to form the German Empire and bring the whole country under their dominion. While other nations were throwing aside kings or reducing their power to a shadow, the Hohenzollerns waxed stronger and stronger, commanding the army with an iron hand, teaching in the schools obedience to kings, and putting down popular uprisings with sternness and cruelty. In theory and in fact Germany was ruled by the German Emperor, King of Prussia, and a handful of generals and barons. The voice of the people was nothing but a voice crying in the night.

The Issue Joined. — It was against a government conceived in military despotism and dedicated to the proposition that kings can do no wrong, that President Wilson asked his country to take up arms. To say that the outcome of the war in Europe was of no concern to the United States was to ignore forty years of German history. Thousands of peaceful citizens, though looking with horror upon the thought of war, were slowly and reluctantly driven by events to the conclusion that a German victory in Europe would imperil democracy in the United States in the coming years. They realized that, with Great Britain beaten and her colonies annexed by Germany, America would not be spared by a power founded on the sword.

They remembered the hundred years of peace which we had maintained with the British Empire; they recalled the three thousand miles of border between this country and Canada, without a fort or battleship or patrol; and they could not bring themselves to believe that with the Hohenzollerns intrenched anywhere in the New World the United States could go on her way undisturbed by German intrigues, spies, and military ambitions. To them the triumph of the German war machine, dominating all Europe, would make vain and foolish two centuries of struggle for popular government, for popular control over the power of kings and aristocracies, for the extension of the suffrage and the advancement of democracy. Accordingly they took up arms to aid in overthrowing militarism and imperialism and in preventing their return to plague the earth's weary multitudes.

SELECTED REFERENCES

D. S. Muzzey, *Thomas Jefferson* (New York, 1918); E. Barker, *Political Thought in England from Herbert Spencer to the Present Day* (New York, 1916); *Out of Their Own Mouths: Utterances of German Rulers* (New York, 1917); J. C. Bracq, *France under the Republic;* Clark, Hamilton, and Moulton, *Readings in the Economics of War* (Chicago, 1918), especially Chaps. i–xv; Treitschke, *Politics* (New York, 1916); H. Croly, *The Promise of American Life* (New York, 1909); Robinson and Beard, *Outlines of European History*, Vol. II, Chaps. vii–ix, xv, and xx, on The French Revolution and Modern France.

PART I. GOVERNMENT IN THE UNITED STATES

CHAPTER II

BUILDING THE AMERICAN SYSTEM OF GOVERNMENT

Colonial Origins. — The foundations of American government were laid during the long colonial period while the English colonists were learning the practical art of managing their own political affairs. The Revolution did not make a breach in the continuity of their institutional life. It was not a social cataclysm, the overthrow of a dominant class, the establishment of a new estate in power. It was rather an expansion of the energy of the American enterprise that burst asunder the bonds which the competing interests in England sought to impose. American shipwrights could build vessels as fleet and strong as any that sailed the seas, and they were determined to conquer by main strength a free place in the world's market. American merchants were as ingenious as those who made England the nation of shopkeepers, and they could ill brook the restraints which condemned them to buy important staples in the marts of Great Britain. America was rich in timber, raw materials, and mineral resources, and American manufacturers chafed under laws compelling consumers to look beyond the seas for commodities which might well have been made in New England or Pennsylvania. It was discontent with economic restrictions, not with their fundamental political institutions, which nerved the Revolutionists to the great task of driving out King George's governors, councilors, judges, revenue officers, and soldiers.

There had long been executive, legislative, and judicial offices in all of the colonies, and the American Revolutionists merely took possession of them. Unlike the French Revolutionists, they did not have to exercise their political ingenuity in creating any fundamentally new institutions. The Revolutionists of Rhode Island and Connecticut, where the governors, councilors, and judges were not appointed by the crown, found their ancient systems of government, based on seventeenth-century charters, so well suited to their needs and ideals that they made no alterations beyond casting off their allegiance to the king of Great Britain. The distribution of representation, the suffrage, the qualifications for office-holders, and the legislative, executive, and judicial institutions of old English origin were continued after the Revolution without many radical alterations.

Even the federal Constitution, in spite of Mr. Gladstone's high praise that it was the most wonderful work struck off at a given time by the brain and purpose of man, was based as far as possible on the experience of the colonies and the states. The very names applied to the Senate, House of Representatives, and President were taken from the institutions of some of the states, while many clauses of the Constitution, such as those providing for the process of impeachment, the presidential message and veto, the origin of money bills in the lower house, and the freedom of each house to determine its procedure under certain limitations, were taken almost verbatim from state constitutions. The powers which the Convention of 1787 vested in Congress were scarcely experimental, for six years' practical experience with the shortcomings of the Articles of Confederation had taught statesmen the inexorable necessity of giving the national government those very powers, and limiting the states in the exercise of the authority which they had previously enjoyed. Nor must it be forgotten that the right later assumed by the Supreme Court to pass upon the constitutionality of laws and declare them void had already been exercised by many state courts.

The dictum of Stubbs that the roots of the present lie deep in the past has now become commonplace; but it is true of American institutions in a very peculiar sense, for they are founded on written documents which, in spirit and form, bear the impress of the political and economic conditions prevailing at the time of their creation. Many state constitutions still reveal distinct traces of Revolutionary days, and the written letter of the federal Constitution, notwithstanding the seventeen amendments and the revolution wrought by the Civil War, remains unchanged so far as the machinery of government and the powers of its three departments are concerned. It is, therefore, from American history alone that one can learn, for instance, why there are two Senators from each state, why the system of checks and balances, so characteristic of American institutions, was adopted, why the President is chosen through an elaborate electoral system, why interstate commerce powers are vested in the federal government, or why certain political practices have sprung up in the attempts to operate our governments, national and state.

The Colonial Governor. — On the eve of the Revolution there were thirteen colonies in America — each with its separate institutions and its peculiar traditions, many of which, it is instructive to remember, were then older than are our national traditions to-day. In form of government, however, especially in its higher ranges, the colonies presented striking similarities. Each had a governor, an assembly, and a judicial system, and the Common Law of England, as far as it was applicable and had not been changed by legislation, was binding everywhere.

In eight of the colonies, — Georgia, North Carolina, South Carolina, Virginia, New Jersey, New York, New Hampshire, and Massachusetts, — the governor was appointed by the king and recognized as the king's personal deputy. He occupied a twofold position. On the one hand, he was the representative of British interests in the colony — the agent through whom the will of the British government was made known to the inhabitants, and the guardian who kept the crown informed on the state of the province. On the other hand, he was the highest executive official in the colony, charged with the conservation of the peace and advancement of the welfare of the colonists.

As the chief executive, he supervised the enforcement of the laws and appointed, usually in connection with the advice of his council, the important civil officers. He could remove councilors and officials for cause, and direct them in administration. By virtue of his position as chancellor, he was head of the highest court in the colony, which entertained appeals from lower tribunals and exercised important original jurisdiction in many matters. Moreover, he granted pardons and reprieves. He was commander-in-chief of the colonial forces, appointed the military officers of high rank, levied troops for defense, and enforced martial law in time of invasion, war, or rebellion. As the king's ecclesiastical representative, he collated to churches and benefices.

In connection with the colonial legislature, the royal governor also enjoyed extensive powers. In all of the eight colonies mentioned above, except Massachusetts, he nominated the council which composed the upper house of the legislature. He summoned, adjourned, and dissolved the assembly; he laid before it projects of law desired by the home government; and he vetoed laws which he thought objectionable. In short, the royal governor enjoyed such high prerogatives in colonial times that the first state constitution-makers, having learned by experience to fear executive authority, usually provided for the supremacy of the legislature and gave their governors very little power.

The royal governor, however, was by no means an unlimited sovereign in his province, for he was bound by his instructions and by the restraints which the assembly imposed through its power of controlling the grants of money. Indeed, in the innumerable disputes which fill colonial history, the assembly often triumphed over an obstinate governor because it was able to keep a firm grip on the purse strings. Toward the eve of the Revolution, his appointing power was curtailed by the claims of the council to a share in the distribution of patronage.

Unlike the other colonies which had governors appointed by the king, Massachusetts had a charter that set forth, among other things, the general organization and powers of the legislature. The governor could adjourn, prorogue, and dissolve the assembly, but he could not appoint the council, or upper house, and he could choose the civil officers only with its consent. However, he enjoyed considerable military authority; he organized the militia, appointed the chief officers, commanded the armed forces, and declared martial law in case of rebellion or invasion. Naturally this division of authority invited conflicts, and it so happened that Massachusetts led the way in throwing off all royal authority.

In Rhode Island and Connecticut the governor occupied a peculiar position. In the first place, he was elected annually by a general assembly composed of the governor, assistants, and representatives chosen by the voters in each " city, town, or place." In the second place, the governor did not stand out as a distinct official; he was little more than a figurehead, his functions being discharged only in coöperation with his assistants, or councilors.

The executive authority in the proprietary colonies of Maryland and Pennsylvania and Delaware stood on a different basis from that in the royal provinces or in Connecticut and Rhode Island. Each of them, as Professor Osgood says, was "a miniature kingdom of a semi-feudal type and the proprietor was a petty king"—a vast estate carved out of the royal domain and granted by the crown to a proprietor who, in theory at least, combined the rights of government with those of landlord, from which he derived large revenues. Nevertheless, under their power to control money grants, the popular branches of the legislature in Pennsylvania and Maryland succeeded, toward the Revolution, in securing a tolerably effective control over the governor in the exercise of his large powers.

Colonial Legislatures. — In all of the colonies, except Pennsylvania, there were two branches of the legislature, and only in Massachusetts, Connecticut, and Rhode Island, was the upper house — to use the term in a general sense — elective. In these three New England colonies, the councilors, or assistants, as they were called, were chosen by the general assemblies, and thus did not occupy the same position of independence over against the representative branch, as did the councilors of the royal colonies. In the provincial colonies, the upper house, or council, was chosen by the king acting through the royal governor, who usually determined the selection himself. In the proprietary colonies, the proprietor or his representative selected the councilors.

In addition to the usual legislative powers, that is, the right to discuss and vote on laws, the council had executive and judicial functions. It advised the governor; in conjunction with him it formed a judicial tribunal; it frequently controlled him in making appointments; and it discharged many of the official duties now vested in higher state officers, such as the secretary and treasurer. In the royal provinces the council became an aristocratic body, sympathizing generally with the governor and king in the contests with the representative branch of the government.

In every colony there was an assembly of representatives chosen by popular vote, subject to many restrictions on the right of suffrage. In New York, for example, voters for members of the assembly — the lower branch of the legislature — were required to be freeholders of lands or tenements to the value of forty pounds free from all encumbrances, except that in New York City and Albany the suffrage was open to all freemen — that is, all men who had been regularly admitted to civic rights. In Virginia the voter had to be a freeholder of an estate of at least fifty acres of land, if there was no house on it; or twenty-five acres with a house twelve feet square; or, if a dweller in a city or town, he had to own a lot or part of a lot with a house twelve feet square. In Massachusetts the voter for member of the legislature, under the charter of 1691, had to be a freeholder of an estate worth at least forty shillings a year, or the owner of other property to the value of forty pounds sterling. In Pennsylvania the vote was restricted to freeholders of fifty acres or more of land " well seated " and twelve acres cleared, and to other persons worth at least fifty pounds in lawful money.

Most of the colonies also followed the example of the mother country in imposing special qualifications on members elected to the legislature. In South Carolina, for example, a member had to own five hundred acres of land and ten slaves or be worth one thousand pounds sterling in land, houses, or other property. New Jersey members had to have one thousand acres freehold, while in Georgia delegates were required to own at least five hundred acres of land. In addition to property qualifications, religious tests were usually imposed on assemblymen.

Following the ancient practice of England, representatives were distributed, in colonial times, among distinct territorial districts rather than among equal groups of people. In New England the town was the unit of representation, and only a slight attempt was made to adjust the representation to the population. In the middle colonies, the county was the unit of representation, and, according to ancient English precedent, each county elected its representatives under the supervision of the sheriff as returning officer. In South Carolina representatives were apportioned among parishes, but they varied so greatly in population that the representation was unequal. In general, it may be said, therefore, that the principle of equal representation was not accepted, but that practical considerations led to a very rough attempt to give special recognition to the more populous areas.

The colonial assemblies constantly maintained that they possessed entire and exclusive authority to regulate their domestic concerns. Especially in the matter of taxation did they stoutly assert their exclusive rights, not only in formal declarations, but also in actual resistance to the royal and proprietary governors. No attempts, however, were made to define and lay down colonial legislative powers in any complete written instruments. Such a procedure was almost unknown to the political practice of England; and no concrete need for it had arisen in the colonies. In the charters, the legislative power conferred was general, not specific. For example, the Massachusetts charter of 1691 provided that the assembly should have "full power and authority from time to time to make, ordain, and establish all manner of wholesome and reasonable orders, laws, statutes, and ordinances, directions, and instructions either with penalties or without (so that the same be not repugnant or contrary to the laws of this our realm of England) as they shall judge to be for the good and welfare of our said province or territory." In addition to this general legislative power, the assemblies usually enjoyed a marked control over the executive department through their power to withhold the salaries of the officials.

Notwithstanding the large legislative rights asserted and enjoyed by the colonial assemblies, there were certain legal limitations on their authority. In the provincial and proprietary colonies, the governor exercised the right to veto laws, and in all colonies except Maryland, Rhode Island, and Connecticut laws had to be sent to England for royal approval. Furthermore a special act of Parliament provided that all laws, by-laws, usages, and customs in the colonies repugnant to laws made in England relative to colonial affairs should be null and void. Later, Parliament distinctly asserted that the colonies and plantations in America were subordinate to and dependent on the crown and Parliament of Great Britain, which enjoyed the power and authority to make laws binding the colonies and people of America in all cases whatsoever. A South Carolina court once went so far as to declare an act of the colonial legislature of 1712, taking away the freehold of one man and vesting it in another, null and void on the ground that it was against common right and Magna Charta. At all events the colonists had long been acquainted with both theoretical and practical limitations on their assemblies, so that, after gaining independence, they acquiesced, though not without contest, in the courts' assumption of power to declare laws null and void on constitutional grounds.

Municipal and Local Institutions. — Although there were in the colonies no cities of importance, measured by modern standards, the foundations of American municipal government must be sought in colonial times. It appears that there were about twenty municipal corporations during that period, each of which received its charter from the colonial governor — New York and Albany in 1686, Philadelphia in 1691, and Trenton, New Jersey, the last, in 1746. The form of organization in general followed old English examples; the governing body was a common council composed of the mayor, recorder, aldermen, and councilors. The striking feature of the colonial municipal system was the fusion of executive, legislative, and judicial functions in the hands of the same body; and it is interesting to note that the commission form of municipal government now being widely adopted throughout the United States is the return to the original principle in so far as it vests administrative and legislative powers in one authority.

In the sphere of rural local government we have departed even less from colonial models than in other branches of administration. The Revolution did not disturb, in any fundamental manner, the institutions of local government which had come down from early colonial times; for, as Professor Fairlie says, " the main features of the old systems continued in the different states. Towns in New England and the middle states and parishes in the southern states remained unaltered; and are in fact not mentioned in most of the constitutions of the revolutionary period." In New England the unit of local administration was the town, which was governed by a meeting of the electors, who chose the town officers, levied taxes, appropriated money, passed by-laws, and reviewed the activities of the various local officers. Counties existed, of course, in New England, but only in a rudimentary form, and principally for judicial purposes. In the middle colonies, notably New York and Pennsylvania, there was a combination of town and county local government. Town meetings were held in New York as in New England. As early as 1691, however, a county board of supervisors, representing the various towns, was created and began to absorb at once the most important local administrative functions. In Pennsylvania, strong county administrative organization overshadowed the town and furnished the model for local government in a large number of western states. In the South, the plantation system led to the formation of scattered settlements, so that local government had to be based upon the county rather than the parish. Thus, for example, in Virginia, " the county became the unit of representation in the colonial assembly and the unit of military, judicial, highway, and fiscal administration. The officers were the county lieutenant, the sheriff (who acted as collector and treasurer), justices of the peace, and coroners. All were appointed by the governor of the colony."

Early Attempts to Unite the Thirteen Colonies. — Although it was the Revolution that welded the thirteen colonies into the union which finally proved permanent, there had been three noteworthy attempts at federation previous to the War of Independence. The first was the New England Confederation formed among Massachusetts Bay, Plymouth, Connecticut, and New Haven in 1643. The united colonies of New England were bound together in a " firm and perpetual league of friendship and amity for offense and defense, mutual advice and succor, upon all just occasions, both for preserving and propagating the truth and liberties of the Gospel and for their own mutual safety and welfare." For some twenty years the Confederation was active, and it continued to hold meetings until 1685, but it left little permanent impress.

The second attempt at union was at Albany in 1754, when on suggestion of the Lords of Trade in England an intercolonial conference was held for the purpose (among other things) of entering into " articles of Union and confederation with each other for mutual defense of his majesty's subjects and interests in North America in time of peace as well as war." Massachusetts, Connecticut, Rhode Island, Pennsylvania, New York,

New Hampshire, and Maryland were represented, and a committee, with Franklin in the lead, reported plans for union. The colonists, however, did not adopt the scheme because they feared that it would give the crown too much power. The crown regarded the plan as too democratic, and so the project fell through.

The introduction of the Stamp Tax bill into Parliament led several of the colonies to protest to the home government; and when the bill was passed in spite of their objections, the Massachusetts legislature recommended a colonial congress and appointed representatives. After no little dispute among the members of other colonial assemblies, the proposed congress, composed of the representatives of nine colonies — all except Virginia, New Hampshire, Georgia, and North Carolina, — convened in New York in 1765. Permanent union, however, was not their purpose. They merely formulated an address to the King, a memorial to the Lords, and a petition to the Commons; and the repeal of the Stamp Act put a stop to the union movement for the time. It required the patriotism aroused by the long war for independence to fuse the colonies into a nation.

Union Forced by the War for Independence. — The American Revolution has two aspects. On the one hand, it was a contest between the government of Great Britain and those colonists who determined, in the beginning of the controversy, to resist the policy of the mother country, and finally to throw off her rule altogether. To bring this contest to a successful issue, the Revolutionists formed committees, assemblies, and national congresses; they raised troops, levied taxes, borrowed money, negotiated with foreign powers, and waged war in the field. On the other hand, when independence was declared, the Revolutionists had to provide some form of united government for the realization of their common purposes, and at the same time to establish permanent state governments. Thus coöperation among the Revolutionists of all the colonies and internal reconstruction within each colony proceeded simultaneously, and the result at the close of the war was a collection of " free, sovereign, and independent states " — each with a constitution of its own — leagued in a " perpetual union " under the Articles of Confederation.

The Revolution was the work of definite groups of men coöperating for specific purposes. In the preliminary stages of resistance to Great Britain, the colonists relied mainly on their regular assemblies as organs for the expression of revolutionary opinion, but as the contest became more heated and acts were performed for which there was no legal sanction, the Revolutionists began to form independent committees to represent them. This was necessary for the purposes of agitation, and later for organized rebellion, especially in those colonies with royal governors.

The germs of these revolutionary organizations which soon widened into state and national governments are to be found in the committees of correspondence — small groups of persons selected by the Revolutionists in parishes, towns, and counties for the purpose of corresponding with one another, comparing views, and finally coöperating in the great task of overturning the old government and setting up a new system. These committees began as local organizations, but spread so rapidly and coöperated so effectively that they soon gathered sufficient force to accomplish the work of the Revolution.

As early as November, 1772, a committee of correspondence was formed in Boston under the direction of Samuel Adams; it held regular meetings, sent emissaries to neighboring towns to organize similar bodies, and carried on a campaign of popular education in opposition to British colonial policy.

Early in the following year the Virginia House of Burgesses appointed a special committee which was charged " to obtain the most early and authentic intelligence of all such acts and resolutions of the British Parliament or proceedings of administration as may relate to or affect the British colonies in America; and to keep up and maintain a correspondence and communication with our sister colonies respecting those important considerations; and the result of such their proceedings from time to time to lay before this house." This official example was speedily followed by other legislative assemblies, so that within about a year there were twelve colonial committees appointed in regular form. Imposing as they seemed, however, they were by no means as active and important as the unofficial local committees representing the Revolutionists directly. These local committees sprang up everywhere under the direction of the county committees, and assumed control of the revolutionary forces. Thus there was organized a government within a government, with the old territorial subdivisions of the colony as a basis.

The First Continental Congress. — The skeleton or framework of the revolutionary machine was therefore well perfected when Samuel Adams in 1774 proposed in the Massachusetts legislature a resolution in favor of calling a congress of delegates from all the colonies to meet at Philadelphia in September. While the messenger of the governor, sent to dissolve the assembly, was thundering at the door, the momentous resolve was passed and the call for united action against Great Britain was issued. The other colonies except Georgia responded to this appeal with alacrity by selecting, in some fashion or another, representatives for the general Congress. The method of choice varied so greatly that the Congress was in every way an irregular and revolutionary body. In Massachusetts, Rhode Island, and Pennsylvania, the representatives were chosen informally by the colonial assembly; in New York practically by the Revolutionists of New York county; in New Jersey, Delaware, Maryland, and Virginia by conventions composed of county delegates, many of whom had been members of the colonial legislatures; in South Carolina by a "general meeting of the inhabitants of the colony," and in North Carolina by "a general meeting of the deputies of the province."

The general purpose of this Congress, ostensibly at least, was stated in the instructions which were given to the delegation of each colony by the body that elected it. These instructions did not speak of union or independence; perhaps it was not thought wise by the leaders to announce any distinctly revolutionary purpose, even if they entertained it. The Massachusetts instructions, for example, authorized the delegates to consult upon the state of the colonies, and to deliberate and determine upon wise and proper measures to be recommended for the recovery and establishment of their just rights and liberties and the restoration of harmony between Great Britain and the colonies. In accordance with the letter of the instructions, the Congress contented itself with remonstrating against British policy, recommending the colonists to join in the non-importation of British goods, and adopting other measures calculated to bring the British government to terms.

This boycott of British goods and the provisions for enforcing it had a marked effect on the course of events. It was agreed by the Congress that a committee should be chosen in every county, city, and town " by those who are qualified to vote for representatives in the legislature, whose business it shall be attentively to observe the conduct of all persons touching this association." These local committees were instructed to publish the names of all citizens who violated the terms of the boycott, to the end that all such foes to American rights might be publicly known and universally contemned. Thus a clear-cut test of allegiance to the revolutionary political system was provided, and tribunals competent to deal with refractory citizens were authorized to apply the test. The Revolutionists, consciously or not, were burning their bridges behind them.

The Second Continental Congress. — The first Congress, furthermore, recommended the call of a second Congress for the purpose of continuing the work thus begun; and, acting on this suggestion, the revolutionary bodies in the colonies, organized in the form of the old assemblies, or conventions, or committees, selected the delegates to a new Congress. This time the instructions were a little more determined in tone, and there was less talk about reconciliation and legal measures.

When this second Congress met in Philadelphia on May 10, 1775, the cause of Revolution had advanced beyond the stage of mere negotiation. Within two months, Ethan Allen's troops took Fort Ticonderoga " in the name of the Great Jehovah and the Continental Congress," the battle of Bunker Hill was fought, and Washington was called to the command of the American troops. In the midst of the crisis, Congress seized and exercised sovereign powers; it assumed the direction of the war; entered into diplomatic negotiations with other countries; issued the Declaration of Independence, regulated common concerns; raised funds; and finally designed a firmer national union in the form of the Articles of Confederation. It was not an assembly of delegates formally chosen and instructed by legally constituted states; it was the central organ, not of colonies or of states, but of that portion of the American population that was committed to the cause of Revolution.

Formation of the Articles of Confederation. — The work of the second Congress had scarcely opened before the boldest of the leaders began to urge that independence was inevitable, and that it should be accompanied by confederation and negotiations with foreign powers. As early as July 21, 1775, the Congress resolved itself into a committee of the whole to take into consideration the state of America, and Dr. Franklin submitted a draft of a plan for confederation. Under the stress of the conflict without, Congress was compelled to postpone the immediate discussion and completion of the union, and it was not until the summer of the following year, June 11, 1776, that a committee was appointed to prepare articles of confederation. The report of this committee made about one month later was then the subject of intermittent and lengthy debates. The final draft was approved in November, 1777. On the day that the agreement was reached, the Articles, accompanied by a long and eloquent letter urging ratification, were submitted to the legislatures of the states.

Notwithstanding the imperative need for a closer coöperation to secure the independence declared in 1776, it was not until noon on March 1, 1781, that the roar of cannon from the ships of war in the Delaware announced to the world that the Union "begun by necessity" had been "indissolubly cemented."

The government provided by the Articles of Confederation, as we shall see, became more famous for its weakness and shortcomings than for its positive achievements. The management of the general interests of the United States was vested under the Articles in a Congress composed of not less than two nor more than seven delegates from each state, appointed as the state legislatures should direct, serving subject to recall at any time, and meeting annually. In this Congress, each state was given one vote and had to assume the expense of maintaining its delegates. No president or permanent executive was provided, but Congress was authorized to appoint a committee to serve during its recesses and discharge such duties as might be intrusted to it. No confederate court was erected, but Congress was authorized to act as a court of appeal in cases of disputes between states, or provide for the creation of a special committee to try such causes on request. With this government, limited in its taxing and commercial powers, the states attempted to conduct their common business for a period of eight years with results that made inevitable a constitutional revolution.

Formation of State Governments. — During the revolutionary conflict the colonial governments, regularly established under the authority of the British crown, broke down or passed into the possession of the popular party. From the royal province, the governor fled before the uprising of the people, and with his departure the executive and judicial branches in their higher ranges went to pieces. Whatever the form, each colony during the Revolution had a legislature, congress, or convention chosen in some fashion by the supporters of the American cause. Sometimes the assembly was elected by popular vote, royalists being excluded; sometimes the members were chosen by local meetings of Revolutionists; and sometimes by town authorities. These provisional assemblies seized on all the powers of government in their respective jurisdictions, made laws, levied taxes, raised troops, and directed the Revolution.

In May, 1776, about two months before the formal Declaration of Independence, Congress, aware that such a step was inevitable, issued a general recommendation " to the respective assemblies and conventions of the United Colonies, where no government sufficient to the exigencies of their affairs has been hitherto established, to adopt such government as shall in the opinion of the representatives of the people best conduce to the happiness and safety of their constituents in particular and America in general." This recommendation met with speedy approval among the Revolutionists, and before the expiration of a year Virginia, New Jersey, Pennsylvania, Delaware, Maryland, Georgia, and New York had drafted new instruments of government as states, not as colonies uncertain of their destiny. Though Virginia and New Jersey completed their constitutions before the Fourth of July, they declared the dominion of Great Britain at an end. Virginia simply repudiated the authority of George III, and New Jersey expressly said in the written instrument that " all civil authority under him is necessarily at an end." Connecticut and Rhode Island, deeming the government they possessed under their ancient charters sufficient for their needs, drew up no new instruments, but merely renounced their allegiance to George III and continued their old systems without any structural change. South Carolina, which had drafted a temporary plan of government in 1776, drew up a new and more complete constitution in 1778, and Massachusetts, with more deliberation, put into effect in 1780 a constitution which in its fundamental principles remains unchanged to-day — the original instrument having never been reorganized. In this way the transition from colonies to states was completed.

Thus America came out of the Revolution a union of thirteen states, loosely bound together under the Articles of Confederation. Each state, except Rhode Island and Connecticut which continued their colonial charters, had a new written constitution based for practical purposes upon the precedents which had been established during colonial times.

The Failure of the Articles of Confederation. — The new government was hardly launched on its career of independence before fatal weaknesses were discovered in the plan of union:

1. The most obvious defect of the government under the Articles was its inability to pay even the interest on the public debt, most of which had been incurred in support of the war.

Indeed, the system of raising money provided by the Articles of Confederation was so constructed as to give creditors no hope that, during its continuance, the long-delayed payments could ever be effected. The confederate Congress had no immediate taxing power: all charges of war and all other expenses were to be defrayed out of a common treasury supplied through levies made by the legislatures of the several states in proportion to the value of the land within each state. Limited to one form of taxation — direct taxation by quotas at that — and dependent upon the will of the state legislatures for all payments, the confederate Congress really could do nothing but recommend contributions, and was in fact compelled to beg from door to door only to meet continued rebuffs, and to sink deeper and deeper in debt from year to year.

Moreover the states vied with each other in delaying the payments of their quotas into the common treasury. During a period of about four years, from November 11, 1781, to January 1, 1786, Congress laid on the states more than $10,000,000 in requisitions, and received in payment less than one-fourth of the amount demanded.

2. The dissatisfaction of the financial interests was more than equaled by the dissatisfaction of traders and manufacturers, both in America and Europe, with the unbusinesslike character of the confederate Congress. It is true that the Congress could regulate foreign commerce by making treaties with foreign powers and that the states were forbidden to lay any imposts or duties which might interfere with certain of these agreements, but in practice the confederate government was unable to enforce treaty stipulations on the unwilling states that insisted on regulating commerce in their own way. The states bid against one another for trade; they laid tariffs on goods entering or passing through their limits, thus stirring up strife among themselves; and, what was no less disastrous, they lost the advantages which a reasonable degree of coöperation would have gained.

3. The monetary system under the Articles of Confederation was even in worse confusion, if possible, than commerce. During the Revolution, Congress had created an enormous amount of paper money, which so speedily declined in value that in 1780 one paper dollar was worth less than two cents in specie, and the states added paper money of their own. It took eleven dollars of this money to buy a pound of brown sugar in Virginia; seventy-five dollars for a yard of linen; and one hundred dollars for a pound of tea. Jefferson records that he paid his physician $3000 for two calls in 1781, and gave $355.50 for three quarts of brandy. After the Revolution, a majority of states continued to issue paper money without any specie basis.

4. Shays' rebellion which broke out in Massachusetts in 1786 showed that grave dangers to public order might arise in any state, and that the duly constituted authorities might be overthrown by violence if no assistance could be secured from neighboring states or the federal authority.

5. The impotence which characterized the confederate government in enforcing measures of taxation and commercial treaties against recalcitrant states extended throughout the whole domain of its nominal authority. It was dependent almost

wholly upon the states for the enforcement of its laws, and yet it had no express power to exact obedience from them or to punish them by pecuniary penalties or suspension of privileges. Whoever argued that such a right was necessarily inherent in every government was met by the contention that the Articles themselves provided " that each state retained every power, jurisdiction, and right not expressly delegated to the United States in Congress assembled." Thus was afforded " the extraordinary spectacle of a government destitute even of a shadow of a constitutional power to enforce the execution of its own laws."

6. This reduction of the confederate government's power to a shadow was the logical result of what Hamilton regarded as the great and radical vice of the Articles of Confederation; namely, the principle of legislation for states in their collective or corporate capacity as distinguished from the individuals of which they were composed. Subject to the rule of apportionment, Congress could demand an unlimited supply of money and men from the states, but in both these important matters, upon which, in final analysis, the foundations of all government rest, Congress could bring no pressure to bear upon any individual. It was practically restricted to transactions with states — corporate entities — represented by transient and often hostile legislatures, so that the complete enforcement of any measure of taxation required the concurrence of thirteen different bodies — a conjuncture which was well-nigh impossible to secure in practice.

The Movement for Constitutional Revision. — The Congress of the Confederation was not long in discovering the true character of the futile authority which the Articles had conferred upon it. The necessity for new sources of revenue became apparent even while the struggle for independence was yet undecided, and, in 1781, Congress carried a resolution to the effect that it should be authorized to lay a duty of five per cent on certain goods. This moderate proposition was not ratified. Two years later Congress prepared another amendment of the Articles providing for certain import duties, the receipts from which, collected by state officers, were to be applied to the payment of the public debt; but three years after the introduction of the measure, four states, including New York, still held out against its ratification, and the project was allowed to drop. At last, in 1786,

Congress in a resolution declared that the requisitions for the last eight years had been so irregular in their operation, so uncertain in their collection, and so evidently unproductive, that a reliance on them in the future would be no less dishonorable to the understandings of those who entertained it than it would be dangerous to the welfare and peace of the Union.

In fact, the Articles of Confederation had hardly gone into effect before the leading citizens also began to feel that the powers of Congress were wholly inadequate. In 1780, even before their adoption, Alexander Hamilton proposed a general convention to frame a new constitution, and from that time forward he labored with remarkable zeal and wisdom to extend and popularize the idea of a strong national government. Two years later, the assembly of the state of New York recommended a convention to revise the Articles and increase the power of Congress. In 1783, Washington, in a circular letter to the governors, urged that it was indispensable to the happiness of the individual states that there should be lodged somewhere a supreme power to regulate and govern the general concerns of the confederation. Shortly afterward (1785), Governor Bowdoin, of Massachusetts, suggested to his state legislature the advisability of calling a national assembly to settle upon and define the powers of Congress; and the legislature resolved that the government under the Articles of Confederation was inefficient and should be reformed; but the resolution was never laid before Congress.

In the same year, however, that the Massachusetts resolution was passed, commissioners, selected by Maryland and Virginia for the purpose of reaching an agreement respecting the navigation of the Potomac, recommended the appointment of a new commission with power to arrange a tariff schedule, subject to the consent of Congress, to be enforced by both states. Thereupon, Virginia invited all the other states to send delegates to a convention at Annapolis to consider the question of duties on imports and commerce in general. When this convention assembled in 1786, delegates from only five states were present, and they were disheartened at the limitations on their powers and the lack of interest the other states had shown in the project. With remarkable foresight, however, Alexander Hamilton seized the occasion to secure the adoption of a recommendation advising the states to choose representatives for another convention to meet in Philadelphia the following year " to consider the Articles of Confederation and to propose such changes therein as might render them adequate to the exigencies of the union."

The proposal of the Annapolis convention was transmitted to the state legislatures and laid before Congress. Congress thereupon resolved in February, 1787, that a convention should be held for the sole and express purpose of revising the Articles of Confederation and reporting to itself and the legislatures of the several states such alterations and provisions as would, when agreed to by Congress and confirmed by the states, render the federal constitution adequate to the exigencies of government and the preservation of the Union.

In pursuance of this call, delegates to the new convention were chosen by the legislatures of the states or by the governors in conformity to authority conferred by the legislative assemblies. The delegates were given instructions of a general nature by their respective states, none of which, apparently, contemplated any very far-reaching changes. In fact, almost all of them expressly limited their representatives to a mere revision of the Articles of Confederation.

The National Constitutional Convention of 1787. — It was a truly remarkable assembly of men that gathered in Philadelphia in May, 1787, to undertake the work of reconstructing the American system of government. It is not merely patriotic pride that compels one to assert that never in the history of assemblies has there been a convention of men richer in political experience and in practical knowledge, or endowed with a profounder insight into the springs of human action and the intimate essence of government. It is indeed an astounding fact that at one time so many men skilled in statecraft could be found on the very frontiers of civilization among a population numbering about four million whites. It is no less a cause for admiration that their instrument of government should have survived the trials and crises of a century that saw the wreck of more than a score of paper constitutions. On the memorable roll of that convention were Elbridge Gerry, Rufus King, Roger Sherman, Alexander Hamilton, Oliver Ellsworth, Benjamin

Franklin, Robert Morris, Gouverneur Morris, William Paterson, James Wilson, George Washington, Edmund Randolph, James Madison, John Rutledge, and the two Pinckneys — to mention only a few whose names have passed indelibly into the records of American history.

All the members had had a practical training in politics. Washington, as commander-in-chief of the revolutionary forces, had learned well the lessons and problems of war, and mastered successfully the no less difficult problems of administration. The two Morrises had distinguished themselves in grappling with financial questions as trying and perplexing as any which statesmen had ever been compelled to face. Seven of the delegates had gained political wisdom as governors of their native states; and no less than twenty-eight had served in Congress either during the Revolution or under the Articles of Confederation. There were men trained in the law, versed in finance, skilled in administration, and learned in the political philosophy of their own and all earlier times. Moreover, they were men destined to continue public service under the government which they had met to construct — Presidents, Vice-Presidents, heads of departments, justices of the Supreme Court were in that imposing body.

Drafting a National Constitution. — The convention had not proceeded very far in the consideration of the problems before it when the question was raised as to whether the delegates were bound by their instructions to the mere amendment of the Articles of Confederation or were free to make a revolution in the political system. Fortunately for the cause of national union, the delegates cast off the restrictions placed upon them by their instructions, and frankly disregarded the fact that they had assembled merely to amend the Articles of Confederation, not to make a new instrument of government. They refused to be bound either by the letter or spirit of the Articles, for they even provided that the new government should go into effect when ratified by nine states, whereas under the Articles unanimous approval was required for any amendment.

A large majority of the convention had determined to establish a strong national government to take the place of the confederate system, and to do this it was absolutely necessary to throw aside the fundamental features of the Articles of Confederation. On May 30, 1787, five days after the opening of the convention, a resolution was adopted in the Committee of the Whole, "that a national government ought to be established consisting of a supreme legislative, executive, and judiciary." The distinction between a "federal and a national supreme government" was clearly explained by Gouverneur Morris. "The former," he said, was "a mere compact resting on the good faith of the parties," while the latter had "a complete and compulsive operation"; and he concluded by adding that "in all communities there must be one supreme power and one only." Madison, in discussing the problem of representation, observed that "whatever reason might have existed for the equality of suffrage when the Union was a federal one among sovereign states, it must cease when a national government should be put in their place." That it was the desire of a majority of the convention to establish a supreme national government is evidenced in nearly every page of the debates.

In devising this national system it was necessary to make many compromises. In the first place, the small states demanded equal representation and the large states representation according to population; a compromise gave the small states equality in the Senate and the large states proportional representation in the lower House. In the next place, the slave states wished to have slaves counted in the apportionment of representation — a demand which was stoutly opposed by the non-slave states; and a compromise was reached by the provision that in apportioning representation and direct taxes only three-fifths of the total number of slaves should be counted. In the third place, the North, having larger commercial interests than the South, wished to give Congress the power to regulate commerce, but the South, being solicitous of the slave trade, feared its prohibition in case unqualified power was vested in Congress; and the result was a compromise authorizing Congress to regulate foreign commerce, but forbidding it to prohibit the importation of slaves before the year 1808.

The Constitution Contrasted with the Articles of Confederation. 1. The Articles of Confederation provided no separate executive department charged with the high function of enforcing federal law. This grave defect was carefully considered by the convention, and warmly discussed by the advocates of the new system. All were agreed that a strong executive power was indispensable, but they were uncertain as to whether such an important authority should be vested in a single person or in a directorate. They also had no little difficulty in deciding on the method by which the chief magistrate was to be elected.

On the point of a single executive armed with large powers, Hamilton argued with great cogency: "Energy in the executive is a leading character in the definition of good government. It is essential to the protection of the community against foreign attacks. It is not less essential to the steady administration of the laws, to the protection of property against those irregular and high-handed combinations which sometimes interrupt the ordinary course of justice, to the security of liberty against the enterprises and assaults of ambition, of faction, and of anarchy. Every man, the least conversant with Roman story, knows how often that republic was obliged to take refuge in the absolute power of a single man, under the formidable title of dictator, as well against the intrigues of ambitious individuals who aspired to the tyranny, and the seditions of whole classes of the community whose conduct threatened the existence of all government, as against the invasions of external enemies who menaced the conquest and destruction of Rome."

Such weighty considerations prevailed in the convention, and an executive department with a single head endowed with large powers was created. To meet the objection of those who were afraid of the excitements of popular elections, it was decided that the President should be chosen indirectly by electors appointed as the legislatures of the several states might determine.

2. No less grave defects were inherent in the Congress created by the Articles of Confederation. Three, in particular, engaged the attention of the convention: the equality of the several states, large and small, in voting power; the instability of a single chamber; and the absence of direct representation of the people in the Congress — the delegates being appointed by their respective state legislatures and thus dependent upon the states as corporate entities rather than upon the people thereof. The convention accordingly decided upon a bicameral legislature: a

Senate affording equal representation to all states and a House composed of representatives apportioned among the states on a basis of population.

3. The crowning defect of the Articles, according to Hamilton, was the want of a central judiciary. The old Congress had no authority to organize courts of general jurisdiction, although it could act as a tribunal of "last resort on appeal in all disputes and differences arising between two or more states concerning boundary, jurisdiction, or any other cause whatever." It therefore had no way of enforcing federal laws by judicial process, and as Hamilton said: "Laws are a dead letter without courts to expound and define their true meaning and operation. The treaties of the United States, to have any force at all, must be considered as a part of the law of the land. Their true import as far as respects individuals, must like all other laws be ascertained by judicial determinations. To produce uniformity in these determinations they ought to be submitted in the last resort to one supreme tribunal." Moreover, Hamilton, fearing the aggression of the legislature, believed that the court should have the power of declaring laws unconstitutional. Accordingly a Supreme Court, and inferior courts to be erected by Congress, were given jurisdiction over all cases arising under the Constitution, federal laws, and treaties — a jurisdiction by later congressional enactment and judicial decision interpreted to include the power of declaring state and federal laws unconstitutional.

4. The financial and commercial objections to the Articles of Confederation were met by two important provisions. The necessity of depending upon the state legislatures for federal funds was entirely eliminated by the clause authorizing Congress to raise revenues by taxes, duties, and excises bearing immediately upon the people as individuals. The continuation of the commercial warfare among the states was prevented by the clause empowering Congress to regulate commerce among the several states and with foreign nations, as well as with the Indians. Provisions for national defense were made in the clauses empowering Congress to raise and support armies and maintain a navy.

No less important for financial and commercial purposes were the restrictions laid upon the powers of the states. They were forbidden to emit bills of credit, make anything but gold and silver coin tender in payment of debts, pass ex post facto laws, lay duties on imports or exports (except with the consent of Congress for specific purposes), lay tonnage duties, or pass any law impairing the obligation of contract.

5. Special effectiveness was given to the new powers conferred upon the national government by authorizing it to deal with individuals instead of thirteen distinct and separate states. Hence it was no longer possible for states to violate and disregard treaties made by the federal government, or to look upon federal laws as mere recommendations to be obeyed if desirable or neglected altogether.

6. Of particular significance was the clause providing for future amendments. The Articles of Confederation had stipulated that no alteration should be made without the approval of Congress and ratification by the legislature of every state. The new Constitution bound every state to an amendment, in case it was approved by two-thirds of both houses of Congress and ratified by three-fourths of the states.

The Ratification of the Constitution. — It is evident from an examination of these departures from the Articles of Confederation that a revolution in our political system was contemplated by the framers of the Constitution. They were doubtless unaware of all the national implications contained in the instrument which they drafted, but they knew very well that the state legislatures, which had been so negligent in paying their quotas under the Articles and which had been so jealous of their rights, would probably stick at ratifying such a national instrument of government. Accordingly they cast aside that clause in the Articles requiring amendments to be ratified by the legislatures of all the states; and advised that the new Constitution should be ratified by conventions in the several states composed of delegates chosen by the voters. They furthermore declared — and this is a fundamental matter — that when the conventions of nine states had ratified the Constitution the new government should go into effect so far as those states were concerned.

After the new Constitution was published and transmitted to the states, there began a determined fight over its ratification. A veritable flood of pamphlet literature descended upon the country, and a collection of these pamphlets by Hamilton, Madison, and Jay, brought together under the title of *The Federalist* — has remained a permanent part of the contemporary sources on the Constitution and has been regarded by many lawyers as a commentary second in value only to the decisions of the Supreme Court. Within a year the champions of the new government found themselves victorious, for on June 21, 1788, the ninth state, New Hampshire, ratified the Constitution, and accordingly, the new government might go into effect as between the agreeing states. Within a few weeks, the nationalist party in Virginia and New York succeeded in winning these two states, and in spite of the fact that North Carolina and Rhode Island had not yet ratified the Constitution, Congress determined to put the instrument into effect in accordance with the recommendations of the convention. Elections for the new government were held; the date March 4, 1789, was fixed for the formal establishment of the new system; Congress secured a quorum on April 6; and on April 30, Washington was inaugurated at the Federal Hall in New York.

SELECTED REFERENCES

H. C. Lodge, *The Thirteen English Colonies in Amercia;* John Fiske, *The Critical Period of American History;* M. Farrand, *The Framing of the Constitution* (1913); Allen Johnson, *Union and Democracy* (Riverside Series, 1915); F. S. Oliver, *Alexander Hamilton: an Essay on American Union* (1907); W. C. Ford, *George Washington* (1900).

CHAPTER III

THE FEDERAL SYSTEM

THE Constitution of the United States provides not only a plan of government but also distributes public functions between the states and the national government and lays down positive limitations on the powers of each. Our government is therefore essentially a government of law. Around the President and Congress and around the legislatures of the states and even the councils of cities the federal Constitution places important restrictions. It is under the rules and regulations — the general principles of the federal Constitution — that all legislative, executive, and judicial authorities must act. This is because federation is founded upon compromise, and compromise implies that power is divided between the national government created by the union and the states which join in forming it; in other words, that each is limited in its sphere.

The State in the Federal System. — It is accordingly an error to regard the federal Constitution as an instrument relating solely to the government which has its seat at Washington. It presupposes the complete organization and satisfactory operation of state governments and prescribes the general sphere in which they may move. Indeed, for a long period in our history it was the state that mainly attracted the interest and concern of the citizen. Jefferson looked upon the national government as principally the agent of the states in the conduct of their foreign affairs; and in the early days of the republic it was quite common for men in politics to leave prominent places in the federal government to accept high offices in their respective commonwealths.

Obviously, fundamental changes have occurred in our federal system since Jefferson's day. The Civil War and the adoption of the Thirteenth, Fourteenth, and Fifteenth Amendments have taken away from the states an enormous domain of power which they previously enjoyed. Our national government has risen in popular esteem; statesmen now look upon local politics principally as a means of advancement to federal honors; the growth of national party organization has subordinated state to national politics, and the failure of state governments to remedy many of the abuses connected with trusts and corporations has led the people to turn to the national government for relief. The supremacy of federal law and the growing practice of corporations and individuals to resort, whenever possible, to federal tribunals in the protection of private property rights, have given a weight to the national government which its founders had slight reason to suspect it would ever secure. Whatever view we may take of the old struggle over states' rights, the fact remains that in law and in political consciousness the nation is now first. The national government is not a light superstructure resting upon the solid foundations of state governments; the national Constitution furnishes the broad legal basis for the whole system, for it is within the sphere marked out by that Constitution and guarded by the federal judiciary that commonwealth governments must operate.

Fundamental Constitutional Limitations on State Governments. — The boundaries and nature of this sphere of power reserved to the several commonwealths are to be understood by an examination of the fundamental limitations on state governments laid down in the federal Constitution, and also the chief judicial decisions interpreting them in practice.

1. The first groups of limitations relate to the taxing power of the state. States cannot lay and collect imposts and duties upon exports and imports—that is, upon articles in the hands of any person who sends them to, or receives them from, foreign countries directly — except to defray expenses incurred in the execution of inspection laws, and then only with the consent of Congress.

2. Analogous to this provision is the clause which forbids any state to lay a tonnage duty without consent of Congress. The word " tonnage " means the entire internal capacity or contents of a vessel or ship expressed in tons of one hundred cubical feet each. States may tax the ships of their citizens as property valued as such; but it is clear and undeniable, the Supreme Court has held, " that taxes levied by a state upon ships and

vessels as instruments of commerce and navigation are within that clause of the instrument which prohibits the states from levying any duty of tonnage without the consent of Congress."

3. No state can lay a tax on the property, lawful agencies, and instrumentalities of the federal government or on federal franchises as such. This principle is not expressed in the Constitution, but it was derived, with his usual logic, by Chief Justice Marshall from the nature of the federal system itself. The power to create implies the power to preserve; the power to tax is the power to destroy, and if wielded by a different hand, is incompatible with the power to create and preserve; therefore if the states could tax federal instrumentalities, they could destroy a union which was meant to be indestructible. The early doctrine that the states cannot in any way touch a federal instrumentality has been modified more recently to the effect that they cannot interfere with such an instrumentality in such a manner as to impair its efficiency in performing the function which it was designed to serve. A state, for example, cannot tax federal bonds, but it may tax the buildings and other property of a national bank chartered by the federal government.

4. In the exercise of its police power and power of taxation a state may not seriously interfere with interstate commerce; but it may pass laws relative to matters which are local in character, even though they do affect in some way such commerce. For example, the Supreme Court sustained a law of Kentucky providing for the inspection of illuminating oils and imposing a penalty upon persons selling oil branded as unsafe by state inspectors — this law being in the interests of public safety — although it certainly interfered with the right of citizens of other states to sell oil freely in that commonwealth. State actions which constitute an invasion of federal power may likewise be illustrated by a concrete case. A law of Minnesota requiring the inspection of all meat twenty-four hours before slaughtering, designed in the interests of pure food, was declared invalid, because it necessarily prevented the transportation, into that commonwealth, of meats from animals slaughtered in other states where, of course, no such inspection could be provided.

5. The state has practically no power over the monetary system. It may charter and regulate state banks, but it cannot

coin money, emit bills of credit, or make anything but gold and silver coin legal tender in the payment of debts. It may, however, authorize a state bank or state banking association to issue notes for circulation, but the exercise of this power is practically prohibited by the act of Congress, passed in 1866, laying a tax of ten per cent upon such notes. The effect of this act was to make it impossible, on account of the weight of the tax, for state banks to issue notes at all.

6. The original Constitution also contains some fundamental limitations on the power of states over criminal legislation. It provides that no state shall pass any bill of attainder — that is, a legislative act which inflicts punishment upon some person without ordinary judicial trial. No state can pass an ex post facto law — that is, one which imposes a punishment for an act which was not punishable when committed; or imposes additional punishment to that prescribed when the act was committed; or changes the rules of evidence so that different or less testimony (to the serious disadvantage of the accused) is sufficient to convict him than was required when the deed in question was committed. This limitation on the states applies only to criminal legislation.

7. To protect citizens in their property rights the Constitution provides that no state shall pass any law impairing the obligation of contracts. The obligation of contract is the body of law existing at the time a contract is made, defining and regulating it, and making provision for its due enforcement. For example, one Crowninshield, on March 22, 1811, gave a note to one Sturges; and shortly afterward the state of New York, in which the note was dated, passed a bankruptcy law under which Crowninshield became a bankrupt, and by paying Sturges a portion of what he owed, claimed the right to be discharged from all of the remainder. This law with reference to all debts contracted *before* its passage was declared invalid by the Supreme Court as impairing the obligation of contract.

The term contract is used in this clause with a far wider meaning than in ordinary private law. It means " a legally binding agreement in respect to property, either expressed or implied, executory or executed, between private parties, or between a commonwealth and a private party or parties; or a grant from one party to another; or a grant, charter, or franchise, from a commonwealth to a private party or private parties." This wide interpretation of the term has given the clause a particular social and economic significance, because it has been applied to the protection of the franchises, charters, and privileges secured by private corporations from state legislatures. The Supreme Court, for example, held that a charter secured by Dartmouth College from King George constituted a contract with that corporation which the state was bound to respect on securing its independence, and that a law of the state of New Hampshire designed to control the college and its funds was an impairment of the obligation of that contract. Under a strict application of this principle, a state legislature having once granted away special privileges to corporations would be bound to maintain them forever if no specific provisions were made in the grant as to times and limitations.

The Supreme Court, however, has refused to extend the term contract to several forms of agreement between a state and its citizens. For example, appointment to a public office for a definite term at a fixed salary is not a contract, and a state impairs no obligation when it abolishes the office. A grant of power to a municipal corporation by a state legislature is not a contract.

It should be noted also that the Court will declare a law invalid as impairing the obligation of contract *only* when it is retrospective, that is, when it applies to contracts made before its passage; and if a state provides in its constitution or laws for future revision of charters, franchises, and other forms of contract, it thereby places, in the body of the law which, as we have seen, constitutes the obligation of contract, a provision securing henceforward the right to alter the terms of new franchises and privileges without violating this clause of the federal Constitution. All the states now safeguard, by this precautionary measure, their right to control privileges once granted. The general tenor of the provisions securing state legislatures from the strangling effect of this clause is illustrated by this extract from the constitution of Wisconsin: " All general laws or special acts, enacted under the provisions of this section [dealing with corporations], may be altered and repealed by the legislature at any time after their passage."

8. By far the most important guarantees for personal and property rights are to be found in the general clauses of the Fourteenth Amendment, which, for practical purposes, place in the hands of the federal judiciary the power of controlling state legislation on most important matters. According to section 1 of that Amendment, no state shall make or enforce any law which may abridge the privileges or immunities of citizens of the United States; no state may deprive any person of life, liberty, or property without due process of law, nor deny to any person within its jurisdiction the equal protection of the law. In order to understand the full import of the several terms employed in this brief but significant section, it is necessary to examine them in the light of judicial decisions, for in themselves they furnish slight clew to the real legal processes which they secure.

The most significant part of the Fourteenth Amendment is a brief sentence which forbids a state to deprive any person of life, liberty, or property, without due process of law. The term "property" is not limited to tangible goods having an exchange value, but it extends to every form of vested right which the possessor has legally acquired.

Of none of these things may any person be deprived without due process of law; but what is due process of law? The Supreme Court has steadily refused to define " due process " in the abstract, and it is not possible to make any very satisfactory generalization. Due process of law, said the Court in one case, is " due process according to the law of the land, and the law of the land is the law of the state." In another case, due process of law was interpreted to mean " a course of legal proceedings according to those rules and principles which have been established in our system of jurisprudence for the protection and enforcement of private rights." And in still another case, the Court declared that there are certain immutable principles of free government which control the law of every state. The best way of ascertaining the full import of this phrase is to examine its application to certain classes of state laws.

(*a*) What is due process of law in criminal cases? On this point the Supreme Court has said: " Any legal proceeding enforced by public authority, whether sanctioned by age and custom, or newly devised in the discretion of the legislative power in furtherance of the general public good, which regards and preserves these principles of liberty and justice [lying at the basis of all our civil and political institutions] must be held to be due process of law."

(*b*) Due process of law in civil matters is defined in a general way as any process which establishes reasonable security, full notice, and satisfactory protection to persons involved in civil suits.

(*c*) In the imposition of taxes states must follow due process; and whenever a tax is imposed according to the valuation of property, due process merely requires general notice to the owner and a hearing of complaints so as to give him a chance to contest his liability; personal notice is not necessary. The right to be heard is not a necessary part of due process in the imposition of poll and license taxes, specific taxes on things, persons, or corporations, or many other kinds of taxes definitely fixed by legislative enactment.

(*d*) It is in legislation controlling corporations and protecting labor, that state legislatures most frequently come into conflict with due process of law as interpreted by the Supreme Court. For example, the legislature of Minnesota created a railway commission with the power to compel any common carrier to fix such rates as the commission should declare to be equal and reasonable, and made no provision for judicial review of the rates and charges so fixed. This law was held unconstitutional on the ground that it deprived a railway company of its right to judicial investigation by due process of law under the forms and with the machinery provided for the judicial investigation of the truth of any matter in controversy, and substituted for this, as an absolute finality, the action of a railway commission which could not be regarded as clothed with judicial functions or possessing the machinery of a court of justice. Whenever a state regulates railway or other rates, its terms must be " reasonable," that is, allow proper returns on investments. To take another example: the legislature of New York passed a law providing that no employees should be required or permitted to work in bakeries more than sixty hours a week or ten hours a day, and the Supreme Court held this law invalid on the ground that it was an unreasonable, unnecessary, and arbitrary interference with the right and liberty to contract in relation to labor — the right and liberty to purchase and sell labor being within the protection of the Fourteenth Amendment.

A state, however, may do, under that vague authority known as the "police power," many things which interfere with life, liberty, and property; but the Court refuses to define the term police power, reserving to itself the right to determine at any time whether any particular act is warranted under that power or not. A broad interpretation of the term police power would give a state the right to do anything designed to promote general welfare as opposed to special privilege. Indeed, the Court once said that the police power is the power " to prescribe regulations to promote the health, peace, morals, education, and good order of the people, and to legislate so as to increase the industries of the state, develop its resources, and add to its wealth and its prosperity." It is evident, however, that such a generous interpretation of the powers of the state might very well nullify the provisions of the Fourteenth Amendment in the hands of any judiciary in sympathy with an increase in the control exercised by the state over private rights in the name of general welfare.

At all events a state, under its police power, may do many definite things. It may, for example, restrict dangerous and objectionable trades to certain localities; it may confine the insane or persons afflicted with contagious diseases; it may regulate, to a limited extent, railways and other common carriers; and it may order the destruction of a building in the path of a conflagration or endangering the health and safety of neighbors and passers-by. It is clear, nevertheless, that police power, like that other vague phrase " due process of law," is wholly within the keeping of the judicial conscience, and its interpretation depends upon the general social and political theories of the judiciary.

The Political and Economic Relation of State and Nation. — The position of the state in the federal system is not only fixed in law, as defined by the federal judiciary. The state forms a section of the great extra-legal party organization which dominates national politics and often subordinates state issues to the exigencies of federal issues. The state is, indeed, the fundamental unit in the national party system. Delegates to the national conventions are assigned to states mainly according to their representation in Congress; federal patronage is distributed with a view to building up the general party organization within the limits of each commonwealth; United States Senators are generally party leaders within their commonwealths, and occupy positions of influence in the national party organization; and ambitious politicians in the state usually regard state offices as stepping-stones to higher things. Thus the great nation-wide party organization, founded on national as opposed to sectional interests, tends more and more to bring the state down from that proud position occupied in the beginning of our history.

The autonomy of the state is furthermore being reduced by the growth of national industries, interstate commerce, and national business organizations known as combinations and trusts. These new forces making for unity and centralization penetrate to the loneliest hamlets in the most thinly populated commonwealths. The regulation of these great interstate interests is confided under the Constitution to the federal government, which is steadily multiplying in number and extent its supervisory activities. The conduct of commerce and industry by corporations increases the amount of legal business which is taken out of the hands of the state judiciary and vested in the federal courts under that clause of the Constitution which gives the latter authority and jurisdiction over suits between citizens of different states.

While enumerating this multitude of restrictions upon the states, we must, at the same time, remember that an enormous and important domain of power is still reserved to them. Article 10 of the amendments provides that the powers not granted to the United States by the Constitution nor prohibited by it to the states are reserved to the states respectively or to the people. The regulation, therefore, of almost all the ordinary affairs of life is left to the states. As Mr. Bryce has put it, " An American may, through a long life, never be reminded of the federal government except when he votes at presidential and congressional elections, buys a package of tobacco bearing the government stamp, lodges a complaint against the post-office, and opens his trunks for a custom house officer on the pier at New York when he returns from a tour in Europe. His direct taxes are paid to officials acting under state laws. The state or local authority constituted by state statutes registers his birth, appoints his guardian, pays for his schooling, gives him a share in the estate of his father deceased, licenses him when he enters a trade (if it be one needing a license), marries him, divorces him, entertains civil actions against him, declares him a bankrupt, hangs him for murder; the police that guard his house, the local boards which look after the poor, control highways, impose water rates, manage schools — all these derive their legal powers from his state alone."

This, however, is too strong a statement of the case, for the individual does come into contact with the federal government far more often than it would lead us to believe — indeed, far more often than when Mr. Bryce wrote his epoch-making work. Although he may not be conscious of the fact, every time he purchases a commodity, smokes a cigar, or has a glass of liquor, the citizen pays tribute to the federal government; whenever he ships a commodity by freight to a point out of his state, he pays rates which are under the supervision of the Interstate Commerce Commission; the rural free mail delivery reaches him on his farm or in his summer camp in the mountains; if he journeys from one state to another, he pays a car fare which is under the regulation of the federal government. If he be a workingman engaged in a strike against some large corporation, the chances are that the injunction against him will come from a federal court, and it will be on an order of that court that he is punished if he disobeys the injunction. If he attempts to send through the mails some publication which the post-office authorities may declare objectionable, he may find himself in the toils of the federal law. It is not necessary to continue the enumeration. The federal government is not so far away from the life of the citizens as it once was, and as the economic organizations of labor and capital increase the extent and strength of their ramifications throughout the social body, the federal government will inevitably come nearer and nearer to the private citizen. Nevertheless, the functions of the state will also increase in importance, and the state as a guardian of fundamental public and private interests should grow in the esteem of the citizen.

The Admission of New States. — The federal Constitution contains no details as to the way in which a new state may be admitted to the Union. It simply provides that new states may be admitted by Congress, and that no new state shall be formed out of another state or by the junction of two or more parts of different states without the consent of the legislatures concerned and Congress as well. A variety of methods have been employed in the admission of new states. Texas, for example, was admitted to the Union in 1845 as an independent republic by resolution of Congress; and California never went through the territorial stage. The inhabitants of that region shortly after the cession from Mexico drew up a constitution, demanded admission to the Union, and Congress yielded.

State Constitutions. — Subject to the limitations of the federal Constitution and to such limitations as may be imposed at the time of admission, the voters of each state may draft the constitution of their commonwealth as they please; and one might naturally expect to discover the greatest divergences among the fundamental laws of the different states. On the contrary, however, we find striking similarities, especially among the constitutions of any particular decade.

A state constitution usually falls into seven or more distinct parts:

I. Taking several of the state constitutions together, we find that a composite view of the bill of rights reveals two somewhat sharply defined parts. The older part contains those ancient and honorable limitations on behalf of private rights so famous in the constitutional history of England and the United States — indictment by grand jury; trial by jury; the free exercise of religious worship without discrimination or preference; the privilege of the writ of habeas corpus save in case of rebellion, invasion, or public danger; prohibition of excessive bails and fines and cruel and unusual punishments; compensation for private property when taken for public use; the right of every citizen to speak freely, write and publish his sentiments on all matters subject to responsibility for libelous publications; and the right peaceably to assemble and petition the government or any department thereof.

In addition to the ancient and some newer principles of civil liberty, there are to be found in several bills of rights curious provisions which belong rather to the sphere of political theory than to constitutional law, but are interesting nevertheless. The constitution of Louisiana, drafted in 1898, declares that "all government of right originates with the people, is founded on their will alone and is instituted solely for the good of the whole; its only legitimate end is to secure justice to all, preserve peace and promote the interest and happiness of the people." The Massachusetts constitution solemnly announces: "It is the right as well as the duty of all men in society, publicly and at stated seasons to worship the Supreme Being, the great creator and the preserver of the universe." While guaranteeing freedom of religious worship, the constitution of Pennsylvania declares, "that no person who acknowledges the being of a God and a future state of rewards and punishments shall, on account of his religious sentiments, be disqualified to hold any office or place of trust or profit under this commonwealth."

II. The second part of a state constitution embraces those sections dealing with the distribution of powers, the frame of government, and the limitations on the authorities of the state. This part usually outlines the form of the central government in considerable detail, and contains more or less explicit provisions in relation to rural and municipal government. It defines the suffrage, provides for the organization of the legislature composed of two houses elected by popular vote, and prescribes the limitations under which it must operate. It provides for the election of the governor and the great officers of state, leaving the construction of the minor administrative offices and boards to the legislature; it creates the judicial system, state and local.

III. The third division of our composite state constitution places fundamental limitations upon the financial power of the state legislature. The provisions are often detailed and complicated, but their general purpose is to fix a debt limit beyond which the legislature cannot go, and to compel that body to make adequate provision for the payment of interest and principal on debts created.

IV. The fourth part of our composite state constitution lays down, with considerable minuteness, the general principles which shall be applied in the regulation of corporations and conditions of labor. The newer constitutions limit very narrowly the activities of corporations. They provide for a corporation commission with large powers in the regulation of rates, charges, and general conduct of corporate business. Oklahoma provides for physical valuation of railways; endeavors to prevent stock watering; fixes a rate of two cents a mile for carrying passengers, subject to change by the legislature and corporation commission; and prohibits the consolidation of competing companies and the establishment of monopolies. On behalf of labor, the Oklahoma constitution provides for a separate state department, prohibits the contracting of convict labor, stipulates an eight-hour day in all public employments, orders the legislature to pass laws protecting the health and safety of employees in factories, mines, and on railroads.

V. The fifth part of our composite constitution contains a large variety of miscellaneous provisions designed to promote general welfare. It usually includes sections relative to the public schools and the state educational system; the Nebraska constitution, for example, requires the legislature to provide free instruction in the common schools of the state for all persons between the ages of five and twenty-five; it sets aside certain revenues for educational purposes; and creates a board of regents for the state university and prescribes their duties. Under these general provisions we also find clauses regulating or prohibiting the manufacture and sale of intoxicating liquors, providing for the care and maintenance of the poor, exempting homesteads from forced sales for debt except under prescribed conditions, fixing the maximum rates of interest, safeguarding public health, creating charitable and eleemosynary institutions, and controlling the care and management of public property.

VI. A sixth part of the state constitution usually relates to the powers of the legislature over the organization of city and local governments and in many instances to the rights of " home rule " to be enjoyed by cities — the management of which is otherwise under the control of the legislature.

VII. The last part of our composite constitution makes provision for future alterations by prescribing the way in which amendments may be proposed and adopted.

Interstate Relations. — The federal Constitution secures to the citizens of each state the privileges and immunities of the citizens in the several states, and the federal judiciary defines and enforces them by proper processes. This means that there are certain great legal rights necessary to free migration throughout the American empire, to the successful conduct of business and industry, and to the enjoyment of property, which no state may take away from a citizen of another commonwealth coming within its borders. It means also that no state may confer civil rights on its own citizens and at the same time withhold them from citizens coming from other states. It does not mean, however, that A. of Illinois, on moving into Indiana, may claim all privileges which he enjoyed in the former state; he is, on the contrary, entitled only to the rights enjoyed by citizens of the latter state. For example, A. enjoys in Illinois the right to sell cigarettes subject to certain restrictions; in Indiana the sale of cigarettes is forbidden by law; consequently A. cannot claim there the privilege which he had in the former state.

To facilitate intercourse among the several states, especially in the transaction of legal business, the Constitution provides that full faith and credit shall be given in each state to the public acts, records, and judicial proceedings of every other state. Congress has provided by law the form in which such acts and proceedings shall be authenticated, and has ordered that, when so authenticated, " such faith and credit shall be given them in every court within the United States as they have by law and usage in the courts of the state from which they are taken."

The extradition of criminals, long an international practice based on treaty stipulations between independent countries, was carried over into the federal Constitution by the provision that any person charged with crime, fleeing from justice and found in another state, shall be delivered up on demand of the executive authority of the state from which he fled to be removed for trial in the state having jurisdiction of the crime. Congress has amplified the constitutional provision by an act declaring that on the demand from the proper authority, " it shall be the duty of the executive authority of the state " to cause the fugitive to be seized and handed over to the agent of the state making the requisition. The words " it shall be the duty " were interpreted by Chief Justice Taney as merely declaratory of a moral duty, not as mandatory and compulsory.

The Supremacy of Federal Law. — Notwithstanding the importance of the states and their indispensable services in the operations of the federal system, it must always be borne in mind that the federal Constitution is the highest law of the land. "This Constitution and the laws of the United States which shall be made in pursuance thereof, and all treaties made or which shall be made under the authority of the United States shall be the supreme law of the land." Federal law is supreme; and, in the last instance, the Supreme Court of the United States is the final interpreter of that law. The decisions of this Court are binding on Congress, the states, and private persons.

The application of this principle may be illustrated by two cases. Congress provided by law that when any civil suit or criminal prosecution was begun against a federal revenue officer in any court of a state, the case could be immediately removed into the federal courts. A federal revenue officer, in the discharge of his duty, killed a man in Tennessee, and his case, against the protest of the state, was removed to a federal court in due form. In discussing the constitutionality of this law, Mr. Justice Strong said of the federal government: "It can act only through its officers and agents, and they must act within the states. . . . No state government can exclude it from the exercise of any authority conferred upon it by the Constitution, obstruct its authorized officers against its will, or withhold from it, for a moment, the cognizance of any subject which that instrument has committed to it."

Another phase of federal supremacy is illustrated by the case involving the constitutionality of a law passed in New York fixing the hours for workmen in bakeries. The owner of a bakery contended that this law violated the principles of the federal Constitution, and on appeal to the Supreme Court his contention was upheld. Thus the state law was set aside by the superior force of the federal Constitution.

The Separation of Powers. — Second in importance to the distribution of power between the state and national governments is the equally famous doctrine that the power conferred upon the federal government must be divided among three distinct departments: legislative, executive, and judicial. According to the traditional account, this doctrine came into our law and practice from Montesquieu, whose treatise on *The Spirit of*

Laws was a veritable political text-book for our eighteenth-century statesmen, and it was derived by that distinguished French author from his study of the English constitution. In point of fact, however, the doctrine, as far as Montesquieu was concerned, was a notion which he acquired during a conflict between the judiciary and king in France in which he participated, and afterwards read into his study of the institutions of England. As a principle of law and government, it is a part of that system of checks and balances and subdivisions of power by which statesmen have sought to prevent the development of that type of democracy that functions through simple legislative majorities. It is explained with great insight by Webster: "The spirit of liberty . . . is jealous of encroachments, jealous of power, jealous of man. It demands checks; it seeks for guards; it insists on securities; it intrenches itself behind strong defenses, and fortifies itself with all possible care against the assaults of ambition and passion."

The doctrine is not expressly stated in a separate article in the federal Constitution, as in several state constitutions, but is thus embodied in the opening sentences of the three articles relating to the legislative, executive, and judicial power: "All legislative powers herein granted shall be vested in a Congress of the United States. . . . The executive power shall be vested in a President of the United States. . . . The judicial power . . . shall be vested in one Supreme Court and such inferior courts as Congress may from time to time ordain and establish." Thus, says Kent, the Constitution has effected the separation of powers "with great felicity of execution, and in a way well calculated to preserve the equal balance of the government."

A close examination of the Constitution, however, shows that the men who framed it were unable to maintain the purity of the principle when they came to prescribing the mode of exercising the powers of government in detail. Indeed, it was thoroughly understood by the framers that a complete separation of powers was impossible, save in the realm of pure theory.

The appointing power of the President is shared by the Senate; so is his treaty-making power. Owing to the amount and variety of executive business, the President must function through departmental offices, and these are created and to some extent controlled by Congress. On the other hand, the President shares in legislation through his veto power and his right to send as many messages as he chooses. Even the Supreme Court which is created by the Constitution lies at the mercy of Congress and the President, for Congress may prescribe the number of the judges and the President may refuse to enforce their decrees.

The Supremacy of the Judiciary. — The crowning feature of the federal system is the supremacy of the judiciary over all other branches of government in matters relating to the rights of persons and property — a supremacy resulting from the power of the courts to declare unconstitutional acts of the other branches of the government. In no European nation, federal or centralized in form of government, is the high authority of declaring null and void the acts of other departments conferred upon a judicial tribunal. This judicial supremacy, says Professor Burgess, is "the most momentous product of modern political science. Upon it far more than upon anything else depends the permanent existence of republican government; for elective government must be party government — majority government; and unless the domain of individual liberty is protected by an independent, unpolitical department, such government degenerates into party absolutism and then into Cæsarism."

It is the Supreme Court, therefore, that stands as the great defender of private property against the attempts of popular legislatures to encroach upon its fundamental privileges. This fact has been so clearly and cogently demonstrated by President Hadley of Yale University, that his statements deserve quotation at length. The theoretical position of property-holders, he says, — " the sum of the conditions which affect their standing for the long future and not for the immediate present — is far stronger in the United States [than in other countries]. The general status of the property-owner under the law cannot be changed by the action of the legislature, or the executive, or the people of a state voting at the polls, or all three put together. It cannot be changed without either a consensus of opinion among the judges, which should lead them to retrace their old views, or an amendment of the Constitution of the United States by the slow and cumbersome machinery provided for that purpose, or, last, — and I hope most improbable, — a revolution.

"When it is said, as it commonly is, that the fundamental division of powers in the modern State is into legislative, executive, and judicial, the student of American institutions may fairly note an exception. The fundamental division of powers in the Constitution of the United States is between voters on the one hand and property-owners on the other. The forces of democracy on one side, divided between the executive and the legislature, are set over against the forces of property on the other side, with the judiciary as arbiter between them; the Constitution itself not only forbidding the legislature and executive to trench upon the rights of property, but compelling the judiciary to define and uphold those rights in a manner provided by the Constitution itself.

"This theory of American politics has not often been stated. But it has been universally acted upon. One reason why it has not been more frequently stated is that it has been acted upon so universally that no American of earlier generations ever thought it necessary to state it. It has had the most fundamental and far-reaching effects upon the policy of the country. To mention but one thing among many, it has allowed the experiment of universal suffrage to be tried under conditions essentially different from those which led to its ruin in Athens or in Rome. The voter was omnipotent — within a limited area. He could make what laws he pleased, as long as those laws did not trench upon property right. He could elect what officers he pleased, as long as those officers did not try to do certain duties confided by the Constitution to the property-holders."

The Structure of the Federal Courts. — The Constitution of the United States makes only slight reference to the structure of the federal courts. It merely provides that the judicial power of the United States shall be vested in one Supreme Court and in such inferior courts as Congress may from time to time ordain and establish. It is thus within the power of Congress to determine the number of judges in the Supreme Court and to create any additional tribunals which may be deemed necessary for the transaction of federal business. Under these constitutional provisions Congress has created the following scheme of courts, the judges in which are appointed by the President and Senate to serve during good behavior:

1. At the head of the system stands the Supreme Court, composed of nine judges. This Court holds its sessions usually from October until May in the chamber of the Capitol formerly occupied by the United States Senate. The most important business that comes before it involves questions of constitutional law brought up from lower federal courts or from state courts on appeal or by writ of error.

2. Immediately under the Supreme Court is a Circuit Court of Appeals in each of the nine great circuits into which the United States is divided. In those circuits which have a large amount of business there are four judges, in the smaller circuits two judges, and in the remainder three judges, appointed by the President and Senate. Each of the Justices of the Supreme Court is assigned to one of the nine circuits.

3. The lowest federal court is the District Court. The whole country is laid out into some eighty or ninety districts, and in each of these there are appointed by the President and Senate one, two, three, or four district judges, according to the amount of business to be transacted. Each of the more sparsely populated states constitutes a single district; other states are divided into two or more districts; and the great state of New York is divided into four districts.

Each large district is usually divided into "divisions," and the law provides the dates and places for holding terms of the District Court within each division. By turning to the law, any one can find in what district he resides and the date and place for the term of court in his district or division, as the case may be. For example, the law of 1911 runs, " the state of New Hampshire shall constitute one judicial district to be known as the district of New Hampshire. The terms of the District Court shall be held at Portsmouth on the third Tuesdays in March and September; at Concord on the third Tuesdays in June and December; and at Littleton on the last Tuesday in August."

In close relation to the judiciary are the Department of Justice and the great army of United States attorneys and marshals in the judicial districts in the states and territories. The head of the Department of Justice is the Attorney-General of the United States, who is the chief law officer of the federal government. "He represents the United States in matters involving legal questions; he gives his advice and opinion when they are required by the President or by the heads of the other executive departments on questions of law arising in the administration of their respective departments; he appears in the Supreme Court of the United States in cases of especial gravity and importance; he exercises a general superintendence and direction over the United States attorneys and marshals in all the judicial districts in the states and territories; and he provides special counsel for the United States whenever required by any department of the government." The enforcement of important federal laws, therefore, depends largely upon the activity of the Attorney-General, or rather upon the pressure brought to bear upon him by the President.

In each of the judicial districts there is a United States district attorney, assisted by a number of deputies, who represents the government in the prosecution and defense of causes arising within his district. There is also in each district a marshal whose duty it is to enforce the orders of the federal courts, to arrest offenders against federal law, and to otherwise assist in the execution of that law. Both of these officers are appointed by the President and Senate.

The Federal Judicial Power. — The jurisdiction of the federal courts is defined in the Constitution. It embraces, on the one hand, cases affecting certain *persons* or *parties* and, on the other hand, cases relative to certain *matters*.

1. In the first place, the jurisdiction of the federal courts covers cases affecting ambassadors, other public ministers and consuls; controversies to which the United States is a party; controversies between two or more states, between a state and citizens of another state, between citizens of different states, and between a state or the citizens thereof and foreign states, citizens or subjects — with the provision that the judicial power shall not extend to any suit in law or equity commenced or prosecuted against one of the United States by American citizens or by citizens of foreign states. When any of these parties are involved in controversies, the case may come under federal judicial power, regardless of the nature of the matter in controversy. So much for the jurisdiction of the federal courts over parties.

2. In the next place, the federal judicial power extends to certain *matters*, regardless of the character of the parties involved in the controversy; that is, to all cases in law and equity arising under the Constitution, the statutes, and the treaties of the United States and to all admiralty and maritime cases.

A case, according to Story, arises "when some subject touching the Constitution, laws, or treaties of the United States is submitted to the courts by a party who asserts his rights in the form prescribed by law." In other words, a case in law or equity comes within the federal judicial power whenever a correct decision of the controversy involves in any way the interpretation of the Constitution or federal laws or treaties.

With the exception of two classes of cases, the Constitution does not say which of the federal courts shall have jurisdiction over any particular matter, but leaves the distribution of the judicial powers to Congress. The two exceptions are cases affecting ambassadors, other public ministers and consuls, and cases in which a state may be a party. Over such cases the Supreme Court, under the Constitution, has original, but not exclusive, jurisdiction; that is to say, whenever any such case arises, it may be taken into the Supreme Court in the very beginning, without having been previously tried in a lower court. Since, however, the Constitution does not confer exclusive jurisdiction in such matters, it is left for Congress to decide whether any other federal court or courts may also try these cases and under what limitations. Over all other cases falling within the scope of the federal judicial power, the Supreme Court has only *appellate* jurisdiction as to law and fact, subject to such exceptions and under such regulations as Congress may make.

SELECTED REFERENCES

Bryce, *The American Commonwealth; The Federalist* (edition in Everyman's Library); A. N. Holcombe, *State Government in the United States* (New York, 1916); W. B. Munro, *The Government of American Cities* (New York, 1912); C. A. Beard, *American Politics and Government* (New York, 1914); E. McLain, *Constitutional Law in the United States* (New York, 1907); J. Story, *Commentaries on the Constitution of the United States* (many editions); Woodrow Wilson, *Constitutional Government in the United States* (New York, 1908); C. A. Beard, *The Supreme Court and the Constitution*.

CHAPTER IV

THE CONGRESS: HOW LAWS ARE MADE

THE Congress of the United States is composed of two houses, a Senate representing the commonwealths in their corporate capacities, and a House of Representatives apportioned among the states according to their respective populations. Two leading motives were responsible for the adoption of this bicameral system. In the first place, it was necessary to secure the support of the smaller states for the new Constitution by granting them equality of power in one branch of the federal government. In the second place, the Fathers believed that some check was necessary upon the impulses and passions of the more popular body. Then, of course, they had before them the examples of the English Parliament and their colonial assemblies.

The House of Representatives: Qualifications and Apportionment of Members. — The number of members in the House of Representatives is fixed by Congress, subject to the limitation that it shall never exceed one for every 30,000 of the population. The first House consisted of sixty-five members, and, with one exception (the reapportionment of 1842) the number has been regularly increased until it has now reached 435. At each recurrence of the decennial apportionment there is a strong pressure on Congress to add more members to the already unwieldy assembly. However, with the growth of population the number of inhabitants in each congressional district has increased enormously, from about 33,000 in 1793 to about 215,000 at the apportionment of 1911. This makes a constituency of great size when compared with the parliamentary district in England or in France.

A member of the House of Representatives must be a citizen of the United States of at least seven years' standing; he must be not less than twenty-five years old and an inhabitant of the state in which he is chosen. He cannot be at the same time a military or civil officer of the United States; and nearly all of the states have, by law or constitutional provision, forbidden their officers to hold positions of trust under the federal government. Some states have gone further and provided that each member must be a resident of the district which he represents; but this restriction is regarded by most lawyers as unconstitutional, because it adds a qualification to those imposed by the federal Constitution. As a matter of fact, however, it is practically an unwritten law that the member must be a resident of his district, although there are a few exceptions, as for example in New York, where downtown constituencies are often represented by men residing in uptown districts.

While it seems clear that states cannot add qualifications to those imposed by the federal Constitution on members of Congress, it is conceded in practice that either house, in the exercise of its constitutional powers to be judge of the elections, returns, and qualifications of its members, may exclude persons on other grounds than those laid down in the Constitution. For example, in 1900, the House excluded Mr. Brigham H. Roberts of Utah on the ground that he was a polygamist. The Constitution also provides that no person holding any office under the United States shall be a member of either house during his continuance in office.

Members of the House of Representatives are apportioned among the several states according to their respective numbers, counting the whole number of persons in each state, exclusive of Indians not taxed — subject, however, to the limitation that each state must have at least one Representative. Until 1842, Congress left the states to their own devices in election methods, but in that year the Apportionment Act provided, " that in every case where a state is entitled to more than one Representative the number to which each state shall be entitled under this apportionment shall be elected by districts composed of contiguous territory, equal in number to the number of Representatives to which said state may be entitled, no one district electing more than one Representative." It is now the rule of Congress to require that congressional districts shall be composed of "contiguous and compact territory containing as nearly as practicable an equal number of inhabitants," each district electing only one Representative, except in the case that, if the state legislature fails to carry out this exact provision, certain or all of the members may be elected at large on a general ticket.[1]

Notwithstanding the intention of Congress to provide for substantially equal congressional districts, our state legislatures have succeeded in creating, principally for partisan purposes, the grossest inequalities. On comparing the total number of votes cast in congressional districts, we find also the greatest discrepancies. For example, in 1906 a Mississippi district with a population of 232,174 cast 1540 votes, while a New York district with a population of 215,305 cast 29,119 votes. In New York in 1906 there were 58,190 voters in the twenty-third congressional district, and only 13,862 voters in the ninth congressional district. These differences, of course, are not due entirely to the gerrymander,[2] for representation is not based on the number of voters, but on the population.

This misuse of the power of creating congressional districts, known as "gerrymandering," has been devised as a means by which a dominant party can make its own vote go as far as possible in congressional elections and cause its opponent's vote to count for as little as possible. This is done by massing the voters of the opposing party in a small number of districts, giving them overwhelming majorities there, while allowing the dominant party to carry the other districts by very small minorities.

The district system under the gerrymander has frequently resulted in the grossest misrepresentation of party strength in the House of Representatives. For example, in 1894, the Republicans, with a vote of 5,461,202, elected 245 Representatives; the

[1] Alaska, Hawaii, and Porto Rico have one delegate each in the House of Representatives, and the Philippine Islands have two delegates. These delegates have seats in the House, and may speak there, but they have no vote.
[2] The term "gerrymander" originated in Massachusetts. It appears that Elbridge Gerry, a distinguished Democratic politician of his day, was instrumental in redistricting his state in such a way that one of the districts had the shape of a lizard. When an artist saw the map of the new district, he declared, "Why, this district looks like a salamander," and gave it a few finishing touches with his pencil. The editor, in whose office the map was hanging, replied, "Say rather a gerrymander," and thus an ancient party practice was given a new name.

Democrats, with 4,295,748 votes, elected 104 Representatives, and the Populists, with 1,323,644 votes, elected 7 Representatives, while the Prohibitionists, with 182,679 votes, elected none. Taking the vote as a whole on a strict basis of equality of representation, the Republican majority of 134 should have been a minority of 7 as against all other parties.

House of Representatives: Terms and Elections of Members. — The term of the members of the House is two years — a short period which has received so much criticism recently that it is difficult for us to understand the necessity that led *The Federalist* to apologize for the action of the Philadelphia convention in not providing for annual elections. Unless there is a special session their term of office is practically half expired when members take their seats; and within a year, if they expect to continue in Congress, they must enter into a campaign for renomination and election. This may have a double effect. It diverts the attention and energy of the member from his official duties, and, if he is defeated, it leaves him disgruntled and more subject to pernicious influences. It is a well-known fact also that no member of Congress can exert a considerable influence during one term of service, since it requires a great deal of practical experience to discover the mysteries of congressional procedure and get a hearing from the leaders in the House.

The time, place, and manner of holding elections for Representatives may be prescribed by the state legislature subject to the provision that Congress may at any time by law make or alter such regulations. For almost a hundred years congressional elections were held at different times and according to the different methods prevailing in the various states — the old system of viva voce voting being retained for a long time in some commonwealths. At length, Congress, by laws passed in 1871 and 1872, provided that congressional elections should be by ballot and that they should occur throughout the Union at the same time, that is, on the Tuesday following the first Monday in November. An exception to the uniformity rule allows Maine to hold its elections somewhat earlier, according to the former custom.

Party machinery has been developed in every state for nominating candidates to the House of Representatives. Where the older methods have not been overthrown by primary legislation, candidates are nominated by district conventions of delegates representing units of local government within the congressional districts, such as counties in the regions more thinly populated, and assembly districts, townships, or wards in the more thickly settled areas. In a large number of states, however, including Wisconsin, Nebraska, New York, Oregon, Kansas, and Oklahoma, the convention system has been abolished altogether, and an official direct primary election is provided for each party. Any member of any party who wishes to be a candidate for Congress must have his name put on the party primary ballot by petition, and at the primary election the party voters are given the opportunity to select from among the several candidates on this ballot. Representatives-at-large are nominated by state conventions or by state primaries.

The House of Representatives and the Senate are the judges of the election, returns, and qualifications of their own members, and therefore contested elections are not determined by a judicial tribunal as in England. The House has committees on elections, whose duty it is to investigate and report on election contests.

The Senate. — The Constitution prescribes that there shall be two Senators from each state, and in the Amendment clause it provides that no state, without its consent, shall be deprived of equal representation in the Senate. This rule of absolute equality grew out of the fear of Maryland, Connecticut, and Delaware that the great commonwealths of New York, Pennsylvania, and Virginia would override them in federal matters; and out of apprehension entertained by the agricultural and slave-owning states that the numerical strength of the manufacturing and commercial states would lead to discriminating legislation. Thus it happens that nine eastern states, Maine, New Hampshire, Vermont, Massachusetts, Rhode Island, Connecticut, New York, New Jersey, and Pennsylvania, with a population of over 21,000,000 in 1900, had only eighteen Senators; while nine western states, Montana, Wyoming, Colorado, Utah, Idaho, Washington, Nevada, Oregon, and California, with a total population of less than 4,000,000, had the same number.

The qualifications of the Senator are fixed by the Constitution. He must be not less than thirty years old, an inhabitant of the state for which he is elected, and a United States citizen of nine years' standing. The same question has arisen here as in the case of the House of Representatives, whether the Senate, under its power to judge of the qualifications of its members, can add any to those fixed in the Constitution. The correct answer to this question seems to have been made in January, 1907, at a time when an attempt to exclude Mr. Reed Smoot of Utah, on the ground that he was a polygamist, was defeated. It was then said that neither the Senate, Congress, nor a state can add to the qualifications prescribed by the Constitution; that the power given to the Senate is merely to judge whether Senators have the qualifications prescribed by the Constitution.

Previous to 1913, Senators were elected by the state legislatures, but in that year a constitutional amendment providing for election by popular vote was adopted. The amendment provides that the two Senators from each state shall be " elected by the people thereof for six years. . . . The electors in each state shall have the qualifications requisite for electors of the most numerous branch of the state legislature. When vacancies happen in the representation of any state in the Senate, the executive authority of the state shall issue writs of election to fill such vacancies: Provided that the legislature of any state may empower the executive thereof to make temporary appointments until the people fill the vacancies by election as the legislature may direct."

The term of the Senator is fixed at six years, and in practice Senators are far more frequently reëlected than members of the House of Representatives. At least five Senators, Benton of Missouri, Morrill of Vermont, Allison of Iowa, Jones of Nevada, and John Sherman of Ohio, served thirty years or more. The tendency toward reëlection was once more marked in the smaller states, perhaps because competition was not so keen.

The terms of all the Senators do not expire at any one time, for the Senate is a continuous body, one-third of the members going out every two years, and, except in extraordinary cases arising from deadlocks, resignation, or death, it seldom happens that a state is called upon to elect two Senators at the same time. At the first session of the Senate in 1789, that body divided its membership by lot into three classes, the seats of the first class being vacated at the expiration of the second year, of the second class at the expiration of the fourth year, and of the third class at the expiration of the sixth year, thus making way for a renewal of only one-third of the Senate biennially.

Privileges of Members of Congress. — Members of the Congress of the United States are entitled to certain privileges by virtue of their position. First among these may be reckoned compensation. The Constitution provides that Senators and Representatives shall receive a compensation for their services, to be ascertained by law and paid out of the treasury of the United States. Up until 1855, it was the custom to pay members a certain per diem allowance; in that year a salary of $3000 per annum was voted. In 1907, the salary of Senators and Representatives was fixed at $7500 per annum, to which is added an allowance for clerk hire, stationery, and traveling expenses.

The second privilege enjoyed by members of Congress is freedom from arrest during their attendance on the sessions of their respective houses, and in going to and returning from the same, in all cases except treason, felony, and breach of the peace. This privilege, as Story points out, exempts Representatives and Senators from all processes, the disobedience of which is punishable by imprisonment. That is, a congressman, during the period mentioned above, cannot be compelled to testify in a court, serve on a jury, or respond to an action brought against him. The term " breach of the peace," however, extends to " all indictable offenses, as well those which are in fact attended with force and violence as those which are only destructive to the peace of the government "; and, therefore, the member of Congress really enjoys no exemption from the ordinary processes of the criminal law. In going to and coming from Congress the member is allowed reasonable delays and reasonable deviations from the nearest course.

The third privilege enjoyed by members of Congress is freedom of speech during debate. The Constitution expressly provides that for any speech or debate no member of either house shall be questioned in any other place. The effect of this privilege is to free the members from the liability to prosecution for libel or slander for anything said in Congress, or in committees, in official publications, or in the legitimate discharge of their legislative duties. Members of Congress also constantly act upon the supposition that the privilege includes the right to circulate their speeches, not only among their own constituents, but anywhere throughout the United States.

The internal organization of each house of Congress is limited by certain provisions of the Constitution. The Vice-President of the United States is made the presiding officer of the Senate; neither house can expel a member for a breach of its rules except on a two-thirds vote, a quorum being present; each house must keep a journal of its proceedings and publish the same from time to time, except such parts as it may deem necessary to keep secret; if one-fifth of the members present in either house demand a record of the yeas and nays upon the journal with regard to any question, that record must be taken by roll-call. Subject to these limitations, each house has the right to elect its own officers, compel the attendance of members, and prescribe rules of procedure and discipline. Each house may also punish its own members for disorderly behavior, and, with the concurrence of two-thirds, expel a member; but it has been held by the Court that the power of Congress to punish its members or private citizens is confined to the session in which the condemnation occurs, and cannot extend beyond imprisonment during the remainder of that session.

The quorum necessary to do business in each house is fixed by the Constitution at a majority of all the members, but a smaller number may adjourn from day to day, and are authorized to compel the attendance of absent members. This question of the quorum is no formal matter. It is necessary to fix the number at a majority of the members in order to prevent " snap " legislation by minorities, but the rule is often attended with serious inconveniences.

For a long time it was a common practice for the minority party in the House of Representatives, whenever it desired to delay business, to refuse to answer the roll-call, and thus frequently compel an adjournment, on the ground that there was no quorum present, until a quorum could be mustered. To stop " filibustering," as such dilatory tactics were called, Speaker

Reed, in January, 1890, held that members present in the House and declining to answer should be counted present in determining the question of a quorum. Shortly afterward the House embodied this principle in a rule authorizing the clerk, on demand of a member or at the suggestion of the Speaker, to count as present those physically present but refusing to answer the roll-call.

The Sessions of Congress. — The Constitution requires an annual session of Congress, and provides that it shall begin on the first Monday in December, unless Congress, by law, shall appoint a different day. Each Congress, therefore, has normally two sessions. The first, known as the long session, begins in December of each odd year, 1919, 1921, 1923, etc., and extends theoretically until the following December, though as a matter of practice it is usually adjourned sometime in the spring or summer — in 1890 the long session was not adjourned until the first of the following October. The second session of each Congress begins in December of each even year, 1918, 1920, 1922, etc., and extends until the following March 4. Every Congress, therefore, expires at noon on March 4 of the odd year, thus giving the President at the very opening of his administration a new Congress. By postponing the session until autumn the President has time to prepare for his legislative duties.

It will be noted that, according to this arrangement, a member of the House of Representatives does not take his seat until more than a year after his election; that is, he is elected in November of the even year, and, unless a special session is called, does not begin his legislative work until one year from the December immediately following. Thus it happens that an expiring House sits for about four months after the election of the members of the new House, and an important measure may be passed by a party which the country has voted down at the preceding election.

Special sessions of Congress may be called by the President under his power to convene either house or both of them on extraordinary occasions. The Senate is often called at the beginning of a new administration to confirm appointments.

The House and Senate Compared. — The difference in the organization of the two houses makes it necessary to say a few words by way of comparison. The Senate is, of course, the smaller body, being composed of ninety-six members, as against 435 members in the House of Representatives. The Senate, generally speaking, is also composed of older men and men of wider political experience. The Senators as a rule have been in some branch of state government or in the House of Representatives. As the term of service is longer and the chances for reëlection greater, the Senate usually contains a relatively larger number of political experts, acquainted not only with the problems of law-making, but also with the inner workings of the federal government. The influence of the Senators is also augmented by their position as party leaders within their respective states. They have, as we have seen, a large power in appointing to federal office; and sometimes they are able to construct political machines of extraordinary strength. They usually have great weight in selecting delegates to national party conventions, and in fact they are largely responsible for the predominance of the federal office-holding element in those assemblies. This command over party resources within their states enables the Senators to bring more or less pressure on the members of their party in the House of Representatives. When the state organization, in close touch with its Senator or Senators, adopts a policy, it is usually wise for the member of the House of Representatives, if he expects further party favors, to fall in line with the policy. The political power of the Senate is greatly augmented by its control over treaties and appointments.

Powers of Congress: Taxation, National Defense, Commerce. — A general view of all the powers of Congress is simply indispensable to an understanding of current politics, for questions of constitutionality underlie all of our political controversies over the powers of the federal and state governments, over centralization and state rights, over national and local reforms. Every student of American government should have definitely and clearly fixed in mind the various powers conferred upon Congress — not as mere rules of law, but as great principles of political practice controlling the national legislature in its manifold relations to the life of the people in every territory and commonwealth of the American empire.

I. In relation to revenue and expenditures, Congress has the power to lay and collect taxes, duties, imposts, and excises, and to appropriate money, in order to pay the debts and provide for the common defense and general welfare of the United States. This power is not unlimited. Indirect taxes, duties, imposts, and excises must be uniform throughout the United States — that is, must be imposed at the same rate on the same article wherever found. Poll taxes, taxes on real and personal property, and other direct taxes, except income taxes from all sources, must be apportioned among the states according to population. Congress cannot tax exports from a state, and under an interpretation by the Supreme Court cannot tax the "necessary instrumentalities" of a state government, such as the salaries of state and local officers, and state and municipal bonds.

II. In respect to national defense, the powers of Congress are practically unlimited, except by the provision that the President shall be commander-in-chief and that military appropriations shall not be made for a greater period than two years. Congress can raise and support armies, create and maintain a navy, and provide for the organization and use of the state militia. Congress also declares war, grants letters of marque and reprisal authorizing officers or private parties to capture property and persons subject to a foreign power; and makes rules concerning captures on land and sea.

III. In respect to commerce and business, Congress may regulate commerce with foreign countries, among the several states, and with the Indian tribes; make uniform laws on the subject of bankruptcy throughout the United States; fix the standards of weights and measures; protect authors and inventors by a system of patents and copyrights; and establish post-offices and post-roads. Commerce not only includes the transportation of commodities; it embraces traffic and intercourse in all of its important branches, such as the transportation of passengers, the transmission of telegraph messages, and the carrying of oil through pipe lines. It is sometimes stated that the power of regulating interstate and foreign commerce is vested exclusively in Congress, but the difficulty of determining when a state law constitutes such a regulation is so great that the mere statement does not carry any very concise information. The power of Congress over bankruptcy is not exclusive; the states may legislate on the subject. The federal law, however, takes precedence in case of a conflict with the provisions of a commonwealth law, and Congress by an act of 1898 has covered the entire domain of bankruptcy.

With regard to weights and measures Congress could, if it saw fit, establish a uniform metric system throughout the United States, but it has only gone so far as to make the use of this system lawful, not obligatory. Meanwhile the regulations of the various states prevail, although the federal government aids in securing scientific exactness by maintaining in the Department of Commerce an important bureau of standards.

The protection of authors and inventors by a system of copyrights and patents is intrusted to Congress; but it is contended by some publicists that this power is concurrent and may be exercised by any state so long as its laws do not contravene the express provision of the federal law. This point, however, has not been authoritatively adjudicated.

For administrative purposes Congress has created a bureau of patents in the Department of the Interior, headed by a commissioner, who administers the patent laws, issues patents for new inventions and improvements, and registers trade-marks, prints, labels, and the like.

The copyright law has been steadily extended to new devices, until it now covers not only books, but also works of art, maps, charts, musical compositions, and the like. For more than a century Congress extended copyright protection only to citizens and residents of the United States, and during that time American publishers, with a few honorable exceptions, regularly " pirated " the works of foreign authors, that is, published them in the United States without paying any royalty or other compensation. Under the act of March 3, 1891, it was at last provided that the citizens of any foreign state which gives to citizens of the United States the benefit of copyright on practically the same basis as their own citizens, may be given the privileges of our copyright laws. As a result, citizens of the United States may claim the protection of foreign countries coming under the terms of the act, and citizens of foreign countries in turn may obtain the protection of our laws.

While the power to establish post-offices and post-roads is

separately conferred upon Congress, it may be regarded, for practical purposes, in connection with the power to regulate commerce. The establishment of post-offices and post-roads is exclusively a federal matter, and it must be noted that the power of the federal government covers the whole domain of mail transportation, within each state as well as among the states.

Powers of Congress: Foreign Relations, Money, Crimes, and Territories. — IV. The direct power of Congress, as a body, over foreign relations is slight, because the President and Senate have the treaty-making power, and the President is our official spokesman in the conduct of all business with foreign countries. Congress, however, may, as we have seen, regulate foreign commerce, including the important branch of immigration; create consular and diplomatic posts abroad and provide the emoluments thereunto attached; define and punish piracies and felonies committed on the high seas and offenses against the law of nations. Congress may also establish a uniform rule by which the subjects of foreign powers may become citizens of the United States. While this power of prescribing the conditions for naturalization is regarded as being vested exclusively in Congress, it must be remembered that the states may, and many of them do, confer on aliens the right to vote.

V. The regulation of the monetary system is vested exclusively in the federal legislature. Congress has power to coin money, regulate its value, and the value of foreign coin. States are forbidden to coin money, emit bills of credit, or make anything but the gold and silver coin of the United States a tender in the payment of debts. There is nothing in the Constitution expressly authorizing Congress to create paper money, but it has exercised this power and has been sustained by a decision of the Supreme Court.

VI. The power of Congress to define crimes and provide punishments for them is narrowly limited. The high crime of treason, as indicated above, is expressly defined in the Constitution: it consists only in levying war against the United States, adhering to its enemies, or giving them aid and comfort. Congress cannot therefore make any offense which it chooses treason. Congress may provide for punishing counterfeiters and persons committing crimes on the high seas or offenses against the laws of nations.

Congress may also define certain crimes against federal laws and provide penalties. For example, it has provided punishment for theft and other offenses connected with the transportation of mail matter.

VII. The government of the territories and districts belonging to the United States is vested in the federal authorities. Congress has the power to dispose of and make all needful rules and regulations respecting the territory or other property belonging to the United States, to exercise exclusive legislation in all cases whatsoever over the District of Columbia, and over all places purchased by the federal government (with the consent of the state legislatures concerned) for the erection of forts, magazines, arsenals, dockyards, and other needful buildings. The right to admit new states and supervise the organization of territories into states is also vested in Congress; and the process to be followed in the admission or organization of a new state is left to the determination of that body.

Powers of Congress: Executive Department and Judiciary. — VIII. Notwithstanding the theory of the separation of powers, Congress may to some extent control the various executive departments by statutes regulating even the minutest duties of the Cabinet officers. As we shall see, the Constitution merely hints at the existence of the executive departments; but the power to determine the number of such departments and to provide for the internal organization of each is, nevertheless, exercised by Congress. How far it may use this authority to control the President's high personal advisers is a matter of dispute that cannot be settled by any abstract definitions; but it may exercise a substantial dominion over executive departments under its power to fix salaries and define duties.

IX. Congress may also exercise in practice a large power over the federal judiciary, notwithstanding the theoretical independence of that branch of the government; because it may determine the number of Supreme Court judges, fix their salaries, subject to certain limits, and define their appellate jurisdiction. The creation of inferior federal courts is subject to its power; and it may define the jurisdiction and procedure of these courts and provide the methods by which cases may be drawn from the state courts into the federal courts.

Powers of Congress: Impeachment. — X. In addition to controlling, to a limited extent, the federal judicial system, Congress itself enjoys the power of removing the civil officers of the United States by the process of impeachment, but in practice this power is of slight importance. In trying cases of impeachment, the Senate acts as the high court. When the President of the United States is being tried, the Chief Justice of the Supreme Court presides. It requires a two-thirds vote of the members present to convict.

The power of preferring and prosecuting charges against offenders is vested in the House of Representatives. In practice, whenever the House decides to bring any federal officer before the bar of the Senate, it adopts, by resolution, articles of impeachment charging the particular offender with certain high crimes and misdemeanors and enumerating with more or less detail his particular offenses. It thereupon chooses leaders to direct the prosecution before the Senate, and the case is then conducted very much in the form of a trial in an ordinary court. The prosecution states its case; witnesses for and against the accused are heard; and attorneys on both sides make their arguments. When the case is fully presented the Senators vote, and if two-thirds of the members present concur in holding the accused guilty, he stands convicted; but in case of failure to secure the requisite two-thirds, he is acquitted.

The penalty which the Senate can impose upon any person convicted in case of impeachment is strictly limited to the removal of the offender from office and the imposition of a disqualification to hold and enjoy any office of honor, trust, or profit under the United States. Any person convicted, however, is still liable, after his removal from office, to indictment, trial, judgment, and punishment for his offense according to law. It is not obligatory upon the Senate to disqualify the convicted person from entering the federal service in the future, but in any case he must be immediately removed from office.

The jurisdiction of the Senate as a court of impeachment extends only over the President, Vice-President, and the civil officers of the United States, and over the offenses of treason, bribery, or other high crimes and misdemeanors. Treason is, of course, defined in the Constitution; and the meaning of the term "bribery" is clear to all. The phrase "other high crimes and misdemeanors," however, is somewhat vague, and Congress might give a loose interpretation to it, even going so far as to treat the neglect of official duty as a ground for impeachment. Nevertheless, a conservative interpretation has generally been placed upon this phrase, so as to limit the offenses, which render an officer liable to impeachment, to crimes and misdemeanors as understood in the ordinary law of the land.

Federal military officers are exempt from this jurisdiction, being subject to courts-martial. Members of Congress are also exempt, for they are not technically "civil officers," and furthermore they are under the control of their respective houses — each house having the power to determine its rules and proceedings, punish its members for disorderly behavior, and, with the concurrence of two-thirds, expel a member.

XI. In carrying into execution the powers vested by the Constitution in the government of the United States or in any department or office thereof, Congress may make all laws which shall be deemed "necessary and proper." The courts have, in general, given a liberal interpretation to this phrase. The Supreme Court has repeatedly declared that Congress possesses the right to use any means which it deems conducive to the exercise of any express power. Said the Court in the case of Juilliard v. Greenman: "The words 'necessary and proper' are not limited to such measures as are absolutely and indispensably necessary, without which the powers granted must fail of execution; but they include all the proper means which are conducive or adapted to the end to be accomplished and which, in the judgment of Congress, will most advantageously effect it."

Party Organization and Leadership in Congress. — I. In attempting to understand the operations of Congress it is first necessary to realize that the working methods of that body are largely determined by the existence of two political parties — one, a majority in control of one or both houses and regarding itself as responsible for the principal legislative policies; the other, a minority, in opposition, bound under ordinary circumstances to criticize and often vote against the measures introduced and advanced by the majority. In England, the political party organization is carried frankly into the House of

Commons, where the majority and minority sit facing each other, and where the government is avowedly that of the predominant party — a government of men, not even theoretically of constitutional law. In the United States, the party rules none the less, but its organization and operations are, as we have seen, unknown to the formal law of the federal Constitution. It is true that the votes on measures in Congress are by no means always cast according to party divisions, but it is likewise true that the principal legislative work of a session is the work of the majority party, formulated by its leaders, and carried through under their direction.

This is not all. Each party in the Senate and the House is organized into a congressional caucus, in which is frequently determined the line of party action with regard to important legislative questions. It is in a party caucus before the opening of each Congress that the majority in the House chooses the Speaker and the minority decides upon its leader whom it formally presents as a candidate for Speaker, knowing full well that he cannot by any chance be elected. It is in the caucus that the majority decides whether it will adopt the rules of the preceding Congress or modify them; and it is seldom that the decision of the caucus is overthrown. The caucus is definitely organized under rules by which party members are expected to abide, although there are often a few "insurgents" who insist on acting independently on some matters.

The Mass of Business before Congress. — II. The second important fact to grasp is that each session of Congress is confronted by an enormous amount of business — from five to twenty times as much as can be considered adequately. Each Congress has to consider from 25,000 to 30,000 bills and resolutions. Any member may introduce as many bills as he pleases by handing them to the clerk if they are of a private nature, or to the Speaker if they are of a public character. He does not have to secure any permission in advance or assume any responsibility for them, even though they may involve heavy charges upon the public treasury.

This looks like a fair, just, and simple matter, but in fact it is largely responsible for the extravagance and confusion that exist in the federal government and for the iron-bound methods that are followed in the procedure of the House. Inasmuch as each member seeks a large number of special appropriations for his own particular district, he is always willing to be generous with the claims of other members in return for a favorable consideration of his own. This practice of coöperating in securing appropriations is known as " log-rolling " — a term derived from pioneer times when frontiersmen helped one another in rolling logs, making clearings, and building cabins. It is owing to this system that national interests are often subordinated to particular and local interests.

It is idle, however, to criticize members of Congress, for they are not individually at fault. Any one of them who refused to join in this general scramble for the division of spoils would find himself speedily retired by the organized element among his constituents, and perhaps by the vote of his constituents, for they are generally prone to measure the achievements of their Representative by the size of the appropriations he secures for the district and the number of bills he introduces and carries. The power to select from the numerous measures before the House must be vested in the hands of some person or group of persons, for the selection cannot be made openly on the floor by any automatic process which brings every measure to the consideration of that body. The persons invested with the power of selection in the House must of necessity be leaders among the majority party, for that party assumes responsibility before the country for the results of a legislative session. In the House these leaders are the Speaker, the committee on rules, and the chairmen of the principal committees to which bills are referred; and the rules provide ways by which they can make selections of business for consideration and limit the amount of time which may be consumed in debate on each measure.

The Rules of the House of Representatives. — III. The rules, therefore, must enable the presiding officer of the House to prevent the consideration of any motion introduced merely for the purpose of delaying business. They must limit, or make provision for limiting, the amount of time which may be consumed in debating any particular matter. They must provide some way in which the party leaders can force the consideration of certain measures whenever they see fit. These principles have slowly been evolved in the development of the House of Representatives, and are now written in the rules of that body.

1. In the first place, the Speaker of the House may refuse to put motions which he regards as dilatory; that is, designed merely to delay business. The immediate cause for the adoption of this principle was the practice of filibustering [1] by the minority or by small groups.

2. In the second place, the Speaker may count as present those members who are physically present but refuse to answer to their names on a roll-call for the purpose of compelling an adjournment in the absence of a quorum.

3. In the third place, the rules provide a method for automatically shortening debate by prescribing that the time occupied by any member in discussing a legislative proposition shall not exceed one hour. This limit was imposed in 1841, and at the time Senator Benton declared that it was " the largest limitation upon the freedom of debate which any deliberative assembly ever imposed upon itself, and presents an eminent instance of permanent injury done to free institutions in order to get rid of a temporary annoyance." It is difficult to see, however, in what way the House could meet the enormous pressure upon it, if any member from among the 435 could talk as long as he pleased on any measure.

4. In the fourth place, in order to enable party leaders to force the consideration of certain measures whenever they see fit, several of the important committees may report on the subjects enumerated practically at any time in the course of the procedure of the House, no matter what may be under discussion.

The Senate also has its code of rules, but it has not adopted any of the drastic methods obtaining in the House. When the Senate rules were revised in 1806, the right to move the previous question, and thus close debate summarily, was omitted, and all attempts to restore it have failed. In 1917, however, the rules

[1] In ordinary use, the word "filibuster" means to act as a freebooter or buccaneer, but in parliamentary practice it means "to obstruct legislation by undue use of the technicalities of parliamentary law or privileges, as when a minority, in order to prevent the passage of some measure obnoxious to them, endeavor to tire out their opponents by useless motions, speeches, and objections." Frequently, the purpose of a filibuster is to call the attention of the country in an emphatic way to the policy of the majority.

were modified in such a manner as to permit a two-thirds majority by due procedure to bring any important matter to a vote.

The direction of business in the Senate is in the hands of the chairman of the majority caucus and his immediate friends. The general direction and coördination of legislative business in both houses is vested in an unofficial " steering committee " composed of several leading Senators and members of the House.

The Committees of Congress. — IV. As a part of the system by which the two houses endeavor to deal with the enormous mass of business coming before them, there has been evolved an extensive scheme of standing committees. The student of our national government should therefore bear in mind the fact that the legislative work of each house is done largely by committees and that every important committee is controlled by a majority of members representing the dominant party.

The committees vary greatly in importance. In the lower house, the leading committees are on ways and means, appropriations, rules, banking and currency, interstate and foreign commerce, rivers and harbors, military affairs, naval affairs, post-office and post-roads, public lands, labor, and pensions. In the Senate, the committees on appropriations, finance, commerce, foreign relations, judiciary, military affairs, naval affairs, interstate commerce, and pensions take high rank.

Formerly all standing committees of the House of Representatives were appointed by the Speaker, but this system was changed in 1910-1911 in favor of an election by the House itself. The difference in practice made by this change in the rules is more apparent than real. Since the beginning of the party system in the United States, the selection of the members of committees has been in the hands of the caucus of each party, under the leadership, and perhaps dominance, of a few men experienced in the arts of management. The minority party chooses representatives on each committee, somewhat in the same manner, but they seldom count for much in the determination of policies.

Every bill, important or unimportant, is sent to the committee having jurisdiction over the subject-matter to which it relates. The recommendations contained in the President's message are likewise so distributed. Quite frequently the committees originate the bills — especially appropriation bills — relating to the matters placed under their jurisdiction.

Thousands of bills which go to committees are not considered at all, but a measure which a committee reports receives an analysis and criticism more or less severe, according to the character of the bill. On a measure of vital importance, papers and documents relating to the subject may be secured from the head of the executive department to whose duties it relates; or the officer himself may be requested to appear personally and answer a multitude of questions propounded by the committee members. Friends and opponents of the measures pending in committees are frequently admitted to state the reasons for their positions; hearings may even be held in various points throughout the country, and witnesses may be required to attend the committee meetings and give evidence very much in the same manner as in a courtroom. With regard to any measure referred to it, a committee may recommend its adoption, amend it, report adversely, delay the report indefinitely, or ignore it altogether. In the House it rarely happens that a member is able to secure the consideration of a bill which the committee in charge opposes; but in the Senate a greater freedom is enjoyed in this respect.

Owing to the pressure of business in the House, it is impossible to consider each bill on its merits and arrive at a vote after searching debate and mature deliberation; and within recent years even very important measures have been forced through as they have come from committee without any serious debate or a single amendment. This, of course, places an enormous power in the hands of committees and changes the House from a deliberative into a ratifying assembly. There has been a great deal of criticism of the committee system, but no acceptable substitute has as yet been suggested.

Leadership in the House of Representatives. — V. In every large body with a great amount of business to transact there must be some directing authority to see that the necessary measures are disposed of promptly, and to prevent procedure from falling into chaos. In England, this leadership is avowedly vested in the Prime Minister, who is the acknowledged head of the cabinet and the majority party in the House of Commons, and is chiefly responsible for the successful realization of the party policy in Parliament. The Speaker of the House of Commons under these circumstances does not feel any responsibility in the matter, and accordingly maintains an attitude of impartiality in his rulings and decisions — at least in theory. In the beginning of our federal government, the Speaker of the House of Representatives was regarded as a mere moderator, but as the House grew in size and the business to be transacted increased enormously, it became impossible for him to sit passively and see the measures of his party delayed or defeated by the dilatory tactics of the minority.

In time it happened that the Speakership of the House in the hands of powerful men like Thomas B. Reed and Joseph Cannon tended to develop into an office akin to that of the Prime Minister. Through the aid of various devices, a perfect system of control over all business of the House was built up by Republican leaders during the long tenure of that party from 1897 to 1911. The Speaker, Mr. Cannon, appointed all of the committees and named the chairman of each; in conjunction with the rules committee and the chairmen of a few powerful committees he completely dominated the procedure of the House.

Against this system the Democrats protested, as a matter of course, for it destroyed their influence in the House; and on securing possession of the House in 1911, they provided that *all* committees should be elected by the House. This change in the machinery for selecting committees was no doubt more nominal than real, because the selection is still made in caucuses as before. The prestige of the Speaker is, however, somewhat reduced, and more power is thus transferred, to other party leaders, particularly the chairman of the ways and means committee.

The Transaction of Legislative Business in the House. — VI. With this preliminary survey of some of the institutions and practices of Congress, we are better able to understand the procedure of this body from day to day. At the opening of a new Congress the House of Representatives is called to order by the clerk of the last House, who calls the roll, and, finding a quorum present, announces that they are ready for nominations for Speaker. The majority and minority put forward their candidates, and after the former's nominee is duly ratified, he takes the oath of office administered by the member longest in continuous service of the House. The roll is called by the clerk, and the Representatives go forward to be sworn in. The other officers are chosen, and the President of the United States and the Senate are informed that the House is ready for business. The question of the adoption of the rules of the preceding Congress is then threshed out, and usually carried in the face of the traditional protests of the minority. In due time the names of the committeemen selected by the caucuses of the parties are read, and approved by the House.

The Senate differs from the House in being a continuous body. At each new Congress only one-third of the members are renewed. The presiding officer, the Vice-President, as required by the Constitution, takes the chair. In case of his absence, his duties are performed by a president *pro tempore*. The newly elected Senators are called in alphabetical order by the secretary of the Senate, and each Senator in turn is escorted to the presiding officer's desk, usually by the colleague from his state, and there takes the oath of office. The President and House are duly notified, and then the Senate is also ready for work.

Bills are introduced in the House in several ways. Any member may introduce any measure he likes by drafting it and depositing it on the clerk's table, or he may introduce a petition for a bill which will be referred to an appropriate committee for drafting. All really important bills, however, such as tariff bills, currency measures, and the like are drafted by the majority members of the committee in charge of the subject-matter. Sometimes, the committee of the House coöperates with the committee of the Senate having charge of similar business, in preparing a bill. If the matter is very important and the President of the United States is interested, he may join with some of the committee members in drafting the bill; and prominent party leaders not in office may be consulted. A caucus of party members may be held on the bill even before it is introduced.

On their introduction, all public bills are referred by the Speaker to the appropriate committees, which may hold hearings and give the matters any amount of attention they see fit. The committee may report the bill to the House favorably un-

THE CONGRESS: HOW LAWS ARE MADE

amended, or it may amend it and report it in such form, or it may report unfavorably, or it may neglect it altogether.

The important committees, which may report at any time, report from the floor, and other committees report by laying their reports on the clerk's table.

Unless it is a highly privileged matter, a bill, when reported, is placed on a calendar for debate according to the rules.

All public bills raising revenue or authorizing the appropriation of money or property are considered in the committee of the whole House. In this form, one hundred constitute a quorum and the Speaker resigns the chair to some other member.

Bills not required to be considered in the committee of the whole House are read a second time when they are reached on the calendar and are then open to discussion and amendment in the House.

The third reading usually takes place by title and the question is put by the Speaker as a matter of course.

When a bill has passed either house, it is transmitted to the other body for consideration. For example, when the Senate has passed a bill, it thereupon dispatches it to the House. If the House passes the measure the Senate is notified; the bill is then signed by the President of the Senate and the Speaker of the House, and is sent to the President of the United States for his signature. If he approves the bill, he notifies the house in which it originated of his action, and sends it to the Secretary of State for official publication. If he vetoes the measure, he returns the bill to the house in which it originated, with a statement of the reasons for his action. A two-thirds vote of each house is necessary to enact a measure into law over the President's veto. If Congress adjourns before the President has acted on a measure, he may simply refuse to sign it or he may veto it and file it away.

SELECTED REFERENCES

Woodrow Wilson, *Congressional Government;* H. J. Ford, *The Cost of Government* (New York, 1910); E. C. Mason, *The Veto Power* (1891); M. P. Follett, *The Speaker of the House of Representatives* (1904); C. R. Fish, *The Civil Service and the Patronage* (1905); H. B. Fuller, *Speakers of the House* (1909); Bryce, *American Commonwealth*, Vol. I; Woodrow Wilson, *Constitutional Government in the United States.*

CHAPTER V

THE PRESIDENT

Nomination and Election. — The framers of the federal Constitution, wishing to remove the office of chief magistrate of the Republic as far as possible from the influence of "popular tumults," provided for his election by a small body of electors chosen as the legislatures of the several states might determine. The original design has been upset, however, by the rise of political parties. It is, therefore, necessary to preface a discussion of the legal provisions regarding the election of the President by a consideration of the extra-legal organization — the national convention — which selects the candidate for whom the electors of each party are morally bound to vote.

The national convention assembles on a call issued by the national committee — an organization composed of one representative from each state and territory. The Democratic convention is composed of delegates from the states and territories. Every commonwealth is allowed two delegates for each of its Senators and Representatives in the Congress of the United States. For example, New York has two Senators and forty-three Representatives — forty-five in all — and it is entitled to ninety members in the national convention. The four delegates corresponding to the representation of the state in the United States Senate are known as delegates-at-large. The Republican convention by rule adopted in 1914 is composed of four from each state, one from each congressional district, and one additional delegate from each district with 7500 or more Republican voters. Each territory also sends a delegation.

In prescribing the methods of electing delegates, the calls of the Democratic and Republican parties differ fundamentally. The former regards the state as the unit of representation, but will in the future require the choice of the delegates at primaries.

The Republican party, on the other hand, definitely stipulates that the delegates-at-large shall be chosen at the state convention and the other delegates from congressional districts. Special provisions are made for the territories, and for the states that prescribe nomination by direct primaries.

In addition to the extensive choice of delegates to the conventions by direct primaries, a new feature was introduced into the campaign of 1912 in a few states, including Massachusetts, New Jersey, Illinois, Nebraska, Oregon, and Wisconsin. In those states the voters of each party were allowed to express at the primaries a preference as to the several aspirants for the presidential nomination, and the delegates (chosen by direct vote) were instructed to record at their respective conventions the preferences of their constituents.

The purpose of the national convention is threefold. It formulates the principles of the party into a platform on which the appeal is made to the voters during the ensuing campaign. It nominates candidates for the presidency and the vice-presidency, and appoints committees to notify both nominees. Finally it organizes a new national committee charged with carrying on the campaign and acting for the party for four years — until the next national convention is held.

The National Convention at Work. — The convention usually assembles in some enormous building where the thousand delegates, and perhaps eight or ten thousand spectators, are seated. Each delegation is arranged around the banner of its state, and has a chairman to direct its part in the convention. Some of the more important delegations are accompanied by brass bands, and often carry curious symbols and transparencies. In the audience are usually gathered the most active politicians who are not serving as delegates, enthusiastic partisans from all over the country, and interested visitors attracted by the spectacular affair. It is indeed a cool-headed politician who is not swept off his feet by the excitement of the hour. Bands play popular airs; party heroes are greeted with prolonged cheering as they appear on the scene; wire-pullers rush here and there among the delegations making and extracting promises; all are apparently intoxicated with enthusiasm and boisterous party zeal.

The convention is called to order by the chairman of the national committee, and a day or two are consumed in the election of officers and adjusting contests among rival delegations contending for seats in the convention. On the second or third day, the convention is ready for the report of the committee on resolutions, which is charged with drafting the platform. This committee begins its sessions immediately after its appointment, and usually agrees on a unanimous report, but sometimes there is a minority report. The platform is not often a statement of the particular things which the party proposes to do if it gets into power; it is rather a collection of nice generalities which will serve to create good feeling and unite all sections around the party standard. It usually contains, among other things, references to the great history of the party, interspersed with the names of party leaders, and denunciations of the policies and tactics of the opposite party. The report of the committee on resolutions seldom meets opposition in the convention, for care is taken by the committee to placate all elements. It is only when there is some very contentious matter, such as the free silver issue in 1896, that there is likely to be a divided report from the committee or any debate on the floor. After the adoption of the platform, the new national committee is named.

About the third or fourth day, the chairman announces that the next order of business is the calling of the roll of the states for the presentation of names of the candidates for President of the United States, and the roll is called in alphabetical order beginning with Alabama. If a state has no candidate to present, it may defer to another further down on the list. This is what happened in both conventions in 1904. When Alabama was called upon in the Republican assembly, the chairman of the delegation said: " The State of Alabama requests the privilege and distinguished honor of yielding its place upon the roll to the State of New York." A representative of the state which is thus named thereupon places a candidate in nomination, in a speech full of high-sounding phrases and lofty sentiments. The first speech may be followed by speeches seconding the nomination, from the representatives of various delegations scattered over the House, if the chairman sees fit to recognize them. The nominations may be closed without calling the full roll of the states, or the calling of the roll may be resumed and each state heard from, as it is reached in regular order.

When the nominations are made, the vote is taken by calling the roll of the delegations, and the chairman of each announces the vote of his group. According to the theory of the Republican party, each member of a delegation may cast his vote as he pleases, although as a matter of fact the delegations are often instructed by the conventions of the states from which they come. The Democratic party, however, does not recognize the right of the individual to vote as he pleases in the convention. It not only permits the state convention to instruct its delegates, but also authorizes the majority in each delegation to determine how the entire vote shall be cast — and cast that vote as a unit. For example, the state of New York has ninety representatives in the national convention, and if forty-six of the delegates agree on the same candidate, the vote of the entire number is cast for him, when the unit rule is applied.

This practice, which is called the application of the " unit rule," is justified by Democratic leaders on the ground that the state, not the congressional district, is the unit of representation; and that greater weight is given to the delegation of a state, in negotiating with the other delegations, by reason of the fact that it can cast the entire number of votes. That is, on account of his ability to deliver the entire vote of the New York delegation, the leader of that state, for example, is able to demand more consideration in the distribution of political favors than if he could only deliver a portion of the vote. The unit rule, therefore, gives more power to the organization of the state than the system of allowing divided delegations. It should be noted, however, that the unit rule is not applied to all state delegations in the Democratic convention. It is left to the states concerned to adopt or reject the principle as they see fit; but if the state does not act in the matter, the delegates may vote as they please.

When the roll of all the states and territories has been called, and the vote of each one has been registered by the tally clerks, the total result is announced. If any nominee in the Republican convention receives a majority of all the votes cast, he is thereupon declared the candidate of the party for the presidency of the United States. In the Democratic convention, however, it is an inflexible rule that the successful nominee must receive a majority of two-thirds — that is, out of the 1000 delegates in the Democratic convention of 1904 in St. Louis, 667 were necessary to a choice. If no nominee receives the requisite majority on the first ballot, the process is repeated until some one secures the proper number of votes. It is the practice of both parties, immediately after the nomination of the presidential candidate, to nominate the candidate for Vice-President in the same manner.

When the convention has chosen its candidates, a separate committee is appointed to convey to each of them a formal notification. Shortly afterward the notification committee waits upon the candidate, and through an official spokesman announces the will of the party. The candidate thereupon replies in a lengthy address, and sometimes follows this by a special letter of acceptance. The acceptance speech is often an important campaign document, for the reason that the candidate may interpret the platform of his party in his own way, going even so far as to modify the spirit, if not the letter, of that pronunciamento. For example, Mr. Taft in his acceptance speech of 1908 elaborated at length the Chicago platform and committed himself personally to many doctrines which had not been specifically indorsed at the convention which nominated him.

The Campaign. — The great work of directing the campaign is intrusted to the national committee, composed, in the Republican and Democratic parties, of one member from each state and territory, who holds office for four years, that is, from one national convention to the next. In 1912, the Democratic convention ordered the election of the future committeeman in each state at party primaries. The principal officers of the national committee are the chairman, secretary, and treasurer. The chairman, who is by far the most important political leader in the national organization, is the choice of the candidate for President. The wishes of the committee and other leaders of the party are, of course, taken into consideration. This power of selecting the chairman is very important to the presidential nominee, because the immediate task of that officer is to conduct the presidential campaign, and it is essential that he and the candidate work together in complete harmony. Upon the officers and advisers of the national committee falls the burden of conducting the long campaign for the election of the candidates nominated by the national convention.

Popular Operation of the Electoral System.—The political activities described above—important as they are in the selection of the President and Vice-President — are wholly unknown to the Constitution. That document, in fact, contains but very few clauses with regard to the actual choice of the President and Vice-President. In the first place it contemplates a system of indirect election: each state shall appoint, in such manner as the legislature thereof may direct, a number of electors equal to the number of Senators and Representatives to which the commonwealth is entitled in Congress. To remove the electors from any direct contact with the federal government, it was added that no Senator or Representative or a person holding any office of trust under the United States should be appointed an elector.

It is to be noted that the electors of each state are to be chosen as the legislature thereof may determine. In the course of our history no less than three distinct methods have been devised. (1) In the beginning, it was often the practice for the state legislatures to choose the electors; but within a quarter of a century the majority of them had abandoned this practice in favor of popular election. (2) Where this more democratic system was adopted it was often the custom at first to have two electors chosen by the voters of the state at large and the remaining electors chosen by congressional districts — thus each voter would have the right to vote for three electors, two at large and one from his own district. (3) It was at length discovered that a state's influence in national politics was greatly increased if all of its electors could be carried by one party or the other, and consequently the system of election by district has been abandoned, in favor of election by general ticket throughout the state at large.

It is necessary, accordingly, for each party in each state to prepare a list of candidates equal to the total number of electors to which that particular commonwealth is entitled. In practice, the presidential electors are generally nominated by the state convention of the party, and very often the office of elector is regarded as a titular honor to be given to distinguished citizens or to partisans willing to make liberal contributions to campaign funds.

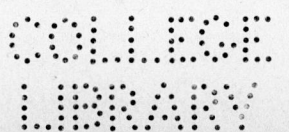

On election day, therefore, the voter does not vote directly for President and Vice-President, although for his information the names of the candidates of all parties appear on the ballot. On the contrary, if he votes a straight ticket, he simply votes for the entire list of electors put forward by his party. There is no point at all in splitting the vote for presidential electors, unless there is a fusion, such as existed for example in some of the western states between the Democrats and Populists whereby each of the two groups was to have a certain share of the electors according to a predetermined arrangement. What happens, therefore, on a general presidential election day is the choice in each state of a certain number of presidential electors — 531 in all. Normally the party which secures a plurality of votes in any state is entitled to all of the electoral votes of that state for President and Vice-President, no matter how large the opposition, though occasionally split tickets occur. No elector would dare to break faith with the party which placed him in nomination, and vote for the candidates of the opposite party. Consequently, the deliberative, judicial, non-partisan system designed by the framers of the Constitution has been overthrown by party practice.

It is sometimes held that through this party practice we have secured popular election of President and Vice-President, but if we mean by popular election, choice by majority or plurality vote throughout the United States, it has not been attained as yet. Indeed, several of our Presidents have been elected by a minority of the popular vote. Lincoln, for example, was chosen President in 1860 by a vote of 1,866,452 against a total of 2,815,617 polled by all of his opponents — the large opposition vote being so divided and distributed as to elect less than a majority of the total number of electors. And two Presidents, Hayes and Harrison, did not even receive a plurality.

This possible contingency of election by a minority of the popular vote cast is due to the fact that when a party carries a state, no matter by how slight a margin, it secures all of the presidential electors to which that commonwealth is entitled. A party, therefore, that wins, although by narrow margins, in a sufficient number of states to obtain a majority of the electors may in fact poll a smaller number of votes than the opposing party which may have carried its states by enormous majorities.

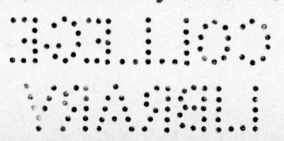

Casting the Electoral Vote. — The methods by which the electors so chosen in each state shall meet and cast their votes are prescribed in the Constitution and in federal and state statutes. It is provided by federal law that the electors of each commonwealth shall convene on the second Monday of January immediately following their appointment at such place as the legislature of the state may direct — in practice, the state capital. When they have assembled, the electors vote by ballot for President and Vice-President, " one of whom at least must not be an inhabitant of the same state with themselves " — that is, for the two candidates, nominated by their party; and they thereupon make distinct lists of the number of votes so cast, and sign, certify, seal, and transmit the lists to the president of the Senate of the United States. With the lists of their votes for President and Vice-President, the electors must transmit their certificates of election as evidence of their power to act — evidence of crucial importance in case of contested elections. When they have cast their votes and transmitted their documents according to law, the electors have performed their whole duty. They are not paid by the federal government, but are regarded as state officers, and must look to the state legislature for remuneration for their services.

The counting of the total electoral vote polled throughout the United States [1] begins in the Hall of the House of Representatives on the second Wednesday in February, following the meeting of the electors in their respective states. It is conducted in the presence of the Senate and the House of Representatives with the president of the Senate in the chair. Two tellers are appointed by the Senate and two by the House of Representatives. The certificates and documents are opened by the president of the Senate, taking the states in alphabetical order beginning with Alabama, and thereupon handed to the tellers who read the

[1] The constitutional clauses relative to counting the electoral vote do not provide for cases of disputed returns from the several states, and in 1876 a grave crisis arose on account of frauds and irregularities in several of the commonwealths. A deadlock occurred and Congress found a way out by creating an electoral commission of five Senators, five Representatives, and five Supreme Court Justices. On all important matters the eight Republicans on the commission voted together, and declared Mr. Hayes elected. See P. L. Haworth, *The Disputed Election*. In 1887 Congress, by an act, provided for settling such disputes. For the details, see the act in Stanwood, *Presidential Elections*, p. 453.

same and list the votes. The candidates having the greatest number of votes for President and Vice-President respectively, if such number be a majority of the whole number of electors appointed, are declared duly elected. Except in case of a contested election, this count is, of course, merely an impressive formality, for the result is ordinarily known three months before.

In case no candidate for President receives a majority of all the electoral votes cast, the House of Representatives thereupon chooses the President by ballot from the three candidates who have received the highest number of votes. It should be noted, however, that, in selecting the President, each state represented in the House is entitled to only one vote; a quorum consists of the members from two-thirds of the states; and a majority of all the states is necessary to choice. Accordingly, the vote of each state for the presidential candidate must be determined by the majority of the Representatives of the commonwealth in the House. In case of the failure of the House to choose a President (whenever the election devolves upon that body) before the fourth of March following, it becomes the duty of the Vice-President to act as President.

There have been only two instances of presidential elections by the House of Representatives — Jefferson in 1801 and J. Q. Adams in 1825. This is due, of course, to the fact that we have two great political parties somewhat equally balanced. If the voters were broken into several parties the election would almost invariably devolve upon the House.

Whenever no candidate for Vice-President receives a majority of all the electoral votes, the election is thrown into the Senate, and the Senators voting as individuals must choose the Vice-President from the two candidates having the highest number of votes. Two-thirds of the whole number of the Senators constitute a quorum for this purpose, and a majority of the whole number is necessary to a choice.

The Inauguration. — It was formerly the practice for Congress, after having made the official count, to select a committee for the purpose of notifying the new President of his election, but this was not uniformly followed, and has now been abandoned altogether. Curiously enough no official notice whatever is given to the President-elect. He is supposed to be sufficiently aware of the fact himself, and on the fourth of March he appears to take the oath of office. He usually arrives in Washington a few days before, and calls upon the retiring President, to pay his respects. On the day of inauguration, the President-elect, in charge of a committee on ceremonies, is conducted to the White House, whence, accompanied by the President, he is driven to the Capitol. Unless the weather prevents, the oath of office, administered by the Chief Justice of the United States, is taken in the open air upon the platform built for the special purpose at the east front of the Capitol. Following the example set by Washington, it is the practice of the President to deliver an inaugural address setting forth his policy. After the administration of the oath of office, the new President is driven back to the White House, where, from a reviewing-stand, he surveys a long procession, which usually takes hours to file past.

The Qualifications of the President. — Certain qualifications for the President are laid down in the Constitution. He must be a natural-born citizen, at least thirty-five years old, and must have been fourteen years a resident within the United States. The same qualifications apply to the Vice-President. The term is fixed at four years and the President can only be removed by impeachment. So far as the Constitution is concerned, the President or Vice-President may be reëlected indefinitely.[1]

To these constitutional requirements, a third has been added by political practice: no person is eligible to the office of President for more than two terms, at least, in succession. This "third term doctrine," as it is called, is supposed to rest upon the example set by Washington in declining reëlection at the expiration of eight years' service. Tradition has it that Washington acted on principle, but this seems to have slight historical foundation. He did not share Jefferson's decided ideas on rotation in office, and there is apparently no reason for believing that he objected to a President's serving three terms or more. In fact,

---

[1] In case of the death or resignation of the President, the Vice-President succeeds. By statute Congress provided, in 1886, that in case of the death or resignation of both the President and Vice-President the following officers shall serve, in the order mentioned: Secretary of State, of the Treasury, of War, the Attorney-General, the Postmaster-General, the Secretary of the Navy, and of the Interior. The President's salary is fixed at $75,000 a year to which is added a large allowance for the executive mansion and contingencies.

his farewell address is filled with reasonable excuses why he in particular ought not to be charged with lack of patriotism or neglect of duty in refusing to serve for another term. Jefferson originally believed that the President should have been given a seven years' term, and then made ineligible for reëlection. Later, however, he came to the conclusion that service for eight years with the possibility of removal at the end of four years was nearer the ideal arrangement. He, accordingly, followed the example set by Washington, and thus the third term doctrine early received such high sanction that it became a political dogma almost as inviolable as an express provision of the Constitution.

The President as a Political Leader and Head of the National Administration. — The functions of the President are prescribed by the Constitution, but his real achievements are not set by the letter of the law. They are determined rather by his personality, the weight of his influence, his capacity for managing men, and the strength and effectiveness of the party forces behind him. As chief executive, he operates through a vast and complicated official hierarchy centering at Washington and ramifying throughout the great American empire and even into foreign countries through the diplomatic and consular services. As political leader he may use his exalted position to appeal to the nation — to sectional, or group interests; he may use his veto power against laws passed by Congress, he may agitate by means of his messages, and he may bring pressure to bear in Congress and within his party through the discriminating use of the federal patronage. By commanding the confidence of the nation he may completely overshadow Congress and compel it to accept his legislative policies. Thus it happens that we do not have the whole office of President before us when we are in the presence of the Constitution and statutes of the United States.

The President is the head of the national administration. It is his duty to see that the Constitution, laws, and treaties of the United States, and judicial decisions rendered by the federal courts, are duly enforced everywhere throughout the United States. In the fulfillment of this duty, he may direct the heads of departments and their subordinates in the discharge of the functions vested in them by the acts of Congress. The exact degree, however, to which he may control an administrative officer is frequently a subject of political controversy, and cannot be set down with precision; it depends more upon the personality of the President than upon any theories of constitutional law.

Some of the departments, however, are made more directly subject to the President's control than others. For example, the Secretary of State, in the conduct of foreign affairs, is completely subject to the President's orders; and the Attorney-General must give an opinion or institute proceedings when required. On the other hand, when the Treasury was organized in 1789, it was definitely understood that Congress had a special control over the administration of that Department.

The Supreme Court has held that the President is bound to see that an administrative officer faithfully discharges the duties assigned by law, but is not authorized to direct the officer as to the ways in which they shall be discharged. Nevertheless, the President has the power to remove the head of a department who refuses to obey his orders, and it is, therefore, rather difficult to see why, in actual practice, he cannot determine, within the lines of the statutes, the general policy to be followed by that officer. When President Jackson wanted the government funds withdrawn from the United States Bank, he removed two Secretaries of the Treasury, and finally appointed a third who was known to be subservient to his will. He had his way in the end.

The President also possesses a large ordinance power — that is, authority to supplement statutes by rules and regulations covering matters of detail sometimes of very great importance. Among other things, he makes rules for the army and navy, the patent office, the customs, internal revenue, consular, and civil services. Under the Overman Act passed in 1918 he can reconstruct and reorganize the great departments and offices of national administration. Sometimes he issues these rules in accordance with provisions of the statutes and sometimes under his general executive power. Many of the army regulations he promulgates as commander in chief. When he makes rules for the civil service, he acts under specific provisions of the civil service law. Thus under his power to remove, to see to the faithful execution of the laws, and to issue ordinances, the President enjoys an administrative authority of no mean dimensions.

As chief executive the President may instruct the Attorney-

General to institute proceedings against any one suspected of violating federal law, and in case of open resistance he may employ the armed force of the United States. Laxness or severity in law enforcement is, therefore, largely within his discretion.

The Power of Appointment and Removal. — In connection with his administrative functions, the President may nominate a large number of federal officers. This is important from the point of view of politics as well as administration.

When considered in relation to the manner of their selection, the civil authorities of the United States — other than the President, Vice-President, presidential electors, Senators and Representatives — fall into two groups: (1) those officers whose appointment is vested by the Constitution or by act of Congress in the President and Senate; and (2) those " inferior " officers, established by law, whose appointment is vested by Congress in the President, the courts of law, or the heads of departments.

The first group embraces most of the important higher officers of the federal government, — the heads of departments, most of the bureau chiefs, judges of the inferior federal courts, many commissioners, such as the civil service and interstate commerce commissioners, revenue officers, and postmasters in large cities and towns. No very consistent rule has been adopted by Congress in defining the term " inferior officers." A few bureau chiefs of great importance — principally in the Department of Agriculture — are " inferior " officers in the view of the law because their appointment is vested in the President or in the head of the department. On the other hand many bureau chiefs are appointed by the President and Senate.

The offices to be filled by the President and Senate may be divided into groups according to the degree of freedom which the President enjoys in making his own selections.

1. Members of the Cabinet, that is, heads of departments, are usually the President's personal selection, although in this matter he is often controlled by preëlection promises or by obligations incurred in engaging the active support of certain prominent men in his party. At all events, the Senate, even when it is in the hands of an opposition party, does not seek to control the ap-

pointments to these offices; it usually ratifies the President's nominations promptly and without objections. The choice of diplomatic representatives is also left largely to the President's discretion, as far as the Senate is concerned; although he often has many party obligations to consider in this connection. Military and naval appointments, especially in times of crisis, are principally subject to presidential control, but political influences are by no means wanting here. It is not often that the Senate blocks appointments to the Supreme Court.

2. A second group of minor offices such as customs offices, filled by the President and Senate, is largely subject to the control of the Senators, as a result of the practice known as " senatorial courtesy." Under its power to advise and consent, the Senate does not officially attempt to suggest nominations to the President, but by a custom which has grown up, it will only ratify appointments which are approved by the Senators (of the President's party) from the state in which the offices in question are located. If, however, they are located in a state not represented by a Senator of the same party, the President is freer to act.[1]

3. A third group of offices filled on presidential nomination is composed of minor positions within congressional districts, such as revenue officers in the smaller cities and towns. It has become a settled custom to allow the Representative, if he is of the President's party, to name the appointees of his district; but if he is not of the President's party, the patronage goes to the Senator or Senators, as in the case of offices within the second group.

The power of removal, so indispensable for the conduct of an efficient administration, has been one of the controverted points of our constitutional law, but it seems now to have been settled with a fair degree of definiteness. The Constitution makes no provision for removal except by way of impeachment, but this is too cumbersome a process to be used often, especially for minor places. It was, therefore, early agreed that the right of removal was constitutionally inherent in the right to appoint, and that the President, without consulting the Senate, could remove the officers whom he nominated. This principle was accepted until 1867, when Congress, then engaged in a bitter contro-

[1] If there is no Senator or Representative from a state, belonging to his party, the President consults party leaders in the state in question.

versy with President Johnson, passed the Tenure of Office Act providing that the President must secure the consent of the Senate in making removals. This law, however, was later modified, and in 1887 repealed altogether, so that the former principle seems to be restored, namely, that the President can remove all officers whom he appoints or nominates in the executive branch of the government. The President can even remove before the expiration of the term for which an officer is appointed, and is not required to assign any causes at all for his action.

The War Powers of the President. — The President is commander in chief of the army and navy and of the state militia when called into the service of the United States. He holds this power in time of peace as well as in time of war. The equipment of the army and navy and the right to declare war, however, belong to Congress, and it is not possible to say just how far into the actual direction of the forces Congress may go under its constitutional authority. Some publicists have even contended that Congress can provide that a particular officer shall be assigned by the commander in chief to a particular division, or that in case a regiment or company has been dispatched to a certain point by presidential order, Congress can countermand the order. If this is true, it is difficult to see why Congress might not in a slow and cumbersome way practically direct the conduct of a campaign. However, it is contended, on the other side, with more reason, that the power of Congress ends with providing and maintaining the army and navy and declaring war; and that the entire command of the military and naval forces is vested in the President, whose guidance, under the Constitution, is the law of nations and the rules of civilized warfare.

The President appoints high military and naval officers by and with the advice and consent of the Senate, — except militia officers who are appointed by the respective states, — and in time of war he may remove them at will. In time of peace, however, they are removed by court martial.

The President is not limited in the conduct of war to the direction of the armed forces; he may do whatever a commander in chief is warranted in doing under the laws of war to weaken and overcome the enemy. It was under this general authority, inherent in his office, that President Lincoln, during the Civil War, suspended the writ of habeas corpus in states that were not within the theater of the armed conflict. It was under this authority that he abolished slavery in many of the states; arrested and imprisoned summarily those charged with giving aid and comfort to the Confederacy; established a blockade of southern ports; and, in short, brought the whole weight of the North, material and moral, to bear in the contest. Greater military power than was exercised by President Lincoln in the conduct of that war it would be difficult to imagine.

Under his war power, the President may govern conquered territory, appoint officers there, make laws and ordinances, lay and collect taxes of all kinds, and, in short, exercise practically every sovereign right, until Congress has acted.

The President may use armed forces in carrying into execution the federal law against resistance that cannot be overcome by ordinary civil process. The United States, under the Constitution, guarantees to each commonwealth a republican form of government, and protects it against invasion, and, on application of the legislature or of the executive (if the legislature is not convened), against domestic violence. By act of Congress, the President is authorized to call forth the militia when aid is asked in due form by the authorities of a state struggling against an insurrection. It is by statutory law also that the President is empowered to use the militia or the army and navy whenever, by reason of obstructions, assemblages, or rebellion, it becomes impracticable, in his judgment, to enforce federal law within any state or territory by the ordinary course of judicial procedure. It was under this authority, and his general obligation to see to the faithful execution of the law, that President Cleveland used federal troops during the Chicago strike in 1894.

The President and Foreign Affairs. — The President is the official spokesman of the nation in the conduct of all foreign affairs, and he is primarily responsible for our foreign policy and its results. It is true, however, that he is controlled in some matters by the Senate and in others by Congress. The Senate must confirm his nominations to diplomatic and consular positions, and must approve his treaties, and Congress alone can create diplomatic and consular positions and provide the salaries attached to them. Congress must also, in many cases, make provision for the execution of treaties, but it has no right to establish and conduct relations with any foreign power independently of the President.

Under the Constitution, the President appoints ambassadors, other public ministers, and consuls, subject to the confirmation of the Senate; he makes treaties with the consent of two-thirds of the Senators present; and he receives ambassadors and public ministers from foreign countries; but his authority is not limited to the formal letter of the law. He may do many things that vitally affect the foreign relations of the country. He may dismiss an ambassador or public minister of a foreign power for political as well as personal reasons, and, if on the former ground, he might take a step leading to war. His power to receive any foreign representative authorizes him to recognize the independence of a new state, perhaps in rebellion against its former legitimate sovereign, and thus he might incur the risk of war. He may order a fleet or a ship to a foreign port under circumstances that may provoke serious difficulty. As commander in chief of the army he might move troops to such a position on the borders of a neighboring state as to bring about an armed conflict. A notable instance of such an action occurred in the case of the opening of the Mexican War, when President Polk ordered our troops into the disputed territory, and, on their being attacked by the Mexicans, declared that war existed by act of Mexico. Again, in his message to Congress the President may outline a foreign policy so hostile to another nation as to precipitate diplomatic difficulties, if not more serious results. This occurred in the case of the Venezuelan controversy, when President Cleveland recommended to Congress demands which Great Britain could hardly regard as anything but unfriendly.

The President may even go so far as to make " executive agreements " with foreign powers without the consent of the Senate. The Constitution requires that only " treaties " shall be confirmed by the Senate, and long practice has shown conclusively that this term does not cover every sort of international arrangement which may be made. Every adjustment of a minor matter with a foreign country is an agreement.

The Power of Pardon. — The President, in addition to his administrative duties, enjoys the power to grant reprieves and pardons (except in cases of impeachment) for offenses against the United States. No limits are imposed on his exercise of this power, and therefore it may be used as he sees fit. He may remit a fine, commute a death sentence to a term of imprisonment, or free the offender altogether; but when forfeiture of office is one of the penalties imposed, he cannot restore the offender to his former position. Though the usual process is to pardon after conviction, a pardon may be granted before or during trial.

In the exercise of his power of pardon, the President relies, of course, largely upon the opinions of others. The application for executive clemency with all the papers attached is sent to the Attorney-General, in whose department there is a pardon-clerk in charge of the preliminary stages. Usually the judge and district attorney under whose supervision the case was first tried are asked to make any statement they may choose about the merits of the case. The Attorney-General indorses on the application his opinion as to what course of action should be pursued, and the papers are then sent to the President for final determination. "If the trial seems to have been fairly conducted," said President Harrison, "and no new exculpatory evidence is produced, and the sentence does not seem to have been unduly severe, the President refuses to interfere. He cannot weigh the evidence as well as the judge and jury. They saw and heard the witnesses, and he has only a writing before him. It often happens that the wife or mother of the condemned man comes in person to plead for mercy, and there is no more trying ordeal than to hear her tearful and sobbing utterances and to feel that public duty requires that she be denied her prayer."

The President and Congress — a Study in Legislative Leadership. — The President's position as chief executive officer is so exalted and the powers of that place are so extensive, that his functions as a legislator, both constitutional and customary, are often lost sight of by commentators. He is required by the Constitution to give to Congress from time to time information of the state of the Union and to recommend such measures as he may judge necessary and expedient. In the exercise of this function, he may recommend laws and even draw bills, which Congress willingly accepts, or which it accepts reluctantly under the feeling that the President has the support of his party throughout the country, or which it modifies or rejects altogether if it disapproves.

The message is the one great public document of the United States which is widely read and discussed. Congressional debates receive scant notice, but the President's message is printed almost *in extenso* in nearly every metropolitan daily, and is the subject of general editorial comment throughout the length and breadth of the land. It is supposed, though often erroneously, to embody in a very direct sense the policy of the presidential party; it stirs the country; it often affects congressional elections; and if its recommendations correspond with real and positive interests of sufficient strength, they sooner or later find their way into law.[1]

Notwithstanding the fact that, in accordance with traditional American political theory, the executive and legislative departments ought to be kept entirely separate, as a matter of practice such separation is not only impossible, but highly undesirable, because it breaks the natural tie which must exist between the body which expresses popular will and the authority charged with carrying that will into execution. Accordingly there has been established in practice a fairly close connection between the executive and legislative departments. This has been accomplished in many ways.

1. In the first place, the party tie, of necessity, binds the President and the members of his party in Congress. Although they may from time to time engage in controversies more spectacular than edifying, yet on fundamental matters of policy, the President and Congress must come into a sort of working agreement. Furthermore, the President is regarded as the leader of his party, and it is to him, rather than to Congress, that his party looks for the enforcement of any specific promises laid down in the platform or made officially during the presidential campaign. Congress cannot, therefore, ignore the leadership of the President, and, however much it may oppose his policy,

[1] The presidential message, at the opening of Congress, was delivered in person to the Senate and House in joint assembly by Washington and Adams; but this was abandoned by Jefferson. From that time forward it was the practice to communicate by means of written messages until President Wilson in 1913 revived the old custom of delivery in person.

it must give heed to those measures in which he has unquestioned national party support.

Within recent years, we have come to recognize more frankly than ever this position of the President as party leader. Mr. Roosevelt was largely responsible for the policies which the Republican party made national issues. As party leader he issued, in 1906, a general letter indorsing the Republican members of Congress and calling upon the country to support them in the coming election; two years later he singled out individual members of Congress and gave them special letters of commendation. Mr. Taft likewise frankly assumed the position of party leadership. He was largely instrumental in the adjustment of differences between the Senate and the House of Representatives over the tariff bill of 1909. Of Mr. Wilson's extraordinary powers of leadership exercised over his party and the country at large it is hardly necessary to speak here — this is the outstanding feature of his two administrations.

2. The party tie is by no means the only bond of union between the executive and legislative departments. By vesting the appointing power to a large number of important offices in the hands of the President and Senate, the Constitution draws the two departments together. The extent to which the President may use his power over appointments to influence his party friends in Congress, or the extent to which the Senate may employ its confirming power to bend the President to its will, depends upon circumstances; but it is perfectly clear that either may take advantage of the opportunity offered by this constitutional connection.

3. The imperative necessity under which Congress is placed of securing information from executive departments with regard to legislative matters, and the desire of executive officers to secure new laws and amendments to old laws, constitute another important bond of union between the executive and the legislature. Congress is constantly making demands upon the executive for papers, documents, and special information of one kind or another, and in so far as the President regards these demands as reasonable and compatible with public interest he complies with them. As a matter of right, Congress may call upon the executive for information, but it has no power, under

the Constitution, to compel him to furnish papers and documents.

In practice, the anxiety of the administration to secure favorable consideration of its own measures in Congress leads it to comply quite readily with requests for information. This is as it should be, for frequently those who have charge of the execution of the laws know more about the actual conditions to which the laws must apply and the actual effect of the laws than do the legislators themselves. Furthermore, it is wise that those who are called upon to execute the laws should know the spirit and intention of those who have passed them.

4. Quite an intimate relation is established between Congress and the executive through the practice of the former in inviting the assistance of departmental chiefs in drafting bills. Very frequently the Attorney-General, who is supposed to be merely the legal adviser of the President, is asked to give his opinion before a committee or to advise members of Congress on some particular matters up for legislative action. It is also sometimes the practice for heads of departments to draft complete measures, transmit them to Congress either through a friend in that body, or even directly, and secure their reference to proper committees and ultimately their passage. It is a matter of common knowledge also that the President from time to time invites to the White House members of Congress who may be of influence in securing the enactment of laws favored by the administration. On the other hand, Congress has in a number of instances even assumed the right to advise the President, by a statute or by a resolution, to adopt some particular executive policy.

5. Another important line of connection is established between the executive and legislature through appropriations. The Treasury Department is by law placed in a special relation to Congress; for Congress has the power to call directly upon that department for financial information without going through the form of making a request to the President. The Treasury Department collects the estimates of the amount of money required by the various executive branches and compiles these estimates in a book which is printed and submitted to Congress at the beginning of each regular session. This is largely perfunctory, for Congress, paying little heed to the Secretary's

estimates, proceeds to make up appropriation bills in its own way. By granting or withholding funds it may exert a powerful influence on the ordinary course of the administration.

Indeed the treatment which the President's recommendations receive, of course, varies according to circumstances. They may be accepted because Congress feels that they are sound in principle or because there is an effective demand for them in the country; or they may be accepted because the President, by his party leadership or personal favors or use of patronage, can bring the requisite pressure to bear on Senators and Representatives to secure their passage.

The Veto Power. — The power of vetoing measures of Congress, like that of sending messages, possesses a legal and a practical aspect. Every bill or joint resolution must be presented to the President; if he signs it, becomes a law; if he disapproves, he must return it to the house in which it originated, with a statement of his objections; and the house must thereupon reconsider it. A two-thirds vote of both houses is sufficient to carry the measure over the executive veto. The same procedure is applied to orders, resolutions, and votes, to which a concurrence of both houses is necessary, excepting questions of adjournment. If the President fails to return a measure within ten days (Sundays excepted) after it is presented to him, it becomes a law without his signature, unless Congress prevents its return by adjourning, in which case it does not become a law. When Congress adjourns leaving many bills to be signed, the President may suppress quietly the bills to which he entertains objections; and this is known as the "pocket veto."

The President does not veto single items in appropriation bills, and Congress has attached other measures — disapproved by the President — to appropriation laws, and thus forced his signature. This practice of attaching "riders" is somewhat discredited, and is seldom employed.

On the question of exercising the veto, different views have prevailed. Jefferson contended: "Unless the President's mind, on a view of everything which is urged for and against the bill, is tolerably clear that it is unauthorized by the Constitution — if the pro and con hang so even as to balance his judgment — a just respect for the wisdom of the legislature would naturally decide the balance in favor of their opinion." General Taylor held that the veto power should never be exercised "except in cases of clear violation of the Constitution, or manifest haste and want of consideration by Congress." President Jackson, however, whose relations to Congress were quite different from those of either Jefferson or Taylor, had his own opinion of what the Constitution was, and alleged unconstitutionality as one of the grounds for vetoing the Bank Bill, although such an institution had been declared constitutional by the Supreme Court. In vetoing a bill, President Grant assigned as his reason the fact that it was "a departure from true principles of finance, national interest, national obligations to creditors, congressional promises, party pledges (of both political parties), and personal views and promises made by me in every annual message sent to Congress and in each inaugural address." Mr. Cleveland expressed his opinion that the veto power was given to the President for the purpose of invoking the exercise of executive judgment and inviting independent executive action.

Certainly the President is expected to safeguard the Constitution by vetoing unconstitutional acts of Congress. This is especially true because many laws can only be brought before the Courts in a collateral way, if at all.

The procedure of the President in dealing with bills has been described by ex-President Harrison. On its passage through Congress, a bill is signed by the President of the Senate and Speaker of the House; it is then taken to the Executive Mansion and usually referred to the head of the executive department to which its subject-matter relates; in case a question of constitutionality arises, the Attorney-General is consulted. The bill then goes to the President with the departmental report upon it, and if he approves he signs the bill, dates it, and sends it to the Department of State for filing and publication. If he disapproves the bill, and Congress is still in session, he returns it to the house in which it originated, with his objections, and perhaps with recommendations for amendment.

The veto power, taken in connection with the message and the appointing power, is an effective political instrument in the hands of the President. By using a threat of the veto, he may secure the passage of bills which he personally favors; and at all times, in considering important measures, Congress must keep in view the possible action of the President, especially where it is a party question and the correct attitude before the country is indispensable. Mr. Roosevelt even went so far as to warn Congress publicly that he would not sign certain measures then before that body — and raised a storm of protest from those who said that he should not veto a bill until it was laid before him.

SELECTED REFERENCES

Ostrogorski, *Democracy and the Organization of Political Parties*, Vol. II, pp. 1–388, for the convention and presidential campaigns; Bryce, *American Commonwealth*, Vol. I, Chaps. v–ix; G. Bradford, *The Lesson of Popular Government*, Vol. I, Chaps. xvi–xvii; Roosevelt, *Theodore Roosevelt: an Autobiography* (New York, 1913); Woodrow Wilson, *Constitutional Government in the United States; The Federalist*, Numbers 67–76.

CHAPTER VI

THE NATIONAL ADMINISTRATION

The Power to Create Federal Offices and Agencies. — The innumerable duties involved in enforcing the federal law under presidential supervision are distributed among ten great departments and certain commissions, established by Congress. Curiously enough, the Constitution makes no direct provision for these branches of the federal administration; but it evidently assumes their existence, for it authorizes the President to require in writing the opinion of the heads of the executive departments, and also gives Congress power to vest in them the appointment of inferior officers. It is on this constitutional basis, therefore, that Congress assumes the power to create departments by law, regulate the duties of their respective heads down to the minutest details, and prescribe their internal organization and the powers and duties of the chiefs of even the minor subdivisions. Occasionally, however, the President takes the initial steps in the organization of a bureau by executive order, and Congress has subsequently sanctioned the act by a special law, or a regular appropriation.

Extraordinary power over the creation, consolidation, and alteration of bureaus, agencies, and offices of the federal administration was conferred on the President by the Overman act, approved May 20, 1918. In the interest of national defense, the successful prosecution of the war, the support and maintenance of the army and navy, the better utilization of national resources, and more efficient administration, the President was authorized to make any redistribution of functions among executive agencies he might deem necessary, including the functions, duties, and powers already conferred by law upon any executive department, commission, bureau, agency, office, or officer. The President was specifically empowered to transfer functions and duties from one office or agency to another, to consolidate offices and agencies, to move employees from one branch to another, to abolish offices, and finally to create an executive agency to control the production of aëroplanes and aircraft equipment. This remarkable measure, intended to give the President the power to eliminate waste, lost motion, and friction in the national administration, was limited, however, to the period of the war and six months after its termination, unless earlier revoked by the President. It was intended to enable the President to cut red tape and to reconstruct at will the many bureaus and agencies of the federal administration for the speedy accomplishment of national purposes. This is a power which the heads of great business corporations have over their respective organizations, and there are many advocates of governmental efficiency who believe that the President should enjoy somewhat similar authority over the details of national administration even in times of peace.

The Heads of Departments. — The head of a federal department occupies a position radically different from that of a cabinet officer in any other country. He is appointed by the President (with the approval of the Senate) and may be removed by him or by impeachment. His duties, however, are prescribed minutely, not in presidential orders, save in certain instances, but in statutes enacted by Congress. He is responsible to the President for the faithful execution of the law; but the President cannot alter or diminish any of the duties laid down by Congress (except under the temporary provisions of the Overman law), and cannot prevent Congress from imposing or taking away duties or from prescribing such minute details as amount to a practical direction of the officer. "The President," said Mr. John Sherman many years ago, "is intrusted by the Constitution and laws with important powers, and so by law are the heads of departments. The President has no more right to control or exercise the powers conferred by law upon them than they have to control him in the discharge of his duties. It is especially the custom of Congress to intrust to the Secretary of the Treasury specific powers over the currency, the public debt, and the collection of the revenue. If he violates or neglects his duty, he is subject to removal by the President or impeachment, . . . but the President cannot exercise or control the discretion reposed by law in the Secretary of the Treasury, or in any head or subordinate of a department of the government." The President, as we have seen, has the power of removal, however, and may exercise it for the purpose of directing his subordinates. In actual practice, therefore, there are many variations from Mr. Sherman's apparently convincing legal argument, especially when a strong-willed President has a firm policy of his own which he is determined to carry out. Indeed, the logical application of his doctrine would amount to a complete decentralization of the administrative organization and a destruction of the President's responsibility.

While it is impossible to give here a full account of the duties of each secretary, it seems desirable to consider some matters which are common to them all.

1. In the first place, a large appointing power to minor offices is conferred by law upon the departmental head, but this is now exercised under civil service rules which restrict his choice, in all except the important subordinate positions, to the candidates who have qualified by examination. The power of removal generally accompanies the power of appointment, although there are some important exceptions by law and by executive order.

2. In the second place, the head of a department enjoys a certain range of freedom in issuing departmental orders, for, by act of Congress, he may " prescribe regulations, not inconsistent with law, for the government of his department, the conduct of its officers and clerks, the distribution and performance of its business, and the custody, use, and preservation of the records, papers, and property appertaining to it."

3. Every departmental chief maintains a more or less definite relation to Congress. He must prepare annually a report of his department, but this is largely a formal compilation, for the matters of policy or detail covered in it have little or no influence in directing legislation. Though Cabinet officers cannot be members of Congress, there is, as we have seen, nothing in the Constitution excluding them from the right to sit and speak there. Custom has decreed, however, that they must bring their influence to bear in circuitous ways. They often appear before Senate or House committees to explain measures or to answer inquiries as to some

legislation relating to their respective departments. There are many instances of heads of departments transmitting to Congress, on their own motion, completed drafts of bills which they would like to see enacted into law. They sometimes establish friendly relations with the chairmen of prominent committees, and thus obtain a hearing for their policies which would otherwise be denied to them.

4. The head of every department is subjected to constant interruptions from outside parties such as can come to the chief of no great business organization. "Washington wishes to see evidence of democracy about the departments," says a former Secretary of the Treasury, Mr. Vanderlip. "Neither Senator nor Congressman is satisfied to cool his heels in an ante-room for any length of time, nor are political leaders who come to the capital on a mission likely to be pleased if the Secretary's engagements are such that an appointment cannot be made without notice or delay. . . . The Secretary of this great department must give heed to innumerable trifles such as would never reach the head of even a comparatively small business organization. Requests come from people of importance, and they must be taken up with the care which the position of such persons demands rather than with any thought of their importance in relation to the administration of departmental affairs."

5. With the multiplication of the official duties connected with immigration, commerce, transmission of mails, and taxation, it has been found necessary to give to the heads of certain departments the high authority of deciding finally upon cases appealed from lower administrative officials. For example, the immigration law provides "that in every case where an alien is excluded from admission into the United States under any law or treaty now existing or hereafter made, the decision of the appropriate immigration officers, if adverse to the admission of such alien, shall be final, unless reversed on appeal to the Secretary of Labor"; and in such cases the decision of the Secretary is conclusive unless it can be made apparent that he has exceeded his jurisdiction or violated the law. Customs officers also are given large powers in appraising the value of imported goods, and the Court has declined to review the appraisements made by the proper authorities, declaring that the interposition of the courts

in the appraisement of importations would involve the collection of the revenue in inextricable confusion and embarrassment. The Postmaster-General may issue fraud orders denying the use of the mails to persons and concerns who in his opinion are engaged in fraudulent transactions; and those affected have no right to appeal to the courts for a review of the facts on which he bases his decisions. In sustaining this conclusion, the Court said: " If the ordinary daily transactions of the departments which involve an interference with private rights were required to be submitted to the courts before action was finally taken, the result would entail practically a suspension of some of the most important functions of government. . . . It would practically arrest the executive arm of the government, if the heads of departments were required to obtain the sanction of the courts upon the multifarious questions arising in their departments, before action were taken in any matter which might involve the temporary disposition of private property. Each executive department has certain public functions and duties, the performance of which is absolutely necessary to the existence of the government, and it may temporarily at least operate with seeming harshness upon individuals. But it is wisely indicated that the rights of the public must, in those particulars, override the rights of individuals, provided there be reserved to them an ultimate recourse to the judiciary."

The Cabinet. — The heads of the various departments compose the President's Cabinet; but this is a matter of custom, not of law, for the Cabinet, as a collective body, has no legal existence or powers. Congress, in creating the first departments in 1789, did not recognize, in any way, the possibility of a Cabinet council composed of the heads. Indeed, the act establishing the Treasury Department was designed, as we have seen, to bring the Secretary under congressional control in many ways. The Senate, being a small body, was then regarded as the real executive council on account of its powers of ratifying treaties and confirming appointments.

Whatever may have been the view of Congress, however, Washington regarded the four chief executive officials, including the Attorney-General, who was not made head of a department until 1870, as his confidential advisers, though the term Cabinet was not immediately applied to them. He also exercised his constitutional right of requiring opinions from the heads of departments, and took them into his confidence in all important matters very soon after the first appointments were made. We have direct evidence of Cabinet meetings as early as 1791, when Washington, having departed on a tour to the South, wrote to the three Secretaries: " I have expressed my wish, if any serious or important cases . . . should arise . . . that the Secretaries for the Departments of State, Treasury, and War may hold consultations thereon, to determine whether they are of such a nature as to demand my personal attendance." During his first administration, Washington, by a gradual process, welded the departmental heads into an executive council, and by 1793 we find the term Cabinet or Cabinet Council applied to this group of presidential advisers.

The Cabinet now meets on call of the President. The meetings are usually secret, and no record is kept of the transactions. As the special business of each department is discussed separately with the President by each officer, only matters of weight relative to the general policy of the administration are brought up for consideration at Cabinet meetings. Any important piece of legislation desired by the President or by a Cabinet officer and about to be submitted to Congress, will very probably be discussed in detail, especially if it concerns party principles. Votes are seldom taken on propositions, and they are of no significance beyond securing a mere expression of opinion. This is illustrated by an incident related of President Lincoln, who closed an important discussion in the Cabinet in which he found every member against him, with the announcement: " Seven nays, one aye, the ayes have it." Nevertheless, Cabinet meetings are of service to the administration, especially in maintaining harmonious coöperation among the departments and in formulating the executive policy.

The Cabinet is the President's council in a very peculiar sense, for, having no legal existence or warrant, it is not subjected as such to congressional control. In the first administration of President Jackson, the Senate requested the transmission of a paper purported to have been read by him to the heads of the executive departments, and he replied in no uncertain language: " The executive is a coördinate and independent branch of the government equally with the Senate, and I have yet to learn under what constitutional authority that branch of the legislature has a right to require of me an account of any communication, either verbally or in writing, made to the heads of departments acting as Cabinet council. As well might I be required to detail to the Senate the free and private conversations I have held with those officers on any subject relating to their duties and my own."

The Departments of National Administration. — The extraordinary agencies created for the prosecution of the war on the Central Powers are discussed below in the chapter on "Government in War Time." The organization and activities of the federal administration under normal peace conditions are indicated by the following table, giving the several departments and their chief offices and subdivisions, as they stood in the summer of 1918. A general notion of the functions intrusted to each department can be gathered from the titles of the agencies which it embraces.

Department of State. — The Secretary and three assistant secretaries; chief clerk; counselor; seven bureaus: diplomatic, consular, indexes and archives, accounts, rolls and library, appointments, citizenship; acting foreign trade adviser, adviser on commercial treaties; and five divisions: far-eastern affairs, near-eastern affairs, western European affairs, Latin-American affairs, and Mexican affairs.

Department of the Treasury. — The Secretary and six assistant secretaries; chief clerk; supervising architect; comptroller of the treasury; auditors for the Treasury, War, Interior, Navy, State (and other departments) and Post-Office Departments; treasurer of the United States; register of the treasury; comptroller of the currency; director of the mint; commissioner of internal revenue; public health service; coast guard; bureau of printing and engraving; federal farm loan bureau; bureau of war-risk insurance; general supply committee, one member of which is drawn from each of the government departments; custom-house.

Department of War. — The Secretary and three assistant secretaries; chief clerk; general staff; adjutant-general in charge of records; inspector-general; chief of the quartermaster's corps (supplies and transportation); surgeon-general; chief of engineers; chief of ordnance; judge-advocate-general; chief signal officer; chief of the bureau of insular affairs; board of engineers for rivers and harbors; division of militia affairs; chief of coast artillery; board of ordnance and fortification; provost marshal general; director of gas service; director of tank corps; war council; war credits board.

Department of Justice. — Attorney-General; assistants; solicitor-general; solicitors for the Departments of State, Treasury, Post-Office, Interior, Commerce, Labor, and internal revenue; chief clerk; division of accounts; attorneys in charge of pardons and titles; appointment and disbursing clerks; superintendent of prisons; chief of division of investigations; assistant attorney-general, customs division; special assistant to attorney-general for war work; librarian.

Post-Office Department. — Postmaster-General and four assistant postmasters-general; chief clerk; assistant attorney-general; purchasing agent; chief inspector; director of postal savings system; divisions of: postmasters' appointments, post-office service, dead letters, correspondence, railway mail service, foreign mails, railway adjustments, finance, stamps, money orders, registered mails, classification, rural mails, equipment and supplies.

Department of the Navy. — Secretary and assistant secretary; chief clerk; eight bureaus: navigation, yards and docks, ordnance, construction and repair, steam engineering, medicine and surgery, supplies, and accounts; judge-advocate-general; solicitor; naval consulting board; office of naval operations; naval militia affairs; navy yard and station, Washington, D.C.; naval medical school; naval hospital; attendance on officers; board for examination of medical officers; board for examination of dental officers; naval dispensary; general board; board of inspection and survey; naval examining board; naval retiring board; board of medical examiners; headquarters of marine corps; marine barracks.

Department of the Interior. — Secretary and two assistant secretaries; chief clerk; commissioner of patents; pensions; general land office; Indian affairs; education; geological survey; reclamation service; mines; national park service; St. Elizabeth's hospital; Columbia Institution for the Deaf; Howard University; Board of Indian Commissioners; Freedmen's Hospital; Alaskan Engineering Commission.

Department of Agriculture. — Secretary and three assistant secretaries; chief clerk; solicitor; bureaus of: farm management, animal industry, weather, chemistry, crop estimates, accounts and disbursements, entomology, soils, biological survey, plant industry; forest service; office of public roads and rural engineering; division of publications; states relations service; bureau of markets; insecticide and fungicide board; federal horticultural board; librarian.

Department of Commerce. — Secretary and assistant secretary; chief clerk; disbursing clerk; divisions of appointments, publications and supplies; bureaus of: foreign and domestic commerce, census, fisheries, navigation, and standards; coast and geodetic survey; lighthouses; steamboat inspection service.

Department of Labor. — Secretary and assistant secretary; chief clerk; disbursing clerk; appointment clerk; division of publications and supplies; conciliation; United States employment service; bureaus of immigration, naturalization, labor statistics and children.

Federal Boards and Commissions. — In addition to the ten departments there are the following boards and commissions:

The Interstate Commerce Commission, seven members, charged with the duty of supervising railways, express companies, and other concerns engaged in interstate commerce, determining the rates which may be charged, and prescribing certain conditions of operation. Government management of many " common carriers " during the war of course materially reduces the authority of this commission which is so powerful in times of peace.

The Civil Service Commission, three members, whose duty it is to administer the laws relative to the examination, selection, appointment, and dismissal of civil employees.

Federal Reserve Board, seven members, administering the banking laws and the system of reserve banks created by the act of December 23, 1913.

Federal Trade Commission, five members, created in 1914 and empowered to investigate the practices of trusts and corporations engaged in interstate commerce.

Federal Farm Loan Board, five members, created in 1916, to enforce the law of that year providing for the loaning of money to farmers and for related activities.

The United States Employees' Compensation Commission, three members, created in 1916, to enforce the law providing for compensation for federal employees injured in the performance of their duties.

United States Shipping Board, organized in 1916, five members, for the purpose of creating, developing, and encouraging a naval reserve and a merchant marine to meet the requirements of the commerce of the United States and to regulate carriers by water engaged in foreign and interstate commerce. The functions of this board were materially altered by the government's shipping activities undertaken shortly after the outbreak of the war (see below, Chapter VIII).

The United States Tariff Commission, six members, created in 1916, to investigate the subject of tariffs and tariff administration and report periodically to Congress.

To the list of federal agencies not embraced in any of the ten great departments may be added the International Bureau of American Republics, under the supervision of a director, charged with fostering trade relations throughout the two Americas, and finally the Government Printing Office.

The Civil Service. — The vast army of civil employees in the executive service of the United States at Washington and throughout the whole American empire is organized into a complicated hierarchy headed by the departmental officers who constitute the President's Cabinet. The head of each department, as noted above, usually has a number of assistants. There are, for example, four assistant postmasters-general and three assistant secretaries of state. The administrative work of each department is distributed among a number of bureaus and divisions, each with a chief officer, generally speaking, responsible to some higher authority. In each of the divisions or bureaus there are a number of clerks, technical experts, and employees serving in a variety of capacities. The officers and employees in the whole executive civil service on June 30, 1916, numbered approximately 462,000. Considering this vast army with regard to methods of appointment, we find that it falls into two groups: 296,000 admitted on examination, or under the merit system, and the remainder appointed without examination.

For a long period in American history the offices now filled by examination were subject to the spoils system — that is, they were given principally to party workers without special consideration for their fitness and without any test of abilities. After some tentative experiments at reforming this spoils system, Congress at length passed, in 1883, the Civil Service Act, which is still the fundamental law governing the federal service. This Act provides for a Civil Service Commission composed of three persons, no more than two of whom shall be adherents of the same party, appointed by the President and Senate, and charged with the duty of aiding the President, as he may request, in preparing suitable rules for competitive examinations designed to test the fitness of applicants for offices in the public service, already classified or to be classified by executive order under the Act, or by further legislation of Congress. The Commission aids the President generally in the execution of the Act.

The Act itself ordered the Secretary of the Treasury and the Postmaster-General to make classifications of certain employees within their respective jurisdictions, and at the same time provided that the heads of certain departments and offices should, at the direction of the President, revise any existing classification or arrangement of their employees and include in one or more of such classes subordinate officers not hitherto classified. In other words, the Act itself brought a few offices under the "merit system," and left the extension of the principle largely to the discretion of the President and future acts of Congress.

When the law went into force it applied to only about 14,000 places which were then included in the classified service. The number has been steadily increased, principally by executive orders, until to-day far more than half of all of the offices in the executive civil service are filled by the process of examination and promotion under the civil service rules. During his administration, President Roosevelt issued a large number of orders extending the merit system. For example, in 1901-02, he extended the application of the rules to the rural free delivery service; in 1902, at the suggestion of the President, the employees in the census office were classified by act of Congress; in 1904, the positions in the forestry service were made competitive; and in 1905, the special agents of the immigration bureau on duty in foreign countries were included within the classified service. This list of Mr. Roosevelt's extensions is by no means complete — it merely illustrates the way in which the President may steadily widen the range of the "merit system" by applying it to one group of government employees after another. When Mr. Roosevelt entered upon his administration there were about 100,000 officials in the classified service, and before the close of his second administration the number had increased to nearly 200,000.

The Operation of the Civil Service Law. — The Civil Service Commission, under the direction of the President, prepares the large variety of examinations required to test the fitness of candidates for the multitude of different offices. There is a chief examiner at Washington, and there are several hundred local boards of examiners scattered among the states and territories for the purpose of supervising local civil service examinations. The Act orders that boards of examiners shall be erected at such points as to make it reasonably convenient and inexpensive for applicants to attend examinations.

The Act requires that such examinations shall be practical in their character, and, so far as may be, relate to those matters which will fairly test the relative capacity and fitness of persons examined to discharge the duties of that branch of the government service to which they seek to be admitted. In preparing the examination papers it is the practice of the Commission to ask the coöperation of the various departments; if a technical position is to be filled, the department concerned usually notifies the

Commission, and very probably prepares the technical questions to test the fitness of candidates for the place.

The preparation of the examination papers for a large number of positions is relatively a simple matter, for about sixty-six per cent of federal offices covered by the merit system are clerical in character. Only about eleven per cent are reckoned as professional, technical, scientific, mechanical, and executive. Nearly as many of the clerical positions are in the postal service as in all the other branches of the federal administration combined.

Any citizen of the United States may apply for an examination admitting him to the federal service. For a long time, owing to the lax methods prevailing, aliens were often admitted to government employment, but within recent years the requirement of citizenship has been quite rigidly enforced. Applicants for examination are not even charged a fee, in spite of the fact that the Civil Service Commission has several times recommended the establishment of a nominal charge for the purpose of excluding the many thousands of ill-prepared persons who take the examinations in a gambling spirit — nothing to lose and possibly something to gain.

Through these examinations the Civil Service Commission must keep its registers of eligibles full, so that it can supply men of the most diverse training and experience when called upon by the several departments. On the same day, there may be demands for clerks, stenographers, expert chemists, patent examiners, draftsmen, interpreters, and postal clerks; and the Commission must be ready at once with a list of persons duly qualified for such positions.

Appointment and Removal of Employees. — When called upon, the Commission selects from the proper register and transmits to the department concerned the names of three candidates at the head of the list, who are (if possible) residents of the state wherein the appointment falls. From this list of three any one may be selected by the appointing officer, and the other names are returned to the Commission to be replaced upon the register. If the appointing officer refuses to accept any one of the three, he must give satisfactory reasons for his action. Every successful candidate is put on probation for a period of six months; then if his record is good his appointment is made permanent.

It should be noted, however, that there are certain exceptions to the operation of the rules in the matter of making appointments. (1) Preference is given to persons honorably discharged from the military or naval service; and, unless by direction of the Senate, no person who has been nominated for confirmation by the Senate shall be required to be classified or to pass an examination. (2) Appointments to the public service in the departments at Washington shall be apportioned among the several states and territories and the District of Columbia upon the basis of population — a principle which it is impossible to carry out in practice. (3) In general, private secretaries to the heads of departments, assistants, bureau chiefs, and attorneys and persons called upon to fill emergency employments are exempt from examination.

The process of removal from the federal service after appointment is a relatively simple matter. The rules require that no person shall be removed from a competitive position, " except for such causes as will promote the efficiency of the service." When the President or head of an executive department is convinced that any employee in the classified service is incapable or inefficient, he may remove such employee without notice. Whenever a subordinate officer recommends to the head of an executive department the removal or reduction in grade of some employee, the head of the department may, at his discretion, require that notice be given to the employee affected and a reasonable time afforded him for answering the same. The Civil Service Commission contends that the complaint frequently heard to the effect that unfit men are protected against removal by the rules is untrue. "On the contrary," says the Commission, "the power of removal for unfitness is with the head of the office. The appointing officer being responsible for the efficient performance of the work of his office, it rests with him to determine whether such cause exists as to require the removal of an employee in order to promote the efficiency or discipline of his office."

The courts do not interfere in cases of removal, on the ground that the right of appointing involves the right of removal and that the Civil Service Act limits the power of removal in only one instance — refusal to contribute money or service to a political party. In practice, however, whenever a large number of employees of the same political faith are removed from office, it is presumed that the removal was for political reasons, and the officer making the removals is required to show that just cause existed for each removal; but the courts will not intervene.

The Political Rights and Duties of Employees. — In making promotions, removals, and reductions in rank it is very difficult to exclude partisan politics from consideration, but attempts have been made by act of Congress and presidential orders to protect employees in the classified service from undue political influence, and also to withdraw them from too great activity in partisan politics. The original Civil Service Act provides that no person in the public service is for that reason under any obligations to contribute to any political fund or to render any political service, and that he shall not be removed or otherwise prejudiced for refusing to do so. Furthermore, no person in the public service has a right to use his authority to coerce the political action of any person. No recommendation by a Senator or a member of the House of Representatives, except as to the character or residence of an applicant, can be lawfully received or considered by any person concerned in making examinations or appointments under the Civil Service Act. Members of Congress and executive, judicial, military, and naval officers are forbidden to be involved in soliciting or receiving political assistance or contributions from any officer employed by the United States or from any person receiving compensation from the United States. The practice of soliciting campaign contributions in the buildings occupied by branches of the federal government is likewise forbidden by law.

Other forms of political activities, however, were left by the Act to the control of the heads of departments, and from time to time executive and departmental orders were issued for the purpose of eliminating abuses arising from the active participation of inferior office-holders in party affairs. At length, in 1907, political activity in the broadest sense was placed under the supervision of the Civil Service Commission by an amendment to the rules, adopted by the President, providing that " all persons who by the provisions of these rules are in the competitive classified service, while retaining the right to vote as they please and to express privately their opinions on all political subjects, shall take no active part in political management or in political campaigns." This rule has been construed by the Commission to forbid the use of official positions for the benefit of any political party; and since its adoption it has been interpreted to prohibit the following types of political activity: "Service on political committees, service as delegates to county, state, or district conventions of a political party, although it was understood that they were not 'to take or use any political activity in going to these conventions or otherwise violate the civil service rules'; continued political activity and leadership; the publication of a newspaper in the interest of a political party; membership in a club taking an active part in political campaigns and management; the circulation of petitions having a political object; service as a commissioner of elections in a community where it was notorious that a commissioner of elections must be an active politician." In 1918, Secretary McAdoo, Director of the Federal Railway Administration, issued a drastic order to railway employees forbidding political activity of all kinds.

As the number of federal employees increases it is obvious that the problem of their rights and duties will become more serious. Questions like the following are already coming up for consideration. Should federal employees organize unions for the purpose of improving their wages and conditions of employment? If so, should they be permitted to use their votes to bring political pressure to bear upon Congress to grant their demands? If workingmen in industries enjoying prosperity under a protective tariff are allowed to use their votes in support of the party that enacts the tariff law under which their wages are increased, why should discrimination be made against other workingmen whose wages depend upon direct governmental action? If the government refuses to grant to federal employees the wages or other concessions which they ask, should they be allowed to leave the service in a body, in other words, "strike" against the government as an employer? If a person has to surrender his political rights on entering the federal service will not able and independent people be deterred from seeking to enter that service? If a federal employee believes in some reform in governmental methods should he be denied the right enjoyed by other citizens to voice his opinions on public questions? It must be admitted that these are questions which cannot be thoughtlessly answered but which must be answered wisely in the not distant future.

The principle of permanent tenure involved in the merit system of appointment also raises the question as to what shall be done with government employees who have passed the age of efficient service. It is possible to keep the civil service up to a high standard only by constantly recruiting it from able young men in the prime of life. This throws upon the officer responsible for administration the unwelcome duty of reducing the pay and the rank of the older men or discharging them altogether. If these older men are kept in service, it is frankly out of a generous appreciation of their condition. They are not only inefficient themselves, but by holding high places which they have won by meritorious services they block the way for the promotion of capable and energetic younger men. " No man," said the quartermaster-general recently, " with the slightest appreciation of the loyalty of these old, tried, and faithful employees will urge that they should be discharged, and a reduction in salary is so disheartening to them as to render nugatory their services after such action. No matter how kindly the necessity is explained to them, reduction is a severe blow. . . . If they are retained in the grades attained by merit in the period when they could and did do all or more than their duty, the effect on the younger clerks who then do the work is depressing in the extreme. Some provision for retiring the old clerks ought to be made. More good effects on administration would probably come through provision for retirement than any other one action that could now be taken, and its effect would doubtless prove as beneficial as did the establishment of the merit system."

President Taft took this view of the situation in his message of December 7, 1909, in which he declared that, in spite of the opposition to the establishment of civil pensions, which had naturally grown out of the heavy burden of military pensions, he was strongly convinced that no other practical solution of the difficulties presented by superannuation in the civil service could be found, than that of a system of civil pensions. No action, however, has been taken on this recommendation.

Problems of Administration. — With the increase in the functions of the national government and the growth in the number and variety of technical civil employees, the following considerations become of prime importance:

I. How can we educate the public up to an appreciation of the necessity for trained and expert service in every branch of the government?

II. How can we so order our public service that it will attract the ablest men and women and guarantee progressive careers to those who prove loyal and efficient?

III. How can we develop a science of public administration in all of its branches?

IV. How can we best train our prospective civil servants in all of the various arts, sciences, and crafts called for by the exigencies of modern government and adjust our curricula and educational methods to the requirements of government recruiting? In other words, how can we best gear up our educational ideals and institutions with the demands of efficient government?

V. How can we continue the training of those admitted to the lower ranges of the public service, while they are in service, thus preparing them for progressive advancement according to talents and aptitudes?

VI. How can we develop our civil service commissions into genuine recruiting agencies capable of supplying the government with exactly the type of service needed at any given moment and maintaining a loyal and efficient personnel? And this is said in no disparagement of the splendid work done by many commissions under the handicaps now imposed by law, custom, and public opinion.

In brief, how can we make our science of government a true science of management rather than a device for distributing party spoils, and at the same time retain and develop those democratic ideals which we have thought worthy of this great nation?

Administration of Territories. — The continental possessions of the United States are now all organized into states duly admitted by Congress to the Union. As regards the outlying territories which have large populations, it has been the consistent policy of America to foster the progressive development of self-government. This policy is well illustrated in the history of the Philippines, the government of which is very complicated, owing to the character of the populations ranging from highly cultured Spaniards to poor and ignorant tribesmen, and owing also to the fact that there are about thirty different peoples speaking about as many different languages or dialects. The government of the Philippines has passed through the following stages: (1) control by American military authorities under the direction of the President of the United States as commander in chief; (2) control by a civil commission under the supervision of Mr. W. H. Taft as civil governor of the islands; (3) the addition of a popularly elected assembly in 1907 to coöperate with the governor and with the civil commission appointed by the President and Senate acting as sort of upper chamber; (4) substitution, in 1916, of a popularly elected Philippine senate to take the place of the civil commission, including a few senators appointed by the governor-general to represent the non-Christian provinces; (5) declaration, in 1916, of the intention of the United States to recognize Philippine independence " as soon as stable government can be established therein."

All other territories of the United States with considerable populations and well-settled life — Hawaii, Alaska, and Porto Rico also enjoy a large measure of self-government on the principles attained in the development of Philippine administration. In each there is a governor-general appointed by the President and Senate of the United States, and a legislature composed of two houses, both elected by popular vote (in Alaska including women).[1]

SELECTED REFERENCES

Fairlie, *The National Administration* (New York, 1905); Roosevelt, *Autobiography* (New York, 1913), Chaps. x–xv; C. R. Fish, *The Civil Service and the Patronage* (1905); Bryce, *The American Commonwealth*, Vol. I, Chap. ix; H. B. Learned, *The President's Cabinet* (New Haven, 1912); G. Hunt, *The Department of State* (New Haven, 1914).

[1] The minor possessions of the United States, Guam, American Samoa, Wake and other islands, and the Virgin Islands (acquired from Denmark in 1916) are under governors appointed by the President pending further action by Congress.

CHAPTER VII

OUR DEMOCRACY: PRIVILEGES AND DUTIES OF CITIZENSHIP

In an absolute monarchy, the responsibility for the government rests upon the monarch and his advisers; in a democracy it rests upon all the voters and in a sense upon all the people who have any share in the formation of public opinion. Although it is customary and proper to associate democratic government with the growth of liberty in the world, it must be remembered that democracy does not mean and cannot mean the right of every citizen to do as he pleases irrespective of the rights of his fellow citizens. In other words the duty and responsibility of understanding and granting the rights of others are the very essence of American government. Democracy cannot imply that each is " free " to follow his own bent and pleasure. On the contrary it implies that the liberty of the individual must be subjected at every turn to the requirements of the common good. In the long and bitter struggle against kingly governments emphasis was laid, as was natural, upon the liberty of the individual as against the tyranny of royal officers. After popular government was established, however, it became evident that while citizens were not to be arbitrarily ordered about by royal agents they were nevertheless under the solemn obligation to sacrifice " liberty to do as they pleased " to the standards of common right. It is necessary therefore to remember that in our democracy there can be no rights without duties; no privileges without responsibility. Unlimited liberty is anarchy.

The Legal Conditions of Citizenship. — In order that it may be definitely known who are entitled to the rights of citizens and subject to the responsibilities of the same, it is necessary to lay down very specifically legal conditions under which American citizenship is enjoyed or may be acquired.

In international law, the term "citizenship" means membership in a nation, but at the time of the formation of our federal Constitution it had received no very definite connotation either in law or popular practice. The Constitution, therefore, speaks of "citizens of the United States" and "citizens of the states"; but a strict usage of the term would require us to speak of citizens of the United States and residents or inhabitants of the states, although this usage might popularly be regarded as a species of pedantry. The state, however, has no power to confer or withhold citizenship, although it may confer many civil and political rights on foreigners. The exclusive right to admit aliens to citizenship is given to the federal government by the clause authorizing Congress to make uniform rules of naturalization.

Citizenship in the United States may be acquired by birth or by naturalization. All persons born in the United States and not subject to any foreign power, excluding Indians not taxed, are *ipso facto* citizens of the United States. This is called citizenship by reason of birth in a particular place, *i.e., jure soli*. To secure civic rights to children born to citizens of the United States, residing abroad, Congress has provided by law that all children born out of the limits of the jurisdiction of the United States, whose fathers are at the time of their birth citizens thereof, shall be deemed citizens of the United States. The rights of citizenship, however, do not descend to children whose fathers never resided in the United States.

Foreigners may be admitted to citizenship by naturalization, either collectively or individually. Collective naturalization may occur when a foreign territory and its inhabitants are transferred to the United States. The manner of this naturalization is generally stipulated in the terms of the treaty transfer. For example, the treaty with France ceding the Louisiana territory provided that the inhabitants of the territory should be incorporated into the Union of the United States and admitted as soon as possible, according to the principles of the federal Constitution, to the enjoyment of all the rights, advantages, and immunities of citizens of the United States.

The process of naturalizing individuals is subject, in all of its details, to the laws of Congress, and it is committed to the charge of certain specified courts. Naturalization can be effected only in a circuit or district court of the United States, or a district or supreme court of a territory, or a court of record of a state having law or equity jurisdiction in cases in which the amount in controversy is unlimited, and having a seal and a clerk. Only white persons and persons of African descent may be naturalized; the Chinese are excluded expressly by law, and this exclusion has been extended to the Japanese on the ground that they are not white persons.

The process of naturalization falls into three stages: (1) At least two years prior to his admission, the alien (who must be at least eighteen years of age) makes a declaration on oath before the clerk of a court stating his intention to become a citizen and renouncing his allegiance to any foreign power. (2) Not less than two years nor more than seven years after this declaration (and after five years' residence in the United States), the alien must file in his own handwriting his petition for citizenship, stating that he is not opposed to organized government, is not a polygamist, intends to become a citizen, and renounces his allegiance to his former country. This petition must be verified by the affidavits of two citizens certifying to the residence and good moral character of the applicant. (3) After ninety days have elapsed from the date of filing the petition, the application is heard by the court. The applicant renews his adherence to the declarations made in the petition, and is then examined by the court. This examination may be formal or thorough and searching, according to the standards of the judge conducting the final hearing. Examining judges are required to satisfy themselves that all the provisions of the law have been complied with, that the applicant has behaved as a man of good moral character, is attached to the principles of the Constitution of the United States, and well disposed to the good order and happiness of the same. When the court is duly satisfied, the certificate of naturalization is issued. A large power of discrimination is thus conferred upon the court, and there are some instances of its being abused by judges personally opposed to the political principles expressed by the alien applicants.

The Right of Suffrage. — Not all citizens have the right to vote. The right of suffrage is restricted by law to certain persons. The Constitution of the United States as originally adopted contained no positive provisions relating to the right to vote, but left the question to the states for solution by stipulating that voters for members of the House of Representatives should have the qualifications requisite for electors of the most numerous branch of the state legislature, and at the same time permitting the state legislatures to decide how presidential electors should be chosen. Accordingly there does not exist in the United States a national suffrage distinct from the suffrage of the respective states. Thus matters stood until the close of the Civil War, when the Fourteenth and Fifteenth amendments were adopted.

The effect of these provisions, however, was not to create one uniform suffrage throughout the Union, but to leave the regulation of the matter to the states, subject to the condition that " when the right to vote at any election for the choice of electors for President and Vice-President of the United States, Representatives in Congress, the executive and judicial officers of a state or the members of the legislature thereof, is denied to any of the male inhabitants of such states, being twenty-one years of age, and citizens of the United States, or in any way abridged, except for participation in rebellion, or other crime, the basis of representation therein shall be reduced in the proportion which the number of such male citizens shall bear to the whole number of male citizens twenty-one years of age in such states "; and to the further condition that the right of citizens to vote shall not be denied or abridged by the United States or by any state on account of race, color, or previous condition of servitude.

Notwithstanding these provisions, a uniform manhood suffrage has not been adopted throughout the United States. Each state provides, usually in its constitution, the limitations on the right to vote. In some states, women are admitted to the suffrage; in others, tax, educational, property, and other qualifications are imposed; and in several states we have the peculiar anomaly of foreigners, who have announced their intention of becoming citizens, being permitted to vote for state and even national officers.

The right to hold office is usually correlative with the right to vote, and as a general principle all those who possess the qualifications prescribed for the exercise of the suffrage may hold any public office within the gift of the people. In the early days of our history it was quite common to impose higher property qualifications on public officers than on voters, but such discriminations are now swept away. The only discrimination now remaining is that of age. The federal Constitution, for example, provides that Representatives must be twenty-five years of age, Senators, thirty, and the President, thirty-five. State constitutions frequently require that certain officers must be older than twenty-one, the limit fixed for voters.

The Right of Citizens to Participate in Government. — In the beginning of our history the right of citizens to share in the government was limited (except in town meetings and on a few occasions) to (1) the choice of public officers to represent them and act in their name and (2) the holding of public offices. Even the first state constitutions as a rule were not submitted to the voters for their approval. In fact, only three of the eighteenth-century constitutions were laid before the electorate for ratification or rejection. Slowly, however, the idea came to be accepted that voters, in a final analysis, had the right to pass upon their own fundamental laws. The New York constitution of 1821 was referred to the electorate, and it further provided that amendments should likewise be submitted to the voters after having received legislative approval. By the middle of the nineteenth century the doctrine of the constitutional referendum was fairly fixed, and most of the constitutions since 1850 have been approved by popular vote. Exceptions are those of Delaware (1897), Mississippi (1890), South Carolina (1895), and Virginia (1902).

The doctrine of popular referendum was early extended to several important matters besides constitutions and amendments. For example, the legislature of New York, in 1849, submitted the proposition of establishing free schools to the decision of the electors; and the question of woman suffrage was laid before the voters of Massachusetts in 1895. It is likewise common to require the reference of special financial measures to popular approval; for example, the constitution of New York fixes a certain debt limit, beyond which the legislature cannot go without receiving the approval of a majority of the electors voting on the proposition. The practice of referring local laws of a special character, such as those selecting county seats and changing county or city boundaries, was also adopted early in our history.

It was not such a long step, therefore, from these and similar practices, to the adoption of a complete system for permitting the voters to participate in the making of ordinary laws as well as constitutions, in other words, to the adoption of the initiative and referendum, whereby the voters may initiate any measure or require the referendum on any legislative act. The initiative is a device whereby any person or group of persons may draft a statute, and on securing the signatures of a small percentage of the voters may compel the state officials, with or without the intervention of the legislature, to submit the same to popular vote; and if the required popular approval is secured, the proposal becomes a law. The referendum is a plan whereby a small percentage of the voters may demand that any statute passed by the legislature (with the exception of certain laws) must be submitted to the electorate and approved by a stipulated majority before going into effect. But as is pointed out below, so many variations in the system are possible that each of the several plans must be studied in detail in order to understand all of its possibilities.

Not less than seventeen states, including South Dakota, Oregon, Idaho, Massachusetts, Missouri, Montana, Utah, Maine, Oklahoma, Nevada, Arkansas, Colorado, California, Washington, Nebraska, Ohio, and Arizona, have established the initiative and referendum in one form or another. During the past few years the spread of the idea has not been so rapid as in the decade before 1912. The scheme has been put into operation a number of times, particularly in Oregon, South Dakota, and Oklahoma, but Oregon has given it the most extensive trial under fair circumstances; and that state has also worked out a complete scheme for educating the voters on measures referred to them. The system was established in Oregon by a constitutional amendment approved in June, 1902. This amendment provided that any legislative measure might be initiated by a petition bearing the signatures of eight per cent of the voters and containing the proposed measure in full. The petition must be filed with the secretary of state not less than four months before election day; it is mandatory upon him to submit it to popular vote, and if the proposal is approved by a majority of all the electors voting on it, it becomes a part of the statutory law of Oregon. Any act passed by the legislature must likewise be referred to the electorate if five per cent of the voters file a duly executed petition within ninety days after the adjournment of the legislature, demanding such a referendum.

A modified form of the initiative was established in Illinois, in 1901, by a law creating what is known as the " Public Opinion System." Under this law twenty-five per cent of the registered voters of any incorporated town, village, city, township, county, or school district may compel the submission of any local question to popular vote; and ten per cent of the registered voters of the state may secure the submission of a proposition to the electorate of the entire commonwealth. The petition for taking public opinion on a question must be filed not less than sixty days before the day of the election at which it is to be submitted. If the voters approve a proposition referred to them, it is understood that public opinion demands its enactment into law; but as the members of the legislature are not pledged to obey the wishes of their constituents, this expression of public opinion is regarded as merely advisory and, therefore, of slight importance.

The system of initiative and referendum is being extended to local as well as to state-wide matters. The constitution of Oklahoma provides that the powers of the initiative and referendum, reserved to the people for the state at large, are also reserved to the voters of every county and district therein as to all local legislative or administrative actions in their respective counties and districts. A Nebraska law of 1897 provides that an ordinance or any other measure may be proposed in counties, cities, and other local divisions by a petition signed by fifteen per cent of the voters and given the effect of law by the approval of a majority. The same statute authorizes local government bodies voluntarily to submit propositions to popular ratification, and requires them to refer any measure to popular vote if it is demanded by a petition bearing the signatures of fifteen per cent of the electors. According to an Indiana statute of 1899, the referendum may be demanded by forty per cent of the voters in an incorporated town within thirty days after the passage of any ordinance to purchase water or light plants or grant franchises; and if any such proposition is rejected on the referendum, no similar ordinance can be enacted within three years. The various local option laws permitting the voters of counties and other units of local government to pass upon the question of licensing saloons may likewise be regarded as a part of the general scheme of initiative and referendum. More than three hundred cities use the initiative and referendum in making charters or municipal ordinances or both.

Undoubtedly, the initiative and referendum, especially for important matters, have found a permanent place among our institutions. In saying this, however, it should be noted that the very terms " initiative " and " referendum " are vague, and the concrete forms which they may take range from extreme radicalism to a conservatism more rigid than the most rigid constitutionalism. The principles behind the initiative and referendum may be worked out into many forms:

I. The initiative may be separated from the referendum, as in the Michigan constitution of 1908, according to which constitutional amendments only could be initiated by petition, and the referendum could be employed only by legislative action.

II. The initiative or referendum may be restricted to statutory enactments, leaving judicial control under the state constitution unaffected.

III. The initiative or referendum may be employed only in the case of constitutional provisions.

IV. The referendum alone may be exercised at the option of the legislature, as was once the case in Massachusetts.

V. The referendum may be set in motion by an initiative petition, — by five per cent of the voters or twenty-five per cent.

VI. The referendum on constitutions and constitutional amendments may be compulsory, as is well-nigh universal in the United States to-day.

VII. The initiative may be coupled with a provision that the legislature may submit in addition to any initiated measure an optional provision, giving the voters a choice between the proposal of the private parties and that which has been debated and digested in the legislature.

VIII. The initiative may be coupled with a provision that any measure initiated which may be adopted by the state legislature in due form shall become a law, unless on a petition of the voters a referendum is required.

IX. The number of voters necessary to initiate a constitutional amendment may be fixed at a definite figure or a percentage of the voters, and a larger number may be required to initiate a constitutional amendment than is required to initiate an ordinary statute. For example, in Oklahoma, eight per cent of the voters may initiate a legislative measure, while fifteen per cent are required to propose amendments to the constitution by petition.

X. A differentiation may be made between the number necessary to initiate a new measure and the number required to sign a referendum petition on an act passed by the legislature.

XI. A large number of variations may be made in the number of votes necessary to the enactment of any particular provision into law. It may be a simple majority of all those voting for or against the measure. It may be a simple majority of those voting for and against the measure, providing that majority is equivalent to a certain percentage of all the votes cast for some particular officer at a general election. A difference may be made between the vote required for the approval of an initiated measure and that required on a legislative enactment referred to the voters on petition; as, for example, in Oklahoma, where a measure referred to the people by the initiative can go into force only when approved " by a majority of the votes cast in such election," while a legislative measure referred to the people by a referendum petition needs to be approved only " by a majority of the votes cast thereon."

XII. The initiative may be restricted, as in a proposed Wisconsin constitutional amendment, by a provision to the effect that it can apply only to measures which have been introduced in regular form in the state legislature — the design of this being to secure a certain amount of legislative consideration of any measure referred to popular approval.

XIII. The initiative may be used to introduce measures into the legislature, as in Ohio, where three per cent of the voters may cause the introduction of a proposal into the legislature. If it is rejected there, an additional three per cent petition may cause the reference of the measure directly to the voters.

XIV. The initiative and referendum may be accompanied by provisions designed to secure general publicity and to educate the voter, as is the case in Oregon.

XV. Finally, the initiative and referendum may take the milder form of a public opinion bill such as was provided by the Illinois law of 1901 authorizing the submission of any question to popular vote on the initiative of a certain percentage of voters, with the understanding that popular approval of the proposal constitutes merely a pious recommendation to the legislature.

The Right to Recall Officers. — Not content with vesting the legislative power in the voters, the advocates of " direct " government have contrived a new device, or rather reconstructed an old institution, known as the recall. The principle upon which it is based is simple, namely, that elected officers are merely agents of the popular will and that the voters should have at all times an opportunity to pass upon the conduct of their representatives. The device itself is a plan whereby a certain number of the voters, whenever they are dissatisfied with the services of a public officer (usually elective officers only), may, on petition, compel the officer in question to stand for a new election and thus submit his claims to the judgment of the electors. The recall began its recent career in the city of Los Angeles, California, where it was introduced in the city charter in 1903. At first it attracted little attention, and then suddenly it sprang into prominence. A state-wide form of the plan was introduced into the Oregon constitution in 1908, and was seized upon by the makers of commission charters for cities as a useful check on the large powers conferred upon the commissioners. California adopted it for state-wide purposes in 1911, Arizona in 1911–1912, Arkansas, Idaho, Washington, Colorado, and Nevada in 1912; and other states have amendments pending.

Although apparently a simple institution, the recall is susceptible of a large number of variations which affect very considerably its character as a practical instrument:

I. The percentage required to force an election to recall an officer may be high or low. It is usually about twenty-five per cent, as in Oregon.

II. The signers of petitions may be secured by solicitors at their homes or places of business, or they may be compelled to appear before a city official.

III. The recall may be used only once against the same officer under some of the provisions, and under others, as in Oregon, it may be used many times against the same officer, if the sponsors for the second and following petitions pay the expenses of the preceding elections.

IV. The vote required to remove an officer may vary. It may be equal to a majority of all the votes cast at the election at which he was elected in the first instance, or it may be simply a majority of those voting at the recall election. Moreover, the recall election may be divided into two parts: the question of removal may be submitted first to popular vote and this followed by an election to fill the vacancy; or the vote on the recall may simply take the form of an election at which the officer against whom the petition is filed may stand if he likes.

V. The recall may be restricted to administrative officers and not applied to the judiciary at all, or it may apply to all elective officers (and in one or two instances attempts have been made to apply it to appointive officers).

Although the recall has been in existence for a number of years, it has not been used very extensively. It was employed in Los Angeles in 1904 and again in 1909 to unseat mayors, and in Seattle in 1911 to oust the mayor. It has been used once against a judicial officer, in San Francisco, to oust a police judge who was charged with being too lenient with the vice elements. There are a few other instances of its use in local government, but it has not been brought into play for a state-wide campaign as yet. Although it has been overdone in one or two western cities, the recall seems to be more of " a gun behind the door," as President Wilson characterized it, to be employed in rare emergencies than for everyday use.

Personal and Property Rights of Citizens and Persons under the Federal Constitution. — The constitutional limitations on the federal government fall into two groups: (*a*) Those designed to protect personal liberty against arbitrary interference on the part of the government, and (*b*) those designed to protect private property against confiscation and irregular action on the part of federal authorities.

I. The limitations on behalf of personal rights which, under the Constitution, run against the federal government may be divided into five classes. In the first place, Congress cannot make any law respecting the establishment of a religion, nor can it interfere with the freedom of religious worship. This does not mean, however, that any person has a right to commit an act, under the guise of a religious ceremony, which transgresses the ordinary law of the land. This point was made by the Supreme Court in a case involving the right of Congress to prohibit polygamy in the territory of Utah and punish offenders who violated the law.

In the second place, Congress has no power to abridge freedom of speech or of the press. It was the purpose of this clause to prevent Congress from establishing a press censorship or enacting any law prohibiting political criticism. In spite of this express provision, Congress passed in 1798 a Sedition Act providing heavy penalties for resisting the lawful acts of the federal officials and for publishing anything bringing or tending to bring the federal government or any of its officers into disrepute. Under this act many American citizens were fined and imprisoned for what would be regarded to-day as harmless criticism of public authorities. When the question of the power of Congress to punish persons libeling the government came before the Supreme Court incidentally, the Court refused to pass upon the constitutionality of the Alien and Sedition law in the abstract. The Espionage Act passed on June 15, 1917 (see below, Chapter VIII), rests upon a different footing because it is a war measure designed to prevent interference with the enforcement of laws necessary to the prosecution of the armed conflict with the enemy.

In the third place, the Constitution guarantees to the people the right to assemble peaceably and petition the government for redress of grievances. This right is upheld against state governments as well as the federal government; but, of course, it does not secure to the petitioners the privilege of having their petition acted upon by the federal authorities.

In the fourth place, the power of the federal government to punish persons is hedged about in many ways. Congress has no power to define treason; it is defined in the Constitution: "Treason against the United States shall consist only in levying war against them or in adhering to their enemies, giving them aid and comfort." Congress cannot, therefore, vindictively declare any act treason which does not meet its approval.

Furthermore, the trial of persons accused of this high crime is carefully safeguarded. No person can be convicted of treason unless on the testimony of two witnesses to the overt act or on confession in open court. In the case of the United States v. The Insurgents, the Court, interpreting a federal statute, ordered that the names of the jurors and a list of witnesses should be furnished the accused; and that a reasonable time be allowed for the defense to prepare its case after receiving this information. The Court, furthermore, declared that until the overt act of treason had been proved by testimony of two witnesses, no evidence relating to the charges could be introduced.

While Congress has the power to provide the penalties for treason, the Constitution expressly stipulates that no attainder of treason shall work corruption of blood or forfeiture except during the life of the person attainted. In old English practice, corruption of blood meant the destruction of all inheritable qualities, so that any attainted person could not inherit lands or other hereditaments from his ancestors nor retain those which he already possessed or transmit them to his heirs. The constitutional provision mentioned above was designed to prevent this punishment of the relatives of traitors; and accordingly no punishment or proceedings may be construed to work a forfeiture of the real estate of a traitor longer than his natural life.

In the fifth place, proceedings against persons charged with crime under the federal law are controlled by several explicit provisions. Congress cannot act as a court by passing a bill of attainder condemning any person to death or to imprisonment or imposing any penalty whatsoever. Congress can pass no ex post facto law; that is, no law making an act a crime which was not a crime when committed, or adding new penalties after a commission of an act, or modifying the procedure in any such way as to make it substantially easier to convict. Federal authorities have no power of arresting wholesale on general warrant; all warrants of arrest must be issued only upon probable causes supported by oath or affirmation and particularly describing the place to be searched and the persons and things to be seized. Indictment by grand jury and trial by jury are secured to all persons coming within the jurisdiction of the federal authorities, except in the insular possessions. The writ of habeas corpus cannot be suspended unless in case of rebellion or invasion, when it may be required by public safety; that is, under all ordinary circumstances any person held by federal authorities has the right to have a speedy preliminary hearing before a proper judicial tribunal. Excessive bail cannot be demanded by federal authorities; in other words, except in capital cases, federal courts must release prisoners on bail, and must not fix the amount at such an unreasonable sum as practically to deny the right. Finally, in general, the federal government must allow due process of law in all of its criminal proceedings: the trial must be open and speedy and in the state and district where the crime was committed; the defendant must be informed of the nature and cause of the charge against him; the witnesses against him must be brought face to face with him; he may force, by compulsory process, the attendance of witnesses in his favor; he cannot be compelled to testify against himself in any criminal case; and he has a right to have the assistance of counsel in preparing and presenting his defense.

II. The limitations on the federal government [1] in behalf of property rights are relatively few in number, but they are fundamental in character. The power to define property is under our system left to the state governments, subject to the one great restriction that slavery and involuntary servitude, that is, property in man, shall not exist. Congress has no power to define property except in the territories not organized into states. Moreover, the Constitution provides some explicit limitations on the power of the federal government to attack the property of private persons: Congress cannot impose duties on articles exported from any state; all direct taxes (except income taxes) must be apportioned according to the population. Duties, imposts, and excises must be uniform, that is, must fall upon the same article with the same weight everywhere throughout the United States.

[1] For federal limitations on state governments in behalf of property, see above Chap. III.

In order to protect the taxpayer, it was provided in the Constitution that revenue bills must originate in the House of Representatives, which is composed of members chosen directly by the voters; but this provision is a dead letter in practice. The Constitution also stipulates that no money shall be drawn from the treasury except under appropriations made by law; consequently the executive authority cannot on its own motion withdraw money from the public treasury.

It is not only by way of taxation that the federal government may approach private property. It enjoys the power of eminent domain; in other words, it may take private property for public use; but it must make just compensation to the owner. In determining what is just compensation, federal authorities must take into account the use for which the property in question is suitable and pay due regard to the existing business or wants of the community and such as may be reasonably expected in the immediate future. The proceedings in ascertaining the value of property taken for public use may be prosecuted before commissioners or special boards or the courts, with or without the intervention of a jury as Congress may determine. All that is required is that the examination into the value of the property shall be conducted in a fair and impartial manner, affording the owner of property in question an opportunity to present evidence as to its value and to be heard on this matter.

The Duties of Citizens. — The obligations imposed upon citizens who enjoy the privileges of American democracy are twofold: legal and moral. The former, by the nature of circumstances, cannot be enumerated here. They range from the duty of rendering military service when called upon to that of driving upon the right side of the road. Such obligations are defined by the law and are enforced by public authorities. They, of course, vary from time to time as new laws are made or old laws are repealed.

The moral obligations are less easily defined, though many of them are quite clear in principle. First among these is the duty of voting when officers are to be elected or measures are submitted on a referendum. The right to vote, as we have seen, is a legal right, and in some countries those who refuse to exercise it are punishable by law. In this country, however, the exercise of the privilege is only a moral obligation resting upon those who have the legal right and they may refuse to vote without incurring any penalties. Those who do refuse are shirking a responsibility and, to that extent, failing to aid in making the government of the people the best possible government.

A second moral obligation, which is closely related to the first, is the duty of being informed about public questions that are ultimately to be decided by the casting of ballots. The citizen who fails to inform himself about the political issues before the people and who merely votes as he is told by some other person is likely to be as dangerous to good government, if not more dangerous, than the citizen who refuses to vote at all. It is for this reason that education is such a vital element in the successful working of the democratic form of government.

In seeking to become informed, the voter will become broader in his views and more inclined to respect the opinions of those from whom he differs. He will learn, with the father of the American Constitution, James Madison, that mankind has a strong propensity "to fall into mutual animosities"; that "landed interest, a manufacturing interest, a mercantile interest, a moneyed interest, with many lesser interests grow up of necessity in civilized nations," and that "the regulation of these various and interfering interests forms the principal task of modern legislation and involves the spirit of party and faction in the necessary and ordinary operations of government." It is by seeking to comprehend the claims and interests of the various parties and factions that the voter obtains the breadth of view and depth of understanding that fit him for wise decisions in matters of public policy.

This leads inevitably to the assumption of a third moral obligation, that of toleration and respect for the opinions of others. This is one of the most difficult but one of the most necessary virtues for the success of democratic government. Where freedom reigns, there will always be differences of opinion, and government by the people, which means government by public opinion, inevitably implies that differences of opinion shall be fairly heard, openly discussed, honestly adjusted. Anything short of this is incompatible with democracy and fatal to the progress of enlightened humanity. As President Wilson has so finely said: "The whole purpose of democracy is that we may hold council with one another, so as not to depend upon the understanding of one man, but to depend upon the counsel of all. For only as men are brought into council and state their own needs and interests, can the general interests of a great people be compounded into a policy that will be suitable to all." Without the toleration involved in common counsel there can be no genuine information; without information the obligations of citizenship cannot be faithfully fulfilled.

SELECTED REFERENCES

Woodrow Wilson, *The New Freedom* (New York, 1913); Burgess, *Political Science and Constitutional Law*, Vol. I, Book ii; J. A. Smith, *The Spirit of American Government* (New York, 1907); Bryce, *The American Commonwealth*, Vol. II; Barnett, *The Operation of the Initiative, Referendum and Recall in Oregon* (New York, 1915); Walter Weyl, *The New Democracy* (New York, 1912); H. Croly, *Progressive Democracy* (New York, 1914); W. H. Taft, *Popular Government* (New Haven, 1913).

CHAPTER VIII

GOVERNMENT IN WAR TIME

Mobilizing the Nation for War. — Never in the history of the United States has there been enacted by Congress a body of legislation so fundamental in its character and so far-reaching in its influence as the group of laws which have been passed since the declaration of war on Germany, April 6, 1917. This legislation provided not only for the raising and equipping of armies, the construction of navies, and supplying materials to fighting forces on the battle line, but it reached out in every direction controlling food supplies, raw materials, railways, mines, forests, and industrial concerns in order to make sure that nothing was left undone that would strengthen the soldiers for the great task before them. That is not all. Provision was also made for war risk insurance designed to place upon the people of the United States rather than upon the soldiers themselves responsibility for those who depend wholly or in part upon the earnings of men withdrawn from civil life to serve in the army and the navy. To the important legislation of the federal government must be added extraordinary measures taken by the legislatures of the several states designed to aid in putting the country in a state of preparedness to meet all of the exigencies arising from the war. Such legislation, national and state, touching every phase and activity of American economic life — farms, mines, mills, and railways — will obviously exert an influence far beyond the purposes of the war itself and long after the treaty of peace has been signed. It therefore deserves careful study because it reveals the earnestness of America's resolve in raising and supporting armies and navies, and it also sets before the people many of the grave problems of reconstruction which will confront them as citizens when the nation returns once more to civilian life.

It is sometimes said that government fixing of prices and government operation of railways and industries constitute a long step toward state socialism. Perhaps, in a serious crisis, it is not worth while to argue about the theoretical nature of the measures necessary to accomplish the great results of defeating the nation's foes on the field of battle, but it is interesting to note that one of the ablest spokesmen of the federal government, Franklin Lane, Secretary of the Interior, warns us against assuming that this body of legislation rests upon socialistic theory:

"Do not confuse this with socialism," he says. "It is diametrically opposed to socialism. Socialism is striving to nationalize industries through common ownership of the capital engaged in industry. What this country is striving to do is to organize the capital and industry owned by individuals for the service of the whole. That is not government ownership but a much larger measure of coördination under government control. . . . We have without realizing it carried individualism to the point of selfishness where it was in danger of defeating itself. Now we will conserve individualism and individual initiative for this country by showing its proper limits as marked by the absolute necessity of coöperation.

"For an illustration, the farmer has been the most individual thing in the United States. We are showing him the way to something far better for himself and his community by means of a recent act of Congress ' to stimulate the production of food ' by means of bringing all the arable public and private land within the reclamation projects of the Department of the Interior under effective cultivation by means of coöperative methods. Hundreds of thousands of acres of land will get the benefit of this, and their output will be a big factor in mitigating the world's food crisis due to the war.

"The plan is to have, on each project, a 'war maintenance corps' equipped with gang plows, harrows and seeders, for the use of which the farmers will be organized, just as soldiers are organized into batteries for the service of the field guns wherever they are needed. These groups are to go from farm to farm, each individual coöperating thereby and not only getting his own work done but helping that of his neighbor. This arrangement with its adequate equipment of machinery will multiply about twenty times the power and ability of each man to get things done. There will be no shortage of labor.

"This experiment, already successfully under way, in the one industry of farming shows the principle of coöperation that must be applied to all our activities throughout the war and for all time after the war. Remember always that there are two kinds of coöperation, the one enforced by the state, and the other voluntarily effected by intelligent men who know what they want for themselves and what they must do for their fellows. To avoid the former we must make successful the latter."

The Declaration of War. — A review of the federal war legislation naturally opens with the declaration of war on Germany. In accordance with the powers conferred upon it by the Constitution of the United States, Congress, by a joint resolution approved by President Wilson on April 6, 1917, resolved, "That the state of war between the United States and the Imperial German Government which has thus been thrust upon the United States is hereby formally declared; and that the President be, and he is hereby, authorized and directed to employ the entire naval and military forces of the United States and the resources of the government to carry on war against the Imperial German Government; and to bring the conflict to a successful termination all of the resources of the country are hereby pledged by the Congress of the United States."

Eight months after this resolution, namely, on December 7, 1917, Congress declared that a state of war existed between the United States and the Imperial and Royal Austro-Hungarian Government and authorized the President to use all the forces and resources of the country to bring that war to a successful termination.

The Selective Draft Law. — It was an old principle of American policy that the responsibility for national defense rested upon every male capable of bearing arms. Occasion had not often arisen in our history, however, to apply this principle. The Mexican wars and the Spanish War made such a slight drain upon our resources that the number of volunteers who rushed to the standards of our country was greater than the government could use. The Civil War also opened with reliance upon volunteers, but as the struggle widened and increased in intensity, it became necessary for the government in 1863 to increase the armies by applying the principle of a draft by lot. In view of the titanic effort called forth by the declaration of war on Germany and Austria, and in view of the fact that these countries drew their entire arms-bearing population into military service, it was obviously unwise that the Government of the United States should brook any delay in raising and equipping armies adequate to the exigencies of the conflict.

Moreover, as President Wilson said in his proclamation fixing registration day — " The power against which we are arrayed has sought to impose its will upon the world by force. To this end it has increased armament until it has changed the face of war. In the sense in which we have been wont to think of armies there are no armies in this struggle. There are entire nations armed. Thus the men who remain to till the soil and man the factories are no less a part of the army that is in France than the men beneath the battle flags. It must be so with us. It is not an army that we must shape and train for war; it is a nation. To this end our people must draw close in one compact front against a common foe. But this cannot be if each man pursues a private purpose. All must pursue one purpose. The nation needs all men; but it needs each man, not in the field that will most pleasure him, but in the endeavor that will best serve the common good.

" Thus, though a sharpshooter pleases to operate a trip-hammer for the forging of great guns, and an expert machinist desires to march with the flag, the Nation is being served only when the sharpshooter marches, and the machinist remains at his levers. The whole Nation must be a team in which each man shall play the part for which he is best fitted. To this end, Congress has provided that the Nation shall be organized for war by selection and that each man shall be classified for service in the place to which it shall best serve the general good to call him.

" The significance of this cannot be overstated. It is a new thing in our history and a landmark in our progress. It is a new manner of accepting and vitalizing our duty to give ourselves with thoughtful devotion to the common purpose of us all. It is in no sense a conscription of the unwilling; it is rather selection from a nation which has volunteered in mass. It is no more a choosing of those who shall march with the colors than it is a selection of those who shall serve an equally necessary and devoted purpose in the industries that lie behind the battle line.

"The day here named is the time upon which all shall present themselves for assignment to their tasks. It is for that reason destined to be remembered as one of the most conspicuous moments in our history. It is nothing less than the day upon which the manhood of the country shall step forward in one solid rank in defense of the ideals to which this Nation is consecrated. It is important to those ideals no less than to the pride of this generation in manifesting its devotion to them that there be no gaps in the ranks.

"It is essential that the day be approached in thoughtful apprehension of its significance and that we accord to it the honor and the meaning that it deserves. Our industrial need prescribes that it be not made a technical holiday, but the stern sacrifice that is before us urges that it be carried in all our hearts as a great day of patriotic devotion and obligation when the duty shall lie upon every man, whether he is himself to be registered or not, to see to it that the name of every male person of the designated ages is written on these lists of honor."

In accordance with the principles laid down by the President, Congress by an act approved on May 18, 1917, declared that the great national army should be impartially chosen from among all males between the ages of 21 and 31 inclusive. That act authorized the President to increase the armed forces of the United States by adding to all organizations of the regular army, by drawing to the service of the United States the National Guard and the National Guard Reserves, and by raising by draft and equipping an additional force of 500,000 men, to be followed by such further increments as the President in his discretion might decide. The President was thus authorized to apply as necessary the terms of a selective draft, to be based upon the liability to military service of all male citizens or male persons (not alien enemies) who have declared their intention to become citizens, between the ages of 21 and 31 years inclusive. Quotas for the several states and territories were determined in proportion to their population. It was specifically provided that no bounty should be paid to induce any person to enlist, and that no person should be permitted to escape service by the payment of money. Federal and state officers, ministers, and a few others were exempted by the law. The act further provided the rate of pay for men and officers, prohibited the sale of intoxicants to officers and members of the military forces while in uniform, and authorized the Secretary of War to make arrangements for surrounding the armed forces of the United States by proper moral conditions. By proclamation June 5, 1917, was fixed as the day for national military registration. From the men so registered soldiers for the national service were selected by law, those being left who were physically unfit or had relatives depending upon their earnings for a livelihood. By act of Congress passed in August, 1918, the period of years was extended to include all men from 18 to 45 years, registration day was fixed on September 12, 1918, and similar principles of selection were applied.

Insurance Act. — In order that the whole burden of the war might not fall upon the soldiers and sailors and those dependent upon them, but might be equitably distributed among all the citizens of the country, Congress, by law enacted October 6, 1917, appropriated $141,000,000 for military and naval family allowances to be paid under appropriate regulation to the families of the soldiers and sailors and those relying wholly or in part upon their earnings; $12,150,000 to compensate officers and enlisted men or their families for death or disability; and $23,000,000 to provide a system of relatively inexpensive insurance for those in active service — such insurance to be voluntary and, of course, in addition to the allowances made regularly by the government. Under this act the government sought to remove from the families of soldiers and sailors at least a considerable portion of the burden which fell upon them as the result of the withdrawal of wage earners, and furthermore, to make it possible for soldiers and sailors to provide through insurance additional safeguards for those left behind. Never in the history of our country has the government taken such a wise and humane view of its responsibilities to those who serve it on the field of battle.

Liberty Loans. — Money affords the sinews of war, and Congress withheld nothing from those responsible for directing the armed conflict. By a law enacted on April 24, 1917, the Secretary of the Treasury, with the approval of the President, was authorized to borrow from time to time amounts totaling $5,000,000,000, in addition to sums authorized by earlier legislation — the bonds to be in such form and subject to such terms as the Secretary of the Treasury might prescribe, providing that the interest should not exceed $3\frac{1}{2}$ per cent per annum. Although the bonds of England and France bearing 5 per cent interest were then selling in the United States far below their par value, at a rate that would produce practically 6 per cent per annum to the investor, the First Liberty Loan bearing $3\frac{1}{2}$ per cent interest was readily oversubscribed.

The Second Liberty Bond issue, of nearly $4,000,000,000, offered in October, 1917, bore the rate of 4 per cent; and for the Third Liberty Bond issue, of $3,000,000,000, offered in the spring of 1918, the rate was increased to $4\frac{1}{4}$ per cent. Owing to the immense amount of bonds issued under the first three loans, there was a slight depreciation on the market; on account of necessity or other reasons many citizens sold their bonds. The First Liberty Loan was depreciated slightly for a short period after its issuance, but owing to the special tax exemption privileges provided by law, it soon recovered and rose above par. The Second and Third loans, however, continue to sell at a discount running as high at one time as approximately 6 per cent. Notwithstanding this fact, the government, knowing that it could rely upon the patriotism of its citizens, asked them to buy at par the Fourth Liberty Bonds, bearing no higher rate of interest than the third, on which $4\frac{1}{4}$ per cent was paid. Although, for example, it was possible for a citizen to buy a $1000 Third Liberty Bond in the open market for approximately $970, considerations of pecuniary gain were put aside, and purchases of the Fourth Liberty Loan of $6,000,000,000 offered in October, 1918, fully met the expectations of the government, for it was largely oversubscribed. The number of subscribers to the different loans affords a true index to the progressive interest of the people in supporting the war.

First Loan	4,500,000 subscribers
Second Loan	9,500,000 subscribers
Third Loan	18,300,000 subscribers
Fourth Loan (est.)	21,000,000 subscribers

Current Revenues for the Support of the War. — Following the policy of distributing in a large measure the burdens of war among those best able to bear them, the revenue law of October, 1917, contained these features:

1. A progressive income tax, imposing a normal tax of 2 per cent on incomes in excess of $2000 a year (single persons $1000) in addition to the old normal tax of 2 per cent on incomes over $4000, with surtaxes rising steadily with the increase of income to 63 per cent of that part of any income in excess of $2,000,000.

2. A progressive inheritance tax rising to 22 per cent on the amount of any estate in excess of $10,000,000.

3. An excess profits tax upon all incorporations and partnerships, rising in amount to 60 per cent of the net income in excess of 33 per cent on the invested capital.

Speaking of this law a distinguished political economist, Professor E. R. A. Seligman, says: "This is the highwater mark thus far reached in the history of taxation. Never before in the annals of civilization has an attempt been made to take as much as two-thirds of a man's income by taxation. In comparing our present income tax with the British, moreover, it is to be noted that our rates are much higher on the larger incomes and much smaller on the lower and moderate incomes. The American scale is an eloquent testimony to the fact, not only that large fortunes are far more numerous here than abroad, but also that there is greater appreciation of the democratic principles of fiscal justice. For the overwhelming trend of modern opinion is clearly in the direction of applying to excessive fortunes the principle of faculty or ability to pay."

National Food and Fuel Control Law. — In order to maintain the successful prosecution of the war and to aid in securing adequate and equitable distribution of foodstuffs and other supplies, Congress enacted a drastic food and fuel control law approved by the President on August 10, 1917. Among other things, this law forbade under appropriate penalties: (1) willful destroying of the necessaries of life for the purpose of enhancing prices; (2) restricting supplies or knowingly committing waste; (3) attempting to monopolize supplies or to limit the facility for producing or transporting supplies; (4) limiting the manufacture of necessaries in order to enhance prices or exact excessive prices, or hoard food. The President was authorized: (1) to requisition food and other supplies for the support of the army and navy; (2) to prescribe regulations governing in whole or in part the conduct of marketing; (3) to fix the price of wheat; (4) to take over and operate, if necessary, factories, mines, packing houses, and other plants; (5) to fix the prices of supplies requisitioned for military purposes; and (6) to fix the price of coal and coke. In order to assure further control over food, the President was empowered to license the importation, manufacture, storage, mining, or distribution of any necessaries with a view to bringing all such operations under strict federal scrutiny. The underlying purpose of this act was to prevent selfish people from taking advantage of the necessities of the nation to increase their private wealth by monopolizing supplies and unduly increasing prices.

Shipbuilding. — Equally important with recruiting the armed forces, raising money, and controlling supplies was the provision of means for transporting men and supplies beyond the seas. For this reason the President was given almost unlimited power to advance shipbuilding. By appropriate legislation he was authorized:

1. To place an order, compliance with which shall be obligatory, with any person for such ships or war materials as the necessities of the government may require and which are of the kind and quantity usually produced by such person;

2. Modify or cancel any existing contract for the building, construction or purchase of war material, and if the contractor fails to comply with the contract as so modified, then to take possession of all or any part of his factory or yards and use the same as may be necessary;

3. Require the owner or occupier of any factory or yards in which ships or war material are built or produced to place at the disposal of the United States all or any part of the output; and

4. Requisition and take over for use and occupation by the government any factory or yard whether or not the United States has any agreement with the owner or occupier. The last provision is not confined to factories or yards for the production of war supplies or materials. Provision is made for just compensation, to be determined by the President in all cases in which the act is called into effect, and if the amount so

determined is unsatisfactory to the person entitled to the same, he shall be paid 75 per cent of such amount and be entitled to sue the United States for such further sum as added to such 75 per cent will constitute just compensation.

In addition, the President is authorized to requisition or take over the title or possession of any ship now constructed or in the process of construction, or hereafter constructed, or any part of or the charter of such ship. Furthermore, he may take over for the United States the possession and title of any vessel within its jurisdiction which at the time of coming therein was owned in whole or in part by any corporation, citizen, or subject of any nation with which the United States is at war, or was under the register of such nation, and may provide for a board of survey to ascertain the actual value of such vessels, the findings to be competent evidence as to any claim for compensation. By an extraordinary measure, approved March 1, 1918, the Emergency Fleet Corporation in charge of the shipbuilding program (see below, p. 158) was authorized to expend $50,000,000 to provide proper housing conditions for fleet workers.

Railroads and Shipping. — Recognizing the vital importance of railway transportation and coastwise shipping in moving troops and supplies to the seaboard for shipment abroad, the leading railway presidents of the United States met in Washington shortly after the declaration of war, namely, on April 11, 1917, and formulated a plan to coördinate their roads in a continental railway system. The direction of this coördinated system was given to the executive committee of the Special Committee on National Defense of the American Railway Association. Under this executive committee, known as the Railroads' War Board, the railroads were operated until December 28, 1917, when they were placed under governmental control by presidential proclamation. Under power vested in the President by the Army bill of 1916, Mr. McAdoo, Secretary of the Treasury, was made director-general of the railroads. In March, 1918, Congress passed a railroad control bill, providing the terms and conditions under which the government was to operate the railways for the period of the war and not to exceed 21 months after the proclamation of peace.[1]

[1] On June 29th, the railroad administration relinquished from federal management the short-line railroads whose control was not deemed needful or desirable.

In a statement issued on June 15, 1918, Mr. McAdoo outlined the general railroad policy as follows:

First: The winning of the war, which includes the prompt movement of the men and the material that the government requires. To this everything else must be subordinated.

Second: The service of the public, which is the purpose for which the railroads were built and given the privileges accorded them. This implies the maintenance and improvement of the railroad properties so that adequate transportation facilities will be provided at the lowest cost, the object of the government being to furnish service rather than to make money.

Third: The promotion of a spirit of sympathy and a better understanding between the administration of the railways and their two million employees, as well as their one hundred million patrons, which latter class includes every individual in the nation, since transportation has become a prime and universal necessity of civilized existence.

Fourth: The application of sound economics, including:

a. The elimination of superfluous expenditures;

b. The payment of a fair and living wage for services rendered and a just and prompt compensation for injuries received;

c. The purchase of material and equipment at the lowest price consistent with a reasonable, but not an excessive, profit to the producer;

d. The adoption of standardized equipment and the introduction of approved devices that will save life and labor;

e. The routing of freight and passenger traffic with due regard to the fact that a straight line is the shortest distance between two points;

f. The intensive employment of all equipment, and a careful record and scientific study of the results obtained, with a view to determining the comparative efficiency secured.

As a result of this legislation, Secretary McAdoo now commands an army of railway workers numbering nearly two millions.

On April 11, 1918, President Wilson issued a proclamation placing in government hands all of the coastwise shipping. The reasons for the action of the government in taking over railways and shipping are briefly summed up in the following statement:

Export business enormously increased, freight piled up, and the roads lost use of cars and yard space;

Much coastwise shipping was diverted to transatlantic service; leaving the railroads to haul much freight that had gone by water before;

· War orders were concentrated in the manufacturing section at first, where congestion is always densest;

The large profits on war orders tempted shippers to use cars for storage, and goods were ordered long before they could be used;

Troop movements were irregular and furnished little or no return load.

Express, Telephone, and Telegraph Companies. — The American Railway Express Company was formed in July, 1918, and given a virtual monopoly of the express business. It represented a combination of four leading express companies. No permanent guarantee of earnings was given. The company is a private corporation acting as the agent of the director-general of the railroads for carrying on the express business. The type of service and the rates are under his control and the government is to share in any profits above 5 per cent on the capital stock. The government likewise gets $50\frac{1}{4}$ per cent of the gross earnings, as the several contracts made by the individual express companies with individual railroads are now superseded by one single contract with the government. The new company was permitted to be capitalized only to the extent of actual property and cash put into the business, and the government refused to permit this to exceed $40,000,000. The employees were made the employees of the government and compensated on a basis arranged by the director-general of railroads instead of on a commission basis as hitherto. The telegraph and telephone systems were taken over August 1, 1918. The operation of the lines was placed by the Postmaster-General in the hands of a special committee of government officials.

The Espionage Act. — For the purpose of preventing interference with the national purpose or national efficiency in waging war by avowed opponents of the war as well as by those seeking to give aid and comfort to the enemy, Congress enacted the Espionage law, approved June 15, 1917. This measure provided appropriate punishment for those who obtained sketches, photographs, or documents, or any information relative to American military preparations with view to using the same to the injury of the United States. A fine of not more than ten thousand dollars, or imprisonment for not more than twenty years, or both, was the punishment established by the law for: (1) those who attempt to communicate to any foreign nation any information, military or otherwise, to be used to the injury of the United States; (2) those who shall willfully make or convey false reports or false statements with intent to interfere with the operation or success of the military or naval forces of the United States or to promote the success of its enemies; and (3) those who shall willfully cause or attempt to cause insubordination, disloyalty, mutiny, or refusal of duty, in the military or naval forces of the United States when the United States is at war, or (4) shall willfully obstruct the recruiting or enlistment service of the United States, to the injury of the service or of the United States.

In a proclamation of April 16, 1917, the President cited the provisions of the Constitution and laws of the United States, and specially warned all citizens as follows:

" The Courts of the United States have stated the following acts to be treasonable: The use or attempted use of any force or violence against the government of the United States, or its military or naval forces;

"The acquisition, use, or disposal of any property with knowledge that it is to be, or with intent that it shall be, of assistance to the enemy in their hostilities against the United States;

" The performance of any act or publication of statements or information which will give or supply, in any way, aid and comfort to the enemies of the United States;

"The direction, aiding, counseling, or countenancing of any of the foregoing acts.

" Such acts are held to be treasonable whether committed within the United States or elsewhere; whether committed by a citizen of the United States or by an alien domiciled, or residing in the United States, inasmuch as resident aliens, as well as citizens, owe allegiance to the United States and its laws.

"Any such citizen or alien who has knowledge of the commission of such acts and conceals and does not make known the fact to the officials named in Section 3, of the penal code, is guilty of misprision of treason.

"And I hereby proclaim and warn all citizens of the United States, and all aliens, owing allegiance to the government of the United States, to abstain from committing any and all acts which would constitute a violation of any of the laws herein set forth; and I further proclaim and warn all persons who may commit such acts that they will be vigorously prosecuted therefor."

Federal Agencies for War Administration. — In pursuance to legislation which we have just reviewed and under the authority vested in the President by the Overman Act, the following important agencies were created to carry on the administration of the functions necessary to keep the country on a war footing and to support adequately our land and naval forces. The changes in bureaus, offices, commissions, and other agencies were so frequent that it is impossible to present here a perfect picture of all branches of administrative activity.

The War Industries Board. — This board was created in July, 1917. It is really a planning and controlling board for industries, empowered to bring all of them under government control, to speed up the production of necessary materials, to distribute the demands for supplies from all the war divisions to the industries best fitted to meet them expeditiously, and to coördinate the work of all to prevent duplication, waste, and delay. It is the greatest centralizing and coöperating agency standing between the government and industries, binding the latter and organizing them to serve the military needs of the former.

The Priorities Board or Division, in the War Industries Board, charged with the duty of guiding industries and governmental agencies in "the production, supply, and distribution of raw materials, finished products, electrical energy, fuel, and transportation," and of laying down rules for giving priority or preference to those materials and activities necessary to meet the war needs of the government in the order of their importance.

United States Railway Administration, under the direction of the Secretary of the Treasury. Supplemented by an Advisory Board. In charge of the administration of the railways taken over by the federal government.

The Emergency Fleet Corporation. — Created for the purpose of drawing together and securing the coöperation of all the shipbuilding interests in the country and creating new shipbuilding forces with a view to the immediate enlargement of the fighting forces on the sea and merchant marine of the United States. The ravages of the submarine and the necessity for an immense tonnage to transport soldiers and then supply them with materials led the government to develop this special agency, which is in effect an extension of the National Shipping Board (see above, p. 118), established before the entrance of the United States into the war.

The Food Administration, created to enforce the provisions of the law of August 10, 1917 (see above, p. 152) and additional rules laid down from time to time in furtherance of the principles therein contained. Federal food administrators are also established in every state.

The Fuel Administration, created to enforce the fuel provisions of the law of August 10, 1917, and rules and regulations relative to the mining, distribution, and price of coal, for war, industrial, and ordinary purposes.

The Aircraft Board, independent organization, supervises (in accordance with requirements of the respective departments), the purchase, production, and manufacture of aircraft and aircraft materials.

National Advisory Committee for Aëronautics, created under act of Congress of March 3, 1915, to direct experimentation and research into the problems of flight and their solution.

The War Labor Board was created in April, 1918, for the purpose of adjusting, by mediation and conciliation, disputes arising between employers and employees in war industries. "In case of an industrial dispute, a local committee or board is first appointed to arbitrate it; failing settlement by the local board, parties to the controversy are summoned before the National Board itself; if the Board members are then unable to agree upon a decision, an umpire is appointed, either unanimously by the Board, or, if the members disagree, then by lot from a list of ten persons nominated for the purpose by the President of the United States. Beyond the decision of this umpire no compulsion is incorporated in the original statement of the Board's powers. The President has, however, commandeered factories of recalcitrant employers, and threatened with exclusion from industry and withdrawal of immunity from the draft striking employees who refuse to return to work after the governmental award. The power of the President and the pressure of public opinion in favor of uninterrupted production make this national experiment in arbitration practically compulsory.

"The Board bases its decisions on the following principles: Workers and employers have the right to organize and to bargain collectively through chosen representatives. Employers are not to discharge workers for membership in trade unions. Workers may not use coercive measures of any kind to induce persons to join their organization. Where the union shop now exists it shall continue to do so, and in establishments where unionists and non-unionists work together and the employer meets only with employees or representatives engaged in his own establishment, the continuance of such conditions shall not be deemed a grievance. This declaration, however, is not intended in any manner to deny the right or discourage the attempt to form labor unions. Safeguards to health shall not be relaxed. Equal pay is allowed for equal work. The basic eight-hour day is recognized as applying in all cases in which the existing law requires it. The right of all workers, including common laborers, to a living wage is declared."[1]

War Labor Policies Board, in the Department of Labor, deals with prin-

[1] *The Nation*, October 26, 1918.

ciples involved in the determination of wages, hours, conditions of labor, government labor policies, and the distribution of labor.

United States Employment Service, in the Department of Labor, manages employment offices throughout the country and aids in the distribution of labor, especially to war industries.

Bureau of Housing, in the Department of Labor, in charge of providing suitable housing conditions in war industries and shipbuilding centers.

The War Trade Board, charged with the functions (1) of conserving for the United States and the Allies the commodities necessary to their economic life and the prosecution of the war, through the control of trade with neutrals as well as the Allied powers and (2) of controlling American merchants in their transactions with foreigners by the publication of the names of enemy corporations or those allied to enemy interests. For example, an agreement was concluded with Switzerland allotting her a certain amount of grain in return for assurances relative to certain trading with the enemy on the part of Swiss citizens.

Board for Vocational Education, created by act approved June 27, 1918, and authorized to plan and execute plans for the training and education of disabled soldiers and sailors so as to fit them for remunerative and congenial employment in civilian life. "Every effort will be made to assist the disabled man toward that occupation in which he is most interested and for which, because of his aptitude and experience on the one hand and his handicap on the other hand, he is best suited." Funds are provided to support the student in training, to assist him in securing desirable employment, and to safeguard his interests after he secures regular employment.

Bureau of War Risk Insurance, in the Treasury Department, with branches throughout the country, charged with the function of executing the provisions of the law (see above, p. 150) relative to allotments to the families of soldiers and sailors and to war risk insurance.

The Council of National Defense, created under act of Congress, approved August 29, 1916, and composed of the six cabinet officers: the Secretaries of War, Navy, Interior, Agriculture, Commerce, and Labor. Its functions are to investigate and to advise Congress and the President as to the best ways in which to mobilize the industrial, transportation, and agricultural interests of the country for immediate concentration and use in national defense. It embraces innumerable committees and subcommittees, which act in an advisory and consulting relation to the war agencies of the government. It endeavors to assist state committees in the prosecution of their work. Much of the planning work of the Council has been taken over by the executive boards herein described.

The Censorship Board, created under the Trading with the Enemy Act, designed to control mail, telegrams, messages, and other communications to neutral countries, which might be intended for enemy countries.

The Committee on Public Information, created to serve as a channel of communication between the government and the people relative to war aims, activities, and accomplishments, and to disseminate in neutral and Allied countries information about the ideals and war aims of the United States.

American National Red Cross, under the presidency of the President of the United States, a relief organization with government sanction assisting the army and the navy in caring for the wounded and suffering.

Alien Property Custodian, empowered to take possession of, manage, and sell the property of enemy aliens and to act as custodian for the funds accumulated.

War Finance Corporation, created by act of Congress signed by the President on April 5, 1918, and supplied with an immense capital for the purpose of aiding banks that make advances to essential war industries, helping savings banks which may be in distress through the competition of federal bonds or otherwise, and loaning money to war enterprises.

Capital Issues Committee, connected with the War Finance Corporation, charged with the duty of supervising the issues of bonds by states, cities, counties, and private corporations with a view to keeping their expenditures down to the minimum, thus securing to the Federal Government money and materials and labor which otherwise might go to local improvements or business extensions not necessary to winning the war.

State War Legislation.[1]— While the Congress of the United States was providing the national legislation in support of the war, the legislatures of the several states were likewise very active in the passage of laws designed to place the country in a condition of preparedness. The volume of legislation has been extraordinary, and it covers a wide range of subjects.

State Councils of Defense. — A number of states passed laws creating state councils of defense, consisting of from 7 to 50 members, appointed by the governor, and representing the manufacturing interests, labor, agriculture, stock raising, the Red Cross and relief societies, the physicians, bankers, railroads, engineers, the women and the citizens generally. The board of public works in West Virginia acts as the state council of defense. Appropriations ranging from $50,000 to $750,000 were made to carry on the work. In Indiana a state council of defense was created by executive action after the adjournment of the legislature of 1917.

Military Census. — Half a dozen states, including Iowa and New York, provided for the taking of a military census to ascertain the resources of the state in men and materials.

Militia Laws. — The federalization of the national guard left the states without adequate military protection, and home guards were therefore created, consisting of able-bodied male persons not subject to conscription, whose term of service is for the duration of the war. For the purpose of guaranteeing state-wide security within its borders, New York also created a state police force. The City of New York is authorized to employ emergency police and temporary firemen. In Connecticut the governor is author-

[1] This section is adapted from an excellent summary of state legislation by Mr. John A. Lapp in the *American Political Science Review*, February, 1918.

M

ized to appoint a military emergency board of three members to perfect and maintain a body of armed troops as a constabulary guard, to be recruited from the unorganized militia of the state, and any town at any annual or special town meeting may appropriate money for the maintenance of military organizations. Many other states took similar precautionary measures.

Registration of Aliens. — A few states, including Connecticut, Florida, and Maine, enacted laws providing for the registration of aliens within a fixed period, usually twenty-four hours after the promulgation of the governor's proclamation, or within twenty-four hours after the alien enters the state. Hotels, boarding houses, and lodging houses are required to supply information as to the residence of aliens therein.

Military Instruction in Schools. — Louisiana passed a law requiring the teaching of military science to all boys above the eighth grade. Maryland and New Jersey appointed commissions to investigate its practicability and methods. New York created a military training commission, consisting of the major-general commanding the national guard, one person appointed by the regents of the state university, and one person appointed by the governor.

Desecration of the Flag. — Several states enacted new or amended old laws prohibiting the desecration, mutilation, or misuse of the national flag. Several states require the flag to be displayed on all schoolhouses while school is in session.

Food Conservation. — The subject of food production, distribution, and conservation has received marked attention and various expedients have been adopted to achieve the desired end. For example, New York created two commissions to deal with the question of food production, food distribution, and food conservation, and the authority of these commissions is extended to comprehend fuel and other necessaries of life. Virginia established a division of markets in the department of agriculture and immigration; West Virginia created a bureau of markets and enacted a law prohibiting speculation for the purpose of cornering the market and controlling the price of foodstuffs, fuel and other necessities of life; Washington created the office of director of farm markets and provided for the production and marketing of farm products; Wyoming provided for the exemption of food from taxation to the value of $100.

Definition of Crimes. — The existence of a state of war has led to the definition of new offenses against the public peace and the dignity of the state and the redefinition of older offenses to secure the loyalty of citizens and provide for the protection of property and human life. Iowa declared the exciting of sedition or insurrection by writing, speaking, or other means a felony and advocating the subversion or destruction of the federal or state government by force, and being a member of or attending a meeting or council of any treasonable organization, society, or order, a misdemeanor. The destruction of armories, gas, electric, telegraph, or telephone plants, sources of food or water supply, dams, reservoirs, canals, trenches, machinery, bridges, docks, quays, fortifications, warehouses, railroads, or other works necessary to the successful prosecution of the war were constituted crimes in Illinois, Maine, Maryland, Rhode Island, and Vermont.

Aid to Dependents. — Prior to the passage of the military insurance act the question of the necessary financial assistance to indigent dependents of enlisted or drafted men was of first-rate importance, and several states enacted laws which afforded partial and temporary relief. In New York, for instance, any county, city, town, or village is authorized to provide financial aid for the dependents of enlisted men, and an agency known as the New York patriotic fund was permitted to incorporate to furnish aid to the dependents of recruits.

Schools. — In New York children are released from school attendance without loss of credit or standing if they are engaged in farm work. In Arizona the state board of education is authorized to close all educational institutions during the continuance of the war if such action be deemed essential. In Connecticut high school pupils over fourteen years of age who volunteer and are accepted for farm work are permitted to reënter school without loss of standing if they maintain the prescribed food standards.

Intoxicating Liquors. — A few states have taken steps to eliminate the sale of intoxicating liquors to soldiers. Maryland prohibits the sale of liquor within two miles of any military camp, and authorizes the appointment of five special police to patrol the dry zone, and prohibits the sale of liquor entirely within Prince George County after November 1, 1917.

Moratorium and Stay Laws. — A few states have provided moratorium and stay laws whereby suits begun against enlisted men during the war are to be suspended until six months after the war has been concluded, and by virtue of which debts due cannot be collected during the continuance of the war. The amount of property owned by enlisted persons and exempted from attachment was increased. Laws of this kind were enacted by Maine, Maryland, and Oregon.

Labor Laws. — Vermont authorized the commissioner of industries, with the approval of the governor, to suspend the operation of the laws relating to the hours of employment of women and children, during the continuance of the war.

Involuntary Labor. — Maryland and West Virginia provide that the governor may order all able-bodied male persons between the ages of sixteen and sixty, not otherwise regularly employed, to be put to work on government contracts.

Discrimination against Soldiers. — Laws designed to prohibit discrimination against soldiers and sailors in theaters, skating rinks, public conveyances, inns, hotels, and other public places were enacted by Maine and Texas.

Miscellaneous. — A large number of miscellaneous laws were enacted. Iowa authorized the construction of armory buildings for the use of reserve officers' training camps. Massachusetts empowered the adjutant-general to receive any aëroplane donated to the state. Several states have provided for calling retired officers back into active service; some amendment was made in the laws regulating the storage of explosives; and provision was made for the appropriation of real estate for military purposes. Illinois authorized the state council of defense to issue and revoke licenses for the solicitation of war relief and charity funds. The governor of Maine is authorized to commandeer buildings, machinery, equipment, horses, wagons, automobiles, aëroplanes, railroad equipment, wharves, ships, boats, fuel and gasoline for use in war purposes.

It is clear from even this incomplete review of America's legislative preparation for war, that no power over the lives or property of citizens deemed necessary for the successful prosecution of the armed conflict was withheld from the duly constituted public authorities. The farmer's wheat, the housewife's sugar, coal at the mines, labor in the factories, ships at the wharves and on the high seas, trade with friendly countries, the vast national railway system, the banks and stores, private riches, lands and houses — all were mobilized and laid under whatever obligations the requirements of waging war made imperative. Never before were labor and capital, land and natural resources so completely subjected to governmental authority in a common enterprise. In this immense extension of public functions are to be found the most difficult problems of the future. To what extent shall the powers exercised in support of the armed conflict be exercised after the war in support of the enterprises of peace? To what extent shall the railways and private business concerns be released from governmental supervision and left to the free course of private initiative? Shall the labor policies adopted and applied by the government be abandoned and direct government efforts to improve living conditions in industrial centers be discontinued? Shall the government withdraw from the promotion of the merchant marine and leave shipping to take its old course? Obviously the problems of reconstruction involved in answering these questions will tax the political and economic genius of the American people.

SELECTED REFERENCES

Clark, Hamilton, and Moulton, *Readings in the Economics of War* (Chicago, 1918), freely used in the preparation of the above chapter; *Important Statutes and Executive Proclamations from April, 1917 to May, 1918* (McKinley Publishing Co., Philadelphia, 1918); Elisha Friedman (editor), *American Problems of Reconstruction* (New York, 1918); Charles W. Wood (editor), *The Great Change: The New America after the War* (New York, 1918).

PART II. GOVERNMENTS OF THE ALLIED NATIONS

CHAPTER IX

THE RISE OF FREE GOVERNMENT IN ENGLAND

I. MEDIEVAL ORIGINS

England's Political Importance. — " England," says a modern historian, " has taken the lead in solving the problem of constitutional government; of government, that is, with authority, but limited by law, controlled by opinion, and respecting personal right and freedom. This she has done for the world, and herein lies the world's chief interest in her history." [1] In turning to the governmental systems of Europe it is natural, therefore, to begin with England — with the nation that has achieved as great distinction in the practice of political democracy as did the Hebrews in religion, the Greeks in sculpture and architecture, and the Romans in law and war. Nowhere else can one observe a political development so orderly, continuous, and prolonged. The governmental forms and agencies of no other state have been studied with greater interest or copied with better results. The public policy of no other organized body of men has been more influential in shaping the progress, social and economic as well as political, of the civilized world. For the American student, furthermore, the approach to the governments of the European continent is likely to be made easier and more inviting by an acquaintance with a system of political institutions which lies at the root of much that is both American and continental. There are, it is true, not a few respects in which the governmental system of the United States to-day bears closer resemblance to that of France, Germany, Switzerland, or even Italy, than to that of England. The re-

[1] Goldwin Smith, *The United Kingdom*, I, 1.

lation, however, between the English and the American is one, in the main, of historical continuity; while that between the French or Swiss and the American is one arising principally from mere imitation or from accidental resemblance.

Early Political Development. — The story of England's political growth from Anglo-Saxon times to the Great War would, if fully told, fill many portly volumes. For students of law and politics it has always possessed a peculiar fascination., Our concern here is chiefly with the English government as it now is, rather than with the long process of its creation. Hence, historical development, prior at all events to the reconstructive seventeenth century, may be disposed of in a reasonably brief summary. The first great epoch in English political history is that of Anglo-Saxon settlement and rule, extending roughly from the fifth to the eleventh century. Although very remote, this period made large and lasting contribution to the governmental forms and usages of the English people. Kingship, at first on an elective basis and strictly limited in power, took firm root; an aristocratic *witenagemot*, or " council of wise men," made laws, levied taxes, and in other ways anticipated the parliament of later ages; local units of government — township, borough, and shire (county) — acquired definite organization and developed a more or less democratic system of lawmaking and administration, in which the principle of representation made an early appearance.

Much more important, however, in the building of the modern constitution was the Norman-Angevin era, extending from the coming of William the Conqueror in 1066 to the death of King John in 1216. The aspect of this period which first arrests attention is the enormous growth of the king's power and the building up of a great centralized administrative system of which the king was the autocratic head. Monarchy in Anglo-Saxon days was weak. But the Norman conqueror was a powerful, aggressive, statesmanlike sovereign who with consummate skill maneuvered the results of his invasion in such a way as to make the king the real master of the country. Feudalism, land tenure, military service, taxation, the Church — all were bent to serve the interests of the crown. Within a generation England became a united, centralized monarchy of the most absolute type. There were certain great gains. Order was kept as never before. Law was rigorously enforced. Jury trial, transplanted from Normandy, became a recognized right. Financial and judicial administration were so organized as to give large opportunity for the growth, locally, of the representative principle. Moreover, absolutism was in practice somewhat tempered by the influence of a body known as the Common, or Great, Council, composed of the chief lords and ecclesiastics of the realm and consulted by the king, as a rule, upon all important questions of legislation, finance, and public policy. This Council was, indeed, of very great importance, for out of it, directly or indirectly, were gradually evolved, not only Parliament, but the cabinet and the principal courts of law.

The Great Charter (1215). — In the hands of able kings like William the Conqueror and his great-grandson Henry II absolute power, although frequently working injustice, was in general beneficent and bearable. But in the hands of weak or vicious rulers like Henry II's sons, Richard I and John, it soon became intolerable. Under John a long accumulation of grievances led the strong men of the country, the barons, into open rebellion; and on June 15, 1215, the king, finding himself without a party and facing the loss of his throne, granted the famous body of liberties commonly known as the Great Charter. No document in the history of any nation is of larger importance than this charter. The instrument contained little that was new. Englishmen had as yet spent practically no effort upon political speculation. When demanding rights and privileges they were quite content to appeal to the ancient laws and customs, without trying to evolve general, abstract principles upon which to base their action. The authors of the Great Charter intended to declare the "law of the land," and to protect that law against invasion; hence they sought merely to gather up within a reasonably brief document those principles and customs which the better kings of England had usually observed, but which in the evil days of Richard and John had been evaded or openly violated. In effect, the Charter was a treaty between the king and his dissatisfied subjects. It was essentially a feudal document, and the majority of its provisions relate primarily to the privileges and rights of the barons. None the less, it contains clauses that affected all classes of society, and it is noteworthy that the barons and clergy pledged themselves in it to extend to their dependents the same customs and liberties which they were themselves demanding of the crown. Taking the Charter as a whole, it guaranteed the freedom of the Church, defined afresh and in precise terms surviving feudal obligations and customs, placed safeguards about the liberties of the boroughs, pledged security of property and of trade, and laid down important regulations concerning government and law, notably that whenever the king should propose the assessment of " scutages " or of unusual financial " aids," he should take the advice of the General Council, composed of the tenants-in-chief, summoned individually in the case of the greater ones and through the sheriffs in the case of those of lesser importance. Certain general clauses, *e.g.*, one pledging that justice should neither be bought nor sold, and another prescribing that a freeman might not be imprisoned, outlawed, or dispossessed of his property save by the judgment of his peers or by the law of the land, emphasized the fundamental principle upon which the political and legal structure was intended to be grounded, that, namely, of impartial and unvarying justice.

The Rise of Parliament. — The age-long contest between royal absolutism and the forces in one way or another representing the nation at large — between the ruler and the ruled — was thus clearly begun. It was destined to go on for many centuries, to become, indeed, the central thread in the country's constitutional history, and to end only when the people had fully established their right to be in all respects their own master. In this tremendous conflict the leading rôle on the side of the people was played by a great institution which did not yet exist in the days of King John, namely, Parliament. The formative period in the history of Parliament was the second half of the reign of Henry III (1216–1272), together with the reign of the legislator-king Edward I (1272–1307). The creation of Parliament as we know it came about through the enlargement of the Norman Great Council by the introduction of representative elements, followed by the splitting of the heterogeneous mass of members into two coördinate chambers. The representative principle was no new thing in the thirteenth century. There were important manifestations of it in the local government of Anglo-Saxon times. As brought to bear in the development of Parliament, however, the principle is generally understood to have sprung from the twelfth-century practice of electing assessors to fix the value of real and personal property for purposes of taxation, and jurors to present criminal matters before the king's justices. By the opening of the thirteenth century the idea was fast taking hold, not only that the taxpayer ought to have a voice in the levying of taxes, but that between representation and taxation there was a certain natural and inevitable connection. In the Great Charter, as has been stated, it was stipulated that in the assessment of scutages and of all save the three commonly recognized feudal aids the king should seek the advice of the General Council. The Council of the early thirteenth century was not a representative body, but it was capable of being made such; and that is precisely what was done. To facilitate taxation it was found expedient by the central authorities to carry over into the domain of national affairs that principle of popular representation which already was doing good service in the sphere of local justice and finance, and from this adaptation resulted the conversion, step by step, of the old gathering of feudal magnates into a national parliamentary assembly. The meeting which in a general way fixed the type for all time to come was Edward I's "Model Parliament" of 1295. To this gathering the king summoned severally the two archbishops, all of the bishops, the greater abbots, and the more important earls and barons; while every sheriff was enjoined to see that two knights were chosen from each shire, two citizens from each city, and two burgesses from each borough. Thus were brought together, in person or by deputy, all of the leading classes or orders of which English society was composed, *i.e.*, nobility, clergy, and commons.

In 1295, and for a long time after, the three estates sat and transacted business separately; and it appeared that, like the Estates-General in France, Parliament would permanently consist of three houses, which would mean that the nobles and clergy would always, as in France, be in a position to outvote the commons. Gradually, however, practical interests led to a different arrangement. The lesser clergy, inconvenienced by attendance and preferring to vote their contributions in the special ecclesiastical assemblages known as the convocations of Canterbury and York, contrived to throw off their obligation of membership. The greater clergy and the greater barons, in the next place, developed sufficient interests in common to be amalgamated with ease in one body. Similarly, the lesser barons found their interests essentially identical with those of the country freeholders, represented by the knights of the shire, and with those of the burgesses. The upshot was a gradual re-alignment of the membership in two great groups, one of which became the House of Lords, the other the House of Commons. By the close of the reign of Edward III (1377) this bicameral, or two-house, organization seems to have been complete.

Growth of Parliamentary Powers. — In the fourteenth and fifteenth centuries Parliament gained steadily in power. Its meetings were irregular and infrequent. But in the all-important domains of finance and legislation it asserted and maintained authority equaling, and at times transcending, that of the king. In finance it forced recognition of the twin principles (1) that the right to levy taxes of every sort lay within its hands, and (2) that the crown might impose no direct tax without its assent, nor any indirect tax save such as might be justified under the customs recognized in Magna Carta. In 1395 appeared the formula employed to this day in the making of parliamentary grants, "by the Commons with the advice and assent of the Lords Spiritual and Temporal;" and in 1407 Henry IV gave formal assent to the principle that money grants should be initiated in the Commons, agreed to by the Lords, and only thereafter reported to the king. Likewise legislation. Originally, Parliament was not conceived of as, in the strict sense, a lawmaking body at all. The magnates who composed the General Council had exercised the right to advise the crown in legislative matters, and their successors in Parliament continued to do the same, but the commoners who were brought in in the thirteenth century were present for fiscal rather than legislative purposes. The distinction, however, was difficult to maintain, and with the continued growth of the parliamentary body the legislative function was recognized eventually to belong to the whole of it. For a time the knights and burgesses were regarded as petitioners for laws (to be made by the king), rather than as true legislators. But at the middle of the fifteenth century procedure was altered in such a way as to enable measures to be introduced in either house in the form of drafted bills. Statutes thereupon began to be made " by the King's most excellent majesty by and with the advice and consent of the Lords spiritual and temporal, and Commons in this present Parliament assembled, and by the authority of the same." And these words comprise the formula with which every act of Parliament to-day begins. Technically, the laws were, and still are, made by the crown; practically Parliament, once merely a petitioning and advising body, had become a full-fledged legislative assemblage.

II. THE CONTEST BETWEEN ABSOLUTISM AND PARLIAMENTARY GOVERNMENT

The Tudor Monarchy. — The salient fact of the Tudor period of English history (1485–1603) is the vigor and dominance of the monarchy. From the long and dreary Wars of the Roses the nation emerged in need, above all other things, of discipline and repose. It was the part of the Tudors to enforce relentlessly the one and to foster systematically the other. The period was one in which aristocratic turbulence was repressed, extraordinary tribunals were erected to bring to justice powerful offenders, vagrancy was punished, labor was found for the unemployed, trade was stimulated, the navy was organized on a permanent basis, the diffusion of wealth and of education was encouraged, the growth of a strong middle class was promoted — in short, one in which out of chaos was brought order and out of weakness strength. These things were the work of a government which was strongly paternal, even sheerly despotic, and, for a time at least, the evolution of parliamentary machinery was utterly arrested. But it should be observed that the question in sixteenth-century England was not between strong monarchy on the one hand and parliamentary government on the other. The alternatives were, rather, strong monarchy and baronial anarchy. This the nation clearly perceived, and, of the two, it preferred the former. " The Tudor monarchy," says an English scholar, " unlike most other despotisms, did not depend on gold or force, on the possession of vast estates, unlimited taxation, or a standing army. It rested on the willing support of the nation at large, a support due to the deeply-rooted conviction that a strong executive was necessary to the national unity, and that, in the face of the dangers which threatened the country both at home and abroad, the sovereign must be allowed a free hand. . . . The Tudor monarchy was essentially a national monarchy. It was popular with the multitude, and it was actively supported by the influential classes, the nobility, the gentry, the lawyers, the merchants, who sat as members of Parliament at Westminster, mustered the forces of the shire as Lords-Lieutenant, or bore the burden of local government as borough magistrates and justices of the peace." [1]

Parliament under the Tudors. — In the eyes of the Tudor monarchs, especially Henry VIII and Elizabeth, Parliament was a tool to be used by the crown rather than an independent, coördinate power in the state. When more or less unpopular changes were to be carried through, such as the breach with the papacy under Henry VIII, it was Tudor policy to have them made in the guise of parliamentary enactments, to the end that they might be given the appearance and sanction of great national measures; and when larger supplies of money were to be obtained it was recognized to be good policy to make them, in similar manner, seem to be the voluntary gifts of the people. It was no part of the Tudor plan, however, that Parliament should be permitted to initiate measures or even to exercise any actual discretion in the adoption, amendment, or rejection of proposals submitted by the kings; and the means employed to keep the body in a purely subordinate position were many and ingenious. One was the practice of convening the houses irregularly and infrequently, and of restricting their sessions to very brief periods. Another was tampering with the freedom of county and borough elections. A third was directing, in the most dictatorial manner, the organization and proceedings of the chambers. Henry VIII bullied his parliaments shamelessly; Elizabeth, by cajolery, flattery, deceit, and other arts of which she was mistress, attained through less boisterous

[1] Prothero, *Select Statutes and other Constitutional Documents Illustrative of the Reigns of Elizabeth and James I*, xvii–xviii.

methods the same general end. Finally, there were well-known and oft-used devices by which the crown could entirely evade the limitations theoretically imposed by parliamentary authority. One of these was the issuing of "proclamations." In the sixteenth century it was generally maintained in royal circles that the sovereign, acting alone or with the advice of the Council, could put forth proclamations with the full force of law and affecting the most sacred liberties of the people so long as such edicts did not violate statute or common law. As a corollary, it was maintained equally that the crown could suspend or dispense with the laws in individual cases and at times of crisis. The range covered by these prerogatives was broad and undefined, and in the hands of an aggressive monarch they constituted a serious invasion of the powers of legislation nominally vested in Parliament. Still another aid to escape from parliamentary control was the relative independence of the king financially, arising from the numerous sources of revenue over which Parliament had as yet no control, and also from the fact that the customs duties and other indirect taxes were still voted at the accession of a sovereign for the whole of the reign.

None the less, Parliament in the Tudor period by no means stood still. The enormous power and independence which the chambers, especially the Commons, showed in the seventeenth century was the result of substantial, if more or less hidden, growth during the previous hundred and fifty years. The popular branch was practically doubled in size; parliaments, instead of being confined to a single brief sitting, began to be kept in existence for years and to be brought together in several successive sessions; both houses started to keep journals, to maintain committees, and in a variety of ways to conduct their business after the manner of modern parliamentary procedure; and, in the Elizabethan portion of the period especially, there took place a very real growth in independence of sentiment and an equally notable advance in consciousness of power on the part of the popular chamber. In 1589 Thomas Smith, a court secretary, published a book entitled *The Commonwealth of England and the Manner of Government Thereof*, in which he laid down the proposition that "the most high and absolute power of the realm of England consisteth in the parliament;"

and there is no record that the enunciation of this doctrine, even by a court official, roused serious protest or difference of opinion.

The Stuarts and the Divine Right of Kings. — In the period which included the reigns of the four kings of the Stuart dynasty (1603–1688) the great issue of autocracy *versus* free government came finally to a head. As every one knows, the doctrine upon which the Stuarts based their rule was the divine right of kings — a doctrine which James I himself, shortly before his accession, formally expounded and defended in a pedantic treatise entitled *The True Law of Free Monarchy*. The sovereign, so ran the argument, rules by the will of God; his subjects have no recourse against him; if tyranny be a menace, anarchy is yet more to be feared; there is no appeal against tyranny save to God. "Monarchy," declared the same king in a speech before Parliament in 1610, " is the supremest thing upon earth. . . . As to dispute what God may do is blasphemy, . . . so is it sedition in subjects to dispute what a king may do in the height of his power." Doctrine of this sort was by no means new in England. James' conception of the royal prerogative was essentially that which had been lodged in the mind of every Tudor, if not of many an earlier monarch; he and his brother, Charles I, expected to maintain the same measure of absolutism which Henry VIII and Elizabeth had maintained — nothing more, nothing less.

There were several reasons why such a purpose could not be realized. The first was the pig-headedness of the rulers themselves. Views which no Tudor would have been tactless enough to avow were proclaimed by the Stuarts from the housetops. The Stuart bluntness, lack of perception of the public will, and habit of insisting on the minutest definitions of prerogative would have alienated seventeenth-century Englishmen under even the most favorable circumstances. A second consideration is the fact, of which the nation was fully cognizant, that under the changed conditions that had arisen there was no longer any real need of strong monarchy. Law and order had long since been secured; all danger of a feudal reaction had been removed; foreign invasion was no more to be feared. Strong monarchy had served an invaluable purpose, but that purpose had been fulfilled.

A third factor in the situation was the long latent, but now obvious and rapid, growth of Parliament as an organ of the public will. In a remarkable document known as *The Apology of the Commons*, under date of June 20, 1604, the popular chamber stated respectfully but frankly to the new sovereign what it considered to be its rights and, through it, the rights of the nation. "What cause we your poor Commons have," runs the address, "to watch over our privileges, is manifest in itself to all men. The prerogatives of princes may easily, and do daily, grow; the privileges of the subject are for the most part at an everlasting stand. They may be by good providence and care preserved, but being once lost are not recovered but with much disquiet. The rights and liberties of the Commons of England consisteth chiefly in these three things: first, that the shires, cities, and boroughs of England, by representation to be present, have free choice of such persons as they shall put in trust to represent them; secondly, that the persons chosen, during the time of the parliament, as also of their access and recess, be free from restraint, arrest, and imprisonment; thirdly, that in parliament they may speak freely their consciences without check and controlment, doing the same with due reverence to the sovereign court of parliament, that is, to your Majesty and both the Houses, who all in this case make but one politic body, whereof your Highness is the head." The shrewdness of the political philosophy with which this passage opens is matched only by the terseness with which the fundamental rights of the Commons as a body are enumerated. Equally significant is a paragraph contained in a petition of the Commons, May 23, 1610, which reads as follows: "We hold it an ancient, general, and undoubted right of Parliament to debate freely all matters which do properly concern the subject and his right or state; which freedom of debate being once foreclosed, the essence of the liberty of Parliament is withal dissolved."

Finally, and most important, the Stuart doctrine ran counter to the fundamental conceptions upon which all English law and government had developed. Chief among these conceptions was the Common Law doctrine that the king, while subject to no man, is always subject to law. As early as the twelfth and thirteenth centuries two great legal writers, Glanvil and Bracton

— both connected with the royal courts — flatly denied that the will of the monarch should have the force of law. Late in the fifteenth century Sir John Fortescue, in a treatise entitled *On the Excellence of the Laws of England*, though himself the titular chancellor of Henry VI, took as his main theme the advantages of a system of government, such as the English, under which the king can make law and lay taxes only with the consent of the three estates of the realm, and in which the judges are sworn to act according to the law of the land even though the king command to the contrary. In the Roman system, Fortescue points out, it is the will of the prince that makes law, while in the English the will of the prince is but a single and subordinate element. Although the despotism of Tudor days made this doctrine seem obsolete, it never died out, and in the reign of James I it was brought into fresh vigor by the great jurist Coke, who from the bench reënforced the rising claims of Parliament by asserting the eternal supremacy of law and denying all claims set up by the king to immunity therefrom.

Monarchy Abolished: the Commonwealth and Protectorate. — During the period 1603–1640 Parliament was convened but seldom, and its sessions were usually terminated by prorogation or dissolution with a view to ending embarrassing inquiries, thwarting protests, or defeating projected measures. Under great disadvantages, however, the House of Commons — now thoroughly alive to the critical nature of the contest — steadily maintained its claims, and even from time to time advanced to new positions. Subsidies were withheld; the power to impeach the king's officers was revived; laws were passed abolishing monopolies granted by the crown; a great Petition of Right was drawn up and forced upon the king; the Star Chamber and other special courts and councils of Tudor origin were swept away as engines of tyranny; proud officers of state were condemned and imprisoned or executed; and finally, by 1640, the distracted Charles I was forced into a position where the only alternative to a complete surrender was war.

Between the political theory of the Stuart kings and that of the parliamentary majority there could be no compromise. The Civil War was waged, in the last analysis, to determine which of the two theories should prevail. It should be emphasized that the parliamentarians entered upon the contest with no intent to establish a government by Parliament alone, in form or in fact. It is sufficiently clear from the Grand Remonstrance of 1641 that what they had in mind was merely the imposing of constitutional restrictions upon the crown, together with the introduction of certain specific changes in the political and ecclesiastical order, *e.g.*, the abolition of episcopacy. The culmination of the struggle, however, in the defeat and execution of the king threw open the doors for every sort of constitutional innovation, and between 1649 and 1660 the nation was called upon to pass through an era of political experimentation happily unparalleled in its history. On May 19, 1649, kingship and the House of Lords having been abolished as equally "useless and dangerous," Parliament, to complete the work of transformation, proclaimed a commonwealth, or republic; and on the great seal was inscribed the legend, "In the first year of freedom by God's blessing restored." During the continuance of the Commonwealth (1649–1654) various plans were brought forward for the creation of a parliament elected by manhood suffrage. But the scheme met with the favor of neither the leaders nor the people at large. In 1654 there was put in operation a constitution — the earliest of written constitutions in modern Europe — known as the *Instrument of Government*. The system for which it provided, which was intended to apply to the three countries of England, Scotland, and Ireland, comprised as the executive power a life Protector, to be assisted by a council of thirteen to twenty-one members, and as the legislative organ a one-house parliament of 460 members elected triennially by all citizens possessing property to the value of £300. Cromwell accepted the office of Protector; and the ensuing six years form the period commonly known as the Protectorate.

Government under the Instrument was but moderately successful. Cromwell and his parliaments quarreled incessantly; in particular, they could not agree as to whether the powers of Parliament should be construed to extend to the revision of the constitution. In 1657 the Protector was asked to assume the title of king. This he refused to do, but he did accept a new constitution, *The Humble Petition and Advice*, in which a step was taken toward a return to the governmental system swept away in 1649. This step comprised, principally, the reëstablishment of a parliament of two chambers — a House of Commons and, for lack of agreement upon a better designation, " the Other House." Republicanism, however, failed to strike root. Shrewder men, including Cromwell, had recognized all the time that the English people were really monarchist at heart, and it is not too much to say that from the outset the restoration of kingship was inevitable. Even before the death of Cromwell, in 1658, the trend was distinctly in that direction, and after the hand of the great Protector was removed from the helm such a consummation was only a question of time and means. On May 25, 1660, Charles II, the third Stuart, having engaged to grant a general amnesty and to accept such measures of settlement of religion as Parliament should agree upon, landed at Dover and was received with general acclamation.

Monarchy Restored: the Later Stuarts. — The years 1660–1689 witnessed a final grand experiment to determine whether a Stuart could, or would, govern constitutionally. The constitution in accordance with which Charles II and James II were expected to govern was that which had been built up during preceding centuries, amended by the important reforms introduced by Parliament on the eve of the Civil War. The settlement of 1660 was a restoration no less of Parliament than of the monarchy, in respect both to structure and to functions. The chambers were reëstablished upon their earlier foundations, and in them was vested the power to enact all legislation and to sanction all taxation. The spirit, if not the letter, of the agreement in accordance with which the Stuart house was restored forbade the further imposition of taxes by the arbitrary decree of the crown and all exercise of the legislative power by the crown singly, whether positively through proclamation or negatively through dispensation. It required that henceforth the nature and amount of public expenditures should, upon inquiry, be made known to the two houses, and that ministers should regularly be held to account for their acts and those of the sovereign.

The easy-going Charles II (1660–1685) contrived most of the time to keep fairly within the bounds that were prescribed for him. His brother and successor, James II (1685–1688), was, however, a man of different temper. He was a Stuart of the

Stuarts, irrevocably attached to the doctrine of divine right and sufficiently tactless to take no pains to disguise the fact. He was able, industrious, and honest, but obstinate and intolerant. He began by promising to preserve " the government as by law established." But the ease with which an uprising in 1685 was suppressed deluded him into thinking that through the exemption of the Catholics from the operation of existing laws oppressing them he might in time realize his ambition to reëstablish Roman Catholicism in England. He proceeded, therefore, to issue decrees dispensing with statutes which Parliament had enacted, to establish an ecclesiastical commission in violation of parliamentary law of 1641, and, in 1687, to promulgate a declaration of indulgence extending to all Catholics and Non-Conformists a freedom in religious matters which was clearly denied by the laws of the land. By this arbitrary resumption of ancient prerogative the compact underlying the Restoration was utterly subverted.

The Revolution of 1688-1689: the Bill of Rights. — Foreseeing no relief from absolutist practices, and urged on by the birth, in 1688, of a male heir to the king, a group of leading men representing the various political groups extended to the stadtholder of Holland, William, Prince of Orange, an invitation to come over to England to uphold and protect the constitutional liberties of the realm. The result was the bloodless revolution of 1688. November 5, William landed at Torquay and advanced toward London. James, finding himself without a party, offered vain concessions and afterwards fled to the court of his ally, Louis XIV of France. By a provisional body of lords, former commoners, and officials William was requested to act as temporary " governor " until the people should have chosen a national " convention." This convention assembled January 22, 1689, decided that James, by reason of his flight, should be construed to have abdicated, and established William and Mary on the throne as joint sovereigns.

The Revolution of 1688-1689 led to the putting into written form of no inconsiderable portion of the English constitution as it then existed. On February 19, 1689, the new sovereigns formally accepted a Declaration of Right, drawn up by the convention; and by act of Parliament, December 16 following, this instrument, under the name of the Bill of Rights, became a part of the law of the land. Specific denial was made in it of a long list of prerogatives to which the last Stuart had laid claim — those, in particular, of dispensing with laws, establishing ecclesiastical commissions, levying imposts without parliamentary assent, and maintaining a standing army under the exclusive control of the crown. In it also were guaranteed certain fundamental rights which during the controversies of the seventeenth century had been repeatedly brought in question, including those of petition, freedom of elections, and freedom of speech on the part of members of Parliament.[1] The necessity of frequent meetings of Parliament was affirmed, and a succession clause was inserted by which Roman Catholics and persons who should marry Roman Catholics were excluded from the throne. In the Bill of Rights were thus summed up the essential results of the Revolution, and, quite as truly, of the entire seventeenth-century liberal movement. The supremacy of Parliament was vindicated; the will of the nation became, in both law and fact, the controlling force in government. Kingship was continued as a natural and useful institution. But thereafter the royal tenure was not by inherent or vested right, but conditioned upon the consent of the nation as expressed through Parliament. Divine right was dead.

SELECTED REFERENCES

G. B. Adams, *The Origin of the English Constitution* (New Haven, 1912); ibid., *Outlines of English Constitutional History* (New Haven, 1918); A. B. White, *The Making of the English Constitution, 449–1485* (New York, 1908); A. D. Innis, *England under the Tudors* (London, 1905); G. M. Trevelyan, *England under the Stuarts* (London, 1904); W. S. McKechnie, *Magna Carta* (Glasgow, 1905); J. N. Figgis, *The Theory of the Divine Right of Kings* (Cambridge, 1896); G. P. Gooch, *History of English Democratic Ideas in the Seventeenth Century* (Cambridge, 1898); G. B. Smith, *History of the English Parliament*, 2 vols. (London, 1892); A. T. Carter, *Outlines of English Legal History* (London, 1899); G. B. Adams and H. M. Stephens, *Select Documents of English Constitutional History* (New York, 1906); G. W. Prothero, *Select Statutes and Other Constitutional Documents Illustrative of the Reigns of Elizabeth and James I* (Oxford, 1898).

[1] In this connection should be mentioned the Habeas Corpus Act of 1679, by whose terms the right of an individual, upon arrest, to have his case investigated without delay was effectually guaranteed.

CHAPTER X

THE ENGLISH CONSTITUTION

I. DEVELOPMENT IN THE EIGHTEENTH AND NINETEENTH CENTURIES

Elements of Stability and of Change. — The framework of the English governmental system was substantially complete by the close of the seventeenth century. The limited monarchy, the ministry, the two houses of parliament, the courts of law, and the local administrative authorities then presented the same general appearance that they present to-day. The fundamental principles, furthermore, upon which the government is nowadays operated were already securely established. Laws could be made only by "the king in parliament"; taxes could be levied only in the same manner; the liberty of the individual was protected by a score of specific and oft-renewed guarantees. In point of fact, however, the English constitution of 1689 was very far from being the English constitution of 1918. The overturn by which the last Stuart was driven from the throne not only marked the culmination of the revolution begun in 1640; it formed the beginning of a more extended revolution, peaceful but thoroughgoing, by which the governmental system of the realm was expanded, carried in new directions, and continuously readapted to fresh and changing conditions. At no time from William III to George V was there a deliberate overhauling of the political machinery as a whole. The American plan of holding specially chosen conventions to revise an entire constitution, or even to make a new one, is quite unknown to English practice. The changes were made gradually, cautiously, sometimes hardly consciously; and, save in occasional parliamentary enactments and judicial decisions, they but rarely found expression in formal documents. Nevertheless, it is hardly too much to say that of the rules and practices which make up the working constitution of the United Kingdom to-day, almost all owe their form and character to developments of the past two hundred years. Before speaking of the characteristics of the constitution as a whole it will be well, therefore, to follow up the historical survey contained in the preceding chapter with an account of a few of the most important of these developments between 1689 and 1900. Equally weighty changes of more recent date will be described in succeeding chapters devoted to the governmental system as it now is.

The Diminished Authority of the Sovereign. — First may be mentioned the gradual eclipse of the king and the establishment of complete and unquestioned ascendancy on the part of Parliament. In consequence of the Revolution of 1688-1689 the sovereign was shorn once for all of a number of important prerogatives. William III, however, was no figurehead, and the monarch was far from having been reduced to impotence. Understanding perfectly the conditions upon which he had been received in England, William none the less did not attempt to conceal his innate love of power. He claimed prerogatives which his Whig supporters were loath to acknowledge, and he habitually exercised in person, and with telling effect, the functions of sovereign, premier, foreign minister, and military autocrat. His successor, Anne, although apathetic, was hardly less attached to the interests of strong monarchy. It was only with the accession of the Hanoverian dynasty, in 1714, that the bulk of those powers of government which the sovereign had hitherto retained slipped finally and completely into the grasp of the ministers and of Parliament. George I (1714-1727) and George II (1727-1760) were not the nonentities they have been painted, but, being alien alike to English speech, customs, and political institutions, they were not in a position to defend the prerogatives which they had inherited. Under George III (1760-1820) there was a distinct revival of the monarchical idea. The king, if obstinate and below the average intellectually, was honest, courageous, and ambitious. He gloried in the name of Englishman, and, above all, he was determined to recover for the crown some measure of the prestige and authority which his predecessors had lost. For a score of years the influence which the sovereign exerted personally upon government and politics exceeded anything that had been known since the days of William III. In 1780 the House of Commons gave expression to its apprehension by adopting a series of resolutions, the first of which asserted unequivocally that "the influence of the crown has increased, is increasing, and ought to be diminished."

After the retirement of Lord North, in 1782, however, the power of the sovereign fell off rapidly, and during the later portion of the reign, clouded by the king's insanity, all that had been gained for royalty was again lost. Under the Regency (1810–1820) and during the reign of the reactionary George IV (1820–1830) the popularity, if not the power, of the king reached its nadir. In the days of the genial William IV (1830–1837) popularity was regained, but not power. The long reign of the virtuous Victoria (1837–1901) served completely to rehabilitate the monarchy in the respect and affections of the British people, an achievement whose permanence more recent sovereigns have done nothing to impair. As will be pointed out in another place, the influence which the sovereign may wield, and during the past three-quarters of a century has wielded, in the actual conduct of public affairs is by no means unimportant. But, as will also be emphasized, that influence is only the shadow of the authority which the king once — even as late as the opening of the eighteenth century — possessed. It is largely personal rather than legal; it is commonly asserted within the domain of foreign relations rather than within that of domestic affairs; and as against the will of the nation expressed through Parliament it is powerless.

Ascendancy of the House of Commons. — A second transformation wrought in the working constitution since 1689 is the shifting of the center of gravity in Parliament from the House of Lords to the House of Commons, together with a notable democratization of the representative chamber. In the days of William and Anne the House of Lords was distinctly more dignified and influential than the House of Commons. During the period covered by the ministry of Robert Walpole (1721–1742), however, the Commons rose rapidly to the position of the preponderating branch. One cause was the Septennial Act of 1716, whereby the life of a parliament was extended from three years to seven, thus increasing the continuity and attractiveness of membership in the Commons. Another was the growing importance of the power of the purse as wielded by the Commons. A third was the fact that Walpole, throughout his extended ministry, sat steadily as a member of the lower chamber and made it the scene of his remarkable activities. The establishment of the supremacy of the Commons as then constructed did not, however, mean the triumph of popular government. It was but a step toward that end. The House of Commons in the eighteenth century was composed of members elected in the counties and boroughs under a severely restricted franchise, or appointed outright by closed corporations or by individual magnates, and it remained for Parliament during the nineteenth century, by a series of memorable statutes, to extend the franchise successively to groups of people hitherto politically powerless, to reapportion parliamentary seats so that political influence might be distributed with some fairness among the voters, and to regulate the conditions under which campaigns should be carried on, elections conducted, and other operations of popular government undertaken. Of principal importance among the pieces of legislation by which these things were accomplished are the Reform Act of 1832, the Representation of the People Act of 1867, the Ballot Act of 1872, the Corrupt and Illegal Practices Act of 1883, the Representation of the People Act of 1884, and the Redistribution of Seats Act of 1885. The nature of these measures, and of their notable successor, the Representation of the People Act of 1918, will be explained presently.[1]

Rise of the Cabinet. — The period under review is further important because it produced the most remarkable feature of the English constitutional system of to-day, *i.e.*, the cabinet. The creation of the cabinet was a gradual process, and both the process and the product are utterly unknown to the letter of English law. It is customary to regard as the immediate forerunner of the cabinet the so-called "cabal" of Charles II, *i.e.*, the shifting group of persons whom that sovereign selected from the Privy Council[2] and took advice from informally, in lieu of the Council itself. In point of fact, by reason principally of the

[1] See pp. 225–236.
[2] That is, the large body of advisers and administrators, historically descended from the Great, or Common, Council.

growing unwieldiness of the Privy Council, the practice of deferring for advice to a specially constituted committee, or inner circle, of that body far antedated Charles II. By some it has been traced to a period as remote as the reign of Henry III, and it is known that not only the thing itself, but also the name "cabinet council," existed under Charles I. The essential justification of the creation of the cabinet was stated by Charles II in 1679 in the declaration that "the great number of the Council has made it unfit for the secrecy and despatch that are necessary in many great affairs." The growing authority of the select circle of advisers was the object of repeated attacks, and the name "cabinet" (arising from the king's habit of receiving the members in a small private room, or cabinet, in the royal palace) was applied at first as a term of reproach. The device met, however, a genuine need, and by 1689 its survival was assured. The Privy Council lived on, and it still exists; but its powers long ago became merely nominal.

Under William III the cabinet rapidly took on the character which it bears to-day. Failing in the attempt to govern with a cabinet including both Whigs and Tories, William, in 1693-1696, gathered about himself a body of advisers exclusively of Whigs, and the principle quickly became established for all time that a cabinet group must be made up of men who are in substantial agreement upon all important matters of state. Before the close of the eighteenth century there was fixed definitely the conception of the cabinet as a body necessarily consisting (a) of members of Parliament (b) of the same political views (c) chosen from the party possessing a majority in the House of Commons (d) prosecuting a concerted policy (e) under a common responsibility to be signified by collective resignation in the event of parliamentary censure, and (f) acknowledging a common subordination to one chief minister. During the eighteenth-century era of royal weakness the cabinet acquired a measure of independence which enabled it to become, for all practical purposes, the ruling power of the realm; and, under the limitation of strict accountability to the House of Commons, it fulfills substantially that function to-day. Its members, as will appear, are at the same time the heads of the principal executive departments, the leaders in the legislative chambers, and the authors of very nearly the whole of governmental policy and conduct.

Beginnings of Political Parties. — A fourth development in the period under survey is the rise of political parties and the fixing of the broader aspects of the present party system. In no nation to-day does party play a rôle of larger importance than in Great Britain. Unknown to the written portions of the constitution, and almost unknown to the ordinary law, party management and party operations are, none the less, of constant and fundamental importance in the actual conduct of government. The origins of political parties in England fall clearly within the seventeenth century, the first groups which can be thought of as essentially analogous to the political parties of the present day, — having continuity of life, fixity of principles, and some degree of compactness of organization, — being the Whigs and Tories of the period of Charles II. Dividing in the first instance upon the issue of the exclusion of James, as a Catholic, from the throne, these two elements in time assumed well-defined and fundamentally irreconcilable positions upon the great public questions of the day. Broadly, the Whigs stood for toleration in religion and for parliamentary supremacy in government; the Tories for Anglicanism and the royal prerogative. And long after the Stuart monarchy was a thing of the past these two great parties kept up their struggles upon these and other issues. After an unsuccessful attempt to govern with the coöperation of both parties William III, as has been stated, fell back upon the support of the Whigs. At the accession of Queen Anne, in 1702, however, the Whigs were turned out of office and the Tories (who already had had a taste of power in 1698–1701) were put in control. They retained office during the larger portion of Queen Anne's reign, but at the accession of George I they were compelled to give place to their rivals, and the period 1714–1761 was one of unbroken Whig ascendancy. This was, of course, the period of the development of the cabinet system, and between the rise of that system and the growth of government by party there was a close and inevitable connection. By the end of the eighteenth century the rule had become inflexible that the cabinet should be composed of men who were in sympathy with the party at the time dominant in the House of Commons, and that whenever the nation elected to the popular branch a majority hostile to the ruling ministry, that ministry should forthwith resign.

The Union with Scotland (1707). — Finally may be mentioned the important changes in the structure of government which arose from the Act of Union with Scotland, in 1707, and the Act of Union with Ireland, in 1801. Except during a brief portion of the period of the Protectorate, the legal relation of England and Wales, on the one side, and the kingdom of Scotland, on the other, was from 1603 to 1707 that simply of a personal union through the crown. Scotland had her own parliament, her own established church, her own laws, her own courts, her own army, and her own system of finance. By the act of 1707 a union was established of a far more substantial sort. The two countries were erected into a single kingdom, known henceforth as Great Britain. The Scottish parliament was abolished, and representation was given the Scottish nobility and people in the British parliament at Westminster. The quota of commoners was fixed at forty-five (thirty to be chosen by the counties and fifteen by the boroughs), and that of peers (to be elected by the entire body of Scottish peers at the beginning of each parliament) at sixteen. All laws concerning trade, excises, and customs were required to be uniform throughout the two countries; but the local laws of Scotland upon other subjects were continued in operation, subject to revision by the common parliament. The Scottish judicial system remained practically unchanged; likewise the status of the established Presbyterian Church.

The Union with Ireland (1801). — The history of Ireland, in most of its phases, is that of a conquered territory, and until late in the eighteenth century the constitutional status of the country approximated, most of the time, that of a non-self-governing colony. During the Middle Ages the Common Law and the institutions of England were introduced in the settled portions of the island (the Pale), and a parliament of the English type began to be developed. But Poyning's Law of 1494, by requiring the assent of the English king and council for the convening of an Irish parliament, by enjoining that all bills introduced in the Irish parliament must first have been considered by the English parliament, and by declaring all existing statutes of the English parliament to be binding upon Ireland, effectually stifled, until its repeal in 1782, Irish parliamentary development. From the middle of the seventeenth century Catholics were debarred from membership, and, from the early eighteenth, from voting at parliamentary elections. The repeal of Poyning's Law in 1782 and the removal of the Catholic disqualification ten years later bettered the situation, yet at the close of the eighteenth century Irish governmental arrangements were still very unsatisfactory. Parliament was independent in the making of laws, but not in the control of administration; and it was in no true sense a national and representative body. The policy urged by Pitt, namely, the establishment of a legislative union on the plan of that which already existed between England and Scotland, gradually impressed itself upon the members of Parliament as more feasible than any other.

An Act of Union creating the "United Kingdom of Great Britain and Ireland" was adopted by the Irish parliament in February, 1800, and by the British parliament five months later; and on January 1, 1801, it was put in operation. Under the terms of this measure the Irish parliament was abolished, and it was arranged that Ireland should be represented in the common parliament by four spiritual lords and twenty-eight temporal peers, chosen by the Irish peerage for life, and by one hundred members (sixty-four sitting for counties, thirty-five for boroughs, and one for the University of Dublin) of the House of Commons. The Anglican Church of Ireland was amalgamated with the established Church of England, although, subsequently, in 1869, it was disestablished and disendowed. The union with Ireland was in the nature of a contract; and while it has been altered in a few respects, its fundamental features stand to-day unchanged. A large part of the Irish people have long been keenly dissatisfied with the status of their country, and the Home Rule movement which has filled so large a place in recent British politics, and which has for some years been at the threshold of victory, aims at arrangements of an entirely different character.[1]

[1] See p. 285.

II. NATURE AND SOURCES OF THE CONSTITUTION

What "Constitution" Means in England. — Writers on government use the term "constitution" in two widely differing senses. Sometimes they mean by it a written instrument of fundamental law which outlines the structure of a governmental system, defines the powers of the governing bodies and officers, and perhaps lays down certain general principles and rules to be observed in carrying on the affairs of state. The document may have been framed by a special, constituent assembly, or drafted by an ordinary legislative body, or promulgated upon the sole authority of a prince or dictator. On the other hand, the writer may employ the term to denote the whole body of laws, customs, and precedents, only partially, or even not at all, committed to writing, which determine the organization and workings of a government. The two usages are equally correct, provided one makes quite clear which is being followed at any given time. Thus the constitution of the United States is the document drawn up at Philadelphia in 1787 and put into operation in 1789, plus the seventeen amendments adopted in subsequent years; *or* it is this instrument taken in conjunction with a great mass of rules, laws, customs, and interpretations, which lose none of their importance, or even of their binding character, because no mention of them can be found in the fundamental document.

Upwards of a century ago a leading French writer, De Tocqueville — author of a valuable work on democracy in America — was led to remark that there is no such thing as an English constitution. As a Frenchman, he was accustomed to consider a constitution as being necessarily a document, or at all events a small group of documents, framed and adopted at a given time, and by some convention or other special agency, and setting forth in logical array the framework and principles of the government operating under it. In England he could find nothing of this sort; nor can one do so to-day. There is, however, it need hardly be affirmed, an English constitution — one which is at once the oldest and the most influential of all constitutions known to history. It is not contained in any single document, nor in a group of documents; a great, though diminishing, portion of it is not in written form at all; it is not the work of any special constitution-framing body or power; far from being adopted at any one time, it is a product of fifteen centuries of political growth, and much of it was never formally " adopted " at all. In short, the term " constitution " as applied to England must always be used in the broader sense indicated above. The English constitution is a complex of elements which one could hope to bring together only by examining intensively a thousand years and more of history, by laying hold of a statute here and of a judicial decision there, by taking constant account of the rise and crystallization of political usages, and by probing to their inmost recesses the mechanisms of administration, law-making, taxation, elections, and judicial procedure as they have been, and as they are actually operated before the spectator's eyes.

Component Elements: the Law of the Constitution. — These elements have been classified in various ways. For purposes of brief enumeration they may be gathered into five main categories. In the first place, there are treaties and other international agreements, which in Great Britain as in the United States are considered parts of the supreme law of the land. In the second place, there is a group of solemn engagements which have been entered into at times of national crisis between parties representing conflicting political forces. Of such character are the Great Charter, the Petition of Right, and the Bill of Rights. A third and larger category comprises parliamentary statutes of such character and importance as to add to or modify governmental powers or procedure. Statutes of this type obviously include the Habeas Corpus Act of 1679, the Act of Settlement of 1701, the Septennial Act of 1716, Fox's Libel Act of 1792, the Reform Acts of 1832, 1867, and 1884, the Municipal Corporations Act of 1835, the Parliamentary and Municipal Elections Act of 1872, the Local Government Acts of 1888 and 1894, the Parliament Act of 1911, and the Representation of the People Act of 1918. In the fourth place there is the Common Law, a vast body of legal precept and usage which through the centuries has acquired binding and almost immutable character. The first three elements mentioned, *i.e.*, treaties, solemn political engagements, and statutes, exist solely, or almost so, in written form. The rules of the Common Law, however, have not been reduced to writing, save in so far as they are contained in reports, legal opinions, and, more particularly, formal decisions of the courts, such as those on the rights of jurymen, on the prerogative of the crown, on the privileges of the houses of Parliament and of their members, and on the rights and duties of the police.

Component Elements: the Conventions of the Constitution. — Finally, there are those portions of the constitution which have been aptly termed by Mr. Dicey "the conventions."[1] The "law" of the constitution, composed of the four categories of elements which have been enumerated, is at all points, whether written or unwritten, enforceable by the courts; the conventions, although they may, and not seldom do, relate to matters of the most vital importance, are not so enforceable. The conventions consist of understandings, practices, and habits which alone regulate a large proportion of the actual relations and operations of the public authorities. They may have been put into written form, but they do not appear in the statute books or in any instrument which can be made the basis of action in a court of law. For example, it is a convention of the constitution that forbids the king to veto a measure passed by the houses of Parliament. If the sovereign were in these days actually to veto a bill, the political consequences would be serious, but there could be no question of the technical legality of the act. It is by virtue of a convention, not a law, of the constitution, that ministers resign when they have ceased to command the confidence of the House of Commons; that a bill must be read three times before being finally voted upon in the House of Commons; that Parliament is convened annually, and that it consists of two houses. The cabinet, and all that the cabinet, as such, stands for, rests entirely upon convention. Obviously, any one seeking to understand the constitutional system as it is and as it operates must fix his attention upon the conventions quite as intently as upon the positive rules of law.[2] The English constitution is indeed, as Lord Bryce has described it, "a mass of precedents carried

---

[1] *Introduction to the Study of the Law of the Constitution,* 8th ed., Chap. xiv.

[2] Convention occupies a large place in most political systems, even in countries which are governed under elaborate written constitutions. Their importance in the government of the United States is familiar. (See Bryce, *American Commonwealth,* 3d ed., I, Chaps. xxxiv–xxxv.)

in men's minds or recorded in writing, dicta of lawyers or statesmen, customs, usages, understandings and beliefs, a number of statutes mixed up with customs, and all covered over with a parasitic growth of legal decisions and political habits." [1] At no time has an attempt been made to collect and to reduce to writing this stupendous mass of scattered material, and no such attempt is likely ever to be made. "The English," as the French critic Boutmy remarks, "have left the different parts of their constitution where the waves of history have deposited them; they have not attempted to bring them together, to classify or complete them, or to make of it a consistent or coherent whole." [2]

Aspects of Continuity and of Change. — In pursuance of what has been said, two observations, representing opposite aspects of the same truth, are pertinent. The first is that in respect to the principles and many of the practices of the English constitution it is profoundly true that, in the familiar phrase of Bishop Stubbs, the roots of the present lie deep in the past.[3] The second is that the English constitution is a living organism, so constantly undergoing change that any description of it that may be attempted is likely to need correction almost before it can be printed. At no time, as the historian Freeman wrote, "has the tie between the present and the past been rent asunder; at no moment have Englishmen sat down to put together a wholly new constitution in obedience to some dazzling theory." [4] On the contrary, each step in the growth of the constitutional system has been the natural consequence of some earlier step. Great changes, it is true, have been wrought. To mention but the most obvious illustration, autocratic kingship has been replaced by a parliamentary government based upon a thoroughgoing political democracy. None the less, transitions have as a rule been so gradual, deference to tradition so habitual, and the disposition to cling to ancient names and forms, even when the spirit had changed, so deep-seated, that the constitutional

---
[1] Bryce, "Flexible and Rigid Constitutions," in *Studies in History and Jurisprudence*, No. 3.
[2] Boutmy, *Studies in Constitutional Law: France — England — United States*, trans. by Dicey, 6.
[3] *Constitutional History of England*, I, prefatory note.
[4] *Growth of the English Constitution*, 19.

history of England presents an aspect of continuity that cannot be paralleled in any other country of Europe.

The letter of a written constitution may survive through many decades unchanged, as has that of the Italian *Statuto* of 1848, and as did that of the American constitution between 1804 and 1865. No constitutional system, however, long stands still, and least of all one of the English type, in which there is little of even the formal rigidity that arises from written texts. Having no fixed and orderly shape assigned it originally by some supreme authority, the constitution of the United Kingdom has retained throughout its history a notable flexibility. It is by no means to-day what it was fifty years ago; fifty years hence it will be by no means what it is to-day. In times past changes have sometimes been accompanied by violence, or, at all events, by extraordinary demonstrations of the national will. Nowadays they are introduced through the ordinary and peaceful processes of legislation, of judicial interpretation, and of administrative practice. Sometimes, as in the case of the passage of the Parliament Act of 1911 altering the position of the House of Lords, they are accompanied by heated controversy and widespread public agitation. Frequently, however, they represent inevitable and unopposed amplifications of existing law or practice, and are hardly taken note of by the nation at large.

Power of Parliament to Alter the Constitution. — In the main, changes are made in the English constitution to-day by act of Parliament. In the United States and in some European countries a sharp distinction is drawn between the powers of constitution framing and amendment and the powers of ordinary legislation. Our Congress may propose a constitutional amendment; but the change can be made only by an affirmative vote of the legislatures of three-fourths of the states.[1] In England powers are not thus divided. All are vested alike in Parliament; and so far as the processes of enactment, repeal, and revision are concerned, there is no difference whatever between a measure affecting the fundamental principles of the governmental system and a statute pertaining to the most petty subject of ordinary

[1] An alternative mode of ratification is by conventions, also in three-fourths of the states. But this plan has never been followed.

o

law. "Our Parliament," observes Anson, "can make laws protecting wild birds or shell-fish, and with the same procedure could break the connection of Church and State, or give political power to two millions of citizens, and redistribute it among new constituencies."[1] The keystone of the law of the constitution is, indeed, the omnipotence of Parliament in the spheres both of constitution-making and of ordinary legislation. In Parliament is embodied the supreme will of the nation; and although from time to time that will may declare itself in widely varying, and even inconsistent, ways, at any given moment its pronouncements are authoritative and conclusive.

It follows that every measure of Parliament, of whatever nature and under whatever circumstances enacted, is "constitutional," in the sense that it is legally valid and enforceable. When an Englishman says of a measure that it is unconstitutional he means only that it is inconsistent with a previous enactment, with an established usage, with the principles of international law, or with the commonly accepted standards of morality. Such a measure, if passed in due form by Parliament, becomes an integral part of the law of the land, and as such will be enforced by the courts. There is no means by which it can be rendered of no effect, save repeal by the same or a succeeding parliament. In England, as in European countries generally, the judicial tribunals are endowed with no power to pass upon the constitutional validity of legislative acts. Every such act is *ipso facto* valid, whether it relates to the most trivial subject of ordinary legislation or to the organic arrangements of the state; and no person or body, aside from Parliament itself, has a right to override it or to set it aside.

[1] *Law and Custom of the Constitution*, 4th ed., I, 358. The fact should not go unmentioned, however, that of late there has been a growing feeling that when fundamental and far-reaching changes are under consideration Parliament ought not to act until after the matter has been put before the people at a general election. It was in deference to this idea that the parliamentary election of December, 1910, was ordered, with the reform of the House of Lords as the one great issue. No fixed rule of the kind, however, has established itself, as is evidenced by the enfranchisement of six million women — not to mention other revolutionary changes in the electoral system — accomplished in the Representation of the People Act of 1918 entirely without formal popular mandate.

SELECTED REFERENCES

A. L. Lowell, *The Government of England* (New York, 1908), I, 1–15; S. Low, *The Governance of England* (new ed., London, 1914), Chap. i; J. A. R. Marriott, *English Political Institutions* (Oxford, 1910), Chaps. i–ii; T. F. Moran, *Theory and Practice of the English Government* (New York, 1908), Chap. i; W. R. Anson, *Law and Custom of the Constitution* (3d ed., Oxford, 1897), Chaps. i–iii; A. V. Dicey, *Introduction to the Study of the Law of the Constitution* (8th ed., London, 1915), Chaps. xiv–xv; H. B. Learned, "Historical Significance of the Term Cabinet in England and America," in *The President's Cabinet* (New Haven, 1912), Chap. i; G. B. Adams, *Outlines of English Constitutional History* (New Haven, 1918); W. Bagehot, *The English Constitution* (new ed., London, 1911); T. E. May, *Constitutional History of England since the Accession of George III*, edited and continued by F. Holland, 3 vols. (London, 1912); M. T. Blauvelt, *The Development of Cabinet Government in England* (New York, 1902); J. A. R. Marriott, *England since Waterloo* (London, 1913); G. B. Adams and H. M. Stephens, *Select Documents of English Constitutional History* (New York, 1906).

CHAPTER XI

THE MINISTRY AND THE CABINET

HAVING seen something of the nature of the English constitution — its antiquity, its diversity of origins, its flexibility, and its elusiveness — we come now to consider the actual governmental system which operates under it. And we may best begin with the great agencies that stand at the head and hold the system together, namely, the king, the ministry, and the cabinet. Parliament, with which these (especially the cabinet), have important relations, will be taken up in two succeeding chapters.

I. THE KING

Title to the Throne — Privileges. — Since the Revolution of 1688 tenure of the English throne has been based exclusively upon the will of the nation as expressed in parliamentary enactment. The statute under which the succession is regulated to-day is the Act of Settlement, passed in 1701. It provided that, in default of heirs of William III and of Anne, the crown and all prerogatives thereto appertaining should " be, remain, and continue to the most excellent Princess Sophia, and the heirs of her body, being Protestants." Sophia, a granddaughter of James I, was the widow of a German prince, the Elector of Hanover; and although in 1701 she was not first in the natural order of succession, she was first among the surviving heirs who were Protestants. It was in accordance with this piece of legislation that, upon the death of Anne in 1714, the throne fell to George I, son of the German Electress. The present sovereign, George V, is the eighth of the Hanoverian dynasty.[1] It would

[1] After the outbreak of the Great War in 1914 the designation "Hanoverian dynasty" was formally discarded and the name "Windsor dynasty" was adopted in its stead. For a century and a quarter the sovereign of Great Britain was also the ruler of Hanover. At the accession of Queen Victoria in 1837, however, the union ended, because the law of Hanover forbade a woman to ascend the throne of that country.

of course be entirely within the power of Parliament to repeal the Act of Settlement and to bestow the crown elsewhere; indeed, Parliament could, if it wished, abolish kingship altogether. Under the established rules of descent the sovereign's eldest son, who bears the title of Prince of Wales, falls heir to the throne when a vacancy arises. If he be not alive, the inheritance passes to his issue, male or female. If there be none, the succession devolves upon the late sovereign's second son, or upon his issue. No Catholic may inherit, nor any one marrying a Catholic; and the act of 1701 prescribed that the sovereign should in all cases "join in communion with the Church of England as by law established."

The king may own land and other property, and may manage and dispose of it precisely as any private citizen. The vast accumulations of property, however, which at one time formed the sovercign's principal source of revenue, have become the possession of the state, and as such are administered entirely under the direction of Parliament. In lieu of the income derived formerly from land and other independent sources, the king has been given for the support of the royal household a fixed annual subsidy — voted under the designation of the "Civil List" — the amount of which is determined afresh at the beginning of each reign. The Civil List was introduced by an act of 1698, and had the effect of separating for the first time the private expenditures of the king from the public outlays of the nation. The amount voted George V at his accession in 1910 was £470,000 a year. The sovereign enjoys large personal immunity. For his private conduct he cannot be called to account in any court of law or by any legal process. He cannot be arrested, his goods cannot be distrained, and as long as a palace remains a royal residence no sort of judicial proceeding against him can be executed in it.

The King's Powers, Theoretical and Actual. — Viewed from a distance, English kingship is still imposing. The sovereign dwells in a splendid palace, sets the pace in rich and cultured social circles, occupies the center of the stage in solemn and magnificent ceremonies, makes and receives ostentatious visits to and from foreign royalty, and seems to exercise far-reaching powers of appointment, administrative control, military command, law-making, justice, and finance. Examined more closely, however, the king's position is found to afford peculiarly good illustration of the contrast between theory and fact which runs so extensively through the English governmental system. On the social and ceremonial side, the king is indeed as important as the observer supposes him to be; indeed, his influence in these directions is commonly underestimated. But his control over public affairs — appointments, legislation, military policy, the Church, finance, foreign relations — is purely incidental. There was a time when his power in these great fields was practically absolute. It was certainly so under the Tudors, in the sixteenth century. But the Civil War cut off large prerogatives, the Revolution of 1688-1689 sundered many more, the apathy and weakness of the early Hanoverians cost much, and the drift against royal control in government continued strong, even under the good monarchs of the last hundred years, — until the king now finds himself literally in the position of one who " reigns but does not govern." Lawyers and students of political science continue to talk much about the powers of the crown; and long chapters will be found in the books upon the subject. This is all proper enough. The powers of the crown, under the English constitution, are numerous, vast, and of transcendent importance. The government could not run an hour if they were not exercised, and they are more extensive to-day than at any time in the past two hundred years. But the point is that the " crown " is no longer the king. If it be asked who or what the crown is, one may reply in the delightfully evasive phrase of Mr. Sidney Low that it is " a convenient working hypothesis; " [1] or one may be a little more definite by saying that it is, in a general way, the supreme executive agency in the government, — once actually the king alone, but now rather the ministers and their subordinates, with the king as a sort of fifth wheel to the wagon. When we say that the crown appoints practically all national public officers we mean that ministers, who themselves are selected by the king only in form, make these appointments. When the king attends the opening of a parliament and reads the Speech from the Throne, the message is one which has been written by these same ministers. " Government " measures

[1] *The Governance of England* (new ed., 1916), 255.

are continually framed and executive acts performed in the name of the crown, though the king may personally be quite ignorant of them or even strongly opposed to them. Two principles, in short, reign supreme and give character to the entire governmental system: (1) the king shall perform no important public act involving the exercise of discretion except through the agency of the ministers, and (2) for every public act performed by or through them these ministers shall be fully responsible to Parliament. The king can "do no wrong," because all of the acts done by him or in his name are chargeable to a minister or to the ministry as a group. But that tends to mean that the king can do nothing; because ministers cannot be expected to shoulder responsibility for acts which they do not themselves originate or favor.

The Real Authority and Service of the Sovereign. — It would be erroneous, however, to conclude that kingship in England is obsolete and unimportant, or even that the king has no real influence in the government. Americans are likely to wonder why an institution which seems so completely to have outlived its usefulness has not been abolished; and Englishmen are free to admit that if they did not actually have a royal house they would hardly set about establishing one. None the less, the uses served by the monarch are considerable; his influence upon the course of public affairs may, indeed, be great. In the oft-quoted phrase of Bagehot, the sovereign has three rights — the right to be consulted, the right to encourage, and the right to warn. "A king of great sense and sagacity," it is added, "would want no others."[1] Despite the fact that during upwards of two hundred years the sovereign has not attended the meetings of the cabinet, and hence is deprived of opportunity to wield influence directly upon the deliberations of the ministers as a body, he keeps in close touch with the premier, and cabinet councils at which important lines of policy are to be formulated are not infrequently preceded by a conference in which the subject in hand is threshed out more or less completely by king and chief minister. Merely because the ancient relation has been reversed, so that now it is the king who advises and the ministry that arrives at decisions, it does not follow that the

[1] *The English Constitution* (rev. ed.), 143.

advisory function is an unimportant thing. Queen Victoria many times wielded influence of a decisive nature upon the public measures of her reign, especially in connection with the conduct of foreign relations. The extent of such influence cannot be made a matter of record, because the ministers are in effect bound not to publish the fact that a decision upon a matter of state has been taken at the sovereign's instance. It is familiarly known, however — to cite a somewhat recent illustration — that Edward VII approved and encouraged the Haldane army reforms, that he sought to dissuade the House of Lords from rejecting the Lloyd George budget of 1909, and that he discouraged the raising, in any form, of the issue of the reorganization of the upper chamber. In other words, while as a constitutional monarch content to remain in the background of political controversy, this king not only had opinions but did not hesitate to make them known; and in the shaping and execution of the Liberal program his advice was at times a factor of importance. His successor, George V, has been similarly active, in relation especially to the Irish question and to the issues of the Great War.

Why Monarchy Survives. — Monarchy in Great Britain is a solid and, so far as can be foreseen, a lasting institution. Throughout the tempestuous years 1909-1911, when the nation was aroused as it had not been in generations upon the issue of constitutional reform, and when every sort of project was being warmly advocated and as warmly opposed, without exception every suggested program took for granted the perpetuation of the monarchy as an integral part of the governmental system. In the general bombardment to which the hereditary House of Lords was subjected hereditary kingship wholly escaped. The reasons are numerous and complex. They arise in part, although by no means so largely as is sometimes imagined, from the fact that monarchy in England is a venerable institution, and the innate conservatism of the Englishman, while permitting him from time to time to regulate and modify it, restrains him from doing anything so revolutionary as to abolish it. That upon certain conspicuous occasions, as in the Cromwellian period, and again in 1688, kingship has owed its very life to the conservative instinct of the English people is well enough known to every student of history. But to-day, as ever, the institution rests upon a basis very much more substantial than a mere national predilection. Monarchy remains impregnably intrenched because it fulfills specific ends which are universally recognized to be eminently worth while, if not indispensable. As a social, moral, and ceremonial agency, and as a visible symbol of the unity of the nation, and especially of the Empire, king and court occupy an immeasurable place in the life and thought of the people; and even within the domain of government, to employ the figure of Lowell, if the crown is no longer the motive power of the ship of state, it is the spar on which the sail is bent, and as such it is not only a useful but an essential part of the vessel.[1] The entire governmental order of Great Britain hinges upon the parliamentary system; and nowhere has that system been reduced to satisfactory operation without the presence of some central, but essentially detached, figure, whether a king or, as in France, a president with the attributes of kingship. It is because the English people have discovered that kingship is not necessarily incompatible with popular government that the monarchy has survived. If royalty had been found standing in the path of democratic progress, it is inconceivable that all the forces of tradition could have pulled it through the past seventy-five or eighty years. As it is, while half a century ago there was in the country a small republican group which was fond of urging that the monarchy was only a source of needless expense, to-day there is hardly a trace of anti-monarchical sentiment in any section of society.

Before turning from this branch of our subject, let us hear what a scholarly English writer, Mr. Edward Jenks, has to say of the uses of kingship in his country. " In the first place," he writes, " the king supplies the vital element of personal interest to the proceedings of government. It is far easier for the average man to realize a person than an institution. Even in the United Kingdom, only the educated few have any real appreciation of such abstract things as parliament, the cabinet, or even ' the crown.' But the vast mass of the people are deeply interested in the king as a person, as is proved by the crowds which collect whenever there is a chance of seeing him;

[1] *Government of England,* I, 49.

and it is possible that the majority of the people, even of the United Kingdom, to say nothing of the millions of India, believe that the government of the Empire is carried on by the king personally. He therefore supplies the personal and picturesque element which catches the popular imagination far more readily than constitutional arrangements, which cannot be heard or seen; and a king or queen who knows how to play this part skillfully, by a display of tact, graciousness, and benevolence, is rendering priceless services to the cause of contentment and good government. . . . Very closely allied to this personal character of the king is the great unofficial and social influence which he wields, and not he alone, but the queen, and, in a lesser degree, the other members of the royal family. Their influence in matters of religion, morality, benevolence, fashion, and even in art and literature is immense. . . . How much good was done in this way by the late Queen Victoria, is a matter of common knowledge; it was one of the striking triumphs of her long reign. And, be it remembered, in such matters the monarch is in no way bound to follow, or even to seek, the advice of his ministers; for such matters lie outside the domain of politics. . . . A king who is fully informed of affairs becomes, in course of time, if he is an able man, an unrivaled storehouse of political experience. Ministers come and go; they are swayed, it is to be feared, by the interests of their party as well as by those of the state; they may have had to make, in order to obtain support, bargains which tie their hands; they have ambitions for the future, which they are loath to jeopardize. Not so the king. He is permanent; he is above all parties; he does not bargain for places and honors; he has nothing in the way of ambition to satisfy, except the noble ambition of securing his country's welfare. So he can say to his ministers, with all the weight of his experience and position: 'Yes, I will, if you insist, do as you wish; but, I warn you, you are doing a rash thing. Do you remember so and so?' Only, the king must not give his warning in public; he must not *seem* to overrule his ministers. But a minister will, unless he is an exceptionally rash person, think many times before disregarding a warning from the king." [1]

[1] *Government of the British Empire*, 37–40.

II. THE MINISTERS AND THE ADMINISTRATIVE MACHINERY

Ministry: Composition and Organization. — It has been made clear that the affairs of state are no longer managed by the king in person. Their management falls rather to the ministry, which therefore becomes the actual working executive or, rather, the directing and controlling part of the executive, since the executive branch, properly considered, includes not only the sovereign and the ministers but the entire body of administrative officials, reaching downwards from the heads of departments and the under-secretaries at London, through the several grades of subordinates, to the humblest revenue and postal employees. The ministers are, in general, the highest of these executive officials: they include the heads of all main departments, some or all of the members of various boards, a considerable group of under-secretaries (assistant secretaries, we would call them in the United States), certain party "whips," a few officers of the royal household, and some dignitaries who really have little or no administrative work to perform. Nominally they are selected and appointed by the king; but actually they owe their positions to the chief, or "prime," minister, whose highly important functions will be described presently. The thing that chiefly distinguishes a minister from any other member of the executive service is his direct responsibility to Parliament; and the ministry may be defined as the group of higher executive officials who are obligated by rigorous custom to resign office at once if Parliament (strictly speaking, the House of Commons) expresses disapproval of their policy. The ministers may therefore be said to have a *political* character not possessed by the mass of the executive officers, who belong rather to the permanent civil service and are not affected in their tenure by the ups and downs of party politics. The number of ministers in the years immediately preceding the Great War fluctuated around sixty. Approximately one-third of them formed the inner circle known as the cabinet, whose importance is such that it will be dealt with at some length in the concluding portions of this chapter.

As is, of course, true in all governments, the work of administration is carried on mainly by and through certain great executive departments. In our own country, the ten executive departments of the federal government (State, Treasury, War, etc.) stand on a common footing and bear much resemblance one to another. All have been created by act of Congress; all are presided over by officials known as secretaries; and all stand in substantially the same relation to the President and to Congress. The executive departments in most continental governments likewise present a generally logical and symmetrical appearance. The English departments, however, are very heterogeneous. In practically all cases, it is true, they are actually presided over by a single responsible minister, assisted by one or more under-secretaries and by a greater or lesser body of non-political officials who carry on the routine work and whose tenure is not affected by the political fortunes of their chiefs. But some of the departments represent survivals of great offices of state of remoter centuries, some are offshoots of the old " secretariat of state," some are boards or commissions established within recent decades. Some were created by Parliament and some were not. Some are directed by persons who do not nominally stand at the head at all.

Treasury, Admiralty, and Lord High Chancellorship. — Of great offices of earlier times from which are descended important ministries there are two, *i.e.*, the Lord High Treasurer and the Lord High Admiral. From the sixteenth century to the death of Queen Anne the principal official of the Treasury was the Lord High Treasurer. Since 1714, however, the office has been in commission; that is to say, the duties connected with it have been turned over to a board composed of certain Lords of the Treasury, and no individual to-day bears the Lord High Treasurer's title. When a new ministry is made up the group of Treasury Lords, five in number, is reconstituted, and as a rule the post of First Lord is taken by the Prime Minister. In point of fact, however, the board is never called together; some of its members have no actual connection whatsoever with the Treasury; and the functions of this most important of all departments are in practice exercised by the Chancellor of the Exchequer, assisted by certain Junior Lords and under-secretaries. The Exchequer, *i.e.*, the department concerned principally with the collection of the taxes, is in fact, although not in name, a branch of the Treasury. Within the Treasury, and immediately under the direction of the Chancellor, is drawn up the annual budget, embodying a statement of the proposed expenditures of the year and a program of taxation calculated to produce the requisite revenue. The Treasury exercises general control over all other departments of the public service, *e.g.*, the Post-Office and the Board of Customs, in which public money is collected or expended.

A second of the ancient offices of state which survives only in commission is that of the Lord High Admiral. The functions of this important post devolve to-day upon an Admiralty Board, consisting strictly of a First Lord, four Naval Lords (naval experts, usually of high rank), and a Civil Lord, with whom, however, sit a number of parliamentary and permanent secretaries. The First Lord is invariably a member of the cabinet, and while legally the status of the six Lords is identical, in practice the position of the First Lord approximates that of the minister of marine in continental countries. Unlike the Treasury Lords, the Lords of the Admiralty actually meet and transact business.

A third survival from early times — and in this case the office still exists very much as it was two or three hundred years ago — is the Lord High Chancellorship. There is in Great Britain no single official who fills, even approximately, the position occupied by the French or Italian Minister of Justice or the American Attorney-General; but the most important of several officers who supply the lack is the Lord Chancellor. "The greatest dignitary," says Lowell, "in the British government, the one endowed by law with the most exalted and most diverse functions, the only great officer of state who has retained his ancient rights, the man who defies the doctrine of the separation of powers more than any other personage on earth, is the Lord Chancellor."[1] The Lord Chancellor is invariably a member of the cabinet. He is the chief judge in the High Court of Justice and in the Court of Appeal. He appoints and removes the justices of the peace and the judges of the county courts and wields large influence in appointments to higher judicial posts. He affixes the

[1] *Government of England*, I, 131.

Great Seal where it is required to give validity to the acts of the crown, and he performs many other more or less formal services. Finally, it is he who presides in the House of Lords.

The Five Secretaries of State. — Five of the great departments to-day are the product of a curious evolution of the ancient secretariat of state. Originally there was but a single official who bore the designation of secretary of state. In the earlier eighteenth century a second official was added, although no new office was created. At the close of the century a third was added, after the Crimean war a fourth, and after the Indian mutiny of 1857 a fifth. There are now, accordingly, five " principal secretaries of state," all in theory occupying the same office, and each, save for a few statutory restrictions, competent legally to exercise the functions of any or all of the others. In practice each of the five holds strictly to his own domain. The group comprises: (1) the Secretary of State for the Home Department, assisted by a parliamentary under-secretary and a large staff of permanent officials, and possessing highly miscellaneous functions — those, in general, belonging to the ancient secretariat which have not been assigned to other departments; (2) the Secretary of State for Foreign Affairs, at the head of a department which not only conducts foreign relations but administers the affairs of such protectorates as are not closely connected with any of the colonies; (3) the Secretary of State for the Colonies; (4) the Secretary of State for War; and (5) the Secretary of State for India, assisted by a special India Council of ten to fourteen members.

The Administrative Boards. — A third general group of departments includes those which have arisen through the establishment in comparatively recent years of a variety of administrative boards or commissions. Two — the Board of Trade and the Board of Education — originated as committees of the Privy Council. Three others — the Board of Agriculture, the Board of Works, and the Local Government Board — represent the development of administrative commissions not conceived of originally as vested with political character. All are in effect independent and coördinate government departments. At the head of each is a president (save that the chief of the Board of Works is known as First Commissioner), and the membership embraces the five secretaries of state and a variable number of other important dignitaries. This membership, however, is only nominal. No one of the Boards actually meets, and the work is performed entirely by the president and his staff, with, in some instances, the assistance of a parliamentary under-secretary. "In practice, therefore, these boards are legal phantoms that provide imaginary colleagues for a single responsible minister." As a rule, the presidents are admitted to the cabinet circle.

The Permanent Civil Service. — One of the many notable features of the English government is the unusual combination of amateur and expert in the work of administration. The ministers are, in general, amateurs. They are drawn from widely differing walks of life; they commonly bring to their posts little experience in administration; the more important ones must give a large part of their time to activities outside their departments; they are frequently shifted from one position to another. All this would mean inefficiency and waste save for the fact that the departments and boards are manned with permanent, non-political officials, who, carefully selected in the first place, have, through long service and close application to duty, become expert in the business which the department or office is expected to carry on. More than that, the great administrative services — the post-office, the customs, the inland revenue, etc. — are completely organized under the plan which we should call in this country the " merit system." It has not always been so; until almost a generation ago England had a civil service question which was almost as serious and as baffling as that with which we have struggled in the United States. Removals were not so frequently made for partisan reasons, but appointments dictated by partisanship and favoritism were very common. Reforms began to be introduced about 1832, — curiously enough, about the time when the United States, under Andrew Jackson's leadership, was rapidly surrendering to the spoils conception of public office; and a great order in council of 1870 practically brought the task to completion. In addition to the ministers, the permanent under-secretaries and assistant under-secretaries and the chiefs of bureaus in the departments still stand outside the protected service. The chief clerks in the departments are recruited mainly by promotion. But practically all officials and employees below these are selected on the basis of competitive examinations, which are thrown open to aspirants almost as generously as are corresponding tests in our own country. The English system provides for even greater security of tenure than does our classified service, and it is applied to positions much higher up the scale than is the competitive system in this country. From this, in part at all events, it arises that the English examinations are shaped mainly with a view to determining the candidate's capacity and general attainments, whereas ours are intended chiefly as tests of the applicant's technical proficiency and present fitness for the kind of work which he seeks. Each system has certain obvious advantages. It need hardly be added that in return for security of tenure and opportunity for promotion in the service, the English appointee must agree, as must the American, to take no part whatsoever in party politics.

III. THE CABINET

Composition. — The fact has been mentioned that a variable number of the most important ministers form an inner group known as the cabinet — a group whose members individually (with two or three exceptions) administer the affairs of the main departments, and collectively shape the policy and direct the conduct of the government as a whole. This is the most unique and characteristic feature of the English system. Nevertheless, the cabinet is still wholly unknown to the law; legally, the cabinet officer derives his administrative function from his appointment to a ministerial post and his advisory function from his membership in the Privy Council.[1] The composition of the cabinet is determined partly by custom, partly by mo-

[1] The Privy Council, once the king's chief agency of government, has completely receded into the background. It is composed of some two hundred men of eminence, including all members of present and past cabinets, holders of certain important non-political offices, and persons prominent in law, literature, science, war, or politics. The body meets nowadays only for formal or ceremonial purposes, and is of slight importance, although certain of its committees, especially the Judicial Committee, perform active service. The fact cannot be escaped, however, that cabinet members have, as such, no legal status except as members of the Council.

mentary considerations of expediency. Certain of the ministers are nowadays sure to be included: the First Lord of the Treasury, the Lord Chancellor, the Chancellor of the Exchequer, the five Secretaries of State, and the First Lord of the Admiralty. Two dignitaries who have no administrative functions, *i.e.*, the Lord President of the Privy Council and the Lord Privy Seal, are likewise always admitted. Beyond this, the make-up of the group is left to the discretion of the prime minister, whose decision as to whether to invite a minister to sit in the cabinet may be determined in deference to the wishes of the minister himself, or by the importance of the office in question at the moment, or by party interest. There has never been a fixed number of members, and the size of the group has steadily increased. Eighteenth-century cabinets contained, as a rule, not above seven to ten members. In the first half of the nineteenth century the number ran up to thirteen or fourteen; the second cabinet presided over by Lord Salisbury, at its fall in 1892, numbered seventeen; and most of the time from 1900 to the outbreak of the Great War there were twenty members. The causes of this increase include pressure from ambitious statesmen for admission to the influential circle, the growing necessity of giving representation to varied elements and interests within the dominant party, the multiplication of state activities which call for organization under new and important departments, and the disposition to give to every considerable branch of the administrative system at least one representative. The effect has been to produce a certain unwieldiness, to avoid which, it will be recalled, the cabinet was originally created; and for some years before the war there was a tendency toward the rise of a small inner circle which should bear a relation to the whole cabinet somewhat analogous to that which the early cabinet bore to the overgrown royal council.

Appointment of the Prime Minister. — When a new ministry — and with it, of course, a new cabinet — is to be made up, the first step is the naming of the prime minister. Technically, the choice rests with the king. But custom, springing from practical necessity, leaves, as a rule, no room whatever for discretion in the matter. Promptly, and as a matter of course, the king sends for the man who is best able to command the support of the majority in the House of Commons, and asks him to proceed to make up a ministry. If the retiring ministry has "fallen," *i.e.*, has been forced out of office by the loss of its parliamentary majority, the new premier is certain to be the recognized leader of the party which formerly has played the rôle of opposition. If there has not occurred a shift in party status, the premiership will be bestowed upon some one of the colleagues, at least upon one of the fellow-partisans, of the retiring premier, nominated, if need be, by the chiefs of the party. Thus, when in 1894 Gladstone retired from office by reason of physical infirmity, the Liberal leaders in the two houses caucused on the question of whether he should be succeeded by Sir William Vernon Harcourt or by Lord Rosebery. They recommended Lord Rosebery, who was forthwith appointed by the Queen. If, by any circumstance, the premiership should fall to the Opposition at a moment when the leadership of this element is in doubt, the crown would be guided, similarly, by the informally expressed will of the more influential party members. While, therefore, the appointment of the prime minister remains almost the sole important governmental act which is performed personally by the sovereign, even here the substance of power has been lost and only the form survives.

Selection of Other Ministers and Cabinet Members. — The remaining members of both ministry and cabinet are selected by the premier, in consultation, as a rule, with leading representatives of the party. Technically, what happens is that the first minister places in the hands of the sovereign a list of the men whom he recommends for appointment to the principal offices of state. The king accepts the list, and there appears forthwith in the London *Gazette* an announcement to the effect that the persons named have been chosen by the crown to preside over the several departments. Officially, there is no mention of the "cabinet." In the selection of his colleagues — whether they are to be simply ministers or cabinet members as well — the premier theoretically has a free hand. Practically he is bound to comply with numerous principles and to observe various precedents and practical conditions. Two principles, in particular, must be adhered to in determining the structure of every cabinet. All of the members must have seats in one or the other of the two houses of Parliament, and all must be identified with the party in power, or at least with an allied political group. There was a time, when the personal government of the king was still a reality, when the House of Commons refused to admit to its membership persons who held office under the crown. With the ripening of parliamentary government in the eighteenth century, however, the thing that once had been regarded as objectionable became highly expedient, if not a necessity. When once the ministers formed the real executive of the nation, it was but logical that they should be permitted to appear on the floor of the two houses to introduce and advocate measures and to explain the acts of the government. Ministers had always occupied seats in the upper chamber; and not only was all objection to their appearance in the lower chamber removed, but by custom it came to be an inflexible rule that cabinet officers, and indeed the ministers generally, should be drawn exclusively from the membership of the two houses. If it is desired to bestow a ministerial post upon a man who is not a member of either house, the difficulty may be got around either by making him a peer, which would entitle him to a seat in the House of Lords, or by procuring his election to a seat in the House of Commons. During the past thirty or forty years cabinet officers have, as a rule, been about evenly divided between the two houses.

Further Considerations Determining Appointment. — A second principle which controls in the making up of both ministry and cabinet is that of party harmony. William III undertook to govern with a cabinet in which there were both Whigs and Tories, but the result was confusion and the experiment was abandoned. Except during the ascendancy of Walpole, the cabinets of the eighteenth century generally embraced men of more or less diverse political affiliations. But gradually the conviction took root that in the interest of unity and efficiency the political solidarity of the cabinet group is indispensable. The last occasion upon which it was proposed to make up a cabinet from utterly diverse political elements was in 1812.[1] The scheme was rejected, and from that day to this cabinets have

[1] This statement must, of course, be qualified by mention of the coalition cabinet organized in 1915 for the carrying on of the war. See p. 218.

regularly been composed, not always exclusively of men identified with a single political party, but at least of men who were in substantial agreement upon the larger questions of policy, and who have expressed willingness to coöperate in the carrying out of a given program. The fundamental requisite is unity. It is the obligation of every cabinet member to agree, or to appear to agree, with his colleagues. If he is unable to do this, he must resign.

In the selection of his co-laborers the premier works under still other practical restrictions. One of them is the well-established rule that surviving members of the last cabinet of the party, in so far as they are in active public life and desirous of appointment, shall be given prior consideration. Members of the party, furthermore, who have come into special prominence and influence in Parliament must usually be included. In truth, as Bagehot points out, the premier's independent choice is apt to find scope not so much in the determination of the cabinet's personnel as in the distribution of offices among the members selected; and even here he will often be obliged to subordinate his wishes to the inclinations, susceptibilities, and capacities of his prospective colleagues. In the expressive simile of Lowell, the premier's task is " like that of constructing a figure out of blocks which are too numerous for the purpose, and which are not of shapes to fit perfectly together." [1]

Ministerial Responsibility. — In its actual operation the English cabinet system, down to the present war at all events, presented three salient features: (1) the responsibility of cabinet ministers to Parliament; (2) the non-publicity of cabinet proceedings; and (3) the close coördination of the cabinet group under the leadership of the premier. Every minister, whether or not in the cabinet, is responsible individually to Parliament, which in effect means to the House of Commons, for all of his public acts. If he is given a vote of censure he must retire. In the earlier eighteenth century the resignation of a cabinet officer did not affect the tenure of his colleagues; the first cabinet to retire as a unit was that of Lord North in 1782. Subsequently, however, the ministerial body so developed in compactness that in relation to the outside world, and even to Parliament, the

[1] *The Government of England*, I, 57.

individual officer came to be effectually subordinated to the group. Not since 1866 has a cabinet member retired singly in consequence of an adverse parliamentary vote. If an individual minister falls into serious disfavor one of two things almost certainly happens. Either the offending member is persuaded by his colleagues to modify his course or to resign before formal parliamentary censure shall have been passed, or the cabinet as a whole rallies to the support of the minister in question and stands or falls with him. This is but another way of saying that, in practice, the responsibility of the cabinet is collective rather than individual. This responsibility covers the entire range of acts of the executive department of the government, whether regarded as acts of the king or of the ministers themselves, and it constitutes the most distinctive feature of the English parliamentary system. Formerly the only means by which ministers could be held to account by Parliament was that of impeachment. With the development, however, of the principle of ministerial responsibility as a necessary adjunct to parliamentary government, the occasional and violent process of impeachment was superseded by continuous, inescapable, and pacific legislative supervision. The impeachment of cabinet ministers may be regarded, indeed, as obsolete.

How a Ministry May Be Overthrown. — A fundamental maxim of the constitution to-day is that a cabinet shall continue in office only so long as it enjoys the confidence and support of a majority in the House of Commons. There are at least four ways in which a parliamentary majority may manifest its dissatisfaction with a cabinet, and so compel its resignation. It may pass a simple vote of "want of confidence," assigning therefor no definite reason. It may pass a vote of censure, criticizing the cabinet for some specific act. It may defeat a measure which the cabinet advocates and declares to be of vital importance. Or it may pass a bill in opposition to the advice of the ministers. The cabinet is not obliged to give heed to an adverse vote in the Lords; but when any of the four votes mentioned is carried in the lower chamber the premier and his colleagues must do one of two things — resign or appeal to the country. If it is clear that the cabinet has lost the support, not only of Parliament, but also of the electorate, the only honorable course for the ministry is to resign. If, on the other hand, there is doubt as to whether the parliamentary majority really represents the country upon the matter at issue, the ministers are warranted in requesting the sovereign to dissolve Parliament and to order a general election. In such a situation the ministry continues tentatively in office. If the elections return a majority prepared to support the ministers, the cabinet is given a new lease of life. If, on the other hand, the new parliamentary majority is hostile, no course is open to the ministry save to retire.

Privacy of Proceedings. — Perpetually responsible to the House of Commons and obligated to resign collectively when no longer able to command a working majority in that body, the cabinet must at all times seek to present a solid and imposing front. Two devices to this end are privacy of proceedings and the leadership of the premier. It is a sufficiently familiar principle that a group of men brought together to agree upon and execute a common policy in behalf of a widespread and diverse constituency will be more likely to succeed if the differences that are sure to appear within their ranks are not published to the world. It is in deference to this fact that the German Bundesrath transacts its business to this day behind closed doors; and it was for an analogous reason that the public was excluded from the sittings of the convention by which the present constitution of the United States was framed. Notices of meetings of the English cabinet and the names of members present regularly appear in the press, but concerning the subjects discussed, the opinions expressed, and the conclusions arrived at, not a word is given out, officially or unofficially. In the earlier part of the nineteenth century brief minutes of the proceedings were preserved. But in later times no clerical employee was allowed to be present, and no formal record whatsoever was kept. For knowledge of past transactions members had to rely upon their own or their colleagues' memories, supplemented at times by privately kept notes. It was, indeed, — so the ex-premier, Mr. Asquith, stated in the House of Commons in 1916 — " the inflexible, unwritten rule of the cabinet that no member should take any note or record of the proceedings except the prime minister." It was made public, however, on this same occasion that a different plan was to be followed in the future, that minutes of the proceedings were to be kept, and that a record of every decision would be sent by the prime minister's secretary to every member of the cabinet, and, if necessary, to any minister or department affected. Cabinet meetings, which are held only as occasion requires (usually as often as once a week when Parliament is in session) are notably informal. There is not even a fixed place for them, the members being gathered sometimes at the Foreign Office, sometimes at the premier's house, or, as circumstance may arise, at almost any convenient spot.

Leadership of the Premier. — The unity of the cabinet is further safeguarded and emphasized by the leadership of the prime minister. Long after the rise of the cabinet to controlling influence in the state the members of the ministerial body continued supposedly upon a common footing in respect to both rank and authority. The habitual abstention of the early Hanoverians from attendance at cabinet meetings, however, left the group leaderless, and by natural development the members gradually came to recognize a virtual presidency on the part of one of their own number. In time what was a mere presidency was converted into a thoroughgoing leadership, in short, into the premier's office of to-day. It is commonly regarded that the first person who fulfilled the functions of prime minister in the modern sense was Sir Robert Walpole, First Lord of the Treasury from 1715 to 1717 and from 1721 to 1742. By the time of the establishment of the ministry of the younger Pitt, in 1783, the ascendancy of the premier among his colleagues was an accomplished fact and was recognized as entirely legitimate. The enormous power of the premier, arising upon the ruins of the royal prerogative, was brought virtually to completion when, during the later years of George III, the rule became fixed that in making up a ministry the king should merely ratify the choice of officials made by the premier.

Not until 1906 was the premier's office recognized by law, but through more than a century no other public position in the nation has been comparable with it in volume of actual ruling power. Within the ministry, more particularly the cabinet, the premier is the guiding force. He presides, as a rule, at cabinet meetings; he advises with colleagues upon all matters of consequence to the administration's welfare; and, although he will shrink from doing it, he may require of his colleagues that they acquiesce in his views, with the alternative of his resignation or theirs. He occupies one of the high offices of state, usually that of First Lord of the Treasury; and, although ordinarily his own portfolio will not require much of his time or energy, he must maintain as close a watch as may be over the affairs of every one of the departments in which his appointees have been placed. The prime minister is, furthermore, the link between the cabinet and, on the one hand, the crown, and, on the other, Parliament. On behalf of the cabinet he advises with the sovereign, communicating information concerning ministerial acts and synopses of the daily debates in Parliament. In the house of which he is a member he represents the cabinet as a whole, makes such statements as are necessary concerning general aspects of the government's policy, and speaks, as a rule, upon every general or important projected piece of legislation. A premier who belongs to the House of Commons is, of course, more advantageously situated than one who sits in the Lords.

The Cabinet's Central Position. — In the English governmental system the cabinet is in every sense the keystone of the arch. Its functions are both executive and legislative, and indeed, to employ the expressive figure of Bagehot, it is the hyphen that joins, the buckle that binds, the executive and the legislative departments together. As has been pointed out, the uses of the sovereign are by no means wholly ornamental. None the less, the actual executive of the nation is the cabinet. It is within the cabinet circle that administrative policies are decided upon, and it is by the cabinet ministers and their subordinates in the several departments that these policies, and the laws of the land generally, are carried into effect. On the other side, the cabinet members not only occupy seats in one or the other of the two houses of Parliament; collectively they direct the processes of legislation. They — primarily the prime minister — prepare the Speech from the Throne, in which at the opening of a parliamentary session the state of the country is reviewed and a program of legislation is outlined. They formulate, introduce, explain, and advocate needful legislative measures upon all manner of subjects; and although bills may be submitted in either house by private members, it is a recognized principle that all measures of large importance shall emanate directly or indirectly from the cabinet. Statistics demonstrate that measures of an important character introduced by private members have but an infinitesimal chance of being passed.

In effect, the cabinet forms a parliamentary committee chosen, as Bagehot bluntly puts it, to rule the nation. If a cabinet group does not represent the ideas and purposes of Parliament as a whole, it at least represents those of the majority of the dominant chamber; and that is sufficient to give it, during the space of its tenure of office, a thoroughgoing command of the situation. The basal fact of the political system is rule by party majority, and within the party majority the power that governs is the cabinet. " The machinery," says Lowell, " is one of wheels within wheels; the outside ring consisting of the party that has a majority in the House of Commons; the next ring being the ministry, which contains the men who are most active within that party; and the smallest of all being the cabinet, containing the real leaders or chiefs. By this means is secured that unity of party action which depends upon placing the directing power in the hands of a body small enough to agree, and influential enough to control." [1]

The War Cabinet, 1916–1918. — It goes without saying that the outbreak of the Great War in 1914 brought upon the cabinet, as upon all parts of the governmental system, an unexpected and terrific strain. By degrees the national administration was transformed almost beyond recognition. New duties fell to the old departments, entailing the creation of new divisions and sections and an enormous increase in the number of officials and the size of the staffs employed. New governmental agencies sprang up on all sides, including the war trade department, the ministry of munitions, and the board of control for the liquor traffic in 1915, the ministries of food control, shipping control, pensions, labor, and blockade in 1916, and the departments of national service and reconstruction in 1917. But the most remarkable changes that took place were those by which the cabinet

[1] *The Government of England*, I, 56.

and the cabinet system were made, temporarily at all events, something totally different from what they had been. The first great step was the formation, in 1915, of a "coalition" cabinet, which got away from the usual party basis and brought together representatives of all parties, who undertook to sink personal and party differences in a common leadership of the nation in its great crisis. The coalition served many useful purposes. But experience showed that a cabinet composed, as the present one was, of twenty-three members was far too cumbersome for the most successful management of a nation's affairs under war conditions, and the upshot was a drastic and spectacular reorganization in December, 1916, whereby the coalition cabinet was replaced by a non-partisan "war cabinet" of five members, headed by Mr. Lloyd George as prime minister. With a membership increased to six, and with a few other minor changes, this war cabinet has since continued at the head of the government. The object chiefly aimed at in the reorganization was, of course, promptness of decision and of action. Hence the cabinet group was made very small; most of the members were either left without ministerial office or assigned to posts that require no administrative activity; the members gave up active work on the floor of Parliament, in order to devote themselves with a free hand to the framing of policy related to the conduct of the war; and, partly because practically all of the ministers now stood outside the cabinet circle, partly because of the necessity of employing the best business methods regardless of precedent, the arrangements for cabinet records and communications already referred to were introduced. Furthermore, in 1917 the prime ministers of the self-governing British colonies, together with representatives of India and of other dependencies, were invited to attend a series of special meetings of the war cabinet; and thus arose the novel and interesting body known as the Imperial war cabinet, which held a second series of meetings in 1918.[1] All of these radical reconstructions were accomplished, in characteristic English fashion, by entirely informal and extra-legal processes. No act of Parliament was passed, and no proclamation or order in council was issued, establishing or even announcing the new machinery.

[1] See p. 322.

How permanent the arrangements will prove is, of course, uncertain. But they are too important to be left out of account by any one who would understand the English governmental system and the processes by which it grows; and one can hardly doubt that their lasting effects will be great.

SELECTED REFERENCES

A. L. Lowell, *The Government of England* (New York, 1909), I, Chaps. ii–viii, xvii–xviii, xxii–xxiii; ibid., *Essays on Government* (Boston, 1889), Chap. i; S. Low, *Governance of England* (new ed., New York, 1914), Chaps. ii–v, viii–ix; T. F. Moran, *Theory and Practice of the English Government* (rev. ed., New York, 1908), Chaps. iv–ix; E. Jenks, *Government of the British Empire* (New York, 1918), Chaps. v, viii–x; W. R. Anson, *Law and Custom of the Constitution* (4th ed., London, 1909–1911), II, Pt. I, Chaps. ii–iii; Bagehot, *The English Constitution* (rev. ed., London, 1911), Chaps. ii, vii–x; R. H. Gretton, *The King's Government* (London, 1913); W. F. Willoughby, and S. M. Lindsay, *Financial Administration of Great Britain* (New York, 1917); Robert Moses, *The Civil Service of Great Britain* (New York, 1913); M. Blauvelt, *Development of Cabinet Government in England* (New York, 1902).

CHAPTER XII

PARLIAMENT AND THE GROWTH OF DEMOCRACY

Importance. — The Parliament which sits at Westminster is not only the chief organ of English democracy but the oldest, the largest, and the most powerful of modern legislative assemblages. Speaking broadly, it originated in the thirteenth century, became definitely organized in two houses in the fourteenth century, wrested the control of the nation's affairs from the king in the seventeenth century, and underwent a thoroughgoing democratization in the nineteenth and twentieth centuries. The range of jurisdiction which, step by step, the two houses have acquired has been broadened until it includes practically the whole domain of government. And within this enormous expanse of political control the competence of the chambers knows, in neither theory nor fact, any restriction. "The British Parliament, . . . " writes Bryce, " can make and unmake any and every law, change the form of government or the succession to the crown, interfere with the course of justice, extinguish the most sacred private rights of the citizen. Between it and the people at large there is no legal distinction, because the whole plenitude of the people's rights and powers resides in it, just as if the whole nation were present within the chamber where it sits. In point of legal theory it is the nation, being the historical successor of the folk moot of our Teutonic forefathers. Both practically and legally, it is to-day the only and the sufficient depository of the authority of the nation; and it is therefore, within the sphere of law, irresponsible and omnipotent."[1] Whether the business in hand be constituent or legislative, whether ecclesiastical or temporal, the right of Parliament to discuss and to dispose is incontestable. In order to understand how England is governed it is, therefore, necessary to give much

[1] *The American Commonwealth* (3d ed.), I, 35–36.

attention to Parliament; and in order to appreciate the fullness of English political democracy one must know something of the long historic process by which this all-powerful Parliament — at all events the House of Commons — has been made completely representative of the people.

I. THE HOUSE OF COMMONS — ELECTORAL REFORMS

Composition. — "When," wrote Spencer Walpole a quarter of a century ago, "a minister consults Parliament he consults the House of Commons; when the Queen dissolves Parliament she dissolves the House of Commons. A new Parliament is simply a new House of Commons." The gathering of the "representatives of the commons" at Westminster is indeed, and has long been, without question the most important single agency of government in the kingdom. The chamber is at the same time the chief repository of power and the prime organ of the popular will. It is in consequence of its prolonged and arduous development that Great Britain has attained democracy in national government; and the influence of English democracy, as actualized in the House of Commons, upon the political ideas and the governmental forms of the outlying world, both English-speaking and non-English-speaking, is incalculable.

The House of Commons consists to-day of 707 members, of whom 492 sit for English constituencies, 36 for Welsh, 74 for Scottish, and 105 for Irish. Fifteen of the members are chosen, under somewhat special arrangements, to represent the principal universities. The remaining 692 are elected in county or borough constituencies — 372 in the former and 320 in the latter — under a newly enacted suffrage law which falls not far short of being the most democratic in the world. The regulations governing the qualifications for election are simple and liberal. There was once a residence qualification. But in the eighteenth century it was replaced by a property qualification, which, however, in 1858 was in its turn swept away. Oaths of allegiance and oaths imposing religious tests formerly operated to debar many from candidacy. But all that is now required of a member is a very simple oath or affirmation of allegiance, in a form compatible with any shade of religious belief or unbelief.

Any male British subject who is of age is qualified for election by any constituency before which he desires to be a candidate, unless he belongs to one of a few small groups — chiefly peers (except Irish); clergy of the Roman Catholic Church, the Church of England, and the Church of Scotland; certain officeholders; bankrupts; and persons convicted of treason, felony, or corrupt practices.

Problem of Electoral Reform in the Early Nineteenth Century. — We have seen that while the United States has achieved a large measure of political democracy, a hundred years ago the suffrage was much restricted, so that the government represented, in a direct way, only a portion of the people.[1] Still more is this true of Great Britain; and it becomes necessary at this point to take account briefly of the series of measures by which the suffrage was there extended and true popular representation in the control of public affairs established. The last great steps, it will be interesting to learn, have been taken since the present war began.

Despite her parliamentary institutions, her traditional principles of local self-government, and her historic guarantees of individual liberty, England at the opening of the nineteenth century was in no true sense a democratic country. Not only was society organized upon a basis that was essentially aristocratic, but government likewise was controlled by, and largely in the interest of, the few of higher station. One branch of Parliament was composed entirely of clerical and hereditary members; the other, of members elected under franchise arrangements which were illiberal, or appointed outright by closed corporations or by individual magnates. Not only the men who made the laws, but the officers who executed them, and the judges in whose tribunals they were interpreted and applied, were selected in accordance with procedure in which the mass of the people had no part. The agencies of local government, whether in county or in borough, were as a rule oligarchical, and privilege and class distinction pervaded the whole of the political system. The ordinary man was called upon to obey laws and to pay taxes voted without his assent, to submit to industrial, social, and ecclesiastical regulations whose making, repeal,

---
[1] See p. 19.

and amendment he had no effective means of influencing — in short, to support a government which was beyond his power to control.

The problem of parliamentary reform was threefold. The first question was that of the suffrage. Originally the representatives of the counties were chosen in the county court by all persons who were entitled to attend and to take part in the proceedings of that body. In 1429, during the reign of Henry VI, an act was passed ostensibly to prevent riotous and disorderly elections, wherein it was stipulated that county electors should thereafter comprise only such male residents of the county as possessed " free land or tenement " which would rent for as much as forty shillings a year above all charges.[1] Even in the fifteenth and sixteenth centuries the number of forty-shilling freeholders was small. With the concentration of land in fewer hands, resulting from the agrarian revolution of the eighteenth and early nineteenth centuries, it bore a steadily decreasing ratio to the aggregate county population, and by 1832 the county electors included, as a rule, only a handful of large landed proprietors. In the boroughs the franchise arrangements existing at the date mentioned were complicated and diverse beyond the possibility of general characterization. Many of the boroughs had been given parliamentary representation by the most arbitrary and haphazard methods, and at no time prior to 1830 was there legislation which so much as attempted to regulate the conditions of voting within them. There were " scot and lot " boroughs, " potwalloper " boroughs, burgage boroughs, corporation or " close " boroughs, and " freemen " boroughs, to mention only the more important of the types that can be distinguished. In some of these the franchise was, at least in theory, fairly democratic; but in most of them it was restricted by custom or local regulation to petty groups of property-holders or taxpayers, to members of the municipal corporations, or even to members of a favored gild. With few exceptions, the borough franchise was illogical, narrow, and non-expansive.

Another phase of the situation was the astounding prevalence of illegitimate political influence and of sheer corruption. Borough members were frequently not representatives of the people at all,

[1] Equivalent in present values to £30 or £40, *i.e.*, $150 or $200.

but nominees of peers, of influential commoners, or of the government. It has been estimated that of the 472 borough members, not more than 137 can be regarded as having been in any proper sense elected. The remainder sat for " rotten " boroughs, or for " pocket " boroughs whose populations were so meager or so docile that the borough might, as it were, be carried about in a magnate's pocket. In the whole of Cornwall there were only one thousand voters. Of the forty-two seats to which that section of the country was entitled, twenty were controlled by seven peers, twenty-one were similarly controlled by eleven commoners, and but one was filled by free election. Bribery and other forms of corruption were so common that only the most shameless instances attracted public attention. Not merely votes, but seats, were bought and sold openly.

The Problem of Redistribution of Seats. — The third question was that of a redistribution of seats. The Constitution of the United States requires a reapportionment of seats in the House of Representatives after each decennial census, and in France there is such a redistribution every five years. The object is, obviously, to preserve substantial equality among the electoral constituencies, so that a vote will count for as much in one place as in another. Curiously, there has never been in England, in either law or custom, a requirement of this kind. Reapportionments have been few and irregular, and most of the time the constituencies represented at Westminster have been very unequal in size. Save that, in 1707, forty-five members were added to represent Scotland and, in 1801, one hundred to sit for Ireland, the constituencies represented in the Commons continued almost unchanged from the reign of Charles II to the reform of 1832. Changes of population in this extended period were, however, enormous. In 1689 the population of England and Wales was not in excess of 5,500,000. The census of 1831 revealed in these countries a population of 14,000,000. In the seventeenth and earlier eighteenth centuries the great mass of the English people lived in the south and east. Liverpool was but an insignificant town, Manchester a village, and Birmingham a sand-hill. But the industrial revolution had the effect of bringing coal, iron, and water-power into enormous demand, and after 1775 the industrial center, and likewise the population center, of the country shifted rapidly toward the north. In the hitherto almost uninhabited valleys of Lancashire and Yorkshire sprang up a multitude of factory towns and cities. In Parliament these fast-growing populations were either glaringly underrepresented or not represented at all. In 1831 the ten southernmost counties of England contained a population of 3,260,000 and returned to Parliament 235 members.[1] At the same time the six northernmost counties contained a population of 3,594,000, but returned only 68 members. Cornwall, with 300,000 inhabitants, had 42 representatives; Lancashire, with 1,330,000, had 14. Among towns, Birmingham and Manchester, each with upwards of 100,000 people, and Leeds and Sheffield, each with 50,000, had no representation whatever. On the other hand, boroughs were entitled to representation which contained ridiculously small populations, or even no settled population at all.

The Reform Act of 1832. — A movement looking toward electoral reform set in during the second half of the eighteenth century. It was checked by the revolution in France and by the long contest with Napoleon, but after Waterloo (1815) agitation was actively renewed. The first notable triumph was the enactment of the Reform Bill of 1832. The changes wrought by this memorable piece of legislation were twofold, the first relating to the distribution of seats in Parliament, the second to the extension of the franchise. There was no general reapportionment of seats, no effort to bring the parliamentary constituencies into precise and uniform relation to the census returns. But the most glaringly inequitable of former conditions were remedied. Fifty-six boroughs, of populations under 2000, were deprived of representation; thirty-one, of populations between 2000 and 4000, were reduced from two members to one; and one was reduced from four members to two. The 143 seats thus made available were redistributed, and the aggregate number (658) continued as before. The redistribution had the effect of increasing greatly the political power of the northern and north-central portions of the country. The alterations made

---

[1] That is to say, the quota of members mentioned was returned by the counties as such, together with the boroughs contained geographically within them.

in the franchise were numerous and important. In the counties the forty-shilling freehold franchise, with some limitations, was retained; but the voting privilege was extended to all leaseholders and copyholders of land renting for as much as £10 a year, and to tenants-at-will holding an estate worth £50 a year. In the boroughs the right to vote was conferred upon all "occupiers" of houses worth £10 a year. The total number of persons enfranchised was approximately 455,000. By basing the franchise exclusively upon the ownership or occupancy of property of considerable value, the reform fell short of admitting to political power the great mass of factory employees and of agricultural laborers, and for this reason it was roundly opposed by the more liberal elements. If, however, the voting privilege had not been extended to the masses, it had been brought appreciably nearer them; and — what was almost equally important — it had been made substantially uniform, for the first time, throughout the realm.

The Representation of the People Acts of 1867 and 1884. — The act of 1832 contained none of the elements of finality. Its authors were, in general, content; but with the lapse of time it became manifest that the nation was not. Political power was still confined to the magnates of the kingdom, the townsfolk who were able to pay a £10 annual rental, and the well-to-do copyholders and leaseholders of rural districts. Whigs and Tories of influence alike insisted that further innovation could not be contemplated, but the radicals and the laboring masses insisted no less resolutely that the reformation which had been begun should be carried to its logical conclusion. The story of the great movement that led up to the next important reform act is too long to be told here. Suffice it to say that in 1867 the third ministry of Lord Derby, whose guiding spirit was Disraeli, carried a bill providing for an electoral reform of a more sweeping nature than any persons save the most uncompromising of the radicals had expected, or perhaps desired. This Representation of the People Act modified, indeed, but slightly the distribution of parliamentary seats. But it broadened the parliamentary suffrage in a very important way. In England and Wales the county franchise was given to men whose freehold was of the value of forty shillings a year, to copyholders and leaseholders of the annual value of £5, and to householders whose rent amounted to not less than £12 a year. The twelve-pound occupation franchise was new, and the qualification for copyholders and leaseholders was reduced from £10 to £5; otherwise the county franchise was unchanged. The borough franchise was modified profoundly. Heretofore persons were qualified to vote as householders only in the event that their house was worth as much as £10 a year. Now the right was conferred upon every man who occupied, as owner or as tenant, for twelve months, a dwelling-house, or any portion thereof utilized as a separate dwelling, without regard to its value. Another newly established franchise admitted to the voting privilege all lodgers occupying for as much as a year rooms of the clear value, unfurnished, of £10 a year. The effect of these provisions was to enfranchise the urban working population, even as the act of 1832 had enfranchised principally the urban middle class. As originally planned, Disraeli's measure would have enlarged the electorate by not more than 100,000; as amended and carried, it practically doubled the voting population, raising it from 1,370,793 immediately prior to 1867 to 2,526,423 in 1871.[1] By the act of 1832 the middle classes had been enfranchised; by that of 1867 political power was thrown in no small degree into the hands of the masses. Only two large groups of people now remained outside the pale of political influence, *i.e.*, the agricultural laborers and the miners.

That the qualifications for voting in one class of constituencies should be conspicuously more liberal than in another class was an anomaly, and in a period when anomalies were fast being eliminated from the English electoral system remedy could not be long delayed. On February 5, 1884, the second Gladstone ministry redeemed a campaign pledge by introducing a bill extending to the counties the same electoral regulations that had been established in 1867 in the towns. The measure passed the Commons, but was rejected by the Lords because it was not accompanied by a bill for the redistribution of seats. By an

[1] It is to be observed that these figures are for the United Kingdom as a whole embracing the results not merely of the act of 1867 applying to England and Wales, but of the two acts of 1868 introducing similar, though not identical, changes in Scotland and Ireland.

agreement between the two houses a threatened deadlock was averted, and the upshot was that before the end of the year the Lords accepted the Government's bill, on the understanding that its enactment was to be followed immediately by the introduction of a redistribution measure. The Representation of the People Act of 1884 is in form disjointed and difficult to understand, but its effect is easy to state. In the first place, it established a uniform household franchise and a uniform lodger franchise in all counties and boroughs of the United Kingdom. The occupation of any land or tenement of a clear annual value of £10 was made a qualification in boroughs and counties alike; and persons occupying a house by virtue of office or employment were to be deemed "occupiers" for the purpose of the act. The measure doubled the county electorate, and increased the total electorate by some 2,000,000, or approximately forty per cent. Its most important effect was to enfranchise the workingman in the country, as the act of 1867 had enfranchised the workingman in the town.

In 1885, the two great parties coöperating, the Redistribution of Seats Act which had been promised was passed. For the first time in English history attempt was made to apportion representation in the House of Commons in something like strict accordance with population densities. The total number of members was increased from 658 to 670, and of the number 103 were allotted to Ireland, 72 to Scotland, and 495 to England and Wales. The method by which former redistributions had been accomplished, *i.e.*, transferring seats more or less arbitrarily from flagrantly overrepresented boroughs to more populous boroughs and counties, was replaced by a method based upon the principle of equal electoral constituencies, each returning one member. This principle was not carried out with mathematical exactness; indeed, considerable inequalities survived the rearrangement. But the situation was made vastly better than before.

Electoral Questions, 1885–1918: Manhood Suffrage, Plural Voting, and Redistribution. — The measures just described stood on the statute book practically without change until 1918. During this long period England properly regarded her government as democratic; and it was so considered by the rest of the world. Nevertheless, even the House of Commons, which was the most democratic part of the national government, was not so broadly representative of the nation as it might have been. Wherein it was lacking will be explained briefly in this and the following section; then will be told how, in the midst of the war, a great parliamentary statute was passed to remedy the situation.

In the first place, the suffrage was defined entirely in terms of relation to property. One voted, not as a matter of inherent (or conferred) individual right, but as an owner, occupier, or user of houses, lands, or other property. The voter did not have to *own* property; and occupational requirements were, as we have seen, comparatively easy to meet. Nevertheless the laws governing the exercise of both the parliamentary and local suffrages were so complicated that only lawyers professed to understand them; and their net effect was to exclude some two million adult males from taking part in the election of parliamentary members. "The present condition of the franchise," wrote Lowell in 1909, "is, indeed, historical rather than rational. It is complicated, uncertain, expensive in the machinery required, and excludes a certain number of people whom there is no reason for excluding; while it admits many people who ought not to be admitted if any one is to be debarred."[1] The first demand of electoral reformers was, accordingly, for a law that would simplify the existing system and at the same time make provision substantially for manhood suffrage.

The second demand was for the abolition of plural voting. The problem of the plural vote was an old one. Under existing laws an elector might not vote more than once in a single constituency, nor in more than one division of the same borough; but aside from this, and except in so far as was not prohibited by residence requirements, he was entitled to vote in every constituency in which he possessed a qualification. In the United States, and in the majority of European countries, a man has only one vote; and any arrangement other than this seems to most people to violate the principle of civic equality which lies at the root of popular government. In England efforts were numerous to bring about the adoption of the rule of "one man, one vote," but for a long time they were not successful. The

[1] *The Government of England*, I, 213.

number of plural voters — some 525,000 — was relatively small. But when it is observed that a single voter might cast during a parliamentary election as many as fifteen or twenty votes, it will not be wondered at that the number sufficed to turn the scale in many closely contested constituencies. An overwhelming proportion of the plural voters belonged to the Unionist party, whence it arose that the Liberals were solidly opposed to the privilege. In 1906, and on two or three occasions thereafter, a Liberal government carried through the House of Commons a bill abolishing plural voting. But the Unionist majority in the House of Lords always blocked the reform.

A third question which aroused much discussion was a fresh apportionment of seats in the House of Commons. In the quarter-century following the act of 1885 the electoral districts again became very unequal. In 1912 the most populous constituency (the Romford division of the county of Essex) had 55,950 voters, while the least populous (the Irish borough of Kilkenny) had but 1690. The populations of the hundreds of county and borough constituencies throughout the United Kingdom fell at all points between these extremes. It was the Liberals who urged abolition of plural voting — because plural voting benefited the Unionists. On the other hand, it was in the main the Unionists who urged a redistribution of seats — because the existing distribution worked advantageously for the Liberals.[1] A Unionist redistribution measure in 1905 did not reach debate; and the several Liberal electoral proposals of the succeeding decade made no provision, beyond somewhat indefinite promises, for the reform.

Electoral Questions, 1885–1918: Woman's Suffrage. — An electoral question which thrust itself into the forefront of public discussion soon after the opening of the present century is woman's suffrage. The history of this issue runs back hardly more than fifty years. The first notable attempt to induce Parliament to bestow the suffrage on properly qualified women was that of John Stuart Mill, who in 1867 vainly urged the adoption of a woman's suffrage amendment to Disraeli's Representa-

[1] This was chiefly on account of the heavy overrepresentation of Ireland, arising from the stationariness of the Irish quota during the nineteenth century while the Irish population was fast declining.

tion of the People Act. A national society to promote the cause was organized in the same year; and in 1869 an act of Parliament conferred the suffrage in municipal elections upon all women taxpayers of England, Wales, and Scotland. From time to time for twenty years thereafter bills on the subject appeared in the House of Commons, but with little chance of success. A new chapter in the history of the movement was opened in 1903 by the organization of the Woman's Social and Political Union, under whose auspices a highly spectacular campaign was carried on in the next decade. The first great object was to persuade or compel a ruling ministry, *i.e.*, " the Government," to introduce a suffrage measure, since bills presented by private members are unlikely to be passed if they deal with controversial matters. This object was not attained until 1918. But meanwhile the cause was advertised, organized, and broadened until it gave promise of bringing the country to a genuine crisis. How the program grew is illustrated by the fact that whereas originally the demand was merely for the removal of the disqualification of women *as women* — in other words, for the enfranchisement of women upon the same terms, in respect to age, residence, and independent ownership or occupancy of property, as men — from about 1909 it was urged that substantially all adult women in the United Kingdom should be made voters. The first plan would have meant the enfranchisement of about two million women; the second, of ten millions. A " conciliation " scheme, incorporated in a great electoral bill in 1910, proposed as a first step to bestow the franchise in parliamentary elections upon such women as already were permitted to vote in municipal and other local elections — approximately one and one-fourth millions. Proposals of every sort were blocked, however, during the pre-war years of the ministry of Mr. Asquith by the inflexible opposition of the premier and several of his colleagues, and by the consequent impossibility of getting before Parliament a government measure on the subject.

The Representation of the People Act, 1918. — On the evening of February 6, 1918, an act which history may pronounce more momentous than any other passed by the British Parliament during the war was given the royal assent. It was not by choice that the ministry and the two houses turned their attention to electoral questions while the nation was yet fighting for its life within hearing of the Channel ports. Rather, they were compelled to do so by the sheer breakdown of the electoral system, caused by wholesale enlistments in the army and by the further dislocation of population arising from the development of war industries. The situation was bad enough in county, municipal, and parish elections. But a parliamentary election under the new conditions would have been a farce. By general consent the life of the parliament chosen in December, 1910, was prolonged, in order to defer, and perhaps to avoid altogether, a wartime election. A general election, however, there must eventually be; and whether before or after the cessation of hostilities, it would demand, in all justice, a radically altered system of registration and voting, if not new franchises and other important changes. Parliament acted wisely, therefore, in addressing itself to this great task in the summer of 1916, and in intrusting the preliminary consideration of a new electoral law to an extraordinary commission, chosen by the Speaker of the House of Commons and presided over by him, and made up with much care to represent in proper proportion not only the parties and groups in Parliament, but the various bodies of public opinion on electoral questions throughout the United Kingdom.

This "Speaker's Conference," consisting of thirty-six members from both houses, began its work October 10, 1916. Its report was presented to the House of Commons in the following March, and on May 5 a bill based upon its recommendations was introduced as a government measure. Debate proceeded intermittently until December 7, when the bill, considerably enlarged, was passed and sent up to the House of Lords. Here, seventeen days were devoted to the project, and on January 30 the measure was returned to the House of Commons with eighty-seven pages of amendments. Pressure of time made for compromise, and on February 6 the houses came into agreement upon a completed bill, which forthwith received the king's assent.

This new Representation of the People Act was primarily a piece of suffrage legislation. Yet it was a great deal more than that. Upon the basis of a doubled electorate it erected an electoral system which was almost entirely new; and the measure itself is to be thought of as a general electoral law, more comprehensive and far-reaching than any kindred act in English history. Effort to adapt electoral machinery to the conditions entailed by the war early convinced the Speaker's Conference that the old practice of defining franchises in terms of relationship to property would have to be discontinued, and that in lieu thereof it would be necessary to adopt the principle that the suffrage is a personal right inherent in the individual. In accordance with this revolutionary decision, the Act swept away the entire mass of existing intricate parliamentary franchises and extended the suffrage to all male subjects of the British crown twenty-one years of age or over, and resident for six months in premises in a constituency, without regard to value or kind.

Many persons supposed that plural voting would now disappear. Events proved otherwise. In the first place, the university franchise, which has long been under fire, and which a government electoral bill of 1912 proposed to abolish, was retained. Indeed it was considerably broadened, first by extending the right of separate representation to several of the younger provincial universities, and, second, by conferring the university franchise upon all persons who have obtained a degree of any kind, rather than, as heretofore at Oxford and Cambridge, merely upon recipients of the degree of M.A. In the second place, a man may acquire a vote in a constituency other than that in which he votes as a resident, by the occupation and use for business purposes of premises worth £10 or more a year. The Conservative elements insisted upon these arrangements as means of preventing the submerging of the more wealthy and more educated part of the electorate. But the Liberals triumphed in so far as to procure a provision that no person may vote at a general election in more than two constituencies.

The main immediate purpose of the Act was to bring back into the electorate the millions of men whose war service temporarily disfranchised them under the old system. Accordingly, full provision was made for the registration of soldiers and sailors as electors in their home constituencies. If within reasonable distance, the elector of this class may personally vote at a general election, receiving and returning his ballot-paper by post. If the distance be such as to involve too great delay, the elector may designate some person at home to act as his proxy and vote in his behalf. Furthermore, the voting age for all men who have rendered military or naval service in the present war was fixed at nineteen, rather than twenty-one. Provision was made, too, for absent voting irrespective of war service, thus liberating from practical disfranchisement many thousands of merchant seamen, commercial travelers, fishermen, and other men whose occupations keep them away from their homes.

The outbreak of the war in 1914 seemed to end all hope of early legislation on woman suffrage. The effect was, however, precisely the opposite. Within two years and a half the conflict brought the suffragists an advantage which no amount of agitation had ever won for them, *i.e.*, the formal backing of the Government, and a few months more carried their cause to a victorious conclusion which might not have been reached in a full decade of peace. There were two main reasons for this turn of events. One was the necessity which the war imposed of undertaking a wholesale revision of the electoral system, leading to the decision to base the franchise upon personal right rather than property relationship, and inevitably suggesting an equality in rights, as individuals, of women with men. But the fundamental reason brought forward by the war for enfranchising women was the great variety and value of women's services to the nation during the conflict. This was the thing that won over thousands of former opponents, from Mr. Asquith down. It soon became manifest that a majority of the Conference, and of both houses of Parliament, stood ready to admit women to the franchise; only the method, the time, and the extent were seriously in dispute. As finally passed, the Act conferred the franchise upon every woman over thirty years of age who occupies a home, without regard to value, or any landed property of the annual value of £5, of which either she or her husband is the tenant. A woman may vote also for a university member if she is a graduate of a university that confers degrees on women, or if she has qualified for a degree in a university that does not admit women to degrees.

The effect of the foregoing legislation is to double the British electorate at a stroke. The reform act of 1832 created half a million new electors, raising the proportion of electors to the total population to one in twenty-four; the act of 1867 created a million electors, raising the proportion to one in twelve; the act of 1884 added two million electors, making the proportion one in seven; the act of 1918 adds eight millions, bringing the proportion up to the remarkable figure of one in three. Of the eight million new voters, one-fourth are men and three-fourths women.

Parliamentary Elections. — Under our American system of government, elections fall at fixed intervals, regardless of the condition of public affairs or the state of public feeling. In England, local elections take place at stated periods, but national elections do not. The only positive requirement concerning the latter is that an election must be ordered when a parliament has attained the maximum lifetime allowed by law. Prior to 1694 there was no stipulation upon this subject, and the king could keep a parliament in existence as long as he liked. Charles II retained for seventeen years the parliament called at his accession. From 1694 to 1716, however, the maximum term of a parliament was three years; from 1716 to 1911 it was seven years; to-day it is five years. In point of fact, parliaments never last through the maximum period, and an average interval of three or four years between elections has been the rule.[1] In most instances an election is precipitated more or less unexpectedly on an appeal to the country by a defeated ministry, and it often happens that an election turns almost entirely upon a single issue and practically assumes the character of a national referendum upon that subject. This was preëminently true of the last general election, that of December, 1910, at which the country was asked to sustain the Asquith government in its purpose to curb the independent authority of the House of Lords. In any event, the campaign by which the election is preceded is brief. Appeals to the voters are made principally through public speaking, the controversial and illustrated press, the circulation of pamphlets and handbills, parades and mass-meetings, and the generous use of placards, cartoons, and other devices designed to attract and focus attention. Plans are laid, arguments are formulated, and leadership in public appeal is assumed

[1] An exception, of course, is the parliament elected in December, 1910, which on account of war conditions has perpetuated its own life down to the date of writing (1918).

by the members of the Government, led by the premier, and, on the other side, by the men who are the recognized leaders of the parliamentary Opposition.

When a parliament is dissolved, a royal proclamation is forthwith issued ordering the election of a new House of Commons, and with this as a warrant, the chancellors of Great Britain and Ireland forthwith issue writs of election, addressed to the "returning officers" of the counties and boroughs, *i.e.*, the sheriffs and the mayors. The eighth day after the proclamation goes forth is, under the new law, election day for all constituencies. Save in one contingency, the only thing that really takes place on that day is the nomination of candidates. So far as the law is concerned, in order to be nominated it is necessary merely to be "proposed" by a registered voter of the constituency and "assented to" by nine other voters. Actually, of course, candidates are usually selected, or at all events approved in advance, by the local, or even the national, committee of the party. The contingency referred to arises when the number of nominees is no larger than that of places to be filled. In this case, the returning officer simply declares the candidate, or candidates, duly elected. The number of such uncontested elections, especially in Ireland, is invariably large, the proportion sometimes reaching one-fourth, or even one-third. If, however, there is a contest, the election is adjourned, in order that a "poll," or count of votes, may be held to decide between the rival candidates. Formerly, the polling — while completed within any one constituency in a single day — dragged out over a period of two weeks or more, making it easy for the plural voter to go about from district to district casting ballot after ballot. Under the law of 1918, however, the polling must take place in all constituencies on the same day, namely, the ninth after the day of nomination. The Australian ballot system is used, and every possible precaution is taken to preserve the purity of elections.

The Regulation of Electoral Expenditures. — From having been one of the most corrupt, Great Britain has become one of the most exemplary of nations in all that pertains to the proprieties of electoral procedure. The Ballot Act of 1872 contained provisions intended to strengthen earlier corrupt practices acts, but the real turning point was the adoption of the comprehensive Corrupt and Illegal Practices Act of 1883. By this measure bribery (in seven enumerated forms) and treating were made punishable by imprisonment or fine and, under varying conditions, political disqualification. The number and functions of the persons who may be employed by the candidate to assist in a campaign were prescribed, every candidate being required to have a single authorized agent charged with the disbursement of all moneys (save certain specified "personal" expenditures) in the candidate's behalf, and with the duty of submitting to the returning officer within thirty-five days after the election a sworn statement covering all receipts and expenditures. And, finally, the act fixed, upon a sliding scale in proportion to the size of the constituencies, the maximum amounts which candidates might legitimately expend. In recent years it has been felt that these amounts were too large, and the Representation of the People Act of 1918 set up a new and reduced scale. In county constituencies the maximum expenditure (aside from a small agent's fee) is 7d. (14 cents) per elector, and in borough constituencies 5d. (10 cents). A further novel and interesting requirement of this new law, intended to prevent an undue multiplicity of candidates, is that every person offering himself for election to Parliament shall deposit £150, to be returned to him if he gets more than one-eighth of the votes recorded, but otherwise to be forfeited. The whole effect of this regulation of expenditures in the past thirty-five years has been to purify politics and to democratize Parliament by making it possible for men of moderate means to stand for election who otherwise would be at grave disadvantage as against wealthier and more lavish competitors.

II. THE HOUSE OF LORDS

Composition. — No sketch of the development of popular government through Parliament in recent decades would give a correct impression which did not take into account the alteration of the powers of the House of Lords made by the Parliament Act of 1911, and the movement for second chamber reform, in which that momentous piece of legislation is likely to stand as only one of several landmarks. With the possible exception of the Hungarian Chamber of Magnates, the British House of Lords is the oldest upper chamber in Europe. It is, furthermore, among second chambers the largest and the most purely hereditary. It contains to-day six groups of members, sitting by various rights and having somewhat different status. The first comprises princes of the royal blood who are of age. The number of these is variable, but never large. The second, and much the most important, comprises the peers (dukes, marquises, earls, viscounts, and barons) with hereditary seats, falling into three divisions: (1) peers of England, created before the union with Scotland in 1707, (2) peers of Great Britain, created between that date and the union with Ireland in 1801, and (3) peers of the United Kingdom created since 1801. Legally, peers are created by the sovereign. In practice, their creation is controlled by the ministry, and the act may be performed for the purpose of honoring men of distinction in law, letters, science, art, statecraft, or business, or with the more practical object of altering the political complexion of the upper chamber. There is no limit to the number of peerages that may be bestowed. A third group of members consists of the representative peers of Scotland, sixteen in number, elected (under the terms of the Act of Union of 1707) for the lifetime of a single parliament by the whole body of Scottish peers. A fourth group consists of twenty-eight representative peers of Ireland, elected (under terms of the Act of Union of 1801) for life, by the whole body of Irish peers. A fifth group is made up of the "lords spiritual," restricted by statute to twenty-six, and composed of the archbishops of Canterbury and York, the bishops of London, Durham, and Winchester, and twenty-one other bishops in the order of seniority. Finally, there are the four lords of appeal in ordinary, or "law lords,"[1] who differ from other peers created by the crown in that they are required to be men of eminence in the legal profession, and in that their seats are not hereditary. The aggregate membership of the chamber varies; in 1911 it was 620, which is almost double the number at the accession of George III, in 1760.

The Breach between the Lords and the Nation. — For upwards

[1] Properly speaking, the "law lords" include also all hereditary peers who hold, or have held, high judicial office.

of a century the "mending or ending" of the House of Lords has been one of the most widely discussed issues of British politics. The question has been mainly one of mending; for persons who have seriously advocated the total abolition of the chamber have been few, and their influence has been slight. The indictments that have been brought by the critics have been based upon the predominantly hereditary character of the membership, upon the meagerness of attendance at the sittings and the small interest displayed by a majority of the members, and upon the hurried and often perfunctory consideration which is given public measures. Fundamentally, however, the attack has had as its impetus the conviction of large numbers of people that the chamber as now constituted stands for interests that are not those of the nation at large. Prior to the parliamentary reforms of the nineteenth century, the House of Commons was hardly more representative of the people than was the upper chamber. Both were controlled by the landed aristocracy, and between the two there was, as a rule, substantial accord. After 1832, however, the territorial interests, while yet powerful, were not so dominant in the Commons, and a cleavage between the Lords, on the one hand, and the Commons, more nearly representative of the mass of the nation, on the other, became a serious factor in the politics and government of the realm. The reform measures of 1867 and 1884, embodying a substantial approach to manhood suffrage in parliamentary elections, converted the House of Commons into a genuine organ of democracy. The development of the cabinet system brought the working executive, likewise, entirely within the range of public control. But the House of Lords underwent no corresponding transformation. It remained, and still is, an inherently and necessarily conservative body, representative, in the main, of the interests of landed property, opposed to changes which seem to menace property and established order, and identified with all the forces that tend to perpetuate the nobility and the Anglican Church as pillars of the state. By simply standing still while the remaining branches of the government were undergoing democratization, the second chamber became, in effect, a political anomaly.

Reform Proposals to 1909. — Projects for the reform of the

House of Lords were not unknown before 1832, but it has been since that date, and more particularly during the past half-century, that the question has been agitated most vigorously. Some of the plans relate to the composition of the chamber, others to its powers and functions, and still others to both of these things. As to composition, the suggestions brought forward most commonly look to a reduction of the aggregate membership, the dropping out of the ecclesiastical members, and the substitution, wholly or in part, of specially designated members for the members who at present sit by hereditary right. In 1869 a bill of Lord John Russell providing for the gradual infiltration of life peers was defeated, and in the same year a project of Earl Grey, and in 1874 proposals of Lord Rosebery and Lord Inchiquin, came to naught. The rejection by the Lords of measures supported by Gladstone's government in 1881–1883 brought the chamber afresh into popular disfavor, and in 1888 the second Salisbury ministry introduced two reform bills, one providing for the gradual creation of fifty life peerages, to be conferred upon men of attainment in law, diplomacy, and administrative service, and the other (popularly known as the "Black Sheep Bill") providing for the discontinuance of writs of summons to undesirable members of the peerage. The measures, however, were withdrawn after their second reading, and an attempt in 1889 to revive the second of them failed. Thenceforward until 1906 the issue remained in the background. During a considerable portion of this period the Unionist party was in power; and between the upper chamber, four-fifths of whose members were Unionists, and the Unionist majority in the Commons, substantial harmony was easily maintained.

With the establishment of the Campbell-Bannerman ministry, in December, 1905, the Liberals entered upon what proved a prolonged tenure of power; and when, in 1906, the Unionist upper chamber began to show a disposition to block the Liberal program relating to educational reform and a number of other important matters, controversy between the two houses quickly assumed a more serious character than at any earlier time. By an overwhelming vote the House of Commons adopted a resolution declaring that, in order to give effect to the will of the people as expressed by elected representatives, the lower chamber ought to be in a position to make any measure law within the life of a single parliament, notwithstanding adverse action taken by the Lords. A bill looking to the reconstruction of the upper house was withdrawn; but the peers themselves were aroused, and in 1908 a committee of their body, presided over by Lord Rosebery (a Liberal), reported a scheme of reform under which (1) possession of a peerage should not of itself entitle the holder to a seat in the chamber; (2) the whole body of hereditary peers, including those of Scotland and Ireland, should elect, for each parliament, two hundred of their number to sit in the upper house; (3) hereditary peers who had occupied certain posts of eminence in the government and the army and navy should be entitled to sit without election; (4) the bishops should elect eight representatives, while the archbishops should sit as of right; and (5) the crown should be empowered to summon four life peers annually, so long as the total should not exceed forty. This scheme failed to meet the Liberal demand, and no action was taken upon it. But it has ever since remained a leading basis of discussion.

Antecedents of the Parliament Act of 1911. — In the autumn of 1909 the issue was reopened in an unexpected manner by the flat refusal of the upper house to pass the Government's Finance Bill (in which were incorporated momentous proposals of the Chancellor of the Exchequer, Mr. Lloyd George, concerning the readjustment of national taxation) until the controversial aspects of the budget should have been submitted to the people at a general election. This act, while clearly within the bounds of formal legality, contravened the long accepted principle of the absolute and final authority of the popular branch in matters of finance, and by most Liberals was pronounced revolutionary. Following as it did the rejection of other important measures which the Liberal majority in the Commons had approved, it raised in an acute form the question of the actual power of the upper chamber over money bills and precipitated a crisis in the relations between the two houses. By a vote of 349 to 134 the lower chamber adopted a resolution to the effect that "the action of the House of Lords in refusing to pass into law the provision made by the House of Commons for the finances of the year is a breach of the constitution, and a usurpation of the privileges of the House of Commons "; while the Asquith ministry came instantly to the decision that the situation demanded an appeal to the country. In January, 1910, a general election took place, with the result that the Government was continued in power, although with a reduced majority; and at the convening of the new parliament, in February, the Speech from the Throne promised that proposals would speedily be submitted " to define the relations between the houses of Parliament, so as to secure the undivided authority of the House of Commons over finance, and its predominance in legislation." The Finance Bill of the year was reintroduced and this time successfully carried through; and resolutions were voted calling for legislation to make it impossible for the House of Lords to defeat or amend a money bill, and also for legislation to limit the chamber's power to impede the passage of measures of other kinds. A bill drawn on these lines was forthwith introduced; while the upper chamber, realizing the force of the attack, brought forward successive proposals for a compromise.

The death of the king, Edward VII, halted consideration of the subject, and through the succeeding summer, hope was centered in the deliberations of a specially organized " constitutional conference," participated in by eight representatives of the two houses and of the two principal parties. Twenty-one meetings, in all, were held; but effort to reach an agreement was futile, and the reassembling of Parliament, at the middle of November, was followed by another dissolution and an appeal to the country. The election of December yielded results almost identical with those of the election of the previous January. The Government secured a majority of 127; and in the new parliament, which met February 6, 1911, the " Parliament Bill " was reintroduced without alteration. On the ground that the measure had been submitted as a clear issue to the people, and had been approved, the ministry demanded its prompt enactment by the two houses; and on May 15 the bill was passed, by a vote of 362 to 241. The upper chamber, jealous of its powers, tried to divert action from that subject to the composition of the chamber. Failing in that, it put forward amendments intended to weaken the Government's bill. But the Liberal ministry would accept no changes touching essentials, and, under threat that enough new Liberal peers would be created to "swamp" the opposition, a group of Unionists sufficient to carry the measure finally joined the handful of Government supporters in a vote not to insist on the proposed amendments. The bill received the royal assent August 18, 1911.

The Parliament Act. — In its preamble the Parliament Act promised further legislation to define both the composition and the powers of a second chamber "constituted on a popular instead of an hereditary basis"; but the act itself related exclusively to the powers of the chamber as it is at present constituted. The general purport of the measure is to define the conditions under which, while the normal methods of legislation remain unchanged, financial bills and projects of general legislation may, nevertheless, be enacted into law without the concurrence of the upper house. The first signal provision is that a public bill passed by the House of Commons and certified by the Speaker to be, within the terms of the act, a "money bill" shall, unless the Commons direct to the contrary, become an act of Parliament on the royal assent being signified, notwithstanding that the House of Lords may not have consented to the bill, within one month after it shall have been sent up to that house. The phrase "money bill" is construed in the act sufficiently broadly to include all measures relating to taxation, supply, appropriations, and public loans. The second important stipulation is that any other public bill (with a few specified exceptions) passed by the House of Commons in three successive sessions, whether or not of the same parliament, and which, having been sent to the House of Lords at least one month, in each case, before the end of the session, is rejected by that chamber in each of those sessions, shall, unless the House of Commons direct to the contrary, become an act of Parliament on the royal assent being signified thereto, notwithstanding the fact that the House of Lords has not consented to the bill. It is required that at least two years shall have elapsed between the date of the second reading of such a bill (*i.e.*, the first real opportunity for its discussion) in the first of these sessions of the House of Commons and the final passage of the bill in the third of the sessions. To come within the provisions of this act the measure must be, at its initial and its final appearances, the "same bill"; that is, it must contain no alterations save such as are rendered necessary by the lapse of time. Finally, the act made provision for increased frequency of national elections by reducing the maximum life of a parliament from seven to five years.

Effects of the Act: the Question of Further Reform. — By these provisions the coördinate and independent position which, in law if not in fact, the British upper chamber, as a legislative body, has occupied through the centuries has been entirely overthrown. Within the domain of legislation, it is true, the Lords may yet exercise much influence. To the chamber must be submitted every project of finance and of legislation which it is proposed to enact into law, and there is still nothing save a certain measure of custom to prevent the introduction of even the most important of non-financial measures first of all in that house. But a single presentation of any money bill fulfills the legal requirement and insures that the measure will become law. For such a bill will not be presented until it has been passed by the Commons, and, emanating from the cabinet, it will not be introduced in that chamber until the assent of the executive is assured. The upper house is allowed one month in which to approve or to reject, but, so far as the enactment of the bill is concerned, the result is the same in any case. Upon ordinary legislation the House of Lords possesses still a veto — a veto, however, which is no longer absolute, but only suspensive. The conditions which are required for the enactment of non-fiscal legislation without the concurrence of the Lords are not easy to bring about, but their realization is not at all an impossibility.[1] By the repeated rejection of proposed measures the Lords may influence public sentiment or otherwise bring about a change of circumstances and thus compass the defeat of the original intent of the Commons; and this is the more possible since a minimum period of two years is required to elapse before a non-fiscal measure can be carried over the Lords' veto. But the continuity of political alignments and of legislative policy in Great Britain is normally such that the remarkable predominance which has been given the popular branch must mean, in effect, little less than absolute law-making authority.

[1] The first measure to become law under the operation of this portion of the Parliament Act was the Welsh Disestablishment Bill of 1914.

The Parliament Act, as has been stated, promises further legislation which will define both the composition and the powers of a second chamber constituted on a popular, instead of an hereditary, basis. No definite action has been taken in this direction as yet (1918), and probably none will be taken until after the war. Even the Unionists, who generally opposed the Parliament Act, may be regarded as committed to some scheme of popularization of the chamber. Many Englishmen to-day are of the opinion that, as John Bright declared, " a hereditary House of Lords is not and cannot be perpetual in a free country." None the less, it is recognized that the chamber as at present constituted contains a large number of conscientious, eminent, and able men; that upon numerous occasions the body has imposed a wholesome check upon the popular branch; and that sometimes it has interpreted the will of the nation more correctly than has the popular branch itself. The most reasonable program of reform would seem to be, not a total reconstitution of the upper chamber upon a "popular" basis, but (1) the adoption of the Rosebery principle that the possession of a peerage shall not of itself entitle the possessor to sit, (2) the admission to membership of a considerable number of persons representative of, and selected by, the whole body of hereditary peers, and (3) the introduction of a substantial quota of life members, appointed or elected by reason of legal attainments, political experience, and other qualities of fitness and eminence. A body so constituted would still incline strongly to conservatism; a Liberal ministry would still have to face in it a Unionist majority. But it may be believed that opposition would be less dogged and less irresponsible than hitherto, and that, coupled with the changes wrought in the powers of the upper house by the Parliament Act, such an alteration would meet all reasonable demands.

The chief difficulty of the plan would be to determine the basis on which the life members (or, possibly, members for ten years or some other long term) should be chosen. In a country organized, as is the United States, on a federal basis, it is easy to make up a second chamber that will not be a replica of the first; the people in small groups can be represented directly in the lower house and the federated states, as such, in the upper. England is not a federal nation, and no logical areas for upper chamber representation exist. But it is not inconceivable that they might be created, — if, indeed, the old historic counties, or special combinations of them, could not be made to serve. However, it is not necessary that the newer elements be composed entirely, or even at all, of men elected by the general mass of voters. Great advantages would arise from a system under which a considerable number should be chosen to represent important special groups or interests, including the great professions. The universities, the learned societies, the principal Non-Conformist bodies, the chambers of commerce, the manufacturers' associations, the bankers, the medical profession, and even the trade unions, come readily to mind in this connection.

It may be assumed that a body composed on the lines thus indicated would be respectable, capable, and vigorous. The only question is whether it would not tend to become too strong a rival of the lower chamber; and therein lies the dilemma of the upper house reformers.

SELECTED REFERENCES

A. L. Lowell, *The Government of England* (New York, 1909), I, Chaps. ix-xi, xxi; S. Low, *Governance of England* (new ed., New York, 1914), Chaps. xii-xiii; T. F. Moran, *Theory and Practice of the English Government* (rev. ed., New York, 1908), Chaps. x-xii; C. Ilbert, *Parliament* (New York, 1911), Chaps. i, ii, ix; Edward Jenks, *Government of the British Empire* (New York, 1918), Chap. vi; J. A. R. Marriott, *English Political Institutions* (Oxford, 1910); W. Bagehot, *The English Constitution* (new ed., New York, 1911), Chaps. v-vi; W. R. Anson, *Law and Custom of the Constitution* (4th ed., London, 1909-1911), I, Chaps. ii, iv-v; T. E. May, *Constitutional History of England*, continued by F. Holland (London, New York, 1912); C. Seymour, *Electoral Reform in England and Wales, 1832-1885* (New Haven, 1915); J. R. M. Butler, *The Passing of the Great Reform Bill* (London, 1914); G. L. Dickinson, *Development of Parliament during the Nineteenth Century* (London, 1895); J. H. Rose, *Rise and Growth of Democracy in Great Britain* (London, 1897); E. Porritt, *The Unreformed House of Commons; Parliamentary Representation before 1832*, 2 vols. (2d ed., Cambridge, 1909); K. Schirmacher, *The Modern Woman's Rights Movement* (New York, 1912), 58-96; W. L. Blease, *The Emancipation of English Women* (new ed., London, 1913); L. O. Pike, *Constitutional History of the House of Lords* (London, 1894); H. W. V. Temperley, *Senates and Upper Chambers* (London, 1910); J. A. R. Marriott, *Second Chambers* (Oxford, 1910); W. S. McKechnie, *Reform of the House of Lords* (Glasgow, 1909); F. Dilnot, *The Old Order Changeth* (London, 1911).

CHAPTER XIII

PARLIAMENT AT WORK

I. MEETINGS, ORGANIZATION, AND PRIVILEGES

Sessions: the Opening of a Parliament. — It is required by law (a succession of " triennial acts," beginning in 1641) that Parliament shall be convened at least once every three years; but by reason of the enormous pressure of business and, in particular, the custom which forbids the voting of supplies for a period longer than one year, meetings are, in point of fact, annual. A session begins ordinarily near the first of February and continues, with brief adjournments at holiday seasons, until August or September. The two Houses must invariably be summoned together. Either may adjourn without the other; and the king can compel an adjournment of neither. A prorogation, which brings a session to a close, and a dissolution, which brings a parliament to an end, must be ordered for the two Houses concurrently. Both take place technically at the command of the king, actually upon the decision of the ministry. A prorogation is to a specified date, and it terminates all pending business; but the reassembling of the Houses may be either postponed or hastened by royal proclamation.

At the beginning of a session the members of the two Houses gather, first of all, in their respective chambers. The commoners are summoned thereupon to the chamber of the Lords, where the letters patent authorizing the session are read and the Lord Chancellor makes known the desire of the crown that the Commons proceed with the choosing of a Speaker. The commoners withdraw to attend to this matter, and on the next day the newly elected official, accompanied by the members, presents himself at the bar of the House of Lords, announces his election, and, through the Lord Chancellor, receives the royal approbation. Having demanded and received a guarantee of the "ancient and undoubted rights and privileges of the Commons," the Speaker and the members then retire to their own quarters, where the necessary oaths are administered. If, as is not unusual, the king meets Parliament in person, he goes in state, probably the next day, to the House of Lords and takes his seat upon the throne, and the Lord Chamberlain is instructed to desire the Gentleman Usher of the Black Rod to *command* the attendance once more of the Commons. If the sovereign does not attend, the Lords Commissioners bid the Usher to *desire* the Commons' presence. In any case, the commoners present themselves, and the king (or, in his absence, the Lord Chancellor) reads the Speech from the Throne, in which the cabinet — for it is the real author of the speech — sets forth its program for the session. Following the retirement of the sovereign, the Commons again withdraw, the Throne Speech is re-read and an address in reply is voted in each House, and " the Government," *i.e.*, the cabinet, begins the introduction of fiscal and legislative proposals. In the event that a session is not the first one of a parliament, the election of a Speaker and the administration of oaths are, of course, omitted.

Physical Surroundings. — From the beginning of parliamentary history the meeting-place of the Houses has regularly been Westminster, on the left bank of the Thames. The last parliament to sit at any other spot was the third Oxford Parliament of Charles II, in 1681. The Palace of Westminster — in medieval times outside, although near, the principal city of the kingdom — was long the most important of the royal residences, and it was natural that its great halls and chambers, together with the adjoining abbey, should be utilized for parliamentary sittings. Of the enormous structure known as Westminster to-day (still technically a royal palace, although not a royal residence), practically all portions save old Westminster Hall were constructed after the fire of 1834. The Lords first occupied their present quarters in 1847 and the Commons theirs in 1850.

From opposite sides of a central lobby corridors lead to the halls in which the sittings of the two bodies are held, these halls facing each other in such a manner that the king's throne at the south end of the House of Lords is visible from the Speaker's chair at the north end of the House of Commons. The room occupied by the Commons is not large, being but seventy-five feet in length by forty-five in breadth. It is bisected by a broad aisle, at the upper end of which is a large table for the use of the clerk and his assistants, and beyond this the raised and canopied chair of the Speaker. " Facing the aisle on each side long rows of high-backed benches, covered with dark green leather, slope upward tier above tier to the walls of the room; and through them, at right angles to the aisle, a narrow passage, known as the gangway, cuts across the House. There is also a gallery running all around the room, the part of it facing the Speaker being given up to visitors, while the front rows at the opposite end belong to the reporters, and behind them there stands, before a still higher gallery, a heavy screen, like those erected in Turkish mosques to conceal the presence of women, and used here for the same purpose."[1] The rows of benches on the gallery sides are reserved for members, but they do not afford a very desirable location and are rarely occupied, save upon occasions of special interest. In the body of the House there are fewer than 350 seats for 707 members. As a rule, not even all of these are occupied, for there are no desks, and the member who wishes to read, write, or otherwise occupy himself seeks the library or other rooms adjoining. The front bench at the upper end of the aisle, at the right of the Speaker, is known as the Treasury Bench and is reserved for members of the ministry. The corresponding bench at the Speaker's left is reserved similarly for the leaders of the Opposition. In so far as is possible in the lack of a definite assignment of seats, members of avowed party allegiance range themselves behind their leaders, while members of more independent attitude seek places below the gangway. " The accident that the House of Commons sits in a narrow room with benches facing each other, and not, like most continental legislatures, in a semi-circular space, with seats arranged like those of a theatre, makes for the two-party system and against groups shading into each other."[2]

The hall occupied by the Lords is smaller and more elaborately decorated than that occupied by the Commons. It contains

[1] Lowell, *The Government of England*, I, 249.   [2] Ilbert, *Parliament*, 124.

cross benches, but in the main the arrangements that have been described are duplicated in it. For social and ceremonial purposes there exists among the members a fixed order of precedence. In the chamber, however, the seating is arranged without regard to this order, save that the bishops sit in a group. The Government peers occupy the benches on the right of the woolsack [1] and the Opposition those on the left, while members who prefer to remain neutral take their places on the cross benches between the table and the bar.

Officers of the House of Commons: the Speaker. — The principal officers of the House of Commons are the Speaker, the Clerk and his two assistants, the Sergeant-at-Arms and his deputies, the Chaplain, and the Chairman and Deputy Chairman of Ways and Means. The Clerk and the Sergeant-at-Arms, together with their assistants, are appointed for life by the king, on nomination of the premier, but the Speaker and the Chairman and Deputy Chairman of Ways and Means are elected for a single parliament by the House.[2] All save the Chairman and his deputy are, strictly, non-political officers. The Clerk signs all orders of the House, indorses bills sent or returned to the Lords, reads whatever is required to be read during the sittings, records the proceedings of the chamber, and, with the concurrence of the Speaker, supervises the preparation of the Official Journal. The Sergeant-at-Arms attends the Speaker, enforces the House's orders, and presents at the bar of the House persons ordered or qualified to be so presented. The Chairman of Ways and Means (in his absence the Deputy Chairman) presides over the deliberations of the House when the body sits as a committee of the whole, and exercises supervision over private bill legislation. Although a political official, he preserves, in both capacities, a strictly non-partisan attitude.

The speakership arose from the need of the House, when it was merely a petitioning body, for a recognized spokesman; and although the known succession of Speakers begins with Sir Thomas Hungerford, who held the office in the last parliament

[1] In the days of Elizabeth the presiding official sat upon a sack actually filled with wool. He sits now, as a matter of fact, upon an ottoman, upholstered in red. But the ancient designation of the seat survives.

[2] In point of fact, the Chairman and Deputy Chairman retire when the ministry by which they have been nominated goes out of office.

of Edward III (1377), there is every reason to suppose that at an even earlier date there were men whose functions were substantially equivalent. The Speaker is elected at the beginning of a parliament by and from the members of the House, and his tenure of office, unless terminated by resignation or death, continues through the term of that parliament. The choice of the House is subject to the approval of the crown; but, whereas in earlier days the king's will was at this point very influential, the last occasion upon which a Speaker-elect was rejected by the crown was in 1679. Although nominally elected, the Speaker is in fact chosen by the ministry, and he is reasonably certain to be taken from the party in power. During the nineteenth century, however, it became customary to reëlect a Speaker as long as he was willing to serve, regardless of party affiliation.

The functions of the Speaker are regulated in part by custom, in part by rules of the House, and in part by general legislation. They are numerous and, in the aggregate, highly important. The Speaker is, first of all, the presiding officer of the House. In this capacity he is a strictly non-partisan moderator whose business it is to maintain decorum in deliberations, decide points of order, put questions, and announce the result of votes. The non-partisan aspect of the English speakership sets the office off in sharp contrast with its American counterpart. "It makes little difference to any English party in Parliament," says Bryce, "whether the occupant of the chair has come from their own or from hostile ranks. . . . A custom as strong as law forbids him to render help to his own side even by private advice. Whatever information as to parliamentary law he may feel free to give must be equally at the disposal of every member."[1] Except in the event of a tie, the Speaker does not vote, even when, the House being in committee, he is not occupying the chair. In the second place, the Speaker is the spokesman and representative of the House, whether in demanding privileges, communicating resolutions, or issuing warrants. There was a time when he was hardly less the spokesman of the king than the spokesman of the Commons, but the growth of independence of the popular chamber enabled him long ago to cast off this dual and extremely difficult rôle. The Speaker, furthermore,

[1] *American Commonwealth*, I, 135.

declares and interprets, although he in no case makes, the law of the House. "Where," says Ilbert, "precedents, rulings, and the orders of the House are insufficient or uncertain guides, he has to consider what course would be most consistent with the usages, traditions, and dignity of the House, and the rights and interests of its members, and on these points his advice is usually followed, and his decisions are very rarely questioned. . . . For many generations the deference habitually paid to the occupant of the chair has been the theme of admiring comment by foreign observers."[1] Finally, the fact should be recalled that the Parliament Act of 1911 gives the Speaker sole power, when question arises, to determine whether a given measure is or is not to be considered a money bill. Upon his decision may hinge the entire policy of the Government concerning a measure, and even the fate of the measure itself. The Speaker's symbol of authority is the mace, which is carried before him when he formally enters or leaves the House, and lies on the table before him when he is in the chair. He has an official residence, and he receives a salary of £5000 a year. Upon retirement from office he is likely to be pensioned and to be raised to the peerage.

Committees of the House of Commons. — Like all important and numerous legislative bodies, the House of Commons expedites business by making large use of committees. The committees regularly employed in recent times are of five main kinds: (1) the Committee of the Whole; (2) select committees on public bills; (3) sessional committees on public bills; (4) standing committees on public bills; and (5) committees on private bills. Until 1907 a public bill, after its second reading, went normally to the Committee of the Whole; since the date mentioned, it goes there only if the House so determines. The Committee of the Whole is simply the House of Commons, presided over by the Chairman of Ways and Means in the place of the Speaker, and acting under rules of procedure which permit almost unrestricted discussion and in other ways lend themselves to the free consideration of the details of a measure. When the subject in hand relates to the providing of revenue the body is known, technically, as the Committee of Ways and

[1] *Parliament*, 140-141.

Means; when to appropriations, it is styled the Committee of the Whole on Supply, or simply the Committee of Supply.

Select committees consist, as a rule, of fifteen members, and are constituted to investigate and report upon specific subjects or measures. It is through them that the House collects evidence, examines witnesses, and otherwise obtains the information required for intelligent legislation. After a select committee has fulfilled the immediate purpose for which it was set up it passes out of existence. Each such committee chooses its chairman, and each keeps detailed records of its proceedings, which are included, along with its formal report, in the published parliamentary papers of the session. The members may be elected by the House, but in practice the appointment of some or all is left to the Committee of Selection, which itself consists of eleven members chosen by the House at the beginning of each session. This Committee of Selection, which appoints members not only of select committees but also of standing committees and of committees on private and local bills, is made up after conference between the leaders of the Government and of the Opposition, and, both theoretically and actually, it ignores party lines entirely in the appointments which it makes. The number of select committees is, of course, variable, but it is never small. A few are constituted for an entire year and are known as sessional committees. Of these, the Committee of Selection is itself an example; others are the Committee on Public Accounts and the Committee on Public Petitions.

Beginning in 1882, certain great standing committees have been created, to the general end that the time of the House may be further economized. In 1907 the number of such committees was raised from two to four; and all bills except money bills, private bills,[1] and bills for confirming provisional orders [2] — that is to say, all public non-fiscal proposals — are required to be referred to one of these committees (the Speaker determining which one) unless the House otherwise directs. It is expected

[1] A private bill is one which has in view the special interest of some locality, person, or group of persons, rather than the general interests of the state.

[2] A provisional order is an order issued by an administrative officer or department of the government authorizing the undertaking of a project in behalf of which application has been made. It is "provisional" because it is not finally valid unless confirmed by Parliament.

that measures so referred will be so fully considered in committee that they will consume but little of the time of the House. Each of the four committees consists of from sixty to eighty members, who are named by the Committee of Selection in such a manner that in personnel they will faithfully represent the composition of the House as a whole. The chairmen are selected (from its own ranks) by a "chairman's panel" of not more than eight members designated by the Committee of Selection. The procedure of the standing committees closely resembles that of the Committee of the Whole; indeed they often serve as substitutes for the larger body.

Organization of the House of Lords. — It is required that the two Houses of Parliament shall be convened invariably together; and one may not be prorogued without the other. The actual sittings of the Lords are, however, very much briefer and more leisurely than are those of the Commons. Normally the upper chamber meets but four times a week, and by reason of lack of business or indisposition to consume time in the consideration of measures whose final enactment is assured, sittings are frequently concluded within an hour; although, of course, there are occasions upon which the chamber deliberates seriously and at much length. A quorum for the transaction of business is three. However, it is but fair to add that if a division occurs upon a bill and it is found that there are not thirty members present, the question is declared not to be decided. Save upon formal occasions and at times when there is under consideration a measure in whose fate the members are specially interested, attendance is always scant. There are members who after complying with the formalities incident to taking a seat, rarely, and in some instances never, reappear among their colleagues. It thus comes about that, despite the fact that nominally the House of Lords is one of the largest of the world's law-making assemblies, the chamber in reality suffers little from the unwieldiness characteristic of deliberative bodies of great size. The efficiency of the House is more likely to be impaired by paucity of attendance than otherwise.

The officers of the House of Lords are largely appointive, although in part elective. Except during the trial of a peer, the presiding official is the Lord Chancellor, appointed by the king on the advice of the premier. The duty of presiding in the Lords, as has been explained, is but one of many that fall to this remarkable dignitary. If at the time of his appointment an incumbent is not a peer, he is reasonably certain to be created one, although there is no legal requirement to this effect. The theory is that the woolsack which comprises the presiding official's seat is not within the chamber proper, and that the official himself, as such, is not a member of the body. The powers allowed him are not even those commonly possessed by a moderator. In the event that two or more members request the privilege of addressing the chamber, the House itself decides which shall have the floor. Order in debate is enforced, not by the Chancellor, but by the members, and when they speak they address, not the chair, but " My Lords." Although, if a peer, the Chancellor may speak and vote as any other member, he possesses as presiding officer no power of the casting vote. In short, the position which the Chancellor occupies in the chamber is purely formal. In addition to " deputy speakers," designated to preside in the Chancellor's absence, the remaining officials of the Lords who owe their positions to governmental appointment are the Clerk of Parliament, who keeps the records; the Sergeant-at-Arms, who personally attends the presiding officer and acts as custodian of the mace; and the Gentleman Usher of the Black Rod, a pompous dignitary whose function it is to summon the Commons when their attendance is required and to play a more or less useful part upon other ceremonial occasions. The one important official whom the House itself elects is the Lord Chairman of Committees, whose duty it is to preside in Committee of the Whole.

Privileges of Members. — On the basis in part of custom and in part of statute, there exists a body of definitely established privileges, some of which appertain to the Commons as a chamber, some similarly to the Lords, and some to the individual members of both Houses. The privileges which at the opening of a parliament the newly-elected Speaker " requests " and, as a matter of course, obtains for the chamber over which he presides include principally those of freedom from arrest, freedom of speech, access to the sovereign, and a " favorable construction " upon the proceedings of the House. Freedom from arrest is enjoyed by members during a session and a period of forty days before and after it, but it does not protect a member from the consequences of any indictable offense nor, in civil actions, from any process save arrest. Freedom of speech, finally guaranteed in the Bill of Rights, means simply that a member may not be held to account by legal process outside Parliament for anything he may have said in the course of the debates or proceedings of the chamber to which he belongs. The right of access to the sovereign belongs to the Commons collectively through the Speaker, but to the Lords individually. With the growth of parliamentary government both it and the privilege of "favorable construction" have ceased to have practical importance. Another privilege which survives is that of exemption from jury duty, although no longer of refusing to attend court in the capacity of a witness. Each House enjoys the privilege—for all practical purposes now the *right* — of regulating its own proceedings, of committing persons for contempt, and of deciding contested elections. The last-mentioned function the House of Commons, however, delegated in 1868 to the courts. A privilege jealously retained by the Lords is that of trial in all cases of treason or felony by the upper chamber itself, under the presidency of a Lord High Steward appointed by the crown. The Lords are exempt from arrest in civil causes, not merely during and immediately preceding and succeeding sessions, but at all times; and they enjoy all the rights, privileges, and distinctions which, through law or custom, have become inherent in their several dignities.

Payment of Members of the House of Commons. — An important step in the democratization of the House of Commons was the passing of an act in 1911 providing for the payment to members of a salary from the national treasury. In the Middle Ages county and borough representatives were given, as a rule, some compensation by their constituents. But in the Tudor era this practice became obsolete, and until the legislation of 1911 no definite arrangement was made in lieu of it. The cost of seeking election and of maintaining oneself as a parliamentary member has always been considerable, and men who were not of independent means had been practically debarred from candidacy for seats. For some years the Labor party was accustomed to provide its needy representatives with the means of maintaining themselves at the capital; but this arrangement affected only a small group of members and was of an entirely private and casual nature. Public and systematic payment of members, to the end that poor but capable men might not be kept out of the Commons, was demanded by the Chartists three-quarters of a century ago, and from time to time after 1870 there was agitation for it. Fresh impetus was afforded by the Osborne Judgment, in which, on an appeal from the lower courts, the House of Lords ruled in December, 1909, that the payment of parliamentary members as such from the dues collected by labor organizations was contrary to law. The announcement of the decision was followed by persistent demand on the part of the labor element for legislation to reverse the ruling. In connection with the budget presented to the House of Commons by the Chancellor of the Exchequer May 16, 1911, the proposition was made, not to take action one way or the other upon the Lords' decision, but to provide for the payment to all non-official members of the House of Commons of a yearly salary of £400 ($2000); and on August 10 a resolution was carried in the Commons providing for " the payment of a salary at the rate of £400 a year to every member of the House, excluding any member who is for the time being in receipt of a salary as an officer of the House or as a minister, or as an officer of His Majesty's Household." Most of the Unionists were opposed to the innovation, and a number of Liberals did not like it. But the Government was bent on carrying it through as the only practicable means of escape from the difficulties in which it was involved with its ally, the Labor party; and the measure in due course became law. The payment of salaries to the members of great elective legislative bodies is not without drawbacks. But it is fundamentally justifiable, and it is interesting to note that Great Britain is but one of several European nations which in recent years have adopted the policy. Germany did so in 1906, and Italy in 1912. The amount of the salary provided by the British legislation of 1911 is not large (although it is far larger than that provided in continental countries); but it is ample to make candidacy for seats possible for numbers of men who formerly could not under any circumstances contemplate a public career.

s

II. FUNCTIONS AND POWERS

Formal and Theoretical Aspects. — The entire political development of England centers around two great facts: the growth of the power of Parliament and the establishment of popular control in the predominant chamber, the House of Commons. Upon the vastness of the powers attained by the two Houses, something has already been said; it has been pointed out that Parliament has long since gained authority to alter or add to the national constitution at will, and that many, if not most, of the great constitutional changes of recent times have come about in that way. Closely following the power of constitutional amendment comes that of general legislation. It will not do to say that Parliament is the author of all English law. The great body of the Common Law has sprung from sources entirely outside legislative halls. But in so far as national laws are *enacted* to-day, it is Parliament, directly or indirectly, that enacts them. And there is no subject upon which Parliament cannot legislate, no sort of law that it cannot put on the statute books, no existing law (written or unwritten) that it cannot modify or rescind. It goes without saying that the volume of legislation enacted by Parliament is enormous. The House of Commons, at all events, is always deluged with urgent business; and while procedure has been expedited by the larger use of committees, and by other devices to be described presently, matters of great importance often lie over for years awaiting a favorable opportunity for their consideration. Similarly, the revenues which accrue to the Treasury and which can be dealt with independently of Parliament would hardly carry on the business of government for a day, and Parliament (in effect, the House of Commons) not only makes possible, by its appropriation acts, the legal expenditure of practically all public moneys; it provides, by its measures of taxation, the funds from which almost all appropriations are made.

Furthermore, Parliament (again, mainly the House of Commons) has full power to inquire into, criticize, and direct the work of administration. An essential feature of the English system is that the ministers shall invariably be members of Parliament, that they shall retain office only so long as they command the support of a majority in the House of Commons, and that the cabinet — the inner circle composed of chief ministers — shall serve practically as an executive committee of Parliament for the general management of the administrative machinery which Parliament sets up and maintains. "Parliament," once declared a leading member of the House of Lords, "makes and unmakes our ministries, it revises their actions. Ministries may make peace and war, but they do so at pain of instant dismissal by Parliament from office; and in affairs of internal administration the power of Parliament is equally direct. It can dismiss a ministry if it is too extravagant or too economical; it can dismiss a ministry because its government is too stringent or too lax. It does actually and practically in every way directly govern England, Scotland, and Ireland."[1]

Loss of Power to the Cabinet and to the Electorate. — All of the great powers thus attributed to Parliament unquestionably belong to it. However, they are actually exercised by the two Houses with not quite so much initiative, continuity, and force as these broad statements would imply; and it becomes necessary to look somewhat beneath the surface to discover the true situation. Such scrutiny reveals the fact that, so far as the actual exercise of its powers is concerned, Parliament has lost, and is losing, on the one side to the cabinet, and on the other to the electorate. For the moment there is something shocking in this discovery; we had been accustomed to think of Parliament as the great organ of popular government, and a diminution of the powers which it wields suggests a back-set for democracy. But reassurance comes when we reflect that loss of power to the cabinet is not necessarily inconsistent with popular government, since the cabinet is made up largely of elected members of Parliament, and is responsible to the House of Commons; while, of course, a loss to the electorate means throwing power back directly into the hands of the people. To this last-mentioned development three things have chiefly contributed. The first is the great increase of popular information and the sharpening of public opinion upon political affairs, made possible by the printing press, the telegraph, and other aids to quick and cheap dissemination of news and ideas. "A debate, a vote, or a

[1] The Duke of Devonshire, quoted in Low, *Governance of England* (new ed.), 57-58.

scene," says Lowell, " that occurs in Parliament late at night is brought home to the whole country at breakfast the next morning, and prominent constituents, clubs, committees, and the like, can praise or censure, encourage or admonish, their member for his vote before the next sitting of the House."[1] Under the constant gaze of his constituents, the member is less free to act and speak and vote as he likes than was his predecessor of a hundred years ago. A second factor in the situation is the growth of the idea of the referendum, or the popular mandate. Legally, Parliament is still free to introduce constitutional changes and to enact ordinary legislation at will. But in the past quarter-century and especially since the sharp political struggles of 1909–1911, the view has come to be widely held that before taking final action on matters of great importance the Houses, through their leaders, ought to consult the nation (ordinarily by means of a dissolution, followed by a national election), so that definitive legislation may be based on a fresh and unmistakable mandate from the people. A third, and more important, factor is the remarkable growth of the power of the cabinet, and the actual supplanting, in a considerable measure, of cabinet responsibility to the House of Commons by cabinet responsibility directly to the electorate. This matter of the cabinet's increased power, as it affects Parliament, calls for some comment.

Cabinet and Parliament in Legislation. — A hundred years ago, and less, the members of the cabinet had comparatively little to do with law-making. They were already, with only an occasional exception, members of Parliament. But their duties were mainly administrative, and they bore no general responsibility for the legislation that was enacted. The public demand, however, that came upon them as administrators for remedial legislation, the growing complexity of the relations between legislation and administration, and the increasing compactness and *morale* of the inner ministerial group — in short, the ripening of the parliamentary system — brought, during the nineteenth century, a totally changed situation. The cabinet of to-day not only actively participates in law-making; it decides what important measures are to be brought before the

[1] *The Government of England*, I, 425.

Houses, puts these measures into form, introduces them, explains them, defends them, presses for their passage, takes full responsibility for them after they are passed, and gives up the attempt to govern if they, or any of them, are definitely rejected by the popular chamber. Every cabinet member has, of course, a seat in one House or the other; and in the House of which he is not a member he — or, more accurately, the administrative department or office over which he presides — has as a rule a spokesman in the person of a parliamentary under-secretary. Measures which are brought forward by the cabinet are known as "Government bills." They are almost certain to be passed. What happens in case one of them is defeated depends on the circumstances; but the fall of the cabinet is not unlikely to be the result. Bills may be introduced by members of the two Houses who do not belong to the cabinet. But little time is allowed for the consideration of these "private members' bills," and few are ever passed — none that are of a far-reaching and controversial nature.

Indeed, the ordinary member plays a distinctly passive rôle. He listens to the speeches of the Government leaders in favor of their bills, and to the rejoinders by the leaders of the Opposition; he may, if he is adroit, manage to take some small part in the discussion himself; and he finally gives his vote one way or the other. How he will vote can usually be told in advance; for his vote helps to decide the fate not only of the bill under consideration, but of the ministry, and therefore the fortunes of his party. Liberal members must vote for the bills introduced by a Liberal ministry or ruin that ministry and drive their own party from power. Only by voting consistently and solidly against the Government's bills can the Opposition hope to make a showing that will attract strength and eventually build up the majority that is necessary to a cabinet overturn in its favor. Nowhere are party lines more sharply drawn than in the House of Commons (conditions in war time are, of course, exceptional); in few legislative bodies does the ordinary member exercise less personal initiative. "To say," concludes the American writer who has made the closest study of this subject, " that at present the cabinet legislates with the advice and consent of Parliament would hardly be an exaggeration; and it is only the right of private members to bring in a few motions and bills of their own, and to criticize government measures, or propose amendments to them, freely, that prevents legislation from being the work of a mere automatic majority. It does not follow that the action of the cabinet is arbitrary. . . . The cabinet has its finger always on the pulse of the House of Commons, and especially of its own majority there; and it is ever on the watch for expressions of public feeling outside. Its function is in large part to sum up and formulate the desires of its supporters, but the majority must accept its conclusions, and in carrying them out becomes well-nigh automatic." [1]

Cabinet and Parliament in Administration. — A similar situation exists in the domain of administration. Most of the members of the cabinet stand at the head of great administrative offices or departments; and, as ministers, their first business is to supervise the work carried on in and through these agencies. Never, save when the Long Parliament, in the Cromwellian era, undertook the administration of public affairs through committees of its members, has Parliament manifested a disposition to draw executive work directly into its own hands. But from the rise of the cabinet system the direct and full responsibility of the ministers to Parliament (actually, the House of Commons) for all of their executive actions has been accepted as axiomatic. The theory is that the ministers are answerable to the elected chamber for all that they do, singly in small or isolated matters, collectively in important ones; that their acts can be examined, criticized, revised, or annulled; and that the great powers which they wield can be stripped from them whenever the House of Commons chooses to withhold from them its support. Any member of the House of Commons may address a question (subject to the Speaker's judgment as to its propriety) to any minister of the crown who is also a member, with a view to obtaining information. Except in special cases, notice of questions must be given at least one day in advance, and half an hour or more is allowed at four sittings every week for the asking and answering of such questions. A minister may answer or decline to answer, but unless a refusal can be shown to arise from legitimate considerations of public interest its political

[1] Lowell, *The Government of England*, I, 326.

effect may be embarrassing. In any event, there is no debate. The asking of questions is liable to abuse, but, as is pointed out by Ilbert, " there is no more valuable safeguard against maladministration, no more effective method of bringing the searchlight of criticism to bear on the action or inaction of the executive government and its subordinates. A minister has to be constantly asking himself, not merely whether his proceedings and the proceedings of those for whom he is responsible are legally or technically defensible, but what kind of answer he can give if questioned about them in the House, and how that answer will be received."[1] Any member may bring forward a motion censuring the Government or any member or department thereof; and a motion of this sort, when emanating from the leader of the Opposition, constitutes a vote of confidence upon whose result may hang the fate of the ministry. By calls upon the Government, or a given department, for information; by the setting up of parliamentary committees, departmental committees, or royal commissions; and, in particular, by taking advantage of the numberless opportunities afforded by the enactment of appropriation bills, the House of Commons may further impose upon the ministers substantial responsibility and control. " A strong executive government, tempered and controlled by constant, vigilant, and representative criticism," is the ideal at which the parliamentary institutions of Great Britain are aimed.[2] After all is said, however, the fact remains that in fifty years scarcely a ministry has been turned out of office by Parliament because of its executive acts. Parliamentary inspection and criticism serve to keep the ministers in a wholesome state of vigilance. But it is mainly to the electorate itself that they look for the signs of approval or disfavor by which to gauge their course.

III. PROCEDURE

Public Bills: Earlier Stages. — The process of converting a bill, whether introduced by the Government or by a private member, into an act of Parliament is long and intricate. The numerous steps that have to be taken are designed to prevent hasty and ill-advised legislation. Some of them have become

[1] *Parliament*, 113–114.   [2] Ilbert, *Parliament*, 119.

mere formalities, involving neither debate nor vote, and the process is undoubtedly more expeditious than it once was. The work of Parliament is still, however, extremely — and, some people think, unnecessarily — slow.

The first formal step is, of course, the drawing up, or "drafting," of the bill itself; for every project for a public act is presented to Parliament in a fixed form, affirming enactment by "the King, Lords, and Commons," and setting forth in regular order, and in numbered clauses, the provisions that are desired. If the bill is a Government measure, and hence sponsored by the cabinet collectively, it is drafted by one of the Parliamentary Counsel to the Treasury (lawyers appointed by the crown for the purpose), or by some independent expert specially engaged. If it is a private member's bill, it is drafted by the member himself or by any one whom he may employ for the purpose. In any case, it bears on its back the name of at least one member of the House, who is formally regarded as its introducer.[1]

The further steps in the enactment of a bill in either House are, as a rule, five: first reading, second reading, consideration by committee, report from committee, and third reading.[2] Formerly the introduction of a measure commonly involved a speech explaining at length the nature of the proposal, followed by a debate and a vote, sometimes consuming, in all, several sittings. Nowadays only very important Government bills are introduced in this manner. In the case of all others, the first reading has become a formality. The member wishing to introduce a measure gives notice to that effect and proceeds to lay the bill on the table, *i.e.*, to have it circulated in printed form among the members of the House. Upon all measures except the most important Government projects, opportunity for debate is first afforded at the second reading, although the discussion at this stage must relate to general principles rather than to details. By the adoption of a motion that the bill be read a second time at some date falling beyond the anticipated limits of the session a measure may be killed at its first reading.

Public Bills : Later Stages. — A bill which survives the second reading is "committed." Prior to 1907 it would go normally to

[1] Jenks, *Government of the British Empire*, 143.
[2] Procedure will here be described as it is in the House of Commons.

the Committee of the Whole. Nowadays it goes there if it is a money bill or a bill for confirming a provisional order,[1] or if, on other grounds, the House so directs; otherwise it goes to one of the four standing committees, assignment being made by the Speaker.. This is the stage at which the provisions of the measure are considered in detail and amendments are introduced. After the second reading, however, a bill may be referred to a select committee, and in the event that this is done a step is added to the process; for after being returned by the select committee the measure goes to the Committee of the Whole or to one of the standing committees. Eventually the bill is reported back to the House. If reported by a standing committee, or in amended form by the Committee of the Whole, it is considered by the House afresh and in some detail; otherwise, the "report stage" is omitted. Finally comes the third reading, the question now being whether the House approves the measure as a whole. At this stage any amendment beyond verbal changes makes it necessary to recommit. The carrying of a measure through these successive stages is spread over, as a rule, several days, and sometimes several weeks, but it is not impossible that the entire process be completed during the period of a sitting. Having been adopted by the originating House, a bill is taken by a clerk to the other House, there to be subjected to substantially the same procedure. If amendments are introduced, it is sent back in order that the suggested changes may be considered by the first House. If they are agreed to, the measure is sent up for the royal approval. If they are rejected and an agreement between the two Houses cannot be reached, the measure falls.[2]

Money Bills: Appropriation and Finance Acts. — Procedure in the handling of money bills differs widely from that described.

---

[1] See p. 253.

[2] The legislative process is summed up aptly by Lowell as follows: "Leaving out of account the first reading, which rarely involves a real debate, the ordinary course of a public bill through the House of Commons gives, therefore, an opportunity for two debates upon its general merits, and between them two discussions of its details, or one debate upon the details if that one results in no changes, or if the bill has been referred to a standing committee. When the House desires to collect evidence it does so after approving of the general principle, and before taking up the details. Stated in this way, the whole matter is plain and rational enough. It is, in fact, one of the many striking examples of adaptation in the English political

Underlying it are two fundamental principles, incorporated in the standing orders of the House of Commons during the first quarter of the eighteenth century. One of them is that no petition or motion for the granting of money shall be considered except in Committee of the Whole. The other forbids the receiving of any petition, or the proceeding upon any motion, for a charge upon the public revenue unless recommended by the crown. Although these principles apply technically only to appropriations, they have long been observed with equal fidelity in relation to the raising of revenue. All specific measures for the expending of money and all proposals for the imposing of fresh taxation or the increase of existing taxation must emanate from the crown, *i.e.*, in practice, from the cabinet. A private member may go no farther in this direction than to introduce resolutions of a general character favoring or opposing some particular kind of expenditure; except that it is within his right to move to repeal or to reduce taxes which the Government has not proposed to modify.

Two great fiscal measures are passed every year: the Appropriation Act, in which are brought together all the grants for the public services for the year, and the Finance Act, in which are included all regulations relating to the revenue and the national debt. Before the close of the fiscal year (March 31) the ministry submits to the Commons a body of estimates for the "supply services," drawn up originally by the government departments, scrutinized by the Treasury, and approved by the cabinet. Early in the session the House resolves itself into a Committee of the Whole on Supply (commonly called simply the Committee of Supply), by which resolutions of supply are discussed, adopted, and reported. These resolutions are embodied in bills which, for purposes of convenience, are passed at intervals during the session. But at the close all are consolidated in one grand Appropriation Act. Upwards of half of the public expenditures, it is to be observed, *e.g.*, the Civil List, the salaries of judges, pensions, and interest on the national

system. A collection of rules that appear cumbrous and antiquated, and that even now are well-nigh incomprehensible when described in all their involved technicality, have been pruned away until they furnish a procedure almost as simple, direct, and appropriate as any one could devise." *The Government of England*, I, 277-278.

debt, are provided for by permanent acts imposing charges upon the Consolidated Fund and do not come annually under parliamentary review.

The Budget. — As soon as practicable after the close of the fiscal year the House, resolved for the purpose into a Committee of Ways and Means, receives from the Chancellor of the Exchequer his budget, or annual statement of accounts. The statement regularly falls into three parts: a review of revenue and expenditure during the year just closed, a provisional balance-sheet for the year to come, and a series of proposals for the remission, modification, or fresh imposition of taxes. Revenues, as expenditures, are in large part "permanent"; yet a very considerable proportion are provided for through the medium of yearly votes. In Committee of Ways and Means the House considers the Chancellor's proposals, and after they have been reported back and embodied in a bill they are carried, with the assent of the crown, though no longer necessarily of the Lords, into law. Prior to 1861 it was customary to include in the fiscal resolutions, and in the bill in which they were embodied, only the annual and temporary taxes. But in consequence of the Lords' rejection, in 1860, of a separate finance bill repealing the duties on paper, it became the practice to incorporate in a single bill — the so-called Finance Bill — provision for all taxes, whether temporary or permanent. In practice the House of Commons rarely refuses to approve the financial measures recommended by the Government. The chamber has no power to propose either expenditure or taxation, and its right to refuse or reduce the levies and the appropriations asked for is seldom used. "Financially," says Lowell, "its work is rather supervision than direction; and its real usefulness consists in securing publicity and criticism rather than in controlling expenditure."[1] The theory underlying fiscal procedure has been summed up lucidly as follows: "The Crown demands money, the Commons grant it, and the Lords assent to the grant;[2] but the Commons do not vote money unless it be required by the Crown; nor impose or augment

[1] *The Government of England*, I, 288.
[2] Since the enactment of the Parliament Bill of 1911, as has been observed, the assent of the Lords is not necessary. See p. 243.

taxes unless they be necessary for meeting the supplies which they have voted or are about to vote, and for supplying general deficiencies in the revenue. The Crown has no concern in the nature or distribution of the taxes; but the foundation of all Parliamentary taxation is its necessity for the public service as declared by the Crown through its constitutional advisers." [1]

Rules of the House of Commons. — " How can I learn the rules of the Commons? " is a question once put by an Irish member to Mr. Parnell. " By breaking them," was the philosophic reply. Representing, as it does, a long accumulation of deliberately adopted regulations, interwoven and overlaid with unwritten custom, the code of procedure under which the business of the House of Commons is conducted is indeed intricate. Lord Palmerston admitted that he never fully mastered it, and Gladstone was on many occasions an inadvertent offender against the " rules of the House." Prior to the nineteenth century the rules were devised, as is pointed out by Anson, with two objects in view: to protect the House from hasty and ill-considered action pressed forward by the king's ministers, and to secure fair play between the parties in the chamber and a hearing for all. Not until 1811 was the business of the Government permitted to obtain recognized precedence on certain days; but the history of the procedure of the Commons since that date is a record of (1) sharp reduction of the time during which private members may indulge in discussion of subjects or measures lying outside the Government's legislative program, (2) increasing limitation of the opportunity for raising general questions at the various stages of Government business, and (3) cutting down of the time allowed for discussing at all the projects to which the Government asks the chambers' assent.

The rules governing debate and decorum are not only elaborate but, in some instances, of great antiquity. In so far as they have been reduced to writing they may be said to consist of (1) " standing orders," of a permanent character, (2) " sessional orders," operative during a session only, and (3) " general orders," indeterminate in respect to the period of application. In the course of debate all remarks are addressed to the Speaker, and in the event that the floor is desired by more than one

[1] May, *Constitutional History of England.*

member it rests with the Speaker to designate, with scrupulous impartiality, who shall have it. When a " division " is in progress and the doors are closed, members speak seated and covered, but at all other times they speak standing and uncovered. A speech may not be read from manuscript, and the Speaker has the right not only to warn a member against irrelevance or repetition but to compel him to terminate his remarks. A member whose conduct is reprehensible may be ordered to withdraw and, upon vote of the House, may be suspended from service. Except in committee, a member may not speak twice upon the same question, although he may be allowed the floor a second time to explain a portion of his speech which has been misunderstood. Undue obstruction is not tolerated, and the Speaker may decline to put a motion which he considers dilatory.

Closure and the Guillotine. — For the further limitation of debate two important and drastic devices are at all times available. One is ordinary closure and the other is " the guillotine." Closure dates originally from 1881. It was introduced in the standing orders of the House in 1882, and it assumed its present form in 1888. It sprang from the efforts of the House to curb the intolerably obstructionist tactics employed a generation ago by the Irish Nationalists; but by reason of the increasing mass of business to be disposed of and the tendency of large deliberative bodies to waste time, it has been found too useful to be given up. " After a question has been proposed," reads Standing Order 26, " a member rising in his place may claim to move ' that the Question be now put,' and unless it shall appear to the Chair that such motion is an abuse of the Rules of the House, or an infringement of the rights of the minority, the Question ' that the Question be now put ' shall be put forthwith and decided without amendment or debate." Discussion may thus be cut off instantly and a vote brought on. Closure is inoperative, however, unless the number of members voting in the majority for its adoption is at least one hundred, or, in a standing committee, twenty.

A more effective device is that known as " closure by compartments," or " the guillotine." When this is employed the House, in advance of the consideration of a bill, agrees upon an allotment of time to the various parts or stages of the measure, and at the expiration of each period debate, whether concluded or not, is closed, a vote is taken, and a majority adopts that portion of the bill upon which the guillotine has fallen. In recent years this device has been regularly employed when an important Government bill is reserved for consideration in Committee of the Whole. Its advantage is economy of time, and also assurance that by a given date final action upon a measure shall have been taken. Prior to the middle of the nineteenth century liberty of discussion in the Commons was unrestrained, save by what an able authority on English parliamentary practice has termed " the self-imposed parliamentary discipline of the parties." The enormous change that has come about is attributable to two principal causes: congestion of business and the rise of obstructionism. The effect has been, among other things, to accentuate party differences and to involve occasional disregard of the rights of minorities.

Votes and Divisions. — When debate upon the whole or a portion of a measure ends a vote is taken. It may or may not involve, technically, a " division." The Speaker or Chairman states the question to be voted on and calls for the ayes and noes. He announces the apparent result and, if his decision is not challenged, the vote is so recorded. If, however, any member objects, strangers are asked to withdraw (save from the places reserved for them), electric bells are rung throughout the building, the two-minute sandglass is turned, and at the expiration of the time the doors are locked. The question is then repeated and another oral vote is taken. If any one still refuses to accept the result as announced, the Speaker orders a division. The ayes pass into the lobby at the Speaker's right and the noes into that at his left, and all are counted by four tellers designated by the Speaker, two from each side, as the members return to their places in the chamber. This method of taking a division has undergone but little change since 1836. Under a standing order of 1888 the Speaker is empowered, in the event that he considers a demand for a division dilatory or irresponsible, to call upon the ayes and noes to rise in their places and be counted; but there is rarely need to resort to this variation from the established practice. " Pairing " is not unknown; and when the question is one of political moment the fact is made obvious by the activity of the party " whips."

Procedure in the House of Lords. — The rules of procedure of the House of Lords are in theory simple, and in practice yet more so. Nominally, all measures of importance, after being read twice, are considered in Committee of the Whole, referred to a standing committee for textual revision, reported, and finally adopted or rejected. In practice the process is likely to be abbreviated. Few bills, for example, are actually referred to the revision committee. For the examination of such measures as seem to require it committees are constituted for the session, and others are created from time to time as need of them appears; but the comparative leisure of the chamber permits debate within the Committee of the Whole upon any measure which the members really want to discuss. Willful obstruction is almost unknown, so that there has never been occasion for the adoption of any form of closure. Important questions are decided, as a rule, by a division. When the question is put those members who desire to register an affirmative vote repair to the lobby at the right of the woolsack, those who are opposed to the proposal take their places in the corresponding lobby at the left, and both groups are counted by tellers appointed by the presiding officer. A member may abstain from voting by taking his station on "the steps of the throne," technically considered outside the chamber. Prior to 1868 absent members were allowed to vote by proxy, but this indefensible privilege was abolished by standing order in the year mentioned and is likely never to be revived.

SELECTED REFERENCES

A. L. Lowell, *The Government of England* (New York, 1909), I, Chaps. xii–xvi; S. Low, *Governance of England* (new ed., New York, 1914), Chaps. iv–v, vii; T. F. Moran, *Theory and Practice of the English Government* (rev. ed., New York, 1908), Chaps. xiii–xv; E. Jenks, *Government of the British Empire* (New York, 1918), Chap. vii; C. Ilbert, *Parliament* (New York, 1911), Chaps. iii, v–vii; W. R. Anson, *Law and Custom of the Constitution* (4th ed., London, 1909–1911), I, Chaps. iii–vi; J. Redlich, *Procedure of the House of Commons; a Study of Its History and Present Form*, 3 vols. (London, 1908); A. I. Dasent, *The Speakers of the House of Commons from the Earliest Times* (New York, 1911); M. MacDonaugh, *The Book of Parliament* (London, 1897); H. Graham, *The Mother of Parliaments* (London, 1910).

CHAPTER XIV

POLITICAL PARTIES: CONSTITUTIONAL ISSUES

I. THE PARTY SYSTEM

Importance and Uses of Party. — It may be set down as an axiom that political parties are not only an inevitable but a necessary and proper adjunct of any scheme of popular government. The moment the people set about deciding upon public policy, or electing representatives to formulate and execute such policy, differences of view appear; and out of these differences of view political parties arise. There is, of course, hardly anything that has been more abused than party organization and spirit. Party principles, party programs, party committees and managers, party treasuries, party propaganda — all have been brought into a certain disrepute; so that, as a writer has wittily remarked, while men may be willing to die for party, they seldom praise it.[1] None the less, political parties afford perhaps a clearer index than anything else of the political capacity and advancement of a nation. "The most gifted and freest nations politically are those that have the most sharply defined parties. . . . Wherever political parties are non-existent, one finds either a passive indifference to all public concerns, born of ignorance and incapacity, or else one finds the presence of a tyrannical and despotic form of government, suppressing the common manifestations of opinion and aspiration on the part of the people. Organized, drilled, and disciplined parties are the only means we have yet discovered by which to secure responsible government, and thus to execute the will of the people."[2]

The uses of political parties in a democracy are fivefold. First, they enable men who think alike on public questions to unite

[1] Low, *Governance of England* (new ed.), 119.
[2] Ray, *Introduction to Political Parties and Practical Politics*, 9–10.

in support of a common body of principles and policies and to work together to bring these principles and policies into actual application. Second, they afford a useful, if not indispensable, means by which men who have the same objects in view may agree in advance upon the candidates whom they will support for office, and recommend them to the general electorate. Third, parties educate and organize public opinion and stimulate public interest, by keeping the public informed upon the issues of the day through the press, platform, and other party agencies. Fourth, they furnish a certain social and political cement by which the more or less independent and scattered parts of the government (in so far as they are under the control of a single party) are bound together in an effective working mechanism. Fifth, the party system insures that the government at any given time will be subject to steady and organized criticism whose effect will usually be wholesome.

Government by Party in England. — In these and other ways parties contribute greatly to the carrying on of government in all democratic nations. Nowhere, however, does "government by party" prevail in the same degree as in England. To understand why this is so it is necessary merely to bring together certain facts, some of which are already familiar. The most important single feature of the English government as it now operates is the cabinet system; and the essentials of this system include (1) the appointment of the ministers from the party which at the given time controls the House of Commons, and (2) the retirement of these ministers whenever they cease to have the support of a parliamentary majority. This system arose out of the warfare of parties; it is inconceivable that it should ever have arisen without parties and party conflict. It is not, however, a matter merely of historical origins; parties are indispensable to the successful operation, and even to the continuance, of the system. The only kind of majority that has sufficient coherence and stability to make it dependable is a majority held together by the powerful ties of party. In the absence of parties the situation would be either that ministries would rise and fall with lightning rapidity because no organized force would be interested in keeping them in power, or that they would go on ruling indefinitely after they had got entirely out of harmony with the popular chamber. There would be no point to the retirement of a ministry, did not an opposing party stand ready to set up a ministry of a different sort and assume full power and responsibility.

The cabinet system and the party system are, therefore, intimately bound up together; indeed, they are but different aspects of the same working arrangement. In the United States parties stand outside the formal governmental system; until within recent decades their activities were not even subject to regulation by law. Many of the great party leaders and managers — for example, the chairmen of the national committees — are not public officials at all, and platforms are made by conventions whose members are usually drawn mainly from private life. In England, however, party works inside rather than outside the governmental system; the machinery of party and the machinery of government are one and the same thing. The ministers — at all events those who sit in the cabinet — are at the same time the working executive, the leaders in legislation, and the chiefs of the party in power. The majority in the House of Commons, which legislates, appropriates money, supervises and controls administration, and upholds the ministers as long as it is able, is for all practical purposes the party itself; while over against the ministry and its parliamentary majority stands the Opposition, consisting of influential exponents of the contrary political faith, who, in turn, lead the rank and file of their party organization, and are ready to take the helm whenever their rivals fall out of favor in the popular chamber.

Two-Party Organization. — Not only is it true that a responsible ministry involves government by party; in order to work smoothly such a ministerial system requires the existence of two great parties and no more — each, in the words of Bryce, " strong enough to restrain the violence of the other, yet one of them steadily preponderant in any given House of Commons." [1] Considerations of unity and responsibility demand that the party in power shall be strong enough to govern alone, or substantially so. Similarly, when it goes out of power, a party of at least equal strength ought to come in. Obviously, this must mean two great parties, practically dividing the electorate

[1] *American Commonwealth*, I, 287.

between them. Any considerable splitting up of the people beyond this point is likely to result in the inability of any single party to command a working majority, with the result that ministries will have to represent coalitions, which will lack unity and responsibility, and will be liable to be toppled over by the first adverse wind that blows. This, as will appear, is precisely the situation in France, Italy, and several other continental countries, which, having copied the outlines of the English cabinet system, are vastly handicapped in operating the scheme by the multiplicity of parties and party groups. Despite the rise forty years ago of the Irish Nationalist group, and later of the now rapidly growing Labor party, it was still true in Great Britain at the outbreak of the present war, as it had been since political parties first made their appearance there, that two leading party affiliations practically divided between them the allegiance of the nation. The defeat of one meant the triumph of the other, and either alone was normally able to govern independently if elevated to power.

II. PARTY HISTORY AND ORGANIZATION

Party History to 1874. — The seventeenth-century origins of English political parties, the relations of Whigs and Tories after the Revolution of 1688–1689, and the prolonged supremacy of the Whigs during the reigns of George I and George II have been mentioned elsewhere.[1] During the eighteenth century the cabinet system slowly took form, aided by the sharp contests of the Whig and Tory elements. The Tories reconciled themselves to the Hanoverian succession with much difficulty, and only after the fall of Lord North's coalition ministry in 1783 did they give up their old ideas and become as loyal to the new dynasty, and to the new cabinet and party system, as were their opponents. From the year mentioned until the resignation of the Duke of Wellington's ministry in 1830 they were almost uninterruptedly in power. In the first half of the nineteenth century the names " Whig " and " Tory," originally applied in abuse, were replaced by the milder titles " Liberal " and " Conservative "; and the change marked the growth of a calmer

[1] See p. 186.

tone in politics, while the appearance of a third, or "Radical," party, though it was ultimately absorbed by the Liberals, showed that the new class of intelligent artisans created by the industrial revolution was determined to have its share in the government of the country.[1]

With the exception of a few brief intervals, the Liberals held office from 1830 to 1874. Without trying to trace the party history of this great era of reform, we may simply take note of the characteristics which the two parties developed, as admirably summarized by an English historian. "The parties of which Gladstone (Liberal) and Disraeli (Conservative) were the chiefs were linked by continuous historical succession with the two great sections or factions of the aristocracy, or hereditary oligarchy, which ruled Great Britain in the eighteenth century. But each had been transformed by national changes since the Reform Bill. The Whigs had become Liberals, the Tories had become Conservatives. The Liberal party had absorbed part of the principles of the French Revolution. They stood now for individual liberty, laying especial stress on freedom of trade, freedom of contract, and freedom of competition. They had set themselves to break down the rule of the landowner and the Church, to shake off the fetters of Protection, and to establish equality before the law. Their acceptance of egalitarian principles led them to adopt democratic ideals, to advocate extension of the suffrage, and the emancipation of the working classes. Such principles, though not revolutionary, are to some extent disruptive in their tendency; and their adoption by the Liberals had forced the Tory party to range themselves in defense of the existing order of things. They professed to stand for the Crown, the Church, and the Constitution. They were compelled by the irresistible trend of events to accept democratic principles and to carry out democratic reforms. They preferred, in fact, to carry out such reforms themselves in order that the safeguards which they considered necessary might be respected. Democratic principles having been adopted, both parties made it their object to redress grievances; but the Conservatives showed a natural predisposition to redress those grievances which arose from excessive freedom of competition, the Liberals were the

[1] Jenks, *Government of the British Empire*, 98.

more anxious to redress those which were the result of hereditary or customary privilege. The harmony of the State consists in the equilibrium between the two opposing forces of liberty and order. The Liberals laid more stress upon liberty, the Conservatives attached more importance to order and established authority." [1]

Party History since 1874. — The next great period in party history, 1874 to 1905, was an epoch of Conservative ascendancy, broken by three intervals (aggregating nine years) of Liberal rule. The chief feature of the Conservative régime was the emphasis placed on foreign relations, working out into a decidedly imperialistic policy which found its logical culmination in the South African war of 1899-1902. From the point of view of strictly party history, however, interest in the period centers around the breach in the ranks of the Liberals in 1886 produced by Gladstone's first bill for Irish " home rule." A large section of the Liberal party, rather than support Home Rule, seceded. For a time it pursued an independent course under the name of the Liberal Unionist party. But eventually it was absorbed into the ranks of the Conservatives, where its influence became such that the older party name was superseded in current usage by the name " Unionist."

The Liberal party survived the shock, and even gained by its new degree of unity. For various reasons, its fortunes declined to a low ebb, however, in the late nineties, and at the opening of the present century the bi-party system seemed in danger of extinction. Then came a rapid Liberal recovery, caused partly by more energetic leadership, partly by popular reaction against Unionist measures connected with the South African war, and partly by division in the governing party upon the question of tariff reform. Foreseeing defeat, the Balfour ministry resigned, in December, 1905; and at the national elections of the following January, the Liberals, under the leadership of Campbell-Bannerman, won such a triumph that they and their allies, the Irish Nationalists and the Laborites, found themselves with a clear majority of 354 in the House of Commons.

From this date until the organization of the coalition cabinet, under stress of war, in 1915, the victorious party continued unin-

[1] S. Leathes, in *Cambridge Modern History*, XII, 30–31.

terruptedly in power;[1] and the period proved one of the most notable in the country's political history. In compliance with popular demand, and in fulfillment of its own campaign pledges, the new government embarked upon a sweeping program of social, economic, and political reconstruction. It stopped the alarming increase of the national debt and made provision for debt reduction at a rate equaled in but two brief periods since the middle of the nineteenth century. It reduced by half the burdensome taxes inherited from the South African war. It remodeled the army on lines that proved highly advantageous when the present war broke out. It procured legislation intended to allay Irish discontent. It carried important labor legislation, including an eight-hour working day in mines, a Labor Exchanges Act, and a Trades Disputes Act. It set up, in 1908, a nation-wide system of old-age pensions, and in 1911 a comprehensive scheme of sickness, invalidity, and unemployment insurance. Upon some of these matters party lines were not clearly drawn. But upon others there was sharp party controversy; and upon still others, including some that were vital to the Liberal program, action was made impossible by unyielding opposition of the Unionist majority in the House of Lords. A bill to abolish plural voting was thus defeated in 1906; a hotly contested measure for the undenominationalizing of the schools, also in 1906; a land values bill, in 1907; a bill for the better regulation of the liquor trade, in 1908; a bill for the reform of elections in London, in 1909; and, finally, the Finance Bill of 1909, whose rejection by the Lords led to a dissolution of Parliament and the ordering of national elections in January, 1910.

This appeal to the nation left the Liberals in power, but shorn of their great majority and dependent upon the help of their allies, the Nationalists and the Laborites. The fiscal reforms provided for in the rejected Finance Bill were made law in 1910. But there was no abatement of party strife; for now the Liberals determined upon the oft-discussed revision of the powers of the House of Lords, and after another national election, in December, 1910, which left the party quotas practically as before, the momentous Parliament Act was put upon the statute book amid controversy almost unparalleled in modern political history.

[1] Campbell-Bannerman was succeeded in the premiership by Asquith in 1908.

Resolved to take immediate advantage of their triumph, the victors started plural voting, Welsh disestablishment, and other contested bills upon the long but now not impossible road to final enactment. In the public mind, however, these measures, important though they were, were soon dwarfed by an issue which, after the contests over the tax reforms and the House of Lords, promptly occupied the center of the political arena, namely, Home Rule for Ireland. The salient facts concerning this question will be stated presently. For the moment it may simply be observed that when, in 1914, the Great War suddenly forced a party truce, the Home Rule question overshadowed all other issues, a Home Rule bill had just been enacted into law, civil war between the Protestant and Catholic elements in Ireland was impending, and Liberals and Unionists were struggling bitterly over a situation whose outcome both feared and neither could foresee.

Party Organization, National and Local. — In view of the antiquity of parties and of their supreme importance in the governmental system, it is not strange that they have developed elaborate machinery for holding their membership together, formulating principles and programs, and nominating and supporting candidates. Such organization is made the more imperative in England by the possibility that the country may be plunged into a campaign at any moment. The party cannot relax in "off years" as the American party does; it must stand at all times fully equipped for combat. More than any other leading people, the English live in a state of perpetual political discussion and unsettlement. It has been pointed out that the party system and the cabinet system arose simultaneously and in the closest possible relations. The earliest party organization was the cabinet, which, indeed, remains to this day the highest authority. The cabinet is, for all practical purposes, the party government, and as such it can brook no control by an outside organization. It, however, needs support; and to secure and maintain this support subordinate party machinery long ago came into existence. The party out of power has, it is true, no cabinet. But it has a group of recognized leaders who, if it were to come into power, would compose the cabinet; and for purposes of party management these men discharge substantially the same functions as if they were in ministerial office.

From the cabinet party organization gradually worked out through the ministry, and through Parliament, to the electorate. In Parliament the Government and Opposition leaders to this day supply all the party machinery that is needed except a small group of " whips " whose business it is, chiefly, to see to it that the party members are in their places when important votes are to be taken. The Government whips, usually four in number, are reckoned as ministers and are paid out of the public treasury, on the theory that it is their function to insure the presence of a quorum so that the appropriations may be voted. The Opposition whips, commonly three in number, are of course private members, named by the leaders, and unsalaried.

Outside of government circles, the earliest party organizations were local committees and societies which began to spring up shortly after the parliamentary reform of 1832. Their purpose was to help new voters register and to see that a full vote was got out at polling time. Both Liberals and Conservatives made extensive use of them; and the doubling of the electorate by the act of 1867 lent fresh impetus. The next step was to bring together these local committees in national federations. In this the Conservatives led by organizing in 1867 the National Union of Conservative and Constitutional Associations. The Liberals followed ten years later by establishing the National Liberal Federation. These two great nation-wide party associations developed on lines broadly similar. The governing body of the Conservative National Union came to be a Conference, meeting annually, and composed of two delegates elected by each dues-paying local association throughout the country, together with the officers of the Union itself. There is also, however, a Council composed in part of ex-officio, and in part of elected, members, and enlarged in 1906 to approximately two hundred persons in order to make it more representative. This Council acts nominally as the party's executive committee. But in point of fact the committee, and the Union itself, is a mere adjunct to the Central Office, composed of the parliamentary leaders and the whips at London and their salaried agents. It is this parliamentary organization, working directly through its own agents or indirectly through the local committees and leaders, that determines party policy, decides whether candidates shall be put in certain constituencies, and dictates who the candidates shall be, or at all events sends down a list of names from which selection must be made. The National Union has the *form* of a great governing party organization; so far as power goes, however, it is a sham.

The situation in the Liberal ranks is substantially the same. The National Liberal Federation, founded by Joseph Chamberlain, has an Executive Committee composed of the officers and some twenty other persons, a General Committee made up of representatives from local associations and all the Liberal members of Parliament (more than a thousand persons in all), and a Council which includes all the members of the two committees with additional delegates from local associations. Formerly the Council seriously undertook to construct platforms at its annual meetings, after the manner of American party conventions. This plan, however, proved embarrassing to the parliamentary leaders, and to-day the Council hears and ratifies, but never opposes, the program which these leaders draw up. The Federation serves a useful purpose in promoting local organization, distributing literature, and gathering information. But its formal acts are cut-and-dried. As among the Unionists, initiative and decision rest with the parliamentary leaders, the whips, and their agents, comprising the Central Office. Even the official leader of each party — the man who when the party comes into power will be premier — is chosen by the party members in Parliament, not by the national organization. The large funds placed at the disposal of the Central Office by the rank and file of the party are administered by the "chief whip."

III. PARTY COMPOSITION: CONSTITUTIONAL QUESTIONS

Liberals and Conservatives (Unionists). — Of the four political parties of Great Britain to-day one, the Irish Nationalist, is localized in Ireland and has for its single purpose the attainment of Irish home rule; another, the Labor party, is composed chiefly of workingmen (mainly members of trade-unions) and exists to promote the interests of the laboring masses; while the two older and more powerful ones, the Liberals and the Conservatives or Unionists, are broadly national in their constituencies and practically universal in the range of their principles and policies. It has been customary for these two major parties to engage in heated combat in Parliament and at the polls, and the casual spectator might suppose that they are separated by a very wide gulf. As a matter of fact, there is no difference between them that need prevent a flexible-minded man from crossing quite readily from one to the other. Even the names "Liberal" and "Conservative" have less significance than might be supposed. During the generation which began with the Reform Act of 1832 the Liberals, indeed, extended the franchise to the middle classes, reformed the poor law, overhauled the criminal law, introduced a new and improved scheme of municipal administration, started public provision for elementary education, enacted statutes to safeguard the public health, removed the disabilities of dissenters, and assisted in the overthrow of the protective régime. In general, they labored to bring the political system into accord with the new conditions caused by the industrial revolution and by the growth of democratic ideas. But if the Conservatives of the period 1830–70 played, in general, the rôle implied by their party designation, their attitude none the less was by no means invariably that of obstructionists; and in the days of the Disraelian leadership they became scarcely less a party of reform than were their opponents. Beginning with the Reform Act of 1867, a long list of progressive, and even revolutionizing, measures must be credited to them; and in late years they and the Liberals have vied in advocating old-age pensions, factory legislation, accident insurance, housing laws, and many other kinds of advanced and remedial governmental action. The differences which separate the two parties are not so much those of principle as those of means or, at the most, of tendencies. It is a claim of the Liberals that they are the more democratic, the more willing to trust the people, the more devoted to the interests of the masses — that they seek the best interest of the working classes from conviction, while their opponents do so only from the desire for votes; but the Unionists enter a strong and, to a degree, plausible denial. It used to be a theory of the Liberals, too, that they fostered peace and economy with more resoluteness than their rivals, and that the Unionists stood for a more aggressive, and even menacing, attitude abroad. There is some historical ground for these assertions. Yet the policy pursued in respect to these matters is likely to be determined, year in and year out, far more by the circumstances that arise and by the temperament of individual ministers than by any deliberate or permanent principle of party. Undoubtedly the Liberals have had more regard for the peculiar interests of Scotland, Wales, and especially Ireland; yet even here the difference is not as great as is often supposed.

Both parties as constituted to-day possess substantial strength in all parts of the kingdom except Ireland, the Liberals being in the preponderance in Scotland, Wales, and northern England, and the Conservatives in the south and southwest. Within the Conservative ranks are found much the greater portion of the people of title, wealth, and social position; nearly all of the clergy of the Established Church, and some of the Dissenters; a majority of the graduates of the universities and of members of the bar, most of the prosperous merchants, manufacturers, and financiers; a majority of clerks and approximately half of the tradesmen and shopkeepers; and a very considerable mass, although not in these days half, of the workingmen. During the second half of the nineteenth century the well-to-do and aristocratic Whig element in the Liberal party was drawn over, in the main, to the ranks of the Conservatives, and to this day the Liberal party contains but a small proportion of the rank and wealth of the kingdom. It draws its strength preëminently from the middle and popular classes.

Recent Party Issues : Miscellaneous Constitutional Questions. — Leaving out of account questions pertaining to foreign relations and to the armed forces of the nation, which in the main are discussed and decided on a non-partisan basis, three great groups of issues may be said to have furnished fuel for controversy between the major parties during the decade preceding the war. The first comprised questions of a constitutional nature; the second, questions of an economic character; and the third, questions of a broadly social bearing. Few, if any, of the issues to be mentioned under these heads have ever been settled. The war crowded some out of the public attention; it increased the urgency of others; all will loom up again after peace is made, perhaps in new guises, but demanding — along with the scores of intricate problems raised by the war itself — the most thoughtful consideration and candid discussion by the leaders and members of all party groups.

Of constitutional questions, two have already been explained, namely, the reform of the House of Lords and the reconstruction of the electoral system. The first has been preëminently a party question. The impetus of the reform movement was supplied by the desire of the Liberals to end the intolerable situation caused by the perpetual dominance of the upper chamber by the Unionists. The Unionists themselves, perceiving that changes were inevitable, proposed various plans for the reconstruction of the chamber on a more popular basis. But the Liberals preferred to get closer to the root of the matter by limiting the power of the Lords to obstruct legislation carried in the lower chamber. This they did in the Parliament Act of 1911. Circumstances have never been favorable since 1911 for the further action promised by this measure with a view to popularizing the upper house. But the question remains; and, notwithstanding the agreement of the parties upon the general ends to be sought, there is likely to be sharp controversy over means and methods whenever the subject shall be taken up.

Throughout the decade the problem of electoral reform absorbed increasing attention. It was not wholly a party question; upon the enfranchisement of women, for example, neither party was able to take a clear stand. But the Liberals were interested mainly in manhood suffrage and the abolition of the plural vote; their opponents talked most about a redistribution of seats. As has been explained, the stress of war unexpectedly forced a general overhauling of the electoral system.[1] To a degree, the task was carried out on non-partisan lines. On certain matters, however, — notably a plan to introduce the principle of proportional representation in the election of some county and borough members — party controversy flared up in a fashion to jeopardize the entire project.

[1] See p. 231.

This plan of proportional representation, to which the Unionist majority in the House of Lords is deeply attached, is likely to become a leading issue between the parties. Even the suffrage is not entirely settled. The National Union of Woman Suffrage Societies has officially announced its purpose to work for the lowering of the age qualification for female voters in parliamentary elections from thirty to twenty-one, thus establishing full equality with men. Inasmuch as this would mean that woman voters would be in a majority throughout the country by about two millions, there will be determined opposition. The question may or may not take on a party aspect.

Incidental mention has been made of the referendum as a political issue. In both parties the idea has slowly developed that Parliament should refrain from drastic changes in the governmental system unless it has a clear mandate from the nation to make them. From this idea it is but a step to the suggestion, — which was first offered officially by Mr. Balfour as leader of the Opposition in the House of Commons during the crisis of 1910, — that *all* great questions shall be referred to the electorate, as a matter of course, and by some fixed process. The Unionist party as a whole has never taken a stand for the referendum as applied to ordinary legislation, but is firmly committed to it as applied to constitutional questions. Individual Liberals think well of the plan; but the party as a whole is not favorably inclined. The difference between the parties on the point is, of course, one of degree rather than of principle.

Irish Home Rule, 1800–1905. — The fiercest party strife of recent decades has centered about another constitutional question, namely, Irish home rule. There has never been a time since the conquest of Ireland by the English in the twelfth century when there was not an " Irish question " of considerable seriousness. By 1850 the question presented three main phases. The first was religious. Descendants of Scotch and English settlers, grouped mainly in five northern and northeastern counties of the province of Ulster, were Protestants (Episcopalians or Presbyterians); the remainder of the population — fully three-fourths — was almost solidly Catholic. Yet the Protestant " Church of Ireland " was the established church throughout the island, to whose support all of the people had to contribute. The second aspect of the question was agrarian. A long series of conquests and confiscations had brought almost all of the land into the hands of English proprietors, and the once independent and prosperous natives had sunk to the level of a poverty-stricken peasantry, living as tenants on the great estates, and enjoying scarcely any rights as against the powerful landlords. The third difficulty was political, arising out of the fact that the island had lost its earlier autonomy and was now ruled from London practically as a crown colony.

The religious grievance was, in the main, removed in 1869 by an act disestablishing and disendowing the Protestant " Church of Ireland "; and the land situation was slowly improved by legislation begun in 1870 and carried forward, by both Liberals and Conservatives, until the present day. The problem of government proved more baffling. As has been explained, Ireland had a separate parliament until 1800, but lost it in that year by acts passed concurrently by the Irish and British parliaments joining the lesser country with England and Scotland in the United Kingdom of Great Britain and Ireland.[1] From the outset the Irish people felt no enthusiasm for the arrangement; and when it became apparent that their interests would suffer at the hands of the united parliament, they bitterly regretted the step that had been taken. Under the leadership of Daniel O'Connell, a peaceful " home rule " movement was set on foot, with a view mainly to the repeal of the Act of Union. The effort was suppressed in 1843 by the authorities; whereupon various insurrectionary movements were launched, with equal lack of success. A new chapter was opened in 1870 by the establishment of a Home Rule Association; for, under the masterful leadership of Charles Stewart Parnell, this organization crystallized sentiment throughout the Catholic portions of the country and built up a new Nationalist party, which in 1874 was able to return to the House of Commons a quota of fifty-nine members. It is this party, mainly, that through all succeeding years has fought the Home Rule battle.

Obviously, the success of the movement was conditioned upon the support of one or the other of the two great English parties. Until the nineteenth century was far advanced, no such support

[1] See p. 187.

was forthcoming. But in 1886, the leader of the Liberals, Mr. Gladstone, was converted to the cause, perhaps in the first instance mainly because his party needed the support of the Nationalist members. Upon becoming prime minister, the new champion brought in a bill setting up a separate parliament at Dublin and withdrawing Irish representation altogether from the House of Commons at Westminster. The measure failed to pass in the Commons, and it permanently disrupted the Liberal party. But the major portion of the party, which remained faithful to Gladstone's leadership, now accepted Home Rule as one of its cardinal tenets; and when, in 1893, Gladstone's last ministry brought in another bill on the subject, the cause met failure only by reason of an overwhelming vote against it by the Unionist majority in the House of Lords. During the ensuing decade of Unionist rule (1895-1905) the question was in abeyance. There was much excellent legislation for Ireland; but the party was unalterably opposed to Home Rule.

Irish Home Rule since 1905. — When the Liberals regained power it was assumed that, sooner or later, they would revive the efforts of 1886 and 1893. That they did not do so for several years was due to the disinclination of the leaders to jeopardize the party's position, to the vast majority in the House of Commons which relieved the party of any need of aid from the Nationalists, and to informal pledges made upon taking office that a Home Rule bill would not be introduced in the parliament elected in 1906. In the course of time the situation changed completely. The parliamentary elections of 1910 stripped the Asquith ministry of its huge majority and left it absolutely dependent upon the votes of the Nationalist group. The latter was duly appreciative of its new importance, and spared no effort to impress upon the Liberal leaders that the price of its support would be a Home Rule bill. Furthermore, whereas formerly such a measure would have been certain to be defeated in the House of Lords, the Parliament Act of 1911 opened a way for its eventual enactment regardless of Unionist opposition. The upshot was that in 1912 the premier introduced a Government of Ireland Bill whereby Ireland, while retaining 42 representatives in the House of Commons at Westminster, was to receive limited rights of self-government, with an elective bi-

cameral parliament — a Senate of 40 members and a House of
Commons of 164 members — at Dublin. The chief executive
would continue to be the lord lieutenant, the king's personal
representative; but he would govern through ministers responsible to the Dublin parliament.

The measure was supported by the Liberals, by the Labor party
(which cared little for Home Rule as such, but wanted the question settled so that social and industrial problems might command
attention), and by the bulk of the Irish Nationalists;[1] and the
Government sought to commend it to the country by putting it
forward as (1) a measure to meet the widely recognized need
of relieving congestion in Parliament by decentralizing both
legislation and administration, and (2) a step toward a reorganization of the entire United Kingdom on federal lines,
involving eventually a parliament for Scotland, and possibly
one for Wales, as well as one for Ireland. The Unionists were
solidly opposed to the bill; and in the five Protestant, Unionist
counties of Ulster opposition arose of a peculiarly spectacular
and menacing character. The Ulster protest was based upon
both economic and religious considerations — upon the fear of
the industrial elements that they would be subjected to undue
taxation by the peasant majority, and upon the apprehension
that the Protestant minority would be oppressed by the Catholic
majority. Countenanced, if not encouraged, by the Unionists
in England, the Ulsterites held excited mass-meetings, signed
solemn covenants never to submit to an Irish parliament, drew
up plans for a provisional government, and made active preparations for a war of resistance.

Twice in the earlier months of 1913 the bill passed the House
of Commons and was rejected in the House of Lords. In May,
1914, it was passed a third time in the lower chamber, although
not until a compromise had been reached whereby the bill was
to be amended before actually going into effect. The details of
this compromise were being worked out when, suddenly, the
scene was completely altered by the outbreak of the Great War.
Political animosities were buried overnight, and Parliament
turned its attention to legislation deemed immediately necessary,

[1] A small group — the so-called Independent Nationalists — opposed the bill
because of certain of its provisions, relating chiefly to finance.

leaving ultimate settlements to a more favorable day. As to Ireland, the Government declared that it would never impose Home Rule on Ulster by force, promised that the Home Rule Act should not take effect for a year (or until the end of the war), and pledged the passage meanwhile of some kind of amending act. Amid dramatic scenes, this program was accepted in both houses; and on September 17, 1914, the long-awaited Government of Ireland Act received the royal assent.[1]

During the first year of the war this status of the matter was undisturbed. But in the spring of 1916 various insurrectionary tendencies came to a head in an uprising of the radical republican elements composing the Sinn Fein ("ourselves alone") Society, who proclaimed the right of Ireland to national independence, set up a provisional republican government at Dublin, and threatened to involve the entire country in civil war. After hard fighting, the rebellion was crushed by British troops, and summary punishment was meted out to the leaders. The Nationalists — whose desire was home rule, rather than independence — disapproved of the course of the radicals. Yet when successive plans of the Government relative to the taking effect of the Home Rule Act failed to be carried out, they formally demanded (March 7, 1917) the immediate execution of the measure as " proof of Britain's sincerity in championship of small nations and democracy." Although the Nationalist leaders avowed the purpose to oppose the Government " by every means " if their demand was not met, and notwithstanding the steady growth of the Sinn Fein movement, the new War Cabinet refused to comply.

Various fresh proposals having failed, an Irish convention was assembled at Dublin, July 25, on suggestion of the Government, to work out a plan. The intention was that the gathering should be representative of all parties; but the Sinn Feiners refused to take part, preferring to hold a convention of their own, at which they drew up a constitution for an independent Irish republic. The report of the loyalist convention, made public April 12, 1918, tried to reconcile conflicting interests by a

[1] It will be observed that the House of Lords did not actually pass the bill; so that the measure became law in conformity with the terms of the Parliament Act of 1911.

scheme for immediate Home Rule with particular privileges of representation for Ulster. But both the extreme Unionists and the extreme Nationalists presented minority reports which showed that no real settlement had been reached. At this juncture the controversy was raised to a new pitch by Lloyd George's proposal to introduce Home Rule and conscription simultaneously. A conscription bill was actually passed by the House of Commons. But the opposition, not only of Irishmen of all groups, but of the majority of the premier's own party, was so bitter that volunteering was substituted for conscription. Matters fell back into their former status, and the fate of Home Rule became as uncertain as before. It is widely felt that the Government of Ireland Act as passed in 1914 will never be put into effect. But it is reasonably certain that the essential purposes of it will be realized without much delay when international peace shall have been restored.

SELECTED REFERENCES

A. L. Lowell, *The Government of England* (New York, 1909), I, Chaps. xxiv–xxxi, II, Chaps. xxxii–xxxvii; Ibid., *Public Opinion and Popular Government* (New York, 1913), Chaps. v–viii; Low, *Governance of England* (new ed., New York, 1914), Chap. vii; T. E. May, *Constitutional History of England*, continued by F. Holland (London, New York, 1912); C. J. H. Hayes, *British Social Politics* (Boston, 1913), Chap. ix; Ibid., *Political and Social History of Modern Europe* (New York, 1916), Chap. xxii; S. Low and S. C. Sanders, *Political History of England, 1837–1901* (London, 1907); J. A. R. Marriott, *England since Waterloo* (London, 1913); M. Ostrogorski, *Democracy and the Organization of Political Parties*, 2 vols. (London, 1902); A. V. Dicey, *Lectures on the Relation between Law and Public Opinion in England during the Nineteenth Century* (2d ed., London, 1914); H. Belloc and G. Chesterton, *The Party System* (London, 1911); H. Cecil, *Conservatism* (London, 1912); L. T. Hobhouse, *Liberalism* (London, 1911); W. L. Blease, *Short History of English Liberalism* (London, 1913); R. S. Watson, *The National Liberal Federation* (London, 1907); W. S. Churchill, *Liberalism and the Social Problem* (London, 1909); E. Childers, *The Framework of Home Rule* (London, 1911); E. Barker, *Ireland in the Last Fifty Years* (London, 1917); F. H. O'Donnell, *History of the Irish Parliamentary Party*, 2 vols. (London, 1910).

CHAPTER XV

POLITICAL PARTIES: ECONOMIC AND SOCIAL ISSUES

I. ECONOMIC AND SOCIAL QUESTIONS

Tariff and Taxation. — The general economic and social reconstruction which will follow the return of peace will be of engrossing interest; and without doubt many great party issues — some new, some merely in new guises — will arise out of it. For present purposes it must suffice to call attention to a half-dozen great economic and social questions, which were at the same time *party* questions, in the years preceding the war. Of economic questions, three were perhaps of chief importance: tariff reform, including colonial preference; taxation; and land reform. The tariff question arose out of a reaction which set in among the Unionists fifteen or twenty years ago against the prevailing system of free trade. Protective tariffs were long ago abolished, by a series of measures dating from the repeal of the Corn Laws in 1842-1849, and carried mainly by the Liberal party. Some interests which stood longest by the protective principle never really underwent a change of heart; and toward the close of the last century the decline in agricultural prices and in industrial profits — coupled with the solitariness of the position which Great Britain as a free-trade nation was compelled to occupy — suggested to many people that the free-trade system ought to be abandoned. In 1903, Joseph Chamberlain, a leading member of the Unionist cabinet, came out for a new tariff system, with two main features: (1) duties on imported foodstuffs, so arranged as to give the products of the British colonies an advantage in rates over those of foreign countries, and (2) duties on imported manufactures to protect British industries against the " unfair competition " of foreign industries. The plan attracted wide attention. Chamberlain resigned in order to give his entire time to advocating his proposals before the country. A Tariff Reform League was organized, and an unofficial Tariff Commission was set to work gathering statistics and preparing reports. The Unionist party was rent asunder on the question, and naturally the Liberals, who assumed with eagerness the rôle of defenders of England's "sacred principle" of free trade, made much capital out of the situation. Indeed it greatly helped them recover power in 1905. Thenceforward until 1914 the question steadily increased in importance as a political issue. The mass of Unionists were gradually won over, and the proposals were fully incorporated into the program of the party; the Liberals stood steadily by free trade; and at the outbreak of the Great War the nation seemed to be permanently, and not very unevenly, divided upon the issue. Since accepting the plan as a party tenet the Unionists had never been in power; but the presumption was that if raised to office they would incorporate in their first budget the fundamentals of their new — or, more accurately, their revived — faith.

It has been remarked by a leading writer that the Unionist party is perhaps chiefly to be distinguished from its leading rival by its benevolent attitude toward certain great interests, of which one is the large landholders.[1] To defray the costs of army reorganization, naval construction, old age pensions, public education, and other great enterprises, vast increases of revenue long ago became imperative. The general fact was recognized by both parties, but upon the mode of obtaining the additional money they were sharply disagreed. The Unionist idea was to tax imports, thereby obtaining revenue while also protecting English agriculture and industry. The Liberal idea was rather to employ income taxes rising in rate as the income grew larger, to make new valuations of land and impose increased taxes upon these values (especially upon unearned increments), and to lay heavy imposts upon inheritances, as well as on motor cars, spirits, and other luxuries — in short, to throw the tax-burden, in far greater measure than hitherto, upon the rich, and especially upon the landlords. This was the purport of the famous Lloyd George budget of 1909; and it was on that account that the Unionist House of Lords refused to pass the finance bill until after its proposals had been submitted to the electorate. In

[1] Lowell, *The Government of England*, II, 120.

successive budgets to 1914 the Liberal ideas were carried out extensively, although not completely; and at the outbreak of the war the parties were as far apart as ever upon the justice and expediency of what had been done. The Unionists still looked to customs duties as a more desirable source of revenue.

Other Economic and Social Questions. — A closely related question which was on the point of becoming an important party issue when the war relegated it to temporary obscurity is that of land reform. The land situation in recent decades has presented many unsatisfactory features: only about twelve per cent of the arable acreage is cultivated by owners; most of the remainder, together with a vast amount of undeveloped land, belongs to rich landlords, who often own whole villages; over sixty per cent of the adult agricultural laborers a few years ago were receiving less that 18*s.* ($4.50) a week; in a half-century the rural population has declined by more than a half-million; though formerly self-sufficing, the country on the eve of the war was producing not more than one-ninth of the wheat consumed within its borders. To the problem thus raised, two principal solutions have been proposed. The Unionist idea has been, in the main, to stimulate agriculture and raise rural wages by protective duties on imported foodstuffs. The Liberal plan has been rather to reach this end by direct and drastic reconstruction of the conditions of land ownership and of rural employment. A Small Holdings and Allotments Act, passed in 1907, made a beginning by enabling thrifty persons to acquire and gradually pay for small tracts of ground. Plans announced by Lloyd George in the winter of 1913–1914 were much more ambitious. They looked to the creation of a ministry of lands, with a large staff of agents to protect the interests of the farm laborer; they involved the reclamation of waste or unused land and the rapid extension of small holdings; and they laid fresh emphasis on accurate valuation as a requisite to equitable taxation. The war cut short a spirited discussion of this great program; but the problem is one of the most serious that England will have to face in coming years. Whenever taken up again, it is likely to become a political issue, since the landholding interests are closely identified with the Unionist party.

The land problem has, of course, extremely important social

bearings; and the attention given it is but one of numberless illustrations of the tendency in recent times to emphasize issues relating to social legislation and reform. From 1905 to 1914 the Liberals used their power mainly to improve the condition of the common man — to protect him against disease, overwork, poverty, unemployment, and accident; to enable him to join more freely with his fellows in trade-unions and other societies; to make better provision for the education of his children; to transfer from his shoulders to those of the rich a considerable share of the burden of public taxation. During these years the Unionists, although differing widely from the governing party upon the nature and methods of such reforms, professed to be no less devoted to the same general end. The Labor party (to be described presently) existed for no other purpose than the promotion of legislation on social and industrial subjects. Among social questions that once stirred sharp party controversy and are certain to come up again are the disestablishment of the Church and the discontinuance of aid from public taxes to schools controlled by sectarian, rather than public, authorities. The Established Church is a bulwark of the Unionist party, while the Non-Conformists, or Dissenters — Methodists, Baptists, Presbyterians, etc. — are to be found mainly in the Liberal ranks. Hence the Unionists opposed a great education bill of 1906, which would have left without public support thousands of schools under Established Church control, and brought about its defeat in the House of Lords. Similarly, they opposed a measure for the disestablishment of the Church in Wales, although in this case the Government was able in 1914, by taking advantage of the Parliament Act, to attain its object.

II. LABOR IN POLITICS

Trade-Unionism and Socialism. — It remains to tell something of the origins, nature, and purposes of a minor, but rapidly growing party — the party of organized labor. As constituted to-day, the Labor party is a product of the twin forces of trade-unionism and socialism. The one, it may be said broadly, has supplied the organization and the funds; the other, the energy and the spirit. Trade-unions, as every one knows, are organizations of workers in particular crafts intended to promote collective bargaining with employers and other concerted action in the laborers' interest. They began to appear in England during the earlier stages of the industrial revolution, and in the nineteenth century they gained control of most of the important industries. Their legal status was always a source of controversy. The earlier restraints of law upon labor combinations were largely abolished in 1871-1876. But in 1901 violent discontent was aroused by a decision handed down by the House of Lords (acting in its judicial capacity) in the Taff Vale case recognizing the right of employers to collect damages from trade-unions for injuries arising from strikes. In 1906 the Liberals rewarded the labor elements for their support by passing a Trade Disputes Act practically exempting the unions from legal process. Again, in the Osborne Judgment of 1909 the House of Lords put pressure on the unions by ruling that they could not legally collect compulsory contributions for the support of labor members of the House of Commons; and once more the Liberals saved the day for their allies, first by the act of 1911 providing salaries for all members of the popular branch of Parliament, and later by a new Trade-Union Act of 1913 which permits trade-union funds to be used for political purposes in so far as they represent contributions made voluntarily for these purposes. The Trade-Union Congress, which holds annual meetings for the consideration of political and industrial questions, represents at the present time approximately three million unionists; and since 1899 there has been a General Federation of Trade-Unions, whose functions are chiefly financial, and which has a membership somewhat exceeding one million, in part duplicating that of the Congress.

Forty years ago men freely predicted that socialism would never take root among the English people. But in point of fact England has of late been hardly less stirred by socialist agitation than Germany and France, and the spirit and ideals of socialism have been injected into parliamentary debates, and even into national and local legislation, quite as prominently as in any of the continental states. The number of organized socialists in the country has never been large; even to-day it does not exceed fifty thousand. But there are many men and women who are thoroughgoing socialists, yet not members of any socialist party or society, and multitudes of others whose minds are saturated with socialist ideas who, however, do not call themselves by the name. The oldest socialist organization of importance is the British Socialist party, which, founded in 1880 as the Social Democratic Federation, maintained absolute independence until 1916, when, with a net numerical strength of only ten thousand, it entered into affiliation with the Labor party. The most famous socialist organization is the Fabian Society, established in 1883, and having a present membership of less than three thousand, but including a long list of scholars, writers, clergymen, and other men of achievement and influence. The most prominent politically of socialist organizations is the Independent Labor party, organized in 1893 as a result of the first serious effort to unite the forces of socialism and labor. This party, whose membership to-day is about thirty thousand, eventually attained a certain amount of success; at the elections of 1906, when the tide of radicalism was running strong, seven of its candidates and sixteen of its members were elected to the House of Commons. It has always been too aggressively socialist, however, to attract the mass of laboring men.

The Labor Party: Composition and Character. — As the nineteenth century drew to a close strong need was felt in labor circles for a broadly based party which should carry on political activities in behalf of labor precisely as the Trade-Union Congress and its subsidiaries carried on activities of a financial and industrial character. This need was met by the organization of the present Labor party. The Trade-Union Congress of 1899, meeting at London, caused to be brought into existence a group of representatives of all coöperative, trade-union, socialist, and working-class organizations that were willing to share in an effort to increase the representation of labor in Parliament. This body held its first meeting at London in February, 1900, and an organization was formed in which the ruling forces were the politically inclined, but non-socialistic, trade-unions. The object of the affiliation was declared to be " to establish a distinct labor group in Parliament, who shall have their own whips and agree upon their own policy, which must embrace a readiness to coöperate with any party which for the time being may be engaged in promoting legislation in the direct interest of labor."

The growth of the new organization was rapid. At the elections of 1906 fifty-one candidates were put in the field, and twenty-nine were elected — forming by far the largest labor group that had as yet appeared on the floor of the Commons. The Liberals now had a majority sufficiently large to make them entirely independent. Yet they were under obligation to the labor elements for past support, and by past pledges, and, furthermore, many of them were not opposed to the more moderate labor demands. Consequently, the political "revolution" of 1906 became the starting point in a new era of labor legislation and labor relief, whose earliest important development was, as has been pointed out, the adoption of the Trades Disputes Act of 1906.

After its great victory the Labor Representation Committee, having attained its immediate object of creating a distinct representation of labor in Parliament, dropped its unassuming name and took that of "Labor party." The constitution of the organization was overhauled, and candidates elected to Parliament were required to agree to be guided completely by the decisions of the party, arrived at in its annual congresses, at least in matters related to the objects for which the party exists. Through its elected central committee the party approves the candidates put forward by the local unions and assists in bringing about their election. Within Parliament the party is compactly organized. Outside, it is simply a loose federation of trade-unions, trades councils, local labor parties, socialist societies, and coöperative societies, having, in 1915, a total membership of somewhat over two millions. This flexibility of organization seems to be a main reason why the party has prospered beyond all other political combinations of labor in the country. An incidental, but extremely important, effect of such flexibility is that men of all social classes and all industrial connections belong to the party — scholars, writers, dramatists, artists, lawyers, teachers, physicians, clergymen, and even employers of labor, equally with the workmen of factory, shop, and farm.

Since 1908 there has been in progress a consolidation of the labor forces represented at Westminster. At the elections of

January and December, 1910, some seats were lost; but the number of labor representatives in the House of Commons since 1910 has fluctuated between forty-two and forty-five. From this point the Labor group occupied a position of power altogether disproportionate to its numerical strength. The Liberal government, having lost the huge parliamentary majority which it obtained in 1906, was utterly dependent upon the support of its allies, the Nationalist and Labor members. Naturally the balance of power thus enjoyed was freely turned to advantage in the promotion of desired legislation. At the same time, it is to be observed that the situation was exceptional, and that in the long run labor can expect to be politically powerful only in one of two ways — by using its votes under some consistent plan within the ranks of the older parties or by building up a third party of sufficient strength to combat its rivals on approximately even terms. The second of these alternatives, although not hopeless, presents great difficulties. The elements from which a great coördinate Labor party would have to be constructed are, and are likely to remain, fundamentally inharmonious, the principal source of friction being socialism. And, even if the tendencies to internal discord could be overcome, there would remain the fact that among the English people the bi-party system is solidly intrenched and that no third party has ever been able to prevent the dissipation of its strength through the continuous re-absorption of its membership into the ranks of the Government and the Opposition.

The New Labor Party and Its Program. — For a time after the Great War broke out the Labor group in Parliament maintained an unsympathetic, and even hostile, attitude toward England's part in the conflict. It regarded the war as the natural fruit of balance of power, secret diplomacy, and other prevailing international concepts and practices, and insisted that England should have remained neutral. When, however, the real nature of the struggle began to appear, sentiment shifted; and eventually full acceptance of the decision by which England had gone in, and full adhesion to the essential program of combat, was given. In the life of the Labor party, as indeed in that of every English organization and every individual Englishman, the years of war have been a period crowded with experience and rich in development. What the party hopes to be and to achieve after peace is restored may best be told at some length in the language of one of its most influential leaders, Arthur Henderson, who in 1915 entered the coalition cabinet as President of the Board of Education and was subsequently a member of Mr. Lloyd George's "war cabinet."

When the war ends, the Labour party, like every other, will be confronted with an unprecedented political situation. No comparison can be made between this situation and any that has arisen out of previous wars. The post-Napoleonic period, following the wars in which this country was involved for twenty years, provides the nearest parallel; but in every essential particular Labour stands to-day, both in relation to world-politics and to national affairs, on an altogether different footing from that of a century ago. The trade-union movement was then strangled by laws which made the combination of workmen, even for purposes of self-protection, illegal. Democracy was rendered abortive by scandalously restricted franchise which concentrated political power wholly in the hands of the landed aristocracy. Social conditions were atrocious. The people were the prey of the profiteering classes, who waxed rich out of the sufferings and privations of the poor.

A generation of political effort on the part of the people brought an extension of the franchise to the commercial and the middle classes, but added nothing to the power of democracy except the right to combine in trade-unions for certain limited purposes, and the privilege of "collective bargaining" with the employers. Everywhere the workers were in revolt against the intolerable conditions under which they were compelled to live and labor. Another generation had to pass before the workmen of the boroughs were enfranchised and a beginning could be made with the organization of political democracy on modern lines. . . . A backward glance at the history of the nineteenth century will show that the people have been steadily extending the range of their influence in politics and affairs, without any very clear notion of what they were doing or how the final stages in the conquest of political power by the organized democracy were to be surmounted. Democracy had to fight hard for every inch of ground it won. It was in the grip of mighty forces it had not learned how to control. It fought these forces blindly, confounding some that were, if properly used, beneficent, with those that were entirely malignant. . . . All this is of the past. The situation to-day is very different. Democracy is awake, and aware of its own power. It sees things in a better perspective, and realizes that at home and abroad the triumph of democratic principles in politics and industry and social life is a matter simply of wise and capable leadership and resolute and united effort on the part of all sections of the organized movement. There never was a bigger opportunity for democracy to achieve its main aims than the one which now offers. It is time that we should begin to think not only of the great social and economic changes that are to take effect in the coming period of reconstruction but of the methods and means of securing them. The war has proved to democracy that a dictatorship, whether with one head or five, is incompatible with its spirit and its ideals even in war-time. It has also revealed many serious defects in the structure of society. And it has shown the need for drastic change in the composition and organization of political parties. It is generally acknowledged that the old party system has irretrievably broken down. Evidence of this is afforded by the clamant call for new parties. The appearance upon the horizon of a National Party and a Women's Party, the probability of separate groups forming in Parliament around the personality of political leaders who have lost or are losing their grip upon the more or less coherent and strongly organized parties of pre-war days, are symptoms of this disintegration. Political power is about to be re-distributed, not only amongst the electors under the Franchise Bill,[1] but amongst the political parties in Parliament which will claim to represent the new democratic consciousness. Minor readjustments designed to adapt orthodox Liberalism or Unionism to the changing psychology of the electorate will not avail. A thoroughgoing transformation of the machinery of the parliamentary parties and a fundamental revision of their programmes are in my judgment not merely timely but necessary.

The Labour party, at any rate, has proceeded upon the assumption that reconstruction is inevitable. It has formulated a scheme which is deliberately designed to give the enfranchised millions full opportunity to express their political preferences in the choice of members to represent them in the Reconstruction Parliament which will have to deal with the vast problems arising out of the war. The outline of the new party constitution is now familiar to every attentive reader of the newspapers. It contemplates the creation of a national democratic party, founded upon the organized working-class movement, and open to every worker who labours by hand or brain. Under this scheme the Labour party will be transformed, quickly and quietly, from a federation of societies, national and local, into a nation-wide political organization with branches in every parliamentary constituency, in which members will be enrolled both as workers and as citizens, whether they be men or women, and whether they belong to any trade-union or socialist society or are unattached democrats with no acknowledged allegiance to any industrial or political movement. We are casting the net wide because we realize that real political democracy cannot be organized on the basis of class interest. Retaining the support of the affiliated societies, both national and local, from which it derives its weight and its fighting funds, the Labour party leaves them with their voting power and right of representation in its councils unimpaired; but in order that the party may more faithfully reflect constituency opinion it is also proposed to create in every constituency something more than the existing trades council or local labour party. It is proposed to multiply the local

[1] The Representation of the People Act, approved February 6, 1918. See p. 231.

organizations and to open them to individual men and women, both hand-workers and brain-workers, who accept the party constitution and agree with its aims. The individually enrolled members will have, like the national societies, their own representatives in the party's councils, and we confidently believe that year by year their influence will deepen and extend. The weakness of the old constitution was that it placed the centre of gravity in the national society and not in the constituency organization: it did not enable the individual voter to get into touch with the party . . . except through the trade-union, the socialist society, or the coöperative society. The new constitution emphasises the importance of the individual voter. It says to the man and woman who have lost or never had sympathy with the orthodox parties, "You have the opportunity now not merely of voting for Labour representatives in Parliament, but of joining the party and helping to mould its policy and shape its future."

Under the old conditions the appeal of the party was limited. It has seemed to be, though it never actually was, a class party like any other. It was regarded as the party of the manual wage-earners. Its programme was assumed, by those who have not taken the trouble to examine its whole propaganda, to reflect the views of trade-unionists not as citizens with a common interest in good government, but as workers seeking remedies for a series of material grievances touching hours of labor, rates of wages, conditions of employment. This misapprehension rests upon a too narrow definition of the term "Labour." On the lips of the earlier propagandists the word was used to differentiate between those whose toil enriched the community, and those who made no productive effort of any kind but lived idly and luxuriously upon the fruits of the labors of others. It is that differentiation we design to perpetuate in the title of the party. The Labour party is the party of the producers whose labor of hand and brain provides the necessities of life for all and dignifies and elevates human existence. That the producers have been robbed of the major part of the fruits of their industry under the individualist system of capitalist production is a justification for the party's claims. One of the main aims of the party is to secure for every producer his (or her) full share of those fruits — and to ensure the most equitable distribution of the nation's wealth that may be possible, on the basis of the common ownership of land and capital, and the democratic control of all the activities of society.

The practice of empirical politics, the effort to secure this or that specific reform, will not suffice; Labour lays down its carefully thought-out, comprehensive plan for the reconstruction of society, which will guarantee freedom, security, and equality. We propose, as a first step, a series of national minima to protect the people's standard of life. For the workers of all grades and both sexes we demand and mean to secure proper legislative provision against unemployment, accident, and industrial disease, a reasonable amount of leisure, a minimum rate of wages. We shall insist upon a large and practicable scheme to protect the whole wage-earning class against the danger of unemployment and reduction of wages, with a consequent degradation of the standard of life, when the war ends and the forces are demobilized and the munitions factories cease work. The task of finding employment for disbanded fighting men and discharged munitions workers we regard as a national obligation: we shall see to it that work is found for all, that the work is productive and socially useful, and that standard rates of wages shall be paid for this work. In the reorganization of industry after the war, the Labour party will claim for the workers an increasing share in the management and control of the factories and workshops. What the workers want is freedom, a definite elevation of their status, the abolition of the system of wage-slavery which destroyed their independence and made freedom in any real sense impossible. We believe that the path to the democratic control of industry lies in the common ownership of the means of production; and we shall strenuously resist every proposal to hand back to private capitalists the great industries and services that have come under government control during the war. This control has been extended to the importation and distribution of many necessary commodities — many of the staple foods of the people and some of the raw materials of industry. More than the great key industries and vital services have come under control; and we do not mean to loosen the popular grip upon them, but on the contrary to strengthen it.

In the field of national finance the Labour party stands for a system of taxation regulated not by the interests of the possessing and profiteering classes, but by the claims of the professional and housekeeping classes, whose interests are identical with those of the manual workers. We believe that indirect taxation upon commodities should not fall upon any necessity of life, but should be limited to luxuries, especially and principally those which it is socially desirable to extinguish. Direct taxation, we hold, upon large incomes and private fortunes is the method by which the greater part of the necessary revenue should be raised; we advocate the retention in some appropriate form of the excess profits tax; and we shall oppose every attempt to place upon the shoulders of the producing classes, the professional classes, and the small traders, the main financial burden of the war. We seek to prevent, by methods of common ownership and of taxation, the accumulation of great fortunes in private hands. Instead of senseless individual extravagances we desire to see the wealth of the nation expended for social purposes — for the constant improvement and increase of the nation's enterprises, to make provision for the sick, the aged, and the infirm, to establish a genuine national system of education, to provide the means of public improvements in all directions by which the happiness and health of the people will be ensured. One step in this direction will be taken when the manufacture and sale of intoxicating drink is no longer left to those who find profit in encouraging the utmost possible consumption. The party's policy in this matter asserts the right of the people to deal with the licencing question in accordance with the opinion of localities; we urge that the localities should have conferred upon them full power to prohibit the sale of liquor within their boundaries, or alternatively to decide whether the number of licences should be reduced, upon what conditions they may be held, and whether they shall be under private or any form of public control. In our relations to other people, whether those of our blood and tongue in the British Empire, or those of other races and languages, we repudiate the idea of domination and exploitation, we stand for the steady development of the idea of local self-government and the freedom of nations. On all these points and the problems underlying them, the Labour party lays down its general principles and policies; and from time to time Labour's representative assemblies will apply these principles to the problems of immediate and pressing importance, and formulate the programme which the electors will be invited to support. In opposition, and presently as we believe and hope in office, Labour will seek to build up a new order of society, rooted in equality, dedicated to freedom, governed on democratic principles.[1]

SELECTED REFERENCES

A. L. Lowell, *The Government of England* (New York, 1909), II, Chap. xxxiii; F. A. Ogg, *Economic Development of Modern Europe* (New York, 1917), Chaps. xix, xxiii; C. J. H. Hayes, *British Social Politics* (Boston, 1913), Chaps. i–viii, x; S. P. Orth, *Socialism and Democracy in Europe* (New York, 1913), Chap. ix; P. Alden, *Democratic England* (New York, 1912); C. Noel, *The Labour Party, What It Is, and What It Wants* (London, 1906); L. T. Hobhouse, *The Labour Movement* (3d ed., London, 1912); A. Henderson, *The Aims of Labour* (New York, 1918); A. W. Humphrey, *A History of Labour Representation* (London, 1912); S. and B. Webb, *History of Trade Unionism* (new ed., London, 1911); C. M. Lloyd, *Trade Unionism* (London, 1915); J. E. Barker, *British Socialism* (London, 1908); H. O. Arnold-Forster, *English Socialism of Today* (3d ed., London, 1908); B. Villiers, *The Socialist Movement in England* (2d ed., London, 1910); E. R. Pease, *History of the Fabian Society* (London, 1916); W. J. Ashley, *The Tariff Problem* (2d ed., London, 1910); S. Walter, *The Meaning of Tariff Reform* (London, 1911); W. Cunningham, *The Case against Free Trade* (London, 1911); C. Turnor, *Land Problems and National Welfare* (London, 1911); H. Harben, *The Rural Problem* (London, 1914); A. H. H. Mathews, *Fifty Years of Agricultural Politics* (London, 1915).

[1] *The Aims of Labour*, 17–26. For a detailed statement of the party's reconstruction proposals, see pages 91–108 of the same volume.

CHAPTER XVI

GREATER BRITAIN: THE SELF-GOVERNING COLONIES

Character of the Empire. — In the forefront of the group of nations that of late have fought in the cause of liberty and democracy stands the British Empire, wielding some degree of control over approximately one-fourth of the earth's habitable surface and also over one-fourth of the world's entire population — by far the most colossal political power known to history. Inasmuch as it is generally understood that the menace to democracy chiefly to be overcome in the war was the ambitions of militarist and conquering empires, some people, in all lands, have been troubled by the rôle assumed by, and even by the very existence of, this vast British dominion. Is not this huge Empire simply the greatest product of that spirit of aggression and conquest against which the free peoples are fighting? The Germans have been wont to describe it as a mighty, greedy tyranny, built up by fraud; to call loudly for Englishmen to release from bondage the millions of India before they talk about liberty; to declare the British naval supremacy a greater danger to the world than German military power could ever be.

Those who believe the British Empire an engine of tyranny have, however, been confronted in these past years with some facts that are difficult to explain away. As stated by an English scholar, writing in 1917, these facts are somewhat as follows: "Over a million volunteer soldiers have come from the great self-governing colonies of the British Empire without any compulsion being imposed upon them. The princes and peoples of India have vied with one another in their generous and spontaneous gifts to the cause, while Indian forces have fought gallantly in all parts of the world, and at the same time India has been almost denuded of British troops. That is not the sort of thing which happens when the masters of a tyrannical dominion find themselves fighting for their very life. Apart from the unhappy troubles in Ireland (which were the work of a small minority) and the rebellion in South Africa (which was promptly put down by the South African Dutch themselves), there has been no serious disturbance in all the vast realms of this Empire during the three years' strain of war. Even the most recently subdued of African tribes have shown no desire to seize this opportunity for throwing off ' the foreign yoke.' On the contrary, they have sent touching gifts, and offers of aid, and expressions of good will. It appears, then, that the subjects of this 'Empire' have, for the most part, no quarrel with its government, but are well content that it should survive." [1]

This describes the situation exactly. Speaking broadly, the peoples living under the British flag to-day are as prosperous, as contented, as free, and as jealous of their rights, as any other great group of peoples in the world. They are scattered all over the earth; they belong to almost every race; they represent every conceivable stage of culture; they have every possible economic interest; the proportion of people of European stock is hardly greater than it was a century and a half ago. Yet the ties that hold the Empire together have been proved infinitely stronger than even the optimists, in ante-war days, supposed them to be. The reasons why they are so cannot be fully considered here. They run the gamut of blood relationship, cultural connections, trade and business advantages, desire for protection, and what not. But at bottom is a great fact, with which we are concerned here, namely, that, on the whole, the British Empire has been, in the past hundred years, wisely, and even beneficently, governed. Great outlying dependencies have been transformed into what are to all intents and purposes free states; peoples upon whom it has not been deemed safe or wise to confer full rights of self-government have been given partial rights; peoples in a still more backward condition have been governed firmly but honestly, and usually to their own great advantage, by English administrators.

From the beginning England, in contrast with other expanding nations, permitted her colonists to have a voice in their government; and yet it was only by bitter experience that even

[1] Muir, *The Character of the British Empire*, 7.

she was made to see that colonial autonomy, far from being inconsistent with true imperial power, may be made its surest basis. It is interesting to note what a scholar (whom we have already quoted), writing from the English standpoint, has to say upon this subject. " When the outpouring of Europe into the rest of the world began, the British peoples alone had the habit and instinct of self-government in their very blood and bones. And the result was that wherever they went, they carried self-government with them. . . . In the eighteenth century, and even in the middle of the nineteenth century, Britain herself and the young nations that had sprung from her loins were almost the only free states existing in the world. It was because they were free that they throve so greatly. They expanded on their own account, they threw out fresh settlements into the empty lands wherein they were planted, often against the wish of the mother country. And this spontaneous growth of vigorous free communities has been one of the principal causes of the immense extension of the British Empire. Now one of the results of the universal existence of self-governing rights in the British colonies was that the colonists were far more prompt to resent and resist any improper exercise of authority by the mother country than were the settlers in the colonies of other countries, which had no self-governing rights at all. It was this independent spirit, nurtured by self-government, which led to the revolt of the American colonies in 1775, and to the foundation of the United States as an independent nation. In that great controversy an immensely important question was raised, which was new to human history. It was the question whether unity could be combined with the highest degree of freedom; whether it was possible to create a sort of fellowship or brotherhood of free communities, in which each should be master of its own destinies, and yet all combine for common interests. But the question (being so new) was not understood on either side of the Atlantic. Naturally, Britain thought most of the need of maintaining unity; she thought it unfair that the whole burden of the common defense should fall upon her, and she committed many foolish blunders in trying to enforce her view. Equally naturally, the colonists thought primarily of their own self-governing rights, which they very justly demanded should be increased rather than restricted. The result was the unhappy war, which broke up the only family of free nations that had yet existed in the world, and caused a most unfortunate alienation between them, whereby the cause of liberty in the world was greatly weakened. Britain learned many valuable lessons from the American Revolution. In the new Empire which she began to build up as soon as the old one was lost, it might have been expected that she would have fought shy of those principles of self-government which no other state had ever tried to apply in its oversea dominions, and which seemed to have led (from the imperialistic point of view) to such disastrous results in America. But she did not do so; the habits of self-government were too deeply rooted in her sons to make it possible for her to deny them self-governing rights in their new homes. On the contrary, she learnt, during the nineteenth century, to welcome and facilitate every expansion of their freedom, and she gradually felt her way towards a means of realizing a partnership of free peoples whereby freedom should be combined with unity. Its success (although it must still undergo much development) has been strikingly shown in the Great War." [1]

The Self-Governing Dominions: General Features. — On the basis of political status the far-flung lands composing the British Empire to-day — aside from the United Kingdom itself — fall into four main groups: (1) the self-governing dominions, (2) the crown colonies, (3) the protectorates, and (4) India, which, while partaking of the characteristics of a crown colony and of a protectorate, is neither, but is rather a "dependent empire," with internal organization and external relationships peculiar to itself. The self-governing dominions are five in number: the Dominion of Canada, the Commonwealth of Australia, the Union of South Africa, the Dominion of New Zealand, and the Colony of Newfoundland. Their aggregate area in 1914 was 7,500,000 square miles, or a little more than one-half of the entire Empire including India, — more than three-fourths if India be left out of the reckoning. Their total white population was about 15,000,000, as compared with 46,000,000 in the United Kingdom.

The student of government discerns at a glance two striking

[1] Muir, *The Character of the British Empire*, 9–12.

facts about these five great regions. The first is that, although they are parts of what custom compels us erroneously to call an Empire, they are, for all practical purposes, independent nations. The second is that all are, in everything but name, republics, — with parliaments elected on democratic suffrages and with responsible executives similar to the working executive in the mother country. They have their own flags, their own armies, their own navies; they amend their own constitutions and make their own laws, with a minimum of interference from London; they appoint their own officers (except the governors-general, whose functions are almost as purely formal as those of the English king); they levy their own taxes; they freely impose protective duties on imports from the mother country and from other parts of the Empire; they make no compulsory financial contributions to the mother country, not even to help pay the interest on indebtedness incurred generations ago in protecting these very colonial possessions; they are not required to contribute to the upkeep of the navy, which is still the great defender of them all; although technically " at war " whenever the United Kingdom is in that state, they are not obliged to send a man or a ship or a shilling. In short, their purely political connection with the mother country is extremely slight. Almost the only tangible evidence of it is their inability to send ministers and consuls of their own to foreign countries and to pursue an independent foreign policy. The right of Parliament to disallow their legislative acts, its right to legislate for them, and even the right of the Judicial Committee of the Privy Council to hear appeals from their courts, are fast becoming obsolete. Indeed, of late the dominions have been allowed to negotiate separate commercial treaties and other international agreements. In view of this increased control over foreign affairs, Canada, in 1909, established a new " ministry of external relations."

The Dominion of Canada. — Having observed these facts about the self-governing dominions in general, we may profitably look a little more closely into the form and character of the governments in three of the principal countries, Canada, Australia, and South Africa. Canada is of particular interest, not only because in both area and population it is the greatest of the dominions, but also because of its nearness to, and its close relations with, the United States. As might be expected, its governmental system affords many points of comparison and contrast with our own. The very first fact to be noted, indeed, is that, like the United States, but unlike England, Canada is organized on a federal plan; that is, the nation [1] is built of co-ordinate provinces, or states, which, while joined together for their common good, have also their own separate governments. In its present form the Canadian confederation dates from 1867, when, at the request of the colonists themselves, the parliament at London passed the British North America Act bringing together four formerly separate colonies — Quebec, Ontario, New Brunswick, and Nova Scotia — in the new "Dominion of Canada." As population spread westward in later decades other provinces were created by the Canadian parliament, very much as our own western states were admitted to the union by Congress; so that since 1905 the Dominion has consisted of nine provinces, besides the Yukon and Northwest territories.

Long before the act of union the original states had obtained representative government; and after 1840 the most advanced ones also got responsible government, *i.e.*, a system under which the ministries became responsible, as the ministry is in England, to the elected legislature. There was, therefore, no question when the plans for the new federation were drawn up as to the general form which the government should take. The English system was made the model; the American was drawn upon at certain points to round out the scheme, and especially to harmonize it with the federal principle. The essential features of the Dominion government can be presented briefly. The formal executive head is the governor-general, who is appointed in London, nominally by the king, but actually by the cabinet, and usually for five years. To him it falls to play substantially the rôle played in the mother country by the sovereign, with the difference that certain powers, *e.g.*, the veto, which have become obsolete in the royal hands are sometimes, although seldom, actually exercised by the colonial dignitary. The working

---

[1] It is convenient to employ this term, although obviously a self-governing dominion, being not independent, cannot be a *nation* in the meaning of international law.

executive is the group of men — 23 in number, in 1917 — comprising technically the privy council, but actually the cabinet, whose members get their places in precisely the same way that English cabinet officers get theirs; that is, the governor-general designates as premier the recognized leader of the majority party in the popular branch of Parliament, and the premier selects his colleagues and assigns them to their posts. Party solidarity, membership and leadership in Parliament, collective responsibility to the popular branch of Parliament, absence of the titular executive from cabinet meetings, the leadership of the premier, even the purely customary basis on which the cabinet system rests — all are exactly as in England; and there are two great opposing parties, Liberal and Conservative, which facilitate the working of the system, just as in the motherland.

Parliament consists of two houses, a Senate and a House of Commons. The Senate contains 96 members, Quebec and Ontario having 24 each, Nova Scotia and New Brunswick 10 each, and other provinces lesser quotas, to as low as three, in approximate proportion to population. It was, of course, suggested when the plan of government was under preparation that the senators should be elected by the people. But, mainly from fear that an elected upper house would encroach on the powers of the lower house, it was decided to give the power to appoint into the hands of the governor-general (in effect, the cabinet). Appointment is for life, although there are several ways, besides death and resignation, by which seats may be voluntarily or involuntarily vacated. Except for the familiar requirement that money bills shall be first considered in the lower chamber, the Senate has identical powers and functions with the House of Commons. Ordinarily, however, the chamber has been content to play the rôle of a diligent but unambitious revising body.

The House of Commons, like its counterpart in the mother country, consists of representatives chosen by the people in single-member districts, with the difference that in Canada there is, as in the United States, a reapportionment following every decennial census. To prevent the total membership from becoming too large, Quebec's quota (65) is stationary, and the quotas of all other provinces are increased or diminished so as to be in proper proportion to it. The allotment of 1914 gave

Ontario 82 seats, Nova Scotia and Saskatchewan 16 each, and other provinces lesser numbers, the total being 234. As in the United States, the suffrage is regulated by the state legislatures, and is, therefore, not uniform. But in seven of the nine provinces manhood suffrage prevails; in the other two — Nova Scotia and Quebec — there are small property or income qualifications. The maximum term is, as in England, five years; but dissolutions take place with sufficient frequency to reduce the average lifetime of a parliament to about four years. The House of Commons is easily the controlling branch of the legislature. All finance bills originate there; most important measures of other kinds are first submitted to it; it is the forum for political controversy, the chamber in which reputations are made and great policies determined. And it must be observed that the powers of the central government are in most directions greater than those of the federal government of the United States. Sixteen clauses of the North America Act define the powers of the provinces; twenty-nine are taken up with a description of those to be exercised by the federal parliament; furthermore, whereas in the United States the powers of the nation are limited and enumerated and those of the states broad and residual, in Canada all powers not exclusively vested in the provinces belong to the government at Ottawa.

Of the governments of the provinces it is impossible to speak, save to say that the nominal executive is a lieutenant-governor appointed by the governor-general (in effect, the Dominion cabinet) for five years; that this official has a cabinet council of four or five members which, under the leadership of a premier, comprises the working, responsible executive; that the legislatures, elected in all cases except two by manhood suffrage, consist also in all cases except two of but one house; that the cabinet system operates substantially as in the national government; and that, in short, the organization of a government at a provincial capital is as near a replica of the government at Ottawa as it can be made. Each of the provinces has its own code for the organization and administration of municipal affairs in counties, villages, towns, and cities. The main point of difference from the English local government system is the larger number of officers elected directly by the people.

The Commonwealth of Australia. — The history of Australia has been said to be as monotonous as the country's scenery. For students of political science, and of public affairs, however, the building of the great federal government which operates to-day in the remote island-continent is filled with interest and instructiveness. Nowhere in the world has English political genius had freer scope in the creation of a nation on virgin soil; nowhere — not even in the United States — have the most modern and radical conceptions of democracy been put in application so completely amidst a vast population and over a broad expanse of territory. The first civil government was set up in the country, in New South Wales, in 1823; and thereafter written constitutions, representative legislatures, and responsible executives were given the various colonies as rapidly as growth of population permitted. By 1860 there were five self-governing colonies (including the island of Tasmania); and a sixth was organized in 1890. Union under a federal government was suggested as early as the middle of the nineteenth century, but fifty years of discussion and experiment proved necessary before the colonies could come into agreement upon a plan. A scheme was at length made ready, in 1899, for the home government's consideration, and in the great Australia Commonwealth Act of the following year Parliament gave the project its assent. The opening day of the twentieth century was accordingly signalized by the proclamation of the new member of the Anglo-Saxon family of self-governing peoples.

The Commonwealth consists of six states, and, further, exercises jurisdiction over the Northern Territory (on the mainland) and over British New Guinea. New states may be admitted by the dominion parliament on such terms as it desires to impose. New Zealand has had opportunity to come in; but, being twelve hundred miles distant, and having very satisfactory governmental arrangements, that country has preferred to remain a separate self-governing dominion. Unlike the Canadian constitution (the North America Act), which was put in operation without popular sanction, the Australian fundamental law (the Commonwealth Act) came direct from the hands of the people; and in contents and arrangement it strongly resembles the Constitution of the United States. The

Canadian instrument can be amended only by act of the Imperial parliament, but the Australian can be changed whenever a majority of the people in a majority of the states so vote, providing the desired amendment has been passed by both houses of the Dominion parliament, or passed twice, at an interval of not less than three months, by one house. The final enactment by the Imperial parliament is purely formal. Amendment is decidedly easier to bring about than in the United States.

The structure of government is so similar to that described in Canada that it need not be dealt with at length. The governor-general, representing the British crown, is the nominal chief executive. The ministers, selected as in Canada, form the actual, working executive. There is no written provision for a cabinet system — no mention, even, of the prime minister. But the system is nowhere more fully operative. Parliament consists of a Senate and a House of Representatives, following the nomenclature of our own Congress. The Senate contains six members from each state, elected directly by the people on a general ticket, and for six years. Representatives are chosen by the people in single-member districts for three years. As in Canada and the United States, a reapportionment follows every decennial census; and undue increase in the size of the house is prevented by the requirement that the lower chamber shall be maintained at practically double the membership of the upper one. As in Canada, the suffrage is controlled by the individual states in so far as the federal government does not impose regulations. Under state law, manhood suffrage prevails everywhere, and most of the states have also bestowed the franchise on women. Following the American plan, the federal government is given only limited powers; residual powers are assigned to the states. The powers definitely conferred upon the federal government are more extensive than in the United States, for the Australians were able to learn from the experience of this country what powers are needed by such a government. But there is far less centralization than in Canada. The history of the Commonwealth in the past fifteen years has been notable for a great succession of measures designed to establish complete political and social democracy. So powerful, indeed, has the working class become that in 1910 the country found itself with a Labor ministry, supported by a Labor majority in the House of Commons, and with a former Scotch coal-miner as premier.

The Union of South Africa. — The latest, and in many respects the most remarkable, triumph of the British policy of colonial unification is the Union of South Africa. At the close of the Boer war, in 1902, Great Britain had, in the late theater of conflict, two self-governing colonies, Cape Colony and Natal, and two conquered territories, the former Boer republics, Orange Free State and the Transvaal, upon which she had promised to confer responsible government of the familiar English type. The pledge to the Transvaal was redeemed in 1906, and that to the Orange Free State (the present Orange River Colony) in the following year. Problems now arose relating to finance, tariff policy, railroad control, and dealings with the natives, which made close coöperation of the colonies imperative. A movement for union under a common government was accordingly set on foot. Boer and English elements alike supported it, and in 1908 a federal constitution was drawn up by a convention of representatives appointed by the several colonial legislatures. Only one colony (Natal) cared to take advantage of the opportunity given for submitting the instrument to a popular vote. Ratified there, the constitution was sent to the home country, where, in the autumn of 1909, Parliament gave it final approval. The new system took effect May 31, 1910.

The main question before the constitution's framers was whether to create a comparatively decentralized union like Australia or a highly centralized one on the plan of Canada. The considerations that made a union necessary at all seemed to require a union of very substantial strength. Hence the decision was for a "unitary," rather than a strictly federal, system. The four component provinces became mere local government areas, with separate legislative and administrative machinery, but with powers reduced far below the level of those of even the Canadian provinces. On the other hand, the Union government was endowed with comprehensive powers, both enumerated and residual. This decision did not in any way interfere with the complete installation of the parliamentary system; indeed, as the experience of Australia shows, pure federalism, at all events if it involves two popularly elected houses of parliament, is likely to raise the troublesome question of cabinet responsibility divided between two legislative bodies. The governor-general represents the crown, the ministers (limited to ten) bear responsibility for all executive acts, and every other essential of parliamentary government appears in its due form. The Senate, preserving a touch of federalism, consists of eight members elected by each provincial council, together with eight appointed by the governor-general, for terms of ten years. The House of Assembly consists of 121 members chosen for five years under suffrage laws that admit practically all male Boer and English residents but exclude native Africans. On account of its numerical preponderance, the "South African," or Boer, party has steadily controlled the government, the first prime minister being General Botha, who less than a decade earlier had ably led the Boer army against the forces of Lord Roberts and Lord Kitchener. However, the larger interests of the Empire suffered nothing thereby. An uprising of discontented Dutch elements in the early months of the Great War caused much apprehension; but it was suppressed by a Union government that was itself Boer, and thereafter South Africa bore a full share in the conflict with the Teutonic powers.

Crown Colonies and Protectorates. — Without exception, the self-governing dominions are inhabited chiefly by people who have the deep-seated instinct of the Anglo-Saxon for self-government, and also his rich traditions of the manner in which to exercise it. In many of the oversea possessions, however, men of European stocks are heavily outnumbered by more or less backward natives; and here it is inevitable that a different plan of government should be employed. The majority of these possessions come under the general designation of "crown colonies," *i.e.*, colonies which are kept under substantial control of the British government at London. Like Bermuda and the Bahamas, they may have an elected lower house and an appointed upper house, or council; like Jamaica and Malta, they may have a partially elected and partially appointed legislative council; like Ceylon and the Straits Settlements, they may have a legislative council that is wholly appointive; like Basutoland and Gibraltar, they may have no legislative council at all. But all of them have a resident governor or other administrator appointed by the British government, who is a real ruler, charged with carrying out the orders of the Colonial Office at London, and not subject to control from within the colony. In other words, while some have partially developed representative institutions, none have responsible government, in the sense in which we have grown accustomed to use that phrase. The executives cannot be forced out of office by the votes of hostile legislatures. It is always possible for a colony to be raised to a higher grade in the political scale; and there has never been an attempt to make these minor possessions a source of tribute to the governing nation. The British method of administering backward regions is based on two main principles — first, the protection of native rights, and second, equality of opportunity (the " open door ") for all trading peoples. British rule in the vast undeveloped parts of Africa, Asia, and Oceanica has not always been free from abuses of power. But there have been no notorious atrocities, and it may be said without exaggeration that to the backward races English authority has meant the suppression of unending slaughter, the disappearance of slavery, the protection of the rights and usages of primitive and simple folk against reckless exploitation, and the chance of gradual improvement and emancipation from barbarism. Everywhere it has meant the reign of law, without which civilization is impossible.

Somewhat different from the crown colonies are the protectorates. In the one, government is largely or wholly in the hands of officials appointed from London, and chiefly Englishmen; in the other, native governments and institutions are kept in operation, but under English supervision. The largest and most important of the protectorates to-day is the ancient land of Egypt, with its dependency, the Egyptian Sudan. Technically, Egypt has been a British protectorate only since 1914. Formerly the country's position was indeed peculiar. It acknowledged Turkish suzerainty; its hereditary prince, the Khedive, was practically immune from Turkish dominance; but from 1879 the land was under substantial control, first of Great Britain and France jointly, and later (after 1883) of Great Britain alone, whose Agents and Consuls-General, while nominally acting only as advisers of the Khedive, in point of fact guided the ministers and law-makers in all that they did. Accordingly, after 1883 the country was to all intents and purposes a British protectorate; and the change was one of form rather than of fact when, in December, 1914, the Khedive (who had openly espoused the cause of Turkey in the war) was deposed, Turkish suzerainty was declared at an end, the khedivial crown was bestowed on a new native dignitary bearing the title of sultan, the British Consul-General became a High Commissioner, and the term protectorate was for the first time officially applied to the country.

The preëxisting system, which has been well described as one of British government "by inspection and advice," will doubtless be continued in all of its essentials. The native prince will be continually counseled by the High Commissioner; the ministers will be selected as London dictates; they will be directed by British financial, judicial, and other special advisers, and the actual work of administration in the departments will be carried on by under-secretaries who are Englishmen; the local authorities, from provincial governor to *omdeh*, or village chief, will be instructed at every turn by British experts; the native army will be drilled and partly officered by British red-coats. Forty years of this sort of control have lifted the country out of a quagmire of political corruption, bankruptcy, ignorance, and misery. The British have sometimes been criticized for not advancing the Egyptians more rapidly toward self-government; and a small but noisy native party has long demanded real autonomy, or even full independence. Much time is required to develop political capacity in a wholly inexperienced and undisciplined people. If there is any value in continuous and forceful object-lessons in good administration, the British have conferred that advantage; besides which they have actually introduced a certain number of self-governing institutions, chiefly a national assembly which was created in 1883, and whose powers were considerably increased in 1913.

The Empire of India.[1] — Another ancient land over which British authority has been extended is India — a country which alone contains four-fifths of the population of the entire British

[1] This has been the official designation of the country since, in 1877, Queen Victoria was proclaimed "Empress of India."

colonial empire. This remarkably vast and rich dependency was brought gradually under control by a great commercial corporation, the East India Company, chartered by Queen Elizabeth in 1600. Toward the close of the eighteenth century the English government began to assert increasing control over the company's affairs, and in 1858, following the famous Sepoy mutiny, all of the corporation's rights and powers were transferred to the crown. The same measure that brought the company's political functions to an end — the Better Government of India Act — vested supreme control of Indian affairs in a new cabinet officer, the Secretary of State for India, assisted by a Council of India, consisting of from ten to fourteen salaried members chosen for seven years by the Secretary, and largely from persons who have had experience in Indian administration. The Secretary and his Council determine large matters of policy; but the actual work of administration must, of course, be left to authorities resident in the dependency. The chief of these is the viceroy, or governor-general, a dignitary appointed by the crown (*i.e.*, the British cabinet) for five years, and ruling from Delhi, the capital of the ancient empire of the Moguls. His court is the center of British power in the country, civil and military, and is maintained in such splendor as to be in keeping with the traditions to which the natives are attached.

In the performance of his numberless duties the viceroy is assisted by two councils: (1) an Executive Council, consisting of five or six high officials appointed by the crown for five years, and serving both individually as heads of departments and collectively as an advisory cabinet, and (2) a Legislative Council, whose recent reorganization constitutes the greatest change introduced in the governmental system of the country since the original legislation of 1858. Formerly the Legislative Council consisted merely of members of the Executive Council, in addition to a variable but small number designated by the viceroy. Under the India Councils Act, passed by the Imperial parliament in 1909, the Legislative Council now consists of 60 members (exclusive of the viceroy and executive councilors) of whom 33 are appointed and 27 are elected directly or indirectly by the people. Not more than half of the members may be crown officials. The representative character of the body is thus greatly emphasized; and while it is to be observed that powers are as yet strictly limited to the proposal and discussion of legislation, it is not unlikely that the final result will be something broadly resembling the British Parliament. Acts of the Legislative Council, unless vetoed by the viceroy, have the force of law throughout the entire country.

Subordinate to the central government are fifteen provincial governments. Their governors, lieutenant-governors, or chief commissioners, are appointed by the crown, but as a rule their legislative councils contain majorities of non-official members, either appointed or popularly elected. Within the provinces the main burden of administration falls on the permanent civil service, a body of officers recruited by severe competitive examination from the most highly educated young men of the United Kingdom and of India itself. These men commonly devote their lives to the service, and they may rise to the responsible positions of provincial governors, or even heads of departments at Delhi. Finally, it must not be forgotten that there are some six hundred "feudatory" states, containing two-fifths of the area and two-ninths of the population of the country. Under treaties individually entered into with the British government, these states are still ruled by their native Hindu or Moslem princes, subject only to British supervision and protection. At important native courts British interests are looked after by a crown official known as a "resident."

During the past fifteen years there has been much fault-finding by both Hindu and Moslem elements of the population, and the Councils Act of 1909 was passed mainly with a view to allaying discontent by giving the government a more popular character. Even the most ardent "nationalist," however, is obliged to admit that all classes of the people have profited enormously by British rule. Until British power was established the country had known nothing but disunion, war, absolutism, conflicts of creed, impermeable barriers of caste, poverty and degradation of the toiling masses. The British have brought the inestimable benefits of substantial political unity, impartial administration of a just and equal system of law, the maintenance of a long and unbroken peace, not to speak of such specific reforms as the construction of railroads and highways, the improvement of sanitation, the irrigation of desert lands, the relief of famines, the abolition of widow-suicide and of infanticide, and the introduction of western learning. The Indian peoples pay not a penny of tribute. They contribute nothing to the upkeep of the British navy. They bear the expense of their own army, but not when the troops are borrowed for service in other parts of the world. British traders enjoy no special privileges in their ports. Protective tariffs may be, and have been, laid with the purpose of restricting imports from the United Kingdom. The whole body of British civil officials in the country does not exceed three thousand, and trained natives are rapidly working their way upwards in the service. In a land where political unity has never existed, where racial and religious cleavages cut to the very bottom of society, where thirty-eight distinct languages are spoken, and where there are no traditions of government save those of absolutism, the establishment of self-government of the sort with which we are familiar is a task not of years but of generations, perhaps of centuries. It is not clear that Britain could thus far have moved more rapidly in India with safety to the fundamental interests involved.

The Problem of Imperial Reorganization. — Sixty years ago it was widely felt in England that colonies were of somewhat doubtful value, and that the English-speaking, self-governing dependencies would eventually claim and obtain full independence. Later came a shift of opinion. Sir John Seeley and other writers roused the nation to a new perception of the glory, power, and importance of the Empire. The unification of Germany and Italy, the rise of Japan, and the growth of the United States brought England, standing alone, into a relatively weaker position than she had been accustomed to occupy. The increase of armaments imposed a burden such as to lead to the suggestion that the colonies, for whose protection in part the new navy was maintained, should regularly bear some share of the cost. The large possibilities of a federal organization of partly autonomous states were revealed by the experience of not only the United States and Germany but, within the Empire, of Canada, and later Australia. The result was that an attitude of indifference gave way to a strong desire to bind the colonies more closely to the mother country, as a means of insuring the Empire's perpetuity, unity, and strength. Ties of sentiment, of common citizenship, and of commercial interest already existed. But no one knew how strong these really were; no one could say precisely what would happen in the event of a serious war in which the mother country should be engaged, but which did not directly touch the colonies' welfare.

The solution seemed to lie in some scheme by which the great self-governing colonies should, without sacrificing their autonomy, and on equal terms one with another, be brought into full copartnership with the mother country; in other words, some plan of "imperial federation." There were several forms which such a federation could take. It might, in the first place, be essentially commercial. That is, the United Kingdom and the self-governing dominions might reciprocally give trade advantages which were denied to the rest of the world. In pursuance of this idea, Canada in 1897 allowed imports from the mother country a reduction of one-eighth of her normal duties, and in three years raised the preference to one-third. South Africa, Australia, and New Zealand took similar action. Thus far, however, the arrangement is one-sided; for the Unionist proposal of "tariff reform" in the mother country has been unavailing, and, having no protective duties to lower or remit, the English government cannot meet the colonial governments halfway. A second possible basis is that of armed defense. It has been pointed out that although the navy is the bulwark of the dominions no less than of the United Kingdom, no one of them, nor yet India, is required to make any contribution to its maintenance. For a decade prior to the outbreak of war in 1914 the English people were staggering under a steadily mounting burden of naval expenditure. The dominions were not blind to the situation, and most of them began making small voluntary grants of aid. New Zealand contributed a battle-cruiser; South Africa voted a small annual money payment; Australia started the building of a modest separate fleet unit; Canada discussed the subject but could not agree upon a plan. By voluntary action, furthermore, three of the dominions furnished land forces for use in the Boer war; and all have put forth unstinted effort in aid of the motherland and her allies in the recent great con-

Y

flict. But, after full acknowledgment of this voluntary assistance has been made, the question remains whether it would not be possible, and desirable, to establish a general Imperial scheme of armed defense based on systematic rather than chance coöperation, and organized under military control.

Any substantial sort of federation must, however, involve more than trade preference and coöperative defense. There must be a certain amount of common *political* action, and, for this, some political machinery. The dominions have not been slow to let it be known that it does not comport with their power and pride to deal with their "copartner" at London simply through the Colonial Office, as a crown colony or other inferior dependency is expected to do; and long ago they asked that affairs of a general imperial interest should be discussed, not in the British cabinet alone, but also in a body in which all the great oversea sections of the Empire were represented. Prior to 1914 no positive steps were taken to meet this demand except the organization of the Imperial Conference. The first Conference was held in 1887 on the occasion of the Queen's jubilee. Others were convoked in 1897, 1902, and 1907; and on the last occasion a permanent organization was adopted, with a view to regular meetings every four years. It was noteworthy that the mother country was represented at the sessions, not by the Colonial Secretary, but by the prime minister, an arrangement which tended to put the dominions — who were also represented by their premiers — on a common footing with her. The Conference had no legal status, but as a deliberative and advisory body it rendered valuable service.

It was inevitable that coöperation in the Great War should bring striking changes in the interrelations of the various parts of the Empire. Chief among these was the rise of an Imperial Cabinet. One of the first acts of the War Cabinet organized late in 1916 [1] was to convoke a special Imperial Conference, at which all the self-governing dominions except Australia, and also India, were represented. During intervals between the Conference's sessions there were held several meetings of a body whose like the nation had never seen before. Into the new and small War Cabinet were brought the premiers and other

[1] See p. 217.

representatives of the dominions, and also two native spokesmen of India — and not as mere witnesses and informal advisers, but as ministers without portfolio, deliberating and voting under the privy councilor's oath. Furthermore, before the delegates sailed for their homes Mr. Lloyd George announced that it was proposed to hold such meetings annually, to be attended by the British premier and such of his colleagues as deal especially with Imperial affairs, by the premiers or other accredited spokesmen of the self-governing dominions, and by a representative of India to be appointed by the Indian government. An Imperial parliament which should bring together legislative delegates from the whole Empire has frequently been proposed, but as often abandoned as impracticable. Under war-time emergency, however, an Imperial Cabinet has become, at least for the time being, a reality. A resolution passed by the Conference of 1917 looks toward a general readjustment of the constitutional relations of the British government at a special Conference to be called after the war; and it contains the interesting declaration that " any such readjustment, while thoroughly preserving all existing powers of self-government and complete control of domestic affairs, should be based upon a full recognition of the dominions as autonomous nations of an Imperial Commonwealth, and of India as an important portion of the same, should recognize their right to an adequate voice in foreign policy and in foreign relations, and should provide effective arrangements for continuous consultation in all important matters of common Imperial concern, and for such necessary concerted action founded on consultation as the several governments determine." [1]

SELECTED REFERENCES

A. L. Lowell, *The Government of England* (New York, 1909), II, Chaps. liv–lviii; E. Jenks, *Government of the British Empire* (Boston, 1918), Chaps. iii–iv; C. J. H. Hayes, *Political and Social History of Modern Europe* (New York, 1916), II, Chap. xxix; C. D. Hazen, *Europe since 1815* (New York, 1910), Chap. xxii; H. E. Egerton, *Federations and Unions within the British Empire* (London, 1911); A. P. Poley, *Federal Systems of the United States and the British Empire* (Boston, 1913); A. B. Keith, *Responsible Government*

[1] Fairlie, *British War Cabinets*, 15.

in the Dominions, 3 vols. (Oxford, 1912); A. Todd, *Parliamentary Government in the British Colonies* (2d ed., London, 1894); C. Lucas, *The British Empire* (London, 1915); Ibid., *Greater Rome and Greater Britain* (London, 1912); C. Dilke, *The British Empire* (London, 1899); E. J. Payne, *Colonies and Colonial Federation* (London, 1905); W. H. Dawson (editor), *After-War Problems* (London, 1917); R. Jebb, *The Imperial Conference*, 2 vols. (London, 1911); Ibid., *The Britannic Question* (London, 1913); J. W. Root, *Colonial Tariffs* (London, 1906); H. E. Egerton and W. L. Grant, *Canadian Constitutional Development, Shown by Selected Speeches and Dispatches* (London, 1907); W. H. Moore, *Constitution of the Commonwealth of Australia* (London, 1902); H. G. Turner, *The First Decade of the Australian Commonwealth* (London, 1911); V. S. Clark, *The Labor Movement in Australasia: a Study in Social Democracy* (London, 1906); R. H. Brand, *The Union of South Africa* (London, 1909); W. B. Worsfold, *The Union of South Africa* (London, 1912); T. W. Holderness, *Peoples and Problems of India* (New York, 1913); C. Ilbert, *The Government of India* (3d ed., London, 1915); Earl of Cromer, *Modern Egypt*, 2 vols. (London, 1908); S. Low, *Egypt in Transition* (London, 1914).

CHAPTER XVII

THE FRENCH CONSTITUTION: PRESIDENT AND MINISTRY

I. ORIGINS OF THE CONSTITUTION

Political Development, 1789-1870. — Among the nations of continental Europe the pioneer of political democracy has been France. The Italian city-republics of the Middle Ages and the Swiss cantons and Dutch provinces of earlier modern times, although republics, were organized on an essentially aristocratic basis. Even in France the beginnings of democracy fall clearly within the period following the summoning of the Estates General at the opening of the Revolution in 1789. The France of the Old Régime was among the most absolute of monarchies. Prior to the Revolution the only organ of popular control in matters of national policy was the Estates General. It, however, consisted of three " orders," or groups, of which only one in any degree represented the people; besides, from 1614 to 1789 it was not once assembled. The local communities had almost entirely lost their earlier right to control their own affairs. " We hold our crown from God alone," reads a royal edict of 1770; " the right to make laws, by which our subjects must be conducted and governed, belongs to us alone, independently and unshared."

The government of the Bourbon kings was extravagant, corrupt, and burdensome; and in 1789 a tide of protest which had long been rising swept over the head of the luckless Louis XVI and engulfed the whole order of things of which he was a part. Already Rousseau and other philosophers had demonstrated that the people was the source of all legitimate authority; and in pursuance of this idea the Estates General of 1789, reorganized as a " National Assembly," enthusiastically adopted a Declaration of the Rights of Man and of the Citizen, in which the great principles of the Revolution were laid down as follows:

(1) that "all sovereignty resides essentially in the nation;" (2) that "law is the expression of the general will;" (3) that "every citizen has a right to take part personally, or through his representative, in the making of law;" and (4) that "law must be the same for all, whether it protects or punishes." These principles underlie the broadly democratic and highly efficient government of the French Republic to-day. How they won full and final acceptance, and how a great system of popular government was erected upon them, makes too long a story to be told here. Suffice it to say that after an exceptionally unsettled political career, during which no form of government lasted continuously as long as twenty years, the country came down at last to the establishment of the Third Republic, which after almost a half-century of orderly progress, and in the fifth year of a racking war, gives every sign of stability and permanence. It is the government of this France of our own day with which we are chiefly concerned.

Collapse of the Second Empire and the Problem of a New Government. — The Third Republic was set up under circumstances that gave promise of even less stability than had been revealed by its predecessors of 1792 and 1848. Proclaimed in the dismal days following the French defeat at Sedan, it owed its existence, at the outset, to the fact that, with the capture of Napoleon III by the Prussians and the utter collapse of the Empire, there had arisen, as Thiers put it, "a vacancy of power." The proclamation was issued September 4, 1870, when the war with Prussia had been in progress but seven weeks. During the remaining five months of the contest the sovereign authority of France was exercised by a Provisional Government of National Defense, with General Trochu at its head, devised in haste to meet the emergency by Gambetta, Favre, Ferry, and other former members of the Chamber of Deputies. Upon the capitulation of Paris, January 28, 1871 (followed by the signing of an armistice), elections were ordered for a national assembly, whose function was to decide whether it was possible to continue the war or necessary to submit to peace, and also what terms of peace should be accepted at the hands of the victorious Germans. There was no time for framing a new electoral system. Consequently the electoral procedure of the

Second Republic, as set forth in a law of March 15, 1849, was revived, and by manhood suffrage there was chosen, February 8, an assembly of 758 members, representative of both France and the colonies. Meeting at Bordeaux, February 12, this body, by unanimous vote, conferred upon the historian and parliamentarian Thiers the title of "Chief of the Executive Power," without fixed term, voted almost solidly for a cessation of hostilities, and authorized Thiers to proceed with an immediate negotiation of peace.

Pending a diplomatic adjustment, the Assembly was inclined to postpone the establishment of a permanent governmental system. But the problem could not long be held in abeyance. There were several possible solutions. A party of Legitimists, *i.e.*, adherents of the old Bourbon monarchy, was resolved upon the establishment of a kingdom under the Count of Chambord, grandson of the Charles X who had been deposed at the revolution of 1830. Similarly, a party of Orleanists insisted upon a restoration of the house of Orleans, overthrown in 1848, in the person of the Count of Paris, a grandson of the citizen-king Louis Philippe. A smaller group of those who, despite the discredit which the house of Bonaparte had incurred in the war, remained loyal to the Napoleonic tradition, was committed to a revival of the prostrate empire of the captive Napoleon III. Finally, in Paris and some portions of the outlying country there was uncompromising demand for the establishment of a permanent republic. In the Assembly the monarchists outnumbered the republicans five to two; and, although the members had been chosen primarily for their opinions as to peace rather than as to constitutional forms, the proportion throughout the nation was probably about the same. The republican outlook, however, was vastly improved by the fact that the monarchists, having nothing in common except opposition to republicanism, were hopelessly disagreed among themselves.[1]

Failure of the Monarchist Programs. — As, from the drift of its proceedings, the royalist character of the Assembly began

[1] Of pure Legitimists there were in the Assembly about 150; of Bonapartists, not over 30; of Republicans, about 250. The remaining members were Orleanists or men of indecisive inclination. At no time was the full membership of the Assembly in attendance.

to stand out in unmistakable relief, there arose from republican quarters vigorous opposition to the prolonged existence of the body. Even before the signing of the Peace of Frankfort, May 10, 1871, a clash occurred between the Assembly and the radical Parisian populace, the outcome of which was the bloody war of the Commune of April–May, 1871.[1] The communards fought fundamentally against state centralization, whether or not involving a revival of monarchy. The fate of republicanism was not in any real sense bound up with their cause; so that after the movement was suppressed, the political future of the nation was as uncertain as before. Thiers continued at the post of Chief of the Executive; and the Assembly, clothed by its own assumption with powers immeasurably in excess of those it had been elected to exercise, and limited by no fixed term, gave not the slightest indication of a purpose to terminate its career. Rather, the body proceeded, August 31, 1871, to pass, by a vote of 491 to 94, the Rivet law, whereby the existing régime was to be perpetuated indefinitely. By this measure unrestricted sovereignty, involving the exercise of both constituent and legislative powers, was declared by the Assembly to be vested in itself. Upon the Chief of the Executive was conferred the title of President of the French Republic; and it was stipulated that this official should thereafter be responsible to the Assembly, and presumably removable by it. A quasi-republic, with a crude parliamentary system of government, thereafter existed *de facto;* but it had as yet no constitutional basis.

This anomalous state of things lasted many months. More and more Thiers, who had begun as a constitutional monarchist, came to believe in republicanism as the kind of government that would divide the French people least, and late in 1872 he put himself unqualifiedly among the adherents of the republican program. Thereupon the monarchists, united for the moment in the conviction that for the good of their several causes Thiers must be deposed from his position of influence, brought about in the Assembly a majority vote in opposition to him on a question of adopting a republican constitution, and so procured his resignation, May 24, 1873. The opponents of republicanism now felt that the hour had come for the termination of a govern-

[1] In March the Assembly had transferred its sittings from Bordeaux to Versailles.

mental régime which all the while they had regarded as being purely provisional. The monarchist Marshal MacMahon was made President, a coalition ministry of monarchists under the Orleanist Duke of Broglie was formed, and republicanism in press and politics was put under the ban. Between the Legitimists and the Orleanists an ingenious compromise was worked out whereby the Bourbon Count of Chambord was to be made king under the title of Henry V and, he having no heirs, the Orleanist Count of Paris was to be recognized as his successor. The whole project was brought to naught, however, by the refusal of the Count of Chambord to give up the white flag, which for centuries had been the standard of the Bourbon house. The Orleanists held out for the tricolor; and thus, on what would appear to most people a question of little importance, the survival of the Republic was for the time determined.

In the hope that eventually they might gain sufficient strength to place their candidate on the throne without the coöperation of the Legitimists, the Orleanists joined with the Bonapartists and the republicans, November 20, 1873, in voting to fix the term of President MacMahon at seven years. The Orleanists assumed that if within that period an opportunity should arise for the establishment of the Count of Paris upon the throne, the President would clear the way by retiring. The opportunity, however, never came, and the septennial period for the French presidency, established thus by monarchists in their own interest, was destined to pass into the permanent mechanism of a republican state.

II. THE CONSTITUTION TO-DAY

Circumstances of Formation. — Meanwhile the way was opening for France to acquire what for some years she had utterly lacked, namely, a constitution. On May 19, 1873, the vice-president of the council of ministers, Dufaure, in behalf of the Government, laid before the Assembly *projets* of two organic measures, both of which, in slightly amended form, passed in 1875 into the permanent constitution of the Republic. On May 24 President Thiers retired, and likewise Dufaure, but in the Assembly the two proposed measures were none the less referred to a commission of thirty. Consideration in committee was sluggish, and the Assembly itself was not readily roused to action. During the twelvemonth that followed several *projets* were brought forward, and there was desultory discussion, but no progress. In the summer of 1874 a new commission of thirty was elected, and to it was intrusted the task of studying and reporting upon all of the numerous constitutional laws that had been suggested. Dominated by a monarchist majority, it contented itself with proposing, in January, 1875, a law providing simply for the continuance of the existing "septennate." Only after earnest effort, and by the narrow vote of 353 to 352 on the first division, were the republican forces in the Assembly able to carry a resolution, introduced January 30, 1875, by the deputy Wallon, making definite provision for the election, term, and reëligibility of the president of the republic. This resolution — which was finally passed by a vote of 425 to 254 — introduced no innovation. It did not formally declare that France should be permanently a republic. But it clearly *assumed* that such was to be the case.

Before the year 1875 was far advanced the Assembly gave up its evasive policy and for the first time in its career turned its effort whole-heartedly to the drafting of a national constitution. To this course it was driven by the agitation of Gambetta and other republican leaders, by fear on the part of the Legitimists and Orleanists that the existing unsettled situation would lead to a Bonapartist revival, and by a new *modus operandi* which was cleverly arranged between the republicans and the Orleanists. Convinced that an Orleanist monarchy was, at least for a time, an impossibility, and preferring a republic to any alternative that had been suggested, the Orleanist members of the Assembly gave their support in sufficient numbers to the program of the republicans to make it possible at last to work out for the nation a conservatively republican constitutional system.

General Features. — Of the organic laws which compose the constitution of France to-day five which date from 1875 are of principal importance : (1) that of February 24, on the Organization of the Senate ; (2) that of February 25 — the most important of all — on the Organization of the Public Powers ;

(3) that of July 16, on the Relations of the Public Powers; (4) that of August 3, on the Election of Senators; and (5) that of November 30, on the Election of Deputies. Collectively, these measures are sometimes referred to as the " constitution of 1875." Other and later constitutional enactments of considerable importance include (1) the law of July 22, 1879, relating to the seat of the Executive Power and of the two Chambers at Paris; (2) the law of December 9, 1884, amending existing organic laws on the Organization of the Senate and the Election of Senators; and (3) laws of June 16, 1885, and February 13 and July 17, 1889, concerning the Election of Deputies.

Springing from the peculiar conditions that have been described, the handiwork of a body in which only a minority felt the slightest degree of enthusiasm for it, the constitution of the French Republic is unlike any instrument of government with which the English-speaking world is familiar. It differs from the British in having been put almost wholly into written form. It differs from the American in that it consists, not of a single document, but of many, and in that it emanated, not from a great constituent assembly, specially charged with the task of formulating a governmental system, but from a law-making body which in truth had never been formally intrusted by the nation with even the powers of general legislation, and had merely arrogated to itself those functions of constitution-framing which it chose to exercise. It consists simply of organic laws, enacted chiefly by the provisional Assembly of 1871–1875, but amended and amplified to some extent by the national Parliament in later years. Unlike the majority of constitutions that went before it in France, it is not orderly in its arrangement or comprehensive in its contents. It is devoid of anything in the nature of a bill of rights,[1] and concerning the sovereignty of the people it has nothing to say. Upon even some of the most essential as-

[1] It is to be observed, however, that many authorities agree with Professor Duguit in his contention that although the individual rights enumerated in the Declaration of Rights of 1789 are passed without mention in the constitutional laws of 1875, they are to be considered as lying at the basis of the French governmental system to-day. Any measure enacted by the national parliament in contravention of them, says Professor Duguit, would be unconstitutional. They are not mere dogmas or theories, but rather positive laws, binding upon not only the legislative chambers but upon the constituent National Assembly. *Traité de droit constitutionnel*, II, 13.

pects of governmental organization and practice it is mute. It contains no provision for annual budgets, and it leaves untouched the entire field of the judiciary. The instrument lays down only certain broad lines of organization; the rest it leaves to be supplied through the channels of ordinary legislation.

Amendment. — It was the desire of all parties in 1875 that the constitutional laws should be easy to amend, and indeed most people expected the new governmental system to undergo, sooner or later, important modification. The monarchists, of course, looked forward to the time when the republican system itself would be overthrown. The process of amendment is laid down in the law of February 25, 1875. Amendments may be formally proposed by the president of the republic or by either chamber of Parliament. Final action upon them falls also to the chambers, so that the same men both enact the ordinary laws and adopt constitutional amendments. The processes, however, differ, for, whereas the work of legislation is carried on by the chambers sitting in separate buildings in the capital, the final consideration of constitutional amendments takes place in a joint meeting of the two bodies — technically the National Assembly — held in the magnificent palace erected by Louis XIV at Versailles. Such a meeting takes place at any time when the chambers vote separately that a revision of the constitutional laws is desirable. Amendments are adopted far more easily and speedily than in the United States, where such proposals, after being put forward by Congress or by a special convention, have to be ratified by the legislatures (or by conventions) in three-fourths of the states. On the other hand, the process differs from the English in that the Parliament at Westminster amends the constitution in precisely the same manner that it enacts ordinary laws. The only restriction that has been laid upon the revising powers of the National Assembly is contained in an amendment of August 14, 1884, which forbids that the republican form of government shall be made the subject of a proposed revision.[1] In point of fact, amendments have

[1] "The minister, Jules Ferry, who took the initiative of this measure, did not, of course, believe that a word inserted in a law could make the constitution eternal. But he wished to put an end to the attacks, then incessantly renewed, of the enemies of the Republic. The practical bearing of this proposition is easily grasped. Any revision which would have for its object the substitution of a monarchical system for

been few; although some, as that of December 9, 1884, modifying the methods of electing senators, that of June 16, 1885, introducing *scrutin de liste*, and those of February 13 and July 17, 1889, reëstablishing single-member parliamentary districts and prohibiting multiple candidatures, have been of great importance.

III. THE PRESIDENT

Election, Qualifications, and Privileges. — At the head of the Republic is the President, who in his capacity of supreme executive is assisted by a ministry and by a numerous and highly centralized body of administrative officials. The presidency, as has been explained, had its origin in the unsettled period following the Prussian war when it was commonly believed that monarchy, in one form or another, would eventually be reëstablished. The title " President of the Republic " was created in 1871; but the office as it exists to-day hardly antedates the election of Marshal MacMahon in 1873. The character and functions of the presidency were determined in no small measure by the circumstance that those who created the dignity intended merely to keep the French people accustomed to visible personal supremacy, and so to make easier the future transition to a monarchical system. Counting Thiers, the Republic has thus far had nine presidents; Adolphe Thiers, 1871-1873; Marshal MacMahon, 1873-1879; Jules Grévy, 1879-1887; F. Sadi-Carnot, 1887-1894; Casimir-Perier, June, 1894, to January, 1895; Félix Faure, 1895-1899; Émile Loubet, 1899-1906; Armand Fallières, 1906-1913; and Raymond Poincaré, 1913 to the present day.

The President is chosen for a term of seven years, and not by the people directly, nor yet, as in the United States, by a college of electors chosen for the purpose by the people, but by the members of the two houses of Parliament meeting jointly (in the same manner as for amending the constitution) at Versailles in National Assembly. The choice is by absolute majority of the combined body. The constitutional law of July 16, 1875,

the Republic would be illegal and revolutionary. The head of the state would have the right, as it would be his duty, to refuse to promulgate such a law if voted." Poincaré, *How France Is Governed*, 163.

stipulates that one month, at least, before the expiration of his term the President shall call together the National Assembly for the election of a successor. In default of such summons, the meeting takes place on call of the president of the Senate two weeks before the expiration; and in the event of the death or resignation of the President the Assembly is required to convene immediately without summons. There is no vice-president, nor any law of succession, so that whenever the presidential office falls vacant there must be an election; and, at whatever time and under whatever circumstance begun, the term of the newly elected President is the full seven years. As upon the occasion of the assassination of Sadi-Carnot in 1894, a vacancy may arise unexpectedly, entailing a hurried election. Even under normal conditions, however, a presidential election in France involves no period of campaigning such as we are familiar with in this country. The candidates, or at all events their friends, are likely to try to line up the parliamentary members in their behalf; they may even make speeches and in other ways appeal to popular sentiment. But the situation is very different from what it would be if the choice lay with the people directly.

So far as the formalities go, an election is likely to be carried through all stages within the space of forty-eight hours. As described by the present President of the Republic, M. Poincaré, the procedure is as follows: " When the Assembly is convoked for a presidential election the members vote without discussion. The urn is then placed in the tribune (the platform from which speakers would address the body if debate took place), and as an usher with a silver chain calls their names in a sonorous voice the members of the Assembly pass in a file in order to deposit their ballot-papers. . . . The procession of voters lasts a long time; there are nearly nine hundred votes to be cast. When the vote is completed the scrutators, drawn by lot from among the members of the Assembly, count the votes in an adjoining hall. If no candidate has obtained an absolute majority of votes, the president [1] announces a second ballot, and so on, if needful, until there is some result. The candidate elected is proclaimed by the president of the Assembly. There is applause, and cries of *Vive la Republique!* and the Assembly

---
[1] The president of the Senate occupies the chair.

dissolves. The new President, accompanied by the ministers, reënters Paris and installs himself in the Palais de l'Élysée."[1]

The qualifications requisite for election are extremely broad. Until 1884 any male citizen, regardless of age, affiliation, or circumstance, was eligible. In the year mentioned members of families that have reigned in France were debarred, and this is still the only formal disqualification. The Assembly can be counted on to elect a man who has long been a member, and has perhaps served as president of one or the other of the two houses, who has had experience in committee work and, as a rule, as a cabinet officer, and who, above all, is not of too aggressive or domineering temperament. A President may be reëlected any number of times; although only one, Grévy, has actually been so honored.

The President receives 1,200,000 francs a year, half as salary, half to cover traveling expenses and the outlays incumbent upon him as the official representative of the country. Besides, the nation furnishes him two residences, the Palais de l'Élysée (the splendid structure on the Champs-Élysées in which Napoleon signed his abdication after Waterloo) and the fine old country place known as the Château de Rambouillet. The President's person and his dignity are protected by special penalties for insult and libel. Like the President of the United States, during his term of office he is exempt from the processes of the ordinary courts; but also like his American counterpart, he may be tried by the Senate, on articles of impeachment presented by the lower legislative chamber. The President of the United States may be impeached for " treason, bribery, and other high crimes and misdemeanors "; the French President may be impeached for treason only. On the other hand, whereas the penalty that may be imposed upon the American President by the Senate is confined to removal from office and disqualification to hold office, the French constitution fixes no limit to the penalty that may be visited upon a President convicted of treason. So far as the law is concerned, he might be condemned to death.

Executive and Legislative Powers. — The constitution bestows upon the President, as head of the state, full executive powers. He promulgates the laws and sees that they are en-

[1] *How France Is Governed*, 168–169.

forced. He appoints to all civil and military offices in the central government and to many in the local governments; and his appointments do not require ratification by the Senate, or by any other body. He may even, by decree, create new offices. He exercises also a power of removal which, except in a few cases, is unlimited. He issues decrees affecting all branches of administrative work, supplementing although not modifying, the laws of Parliament. Like the American President, he represents the nation on ceremonial occasions, and sends and receives all ministers, ambassadors, envoys, and consuls. He also negotiates and approves treaties. Treaties of peace and commerce, treaties which involve the finances of the state, and those which affect the personal status and the rights of property of French persons abroad require ratification by the two chambers (not simply the Senate, as in the United States); and, with or without a treaty, no cession, exchange, or addition of territory can be made without parliamentary sanction. The exceptions are so inclusive that there are not many foreign agreements that can be made effective by action of the executive alone. However, military conventions, and even treaties of alliance, fall in this category, so long as they do not require appropriations from the national treasury. The President, furthermore, is commander in chief of the armed forces of the nation, military and naval. He cannot declare war without the consent of the chambers; but through the conduct of foreign affairs he may at any time, very much as may the President of the United States, create a situation making war inevitable. Finally, the President is vested with the powers of pardon and reprieve, although amnesty may be granted only by parliamentary act.

On the side of legislation the President's powers are impressive. In the first place, he convokes the two houses of Parliament in both regular and extraordinary sessions (subject to the constitutional requirement that they shall assemble each year in January whether convoked by the President or not) and adjourns them for any period not exceeding one month; and, with the consent of the Senate, he can dissolve the Chamber of Deputies before the expiration of its term, thereby bringing on a national election. He cannot veto measures in the same fashion as the President of the United States, but he can refuse to promulgate them until they have been reconsidered by the chambers. If upon reconsideration a bill is again passed, even by bare majorities, the President must proclaim it and enforce it. A further important power is the promulgation of ordinances (*décrets*) having the character and effect of supplementary legislation. Finally, the President is given, by the constitutional law of February 25, 1875, the power to initiate, *i.e.*, to propose, laws, concurrently with the two houses. Formally, the President of the United States has no such power; actually, as every one knows, he not only possesses it but makes it a chief means of leadership in the affairs of his administration.

IV. THE MINISTRY

Relation to the President. — " There is," says an English writer of the last generation, " no living functionary who occupies a more pitiable position than a French President. The old kings of France reigned and governed. The Constitutional King, according to M. Thiers, reigns, but does not govern. The President of the United States governs, but he does not reign. It has been reserved for the President of the French Republic neither to reign nor yet to govern." [1] The weakness of the French President's actual position arises from two clauses of the constitutional law of February 25, 1875. One of them stipulates that " every act of the President of the Republic shall be countersigned by a minister." The other provides that " the ministers shall be collectively responsible to the chambers for the general policy of the government, and individually for their personal acts." Under the operation of these principles the ministry becomes, as in England, the real executive; and, as will appear more fully, it also emulates the example of the English cabinet group in seeking to lead and control in legislation. Aside from various formalities, largely of a social nature, the President performs no functions and exercises no powers independently. Instead, his acts are limited to those for which the ministers are prepared to bear responsibility before Parliament and the nation; and in practice this means, precisely as it means in England, that it is the ministry itself, and not the formal head of the state, that makes decisions, issues orders, and formulates policies.

[1] Maine, *Popular Government*, 250.

We say that the President appoints to and removes from office; actually, it is, with few exceptions, the ministers, collectively or singly, who do this. Similarly, it is the ministers who enforce the laws, conclude treaties, manage the army and navy, introduce " government " bills in Parliament, and promulgate ordinances. The President's position is, therefore, totally different from that of the President of the United States, who personally directs the entire work of one great branch of the government and has relations of the highest importance with the other two branches. The analogy that at once suggests itself is the position occupied by the sovereign in England. The resemblance, however, is not so close as might be supposed. The French President, being an elected official with no halo of royalty about his head, fills no such place in the general scheme of things as does the English king. But he has closer personal contact with the officers and affairs of state. He, for example, sits with and presides over the ministry at its frequent meetings for the consideration of purely administrative business. The influence which he wields upon administration, law-making, and foreign policy depends very largely upon his own capacity, interests, and activity. M. Fallières was an amiable gentleman who was content to leave the business of state to others; he contributed little to the policies and achievements of his time. M. Poincaré, a scholar and man of affairs, has played a much more active rôle, and has supplied impressive leadership of the nation in its supreme hour of trial.

Ministerial Organization and Functions. — In the absence of constitutional provision on the point, the administrative departments presided over by the ministers are created by executive decree; although, obviously, Parliament must give its approval, since a new ministry could not long survive without grants of supplies. The number of ministries has grown slowly. In 1875 there were nine. In 1879 a tenth was created. Between 1881 and 1887 there were eleven. In 1914, on the eve of the war, there were twelve, as follows: (1) Interior; (2) Finance; (3) War; (4) Justice and Public Worship; (5) Marine; (6) Colonies; (7) Public Instruction and the Fine Arts; (8) Foreign Affairs; (9) Commerce; (10) Agriculture; (11) Public Works and Posts, Telegraphs, and Telephones; and (12) Labor.

THE FRENCH CONSTITUTION

The first step in the making up of a new ministry is the selection of the prime minister. The choice rests with the President; and inasmuch as the parliamentary system prevails, nominally at least as in England, it theoretically falls to that officer merely to call in the recognized leader of the parliamentary majority and ask him to make up a ministry. In England, as we have seen, this action as performed by the sovereign is usually a mere formality. In France the case is otherwise, for the reason that there, as will be explained, parties are so numerous that no one of them can ever have a parliamentary majority alone. It often therefore becomes a matter of difficulty to find a man who can succeed in bringing together a ministry that will command majority support in the popular chamber. Sometimes the post is tendered to half a dozen men before the right one is found. Under even the most favorable circumstances there is likely to be much uncertainty as to who will be appointed, and whether after a man is appointed, he will prove equal to the demands of the occasion. This means that the President has far more discretion and actual power in the selection of a premier than does the sovereign in England. By custom, he looks for information and advice to the presidents of the Senate and Chamber of Deputies and to the chiefs of the recognized party groups; but the task of finding the proper man is one which he cannot delegate or evade.

After the new premier is finally found, he selects the remaining ministers and assigns them to their posts, after taking for himself whatever portfolio he desires. This, as has been intimated, is no simple matter. "There is no majority in the English and American sense with its recognized leaders to whom he may turn. He is under the necessity, therefore, of creating a majority through a judicious distribution of portfolios among a certain number of groups so that each member will bring to the support of the cabinet a body of adherents. . . . During the exciting days of a ministerial crisis, the Parisian journals give detailed accounts of the hurried visits of the newly appointed premier to the houses of prominent politicians, of his interviews, pourparlers, overtures, solicitations, and possible combinations, and each day there is a summary of his successes and failures. Sometimes his *démarches* are prolonged through a period of several weeks before the cabinet is finally completed; not infrequently at the last moment, after the list has been sent to the *Journal Officiel*, for publication, the combination is upset by withdrawals."[1] In form, all of the ministers are appointed by the President; but in practice the premier is free to choose his colleagues as best he can under the circumstances described. Usually, although not necessarily, the ministers are members of the Senate or of the Chamber of Deputies, principally the latter. Whether members or not, they have a right to attend all sessions of both chambers and to take a privileged part in debate. Ministers receive annual salaries of 60,000 francs and reside, as a rule, in the official mansions maintained for the heads of the departments they control.

Collectively the ministers possess two sets of functions which are essentially distinct. The one they fulfill as a " council "; the other as a " cabinet." In the capacity of a council they exercise a general supervision of the administration of the laws, to the end that there may be efficiency and unity in the affairs of state. In the event of the President's death, incapacitation, or resignation, the Council is authorized to act as head of the state until the National Assembly shall have chosen a successor. As a cabinet the ministers formulate the fundamental policies of the Government and represent it in the chambers. The Council is administrative and is expressly recognized by law; the Cabinet is political and is not so recognized. In the meetings of the Council, commonly held twice a week, the President of the Republic not only sits, but presides; in those of the Cabinet, normally once a week, he rarely even appears. Aside from the President, however, the two bodies, in personnel, are identical. Neither keeps minutes of its proceedings.

The Parliamentary System: Contrast with England. — On paper France has a parliamentary system of government copied from, and substantially like, that of Great Britain. There is a politically irresponsible titulary of the executive power. The real executive consists of the ministers. The ministers are responsible, collectively in general matters and individually in particular ones, to the chambers — in reality to the Chamber of Deputies. When defeated on any important proposition, they

[1] Garner, "Cabinet Government in France," *Amer. Polit. Sci. Review*, VIII, 366.

resign as a body. The right of dissolution as a means of terminating conflicts between the executive and legislative departments is duly provided for.

In practice, parliamentary government in France means, however, something very different from what it means across the Channel. It presents an appearance such that some observers have been led to apply to it the designation "parliamentary anarchy," its outstanding characteristics being the instability of ministries, the frequency of ministerial crises, and the recurring conflicts between the chambers and the Government. From the middle of the nineteenth century to the outbreak of the Great War in 1914 England had but twelve prime ministers; France had as many between 1900 and 1914. From 1873 to 1914 England had but eleven different ministries; France had fifty. Between 1875 and 1900 only four years passed in the latter country without at least one change of ministry. Only four of the fifty ministries since 1873 held power for a longer period than two years, while most of them were in office only a few months, the average tenure for the whole period being, indeed, less than eight months.[1] It is of the essence of parliamentary government that the tenure of the ruling ministry shall be determined entirely by the continuance of good relations with the popular chamber. No ministry, even in England, has any definite assurance as to its lifetime. The statistics cited show, however, that in the latter country a ministry has a reasonable expectation of several years in which to carry out its policies. In France, a ministry can be morally certain that it will not last long. Following custom, it begins by issuing a "declaration" setting forth an extensive program of reforms; but it knows in its heart that it will never survive to fulfill any large part of its promises. The work of government tends to become a wearisome succession of starts and stops; great measures hang in the balance for years; politicians of mediocre ability — men who in England would not be considered fit for ministerial posts — troop through the great offices in rapid succession.

Causes of Ministerial Instability. — The reasons why the parliamentary system works so much less smoothly than in

[1] Garner, *ibid.*, 368–369.

England are not difficult to discover. There is, of course, the underlying fact that whereas the system is in the one country a product of long evolution and adaptation, in the other it is an importation, but imperfectly understood by those who a century ago brought it in, and never wholly suited to its new environment. Of more specific reasons for the failure of the system to work as in England, the most important is undoubtedly the condition of political parties. In Great Britain, while in recent decades minor political groups have sprung up to complicate the situation, the political life of the nation is still very largely confined to two great rival parties, each of which has sufficient strength, if raised to power, to support a homogeneous and sympathetic ministry. In France, on the contrary, there is a multiplicity of parties, and no one of them is likely ever to be in a position to operate the government alone. The election of 1910 sent to the Chamber of Deputies representatives of not fewer than nine distinct political groups. As has been observed, no ministry can be made up with any hope of being able to command a working majority in the Chamber unless it represents in its membership a coalition of several parties. A government so constituted, however, is almost certain to be vacillating and short-lived. It is unable to please all of the groups and interests upon which it depends; it dares displease none; it commonly ends by displeasing all.

A second cause of ministerial instability is Parliament's insistence upon the exercise of a close and continuous control over the ministers, not only in the shaping of policy, but in matters of administrative detail. In England, as has been pointed out, the cabinet leads and dominates, in both legislation and administration. Parliament holds it to a general responsibility, but in practice allows it free scope, especially on the side of administration. The French Parliament is content to play no such passive, trustful rôle. It displays a regrettable eagerness to dictate appointments and promotions, issue orders, and meddle generally in matters that do not properly concern it. " Not content with depriving the chief of state of his constitutional prerogatives and reducing him to the position of a figurehead, the French chambers insist upon throwing the ministers out upon trivial questions, and this notwithstanding the constitutional prescription that they shall be responsible only for their *general* policies." [1]

The position occupied by French ministries is made the more precarious by the parliamentary device of interpellation. As in Great Britain, every member of the two chambers has the right at any time to put to an executive head a direct question concerning any affair of state which, without impropriety, may be made the subject of open discussion. A minister may not, however, be questioned without his consent, and the incident ordinarily passes without debate. In France, however, any member may also direct at a minister an " interpellation," which is often designed not to obtain information, but to put the Government on the defensive and to precipitate a debate that may end in the overthrow of the ministry on some mere technicality or other matter in itself of but slight importance. The interpellation is a challenge. It is reduced to writing and is made the special order for a day fixed by the chamber, and it almost invariably results in a debate and in a vote to test the " confidence " of the chamber. If the vote is unfavorable and the general policy of the ministry is involved, the ministry as a body resigns. Observers agree that the practice lends itself too readily to the ends of sheer factiousness to be considered a valuable feature of parliamentary procedure.

A final consideration is the practical ineffectiveness of the constitutional provision for parliamentary dissolutions. The power to dissolve the Chamber of Deputies is formally vested in the President, and would normally be exercised by the ruling cabinet. It is subject, however, to a restriction which has no parallel in England: a dissolution can take place only with the consent of the upper chamber. Furthermore, the dissolution which was carried out in 1877 was so unwise, if not actually unconstitutional, as to bring the practice into lasting disfavor. The consequence is that there has not been a dissolution since that date, and the power is for practical purposes obsolete. The effect of this is obvious. In England, when disagreement arises between the cabinet and Parliament the ministers may resign; but, on the other hand, they may dissolve Parliament, order a general election, win a parliamentary majority, and

[1] Garner, "Cabinet Government in France," *Amer. Polit. Sci. Review*, VIII, 366.

remain at the helm. This is precisely what happened at the two national elections of 1910. But in France, it is the ministry that must give way in any conflict with Parliament; dissolution is, practically, not available as a mode of ministerial vindication. In other words, the ministry is responsible to Parliament alone and not to the nation; it cannot appeal over the head of Parliament to the electorate, or ask the people to sustain it by electing a Parliament of a different complexion. As has been explained, development in England has been of precisely the opposite sort. There, unless the circumstances are very unusual, the ministry refuses to yield to an adverse parliamentary majority unless the people back up that majority at the polls.

Elements of Continuity. — " The chronic inability of the French to produce the two-party system," says an English writer, " is in itself a sure sign of their incapacity for parliamentary government." [1] This judgment is much too drastic. Failure to develop a two-party system (and there is no indication that such a system will arise) unquestionably means that France cannot have parliamentary government *of the English type*. It may very well mean that her government must continue to be in some respects inferior to the English. But it does not mean that the French system is impossible, objectionable, or more than ordinarily inefficient. In point of fact, French government is exceptionally democratic, economical, and effective. It is also far more stable and continuous than might be inferred from the kaleidoscopic succession of ministries; and this for two main reasons. In the first place, in each executive department there is, as in England, a corps of highly trained officials who carry on the actual work of administration and who do not change with the rise and fall of their chiefs. And in the second place, a ministerial " crisis " involves as a rule no very great upset. Defeated in the Chamber of Deputies, or unable to make progress, a ministry as a body resigns. But it is altogether probable that many of the members will be immediately reappointed, with perhaps an exchange of portfolios. In England a change of ministry usually means not only a new personnel throughout, but a complete shift of policy. In France many familiar faces reappear, and the change of policy is apt to

[1] Bodley, *France*, II, 176.

be microscopic. In her own way — which is not necessarily the best way, but the only way *for her*, considering the conditions — France contrives to get most of the great advantages of parliamentary government. And if the political surface seems unduly ruffled, it is but the ripples that reach the eye; the current runs deep and steady beneath.

SELECTED REFERENCES

A. L. Lowell, *Governments and Parties in Continental Europe* (Boston, 1896), I, Chaps. i–ii; R. Poincaré, *How France Is Governed* (New York, 1914), Chaps. vi–viii; H. A. L. Fisher, *The Republican Tradition in Europe* (New York, 1911), Chaps. v–vi, viii, xi; C. D. Hazen, *Europe since 1815* (New York, 1910), Chap. xv; C. J. H. Hayes, *Political and Social History of Modern Europe* (New York, 1916), II, Chap. xxiii; J. W. Garner, " Cabinet Government in France," *Amer. Polit. Sci. Review*, VIII, 353–374; J. T. Shotwell, "Political Capacity of the French," *Polit. Sci. Quar.*, XXIV, 115–126; J. C. Bracq, *France under the Republic* (New York, 1910); C. H. Wright, *History of the Third Republic* (Boston, 1916); A. L. Guerard, *French Civilization in the Nineteenth Century* (London, 1914); E. A. Vizetelly, *Republican France, 1870–1912* (Boston, 1912); G. Hanotaux, *History of Contemporary France, 1870–1882* (trans. by J. C. Tarver, 4 vols., London, 1903–1909); W. F. Dodd, *Modern Constitutions* (Chicago, 1909), I, 286–319, for texts of organic laws of 1875; F. M. Anderson, *Constitutions and Other Select Documents Illustrative of the History of France, 1789–1907* (2d ed., Minneapolis, 1908).

CHAPTER XVIII

PARLIAMENT AND PARTIES IN FRANCE

I. COMPOSITION OF PARLIAMENT

The Bicameral System.— With the break-up of the Estates General in 1789, France definitely abandoned the plan of a national assembly based on the medieval principle of orders or estates. For upwards of a hundred years, however, the scheme of parliamentary organization to be substituted continued uncertain. During the Revolution ultra-democratic reformers favored a national assembly of but one house, and it was only when the constitution of 1795 was promulgated that a frame of government making provision for a legislature of two houses was put in operation. The bicameral system of 1795–1799 was succeeded by the anomalous legislative régime of Napoleon; but under the Constitutional Charter of 1814 the two-house principle was revived and continuously employed for thirty-four years. The legislative organ of the Second Republic (1848–1852) was a unicameral assembly. But an incident of the transition to the Second Empire was the revival of a Senate; and throughout the reign of Napoleon III the legislative chambers were nominally two in number, although only in 1870 was the Senate as a legislative body made coördinate with the *Corps législatif*. On the whole, it can be said that when the constitution of the Third Republic was drawn up, the political experience of the nation had proved the bicameral system to be the more natural, the safer, and the more effective. The opening stipulation of the Constitutional Law on the Organization of the Public Powers, adopted February 25, 1875, was that the law-making power should be exercised by a national parliament consisting of a Chamber of Deputies and a Senate. The one was intended to rest upon a broadly democratic basis. The other was planned, as is customary with second chambers, to stand somewhat removed from the immediate control of the voters of the country. But both were charged with the duty of enacting into law the will of the people, in whom the sovereignty of the French nation is clearly lodged. And any one who observes the French governmental system as it operates to-day will be impressed with the fact that the structure and organization of the parliamentary body have lent themselves to the usages of a democratic state in a measure even exceeding that intended by the founders of the existing order.

The Senate. — Having determined that parliament should consist of two branches, the National Assembly, in 1875, faced the difficult problem of constituting an upper chamber that should not be a mere replica of the lower, and yet should not inject into a democratic constitutional system an incongruous element of aristocracy. The device hit upon was a chamber in which seats should be wholly elective, yet not at the immediate disposal of the people. By the constitutional law of February 24, 1875, it was provided that the Senate should consist of three hundred members, of whom two hundred twenty-five should be elected by the departments and colonies and seventy-five by the National Assembly itself. The departments of the Seine and of the Nord were authorized to elect five senators each, the others four, three, or two, as specified in the law. The senators of the departments and of the colonies were to be elected by a "college" meeting at the capital of the *département* or the colony, composed of the deputies and general councilors of the department, the councilors of arrondissements, and delegates elected, one by each municipal council, from among the communal (*i.e.*, municipal) voters.[1] Senators chosen by the Assembly were to be elected by an absolute majority of votes. No one should be chosen who had not attained the age of forty years, and who was not in enjoyment of full civil and political rights. The seventy-five elected by the Assembly were to retain their seats for life, vacancies being filled by the Senate itself. All other members were to be elected for nine years, being renewed by thirds every three years.

The system thus devised continues, in the main, at the present

[1] The department is the largest area for purposes of local government. It is divided into *arrondissements*, and these, in turn, into *communes*.

day. The principal variations from it are those introduced in a constitutional law of December 9, 1884, which provided (1) that the coöptative method of election should be abolished, and that, while present life members should retain their seats as long as they lived, all vacancies thereafter arising from the decease of such members should be filled within the departments in the regular manner, and (2) that the electoral college of the department should be broadened to include not merely one delegate from each municipal council, but from one to twenty-four (thirty in the case of Paris), according to the number of members in the council. By the same law members of families that have reigned in France were declared ineligible; and by act of July 20, 1895, no one may become a member of either branch of Parliament unless he has complied with the law regarding military service.

The Senate consists to-day of three hundred members apportioned among the departments in approximate accordance with population and chosen in all cases by bodies of electors all of whom have themselves been elected directly by the people or are delegates of those so elected. Election is thus indirect, as was the election of senators in the United States prior to the adoption of the Seventeenth Amendment in 1913. But the method is justified by the results, and there has been little demand for a system of election by the people directly. The present apportionment gives to the department of the Seine ten members; to that of the Nord, eight; to others, five, four, three, and two apiece, down to the territory of Belfort and the three departments of Algeria, and the colonies of Martinique, Guadeloupe, Réunion, and the French West Indies, which return one each. From having long been viewed by republicans with suspicion, the Senate has come to be regarded by Frenchmen generally as perhaps the most perfect work of the Republic. In these days its membership is recruited heavily from the Deputies, so that it includes not only many men of distinction in letters and science but an unusual proportion of experienced debaters and parliamentarians. A leading American authority has said that it is " composed of as impressive a body of men as can be found in any legislative chamber the world over." [1] The sittings

[1] Lowell, *Governments and Parties in Continental Europe*, I, 22.

of the Senate, since 1879, have been held in the Palais de Luxembourg, a splendid structure on the left bank of the Seine dating from the early seventeenth century.

The Chamber of Deputies: Composition and Qualifications.
— The 602 members of the lower branch of the national legislature are chosen directly by the people, under conditions determined by a series of electoral measures, principally the organic law of November 30, 1875. The franchise is extended to all men who have attained the age of twenty-one, and who are not convicts, bankrupts, under guardianship, or in active military or naval service. Of educational or property qualifications there are none. The only requirements are that the voter shall have his name inscribed on the electoral lists and shall be able to prove a residence of six months in the commune in which he casts his ballot. Notwithstanding the fact that manhood suffrage has prevailed since the revolution of 1848, there has been no such demand for the enfranchisement of women as has stirred both England and the United States; and no legislation upon the subject has been enacted. Indeed, in 1913 the Chamber of Deputies overwhelmingly rejected a woman's suffrage amendment to the national constitution. The terms upon which the suffrage is exercised are fixed by national law. But the keeping and the annual revision of the electoral lists devolve upon the authorities of the commune; and the lists are identical for communal, district, departmental, and national elections. The registration system is notably effective.

The area from which members are elected to the Chamber of Deputies is the *arrondissement*, an administrative subdivision of the department. Each *arrondissement* returns one deputy, unless its population exceeds 100,000, in which case it is divided into single-member constituencies, one for each 100,000 or remaining fraction thereof. A fresh apportionment is made after each quinquennial census. The present method of election, under which the individual elector votes within his *arrondissement* for one deputy only, is known as the *scrutin d'arrondissement*. Established in 1876, the *scrutin d'arrondissement* was employed until 1885, when a system was adopted under which deputies for an entire department were voted for on a general ticket, as, for example, presidential electors are voted for in an American state. This system — called *scrutin de liste* — was kept in operation only until 1889, when the *scrutin d'arrondissement* was reëstablished.

The full membership of the Chamber is elected simultaneously for a four-year term. Theoretically, as has been observed, the Chamber may be dissolved at any time by the President, with the assent of the Senate. But there has been only one such dissolution (1877), and a newly elected chamber is now practically certain to fill out its full four years. Parliamentary elections therefore take place with the same regularity as congressional elections in our own country, although only half as frequently. Members of the Chamber are required to be voters and not less than twenty-five years of age; and by law of June 16, 1885, members of families who have ever reigned in France are debarred. All that is required of a person who, possessing the requisite legal qualifications, wishes to be a candidate is that five days before the election he shall deposit with the prefect of the department within which the polling is to take place a declaration, witnessed by a mayor, of the name of the constituency in which he proposes to seek election. Even this trifling formality was introduced only by the Multiple Candidature Act of 1889, by which it is forbidden that a person be a candidate in more than one district. Members represent districts other than those in which they live considerably less frequently than in England, but more frequently than in the United States.

Electoral Procedure. — The electoral process is simple and inexpensive. Voting is by secret ballot, and the balloting lasts only one day. As a rule, the polling takes place in the *mairie*, or municipal building, of the commune, under the immediate supervision of an electoral bureau consisting of a president (usually the mayor), four assessors, and a secretary. The count is public and the result is announced without delay. If it is found that no candidate within the district has polled an absolute majority of the votes cast, and at the same time a fourth of the number which the registered voters of the district are legally capable of casting, a second balloting (the so-called *ballotage*) is ordered for two weeks from the ensuing Sunday. No one of the candidates voted for drops out of the contest, unless by voluntary withdrawal; new candidates, at even so late a day, may enter the race; and whoever, at the second balloting, secures a simple plurality is declared elected. The second ballot is a familiar device in continental countries. It is most advantageously used, however, to ascertain the preference of the voters as between the *two* candidates who stood highest at the first ballot — in other words, to secure a majority election. As employed in France, it is of doubtful value.

Formerly the conduct of elections was considerably less satisfactory than it is to-day. The chief difficulty was the lack of adequate protection of the secrecy of the ballot. The constitutional law of November 30, 1875, stipulated that voting should be secret, but it unfortunately did not set aside a decree of 1852 which provided that ballots should be marked outside the voting hall and that they should be handed by the voter to the president of the electoral bureau (usually the mayor), who should deposit them in the urn. As was true in England until 1918, and as is still true in most European countries, the ballot-papers were supplied, not by the state, but by the candidates; and many times they were distributed to the voters in their homes by the candidate or his agents several days before the election was to take place.[1] The requirement that all ballots should be made of white paper and should be without any outward signs or marks did not, in practice, prevent the papers from being so prepared (as to size, shape, or texture), that the election officer, and even the bystanders who under French usage are freely admitted to the polling places, could readily distinguish between those of the different candidates. The situation was like that which we had in our own American states before they adopted the Australian ballot system, whose cardinal feature is the issuing of ballot-papers only under authority of the state, and to the voters as they actually use them at the polls. Measures designed to secure genuine secrecy of the ballot, and to remedy various electoral abuses, received much attention in Parliament after 1900, but it was only in 1913 that the chambers could come into agreement upon a bill. A law promulgated July 29 provided (1) that when the voter presents himself at the polls he shall be given an official ballot and an opaque envelope furnished by the prefectural authorities, (2) that he shall retire to a private booth

[1] Garner, "Electoral Reform in France," *Amer. Polit. Sci. Review*, VII, 531.

and there seal his ballot in the envelope, and (3) that he shall personally deposit the envelope in the electoral urn. These regulations have at last made it possible for an elector to vote in complete secrecy if he desires to do so. The safeguarding of the purity of elections by a general corrupt and illegal practices act, such as exists in England and in our American states, remains to be undertaken; although moderately effective laws against bribery and similar offenses have been passed. It may be added that the central government, through its local agents, exerts much influence in parliamentary elections. But all of the more important political groups have profited at one time or another by the practice, and it is not generally condemned.

Electoral Reform: Scrutin d'arrondissement and Scrutin de liste. — In the decade preceding the war there was much discussion, in Parliament and throughout the country, of other questions pertaining to the remodeling of the electoral system. Indeed, it may be said that after the relations of church and state were finally fixed by the great separation law of 1905 electoral reform took the place of the religious question as the paramount issue in French domestic politics. The questions under consideration related only incidentally to the franchise. The country already has manhood suffrage. There is no plural voting. The only possible franchise question is the extension of the suffrage to women, for which, as has been said, there has been less demand in France than in Great Britain, the United States, and a number of other countries. The questions which, up to the war, assumed political importance were rather such as related to the conditions under which the existing scheme of manhood suffrage should be operated.

Those who criticize the electoral system as it is are by no means agreed as to the changes that ought to be made; but, in general, there are two principal programs. One calls simply for the substitution of *scrutin de liste* for *scrutin d'arrondissement*. The other proposes both a return to *scrutin de liste* and the adoption of a plan of proportional representation. The *arrondissement*, many persons contend, is too small to be used to advantage as an electoral unit. Within a sphere so restricted the interests of the nation are in danger of being lost to view, and political life is prone to be reduced to a wearisome round of compromise, demagogy, and trivialities. If, it is contended, all deputies from a department were to be elected on a single ticket, the voter would value his privilege more highly, the candidate would be in a position to make a more dignified campaign, and issues which are national in their scope would less frequently be obscured by questions and interests of a petty and purely local character. Professor Duguit, of the University of Bordeaux, who is one of the ablest exponents of this proposed reform, contends (1) that the scheme of *scrutin de liste* harmonizes better than does that of *scrutin d'arrondissement* with the fundamental theory of representation in France, which is that the deputies who go to Paris do so as representatives of the nation as a whole, and not of a single locality; (2) that the *scrutin d'arrondissement* facilitates corruption through the temptation which it affords candidates to promise voters favors, appointments, and decorations; and (3) that the prevailing system augments the more or less questionable influence which the Government brings to bear in the election of deputies.[1] It does not appear that in the period 1885-1889 when the *scrutin de liste* was in operation the ends now expected to be attained by a restoration of it were realized; indeed the system lent itself more readily to the menacing operations of the ambitious Boulanger than the *scrutin d'arrondissement* could possibly have done. It is but fair, however, to observe that the trial of the system was very brief and that it fell in a period of unusual political unsettlement.

Electoral Reform: Proportional Representation. — " Elected assemblies," declared Mirabeau, more than a century ago, " may be compared to geographical charts, which ought to reproduce all the elements of the country with their proportions, without allowing the more considerable elements to eliminate the lesser;" and in the judgment of many French reformers to-day a simple enlarging of the electoral unit, however desirable in itself, would be by no means adequate to place the national parliament upon a satisfactory basis. There is a growing demand for the adoption of some scheme whereby minorities in the several departments shall become entitled to a proportionate voice in the Chamber at Paris. Hence a second program of reform is that calling not merely for the *scrutin de liste*, but also for proportional repre-

[1] Duguit, *Traité de droit constitutionnel*, I, 375-376.

sentation. Within the past two decades the spread of the proportional representation idea in Europe has been rapid. Beginning in 1891, the device has been adopted by one after another of the Swiss cantons, until now it is in use in about half of them. Since 1899 Belgium has employed it in the election of all members of both chambers of her parliament. In 1906 it was adopted by Finland and by the German state of Württemberg. In 1908 Denmark, which has employed the system in the election of members of the upper chamber since 1867, extended its use to election in the municipalities; and in 1915 it was introduced in the election of members of the lower parliamentary chamber. In 1907 an act of the Swedish parliament (confirmed after a general election in 1909) applied it to elections for both legislative chambers, all parliamentary committees, and provincial and town councils.[1] In France there was organized in 1909 a Proportional Representation League which started vigorous and widespread propaganda. The principal arguments employed by the advocates of the proposed reform have been (1) that the effect of its adoption would be to increase greatly the aggregate vote cast in parliamentary elections, since electors belonging to minority parties would be assured of actual representation; (2) that it would no longer be possible, as is now usually the case, for the number of voters unrepresented by deputies of their own political faith to be in excess of the number of electors so represented;[2] and (3) that a parliament in which the various parties are represented in proportion to their voting strength can be depended upon to know and to execute the will of the nation with more precision than can a legislative body elected under the majority system.

The Government and Electoral Reform. — After 1905 the successive ministries were committed, more or less explicitly, to the cause of electoral reform. In 1907 a special committee of

[1] The first English-speaking state to adopt the system was Tasmania, where, after being in partial operation in 1896–1901, it was brought fully into effect in 1907. By an electoral law of 1900 Japan adopted it for the election of the members of her House of Commons. The plan was put in operation in Cuba April 1, 1908, and was authorized in Oregon by a referendum of June 1, 1908.

[2] It is the assertion of M. Benoist, founder of the League, that this situation has existed uninterruptedly since 1881. An interesting fact cited is that the Separation Law of 1905 was adopted in the Chamber by the votes of 341 deputies, who represented in the aggregate but 2,647,315 electors in a national total of 10,967,000.

the Chamber of Deputies reported a scheme of proportional representation, and in 1909 the Chamber passed a resolution favoring the adoption of the principle in some form. It will be observed, of course, that while *scrutin de liste* might be set up without proportional representation, any plan of proportional representation would make necessary the enlarging of the electoral area and the choice of deputies on a general ticket. At the parliamentary elections of April–May, 1910, the issue of electoral reform overshadowed all others. According to a tabulation by the Ministry of the Interior, of the 597 deputies chosen at this time, 94 had not declared themselves on electoral reform, 35 were opposed to the introduction of any change in the existing system, 32 were in favor of a slightly modified *scrutin d'arrondissement*, 64 were in favor of *scrutin de liste* on a majority basis, 272 favored *scrutin de liste* combined with proportional representation, and 88 were known to be friendly to electoral reform although not committed to any particular program.

On at least four occasions in the next two years the Chamber elected in 1910 declared by heavy majorities in favor of reform; and it almost constantly had under consideration some measure upon the subject. The ministry of M. Poincaré, established at the beginning of 1912, asserted that the nation had unmistakably expressed its desire for reform and promised to take steps forthwith to obtain a law that would " secure a more exact representation for political parties and would confer upon deputies the freedom that is required for the subordination of local interests in all cases to the national interest." During ensuing months consideration of the subject was pressed in the Chamber of Deputies, and on July 10 the Government's Electoral Reform Bill, providing for both *scrutin de liste* and proportional representation, was carried by a vote of 339 to 217. In the Senate the bill encountered determined opposition. It was referred to a commission, whose report was unfavorable; and under the persuasive leadership of Clémenceau and Combes, who contended that the representation of minorities would operate to strengthen the clerical elements, the house finally rejected the measure. The deadlock between the two houses which followed the bill's defeat caused the fall of the Briand ministry, in February, 1913. The new Barthou ministry promised to work out a plan of compromise. But for a time the question was overshadowed by protracted parliamentary contests over army legislation and fiscal policies; and when, in the summer of 1914, the way was fairly clear for a resumption of electoral discussion, the subject was thrown instantly into the background by the outbreak of the war. There, for the time being, the matter rests.

II. PARLIAMENT AT WORK

Sessions and Organization. — The constitutional law of July 16, 1875, requires that the Chamber of Deputies and the Senate shall assemble annually on the second Tuesday of January, unless convened at an earlier date by the President of the Republic, and that they shall continue in session through at least five months of each year. The President may convene an extraordinary session, and is obliged to do so if at any time during a recess an absolute majority of both chambers request it. The President may adjourn the chambers, but not more than twice during the same session, and never to exceed one month. The sessions of the Deputies are held in the Palais Bourbon, situated in the neighborhood of a group of ministerial buildings at the end of the Boulevard St. Germain, directly across the Seine from the Place de la Concorde; those of the Senate, as has been stated, in the Palais de Luxembourg. Sessions are required by law to be public; under stipulated conditions the doors may be closed, but the right has fallen into disuse. The public is admitted as long as there are vacant seats in the galleries; and the publication of reports of debates by the press is unrestricted. Since January 1, 1907, deputies have received 15,000 francs a year (increased by law of November, 1906, from 9000); and they are entitled, on payment of a nominal sum, to travel free on all French railways. The emoluments of senators are the same as those of deputies.

The presiding officer of the Chamber of Deputies is known as the president. He is elected by the Chamber and, far from being a mere moderator, as is the Speaker of the British House of Commons, is ordinarily an aggressive party man, not indisposed to quit the chair to participate in debate, and therefore bearing an interesting resemblance to the Speaker of the American House of Representatives. Besides the president, there are four vice-presidents, eight secretaries, and three questors, all chosen by the Chamber. The vice-presidents replace the president when necessary; the secretaries (of whom half must always be on duty when the Chamber is in session) supervise the records of the meetings and count the votes when there is a division; the questors have charge of the Chamber's finances. Collectively, this group of sixteen officials forms what is known as the "bureau" of the Chamber. It manages the business of the body during a session and, if need be, acts in its name during a recess.

Every month during a session the entire membership of the Chamber is divided by lot into eleven other bureaus of equal size. These bureaus meet from time to time separately to examine the credentials of members, to give formal consideration to bills which have not yet been referred to a committee, and, most important of all, to select one of their number to serve on each of the committees of the Chamber. In the case of very important committees, the bureaus may be instructed by the Chamber to designate two members, or even three, each. Thus, the Budget Committee contains three representatives of each bureau. This committee and another constituted to audit the accounts of the Government are created for a year. Others serve a single month. Theoretically, indeed, every measure is referred to a committee specially constituted for the purpose; but practically the result of such procedure would be endless confusion, so that the greater committees, as those on labor, railways, and the army, are allowed to acquire substantial permanence. Committee positions are objects of lively barter among party groups and leaders.

Powers and Procedure. — The functions of the French Parliament are threefold — to amend the constitution, to elect the President, and to enact laws. The mode of exercising the first two has been sufficiently described.[1] The chambers have concurrent powers in all that relates to the initiation, enactment, and amending of laws, save that money bills must be introduced in and passed by the Chamber of Deputies before being considered in the upper branch. Except for this limitation, measures may be introduced in either house, by the ministers

[1] See pp. 332–335.

or by private members. The vast fabric of Napoleonic law which has survived has narrowed the range of legislative activity under the Republic, and during the first generation after 1871 few great statutes were passed, save those of a constitutional character. In our own day, however, the phenomenal expansion of social and industrial legislation, which has been a striking feature of the public life of most European nations, has imparted a new vigor and productiveness to French parliamentary activity.

Each of the chambers has certain functions peculiar to itself. Aside from the prior consideration of money bills, the principal such function of the Deputies is the bringing of impeachment charges against the President for high treason, or against the ministers for crimes committed in the exercise of their functions. As in the United States, the Senate sits as a court of justice in cases of this character. Furthermore, by decree of the President, issued in the council of ministers, the Senate may be constituted a court to try any persons whatsoever who are accused of attempts upon the safety of the state; and every year the house elects a commission which, should a case of this kind arise, would conduct the inquiry. Finally may be mentioned the fact that the Senate is empowered to assent or refuse to assent when the President proposes to dissolve the Chamber of Deputies before the expiration of its term.

Immediately upon assembling, each chamber validates the elections of its own members, chooses its " bureau " of president, vice-presidents, secretaries, and questors, and adopts its own rules of procedure. At an early date the premier communicates orally a " ministerial declaration," corresponding to the Speech from the Throne in England. In it the cabinet announces its policies and plans, and calls for the consideration of various matters specified. Private members have larger opportunity than in England to introduce and advocate bills; yet most of the chambers' time is devoted to discussion of the projects submitted by the Government. The hall in which each body sits is semi-circular, with as many seats and desks as there are members to be accommodated. In the center stands a raised armchair for the use of the president, and in front of it is a platform, or " tribune," which every member who desires to speak is required to mount. On either side of the tribune are stationed stenographers, whose reports of the proceedings are printed each morning in the *Journal Officiel*. The first tier of seats in the semicircle, facing the tribune, is reserved for the Government, *i.e.*, the members of the ministry; behind are ranged the remaining members of the chamber, with the radicals on the president's left and the conservatives on his right.

Of the bureaus into which, at the beginning of each month, the members of each chamber are divided, there are, as has been said, eleven in the Deputies; in the Senate there are nine. When a bill is introduced it is referred first of all to these bureaus, each of which designates one or more commissioners; these persons acting as a committee, are expected to make a careful examination of the measure. The report of the committee is printed and distributed, whereupon general discussion begins in the chamber. Every measure must pass two readings in each chamber, with an interval of five days, unless otherwise ordered by a majority vote. A member wishing to take part in the debate indicates his desire by inscribing his name on lists kept by the secretaries. On the motion of any member, the closure may be applied and a vote ordered. The division may be taken by a show of hands, by rising, or by a ballot in which a white voting paper denotes an affirmative, and a blue one a negative, vote. No decision is valid unless an absolute majority of the members (151 in the Senate and 279 in the Deputies) has participated in the vote. In the upper branch proceedings are apt to be slow and dignified; in the lower they are more animated, and frequently tempestuous. The duty of keeping order falls to the president. In serious cases he is empowered, with the consent of a majority of the chamber, to administer a reprimand carrying with it temporary exclusion from the deliberations.

III. POLITICAL PARTIES SINCE 1871

Origins: Republicans, Conservatives, and Radicals. — Up to a certain point, the alignment of political parties in France to-day dates from the middle of the nineteenth century. In the National Assembly of 1848 — the first representative body elected in France by direct universal suffrage — the line was sharply drawn between the republicans of the Left, who wished to perpetuate the Second Republic and with it a liberal measure of democracy, and the reactionaries of the Right, who began by insisting upon a restoration of clerical privilege and bourgeois rule and ended by clamoring for a restoration of monarchy itself. After Napoleon III's *coup d'état* of 1851, which practically brought an end to the Second Republic, both groups were silenced, although even in the stagnant era of the early Empire they did not altogether lose their identity. With the revival, however, after 1860, of a vigorous political life the two worked together, and with success, to accomplish the overthrow of the personal government of Napoleon III. Upon the collapse of the Empire in 1870 the original cleavage reappeared. The National Assembly elected in 1871 was divided broadly into Republicans and Conservatives (which name gradually replaced that of Reactionaries), and during the five years covered by the life of this extremely important body these two great groups struggled continuously over the supreme question of the day, *i.e.*, the style of government to be adopted permanently for France. Each of the groups embraced a variety of elements. To the Republicans belonged the Radical Extreme Left of Gambetta, the Left of Grévy, Freycînet, and Loubet, and the Center Left of Thiers and Jules Simon. To the Conservatives belonged the Legitimist Extreme Right, an Orleanist Center Right, and eventually, the Imperialists; they were, therefore, the monarchists. Following the definite establishment, in 1875, of the republican constitution, the lines by which these various elements had been marked off grew less distinct, and Republicans and Conservatives each acquired a more homogeneous character.

After the first election under the new constitution (that of 1876) the Senate remained in the control of the monarchist Conservatives, but the Chamber of Deputies was found to contain a Republican majority of more than two to one; not until 1882 did the Republicans command a majority in the upper house. During the early eighties there sprang up a flourishing group which, reviving the original program of Gambetta, assumed the name Radical; and in the elections of 1885 this group acquired such a quota of seats in the Chamber (150) as to render it impossible for the Republicans alone to retain control. Thereafter there were three principal party groups.— the Conservatives and the two republican groups, the Republicans proper and the Radicals. No one of the three being sufficiently strong to obtain a majority that would enable it to rule alone, the politics of a long period turned upon the adoption of one or the other of two lines of tactics — the coalition of the two republican divisions to the end that they might rule as against a Conservative minority (the so-called policy of "republican concentration"), and the alliance of one of these groups with the Right against the other republican group (spoken of commonly as a "pacification").

The Party Situation since 1900. — There is no need to follow through all of its stages the tortuous story of French party development. Rather it will be profitable to survey the party grouping of comparatively recent times, to sum up certain significant aspects of party life, and to call attention to the extraordinary growth of radicalism, especially as it finds expression in organized socialism. The first thing to be observed is that the old alignment of Conservatives and Republicans, if indeed it can be said nowadays to exist, means something totally different from what it meant in the formative era of the Republic. There is no single party which bears either name. There are "conservatives," but few of them are monarchists; there are republicans, but they include most of these conservatives and, indeed, almost everybody else. The party situation can be made most concrete by viewing it in terms of the various groups of members as they sit in front of the presiding officer of the Chamber of Deputies; because, in accordance with continental custom, they there occupy places which denote both the general character of their tenets and the relationship which they bear to other political elements. At the president's extreme right sit the ultra-conservatives, at his extreme left the ultra-radicals; whence arise the terms Right and Left, as used to denote the membership of conservative and radical temperaments respectively. Groups whose views are intermediate occupy middle positions in the hall.

As matters have stood for upwards of two decades, the extreme right has been occupied by the Monarchists, and next to them has sat the members of the *Action Libérale* (Liberal Action). The Monarchist members at the outbreak of the war numbered only twenty-six. Some supported a Bourbon pretender, some a Bonapartist claimant; none were taken very seriously either inside or outside the chamber. The *Action Libérale* was organized in 1901, when the great conflict over the relations of church and state was approaching a crisis; and its object was to reconcile clericalism, *i.e.*, in a general way, the interests of the Catholic Church, with republicanism. Its members fully support the present form of government, but they demand the repeal of the anti-clerical legislation of 1901-1917. The existing electoral system works to their disadvantage; hence they are ardent supporters of *scrutin de liste* and proportional representation. And they seek to compete with the Socialists for the votes of the working classes by advocating new labor laws, trade-unionism, and social insurance. That their appeal is not fruitless is indicated by the fact that in 1914 they polled 1,350,000 votes, which, however, were so scattered over the country that only 34 of the party's candidates were elected. Considering that the Unified Socialist party in the same election obtained 102 seats on a basis of one hundred thousand fewer votes, largely because of their concentration in industrial constituencies, it is not difficult to see why the *Action Libérale* favors proportional representation and the Socialists oppose it.

At the extreme left of the Chamber sit the Socialists, whose rise to prominence will be described presently. Between the Monarchists and *Action Libérale* and the Socialists sat from 1900 to 1910 a number of groups descended more or less directly from the old Republican party, and organized, in this decade, in a *bloc* which was able to control the ministries, dominate the Chamber, and shape the policies of the Republic. " Reckoned from Right to Left," as a recent writer has described it, " the *bloc* included (1) the Progressist Republicans, headed by Paul Deschanel . . ., recruited from the upper middle class and from the small propertied class, devoted to the individual rights and liberties proclaimed by the Revolution, especially to the basic right of private property; (2) Radicals of varying titles, the core, and by far the most numerous, of the *bloc*, true disciples of Gambetta, shapers of bourgeois policies, intellectual radicals, most stalwart anti-clericals, including in 1910 such influential politicians as Senators Clémenceau and Combes and Deputy Caillaux; and (3) Radical Socialists, or, as would be more accurately descriptive, the ' socialistically inclined Radicals,' a remarkable group, who with pronounced anti-clericalism combined a determination to drag their more or less unwilling allies along the path of social reform and to do for the working classes what the French Revolution did for the bourgeoisie, a ' bourgeois party with a popular soul,' championing not only strict governmental regulation of industry but government ownership of all means of communication and transportation, likewise of national resources like mines, forests, oil fields, etc. Among the Radical Socialist group were to be counted several brilliant men, such as Briand, Millerand, and Viviani, who called themselves plain Socialists, but who were read out of the regular Socialist camp because of their willingness to enter coalition ministries with representatives of non-Socialist groups." [1]

The great issue that held the *bloc* together was anti-clericalism; and during the decade the anti-clerical program was carried forward rapidly: the religious orders were expelled from the country, church and state were separated, and larger provision was made for secular education. Then new questions pushed into the foreground — the taxation of incomes, electoral reform, the revival of a three-year term of military service, and several aspects of further social reconstruction. The groups in the *bloc* by no means thought alike on these matters, and after 1910 the combination gradually dissolved. At the elections of April–May, 1914, the *Action Libérale* on the one side and the Socialists on the other made substantial gains; while the bourgeois groups that had composed the *bloc* fared, in the words of the writer already quoted, as follows: " The Progressists adhered to their earlier principles and maintained their strength practically unimpaired. But the Radicals and Radical-Socialists were split up into a number of groups, which tended, both in the parliament and in the country at large, to gravitate toward one or other of two new and rival combinations. The first was the Unified Radicals, including such men as Caillaux, Combes, and Clémenceau, bent upon the vigorous prosecution of more extreme anti-clerical legislation, especially against private church schools, generally hostile to electoral reform, and lukewarm in the cause of labor legislation. The second new coalition was the Federation of

[1] Hayes, *Political and Social History of Modern Europe*, II, 365.

the Left, whose principles were championed by Briand and by Poincaré, who had been elected to the presidency in January, 1913; it urged both labor legislation and parliamentary reform, and while not favoring any repeal of anti-clerical legislation, it was unwilling further to open the breach between Catholics and non-Catholics."[1] Following the election, cabinets rose and fell in swift succession; the main source of discord being the demand of the Socialists and other radical elements for immediate repeal of the three-year service law. With fine irony, the Great War cut short this controversy; and every important political group forthwith turned its full strength into the channels of national defense.

General Features of French Party Politics. — As may be inferred from what has been said, political parties of the sort with which Americans and Englishmen are familiar hardly exist in France. Certain fundamental *tendencies* exist — reactionary, moderate, radical, socialist, syndicalist; and it is they, rather than formal party organizations, that endure from year to year and from decade to decade. The groups that spring up around some inspiring leader, and for a time give these tendencies expression, dissolve almost as readily as they form. They exist rather in Parliament than in the nation, and are apt to take shape rather *after* a Parliament has come into session than before. Between sessions — and yet more, between quadrennial elections — the political scene may change completely. Deputies and senators pass readily from one group to another, sometimes belonging to two simultaneously; and the groups show hardly more stability in their affiliations one with another than in their internal composition and organization. Party organization and party discipline throughout the country can hardly be said to exist. Candidates for Parliament announce themselves, or are announced by their friends; they make their own platforms and conduct their own campaigns. Occasionally a great issue, such as clericalism, dominates in an electoral contest to such a degree that the will of the nation can be clearly tested. But as a rule the issues are so numerous, localized, personal, and confused that a study of the electoral returns leaves only a blurred impression. This was eminently true of the elections of 1910, and scarcely less so of those of 1914.

[1] Hayes, *Political and Social History of Modern Europe*, II, 367.

All of this does not mean a lack of interest in public affairs. The Frenchman, however, as has been pointed out by Lowell, is theoretical rather than practical in his politics. "He is inclined to pursue an ideal, striving to realize his conception of a perfect form of society, and is reluctant to give up any part of it for the sake of attaining so much as lies within his reach. Such a tendency naturally gives rise to a number of groups, each with a separate ideal, and each unwilling to make the sacrifice that is necessary for a fusion into a great party. In short, the intensity of political sentiment prevents the development of real political issues. To the Frenchman, public questions have an absolute rather than a relative or a practical bearing, and therefore he cares more for principles and opinions than for facts. This tendency is shown in the programs of the candidates, which are apt to be philosophic documents instead of statements of concrete policy, and, although published at great length, often give a comparatively small idea of the position of the author on the immediate question of the day. . . . The inability to organize readily in politics has this striking result, that vehement as some of the groups are, and passionate as is their attachment to their creeds, they make little effort to realize their aims by associating together their supporters in all parts of the country for concerted action."[1]

These words were written a quarter of a century ago; and as applied to very large sections of French political life they still state the situation perfectly. It is important to observe, however, that of late there has been considerable development in the direction of stable parties with a nation-wide organization. At one extreme of the political scale the *Action Libérale* has built up, through seventeen years, a party with a coherent program, an executive committee, a dues-paying membership, and a well-filled treasury. At the other extreme the Socialists have, in a somewhat briefer period, set up a united party whose successes — at parliamentary elections, on the floor of the chambers, and, indeed, within the cabinet circle — have been a source of constant surprise. To this Socialist achievement we must now turn.

Socialism to 1905. — France is the land that gave modern socialism birth. After a feverish outburst during the revolution

[1] *Governments and Parties in Continental Europe*, I, 105–107.

of 1848, however, propaganda practically ceased for a generation. There continued to be socialists, and there was a certain amount of socialist discussion and writing; but there was no socialist party or "movement." Unrest among the laboring masses was partially allayed by a measure of 1864 legalizing strikes, and another of 1868 tolerating trade-unions, and although the war with Prussia in 1870-1871 deeply stirred the working people, the Paris uprising known as the Commune caused most exponents of socialist doctrine to be expelled from the country and left the cause leaderless. The revival may be said to have begun with the return, in 1876, of the political exile Jules Guesde, an able journalist, who began by establishing a new and widely read socialist journal, *L'Égalité*, and by persuading the third French labor congress, convened at Marseilles in 1879, to declare for socialism and, indeed, to take the name of Socialist Labor Congress. Henceforth the trade-union movement was dominated by socialist organizers and leaders, who, however, could not agree among themselves; so that both the socialist and the trade-union ranks broke into petty, contending factions whose bickerings it would be wearisome to describe. By 1890 there were five well-defined socialist groups, counting in their membership some of the most brilliant journalists, scholars, and lawyers of the country. At the elections of 1893 almost half a million socialist votes were cast, and forty socialist deputies were returned to the Chamber; and since, under the leadership of the scholar and orator Jaurès the group was able to perfect a working organization, the beginning of socialism as a factor in parliamentary proceedings may be dated from this point. Presenting the group to the new Chamber, Jaurès declared that its guiding motives would be "allegiance to the Republic and devotion to the cause of humanity." Throughout the period covered by this parliament (1893-1897) the program of socialism was first expounded authoritatively in the Chamber, and put before the country with clearness and power. The division of forces, however, persisted; and strong effort had to be made to build up real party unity. Just when in 1898-1899, the outlook for union was bright, fresh dissensions arose over the attitude to be taken toward the Dreyfus affair and over the acceptance by one of the leaders, Millerand, of the portfolio of Commerce in the ministry of Waldeck-Rousseau. The parliamentary group was completely disrupted, and an international socialist congress at Paris in 1900 was compelled by the resulting situation to devote its time principally — and fruitlessly, as it proved — to consideration of the " cas Millerand."

Throughout the years 1900-1905 the socialist forces continued to have no unity, even in form. On the contrary, the bickerings of the various groups were being constantly aired before the country and before the world, to the chagrin of socialist leaders in other lands. There were now two principal factions, or so-called parties. One was the *Parti Socialist de France*, or Socialist party of France, composed principally of the Guesdists. The other was the *Parti Socialist Français*, or French Socialist party, made up mainly of the followers of Jaurès. The policy of the one was to stand by the doctrine of Karl Marx and refuse to compromise or to coöperate with any group having less orthodox ideas or less fixedness of purpose than itself. The policy of the other was to "penetrate the democracy with the ideas of socialism," and to do it, in the words of Jaurès, "by collaborating with all democrats, yet vigorously distinguishing one's self from them."

Jaurès and the Plea for Opportunism. — Acknowledging freely, in a remarkable speech at the Bordeaux congress of 1903, that the policy of opportunism was complicated, awkward, and certain to create serious difficulties at every turn, Jaurès contended, none the less, that in it alone lay hope of the achievement of the socialist purpose. "Guesde is wrong," he declared, "in thinking . . . that the state is exclusively a class-state, upon which the too feeble hand of the proletariat cannot yet inscribe the smallest portion of its will. In a democracy, in a republic where there is universal suffrage, the state is not for the proletarians a refractory, hard, absolutely impermeable and impenetrable block. Penetration has begun already. In municipalities, in parliament, in the central government, there has begun the penetration of socialistic and proletarian influence. . . . It is in part penetrated by this democratic, popular, socialistic force, and if we can reasonably hope that by organization, education, and propaganda this penetration will become so full, deep, and decisive, that in time by accumulated efforts we shall find the proletarian and socialistic state to have replaced the oligarchic and bourgeois state, then perhaps we shall be aware of having entered the zone of socialism, as navigators are aware of having crossed the line of a hemisphere — not that they have been able to see as they crossed it a cord stretched over the ocean warning them of their passage, but that little by little they have been led into a new hemisphere by the progress of their ship." [1]

This was clearly evolutionary, not revolutionary, socialism; and it differed from the socialism of the Marxists in France quite as profoundly as the socialism of the Revisionists differs from that of the Marxists in Germany. At the International Socialist Congress at Amsterdam in 1904 Jaurès was compelled to enter the lists against Bebel in defense of his ideas, and there occurred one of the most notable debates — "a titanic international duel," it has been aptly designated — in the history of the socialist movement. The burden of the French leader's argument was that, notwithstanding the fact that the socialists of Germany in congress at Dresden in 1903 had voted overwhelmingly against revisionism, it was not possible to pursue an identical policy in all countries, and as matters were in France, where the proletariat was in a position already to exercise control over the government, the policy of opportunism was not only permissible but fundamentally necessary. The logic of Bebel, however, prevailed, and the congress voted a revised resolution against opportunism based upon that adopted by the Germans at Dresden.

The Unified Socialist Party. — The outcome of the Amsterdam meeting cleared the way for socialist unification in France. The congress, indeed, voicing the desire of the socialists of all lands, urged, and practically enjoined, that the French factions drop their quarrels and combine in a single party. The Guesdist element had stood with Bebel and the non-opportunist forces. Jaurès and his followers had put forth their best effort and had been defeated, and they now accepted the decision loyally. In 1905, at the congress of Rouen, took place the long deferred fusion of the two groups in the *Parti Socialist Unifié*, or Unified Socialist party, of the present day, designated officially as the

[1] Quoted in Hunter, *Socialists at Work*, 74.

Section Française de l'Internationale Ouvrière, or French Section of the International Workingmen's Association.

The instrument of agreement between the contracting groups contained the following notable declarations: (1) " The Socialist party is a class party which has for its aim the socialization of the means of production and exchange, that is to say, to transform the present capitalistic society into a collective or communistic society by means of the political and economic organization of the proletariat. By its aims, by its ideals, by the power which it employs, the Socialist party, always seeking to realize the immediate reforms demanded by the working class, is not a party of reforms, but a party of class war and revolution. (2) The members of Parliament elected by the party form a unique group opposed to all the factions of the bourgeois parties. The Socialist group in Parliament must refuse to sustain all of those means which assure the domination of the bourgeoisie in government and their maintenance in power; must therefore refuse to vote for military appropriations, appropriations for colonial conquest, secret funds, and the budget. In Parliament the Socialist group must consecrate itself to defending and extending the political liberties and rights of the working classes and to the realization of those reforms which ameliorate the conditions of life in the struggle for existence of the working class. (3) There shall be complete freedom of discussion in the press concerning questions of principle and policy, but the conduct of all the Socialist publications must be strictly in accord with the decisions of the national congress as interpreted by the executive committee of the party." [1]

The united party grew rapidly in membership and in influence. Although founded in reaction against opportunism, it has steadily pursued a political policy. It has consistently sought to increase its strength in the Chamber of Deputies, and its members have had no hesitation in accepting municipal, departmental, and national office. When, in 1906, two socialists, Réné Viviani and Aristide Briand, accepted posts in the ministry of Clémenceau, the event was taken quite as a matter of course.[2] In 1885, when

[1] Orth, *Socialism and Democracy in Europe*, 289-291.
[2] Even Jules Guesde, arch-opponent of all coalition with non-socialist ministries, entered the cabinet almost immediately after the outbreak of the Great War.

the French socialists made their first concerted effort to influence the results of a parliamentary election, the aggregate number of votes polled by their candidates was but 30,000. In 1889 their popular vote was 120,000, and in 1898, 700,000, or almost twenty per cent of the total. In 1910 the vote was 1,200,000, and the number of socialist deputies was raised to 105, of whom 75 were identified with the Unified party. At the elections of 1914 the total socialist quota became 132. Of these members, 102 belonged to the Unified party, which alone cast 1,250,000 votes; the other 30 were "Independent Socialists." The Unified party now either has a majority or lacks but little of it in most of the cities and large towns throughout the country.

General Aspects of French Socialism in Recent Years. — Memories of the differences between the Guesdist and Jaurèsite groups could not be instantly obliterated. They have not yet wholly disappeared. But since 1905 the unity of the party, although at times severely tested, has withstood every strain that has been put upon it. Not that the Unified party includes all French socialists. There are the Independent Socialists; also the Radical Socialists — men like Briand, Viviani, and Millerand, who, as has been said, consider themselves socialists, and who, in other countries, would be identified with organizations of a strictly socialist character. The hope of organized socialism in France lies, however, with the Unified party. As is true of the German Social Democracy, the number of bona fide, dues-paying members of this party is very much smaller than the number of votes polled by the candidates whom it places in the field. In 1905, the date of unification, the number of dues-paying members was only 27,000. By 1908 the number had risen to 52,000, and in 1914 it was 68,900. The principal reason for such slowness of growth is to be found in the policy of the trade-unions, which, while not discouraging their members from casting their votes for socialist candidates, have of late held aloof from the socialist organizations. The party is governed by a congress, meeting annually in some important town; and there is a committee to administer affairs during intervals between sessions.

The party program lays stress principally upon the socialization of the instrumentalities of production and exchange, involving the supplanting of the capitalistic by a collectivist organization of the state; and the means to be employed to this end is the acquisition of control over the state through the unification of the industrial classes in support of the party's policies. That, despite its opportunism, the party stands by its traditional ideal is indicated by a resolution adopted by the congress at Limoges in 1907. " The congress," it was affirmed, " considering that any change in the personnel of a capitalist government could not in any way modify the fundamental policy of the party, puts the proletariat on its guard against the insufficiency of a program, even the most advanced, of the ' democratic bourgeoisie ' ; it reminds the workers that their liberation will only be possible through the social ownership of capital, that there is no socialism except in the socialist party, organized and unified, and that its representation in Parliament, while striving to realize the reforms which will augment the force of the action and the demands of the proletariat, shall at the same time oppose unceasingly, to all restricted and too often illusory programs, the reality and integrity of the socialist ideal."

A striking aspect of socialism in France is the extent to which the creed permeates all social classes and all professions. In England members of the educated classes belong mainly to one of the two great political parties, and in Germany there have ordinarily been no socialists in the governing class and comparatively few in the professions. In France, on the other hand, many men of education, wealth, and social standing have been willing to associate themselves with the masses, not only as leaders, but as private advocates of the enthronement of the people. Most of the leaders, indeed, are of bourgeois extraction. A recent writer has pointed out that among the representatives of the Unified party in the Chamber of Deputies after the elections of 1910 there were only thirty workingmen and trade-union officials, while there were eleven professors and teachers, seven journalists, seven lawyers, seven farmers, six physicians, and two engineers.[1] This very cosmopolitanism of the present movement leads one to doubt whether there is any chance that the more radical portions of the party program will ever be realized. Certainly many men who at present lend their support to the party are in sympathy with its ultimate ideal in only a

[1] Orth, *Socialism and Democracy in Europe*, 116.

broad and theoretic way. And it may be added that the temper of the French people as a whole runs counter to the socialistic aspiration. For while, as has been demonstrated on many historic occasions, no people is more ready to theorize and to talk radicalism, it is just as true that no people clings more tenaciously to its property and its property rights. The French are a nation of small farmers and shopkeepers, and while they have been ready to accept the nationalization of railways and various other forms of collectivism, they would be loath indeed to divest themselves of their traditional and treasured rights of private property.

SELECTED REFERENCES

A. L. Lowell, *Governments and Parties in Continental Europe* (New York, 1896), I, Chaps. i–ii; R. Poincaré, *How France Is Governed* (New York, 1914), Chap. ix; J. C. Bracq, *France under the Republic* (New York, 1910), Chaps. i–ii; J. S. Schapiro, *Modern and Contemporary European History* (Boston, 1918), Chap. xi; F. A. Ogg, *Economic Development of Modern Europe* (New York, 1917), Chap. xxiii; A. P. Usher, " Procedure in the French Chamber of Deputies," *Polit. Sci. Quar.*, Sept., 1906; J. W. Garner, " Electoral Reform in France," *Amer. Polit. Sci. Review*, Nov., 1913; S. P. Orth, *Socialism and Democracy in Europe* (New York, 1913), Chap. v; R. Hunter, *Socialists at Work* (New York, 1908), Chap. iii; L. Levine, *Syndicalism in France* (New York, 1916); M. Pease, *Jean Jaurès* (New York, 1918).

CHAPTER XIX

JUSTICE AND LOCAL GOVERNMENT IN ENGLAND AND FRANCE

It is of much concern to the citizen that the laws of the nation be wisely made, and that they be fully and impartially executed. But it is of even greater moment that his life, liberty, and property be protected by a correct interpretation and a due enforcement of law in the courts, and that the agencies of government in his own community, with which he is brought into contact every day that he lives, be adequately organized, efficient, and responsive to the public will. Before passing from the two great European democracies, England and France, it will be well, therefore, to look somewhat into the nature of their judicial systems and of their machinery of local government.

I. ENGLISH LAW AND JUSTICE

Character and Form of the Law. — "Nothing," says a recent writer, "has contributed more to the stability of the British Empire, or the respect in which it is held, than the even-handed dispensing of justice which has distinguished its tribunals, from the highest to the lowest, for the last two hundred years."[1] The fundamental principle of the English political system may, indeed, be said to be the rule of law, which means, in effect, two things: first, that no man may be deprived of liberty or property save on account of a breach of the law proved in court and, second, that no man stands above the law, and that for every violation of the law reparation may be obtained, whatever the station or character of the offender. Upon these great guarantees has been erected through the centuries a fabric of personal liberty which lends the British nation one of its chief distinctions. The influence of English concepts and forms of law has counted for

[1] Jenks, *Government of the British Empire*, 246.

much, furthermore, in the shaping of continental legal systems; and outside of Europe, and especially in the English-speaking countries of both hemispheres, the law of England has made, within modern times, exceedingly important contributions to legal development.

From at least the seventeenth century, law has been conceived of in England as the body of rules, of whatsoever origin or nature, which can be enforced in the courts. As it has taken form, it falls into two principal categories. The one is statute law, the other is the Common Law. Statute law consists of specific acts of Parliament, supplemented by by-laws, rules, and regulations made under parliamentary sanction by public officials and bodies. Chronologically, it begins in 1235, in the reign of Henry III; and inasmuch as it is amended and amplified at every parliamentary session, its bulk has come to be enormous. The more comprehensive and fundamental part of English law, however, is, and has always been, the Common Law. The Common Law is a product of growth rather than of legislation. No definite time can be assigned for its beginning, for at as early a period as there are reports of judicial decisions the existence of a body of law not emanating from law-makers was taken for granted. Long before the close of the Middle Ages the essentials of the Common Law acquired not only unquestioned sanction but also thoroughgoing coherence and uniformity. Despite the greatly increased legislative activity of modern times, it may still be said that the rules of the Common Law are fundamental, the laws of Parliament but incidental. Statutes simply *assume* the principles of the Common Law, and are largely, as one writer has put it, " the addenda and errata " of this law, incomplete and meaningless save in coördination with the legal order by which they are supported and enveloped.[1] Thus no act of Parliament enjoins in general terms that a man shall pay his debts, or fulfill his contracts, or pay damages for trespass or slander. Statutes define the *modes* by which these obligations shall be met, but the obliga-

[1] Geldart, *The Elements of English Law*, 9. This author further remarks: "If all the statutes of the realm were repealed, we should have a system of law, though, it may be, an unworkable one; if we could imagine the Common Law swept away and the Statute Law preserved, we should have only disjointed rules torn from their context, and no provision at all for many of the most important relations of life."

tions themselves are derived entirely from the Common Law. It is, however, a fixed rule that where statutes fall in conflict with the Common Law the statutes prevail. The limitless power of Parliament involves the right to set aside or to modify at any time any Common Law principle or practice; while, on the other hand, no development of the Common Law can repeal a parliamentary statute.

Statute law, of course, invariably takes written form. The acts of Parliament are to be found in imposing printed collections, to which a substantial volume is added every year. Of the Common Law, however, there is no single or authoritative text. The Common Law grew up originally as unwritten law, and in a large measure it retains that character. The sources, however, from which knowledge of it must be drawn are mainly in writing or in print. The most important are (1) the decisions of the judges of the English courts, which from at least the sixteenth century acquired weight as precedents and are nowadays practically decisive in analogous cases; (2) the decisions of courts of other countries in which is administered a law derived from the English, such decisions being, of course, not binding, yet highly influential; and (3) certain " books of authority " written by learned lawyers of earlier times. Some small branches of the Common Law have, indeed, been codified in the form of statutes, among them the law of partnership, that of sales, and that of bills of exchange.

Criminal Justice and Its Agencies.[1] — It would be wearisome to describe one by one the many offices and courts that make up the English judicial system. The essential facts may better be brought out in another way, namely, by sketching the great processes by which criminal and civil justice is actually administered. For practical purposes, all cases that come before English courts of justice may be classed as either criminal or civil; and the arrangement of the courts, and their procedure, are largely based on this distinction. By criminal cases is meant those in which the king (that is to say, in these days, the *government*), acting in the double capacity of accuser and judge, " prosecutes "

[1] This section and the succeeding one represent practically a condensation of Jenks, *Government of the British Empire*, Chap. xi. It should be noted that the judicial system described is that of England alone. The systems existing in Scotland and Ireland differ from it at many points.

a person who is alleged to have committed an offense, such as murder, theft, or forgery, in order that the offender may be punished. The difficulty which would naturally arise from the double capacity of the king in such cases, if he acted in person, is got over by the fact that he has long ceased so to act, and that his duties in each capacity are now performed by totally distinct officials — by the law officers of the crown or other prosecutors on the one side, and by " His Majesty's judges " on the other.

When a man is accused of having committed an offense he is formally summoned, or arrested and brought, first of all, before the " magistrates," *i.e.*, one or more of the justices of the peace. The office of justice of the peace dates from the thirteenth century and has filled a large place in the development of administrative and judicial practice. The normal area of jurisdiction of the justices is the county, although there are also borough justices; and, aside from various persons who attain the office on an *ex-officio* basis, the justices in any given county are appointed, " at the pleasure of the crown," by the Lord High Chancellor, usually on recommendation of the lord lieutenant of the county. In many counties the list of justices contains three or four hundred names. But some of the appointees do not take the oath required to qualify them for magisterial service, and the actual work is performed in each county by a comparatively small number of persons. The justices serve without pay, but the office carries much local distinction, and appointments are widely coveted. A large proportion of the appointees would be classed as country gentlemen.

When the accused is brought before the justice of the peace the duty of the latter is, in the first place, merely to see whether there is a *prima facie* case against him. For this purpose, the magistrate hears the evidence, usually sworn testimony, of the prosecutor and his witnesses. There is no jury, and the accused need not make any statement or offer any defense unless he likes. If, after the hearing, the justice feels that no *prima facie* case has been made out, *i.e.*, that no jury would convict even if the prosecutor's evidence were unchallenged, he dismisses the charge, and the accused goes free. If, however, he thinks that a *prima facie* case has been established, he " commits the prisoner for trial," and decides whether to let him out on bail or to have him confined to await further proceedings. If the privilege of bail is refused the prisoner may apply, by a writ of *habeas corpus*, to a judge of the High Court for an order compelling it to be granted. The court in which the trial will take place is determined mainly by the seriousness of the case. A large and increasing number of offenses, including petty assaults and thefts, small breaches of public order, and other minor misdemeanors — and even graver offenses if the accused wishes, or if it is a first charge, or if he is under age — are " punishable on summary conviction." The court of summary conviction is composed of at least two justices of the peace (usually resident in the immediate neighborhood), and is known as " petty sessions." The trial is public and without a jury, and the accused is given full opportunity to be heard and to introduce counsel. If the court finds the man guilty it imposes a fine or a limited period of imprisonment; but he may appeal to the "quarter sessions" of all the justices of the county, who will hear his case again from beginning to end.

In graver cases the accused is proceeded against by formal " indictment," or written statement accusing him of a definite crime committed in a particular way; and he is entitled to a copy of this indictment before his trial. An indictment case is tried either before quarter sessions or before a judge of the High Court " at assizes," in open court, usually in the county in which the offense is alleged to have been committed, and invariably by jury. Quarter sessions are so called because they are held four times a year. In the counties they comprise all the justices of the peace for the county who care to take part; and all who sit are entitled to vote on the decisions. The assizes courts are held three times a year in all counties and four times in certain cities; and, as has been said, they are presided over normally by a judge of the High Court who goes out " on circuit " for the purpose. Wherever the trial takes place, the accused is entitled to have his fate decided by a jury of twelve of his countrymen, chosen at random by the sheriff from a list of householders compiled by the local authorities; and he has an almost unlimited right to " challenge," *i.e.*, to object to, the jurors selected. It is the business of the judge (or judges) throughout the trial to see that the rules of procedure and evidence are followed; and after counsel for both sides have completed the examination of witnesses and have addressed the jury, the presiding judge sums up the case and gives the jurors any instructions about the law that may be necessary to enable them to arrive at a verdict on the facts. If the jury finds the prisoner not guilty, he is discharged at once; and he can never be tried on the same accusation. If it finds him guilty, the judge pronounces the sentence provided by law; although, except in " capital " cases, he has considerable discretion within fixed limits. If the jury cannot agree, there may be a new trial, with a different set of jurors.

Formerly there was no appeal from the verdict of a jury in a criminal trial, although appeal lay to the House of Lords on points of law involved. An act of 1907, however, set up a Court of Criminal Appeal, consisting of not fewer than three judges of the King's (or Queen's) Bench; and a convicted person may now, as a matter of right, appeal to this tribunal on any question of law, and (with the permission of either the judge at the trial or the Court of Criminal Appeal itself) on any question of fact, *e.g.*, that the verdict of the jury was not justified by the evidence. If the appellate court thinks there has been a serious miscarriage of justice it can modify the sentence, or even quash the conviction altogether. There can be no further appeal from the Court of Criminal Appeal, except to the House of Lords upon a point of law which one of the " law officers of the crown," the Attorney-General, certifies to be of public importance. Under no circumstances can the prosecutor appeal.

Civil Proceedings. — A civil action is a proceeding brought by a private citizen, or by an official in his private character, to obtain redress against another person, official or private, for a wrong — slander, trespass, breach of contract, infringement of patents, and the like — alleged to have been committed against the bringer of the action, or " plaintiff," by the person against whom the action is brought, or " defendant." In matters of this kind the function of the public authorities is merely to judge, *i.e.*, to determine the merits of the controversy. The parties may at any time agree to compromise and end the controversy out of court, as can never be done in criminal proceedings. Under the English system the court in which a civil action will be brought depends, in the first instance, on the amount of the claim. If it is less than £100, or if, in certain cases, the value of the property about which the dispute arises is not more than £500, the suit will probably be instituted in a county court. The county courts of the present day, established by act of 1846, replace, although they are not historically descended from, the ancient courts of the hundred and county. They are known as county courts, but in point of fact the area of their jurisdiction is a district which not only is smaller than the county but bears no relation to it. There are in England at present some five hundred of these districts, each with its own "court house"; the object being to bring the agencies of justice close to the people and so to reduce the costs and delays incident to litigation. The volume of business to be transacted in a district is normally insufficient to occupy a judge during any large part of his working time, and the districts are grouped in some fifty circuits, to each of which is assigned by the Lord Chancellor one judge who holds court in each district of his circuit approximately once a month. The judges are paid out of the national treasury and hold office during good behavior. Procedure in the county court is simple, and frequently the case is conducted by the parties in person. Where the amount in dispute exceeds £5 either party may demand a jury (which for this purpose consists of eight persons); but this is rarely done. Where there is a jury it finds a verdict on the facts proved, under the direction of the judge; where there is none the judge decides on the facts and on the law, and in either case gives a judgment for the plaintiff or the defendant, which is enforced by seizure of the property of the party who fails to obey it, or even by imprisonment. The object of civil proceedings is, however, compensation, not punishment. There can be no appeal from the court's decision on a question of fact; but on a point of law appeal lies to a "divisional" sitting of the High Court of Justice, at which two judges are present. In cases arising out of workmen's compensation and some other matters, appeals on questions of law may go to the Court of Appeal, and, ultimately, to the House of Lords.

Where the plaintiff's claim exceeds the jurisdiction of the county court he must, and, even if it does not, he may, bring his action in the High Court of Justice. This High Court is the lower chamber of the Supreme Court of Judicature established in 1875. It is organized in three "divisions" — Chancery, King's Bench, and Probate, Divorce, and Admiralty. In theory, any kind of civil action can be begun in any one of these divisions; and there is no limit to the importance of the actions that may be tried there. In practice, each division retains the kind of business it inherited from the tribunals out of which it was formed. The judges, whose number is variable, are appointed by the crown on nomination of the Lord Chancellor and hold office during good behavior. Under varying conditions, too complex to be stated here, they sit singly and in groups (although never as one body), at the capital and on circuit. There is no appeal on a question of fact from the judge (or jury, if there be one), although on various grounds, *e.g.*, that the verdict was unwarranted by the evidence, application for a new trial may be made to the Court of Appeal, which is the upper chamber of the above-mentioned Supreme Court of Judicature. Appeals on points of law go to this same tribunal. The Court of Appeal consists of the Lord Chancellor, three other high judicial personages sitting by *ex-officio* right, and six Lords Justices of Appeal specially appointed by the crown on recommendation of the Lord Chancellor; and while it is technically a single court it usually sits in two sections, each actually consisting of three of the specially appointed justices. The sittings are held exclusively at London; no witnesses are heard, and there is no jury; and the business, chiefly hearing appeals in civil cases from the High Court, is exclusively appellate; the decisions take the form of affirmation, reversal, or alteration of the judgment of the lower court.

The dissatisfied litigant has still one more appeal, if he can stand the delay and expense, *viz.*, to the House of Lords. Starting with control, through appeal, over the courts of common law in England, this body in time acquired a similar supremacy in both civil and criminal actions over all British and Irish tribunals except those of an ecclesiastical character. In 1875 it was proposed to abolish this control, and an act to that effect was passed. But, on the understanding that there would be an alteration of the composition of the chamber when sitting as a court of appeals, the measure was repealed before it had been put into effect. Provision was thereupon made for two (later three, and eventually four) salaried life peers to be selected from men of legal eminence, and to be known as Lords of Appeal in Ordinary. No judgment can be rendered on an appeal unless at least three " law lords " (these life members, together with all hereditary peers who hold, or have held, high judicial office) have been present at the hearing of the arguments, and have taken part in the decision. Normally, judicial business is transacted by the chamber as a whole, and every member has a right not only to be present but to participate in the decisions. Actually, it is transacted by the little group of law lords under the presidency of the Lord Chancellor; and the unwritten rule which prohibits the presence at judicial sessions of any persons save the law lords is quite as strictly observed as is any one of a score of other important conventions of the constitution. The law lords may sit and pronounce judgments in the name of the House at any time, regardless of whether Parliament is in session. A sitting of the Court is, technically, a sitting of the House of Lords, and all actions are entered in the Journal as a part of the chamber's proceedings.[1]

II. FRENCH LAW AND JUSTICE

Law: the Codes. — The law of France is, in an exceptional degree, composite. Its sources lie far back in the Roman law, the canon law, and the Germanic law of the Middle Ages. As late as 1789 there had been no attempt at a complete codification of it. Royal ordinances, it is true, had brought about a reasonable degree of uniformity in criminal law, civil and criminal procedure, and commercial law. But the civil law still existed in the form of

[1] A tribunal of great and growing importance, although, practically speaking, it does not hear appeals from British or Irish courts, is the Judicial Committee on the Privy Council. This court was created in 1833 to take over jurisdiction (mainly, but, not exclusively, civil) formerly exercised, in a rather loose manner, by the Council as a whole. The members include the Lord President of the Privy Council, the Lord Chancellor, the four Lords of Appeal in Ordinary, such additional members of the Council as hold (or have held) high judicial office, and not more than seven judges of the superior colonial courts, and two of the superior Indian courts, provided they are members of the Privy Council. The Committee's function is to hear appeals from the ecclesiastical courts, from courts in the Channel Islands and the Isle of Man, from the courts of the colonies and dependencies, and from English courts established by treaty in foreign countries. Its decisions are tendered under the guise of "advice to the crown," and, unlike the decisions of the Lords, must represent a unanimous opinion of the judges (not under three) that have heard the case. The Committee is assuming, more and more, an imperial character, and the appeals that come to it are of the most varied nature and involve a knowledge of the most diverse systems of law.

"customs" (*coutumiers*), which varied widely from province to province. A uniform code of civil law was earnestly demanded in the *cahiers* of 1789, and was definitely promised in the constitution of 1791.

Some steps toward a codification were taken by the first two Revolutionary assemblies, but the development of a coherent plan began only with the Convention, in 1793. In the period of the Consulate (1799–1804) the task was continued and progress was rapid. The drafting of the codes was intrusted to a special commission, appointed by the First Consul, Napoleon; and the ultimate decision of difficult or controverted questions fell to the Council of State, over whose deliberations Napoleon frequently presided in person. On March 31, 1804, — less than two months before the proclamation of the Empire, — the new *Code Civil des Français* was promulgated in its entirety. In arrangement the Code resembles the famous Institutes of Justinian; in content it represents a very successful combination of the two great elements with which the framers had to deal, *i.e.*, the ancient heterogeneous law of the French provinces and the new uniform law which flowed from the deliberations of the successive Revolutionary assemblies.

With the progress of time certain defects appeared in the Code, and since 1871 more than a hundred modifications have been introduced in it. Upon the occasion of the celebration, in 1904, of the centenary of its promulgation, an extra-parliamentary commission was created to undertake a revision of the instrument. In the main, the faults to be corrected were those which had inevitably arisen from the growth of new interests and the development of new conditions since 1804, in respect, for example, to insurance and to labor. In Belgium the *Code Napoléon* [1] survives to this day; and the codes of Italy, Spain, Portugal, Holland, and many of the Latin-American states are modeled upon it.

Aside from the revised Civil Code of 1804, containing an aggregate of 2281 articles, the larger part of the law of France to-day is to be found in four great codes, all drawn up and promulgated during the era of the Consulate and the Empire. These are: (1) the Code of Civil Procedure, of 1042 articles, in 1806; (2) the Code of Commerce, of 648 articles, in 1807; (3) the Code of

[1] This was the name borne by the Civil Code from 1807 to 1818.

Criminal Instruction, of 648 articles, in 1808; and (4) the **Penal Code**, of 484 articles, in 1810. The last two codes were submitted to a general revision in 1832; and various supplementary codes, — *e.g.*, the Forest Code, of 226 articles, in 1827, — have been promulgated. But the modifications introduced since Napoleon's day have involved hardly more than details and the addition of subjects not originally dealt with. No one of the codes represented at the time of its promulgation a new body of law. On the contrary, all of them, and especially the fundamental Civil Code, merely reduced existing law to systematic, written form, introducing order and uniformity where previously there had been diversity, and even chaos. The law of the country was thus given a measure of unity and precision which it had never before possessed, with the disadvantage, however, that it lost the flexibility and dynamic character that once had characterized it. Throughout the past hundred years the whole of France has been a country of one written law — a law so comprehensive in both principles and details that, until the great economic and social transformations of recent times, there seemed to be little reason for changing it. As has already been pointed out, this completeness of the country's law has considerably narrowed the field of legislation left to be occupied by the parliament of the Third Republic.

Appointment and Tenure of Judges. — No part of the French governmental system called more loudly for reform when the Estates General assembled in 1789 than the judiciary. Judicial positions were frequently disposed of by the government to the highest bidder; some became hereditary; sometimes the offices were sold by the holders themselves to their successors. Having paid well for their positions, the judges were prone, furthermore, to recoup themselves by accepting gifts, often in money, from parties to suits. The Revolution swept these conditions away and brought in a régime whose aim was equal and exact justice for all. The first idea was to have the judges elected by the people, as they commonly are in our American states. Experience proved, however, that popular election has certain drawbacks, especially that of involving the judges in politics; hence it became the plan to have them appointed by the executive power, but protected against arbitrary removal by guarantee of a tenure lasting during good behavior. " Thus," says an eminent French writer, "saved from any dangers of a forcible dismissal, having no reason to fear disgrace or arbitrary action, they have a greater liberty of judging according to their consciences the causes which are submitted to them."[1] All judges attached to the ordinary tribunals to-day are appointed by the President of the Republic, on the recommendation, and under the responsibility, of the Minister of Justice. With the exception of justices of the peace in France, and of judges of all grades in Algeria and the colonies, tenure of judicial office continues during good behavior; and, outside of the classes mentioned, no judicial officer may be dismissed without the consent of the Court of Cassation.[2] There is, however, an age limit, varying with the official grade, at which retirement is expected and virtually required. Justices of the peace and Algerian and colonial judges may be dismissed by the President. Salaries range from 1600 francs per year for the justice of the peace to 30,000 for the President of the Court of Cassation; and it need hardly be added that a judge who should accept any money or other gift from a litigant would expose himself to heavy penalties. Cases are normally tried, and all sentences must be pronounced, in open court. And not only are the courts open to all; the state, since 1851, has provided means whereby the poor may obtain legal assistance in establishing their rights at law.

The Ordinary Courts. — In French practice the distinction which is drawn between private law and public law is so sharp that there have been built up two systems of courts — the ordinary and the administrative — each of which maintains practically exclusive jurisdiction within an independent field. The ordinary courts comprise civil and criminal tribunals, together with certain special tribunals, such as the *tribunaux de commerce*. At the bottom stands the court of the justice of the peace (*juge de paix*) of the canton. This tribunal was created in 1790 and has existed continuously to the present day. The justice of the peace takes cognizance of disputes where the amount involved does not exceed 600 francs, and of violations of law punishable by a fine not exceeding fifteen francs or imprisonment not beyond five days. In civil cases involving more than 300 francs, and in criminal cases involving imprisonment or a fine exceeding five

---

[1] Poincaré, *How France Is Governed*, 235.   [2] See p. 386.

francs, appeal lies to the next higher tribunal, the "court of first instance." It should be added, however, that the oldest, and perhaps still the most important, function of the justice of the peace is to *prevent* lawsuits rather than to hear them. He is expected to persuade the parties appearing before him, if he can, to accept a friendly settlement; and inasmuch as they are often his own neighbors, he is not unlikely, if he is a man of tact and probity, to succeed in this somewhat delicate undertaking.

Next above the court of the justice of the peace stands the *tribunal de première instance*, or *tribunal d'arrondissement*. Of such courts there is, with a few exceptions, one in each *arrondissement* or district. Each consists of a president, at least one vice-president, and a variable number of judges, three of whom form a court with full powers. To each is attached a *procureur*, or public prosecutor. This tribunal takes cognizance of all kinds of civil cases. In appeals from the justices of the peace, actions relating to personal property to the value of 1500 francs, actions relating to land to the value of sixty francs per year, and all cases of registration, there is no appeal from its decisions. The jurisdiction of the court in penal cases extends to all offenses of the class known as *délits* (misdemeanors), *i.e.*, offenses involving penalties heavier than those attached to the wrongful acts dealt with by the justices of the peace, yet less serious than those prescribed for crimes. When sitting as a criminal court, the court of first instance is known as a *tribunal correctionnel*, or "correctional court." All of its judgments in criminal cases are subject to appeal.

Above the courts of first instance are twenty-five *cours d'appel*, or courts of appeal, each of which exercises jurisdiction within a region consisting of from one to five departments. At the head of each is a president, and each maintains an elaborate *parquet*, or permanent staff of officials, in which are included several *procureurs-généraux* and *avocats-généraux*. For the transaction of business the court of appeal is divided into chambers, or sections, each consisting of a president and four *conseillers*, or judges. The principal function of the court is the hearing of appeals, in both civil and criminal causes, from the courts of first instance. Original jurisdiction is limited and incidental. The decisions of the court are known as *arrêts*.

Closely related to the courts of appeal are the *cours d'assises*, or courts of assize. These are not separate or permanent tribunals. Every three months there is set up in each department, ordinarily in the chief town, a court of assize consisting of a specially designated member of the court of appeals within whose jurisdiction the department lies and two other magistrates, who may be chosen either from the remaining *conseillers* of the court of appeals or from the justices of the local court of first instance. The courts of assize are exclusively occupied with serious offenses, such as are classified in the Penal Code as crimes. In them, and in them only among French tribunals, is a jury regularly employed. A jury consists of twelve men, whose verdict is rendered by simple majority. As in Great Britain and the United States, the jurors determine the fact but do not apply the law.

At the apex of the hierarchy of ordinary tribunals is the Court of Cassation, created in 1790. This court sits at Paris, and in all matters of ordinary private law it is the supreme tribunal of the state. It consists of a first president, three sectional presidents, and forty-five judges. Attached to it are a procurator-general and six advocates-general. For working purposes it is divided into three sections: the *Chambre des Requêtes*, or Court of Petitions, which gives civil cases a preliminary hearing; the Civil Court, which gives them a final consideration; and the Criminal Court, which disposes of criminal cases on appeal. The Court of Cassation can review the decisions of any tribunal in the country, save those of an administrative character. It passes not upon fact, but upon the principles of law involved and upon the competence of the court rendering the original decision. A decision which is overruled is said to be *cassé, i.e.*, quashed. No substitute decision is offered; rather, the case, with a statement of the law, is referred back to a tribunal of the same grade as that whose action has been annulled. The pronouncements of the Court have much weight with the judges at large, and they have the important effect of establishing a common basis of action in cases of an analogous character. The tribunal thus not only furthers the interests of justice, but preserves and develops the unity of French jurisprudence.

Administrative Law and Administrative Tribunals. — Actions at law arising out of the conduct of administration are brought, not in the regular courts connected with the Ministry of Justice, but in special administrative tribunals connected with the Ministry of the Interior. Administrative courts exist for the application of administrative law; and administrative law may be defined in brief as that body of legal principles by which are determined the status and liabilities of public officials, the rights and liabilities of private individuals in their dealings with the official representatives of the state, and the procedure by which these rights and liabilities may be enforced. The idea underlying it is that the government, and every agent of the government, possesses a body of rights, privileges, and prerogatives which are sharply marked off from those of the private citizen, and that the nature and extent of these rights and privileges are to be determined on principles essentially distinct from those which govern in the fixing of the rights and privileges of citizens in relation one to another. In some states, as Belgium, the rules of administrative law are interpreted and enforced by the ordinary courts; but in others, as in France, they are dealt with by an entirely separate hierarchy of tribunals, made up of officials in the service of the government and dismissible at any time by the head of the state. "In France," as one writer puts it, "there is one law for the citizen and another for the public official, and thus the executive is really independent of the judiciary, for the government has always a free hand, and can violate the law if it wants to do so without having anything to fear from the ordinary courts."[1] Although not without precedent in the Old Régime, the distinction between ordinary and administrative law in France was first clearly established by Napoleon in the constitution of 1799, and the system of administrative courts erected under that instrument has survived in large measure to the present day.

The most important of the administrative tribunals is the *Conseil d'État*, or Council of State, a body which once had large functions of an executive and legislative character, but whose influence to-day arises almost exclusively from its supreme administrative jurisdiction. The Council of State is composed of 35 councilors *en service ordinaire*, 21 councilors *en service extraordinaire* (government officials deputed to guard the interests of the various executive departments), 37 *maîtres des*

[1] Lowell, *Governments and Parties in Continental Europe*, I, 58.

requêtes, and 40 auditors. All members are appointed by and dismissible by the President. For purposes of business the body is divided into four sections, each corresponding to a group of two or three ministerial departments, and a fifth section which deals more directly with questions of administrative law. It is the function of the Council to consider and make reply to all questions relating to administrative affairs which the Government lays before it; and in all administrative cases at law it is the court of last resort. Below it stands in each department a *conseil de préfecture*, or prefectural council, which is the court of first instance in all litigation arising out of the application of administrative law. A special function of the prefectural council is the determining of the validity of arrondissement and municipal elections.

III. LOCAL GOVERNMENT IN ENGLAND

Historical Development: the Agencies of Central Control. — The history of local institutions in England covers an enormous stretch of time, as well as a remarkable breadth of public organization and activity; and by no means its least important phases are those that have appeared in comparatively recent times. Speaking broadly, it may be said to fall into four unequal periods. The first, extending from the settlement of the Saxons to the Norman Conquest, was marked by the establishment of the distinctive English units of administration — shire, hundred, township, and parish — and by the fixing of the principle of popular local control. The second, extending from the Conquest to the fourteenth century, was characterized by a general increase of centralization and a corresponding decrease of local autonomy. The third, extending from the fourteenth century to the adoption of the Local Government Act of 1888, was preëminently a period of aristocratic control of local affairs, of government by the same squirearchy which prior to 1832, if not indeed 1867, was accustomed to dominate Parliament. The last period, that from 1888 to the present time, has been notable in a special degree for democratization and simplification of local governing arrangements. The system as it operates to-day is less symmetrical, and less easy to describe, than that of France, Italy, and other continental states; it is considerably more complicated than that of most parts of the United States. But, as a result of the great reforms of the fourth period mentioned, it has an orderliness and a simplicity that were altogether lacking a generation ago. The variety of areas of administration has been lessened, the number of officials has been reduced and their relations have been made more clear, the guiding hand of central authorities in local affairs has been strengthened. Stated briefly, the situation is as follows: the entire kingdom is divided into counties and county boroughs; the counties are subdivided into districts, rural and urban, and boroughs; these are subdivided further into parishes, which are regrouped in poor-law unions; while the city of London is organized after a fashion of its own. In order to make clear the essentials of the system it will suffice to allude briefly to the connection between the local and central administrative agencies, and to point out the important features of each of the principal governmental units named.

In most stages of its history English local government has been carried on with a smaller amount of interference and of direction on the part of the central authorities than have the local governments of the various continental nations. Even to-day the general government is not present in county or borough in any such sense as that in which the French government, in the person of the prefect, is present in the department, or the Prussian, through the agency of the "administration," is present in the *Regierungsbezirk*, or district. A noteworthy aspect of English administrative reform during the past three-quarters of a century has been, nevertheless, a large increase of centralized control, if not of technical centralization, in relation to poor relief, education, finance, and the other varied functions of the local governing agencies. There are to-day five ministerial departments which exercise, in greater or lesser measure, this kind of control. One, the Home Office, has special surveillance of police and of factory inspection. A second, the Board of Education, directs and supervises all educational agencies which are aided by public funds. A third, the Board of Agriculture, supervises the enforcement of laws relating to markets and to diseases of animals. A fourth, the Board of Trade, investigates and approves enterprises relating to the supply of water, gas, and electricity, and to other forms of "municipal trading." Most important of all, the Local Government Board directs in everything that pertains to the execution of the poor laws and to the activities of the local health authorities, oversees the financial operations of the local bodies, and fulfills other supervisory functions too extensive to be enumerated. The powers of these departments in relation to local affairs are exercised in a number of ways, but chiefly through the promulgation of orders and regulations, the giving or withholding of assent to measures passed or proposed by the local bodies, and the giving of expert advice and guidance. It need hardly be added that the powers and functions of the local authorities are subject at all times to control by parliamentary legislation.

Rural Areas of Local Government: the County. — Since the Local Government Act of 1888 was passed there have been two kinds of counties in England. There are, in the first place, the historic counties, fifty-two in number, which survive as areas for parliamentary elections, the organization of the militia, and the administration of justice. Their officials — the lord lieutenant, the sheriff, and the justices of the peace — are appointed by the crown. Much more important, however, are the administrative counties, sixty-four in number, created and regulated by local government legislation of 1888 and 1894. Six of these administrative counties coincide geographically with ancient counties, while most of the remaining ones represent no wide variation from the historic areas upon which they are based. They do not include the seventy-four county boroughs which are situated within them, but they do include all non-county boroughs and all urban districts, so that they are by no means altogether rural. They are extremely unequal in size and population, the smallest being Rutland with 19,709 inhabitants and the largest Lancashire with 1,827,436.

The governing authority of each administrative county is the county council, a body composed of (1) councilors elected for a term of three years in single-member electoral divisions, under very liberal suffrage arrangements applying to both men and women, and (2) aldermen chosen for six years by these popularly elected councilors, either from their own number or from outside.[1] The aldermen are one-third as numerous as the other councilors,

[1] If a councilor is made an alderman his seat as an ordinary councilor becomes vacant and is filled again at a special election.

and half of them retire triennially. There is no distinction of power or function between the two classes of members. In the choice of councilors party feeling seldom displays itself, and elections are often uncontested. Members are drawn mainly from the landowners, large farmers, and professional men, although representatives of the lower middle and laboring classes are now more frequently appearing. The councils vary greatly in size, but the average membership is approximately seventy-five. It is not easy to bring together so many men at brief intervals, and the bodies do not assemble ordinarily more than the four times a year required by law. The mass of business devolving upon them is transacted largely through committees. Of these, some — as the committees on finance, education, and asylums — are required by law; others are established as occasion arises. The continuous work of administration is performed by a group of officials — the clerk, the chief constable, the treasurer, the surveyor, the public analyst (chemist), and others — chosen in most instances by the council and having substantial permanence of tenure.

The powers and duties of the council are many and varied. In the act of 1888 they are enumerated in sixteen categories, of which the most important are the raising, expending, and borrowing of money; the care of county property, buildings, bridges, lunatic asylums, reformatory and industrial schools; the appointment of inferior administrative officials; the granting of certain licenses other than for the sale of liquor; the care of main highways and the protection of streams from pollution; and the enforcement of various regulations relating to animals, fish, birds, and insects. The Education Act of 1902 made the council also the school authority throughout the county except in the urban sections. It must see that adequate provision is made for elementary schools, and it may assist in the maintenance of agencies of education of higher grades. The control of police within the county devolves upon a joint committee representing the council and the justices of the peace. Finally, the council may make by-laws for the county, supervise in a measure the minor rural authorities, and perform the work of these authorities when they prove remiss.

Other Rural Areas of Local Government. — The administrative county contains four kinds of local government areas —

rural districts, rural parishes, urban districts, and municipal boroughs. Of rural districts there are, in England and Wales, 672. They are coterminous, as a rule, with rural poor-law unions, or with the rural portions of unions which are both rural and urban; but they cannot comprise parts of more than one county. The governing authority of the district is a council, composed of persons (women being eligible) chosen in most instances triennially by the rural parishes in proportion to population. As a rule, one-third retire each year. The council meets at least once a month, and is chiefly responsible for the enforcement of public health acts and for the care of highways which are not classed as "main roads." To meet in part the costs of this administration it is empowered to levy district rates, or taxes. The principal salaried and permanent officials of the district, chosen by the council, are a clerk, a treasurer, a medical officer, a surveyor, and a corps of sanitary inspectors.

Of parishes there are two types, the rural and the urban, and their aggregate number in England and Wales is approximately 15,000. The urban parishes have no administrative importance, and further mention need not be made of them. Under the act of 1894 the rural parish, however, has been revived from the inert condition into which it had fallen, and it to-day fills an appreciable, if humble, place in the rural administrative scheme. Its organization is dependent to a degree upon its population. But in every parish there is " a parish meeting " in which all persons on the local government and parliamentary registers (including women) have a right to participate. What this meeting — which is, of course, a primary assembly, and not a representative body — does depends upon whether the parish has or has not a council. Parishes having a population of three hundred or more must have councils, and others may do so if they desire. The council is composed of from five to fifteen members (women being eligible), elected as a rule for a term of three years. If there is a council, the parish meeting has little to do except choose the councilors and criticize their work. In this case it meets but once a year. But if there is no council, the meeting chooses a group of overseers to represent it in carrying on the routine work; and in this case it meets twice a year. Whatever the organization, the powers of the parish authorities make an extended, if not imposing, list.

They include the management of civil parochial property, the provision of fire protection, the inspection of local sanitation, the maintenance of foot-paths, and the appointment of trustees of civil charities within the parish. The meagerness of the population of large numbers of the parishes, however, together with the severe limitations imposed both by law and by practical conditions upon rate-levying powers, usually prevent the authorities from undertaking many or large projects.

For the administration of poor relief there have existed since 1834 poor-law unions, consisting of parishes grouped together, usually without much effort to obtain equality of size or population. The administrative agency is a board of guardians, composed of the district councilors representing the various parishes within the union. The unions, however, often contain both rural and urban parishes, and in cases of this kind the board of guardians is composed of the persons elected as district councilors in the rural parishes of the union, together with other persons who are specially elected as guardians in the urban parishes and have no other function. The conditions under which poor relief is administered are minutely prescribed in regulations laid down by the Local Government Board at London, so that, save in the matter of levying rates, the range of discretion left to the boards of guardians is very narrow.

Urban Areas of Local Government: the Urban District and the Borough. — Aside from London, which has a complicated system of government peculiar to itself, the urban portions of the country are organized under three chief forms, *i.e.*, the urban district, the municipal borough, and the county borough. Little need be said about the urban district. It comprises simply a section of a county which presumably has a somewhat dense population, and is on the road to becoming a borough, and in the meantime is given a government adapted to its peculiar needs. Its organization hardly differs from that of the rural district; it has a council, elected for three years, and holding meetings once a month; and its work — chiefly the control of sanitation and highways — is carried on by committees, assisted by permanent salaried officials whom the council elects. The standard municipal unit is, rather, the borough, which differs from the urban district mainly in having a charter granted by the central government at London, and in being vested with numerous powers belonging to no inferior urban area. The distinction between municipal boroughs and county boroughs need not detain us. All boroughs are of course, properly speaking, municipal; all have substantially the same organization. The county boroughs — now upwards of eighty in number — are simply those that have been withdrawn from the jurisdiction of the administrative counties in which they lie, and have themselves been endowed with the powers of such counties; under the Local Government Act of 1888 boroughs are so withdrawn automatically when they attain a population of fifty thousand. Ordinary municipal boroughs are those that still form parts politically, as well as geographically, of the counties in which they are situated.

The Municipal Corporations Act of 1835, which put municipal government in England upon its present basis, was immediately applied to 178 boroughs in England and Wales; and the number covered has been increased, as new boroughs have been created, to upwards of four hundred. Every borough has a charter, which creates a corporation (consisting of the " mayor, aldermen, and burgesses "), and, in conformity with the Municipal Corporations Consolidation Act of 1882, prescribes a form of government and defines a body of powers similar to, although not in all details identical with, those possessed by other boroughs. Charters are normally issued, on petition of the inhabitants, by the Local Government Board, acting in the name of the crown. If a petition raises controversy, the final decision is likely to be made by Parliament.

Borough government is constructed on the characteristic English plan of throwing substantially all authority into the hands of a single elected body, a council; the doctrine of separation of executive and legislative powers finds no more acceptance in municipal than in county and other local organization. The borough council consists of councilors, aldermen, and a mayor, sitting as one body. The councilors, varying in number from nine to more than a hundred, are elected by practically the entire adult population, male and female, for terms of three years, one-third retiring annually. In small boroughs they are usually elected on a general ticket, in large ones by districts or wards. Since 1907 women have been eligible, and many have been elected. The aldermen, to the number of one-third of the councilors, are chosen by the council for six years, one-half retiring triennially. They may be taken from outside the council, but most of them are selected from the more experienced councilors, making it necessary to hold " by-elections " to fill the vacancies. Legally the aldermen differ from the ordinary councilors only in the manner of their election and the length of their term. Being, however, as a rule more experienced, they are likely to hold the principal committee chairmanships and to have exceptional influence in the shaping of policies. The system makes it possible, also, to draw into the council men of high qualifications who would not seek election, or be likely to be elected, by the people at large. The mayor is elected for one year by the council, either from its own membership or from outside. He is not the head of a separate branch of government, as is the mayor of an American city, but merely the presiding officer of the council and the official representative of the borough on state occasions. He cannot appoint or remove officers, control the departments, or veto ordinances. Hence he need not be a man of executive ability or experience. As matters go, it is far more important that he be a person of some wealth, and of leisure; for the chief demands upon him will be of a social and philanthropic nature, and a salary is rarely provided. If he is willing, he is likely to be reëlected a number of times. Reelections of councilors and aldermen are also numerous, resulting in a continuity of service and an accumulation of experience quite unknown to the American city council, where the doctrine of rotation in office is still popular.

The council meets in the town hall monthly, fortnightly, or weekly, according as the amount of business demands. The larger part of its work, however, is transacted through committees, which are elected by the council, and presided over by chairmen whom the committees themselves choose. Under national law there must be a " watch," *i.e.*, police, committee and a committee on education. Others are created at the council's discretion, and the number varies from six or seven in small boroughs to twenty or twenty-five in large ones. Practically all matters brought up in the council are referred to some committee; and since they are there considered in all due detail, and normally by the councilors who are best informed on the subject in hand, committee recommendations are almost certain to be adopted.

The council comprises, in the fullest sense, the government of the borough; hence it exercises substantially all of the powers (save that of electing the councilors themselves) that come to the borough from the Common Law, from general and special acts of Parliament, and from the provisional orders of the Local Government Board. These powers fall into three main classes: legislative, financial, and administrative. The council makes by-laws, or ordinances, relating to all sorts of matters — streets, police, health, traffic control, etc. — subject only to the power of the Local Government Board to disallow ordinances on public health and a few other subjects if that authority finds them objectionable.

The council acts as custodian of the "borough fund" (consisting of receipts from public property, franchises, fines, fees, etc.); levies "borough rates" of so many shillings or pence per pound on the rental value of real property, in order to obtain whatever additional revenue is needed; draws up and adopts the annual budget; makes all appropriations; and borrows money on the credit of the municipality in so far as the central authorities permit. Finally, the council exercises control over all branches of strictly municipal administration. This it does, first by appointing, on a non-partisan basis, the staff of permanent salaried officials — clerk, treasurer, engineer, public analyst, chief constable, medical officer, etc. — who carry on the daily work of the borough government, and, second, by constant supervision of these officials and their subordinates, exercised through the committees having to do with the various branches of business. Thus the education committee not only receives and considers legislative proposals relating to education; it interviews candidates for educational positions, makes nominations to the council, and in the name of the council inspects and directs the work of the educational authorities. The rôle of committees thus becomes something very different from, and much more important than, anything of the kind in the government of the cities of the United States.

IV. LOCAL GOVERNMENT IN FRANCE

Historical Development: Democracy and Centralization. — Students of political science are familiar with the fact that governmental systems are, as a rule, less stable at the top than at the bottom. Local institutions, imbedded in the interests of the community and supported by the native conservatism of the ordinary man, strike root deeply; the central, national agencies of law-making and of administration are played upon by larger, more unsettling forces, with the consequence of greatly increased likelihood of change. Of this principle the history of modern France affords notable illustration. Throughout a century and a quarter of remarkable instability of central government the scheme of local government in use at the present day has been preserved almost intact. The origins of it, it is true, are to be traced to revolution. In most of its essentials it was created by the National Assembly of 1789 and by Napoleon, and it rose upon the wreckage of a system which had lasted through many centuries of Capetian and Bourbon rule. Once established, however, it proved sufficiently workable to be perpetuated under every one of the governmental régimes which, between 1800 and the present day, have filled their successive places in the history of the nation.

When the National Assembly, in 1789, addressed itself to the reformation of local government it did so in no faltering spirit. The communes — the little semi-political, semi-social *community* groups that had grown up through the centuries — were allowed to stand, to the number of some forty thousand. But the old provinces and *généralités* were abolished and in their stead was erected a system of departments, districts, and cantons. Eighty-three departments, of approximately equal size, were created. In each there were on an average six or seven districts, and in each of these eight or nine cantons. The cantons, in turn, were made up of varying numbers of communes. The most striking features of the system were its symmetry and its detachment from history and tradition. The departments were so laid out as to be substantially equal in size; and little attention was paid to ancient boundary lines and social cleavages, or to physical demarcations. " The new departments, districts, and cantons had no history, no associations, no inner life or bond of common feeling, and presented a smooth blank surface upon which the legislator might impress whatever pattern he thought proper." [1] Such a deliberate blotting out of the old areas of local government would be unthinkable in England. But it was characteristic of the French Revolution that the newly emancipated people found pleasure in destroying even the names and forms that reminded them of the past.

For the time being, furthermore, ultra-democratic ideals were in the ascendant, and the measures of 1789, reënforced by the constitution of 1791, transferred at a stroke the entire administration of local affairs from the agents of the crown to the elected representatives of the new governmental units. A little experience proved, however, that in the direction both of democracy and of decentralization the reformers had gone too far. Hence in 1795 local affairs were brought under more direct supervision of the national authorities; and under the Napoleonic régime centralization was made once more complete. By law of 1800 there was established in each department a prefect, appointed by the First Consul (after 1804, the Emperor), responsible only to him, and endowed with almost absolute powers; while the communal and departmental councils ceased to be elective and became appointive. At the same time the departments were freshly subdivided into *arrondissements*, also with an appointive council.

This Napoleonic administrative system — simple, symmetrical, bureaucratic, and centralized to the last degree — has persisted in large measure to the present day.[2] Such modifications as have been introduced in it have arisen chiefly from the cautious revival of the elective principle in connection with the several councils, followed by a gradual expansion of the electorate until nowadays all of the bodies are chosen by manhood suffrage.

---

[1] *Cambridge Modern History*, VIII, 190.

[2] Its influence upon the administrative systems of other countries — Belgium, Italy, Spain, and even Greece, Japan, and various Latin-American states — has been profound. "Judged by its qualities of permanence and by its influence abroad, the law of 1800 is one of the best examples of Bonaparte's creative statesmanship, taking rank with the Code and with the Concordat among his enduring non-military achievements. If, in the nineteenth century, England has been the mother of parliaments and has exercised a dominant influence upon the evolution of national governments, France has had an equally important rôle in molding systems of local administration among the nations." Munro, *Government of European Cities*, 7.

During the unsettled period ushered in by the Franco-German war, when the liberal elements were successfully striving for a total reorganization of the machinery of national government, little desire was expressed for a decentralized system of local administration. At the most, what was asked was autonomy for the communes, while the cantons, *arrondissements*, and departments should continue to be administered by, and largely in the interest of, the national government. By law of March 28, 1882, the demand in behalf of the communes was met. Every commune, large and small (except Paris), obtained the privilege of choosing its entire quota of administrative officials. Departments and *arrondissements*, however, continued to be primarily spheres within which the general government, acting through its own agents, brought home to the people the force and beneficence of its authority. And to this day France presents the curious spectacle of a nation broadly democratic in its constitution, its central government, and its local organs of legislation, yet more highly centralized in its administrative arrangements than any other principal state of western Europe. Not only is central control far greater than in England; it is not split up among a half-dozen scattered branches of the national government, as it there is, but is gathered in the hands of a single great directing agency at Paris, the Ministry of the Interior.

Local Government To-day: Department, Arrondissement, and Canton. — At the head of each of the departments is a prefect, appointed and removed nominally by the President of the Republic, but in reality by the Minister of the Interior. The prefect, who is far the most important of all local officials, is at the same time an agent of the general government and the executive head of the department in the administration of local affairs. As agent of the general government he acts, in some instances, upon detailed instructions; in others, he enjoys a wide range of discretion. His powers extend to practically all public matters affecting the department. He supervises the execution of the laws; maintains a vigorous control over all administrative officials of the department, even to the extent of annulling their acts; gives the authorities at Paris information and advice concerning the affairs of the department; nominates to a variety of subordinate offices; exercises an oversight of the communes, some of whose measures become effective only after receiving his assent; issues by-laws, or ordinances; and, in certain instances indicated by law, acts as a judge. His discretion is not so broad as it once was, but even to-day there are few, if any, local officials in any country whose authority is so great. Being essentially a political officer, the prefect is liable to sudden termination of his tenure by a change of ministries at Paris. Ordinarily, however, such changes have little effect outside the capital. Visiting the chief town of a department, one can hardly fail to observe an imposing, well-kept building before which the tricolor is flying, and which bears in large letters the word "Prefecture"; and it is in this departmental capitol that one will find the quarters of the prefect and the various offices or bureaux of the prefecture.

Here one will find, also, the hall used by the *conseil général*, or general council, a body elected by manhood suffrage under a scheme which gives each canton one representative. The term of members is six years, and half retire triennially. All are unpaid. The powers of the assembly are not extensive; aside from apportioning the direct taxes among the *arrondissements*, they relate mainly to the construction and upkeep of highways, bridges, canals, school-buildings, and asylums. Under law of 1871 a council may not vote upon any question of a political character — a fact of which the prefect is likely to remind the members if their discussions indicate that they have forgotten it. There are but two regular sessions a year. The first, held soon after Easter, is devoted to general matters, and is limited to fifteen days; the second, held in the early autumn, is devoted to the budget, and may last a month. During the intervals between sessions the council is represented by a *commission départementale*, or permanent delegation, of from four to seven members, which meets once a month to deal with current affairs. The measures of both the council and this commission may be vetoed by the central government; and under certain conditions the council can be dissolved by the same authority. As the status of the council abundantly proves, the department remains an essentially artificial unit, valuable chiefly as a subsidiary of the central administration. During the century and a quarter of its existence it has not become — indeed has been deliberately prevented from becoming — a sphere of forceful, independent governmental activity.

Next to the departments stand the *arrondissements*, or districts, of which there are to-day 362. Except those in the department of the Seine, and the three containing the capitals of departments elsewhere, each has in its chief town a sub-prefect, who serves as a district representative of the prefect. Every one has a *conseil d'arrondissement*, or *arrondissement* council, consisting of at least nine members, elected by manhood suffrage for a term of six years. But since the *arrondissement* has no corporate personality, no property, and no budget, the council has but a single function of importance, that, namely, of allotting among the communes their quotas of the taxes assigned to the *arrondissement* by the general council of the department. The *arrondissement* is, however, the electoral district for the Chamber of Deputies, and also normally the seat of a court of first instance.

The canton is an electoral and a judicial, but not strictly an administrative, unit. It is the area from which the members of both the departmental general council and the council of the *arrondissement* are chosen, and it constitutes the jurisdiction of the justice of the peace. The total number of cantons is 2911. Most of them contain about a dozen communes, although a few of the larger communes are divided into a number of cantons.

Local Government To-day: the Commune. — From the point of view of popular self-government the most important local division of France, and the only one whose origins antedate the Revolution, is the commune. The commune is at the same time a territorial division and a corporate personality. "On the one hand," says a recent writer, "it is a tract of territory the precise limits of which were defined by the law of December 22, 1789, or by some subsequent law or decree; for by the law of 1789 all local units which had a separate identity during the old régime were authoritatively recognized as communes, and since that enactment there have been a number of suppressions, divisions, consolidations, and creations of communal units. On the other hand, the commune is an agglomeration of citizens united by life in a common locality and having a common interest in the communal property. A commune ranks as a legal person: it may sue and be sued, may contract, acquire, or convey property, — it may, in general, exercise all of the ordinary rights of a corporation." [1]

[1] Munro, *Government of European Cities*, 15.

Of communes there are, in all, under the territorial land survey of 1909, 36,229. In both size and population they vary enormously. Some consist of diminutive hamlets of two or three score people; others comprise cities like Bordeaux, Lyons, and Marseilles, with populations in excess of a quarter of a million. At the census of 1911, 27,000 communes had a population of less than one thousand; 17,000, of less than five hundred; 9000, of less than three hundred; 137, of less than fifty. On the other hand, 250 contained a population of more than ten thousand, and fourteen of more than one hundred thousand. In area they vary all the way from a few acres to the 254,540 acres of the commune of Arles.

Except Paris and Lyons, all communes are organized and governed in the same manner. Each has a council, whose members are elected by manhood suffrage (usually by *scrutin de liste*), for a term of four years. All members are elected at the same time, *i.e.*, on the first Sunday in May in every fourth year. In communes whose population is under five hundred the number of councilors is ten; in those whose population exceeds five hundred the number is graduated on a basis such that a commune of sixty thousand people has a council of thirty-six, which is the maximum. The council holds four ordinary sessions a year — in February, May, August, and November. Special meetings may be convoked at any time by the prefect, the sub-prefect, or the mayor. Sessions are held in the *mairie*, or municipal building, and are open to the public. Except the May session, at which the budget is considered, a regular meeting may not be prolonged beyond fifteen days, save with the consent of the sub-prefect. The maximum duration of the May sitting is six weeks. In contrast with both English and American usage, which involves frequent but short council meetings, the French plan thus calls for sessions held at long intervals but extended, as a rule, over a number of days.

Speaking broadly, the functions of the council comprise the administration of the purely local affairs of the commune and the formulation and expression of local needs and demands. In the municipal code of 1884 the powers of the body are defined with exceeding minuteness. Some are purely advisory, to be exercised when the council is called upon by the higher administrative authorities for an expression of local interest or desire concerning a particular question. Advice thus tendered may or may not be heeded. Other powers involve the initiation by the council of certain kinds of measures, which, however, may be carried into effect only with the assent of the higher authorities. Among the thirteen such measures which are enumerated in the code the most important are those pertaining to the purchase, sale, or other legal disposition of property belonging to the commune. Finally, there is a group of powers — relating principally to the various communal services, *e.g.*, parks, fire-protection, etc. — which are vested in the communal authorities (council and mayor) independently. But the predominating fact is that even to-day the autonomy of the commune is subject to limitation at every turn. Many communal measures become valid only upon receiving the approval of the prefect, and practically any of them may be suspended or annulled by that official. Some require the consent of the departmental council, or even of the President of the Republic; and by decree of the President the council itself may be dissolved at any time.

The executive head of the commune is the *maire*, or mayor, who is elected by the municipal council, by secret ballot, from its own membership, for a term of four years. Associated with the mayor is, in communes of 2500 inhabitants or fewer, an *adjoint*, or assistant, similarly chosen. In communes of 2500 to 10,000 inhabitants there are two assistants, and in those of over 10,000 there is an additional one for every 25,000 people in excess of the figure named. Except in Lyons, however, where there are seventeen, the number may not exceed twelve. The mayor plays the dual rôle of executive head of the commune and representative (although not the appointee) of the central government. The powers which he exercises vary widely according to the size and importance of the commune. But in general it may be said that he appoints to the majority of municipal offices, publishes laws and decrees, issues *arrêtes*, or ordinances, supervises finance, organizes and controls the local police, executes measures for public health and safety, safeguards the property interests of the commune, represents the commune in cases at law and on ceremonial occasions, and acts as the agent of the central government in the supervision of census-taking, the preparation of the electoral lists, the enforcement of military service, and the keeping of complete records of births, deaths, and marriages.

The functions of the mayoral office are in practice distributed by the mayor among the assistants, to each of whom is assigned a particular department, such as that of streets, of sanitation, or of fire-protection. As a rule, the mayor reserves to himself the control of police. For the acts of the assistants, however, he is directly responsible; and all acts, whether of the mayor or of the assistants, which relate to the interests of the general government are performed under the strictest surveillance of the prefectural authorities. The mayor may be suspended from office for a month by the prefect, or for three months by the Minister of the Interior; and he may be removed from office altogether by order of the President.

Despite the restrictions by which it is hedged about, the commune remains the true focus of local life. Its activities, on a petty scale though they frequently are, run the gamut of finance, commerce, industry, education, and politics. So strong is the communal spirit that public sentiment will but rarely accede to the suppression of a commune, or even the union of two or more diminutive ones; and, in truth, the code of 1884 recognized the fixity of communal identity by permitting changes of communal boundaries to be undertaken by the departmental authorities only after an *enquête* designed to ascertain local feeling on the subject. Save by special decree of the President of the Republic, not even the name of a commune may be altered.

SELECTED REFERENCES

A. L. Lowell, *Government of England* (New York, 1909), II, Chaps. xxxviii–xlvi, lix–lxii; E. Jenks, *Government of the British Empire* (New York, 1918), Chaps. xi, xiii–xiv; *Ibid.*, *Short History of the English Law* (Boston, 1912); J. A. R. Marriott, *English Political Institutions* (Oxford, 1910), Chaps. xiii–xiv; W. B. Munro, *Government of European Cities* (New York, 1909), Chaps. i, iii; P. W. L. Ashley, *Local and Central Government* (London, 1906); R. Poincaré, *How France Is Governed* (New York, 1914), Chaps. ii–iii, x; W. M. Geldart, *Elements of English Law* (London, 1912); A. T. Carter, *History of English Legal Institutions* (4th ed., London, 1910); O. W. Holmes, *The Common Law* (Boston, 1881); C. A. Beard, *The Office of Justice of the Peace in England* (New York, 1904); J. Brissaud, *History of French Private Law* (Boston, 1912); J. Redlich and F. W. Hirst, *Local Government in England*, 2 vols. (London, 1903).

CHAPTER XX

DEMOCRACY IN ITALY

HAVING described at some length the governmental systems of two of the great nations which have fought shoulder to shoulder with the United States in the cause of freedom and democracy, we may now pass in rapid review the cardinal facts about the political organization of two of our smaller but equally valiant co-belligerents. The merest summary would show that these states — Italy and Belgium — have equal reason with ourselves for the stand that has been taken against the purposes and methods of autocracy as embodied in the governments of the Teutonic powers.

Italian Unification: the Constitution. — The dominant forces in the politics of Europe since the French Revolution have been the twin principles of nationality and democracy; and nowhere have these principles brought greater things to pass than in the long disrupted, inert, and misgoverned peninsula of Italy. The awakening of the Italian people to a new consciousness of unity and strength, and to new aspiration and hope, may be said to date from the Napoleonic invasion of 1796; and the first stages of the *Risorgimento*, or "resurrection," belong to the period of French domination which continued, speaking broadly, to the collapse of Napoleon's power in 1814. At the outset, republics were erected by the conqueror on the ruins of Austrian and Spanish power, as well as on those of the independent native monarchies; and extensive reforms were introduced in law, administration, finance, education, and industry. The republics, however, were short-lived. From the beginning they were tributary to France; and after the establishment of the Napoleonic empire in 1804 Italy was fast assimilated politically to that nation. Early in 1805 the Emperor was crowned king of Italy; and monarchy, long veiled, appeared again in the open. Reforms on economic and social lines continued for years, however, to be carried forward.

When, in 1815, Napoleon was finally overthrown, Italy relapsed largely, although not wholly, into the condition prevailing in the eighteenth century. After the Congress of Vienna completed its readjustments the peninsula was found to contain ten states, of which several were dominated directly or indirectly by Austria; Italy was still, as Metternich declared, only " a geographical expression." Furthermore, such traces of liberal government as had survived Napoleon's increasingly autocratic régime totally disappeared. Not one of the states now had a constitution, a parliament, or any means of popular control over its ruler. Napoleon, however, had sowed the seeds of national unity; indeed, from St. Helena he predicted that one day the Italians would form a single nation, with Rome as their capital. Notwithstanding the active agitation carried on, under discouraging conditions, by eloquent leaders like Mazzini and by daring organizations like the Carbonari, the prophecy seemed for some decades unlikely to be fulfilled. A turning point came, however, with the mid-century era of revolution. In the course of the popular uprisings of 1848–49 several constitutions were granted by Italian princes; and one — that promulgated March 4, 1848, by King Charles Albert of Piedmont — unlike the rest, was never revoked, but instead became, and is to-day, the fundamental law of the united Italian nation. After 1848 the building of modern Italy became preëminently the work of Piedmont, and when finally, in 1870, the task was completed, the result stood a monument to Piedmontese organization, leadership, conquest, and expansion. The principal steps in the process — the alliance with France in 1855; the war with Austria and the conquest of Lombardy in 1859; the annexation of Tuscany, Modena, Parma, Romagna, Umbria, the Papal Marches, Naples, and Sicily in 1860; the proclamation of the kingdom of Italy in 1861; the incorporation of Venetia in 1866; the occupation of Rome in 1870, and the removal of the capital thither from Florence in 1871 — are familiar to every student of nineteenth-century history.

As has been stated, the formal constitution of the kingdom of Italy to-day is the *Statuto fondamentale del Regno* granted in

1848 by Charles Albert to his Piedmontese subjects. To each of the territories successively annexed to the Piedmontese kingdom this instrument was promptly extended, on the basis of popular ratifications, or plebiscites; and when, in 1861, the kingdom of Piedmont was converted into the kingdom of Italy, the fundamental law, modified in only minor respects, was continued in operation. The *Statuto* was granted originally as a royal charter, and its author seems to have expected it to be final, at least until it should have been replaced as a whole by some other instrument. At all events, no provision was made in the document for its own amendment; and none has ever been added. Upon a number of occasions since 1861 modifications of the text have been suggested, and even debated, but no one of them has been adopted. Of course, this does not mean that the constitutional system of Italy has stood all this time unchanged. On the contrary, it has shown remarkable vitality, growth, and adaptive capacity. In Italy, as in other nations, the written constitution undergoes constant amplification, and — so far as actual practice is concerned — substantial modification, by custom and also by ordinary legislation. The country's jurists have long since become agreed that custom is a genuine source of public law; while the power of Parliament to introduce changes in the constitutional system, *e.g.*, by the organization of the judiciary in 1865 and by the suffrage laws of 1882, 1895, and 1912, is recognized as scarcely inferior to that of the British Parliament. Care is exercised to make such fundamental enactments conform to the public will; in practice they are rarely brought to a final vote until the country has been given an opportunity to pass upon them at a general election.

The *Statuto*, in eighty-four articles, is an instrument of considerable length. It deals, successively, with the crown, the rights and duties of citizens, the Senate, the Chamber of Deputies, the ministers, the judiciary, and matters of a miscellaneous character. The bill of rights contained in Articles 24–32 solemnly guarantees equality before the law, liberty of person, inviolability of domicile and of property, freedom of the press, exemption from national taxation not voted by Parliament, and, with certain qualifications, freedom of assembly. It is constantly to be borne in mind, however, that, so overlaid is the *Statuto* with legislative enactments and with custom that one cannot lay hold upon the working constitution of the kingdom to-day, in respect to either general principles or specific governmental organs, through an examination of this document alone. In the language of an Italian publicist, the Italian constitution no longer consists of the *Statuto* of Charles Albert. This forms simply the beginning of a new order of things. Many institutions have been transformed by laws, decrees, usages, and neglect, whence the Italian constitution has become cumulative, consisting of an organism of law grouped about a primary kernel which is the *Statuto*.[1]

The Governmental System. — Italy is to-day a constitutional monarchy, in which the powers of the crown are closely restricted and the parliamentary system, while hampered as in France by the multiplicity of political parties, operates with sufficient facility to insure effective control of the executive by the legislative branch of the government. As in Great Britain and France, the ministers form the working executive and the functions of the nominal chief executive are incidental and ornamental. The ministers are members of Parliament, and they are responsible to the Chamber of Deputies for every act which, in the name of the king, they perform. Parliament consists of two houses, the Senate and the Chamber of Deputies. The Senate is composed entirely of members appointed for life by the crown. It stands, therefore, midway between the British House of Lords, which consists predominantly of hereditary peers, and the French Senate, whose members are wholly elective. There is no restriction upon the power to appoint men to the Senate, save that every appointee must be taken from one or another of twenty-one stipulated classes of citizens, including high officials of church and state, men of distinction in science, literature, or public service, and the larger taxpayers. There are usually about 385 members. Whether or not in consequence of the method by which it is recruited, the Senate is not a factor of large weight in the conduct of public affairs. Few legislative measures originate in it, and rarely does it exhibit much independence of judgment upon the projects which come up to it from the Chamber of

[1] Ruiz, "The Amendments to the Italian Constitution," *Annals of Am. Acad. Polit. and Soc. Sci.*, Sept., 1895, 57.

Deputies. In recent years it has recognized its weakness, and in 1910 a commission of nine members, to which the question had been referred, brought in a report proposing that approximately two-thirds of the senators should be elected by university professors, chambers of commerce, agricultural societies, and other special " colleges " so constituted that they would represent actual and varied groups of interests throughout the nation. The remaining third should be appointed, as all members now are, by the king. Thus far, no plan of reform has been adopted. But prior to the outbreak of war in 1914 the subject continued to receive intermittent attention in Parliament and in the press, and it is probable that before long some plan of popularization such as that which the commission of 1910 suggested will be put into effect.

The Chamber of Deputies is composed of 508 members chosen simultaneously by direct vote, and by secret ballot, in single-member districts. The term is five years; but a dissolution is practically certain to befall before the end of the full period, and the average interval between elections is nearer three years than five. Deputies are not required to be residents of the districts which they represent, but they must be citizens not less than thirty years of age, in possession of full civil and political rights, and not members of certain classes (chiefly clergymen and salaried government officials) specially debarred. In late years a system of nomination of parliamentary candidates by petition has been introduced; and in 1912 provision was made for the first time for payment of a salary to members, amounting to 6000 lire ($1200) annually.

Electoral Arrangements to 1912. — A main problem of Italian domestic politics during the past fifty years has been the parliamentary franchise; and one of the most notable events in the recent history of democratic government was the introduction of manhood suffrage in Italy, almost tripling the electorate at a stroke, by the electoral law of June 30, 1912. The history of the suffrage since the establishment of the present kingdom falls into three periods, separated by the legislation of 1882 and 1912. Under law of 1860 the suffrage was restricted to male property-holders who were able to read and write, who had attained the age of twenty-five, and who paid an annual tax of at least forty lire ($8) — qualifications which not more than two and one-half per cent of the population could meet. In 1882, after prolonged consideration of the subject, the ministry carried through Parliament a series of measures reducing the property qualification from forty lire to nineteen lire eighty centesimi (about $3.95) and lowering the age limit to twenty-one years. The disqualification of illiteracy was retained, and a premium was placed upon literacy by the extension of the franchise, regardless of property, to all males over twenty-one who had received a primary school education. The net result was to raise the number of voters from 627,838 to 2,049,461, about two-thirds of the new electors obtaining the franchise by reason of their ability to meet the educational qualification. An incidental effect of the reform was to augment the political influence of the cities, because in them the proportion of illiterates was smaller than in the country districts. Small landed proprietors, although of a more conservative temperament, and frequently of a better economic status, than the urban artisans, were usually unable to fulfill the educational qualification. Originally, deputies were elected in single-member districts. The law of 1882 provided for elections by general ticket, *i.e.*, on the principle of *scrutinio di lista*. An act of May 8, 1891, however, abolished the general ticket and created a commission by which the country was divided into 508 single-member districts; and during the past quarter-century this system has been adhered to uninterruptedly.

As the system stood prior to the electoral law of 1912, voters generally were required to have the following qualifications: (1) Italian citizenship; (2) minimum age of twenty-one; (3) ability to read and write; (4) passage of examinations in the subjects included in the course of compulsory elementary education. The last-mentioned qualification was not, however, required of public officials, graduates of colleges, professional men, persons who had served two years in the army, citizens who paid annually a direct tax of not less than nineteen lire eighty centesimi, those who paid an annual agricultural rental of 500 lire, those who paid house-rent of from 150 lire in communes of 2500 people to 400 lire in communes of over 150,000, and certain less important classes. Through the operation of the literacy test the system provided an avenue for an indefinite increase of the number of voters, although the obstacles to universal elementary education continued to be so numerous and so weighty that the democratization of the state proceeded with extreme slowness. In 1904 the number of enrolled electors was 2,541,327, exclusive of 26,056 temporarily disfranchised because of being engaged in active military service. This was but 29 per cent of the male population over twenty-one years of age, and 7.67 per cent of the total population. In June, 1912, immediately before the enactment of the law establishing manhood suffrage, the number of voters was 3,247,772, in a total population of 34,671,377. It is to be observed, furthermore, that the proportion of registered electors actually voting was ordinarily astonishingly small. At the elections of November, 1904, the number who went to the polls was 1,593,886, which was but 62.7 per cent of those who had a right to do so. In individual cities and provinces the proportion sometimes fell as low as thirty, or even twenty, per cent.

The Electoral Law of 1912. — So ominous was the menace of illiteracy that only within comparatively recent years was there serious thought of introducing a system of manhood suffrage. After 1900, a movement in this direction began to gather strength. It found support, not only among the Socialists and other radicals, but among men who felt that the illiberality of the existing franchise branded the nation in the eyes of the world as backward and inferior. The question of electoral reform became paramount in party politics; ministries rose and fell because of their attitude upon it. There was much discussion, — official, academic, and popular, — although not so much candid weighing of the advantages and disadvantages of the proposed change as there should have been. Finally, in June, 1911, the third Giolitti ministry laid before Parliament a measure in which the demands of the franchise extensionists were met more satisfactorily than in previous projects, and on May 29, 1912, the bill was passed in the Chamber of Deputies by the decisive vote of 284 to 62. After some weeks the Senate acted upon it favorably, and on June 30 the law was formally approved.

The measure bestows the suffrage upon substantially all adult male citizens, who are divided for the purpose into three categories. One comprises literates of a minimum age of twenty-one, without regard to property or other qualification. A second comprises, similarly, illiterates of a minimum age of thirty. The third consists of persons who have rendered service in the army or navy, without regard for education, property, or age. The number of electors was thus raised from 3,247,722 to 8,635,148, more than half of whom, it is estimated, cannot read or write. Opportunity to test the new arrangements was afforded by the parliamentary elections of 1913, which were hailed by enthusiasts as the first elections of a truly national character in Italian history. The results were not altogether reassuring. The five million illiterates upon whom the franchise had been conferred availed themselves of their new and unfamiliar privilege sparingly. Despite the efforts of the various parties to enlist as many as possible of the new voters, the percentage of the electors who went to the polls was, in many districts, smaller than at the elections of 1909. In Rome the percentage in 1909 was fifty, while in 1913 it was but thirty-five. The stolid assumption of the mass of the newly enfranchised that the intricacies of the electoral process were not to be mastered, or were not worth mastering, afforded striking evidence of the nation's unpreparedness for manhood suffrage, and therefore of the dubiousness of the law by which the innovation was introduced. In thirty years Italy has achieved a record of economic growth and of social reform of which a nation may be proud. The Italian aptitude for orderly politics is, however, imperfectly developed, and much time will be required to build up a political *morale* equal to the English or the French. On the whole, however, it may prove not disadvantageous that opportunity has been provided for the mass of the people, rich and poor, literate and illiterate, to acquire their political experience and political acumen through the exercise of common privileges and responsibilities.

Quirinal[1] **and Vatican.** — As in other countries, the actual operation of the machinery of government is profoundly influenced by party organization and programs; and these, in turn, are much affected in Italy by a peculiar circumstance which must at this point be explained. The capital of the kingdom is

---

[1] The palace occupied by the royal family. It was formerly a papal residence. The name is sometimes used figuratively, as it is here, to denote the civil, secular power in Italy as distinguished from the papal power.

likewise the capital of the Catholic world, the administrative seat of a government which not only is absolutely independent of the government of the Italian nation but is avowedly antagonistic to it. This state of things dates from 1870, when the armed forces of King Victor Emmanuel II crossed the borders of the little papal dominion around Rome, entered the city, and by a few sharp strokes beat down all forcible opposition to the sovereignty of the united Italian nation. The purpose was not to drive the Pope from the Eternal City, not to interfere with the free exercise of his spiritual functions, but simply to bring into the new kingdom a territory that was essential to its unity, and to make possible the removal of the seat of government to the one logical and necessary location, *i.e.*, Rome. With a view to compensating the head of the Church for his losses and assuring him of future independence and security, Parliament enacted, early in 1871, a comprehensive Law of Papal Guarantees, which stands on the statute book to this day. The Pope was to retain full sovereign rights on an equality with the king; his person was to be inviolate, and he might send and receive diplomatic representatives and maintain separate postal and telegraph services. He was to have permanent possession of the Vatican and Lateran palaces, with all appurtenant buildings, museums, libraries, gardens, and lands (including the church of St. Peter's), together with the villa of Castel Gandolfo, seventeen miles southeast of Rome, near Albano. As compensation for the loss of his temporal possessions, he was to receive perpetually the sum of 3,225,000 lire ($645,000) a year. Finally, he was to be immune from all interference by the government or its agents with his spiritual activities.

To Victor Emmanuel and his advisers this seemed a reasonable settlement. But Pope Pius IX flatly refused to accept it. He felt that he had been robbed of his rightful possessions and of his real independence, and, although helpless to get them back by his own efforts, he hoped, and for a good while expected, to do so with the aid of some Catholic power, probably France. To accept the Law of Guarantees would be tantamount to a recognition of the despoiler. Hence the pontiff refused to take any of the money voted him, and shut himself up as a "prisoner" in the Vatican, so that he should not even so much as set foot on soil ruled over by the king. Consequently, what was intended as a treaty arrangement effecting a compromise became, rather, a one-sided *modus vivendi* steadily adhered to by the government, but altogether disregarded by the papal authorities. Successive appeals to the Catholic powers having failed to bring relief, the Vatican eventually fell back upon a policy of obstruction, and in 1883 Pope Leo XIII promulgated a decree, designated *Non Expedit*, declaring it undesirable for Catholics to vote at parliamentary elections or to hold office under the royal government. Twelve years later a decree of the same Pope, *Non Licet*, went a step farther by expressly prohibiting political activities formerly pronounced simply "inexpedient." The object was, of course, to embarrass the government and to weaken its popular support. The effect was not as great as was desired; the decrees were warmly resented by many loyal Catholics, and they were never generally observed. They tended, however, to draw a sharp line between loyal patriots and faithful Catholics. "On the one side, while the bulk of Italians continued to describe themselves as Catholics, the Church by combating nationalism weakened its hold upon them. On the other side, the conscientious abstention of many good and honest people from politics left the Italian government in the hands of men indifferent, if not opposed, to religion, and weakened the state."[1]

Political Parties. — The conflict of Quirinal and Vatican, and the effort of the latter to frustrate the normal operation of the government, added to the political inexperience of the Italian people, the traditions of localism, and the innate tendencies to factionism, have brought it about that in the kingdom to-day, as in France, political parties are numerous, and their memberships and programs are subject to swift and bewildering fluctuation. From 1870, when the country's unification was completed, to 1876 the nation's affairs were controlled by an ill-defined group of Conservatives, composing the "Right," whose strength lay in Tuscany and the regions northward, and whose vigorous and sometimes arbitrary management disclosed a distrust of democracy for which the illiteracy and backwardness of the masses were not entirely responsible. During the next twenty years the Left was in the ascendancy. Its leaders — Depretis,

[1] Hayes, *Political and Social History of Modern Europe*, II, 372.

Crispi, and others — were men of the south; they favored democracy, and hence became the authors of the electoral law of 1882; and, while the successive ministries ruled with the support rather of an incoherent group of factions than of a party in any true sense, they succeeded in giving the nation's course a decided bent both toward democracy and toward a bolder international policy. After 1896 came an era — which has lasted to this day — in which the growing multiplicity of parties bore fruit in cabinets of amazingly composite character. Nothing would be gained by telling the story of these cabinets here. Certain aspects of the party situation as it had come to be by 1914 may, however, be pointed out.

"From the beginning," says an Italian writer, "the constitution of our parties has been determined, not at all by great historical or political considerations, but by considerations of a purely personal nature, and this aspect has been accentuated more and more as we have progressed in constitutional development. The natural conditions surrounding the birth and growth of the new nation did not permit the formation of a true conservative party which could stand in opposition to a liberal party. The liberal party, therefore, occupying the entire field, divided into groups, somewhat arbitrarily called Right and Left, in accordance with simple distinctions of degrees and forms, and perchance also of personal disposition." [1]

The preponderating facts, in short, concerning political parties in Italy are two: (1) the absence of any genuinely conservative party such as is to be found in most continental countries, and (2) the splitting of the liberal forces, which elsewhere are compelled to coöperate in some degree against the conservatives, into a number of factional groups, dominated largely by ambitious leaders, and unwilling to unite save in occasional coalitions for momentary advantage. The lack of a real conservative party is to be explained largely by the anomalous situation which has existed since 1870 in respect to church and state. Until late years that important element, the clericals, which normally would have constituted, as does its counterpart in France, the backbone of a conservative party, has persisted in the purely passive policy of abstention from national politics. In the

[1] Cardon, *Del governo nella monarchia constituzionale*, 125.

evolution of party groupings it had no part, and in Parliament it was without representation. All active party groups were essentially "liberal," and rarely did any one of them put forward a program which distinguished it sharply from its rivals. Each was little more than a faction, united by personal ties, fluctuating in membership and in leadership, fighting with such means as for the moment appeared dependable for the perquisites of office. Of broadly national political issues there were none, just as indeed there were no truly national parties.

Of late, however, there has been a certain development in the direction of national parties and of stable party programs. This is coming about primarily through the growth of the Extreme Left, especially of the Socialist wing. Although the effects are not yet such as to save the country from the somewhat chaotic conditions inherent in the group system, the development of the *partiti populari* which compose the Extreme Left, *i.e.*, the Republicans, the Radicals, and the Socialists, is an interesting political phenomenon. The Republicans are not numerous or well organized. Quite impotent between 1870 and 1890, they gained a good deal of ground during the stormy ministries of Crispi; but the rise of socialism has weakened them, and they are now practically confined to Freemason and other special circles. The royal family is popular throughout the country; monarchy, as it is organized, in no way interferes with the fullest development of democracy; and there is no reason to expect the early conversion of the country into a republic. It already has the essentials of republican government. To employ an espressive phrase of the Italians themselves, the Republicans are but *quattro noci in un sacco*, "four nuts rattling in a bag." The Radicals are stronger, and their outlook is more promising. They are monarchists who are dissatisfied with the government of the older parties, but who distrust socialism. They draw especially from the artisans and lower middle class, and are strongest in Lombardy, Venetia, and Tuscany.

The Growth of Socialism. — Of far greater importance are the Socialists. The remoter origins of socialism in Italy can be traced to the first half of the nineteenth century; but until comparatively late socialism in the peninsula was hardly distinguishable from Bakuninian anarchism. The franchise law of

1882, tripling the electorate, influenced many anarchists to accept the parliamentary method of reform and to become simple socialists; and gradually a line of cleavage was drawn between the two creeds. In 1885 a socialistic workingmen's party, which soon numbered forty thousand members, was organized at Milan. The anarchists, however, captured the organization, and in the following year it was suppressed. In 1891 a socialist fortnightly review, *La Critica Sociale*, was founded at Milan; and in the same year was held, in the same city, the first Italian congress which was distinctively socialist. This congress, containing representatives of one hundred and fifty workingmen's societies, organized a party that may be regarded as the immediate forerunner of the Italian Socialist party of the present day. In 1892, at the congress of Genoa, came the final break with the anarchists, and since this date the socialism of Italy has differed in no essential regard from that of France or Germany.

Between 1891 and 1893 the new party acted with the Right; but the policy of repression pursued by Crispi in 1894-1895 and by Rudini and Pelloux in 1898-1899 had the effect of gradually driving the radical groups, Republicans, Radicals, and Socialists, into alliance; and it is to this period that the origins of the present coalition of the groups of the Extreme Left are to be traced. During the years 1895-1900 the Socialists became, in effect, the advanced wing of a great parliamentary party, with a definite program of political and social reform. Included among the most essential features of this " minimum program " (dating from about 1895, and revised in 1900) were universal suffrage for adults of both sexes, salaries for deputies and for members of municipal councils, a more humane penal code, the substitution of a national militia for the standing army, improved factory legislation, compulsory insurance against sickness, reform of the laws regulating the relations of landlords and tenants, nationalization of railways and mines, extension of compulsory education, abolition of duties on food, and a progressive income tax and succession duty.

The widespread dissatisfaction of Italians with the older parties, the practical character of the Socialist program, and the comparatively able leadership of the Socialist forces have combined to give socialism an extraordinary growth in the past twenty years. In 1895 the party polled 35,000 votes and returned twelve members to the Chamber of Deputies. In 1897 it polled 108,000 votes and returned sixteen members. In 1904 it polled 301,000 votes (about one-fifth of the total number) and returned twenty-six members. Finally, in the elections of 1913 there were no fewer than 376 Socialist candidates, the popular vote rose to almost a million, and the party increased its quota in the Chamber from 41 to 78. Among features which Italian socialism in late years has had in common with the socialism of France, Germany, and other lands, is the conflict between wings or factions of opposing tendencies, and most notably between the moderate, evolutionary, " reformist " group led by Turati and the uncompromising, revolutionary group led by Enrico Ferri and the syndicalist Arturo Labriola. The question of " reformism " *versus* revolutionism was debated as early as the congress of Imola in 1902, and the friction between the two tendencies became especially acute in 1904, when the revolutionists organized a general strike, which failed. In 1902 the reformists carried the day, but during the years 1904-1908 the revolutionists, largely in consequence of the eloquence and leadership of Ferri, were in the ascendant. At the congress of Florence in 1908 the reformists regained control, and with slight interruptions they dominated the councils of the party until 1913. In the elections of that year, however, the revolutionists obtained 58 in a total of 78 Socialist seats and acquired complete dominance of the parliamentary group. The further fact may be noted that in no European country has socialism gained a larger hold upon the section of the population which as a rule is least appealed to by it, namely, the agricultural laborers.

An extremely important result of the steady progress of socialism and other forms of radicalism has been a new attitude on the part of the Holy See toward the participation of Catholics in politics. In the elections of 1904 many Catholics who hitherto had abstained from voting joined with the Government's supporters at the polls in an effort to check the growing influence of the radical groups, justifying their action by the argument that the combating of socialism is a fundamental Catholic obligation. Pope Pius X was ready to admit the force of the contention, and in June of the following year he issued an encyclical which made it the duty of Catholics everywhere, Italy included, to share in the maintenance of social order, and permitted, and even enjoined, that they take part in political contests in defense of social order whenever and wherever it was obviously menaced. At the same time, such participation must be, not indiscriminate, but disciplined. It must be carried on under the direction of the ecclesiastical hierarchy, and with the express approval of the Vatican. Theoretically, and as a general rule, the *Non Expedit* remains. But where the rigid application of the law would open the way for the triumph of the enemies of society and of religion (as, from the papal point of view, socialists inevitably are), the rule, upon request of the bishop and sanction by the Holy See, is to be waived. A corollary of this new policy is that, under certain circumstances, Catholics may not merely vote but also stand for parliamentary seats. By the encyclical it is prescribed that such candidacies shall be permitted only where absolutely necessary to prevent the election of an avowed adversary of the Church, only where there is a real chance of success, and only with the approbation of the proper hierarchical authorities; and even then the candidate shall seek office not *as* a Catholic, but *although* a Catholic.

The partial lifting of the *Non Expedit* has had two clear effects. In the first place, it has considerably stimulated the political activities of the Catholics. In the elections of 1909 and 1913 the number of Catholic voters and of Catholic candidates was larger than ever before, and in the Chamber of Deputies the group of Clerical members — raised in 1913 to 35 — gives promise of attaining real importance. Besides denouncing socialism, and condemning infringements by the state upon the liberties of the papacy and of the church at large, this newer Clerical party urges social reform, *e.g.*, factory legislation, workingmen's insurance, coöperative enterprises, and a wider distribution of land, with all the arguments, if not with all the vehemence, of the Socialists. A second result of the relaxation of the papal ban has been, on the other hand, a quickening of the anti-clerical spirit, and a perceptible strengthening of the Radical-Republican-Socialist *bloc*. By providing the Left with a solidifying issue the papacy may yet prove to have rendered a service unwittingly to the very elements against whom it has authorized its adherents to wage relentless war.

SELECTED REFERENCES

W. F. Dodd, *Modern Constitutions* (Chicago, 1909), II, 5-16, containing text of constitution; A. L. Lowell, *Governments and Parties in Continental Europe* (Boston, 1896), I, Chaps. iii-iv; B. King and T. Okey, *Italy To-day* (2d ed., London, 1909), Chaps. i-iii, xiii-xiv; F. M. Underwood, *United Italy* (London, 1912), Chaps. v-viii, xi-xii; C. D. Hazen, *Europe since 1815* (New York, 1910), Chap. xvi; B. King, *History of Italian Unity, 1814-1871*, 2 vols. (London, 1899); W. R. Thayer, *Count Cavour*, 2 vols. (Boston, 1911); W. J. Stillman, *Francesco Crispi* (London, 1899); M. Prichard-Agnetti (trans.), *Memoirs of Francesco Crispi*, 3 vols. (New York, 1912-1914); F. Nielsen, *History of the Papacy in the Nineteenth Century* (London, 1906).

CHAPTER XXI

THE GOVERNMENT OF BELGIUM

The Nation and Its Constitution. — With a view to erecting a northern barrier against French aggression, and at the same time compensating Holland for colonial losses recently suffered in the East, the Congress of Vienna, in 1815, agreed to incorporate in the Dutch kingdom the old Austrian Netherlands, the bishopric of Liège, the duchy of Limburg, and the duchy (henceforth to be known as grand-duchy) of Luxemburg. The union, however, was purely artificial; the Dutch and the Belgians were unlike in racial descent, language, religion, and economic interests; King William I's government was autocratic, partisan, and stupid; and in 1830 the whole arrangement was broken up by a war of independence waged by the Belgians under the not altogether disapproving eyes of the powers that had been responsible for the union fifteen years before. An international agreement reached at London in 1831 recognized both the independence and the neutrality of the new nation, although on account of the refusal of William I to evacuate certain territories claimed by the Belgians the final settlement was delayed eight years. On April 18, 1839, the treaty that regulated Belgium's international status down to August 3, 1914, was signed at London; the country's neutrality being unreservedly guaranteed by Great Britain, France, Russia, Austria, and Prussia.[1]

Meanwhile a constitution was framed for the new state by an appointed commission and ratified by a national congress of two hundred elected delegates; and on July 21, 1831, the first independent Belgian sovereign, Leopold I, took oath to observe and maintain it. Circumstances combined to give the instrument an exceptionally liberal character. Devised in the midst of a revolution brought on principally by the autocratic rule of

[1] This treaty is the "scrap of paper" contemptuously referred to by the German chancellor, von Bethmann-Hollweg, in the early days of the Great War.

William I, it is, and was intended to be, uncommonly explicit in its limitations on the royal prerogative. There were Belgians in 1831, indeed, who advocated the establishment of a republic. Against such a course various considerations were successfully urged; but the monarchy that was set up, depending for its very existence upon popular approval, is of the strictly limited, constitutional type. "All powers," it is expressly declared in the fundamental law, "emanate from the people." The principles of liberalism are the more in evidence by reason of the fact that the framers of the constitution deliberately accepted as models the French instruments of 1791 and 1830, and were likewise influenced greatly by their admiration for the governmental system of Great Britain.

A striking testimony to the thoroughness with which the work was done, and to the liberal character of the government established, is the fact that the text of the Belgian fundamental law operated for more than half a century absolutely unchanged, and, further, that when in our own day the work of amendment was actively taken up, not even the most ardent revisionists cared to insist upon more than the overhauling of the arrangements concerning the franchise. The instrument is to-day the oldest written constitution in force on the continent, except the Dutch. Leopold I (1831–1865), and Leopold II (1865–1909), frankly recognized the conditional basis of the royal tenure and, although conspicuously active in the management of public affairs, gave little occasion for popular criticism or disaffection. Even the revolutionary year 1848 passed without producing in Belgium more than a ripple of unrest. In 1893 the constitution was amended to provide for universal male suffrage, and in 1899 a further amendment introduced a system of proportional representation. Otherwise, the instrument stands to-day practically as it was put into operation in 1831. It need hardly be remarked that, in Belgium as elsewhere, the written constitution does not by any means contain the whole of the actually operative political system. Numerous aspects of parliamentarism, and of other well-established governmental forms and practices, depend for their sanction upon the conventions, rather than upon the law, of the constitution; but they are none the less real and enduring.

The written instrument is comprehensive in scope. It comprises an extended bill of rights; a detailed definition of the framework of the national executive, legislative, and judicial departments; special provisions relating to finance and the army; and an enumeration of the principles underlying provincial and communal administration. The process of amendment is calculated to ascertain the public will unmistakably before any change in the fundamental law is actually made. When both houses of Parliament vote favorably upon a proposed amendment they are forthwith dissolved, and a national election takes place. If the new chambers approve the proposition by a two-thirds vote, and the sovereign gives his assent (this being a mere formality), it is declared adopted.

In the forthcoming brief description of the Belgian governmental system it will be necessary to allude to certain features that hitherto have obstructed the fullest expression of democracy. It is the more desirable, therefore, at this point to emphasize the fact that so far as the legal rights and personal liberties of the individual go, there is hardly a country in the world in which the laws afford better protection than in the Belgium of earlier and happier days. Let a great Belgian lawyer himself state the situation. "Freedom reigns among us," he says, "without flaw and without infringement. It takes every form; it sustains every right. I have freedom of the person; and I can only be arrested in the prescribed manner. I have freedom of the home; and my dwelling is inviolable, subject to the rule of law. I have freedom of property; and I am guaranteed against expropriation, confiscation, and arbitrary taxes, as well as the forfeitures which have been abolished. I have freedom of activity; I am free to work, to choose my trade, to enter into industrial contracts. I have freedom of opinion; for all the channels of the press and of publication are open to me. I have freedom of speech; for I can speak freely, whether in Parliament, in the pulpit, in the police court, at the bar, and in whatever language. I have freedom of thought; for no one may violate the privacy of my letters, and the law lays no hand on my thoughts, even my guilty thoughts. I have freedom of worship; for my conscience is free, the ministers of my religion are independent, I may let it exert its full influence and efficacy for me. I have freedom of instruction; for I am allowed to teach and to learn, where I like and at every stage, what is known and what is believed. I have freedom of movement; for every barrier has disappeared within the country, and the protection of foreigners is assured. I am free to seek help, to claim justice, to make my voice heard against any oppression; for I can use when I please the right of petition." [1]

The Governmental System. — The general scheme of government represents a constitutional monarchy modeled on early nineteenth-century England and the France of Louis Philippe, and superimposed upon, and cleverly articulated with, the historic governmental usages of the old Belgian provinces and cities. Executive power is vested nominally in the king, who, however, can act only through the responsible ministers. So far as the actual conduct of the government is concerned, the king's personal position differs in no important respect from that of the English sovereign. The ministers are eleven in number. Individually, they preside over the eleven executive departments; collectively, they form an advisory and deliberative body which determines policy, leads in legislation, and looks after the interests of the party to which the members belong. They are selected precisely as in England and France; all belong to the party (or party coalition) which is at the time in power; with only an occasional exception, all have seats in Parliament, and usually in the lower house; all go out of office together when a working majority in the lower chamber fails them. In England a minister can appear and speak in only the house of Parliament of which he is a member. In Belgium, on the contrary, ministers are entitled to be heard, upon their own demand, in either chamber, although of course they can vote only in the body to which they belong. Either chamber can, in fact, demand a minister's presence, in order to interrogate him. On the responsibility of ministers the constitution is very explicit. "No decree of the king," it is stipulated, "shall take effect unless it is countersigned by a minister who, by that act alone, renders himself responsible for it." Furthermore, "in no case shall the verbal or written order of the king relieve a

---

[1] M. Charles Faider, in a speech before the Court of Cassation. Quoted in Ensor, *Belgium*, 163–164.

minister of responsibility." Ordinarily the enforcement of this responsibility takes the course that is customary under the cabinet system; but, in addition, ministers can be arraigned by the lower chamber before a supreme tribunal, the Court of Cassation, and a minister sentenced by the tribunal cannot be pardoned by the king save upon request of one of the two legislative houses. On the whole, there is no continental country in which the parliamentary system, in the technical meaning of the phrase, approaches so closely, in its actual operation, that of England.

Parliament consists of two houses, both elective and both representative of the nation as a whole. The upper house, or Senate, is composed of 112 members, chosen for a term of eight years, half retiring every four years. On the basis of method of election, the members fall into two categories. Under a constitutional amendment of 1893 a number of senators equal to one-half the number of members of the House of Representatives is chosen directly by the people in twenty-one large constituencies. The electorate which returns these senators is identical with that which returns the deputies except that it is confined to voters who are thirty years of age and upwards; and by amendment of 1899 the elections are on the plan of proportional representation. A second group of members consists of those elected by the councils of the several provinces, to the number of two for each province having fewer than 500,000 inhabitants, of three for each province having from 500,000 to 1,000,000 inhabitants, and of four for each province having more than 1,000,000 inhabitants. The proportion of senators elected directly by the people is approximately three-fourths. There is no hereditary element except the sons, or the heir-apparent, of the king; these become nominal members at eighteen, and voting members at twenty-five. All elective senators must be Belgian citizens and residents, at least forty years of age, and either payers of as much as 1200 francs of direct national taxes, or proprietors or lessees of Belgian real estate of an assessed income of at least 12,000 francs. All are unsalaried.

The House of Representatives is wholly elected by direct popular vote, in twenty-nine large constituencies. The number of seats — at present 166 — is fixed by law, under the constitutional requirement that a member must represent a quota of not less than 40,000 inhabitants. The term is four years; but only half of the constituencies elect their representatives at a given time, so that there is a parliamentary election in half of the country every two years. In the event of a dissolution, the entire chamber is renewed at one time; but dissolutions are rare. Any one who can vote at parliamentary elections is qualified to be elected to a seat. Representatives are paid 4000 francs a year.

From the essentially democratic character of the Belgian government it follows that the powers of the legislative chambers are comprehensive. The functions of legislation are vested by the constitution conjointly in the king and the two houses, but in practice they belong to the houses alone; the right of initiative is exercised wholly through the ministers; that of veto is not exercised at all. All laws relating to the revenues or expenditures of the state, or to military contingents, must be voted first by the House of Representatives. Authoritative interpretation of the measures enacted is confided exclusively to the legislative power, and, as has been pointed out, each house has full right to inquire into the conduct of public affairs and to compel the attendance of ministers for the purpose of interpellation. The lower house alone, however, has power to formulate charges against public officials and to arraign them before the Court of Cassation.

Electoral Reform: the Suffrage. — The election of members of the House of Representatives presents three principal features, all attained by stages since the original electoral system was devised. The first is manhood suffrage; the second is plural voting; and the third is proportional representation. The franchise set up for the lower chamber in 1831 was narrow, being based on high tax-paying qualifications. The urban electorate, composed of men paying seventy florins ($28) in taxes, was particularly restricted. In 1848 the requirement was reduced to twenty florins, doubling the electorate; and on this basis all elections were held down to 1894. That the system was highly undemocratic is sufficiently evidenced by the fact that in 1890, when the population of the country was six millions, there were only 135,000 parliamentary voters. As early as 1860 the Liberal party urgently demanded a constitutional amendment on the subject; and after 1885 effort was reënforced by persistent and at times violent agitation carried on by a new Labor party and by other socialist organizations.

In 1890 the conservative Catholic party,[1] which had long blocked reform, recognizing in part the justice of the demand, and preferring, if there was to be revision, to carry it through, rather than to incur the risk of having it carried through by a radical government, yielded to the pressure, and the ministry consented to the formal consideration of the electoral question upon the floors of the two chambers. Three years of intermittent, but animated, discussion followed. At length, in May, 1892, the chambers were able to agree upon the primary proposition that some sort of revision was necessary. Then came the dissolution which is required by the constitution in such a case, followed by a general election. The newly chosen chambers, which for the purpose in hand comprised practically a constituent convention, entered upon their task later in the same year. In both the Catholics still had a majority, but by reason of the requirement of a two-thirds vote for the adoption of a constitutional amendment, they were none the less obliged to rely upon their Liberal opponents for a certain amount of support. To the scheme of revision which was finally adopted all parties made substantial contribution.

No fewer than fourteen distinct programs were laid before the chambers. The conservatives, in general, desired a system

[1] The division between Liberals and Catholics has existed since the earliest days of Belgian independence, and is primarily religious. The Catholic party has represented the interests of ecclesiasticism — interests of a very extensive and complicated kind, since the Roman Church, through its various organizations, is the largest property-owner of the country. The party's insistence upon clerical control of the schools delayed the establishment of compulsory elementary education until 1914. On the other hand, the party has been the author of a large amount of important social legislation; although it must be added that some of this legislation was passed reluctantly as a means of keeping the party in power, and other portions have been designed primarily to increase the hold of the Church upon the people. The Catholic party has found its main strength in the northern provinces, which before the war were peopled by about four million "Flemings" of Teutonic stock, speaking a Dutch dialect, and living mainly by agriculture. The Liberals, on the other hand, have prospered chiefly in the southern provinces, which were inhabited by three million "Walloons" of Celtic origin, speaking French, and living almost entirely by industry. The northerners were devoted to the Church; the southerners were deeply affected by French anti-clericalism.

based upon occupation, combined with the payment of taxes; the majority of the Liberals sought to secure special recognition for electors of approved capacity — in short, an educational qualification; the Radicals inside, and the Socialists outside, Parliament carried on ceaseless propaganda in behalf of universal, direct, and equal suffrage. The rejection in committee (April, 1893) of a plan of universal suffrage led to popular demonstrations which required the calling out of the military; and when it was at one time proposed to go no farther than to reduce the age limit for voters there were threats of a universal industrial strike. In the end all elements wisely receded from their extreme demands, and it was found possible to effect a compromise. A Catholic deputy — Albert Nyssens, professor at the University of Louvain — came forward with a scheme for manhood suffrage combined with plural voting, and on September 3, 1893, the plan was adopted.

By the terms of the new law one vote is allotted to every male Belgian citizen who has reached the age of twenty-five years, who is in unrestricted enjoyment of his civil and political rights, and who has been resident at least one year in the same commune. There is nothing whatsoever in the nature of either an educational or a property qualification. Having conferred, however, upon the mass of male citizens the right to vote, the law proceeds to define the conditions under which a citizen may be entitled to two votes, or even three. One supplementary vote is conferred upon (1) every male citizen over thirty-five years of age, married or a widower, with legitimate offspring, and paying to the state as a householder a tax of not less than five francs, unless exempt by reason of his profession, and (2) every male citizen over twenty-five years of age owning real estate to the assessed value of 2000 francs, or possessing income from land corresponding to such valuation, or who for two years has derived a minimum interest return of one hundred francs a year from Belgian funds, in the form of either government bonds or obligations of the Belgian government savings bank. Two supplementary votes are conferred upon citizens over twenty-five years of age who (1) hold a diploma from an institution of higher learning, or an indorsed certificate testifying to the completion of a course of secondary education of the higher grade; or (2) occupy or have occupied a public office, hold or have held a position, practice or have practiced a profession, which presupposes the knowledge imparted in secondary instruction of the higher grade — such offices, positions, and professions to be defined from time to time by law.

What, therefore, the law of 1893 does is, broadly, to confer upon every male citizen one vote and to specify three principal conditions under which this basal voting power may be augmented. As the head of a family, the citizen's suffrage may be doubled. By reason of his possession of property or of capital, it likewise may be doubled. On the basis of a substantial educational qualification, it may be tripled. Under no circumstances may an individual have more than three votes. The plural vote of Belgium differs, therefore, from that of Great Britain prior to 1918, not only in that it is based upon a variety of qualifications of which property relationship is but one, but also in that there is fixed an absolute and reasonably low maximum of votes. In Great Britain to-day, as has been pointed out, this maximum is two. There is the further difference that whereas in Great Britain the plural voter casts but one ballot in any one constituency, in Belgium the plural voter casts two or three ballots at one place and for one set of candidates.

The effect of the extension of the suffrage was to raise the number of voters at the 1894 elections from 137,772 to 1,350,891; and as a result of the plural-voting provision this enlarged electorate cast 2,085,605 votes. In the registration year 1912–1913 the number of electors and the number of plural votes for both Senate and House of Representatives were as follows:

	SENATE	HOUSE
No. of voters	1,483,994	1,745,666
No. with 1 vote only	761,864	1,005,094
No. with 2 votes	402,444	412,471
No. with 3 votes	319,686	327,851
Total no. of votes	2,525,810	2,814,089
Excess of votes over voters	1,941,816	1,068,423
Excess per cent	70	61

The plural voter wields more control over the Senate than over the lower chamber, and this is one of the reasons why the Senate is the more conservative body. But even in the House of Representatives the effects of plural voting are very perceptible. Thus, whereas the people who have but one vote — including the entire propertyless class of manual workers in the towns — comprise almost 59 per cent of the total electorate, they have only 36 per cent of the voting power. It is not strange, therefore, that the law of 1893 was hardly adopted before the Socialists and other radical elements announced their purpose to wage unremitting war on the plural-voting feature. Demanding the rule of *un homme, un vote*, " one man, one vote," and a reduction of the age limit to twenty-one, the Socialists kept up a steady agitation for twenty years. The Liberals were also, in the main, opposed to the new system. But on account of the inability of the two elements to work together it proved possible for the conservative forces to stave off a change. When the Great War came on, in 1914, however, reform seemed not far distant; and one may venture the prediction that in the reconstruction of the despoiled country after the restoration of peace plural voting will finally disappear.

It is of interest to observe that every elector qualified to vote is compelled by law under penalty to do so. Failure to appear at the polls, without adequate excuse made to the election officer, is a misdemeanor. The citizen may, if he likes, evade the purposes of the law by depositing a blank ballot. But he must deposit a ballot of some sort.

Electoral Reform: Proportional Representation. — Contrary to general expectation, at the first election held under the new law (in 1894) the conservative Catholic party, which already had been in power for ten years, won an overwhelming victory. It obtained 104 seats, the Liberals only 19; while the Socialists, who had previously had no representation, secured 29. At the succeeding elections of 1896 and 1898 the Catholics so increased their parliamentary majority that all of their rivals combined could muster only 40 votes in the lower house and 31 in the upper one. The Liberal party was threatened with extinction. Its strength throughout the country was, however, still considerable; and from both Liberals and Socialists arose demand for some system that would give the various parties seats in the lawmaking bodies in proportion to their popular vote.

The suggestion was not so novel as it sounded. No European country had as yet a general system of proportional representation; but the subject had been discussed in the Belgian lower chamber as far back as 1866; and at the time of the reform of 1893 the ministry had favored adoption of the principle. Following a short contest, a constitutional amendment was pressed upon the somewhat divided Catholic forces, and late in 1899 it became law. Under its provisions representatives and the popularly elected senators continue to be chosen in the large electoral divisions by *scrutin de liste*. Within each electoral area the seats to be filled are distributed among the parties in proportion to the party strength as revealed at the polls, the allotment taking place in accordance with the " list system " devised by Victor d'Hondt, of the University of Ghent. The number of representatives elected in a district varies from three to twenty-one. When an elector appears at the polls he presents his official summons and receives from the presiding officer one, two, or three ballot-papers, according to the number of votes to which he is entitled. He takes these papers to a private compartment, marks them, places them in the ballot-box, and receives again his letter of summons stamped in such a way as to show that he has discharged his civic duty. The candidates of the various parties are presented in lists, and ordinarily the task of the elector is merely to indicate his approval of one list for each of the votes which he is entitled to cast. This he does, not by making a cross as in England or the United States, but by blacking out a white spot in the center of a black square. He may pencil only the spot at the head of a list, thereby approving the order in which the candidates have been arranged by the party managers; or, by marking spaces opposite names of candidates, he may indicate his preference for a different order. Experience shows that under this system, as under those prevailing in the United States, almost all electors vote a " straight ticket."

How after the votes are counted the seats are allotted may best be explained by a hypothetical case. Assume that in a given district four lists of parliamentary candidates have been presented and that an aggregate vote of 33,000 is distributed as follows: Catholics, 16,000; Liberals, 9000; Socialists, 4500; and Christian Democrats, 3500. Assume, further, that the district is entitled to eight seats. The first step is to divide the total number of votes for each list successively by 1, 2, 3, 4, etc., arraying the results thus:

	Catholic List	Liberal List	Socialist List	Christian Democrat List
Divided by 1	16,000	9,000	4,500	3,500
Divided by 2	8,000	4,500	2,250	1,750
Divided by 3	5,333	3,000	1,500	1,166
Divided by 4	4,000	2,250	1,125	875
Divided by 5	3,200	1,800	900	700

The eight highest numbers (eight being the number of seats to be filled) are then arranged in order of magnitude as follows:

> 16,000
> 9,000
> 8,000
> 5,333
> 4,500
> 4,500
> 4,000
> 3,500

The lowest of these numbers, 3500, becomes the common divisor, or the "electoral quotient." The number of votes cast for each list is divided by this quotient, and the resulting numbers (fractions being disregarded) indicate the quota of seats to which each of the parties is entitled. In the case in hand the results would be:

> 16,000 divided by 3,500 = 4 Catholic seats
> 9,000 divided by 3,500 = 2 Liberal seats
> 4,500 divided by 3,500 = 1 Socialist seat
> 3,500 divided by 3,500 = 1 Christian Democrat seat

Lists of candidates are made up, and the order in which the names of candidates appear is determined, by the local organizations of the respective parties. In order to be presented to the electorate a list must have the pledged support of at least one hundred electors. A candidate may stand as an independent, and his name will appear in a separate "list," provided his candidacy meets the condition that has been mentioned; and any organization or group, political or non-political, has a right to place a list before the electorate. The power of the organization responsible for the presentation of a list to fix the order of candidates' names is not a necessary feature of the proportional system, and it has been the object of much criticism; but it is not clear that serious abuse has arisen from it. Candidates whose names stand near the top of the list are, of course, more likely to be elected than those whose names appear farther down, for, under the prevailing rules, all votes indicated in the space at the head of a list form a pool from which the candidates on the list draw in succession as many votes as may be necessary to make their individual total equal to the electoral quotient, the process continuing until the pool is exhausted. Only by receiving a large number of individual preferential votes can a candidate be elected to the exclusion of a candidate whose name precedes his.

The first parliamentary election under the proportional system — that of May, 1900 — yielded the Socialists small advantage. But it brought the almost defunct Liberal party into a position of some strength and influence. The Catholics, however, retained control of the chamber; and, contrary to common expectation, this control was held uninterruptedly until the Great War, at whose outbreak a coalition ministry, representing all parties, was set up. Instead of the overwhelming majorities of earlier days, however, the margin in this period averaged not more than fifteen votes, and after the elections of 1910 it fell to six. A salutary result was therefore that the government was kept continually on its mettle; and a good amount of legislation was enacted that had a decidedly liberal slant. Notwithstanding the failure of the system to bring the liberal and radical elements into power, all parties are committed to its continuance. The Socialists, in particular, feel that the objectionable feature of the existing electoral system is plural voting, not "P. R."; and it was with a view exclusively to forcing the establishment of universal and equal suffrage that they carried out great, though unsuccessful, strikes in 1902 and 1913.

Further electoral reform as a feature of Belgian reconstruction was promised by King Albert in a speech from the throne in Parliament, November 22, 1918. "The government proposes to the chamber," he said, "to lower, by patriotic agreement, the ancient barriers, and to make the consultation of the nation a reality on the basis of equal suffrage for all men of the mature age required for the exercise of civil rights."

SELECTED REFERENCES

W. F. Dodd, *Modern Constitutions* (Chicago, 1909), I, 126–148, containing text of constitution; *Cambridge Modern History* (London, 1902–1910), X, Chap. xvi, XI, Chap. xxiii, XII, Chap. ix; R. C. K. Ensor, *Belgium* (London, 1915), Chaps. vii–viii; S. P. Orth, *Socialism and Democracy in Europe* (New York, 1912), Chap. vi; J. Humphreys, *Proportional Representation* (London, 1911); *Ibid.*, "Proportional Representation in Belgium," in *Contemporary Review*, Oct., 1908; D. C. Boulger, *History of Belgium*, 2 vols. (London, 1909).

PART III. GOVERNMENT IN THE TEUTONIC STATES

CHAPTER XXII

THE GERMAN EMPIRE AND ITS CONSTITUTION

ONE can say without exaggeration that in all of the countries whose governmental systems we have thus far considered — the United States, Great Britain, France, Italy, and Belgium — it is the people who rule. There are, of course, practical limitations upon the actual workings of democracy in these, and in all other, lands. Men of indubitable liberality of mind are, indeed, by no means agreed upon the measure of democracy that it is desirable to seek to attain. But every one of these countries is in form or to all intents and purposes a republic; each intrusts its larger interests to lawmakers and administrators who are popularly elected; all have manhood suffrage (two have woman suffrage, in a large measure, as well) and direct and substantially equal voting; all have governments that are promptly and fully responsive to the public will. We come now to examine certain governmental systems — those of the German Empire, of the kingdom of Prussia, and of the Dual Monarchy, Austria-Hungary — which are based upon different principles; systems in which the form of popular control exists to a certain degree, but in which the substance of democratic government is, speaking broadly, not to be found. These are the states against which an allied world has been in arms, the states whose irresponsible despotism and aggression must be curbed before the world can be considered safe for democracy.[1]

[1] The following description of the German and Austro-Hungarian governments was written before the political changes (including the abdication of Emperor William II) which attended the signing of the armistice of November 11, 1918. As these pages go to press no one can foresee what governmental systems will arise in the Teutonic countries. The present purpose, however, will be served by a survey of the systems that have operated to our own day, and especially by a

The German Political Heritage. — "Liberty, that lovely thing," wrote the French critic Montesquieu in the eighteenth century, "was discovered in the wild forests of Germany." Like most glittering statements, this is but a half-truth. Before the Germanic peoples are heard of in history very substantial liberty was attained in the Greek world, and to a less extent among the early Romans. None the less, by all accounts the Germanic peoples who, between the fifth and tenth centuries, poured into the lands we now know as England, France, Italy, and Spain, and there contributed powerfully to the creation of new racial stocks and new political forms, were above all things jealous of their personal, family, and tribal freedom. Similarly notable for their strong sense of independence and equality were the kinsmen who remained north of the old Rhine-Danube frontier and became the direct ancestors of the Bavarians, Badeners, Württembergers, and Prussians of the present day. It was not to be expected that these peoples — Franks, Saxons, Burgundians, and later Norsemen — would, on account of their impatience of restriction, set up, in either their old or their new homes, republican governments. Wholly apart from the consideration that republican government calls for a high degree of political experience and capacity, the conditions of disorder, war, conquest, and feudal rivalry prevailing throughout the Middle Ages made inevitable the development of kingship and, indeed, the gathering of governmental power largely into autocratic hands. In England, however, this development never went so far as to extinguish all popular elements in the control of public policy and the administration of public business. Even under the strong government of the Norman-Angevin kings, the representative principle made steady headway in justice and finance, and gained a footing which enabled it presently to become the cornerstone of the scheme of national legislation. In France likewise — although the popular element failed to maintain itself as a working factor outside the domain of local affairs — the idea that the people should have a voice in the determination of national policy repeatedly flared up, notably

comparison of them with the systems operating in the United States, Great Britain, France, and Italy. It is of prime importance that the world shall not soon forget either the nature or the baleful effects of Teutonic autocracy.

during the Hundred Years' War (1340-1453), and again in the eighteenth century.

The Germany of the later Middle Ages and of early modern times was by no means without manifestations of a surviving spirit of liberalism. At the close of the fifteenth century there were vigorous attempts to reorganize the Holy Roman Empire (now consisting practically of the German states) on a more popular basis. During the Lutheran Revolt certain elements, especially the peasants of the south, loudly demanded freer forms of government. In the eighteenth century the most illustrious and influential of Prussian kings, Frederick the Great, wrote three treatises admonishing his brother princes that they were not in their positions by any special favor of God, assuring them that the only justification for their occupancy of their thrones was the contribution they could make to the welfare of their subjects, scoffing at the prevailing notion that the people were merely the private property of the prince, and sharply attacking the Machiavellian doctrine that the ruler is not to be bound by the ordinary principles of morality in promoting the ends of the state. The practical effect of these various movements and arguments, however, was *nil*. The effort to put the Empire on a more popular basis totally failed. The peasant reformers of 1524 were ruthlessly suppressed, Luther himself openly encouraging the princes in the bloody business. There is no record that any ruler was led to mend his ways by Frederick's lecturings; while the latter, by a remarkable series of high-handed acts during his prolonged reign (1740-1786) cast grave doubts upon his own sincerity. The condition in which Germany came down to the nineteenth century was, indeed, deplorable. The Holy Roman Empire lost all vitality, and the German-speaking world was left without the semblance of unity. The three hundred or more states were ruled by despots, petty and great, who cynically disregarded all demands for popular participation in government and ferociously resisted all suggestions that they subordinate their interests to those of a united nation. Economic life was shackled by a network of gild, town, provincial, and royal regulations. Fully half of the people were serfs. Militarism and bureaucracy blocked every avenue of reform; popular ignorance and apathy were, if possible, even greater obstacles. All told, the political heritage which the German people carried into the new century afforded scant basis for governmental development of the sort which already was far advanced in England, and which had been so dramatically inaugurated in the past decade in France.

Autocracy *versus* Liberalism, 1815-1848. — Interest in German political history in the first half of the nineteenth century centers around two interrelated movements, the one looking toward national unity, the other toward constitutional government. The period of the Napoleonic wars made some contribution in both directions. The ground was cleared for a future unification, first by the extinction of more than five-sixths of the petty states of earlier times, and second, by the replacing of the nondescript and obsolete Holy Roman Empire (terminated by decree of Napoleon in 1806) by a German Confederation created by the Congress of Vienna in 1814-1815. It is true that the immediate effect of reducing the number of states was merely to strengthen the surviving kingdoms and duchies and stiffen them against any attempt to establish an effective common control. It is true, also, that the new Confederation, whose *Bundestag*, or Diet, was hardly more than a congress of ambassadors, was so weak as to be ridiculous. Nevertheless, if the German-speaking world was ever to be united, the number of independent states must be gradually reduced, and a common German government must be set up, which, although at first a sham, might be capable of conversion by degrees into a reality.

The contribution of the Napoleonic period to the cause of liberal government in Germany took the form chiefly of a great Prussian Municipal Edict of 1808 sweeping away the gild oligarchies, broadening the suffrage, and setting up elective executive boards and town councils, at the same time giving the municipalities a larger degree of independence in the management of their own affairs. It is interesting to note that Baron von Stein, who was the author of this reform, desired to introduce the representative principle in the central, as well as the local, government; and he proposed a national elective congress with fairly extensive legislative powers. But the plan met with no favor in princely circles.

The Germany of 1815 was, then, a confederation of thirty-nine practically independent states, united under the perpetual presidency of Austria, having no common organ of discussion except an impotent Diet, and having no common administrative authority at all. Government was in all cases autocratic, and the outlook for both national unity and political liberty was dark. During the next three decades substantial economic unity was attained through the building up, under Prussian leadership, of a great *Zollverein*, or Customs Union; and this made political unification in later days somewhat easier. But liberalism advanced slowly, and with much difficulty. The Final Act of the Congress of Vienna (1815) provided not only that " diets should be held in the various federal states " of Germany, but that all of the members of the Confederation should promulgate written constitutions. Beginning in 1816, constitutions were actually granted in one state after another — fundamental laws which in a number of instances are still in operation. But most of these instruments were illiberal; none were based upon the doctrine of popular sovereignty; and the two most important states, Austria and Prussia, granted no constitutions at all. Throughout Germany there were numbers of men of liberal inclination, who wanted not only written constitutions but parliaments with real powers, and an end of absolutism; and the disappointment of these elements found expression in numerous outbursts at the universities and in more or less violent demonstrations in other quarters. The malign influence of the reactionary Austrian minister, Prince Metternich, rested, however, like a blanket upon all central Europe, and liberalism was effectually crushed wherever it dared show its head. The Prussian king, Frederick William III, repeatedly promised to give a written constitution to his people and to convoke the old " estates," or " orders," with a view to the creation of a national assembly. But the years passed and neither thing was done. The most that the reactionary monarch could bring himself to do was to create local diets in each of the eight provinces of the kingdom. In 1847 his son, Frederick William IV, went so far as to summon a *Vereinigter Landtag*, or " United Diet," comprising all members of the provincial assemblies, and organized in two chambers — a house of lords and a house containing the three estates of the knights, burghers, and peasants. But when the members fell to discussing constitutions and legislative privileges the king reminded them that he was better able to judge political institutions than they were and sent them home. Never, he declared, would he allow " to come between Almighty God in heaven and this land a blotted parchment, to rule us with paragraphs, and to replace the ancient, sacred bond of loyalty."

The Liberal Failure of 1848. — Shortly before the middle of the century Germany, and in particular the kingdom of Prussia, came to the parting of the political ways. Liberalism, driven to cover in the first decade following the restoration of 1815, had none the less deepened and broadened, and awaited only a favorable opportunity to demonstrate its real strength. In the smaller states of the south it was fighting kings and ministers on practically even terms; in Prussia it had permeated the masses to a degree undreamt of in 1815; even in reactionary Austria it had stirred the populace of Vienna and other cities, and had roused the subject nationalities to fresh protests and demonstrations. Not all liberals were agreed upon a program; and this fact proved their undoing when their opportunity came. Originally the most that they hoped for, or indeed desired, was constitutional monarchy; and in 1848 the larger portion would still have been satisfied with that form of government, providing a flexible constitution left the way open for such redistributions of power as might prove desirable. But there was now an advanced wing of the party which demanded nothing less than a republic, and in many cases some sort of socialistic organization of the state as well. " There was, indeed, a painful lack of unity and distinctness in the political ideals of the reformers. Some wished to include German Austria in the new state, others to exclude it; some dreamed of a revival of the old Empire in a modern vesture of constitutional rights and liberties, others of a central directory; some thought of the Germany of the future as a federation upon the American model, others as a strong and united republic; but the great central body of the nation, holding that no project could succeed without the support of the princely governments, did not advance beyond the conception of a federation of constitutional monarchies."[1] Professors, students, poets, philosophers, scattered knots of artisans nowhere very numerous save in Baden and the Bavarian Palatinate — these were the chief exponents of the ultimate democratic ideal.

The event that brought matters to a head was the revolution at Paris which overwhelmed Louis Philippe's government in February, 1848. Within a month a third of all Germany was in turmoil. The princes, in a panic, began making concessions right and left, and when a *Vorparlament*, convened at Frankfort, called upon the states to send delegates to a special convention to revise the Act of Federation of 1815 " on really national lines," no strong objection was interposed. The Parliament which met in the Pauluskirche at Frankfort, May 18, 1848, in response to this invitation was a body such as Germany had never seen before. Its 586 members were elected by manhood suffrage, one for every 50,000 inhabitants, and represented all the lands from the Vosges to the Vistula, and from the Baltic to the Alps. There were no princes or princes' delegates; and the body was immune from governmental interference. Stated simply, the problem to be worked out was, how to convert a loose confederation of despotically governed states into a constitutional, liberal, federal nation. Compared with this, the task of our own constitutional convention at Philadelphia in 1787 was easy, and we should not censure too severely the men who failed to find the right solution. But they were partly at fault. In the first place, they allowed their differences of view (they fell into at least eleven distinct " parties ") to involve them in unnecessary conflicts, often over irrelevant matters. In the second place, being largely idealists and enthusiasts, they looked too much to theory and not enough to fact. In the third place, they ignored the big, essential difficulty, *i.e.*, the rival ambitions of Austria and Prussia — failure to remove which, as one writer has said, " cost Germany two great wars, the Bismarckian régime, and its present constitution." Finally, the members seem to have been oblivious to the flight of time. The upshot was that by the time when, in 1849, the Parliament brought forward its plan, the princes had largely suppressed their rebellious subjects and were in a position to frown down

[1] Fisher, *The Republican Tradition in Europe*, 259.

the new scheme. Notwithstanding that there were two hundred men in the convention who called themselves republicans, the plan provided for a constitutional empire, with a parliament of two houses, direct manhood suffrage, and a responsible ministry.

It fell to Frederick William IV of Prussia to administer the fatal blow by refusing the new Imperial crown when Parliament solemnly tendered it to him. Crowns, he said, were for him and his peers to give, not to take from any gathering of mere commoners; although it is not unlikely that his decision was dictated chiefly by his desire to avert a war with Austria. The project was approved by a large majority of the states, but by none of those — Austria, Prussia, Bavaria, Saxony, Württemberg — whose assent was indispensable to its success. Accordingly, it collapsed. Thus was enacted a political tragedy. For never again did liberalism have so good an opportunity to lay the foundations for a new, enlightened, and humane Germany. Years afterwards Bismarck wrote that even in the most unsettled days of 1848 the political situation from his point of view had never been " unfavorable," since the real " barometer " of the situation was not " the noise of parliaments great and small," but " the attitude of the troops." [1] It was, unfortunately, through the use of the troops — by " blood and iron " — that the Germany of our day was destined to be made.

Prussian Autocracy Assumes Leadership. — The one tangible gain coming from the revolutionary movement of 1848 in Germany was the constitution granted in Prussia, in 1850, by Frederick William IV.[2] This instrument was disappointing to the liberals. Yet it substituted a bicameral parliament for the outworn " estates," conferred the suffrage on a large portion of the adult male population, and purported to guarantee numerous individual liberties. It has remained the fundamental law of the Prussian kingdom to this day. More and more, after 1850, the hopes of the German patriots were centered in Prussia, as leader both in national unification and in the establishment of liberal government. The only other state in the Confederation that was of sufficient size and strength to be a leader was Austria. But Austria, while herself mainly German, was so

---

[1] *Reflections and Reminiscences*, I, 66–67.   [2] See p. 439.

enmeshed in racial complications that she could never be expected to pursue a purely German policy. Prussia was thoroughly German. Besides, she had not only acquired a constitution, but had succeeded, as Austria had not, in building up an economic union (the *Zollverein*) which afforded an obvious stepping-stone to political unification. By 1860 forward-looking Germans were convinced that the old Confederation would have to be dissolved; that the new Germany would have to be the creation, not of the democratic elements working without the princes, but of one of the great princely states; and that Prussia was the only state prepared to play the rôle. German unification — and for a time German liberalization as well — became synonymous with Prussian success.[1]

With the elevation of Otto von Bismarck, in 1862, to the presidency of the Prussian ministry, events began to move toward the inevitable conclusion. Already King William I — himself a soldier to the core — had been seeking to reorganize the national army, with a view to making it the strongest in western Europe. Opposition in the lower house of Parliament had partially thwarted his plans, and he had been on the point of abdication when, at the advice of friends, he called in Bismarck and told him to save the situation if he could. As a hater of democracy, a believer in divine right, and an ardent supporter of the Hohenzollern dynasty, the new minister stepped into a full control of Prussian affairs which was never relaxed until the Emperor William II chose, in 1890, to dispense with his services. How he told the Budget Committee of the lower chamber that it was "not by speeches and resolutions of majorities, but by blood and iron (*durch Blut und Eisen*), that the great questions of the time were to be decided; how he cajoled, threatened, and finally defied, the refractory *Fortschrittspartei*, or Progressist majority, and, in order to carry out the king's plans for the army, ruled for four years without budgets or parliaments; how he planned a war for the ejection of Austria from the Confederation, and cynically began by dragging the future victim, as an ally, into war, in 1864, with Denmark; how he refused in 1863 to countenance a discussion, under Austrian auspices, of the reorganization of the Confederation, and then,

[1] Hayes, *Political and Social History of Modern Europe*, II, 180.

when, in 1866, all was in readiness, threw a bombshell into the political arena by proposing to the Diet his own scheme of reform, the most important features of which were the exclusion of Austria and the election of a German national parliament by manhood suffrage; and how, upon Austria's inevitable refusal, he declared the Confederation dissolved and hurled the Prussian army against the tottering Habsburg dominion — all this is history which cannot be related in detail here.

The North German Confederation. — The war of 1866 was short and victory decisive. The new Prussian army cut its way into Austrian territory and practically broke down all resistance in the one great battle of Sadowa, or Königgrätz. The terms which Bismarck extended were far more moderate than the king and most other Prussians desired. But they attained the essential object: the proud Habsburg monarchy was compelled not only to acknowledge that the old Confederation was no more, but also to agree to the establishment of a new confederation north of the river Main, which Prussia should lead and in which Austria should have no part. The path was now cleared for a real German unification under Prussian leadership. Taking advantage of her military triumph over the lesser states which had fought on the side of Austria, Prussia now annexed Hanover, Hesse-Cassel, Nassau, and Frankfort (in addition to the disputed duchies of Schleswig and Holstein), giving the kingdom five million new inhabitants, and also lands, including the future naval base of Kiel, of the highest strategic value. In the second place, the Berlin government concluded a series of secret military alliances with the now detached states — Bavaria, Baden, Württemberg, and Hesse-Darmstadt — south of the Main; these being followed by economic agreements looking to the early inclusion of the states in the reorganized *Zollverein*.

Finally, the new and long-talked-of confederation made its appearance. As soon as the terms of peace were settled, in 1866, Bismarck invited the states north of the Main to send delegates to Berlin to discuss plans for the union. All accepted, and the delegates appeared at the Prussian capital in December. A constitution which Bismarck had himself drafted (he is reported to have dictated it to his secretary in a single evening) was provisionally adopted, February 2, 1867, and ten days later a "constituent Bundestag" was elected, by manhood suffrage and secret ballot, to deliberate upon the instrument. After seven weeks of discussion, this body gave its approval, by a vote of 230 to 53. The diets or parliaments of the twenty-two states then ratified the instrument; and on July 1 it went into effect. The principles upon which the system was based were, in brief, autonomy for the individual states; control of foreign relations mainly by the *Bund*, or Confederation; Prussian supervision of the military establishments in peace and war; and a limited participation of the people in decisions upon public policy. The main organs of government were four: (1) the *Praesidium*, or Presidency, to be hereditary in the royal family of Prussia; (2) a *Bundeskanzler*, or Federal Chancellor, to assist the President; (3) a *Bundesrath*, or Federal Council, composed of representatives of the governments of the states; and (4) a *Bundestag*, or Diet, consisting of deputies elected by direct vote of the people, and by manhood suffrage. In this scheme appeared all the essential features of the later Imperial government; so that from 1867 the German Empire, under the hegemony of Prussia, was to all intents and purposes, though not in form or name, a reality.

A question that is likely to suggest itself is, why did Bismarck, an arch-conservative, include in his scheme a popularly elected representative body? The answer was given by himself to certain of his critics at the time. The real radicals, he said, belonged mainly to the middle, bourgeois classes — the professors and other teachers, lawyers and other professional folk, traders and travelers. The masses bade fair, he thought, to prove the real conservatives, the people who would be willing to be led, the most dependable supporters of a militaristic state. Besides, the powers assigned to the representative chamber were so modest that not much was being risked by bringing it into existence. The general state of good feeling following the late triumphs, marked by the resumption of normal parliamentary activities in Prussia, and by a vote of the hitherto obstructionist lower chamber indemnifying Bismarck for all his high-handed acts during the past four years, undoubtedly was not without effect upon the minister's policy.

The Empire Established: the Constitution. — For the time being, the states south of the Main were left to their own devices, although the constitution of the *Bund* was carefully shaped to permit, and even to encourage, the accession of new members. The patriotic fervor aroused by the war with France in 1870–1871 completed a transformation which economic agreements and military alliances had begun. Contrary to the expectation of Napoleon III, the states of the south contributed troops and otherwise coöperated vigorously with the Prussians throughout the contest, and before its close they let it be known that they were ready to become members of the Confederation. On the basis of treaty arrangements, concluded in November, 1870, it was agreed that the North German Confederation should be replaced by a German Empire, and that for the title of President, borne by the Prussian sovereign, should be substituted the title *Deutscher Kaiser*, " German Emperor." Bismarck found it no easy task to persuade the simple-minded old king to accept the new dignity. William wanted his house to keep up the habits of industry and plain living that he had followed from his youth, and he feared that an imperial title would have a seductive influence. Bismarck believed, however, that " by its reminder of days when it meant theoretically more but practically less than now " the title would " constitute an element making for unity and concentration." Consequently he prompted the princes, and also the Prussian parliament, to make a formal request that the ancient title be revived, and the sovereign felt obliged to waive his personal objections. The ceremony of proclamation took place, January 18, 1871, in the Hall of Mirrors in the richly adorned palace of Louis XIV at Versailles, in the presence of the Prussian military and civil leaders and representatives of most of the reigning families of the new Empire, while the cannon were still pounding the beleaguered and fast-weakening city of Paris.

As ordained in the treaties of November, 1870, ratified subsequently by the *Bundesrath* and the *Bundestag* of the Confederation, and by the legislative assemblies of the four incoming states, the German Empire came legally into existence January 1, 1871. It consisted fundamentally of the Confederation, which in the process of expansion did not lose its corporate identity, together with the four states whose treaties bound them severally to it.

The *Bund* was conceived of technically, not as replaced by, but rather as perpetuated in, the new Empire. The accession of the southern states, however, necessarily involved a considerable modification of the original character of the union; and the innovations that were introduced called for a certain amount of change of the fundamental law upon which the enlarged structure was to be grounded.

The elements at hand for the making of the constitution of the Empire were four: (1) the constitution of the North German Confederation, in operation since 1867; (2) the treaties of November 15, 1870, between the Confederation, on the one hand, and the grand duchies of Baden and Hesse on the other; (3) the treaty of November 23, 1870, which arranged the adhesion of the kingdom of Bavaria; and (4) the treaty of November 25, 1870, between the *Bund*, Baden, and Hesse, on the one side, and the kingdom of Württemberg on the other. Each of these treaties laid down the precise conditions under which the new affiliation should be maintained, these stipulations comprising, in effect, so many projected amendments of the original constitution of the *Bund*. At the initiative of the Emperor there was prepared, early in 1871, a revised draft of the constitution, and in it were incorporated such modifications as were made necessary by the adhesion of the southern states and the creation of the Imperial title. On March 31 the Reichstag was convened in Berlin, and the constitutional *projet* was laid before it; already the Bundesrath had given its assent. On April 14 the instrument was approved by the popular chamber, and two days later it was promulgated as the supreme law of the land.

As it came from the hands of its framers, the new constitution comprised a judicious amalgamation of the various fundamental documents that have been mentioned, *i.e.*, the constitution of the Confederation and the treaties. Within the scope of its seventy-eight articles most subjects which are ordinarily dealt with in such instruments find ample place: the nature and extent of the legislative power; the composition, organization, and procedure of the lawmaking bodies; the privileges and powers of the executive; the adjustment of disputes and the punishment of offenses against the national authority; the process of constitutional amendment. It is a peculiarity of the German constitution, however, that it contains elaborate provisions relating to a variety of things concerning which constitutions, as a rule, are silent. There is an extended section upon customs and commerce; another upon railways; another upon posts and telegraphs; another upon navigation; another upon finance; and an especially detailed one relating to military organization. In part, the elaboration of these essentially legislative subjects in the constitution is to be attributed to the federal character of the Empire, which entails a more or less minute enumeration of powers. In a greater measure, however, it arose from the purpose of Bismarck and of William I to smooth the way for the conversion of Germany into the premier military power of Europe. In such matters as transportation, taxation, telegraph service, and, most of all, military administration, no chance must be left for the states to obstruct the great purposes and projects upon which the Empire might later embark. The constitution is, on the other hand, notable for its silence on the status and privileges of the individual. There is provision for a common citizenship, and a guarantee of equal protection for all citizens as against foreign powers. But that is all. There is no bill of rights, and no enunciation of abstract principles. Among instruments of its kind, none is of a more thoroughly practical character.

"I credit to our constitution," declared Bismarck in 1877, "the capacity to develop just as the English constitution has developed." To promote such growth a simple process of formal amendment was provided. Clauses securing special rights to particular states cannot be changed without the consent of the states affected; but any other part of the written instrument can be rescinded or amended by a procedure identical with that of ordinary legislation, *i.e.*, by being adopted, by simple majority, in the Bundesrath and the Reichstag and duly promulgated by the Emperor. From one point of view, the process is extremely easy. No special machinery has to be called into play, no "ratification" to be awaited. However, it is also provided that any amendment against which as many as fourteen votes are cast in the Bundesrath is to be considered rejected. Since Prussia alone has seventeen votes in that body, and controls three others, her government can absolutely block any proposed amendment of which it disapproves. The constitution is, accordingly, easy to amend so long as Prussia is willing, but impossible to amend whenever she opposes. It would require the votes of several states — at a minimum, the six votes of Bavaria, the four of Saxony, and the four of Württemberg — to defeat an amendment that Prussia wanted. Between 1873 and 1914 the text of the fundamental law was amended eleven times, the last change being the admission of Alsace-Lorraine to representation in the Bundesrath, under certain restrictions, in 1911. But, as in all nations, the actual governmental system changes in other ways besides formal constitutional amendment, chiefly through ordinary legislation, through interstate agreements, and through custom. Thus it is by ordinary legislation that the several ministries and the Imperial courts exist; by interstate agreement that Prussia has the administration of the state of Waldeck; and by custom that the Emperor possessed the power to initiate legislation, and that the Bundesrath, instead of meeting periodically, is in continuous session.

Federal Character of the Empire. — The political system of Germany to-day is the product of centuries of particularistic statecraft, capped, in 1871, by a partial centralization of sovereign organs and powers. The Empire is composed of twenty-five states: the four kingdoms of Prussia, Bavaria, Saxony, and Württemberg; the six grand-duchies of Baden, Hesse, Mecklenburg-Schwerin, Saxe-Weimar, Mecklenburg-Strelitz, and Oldenburg; the five duchies of Brunswick, Saxe-Meiningen, Saxe Altenburg, Saxe-Coburg-Gotha, and Anhalt; the seven principalities of Schwarzburg-Sonderhausen, Schwarzburg-Rudolstadt, Waldeck, Reuss Älterer Linie, Reuss Jüngerer Linie, Lippe, and Schaumburg-Lippe; and the three free cities of Hamburg, Bremen, and Lübeck. These states vary in size from Prussia, with 134,616 square miles, to Bremen, with 99; and in population, from Prussia, with 40,163,333, to Schaumburg-Lippe, with 46,650. There has been, in addition, the *Reichsland*, or Imperial domain, of Alsace-Lorraine, whose position until 1911 was that of a purely dependent territory, but which by act of the year mentioned was raised to quasi-statehood.

Prior to the formation of the North German Confederation, each of the twenty-five states was sovereign and essentially independent. Each had its own governmental establishment, and in many instances the existing political system was of considerable antiquity. With the organization of the *Bund*, those states which were identified with the federation yielded their independence, and presumably their sovereignty; and with the establishment of the Empire, all gave up whatever claim they as yet maintained to absolute autonomy. Both the *Bund* and the Empire were creations, strictly speaking, of the states, not of the people; and, to this day, as a great German jurist has put it, the Empire is " not a juristic person composed of fifty-six million members, but of twenty-five members." [1] At the same time, it is not what the old Confederation of 1815 was, *i.e.*, a league of princes. It is a state established by, and composed of, states. The Germans are not themselves altogether agreed concerning the precise location of sovereignty; but it is reasonably clear that sovereignty, in the ultimate meaning of that much misused term, is vested in the government of the Empire, and not in that of any state. The embodiment of that sovereignty, as will appear, is not the national parliament, nor yet the Emperor, but the Bundesrath, which represents the " totality " of the affiliated governments.

The Empire and the States: Division of Powers. — The federal character of the Empire calls for a division of the powers of legislation, administration, and justice between the Imperial governmental establishment and the states. As in our own country, the powers of the federal government are specific, and enumerated; while those of the states are broad, undefined, residual. It is inconceivable that the lesser states would have entered a union formed, and likely to be dominated, by Prussia on any other terms. Through constitutional amendment, and even through legislation and custom, the Imperial government can bring about an enlargement of the powers that have been confided to it; but until it does so in any particular direction the power of the state governments in that direction is unlimited. On the one hand, there is a considerable field of legislative activity — in respect to citizenship, tariffs, weights, measures, coinage, patents, military and naval establishment of the Empire, etc. — in which the Empire, by virtue of constitutional

[1] Laband, *Das Staatsrecht des deutschen Reiches* (2d ed.), I, 91.

stipulation, possesses exclusive power to act. On the other, there is a no less extensive domain reserved entirely to the states — the determination of their own forms of government, of laws of succession, of relations of church and state, of questions pertaining to their internal administration; the framing of their own budgets, police regulations, highway laws, and laws relating to land tenure; the control of public instruction. Between lies a broad and shifting area, which is shared by the two. "The matters over which the states preserve control," says the German jurist above quoted, "cannot be separated completely from those to which extends the competence of the Empire. The various powers of government are intimately related one to another. They run together and at the same time impose mutual checks in so many ways, and are so interlaced, that one cannot hope to set them off by a line of demarcation, or to set up among them a Chinese wall of division. In every sphere of their activity the states encounter a superior power to which they are obliged to submit. They are free to move only in the circle which Imperial law-making leaves open to them. That circle does exist. It is delimited, but not wholly occupied, by the Empire. . . . In a certain sense it may be said that it is only by suffrance of the Empire that the states maintain their political rights at all, and that, at best, their tenure is precarious."[1]

It may be observed that there is, in fact, a distinct tendency toward the reduction of the sphere of authority formerly left to the states. One of the means by which this has been brought about is the establishment of uniform codes of law throughout the Empire, containing regulations upon a multitude of subjects which otherwise would have been dealt with by the states alone. Most important among these is the great Civil Code, which went into effect January 1, 1900. Another means to the same end is the increase in recent years of Imperial legislation relating to workingmen's insurance, factory regulations, industrial conditions, and other matters of a social and economic nature. Furthermore, there is no power in the courts to pass upon the constitutionality of Imperial laws and acts, and thereby keep the Imperial authority within bounds. Many times in the past

[1] *Ibid.*, 102–103.

fifteen or twenty years the states, or some of them, raised protest against this centralizing tendency, and especially against the " Prussianization " of the Empire which it seemed clearly to involve. In many states, especially those south of the Main, the separatist tradition is still strong. In Bavaria, more than anywhere else, is this true, and in 1903 a new premier of that country was able to arouse genuine enthusiasm for his government by a solemn declaration before the diet that he and his colleagues would combat with all their might " any attempt to shape the future of the Empire on lines other than the federative basis laid down in the Imperial constitution."

The functions of a legislative character which are delegated to the Imperial government are numerous and comprehensive, and in practice they tend constantly to be increased. Functions of executive and judicial character are very much more restricted. In respect to foreign relations, the navy, and the postal and telegraph service, administration is absolutely centralized in the organs of the Empire; in respect to everything else, administrative functions are performed entirely, or almost entirely, through the agency of the states. Military administration is, indeed, centralized; but in the hands of Prussia rather than in those of the Empire. In the United States the federal government is essentially complete within itself. It has its own lawmakers, administrators, and judges, who carry on the national government largely independently of the governing agencies of the various states. In Germany, where the state as such occupies a more exalted position in the federation than does its counterpart in America, the central government, in respect to all save the fields that have been mentioned, depends for the execution of its measures upon the officials of the states not as a matter of constitutional requirement, but merely out of considerations of convenience. The Empire establishes taxes and customs duties, but the states collect them. Similarly, justice is rendered, not in the name of the Empire, but in the name of the state, and by judges in the employ of the several states.

In respect to machinery, the Imperial government is, therefore, but a part of a government. Alone, it could not be made to operate. It lacks a judiciary; likewise the larger portion of the administrative agencies without which powers of legislative enactment are futile. To put the matter succinctly, the working government of the Empire comprises far more than the organs and functions that are purely Imperial; it comprises the federal organs and functions possessed by the individual states as well.

The Privileged States. — Legally, the union of the German states is indestructible. The Imperial government is vested with no power to expel a state, to unite it with another state, to divide it, or in any way to alter its status in the federation without its own consent. On the other hand, no state has a right to secede, or to modify its powers or obligations within the Empire. If a state violates its obligations or refuses to be bound by the authority of the Empire, the federal army, on decision of the Bundesrath, may be mobilized by the Emperor against it.

Among the states, however, there is no pretense of equality of status and privilege. When the Empire was formed the federated states differed widely in area, population, and traditional rights, and there was no attempt to reduce them to an absolutely uniform footing. Prussia, besides being the moving spirit in the new affiliation, contained a population considerably in excess of that of the other twenty-four states combined. The consequence was that Prussia inevitably became the preponderating power in the Empire. The king of Prussia is *ex-officio* German Emperor; the Prussian votes in the Bundesrath can defeat any proposed amendment of the constitution, and likewise any measure looking toward a reduction of the army or navy or a decrease of the taxes; and Prussia controls the chairmanship of all standing committees in the Bundesrath except the committee on foreign affairs.

Other privileges Prussia possesses by virtue, not of the constitution, but of agreements with her sister states. The most important of these relate to the army. By the constitution it was provided at the outset that the armed forces of the Empire should be organized into a single establishment, to be governed by Imperial law and to be under the supreme command of the Emperor. In respect to the appointment of minor officers, and some other matters, powers of jurisdiction were left, however, to the individual states. These powers were in themselves worth little, and in the course of time all of the states save Bavaria, Saxony, and Württemberg were brought to the point of yielding to Prussia the slender military authority that remained to them.

In this manner Prussia acquired the right to recruit, drill, and officer the contingents of twenty-one states — a right which appreciably increased her already preponderant authority in all matters of a military character. As matters stood prior to 1914, there was, technically, no *German* army, just as there was no *German* minister of war. Each state maintained its own contingent, and the contingent maintained by the state was normally stationed within that state. By virtue of the treaties, however, all contingents save those of Bavaria, Saxony, and Württemberg were administered precisely as if they comprised integral parts of the Prussian establishment, organized on the same principles.

Prussia, however, is not the only state that enjoys privileges under the Empire peculiar to itself. When the states of the south became members of the federation all of them put forward certain *Sonderrechte*, or reserved rights, whose acknowledgment was made the condition upon which they came into the union. Württemberg and Bavaria retain on this basis the administration of posts and telegraphs within their boundaries, and Württemberg, Bavaria, and Baden have exclusive right to tax beers and brandies produced within each state respectively. Bavaria retains the administration of her own railways.

At one time it was feared that the special privileges given the southern states would prove a menace to the stability of the Empire. Such apprehension, however, has proved groundless. In this connection it may be pointed out that under the Imperial constitution the right to commission and dispatch diplomatic (although not consular) agents is not withdrawn from the individual states. In most instances, however, the maintenance of diplomatic representatives abroad has long since been discontinued. Saxony, Bavaria, and Württemberg retained in 1914 only their posts at Vienna, St. Petersburg, and the Vatican.

SELECTED REFERENCES

A. L. Lowell, *Governments and Parties in Continental Europe* (Boston, 1896), I, Chap. v, II, Chap. vii; B. E. Howard, *The German Empire* (New York, 1906), Chaps. i–ii; F. K. Krüger, *Government and Politics of the German Empire* (Yonkers, 1915), Chaps. i–iv; C. D. Hazen, *Europe since 1815* (New York, 1910), Chap. xiv; C. J. H. Hayes, *Political and Social History of Modern Europe* (New York, 1916), Chap. xxiv; *Cambridge Modern History* (London, 1902–1910), IX, Chap. xi; XI, Chaps. iii, vi–vii, xv–xvii; XII, Chap. vi; E. Henderson, *Short History of Germany* (new ed., New York, 1916), II, Chaps. viii–x; H. Perris, *Germany and the German Emperor* (New York, 1912), Chaps. v–vi; J. P. Lichtenberger, *Germany and its Evolution in Modern Times* (New York, 1913), Book II, Chaps. i–iii; J. W. Headlam, *Bismarck and the Founding of the German Empire* (New York, 1899); J. H. Rose, *Political History of Germany in the Nineteenth Century* (Manchester, 1912); G. B. Malleson, *The Refounding of the German Empire* (2d ed., London, 1904); P. Bigelow, *History of the German Struggle for Liberty* (New York, 1905); Bismarck's *Reflections and Reminiscences*, trans. by A. S. Butler, 2 vols. (London, 1899); W. F. Dodd, *Modern Constitutions* (Chicago, 1909), I, 325–351, for text of the Imperial Constitution.

CHAPTER XXIII

THE IMPERIAL GERMAN GOVERNMENT[1]

I. THE EMPEROR

Status and Privileges. — Under the North German Confederation of 1867–1871 the king of Prussia had supreme command of the federal army and navy, and also numerous purely governmental powers, including control over the sessions of the Bundesrath and Bundestag, the appointment of the Chancellor and of other federal officials, the publication of the federal laws, and a general supervision of the federal administration. These powers were exercised by the king partly in the capacity of *Bundesfeldherr*, or commander in chief of the federal forces, partly in the capacity of *Bundespräsident*, or principal magistrate. Upon the accession of the south German states in 1870–1871, Bismarck, as has been related, determined to bring into use again the title of Emperor, although he was the first to recognize that between the empire that was now assuming form and the empire that had been terminated in 1806 there was no historical connection. The constitution of April 16, 1871, accordingly stipulates that "to the king of Prussia shall belong the presidency of the Confederation, and he shall bear the title of *Deutscher Kaiser* (German Emperor)."

The revival of the Imperial title and dignity was intended to make no change in the status of the Bundespräsident, except in respect to his official designation and certain of his personal privileges. It will be observed that the title adopted was not "Emperor of Germany." That would imply direct sovereignty over the entire country, whereas the purpose was that the Emperor, while a *German* Emperor, should be only what the Bundespräsident had been, *i.e., primus inter pares* in a confederation of *Landesherren*, or territorial princes. He was himself to be a territorial sovereign only in Prussia. The title, therefore, does

---

[1] This chapter describes the national government of Germany as it was up to the changes which immediately preceded the armistice of November 11, 1918.

not denote a monarchy of the usual sort. There is no Imperial crown, no Imperial civil list, no Imperial " office " as such. The king of Prussia, in addition to his purely Prussian prerogatives — and they are very great — is by the Imperial constitution vested with the functions of the old Bundespräsident, plus the function of bearing the Kaiser title; that is all. Apart from the Prussian crown, the Imperial function does not exist; from which it follows that there is no law of Imperial succession apart from the Prussian law regulating the tenure of the Prussian throne, and that in the event of a regency in Prussia the regent would, *ipso facto*, exercise the functions of Emperor. Chief among the privileges which the constitution or subsequent law bestows upon the Kaiser as such are special protection of person and family, and absolute exemption from legal process. Responsible to no superior earthly authority, the Emperor may not be brought for trial before any tribunal, nor be removed from office by any judicial proceeding. Assaults upon his person are punishable with death, and attacks in speech or writing, which constitute *lèse majesté* are subject to special and severe penalties.

Legislative, Judicial, and Executive Powers. — The king of Prussia being *ipso facto* Emperor, the royal and Imperial functions which are combined in the hands of the one monarch are of necessity closely interrelated. Some powers belong to him solely by virtue of his position as king of Prussia. Others, of an Imperial nature, he possesses by reason of the fact that, being king of Prussia, he is also Emperor. In practice, if not in law, there are still others which arise from the preponderance of the Prussian kingdom as a state within the Empire — the power, in general, of imparting a bent to Imperial policy such as would not be possible if, for example, the king of Württemberg were Emperor, rather than the king of Prussia.

The powers that go with the Imperial title fall into three general classes — legislative, judicial, and executive. The constitution, in the first place, gives to the Emperor the right to convene the Bundesrath and the Reichstag, and to open, adjourn, and close them; although it is to be observed that for many years the Bundesrath has been, as a matter of fact, almost continuously in session. Under the letter of the law the Reichstag can be dissolved (entailing a general election within sixty days) only by the Bundesrath; but in practice dissolution is ordered by the Emperor with the Bundesrath's consent. In the second place, bills passed by the Bundesrath are laid before the Reichstag in the name of the Emperor. So far as the law goes, the Emperor, as such, has no right of initiative in legislation, but practically such a right has long been freely exercised. In the third place, it falls to the Emperor to promulgate the laws after they are duly passed. As Emperor he has no general right of veto. He may refuse to publish a law on the ground of alleged irregularity in its enactment, but he is given no power to withhold a measure because of its contents. However, as king of Prussia he controls enough votes in the Bundesrath to impose an absolute check upon constitutional amendments and to impede other kinds of legislation to which he is opposed. Finally, in so far as is permitted by the constitution and the laws, he may issue ordinances under the countersignature of the Chancellor. Of judicial powers, two are of chief importance. On motion of the Bundesrath, the Emperor appoints (although he cannot remove) the members of the *Reichsgericht*, or Imperial Court; and the Code of Criminal Procedure stipulates that in cases in which the Imperial Court shall have rendered judgment as a tribunal of first instance, he shall possess the power of pardon. The pardoning power is extended likewise to cases decided in consular courts, prize courts, and other tribunals specified by law.

Finally, the execution of the Imperial laws is intrusted to the Emperor; with, however, this important qualification, that since under the German system the execution of law falls largely to the states and the officials thereof, all measures of the Imperial government whose execution is not otherwise provided for by the constitution and the laws are presumably carried into effect by the authorities of the states. There are, however, Imperial agents whose business it is to inspect the execution of Imperial measures by the states and to report to the Emperor infractions or omissions. When such delinquencies are deemed sufficiently serious, the Emperor may bring them to the attention of the Bundesrath, and that body may order an "execution," *i.e.*, a show of military force to coerce the erring state. The carrying out of the "execution" is intrusted to the Emperor. Incident to the general executive function is the power to make appointments. The constitution stipulates that the Emperor, in addition to appointing the Imperial Chancellor, shall appoint Imperial officials, require of them an oath to the Empire, and, when necessary, dismiss them. The position which the Chancellor occupies in the Imperial administrative system is such that the power of appointing to, and of removing from, the chancellorship is in itself of the utmost importance; and the Kaiser's control of administration is still further increased by his power to appoint and remove subordinate officials. Practically, the administrative hierarchy, from the Chancellor down, is in his hands.

Control of Foreign Relations and the Military Establishment. — " The Kaiser," says the Imperial constitution, " shall represent the Empire in international matters and in the name of the Empire shall declare war and make peace, shall enter into alliances and treaties with foreign states, and shall accredit ambassadors and receive them." The control which this clause gives over foreign relations is practically unlimited. The Emperor appoints and receives all Imperial ambassadors and ministers; and, as has been observed, only the Imperial, not the state, diplomatic representatives are now of importance. The consuls, also, are appointed exclusively by the Emperor, in consultation with the Bundesrath committee on trade and commerce. The unrestricted power to appoint ambassadors and ministers has been systematically employed by William II to prepare the way for German world dominion. One need only instance the selection of the crafty Baron Wangenheim to bring Turkey completely under German control, and of the mild-mannered Prince Lichnowsky (although he seems to have been an innocent tool) to lull England into a false sense of security. No treaty can be made without the Emperor's assent; and, in the main, the initiative in treaty-making lies with him. The only restriction is the provision of the constitution that, so far as treaties relate to matters which are to be regulated by Imperial legislation, " the consent of the Bundesrath is required for their conclusion, and the approval of the Reichstag is necessary to make them valid." The power to make war and peace is qualified in the constitution by the stipulation that war may be declared only with the consent of the Bundesrath, " unless an attack is made upon the federal territory or its coasts." It is necessary to observe, however, in the first place, that, as king of Prussia the Emperor absolutely controls upwards of one-third of the votes in the Bundesrath and, second, that if the Emperor wants war it is a matter of no great difficulty to bring about an international situation such that it can be alleged that an attack is going to be made upon the "federal territory or its coasts." This is precisely what was done in 1914.

Finally the Emperor is commander in chief of the armed forces of the Empire. The case of the navy is perfectly simple. When the North German Confederation was formed, no state entering the union had a navy except Prussia. This Prussian navy was, of course, taken into the *Bund*, and eventually into the Empire. The other states began to contribute to its support; but it continued under the absolute control of the Prussian king, now Emperor, and it was never anything but a unitary establishment. Until 1889 the commanding admiral was an appointee of the Emperor; after that date the Emperor, himself. Naval affairs are administered through the Imperial Naval Office at Berlin, presided over by a secretary of state who, although nominally responsible to the Chancellor, has always enjoyed a large amount of independence. From 1897 to 1916, this post was filled by the author of Germany's submarine campaign in the Great War, Grand-Admiral von Tirpitz. The case of the army is more complicated. Each member of the *Bund*, prior to 1867, had its own army, organized and equipped under its own laws. Each now placed its army, as a contingent, at the service of the federation, yet without surrendering it completely; and to this day the organization presents a unique combination of unitary and federal features. Technically, each state has its own army, and the rulers of the several states are the heads of their respective contingents. But these contingents are recruited, organized, equipped, and drilled under Imperial law; their strength is fixed by the Imperial legislative bodies; all expenses of maintenance are paid out of the Imperial treasury; and the Emperor is commander in chief, with full powers of inspection, appointment, and mobilization in time of peace, and with unlimited authority in time of war. The only contingents which retain special privileges are those of Bavaria, Württemberg, and Saxony. In so far as military administration is centralized, it is carried on through the Prussian ministry of war; for just as, in the eye of the law, there is no Imperial army, so there is no Imperial war ministry. If, however, the law knows no Imperial army, but only a combination of state contingents, these contingents none the less form, as all the world has good reason to know, a wholly unified fighting force under the Imperial command. With the world's second navy at his absolute call, with a military system which aimed to pass the whole able-bodied male population of the Empire through the army, with power to mold this army on almost any pattern, with all officers and men under personal oath of allegiance to him, and with means of turning both army and navy loose upon the world almost at will, the Kaiser had indeed become, by 1914, the chief war lord of modern times.

II. THE CHANCELLOR AND THE MINISTERS

The Chancellor: Functions. — Within the domain of Imperial government the place filled in other political systems by a ministry or cabinet is occupied by a single official known as the *Reichskanzler*, or Chancellor. When the constitution of 1867 was framed Bismarck sought to secure for the new federal government a high degree of administrative unity, and at the same time to provide for himself a place of becoming dignity and power, by giving the Chancellor no colleagues, and by making him responsible solely to the Bundespräsident. The plan tended, of course, toward a thoroughgoing centralization in Imperial affairs and an utter negation of anything in the nature of cabinet government. The subject was reopened for discussion in 1871, and the liberal elements in the constituent Reichstag forced a modification, of such a sort that when the constitution assumed final form it contained not merely the stipulation, "The Imperial Chancellor, to be appointed by the Emperor, shall preside in the Bundesrath and supervise the conduct of its business," but also the following provision: "The decrees and ordinances of the Emperor shall be issued in the name of the Empire, and shall require for their validity the countersignature of the Imperial Chancellor, who thereby assumes the responsibility for them."

Before alluding further to this matter of responsibility it will be well to state briefly who the Chancellor is and what his part is in carrying on the work of government. As has been indicated, he is appointed by the Emperor, and he must be a member of the Bundesrath; although if the Emperor desires to appoint a man who at the moment has not a seat in that body, he can easily do so, since as king of Prussia he also names Prussia's Bundesrath delegates. Speaking broadly, the functions of the Chancellor are twofold. The first arises from his position within the Bundesrath. Not only does he represent in that body, as do his Prussian colleagues, the king of Prussia; he is vested with the chairmanship of it and with the supervision of its business. He fixes the dates of its sessions. Through his hands pass all communications and proposals, from the states as well as from the Reichstag, addressed to it, and he is its representative in all of its external relations. In the name of the Emperor he lays before the Reichstag all measures enacted by the Bundesrath; and as a member of the Bundesrath, although not as Imperial Chancellor, he appears on the floor of the Reichstag to advocate and explain proposed legislation. Measures which have been enacted into law are binding only after they have been proclaimed by the Chancellor, in the name of the Emperor, such proclamation being made regularly through the official organ known as the *Reichsgesetzblatt*.

A second function, so inextricably intertwined with those just mentioned as to be in practice sometimes not clearly distinguishable from them, is that which arises from the Chancellor's position as the principal administrative official of the Empire. As has been pointed out, the work of administration under the German system is largely decentralized, being left to the states; but the ultimate administrative *authority* is very highly centralized, being gathered in the hands of the Chancellor in a measure not paralleled in any other nation of western Europe. As an administrative official the Chancellor has been described with aptness as the Emperor's " other self." He is appointed by the Emperor; he may be dismissed by him; he performs his functions solely as his agent and assistant.

Prior to 1870 the administrative functions of the Confederation were vested in a single department, the *Bundeskanzleramt*, or Federal Chancery, which was organized in three sections — the " central office," the postal office, and the bureau of telegraphs.

For the time being, affairs pertaining to the army, the navy, and foreign relations were confided to the care of the appropriate ministries of Prussia. In 1870 a separate federal department of foreign affairs was created, and in the following year a federal department of marine. One by one other departments were established, until in 1879 the process was completed by the conversion of what remained of the *Bundeskanzleramt* into a department of the interior. The status of these departments, however, was from the outset totally unlike that of the corresponding branches of other governments. They were, and are, in effect only bureaus of the Imperial Chancellery, and their heads form in no sense a collegiate ministry or cabinet. Each official in charge of a department owes his position absolutely to the Chancellor, to whom — rather than to either the Reichstag or the Emperor — he is directly responsible. Some of the more important officials bear the title of "secretary of state," but in any case they are legally nothing more than expert and essentially non-political functionaries of the administrative hierarchy, answerable to the Chancellor for all that they do.[1] Of principal departments there are at present seven: the Foreign Office, the Colonial Office, the Home Office, the Department of Justice, the Treasury, the Admiralty, and the Post-Office. In the nature of things some are more important than others; and in addition there are several Imperial bureaus, notably those of Railways, the Bank, and the Debt Commission. Throughout all branches of the Imperial administrative service appointments and dismissals are made by the Chancellor, in the name of the Emperor; and by the same authority all administrative regulations are promulgated.

Absence of Ministerial Responsibility. — As has been pointed out, the Imperial constitution says that the decrees and ordinances of the Emperor require for their validity the countersignature of the Imperial Chancellor, "who thereby assumes the responsibility for them." German writers on constitutional law have produced a small library of monographs on the subject of

[1] At the same time it is to be observed that, in practice, the more important state secretaries are apt to sustain a relation with the other organs of government which is somewhat closer than might be inferred from what has been said. Occasionally they sit in the Bundesrath, and by reason of that fact are privileged to defend their measures in person on the floor of the Reichstag. Frequently, too, they are members of the Prussian ministry.

the Chancellor's responsibility. Some regard it as a legal responsibility, some as political, some as only moral. Furthermore, to whom does responsibility lie? The constitution makes no answer, and various views have been put forward. How is responsibility to be enforced? Again the constitution is silent, and the commentators disagree.

The truth is that most of the discussion merely befogs a situation which to the unbiased observer is perfectly clear. The clause cited is an excrescence upon the real, organic constitution of 1867, devised merely to allay criticism, and having no actual worth or meaning. It was appropriated almost bodily from the constitution of the kingdom of Prussia, where also the provision was, and is, of little real import. In the sense in which the ministers of England and France are responsible, the German Chancellor is not responsible at all. He is answerable in all matters to his Imperial master, who can instruct, admonish, censure, or remove him at any moment. But, whatever theories may be spun upon the subject, other responsibility, in practice, he has none. Hence it matters very little whether his hypothetical responsibility — to Bundesrath, to Reichstag, or to some other agency — is legal or political. No machinery whatsoever is provided for the enforcement of responsibility to *any* authority except the Emperor. The ministers in turn, being subject to the full and direct control of the Chancellor, bear likewise no responsibility except to him, and through him to the Emperor. " In Germany," declared Chancellor von Bülow in 1906, " the ministers are not organs of the Parliament and of its temporary majority, but they are the intrusted representatives of the Crown." In an impassioned speech in the Reichstag in 1912, prompted by a storm of protest against the Emperor's alleged threat to withdraw the newly granted constitution of Alsace-Lorraine, Chancellor von Bethmann-Hollweg stated the theory and fact of his office thus: " No situation has been created for which I cannot take the responsibility. As long as I stand in this place I shield the Emperor. This not for the courtier's considerations, of which I know nothing, but as in duty bound. When I cannot satisfy this my duty you will see me no more in this place." These several statements were literally true, and never more so than in the days of the chancellors who uttered them. Bismarck enjoyed a large measure of independence. But William II's chancellors have been mere personal secretaries, with very little power of initiative. To do the Kaiser's bidding has been almost their sole function.[1]

The cabinet system of government, whose cornerstone is the full and continuous responsibility of the executive to an elected parliamentary assembly, does not exist within the length and breadth of Germany. There has long been strong demand for it by the liberal elements, including in later days the Liberal, Radical, and Social-Democratic parties; and observers have sometimes thought that they detected signs of its development. But the Imperial government has always been able to do business without for a moment admitting the right of the Reichstag to unseat the Chancellor or any of his subordinates by an adverse vote. The Chancellor, may of course, be criticized, and the proposals which he introduces may be defeated; expediency may even require his removal by his Imperial master; but he has never felt obliged to retire merely by reason of lack of support in the legislative chamber, as would a British or a French minister similarly situated. This does not mean that the blocking of a government program may not tend to produce the practical effect of a parliamentary vote of "want of confidence." It means simply that the Chancellor, in such a case, is under no admitted obligation to resign. The retirement of Chancellor von Bülow in 1909 was more nearly involuntary than that of any of his three predecessors; but persons most conversant with the circumstances agree that it was intended to involve no acknowledgment of responsibility to the nation's elected representatives. The situation was simply one in which legislation had become impossible because the Chancellor was unwilling to enter into a compromise with the Conservative-Clerical majority in the Reichstag on his proposed taxation of inheritances and other financial reforms.

III. THE BUNDESRATH

If the chancellorship is without a counterpart among modern governments, no less so is the Federal Council, or Bundesrath. No feature of the German political system is more extraordinary;

[1] Shepard, "Tendencies toward Ministerial Responsibility," *Amer. Polit. Sci. Review*, V, 59.

none, as one writer has observed, is more thoroughly native.[1] The Bundesrath is not an "upper house," nor even, in the ordinary sense, a deliberative chamber at all. On the contrary, it is the central institution of the whole Imperial system, and as such it is possessed of a broad combination of functions which are not only legislative, but administrative, consultative, judicial, and diplomatic.

Origins and Composition. — The Bundesrath is composed of delegates appointed by the princes of the monarchical states and by the senates of the free cities. The original Imperial constitution required that the fifty-eight votes to which the twenty-five states of the confederation are entitled should be distributed in such a manner that Prussia should have seventeen, Bavaria six, Saxony four, Württemberg four, Baden three, Hesse three, Mecklenburg-Schwerin two, Brunswick two, and the seventeen other states one apiece. Save for the increase of the Bavarian quota from four to six, and of the Prussian from four to seventeen, these numbers were simply carried over from the Diet of the Confederation of 1815. The Prussian increase arose, in 1866, from the absorption of Hanover, Hesse-Cassel, Holstein-Lauenburg, Nassau, and Frankfort; the Bavarian, from a customs union treaty of July 8, 1867. Subsequent to the adoption of the constitution of 1871 Prussia acquired, by contract, the vote of the government of Waldeck; also, through the establishment in 1884–1885 of a perpetual Prussian regency in Brunswick, the two votes to which that state is entitled; so that the total of the votes controlled by the government of Prussia has been raised, for all practical purposes, to twenty. Under the Alsace-Lorraine Constitution Act of 1911 the former *Reichsland* is entitled to three votes in the Bundesrath, bringing up the total to sixty-one. These votes are cast by delegates appointed by the *Statthalter*, or governor, of the territory; and since he is appointed by the Emperor, the votes would normally be subject to control by Prussia. The law provides, however, that the Alsatian votes shall not be counted in favor of Prussia unless she would have a majority without them, and that they shall in no case be counted upon constitutional amendments or in case of a tie.

It may be observed that the allotment of votes for which pro-

[1] Lowell, *Governments and Parties*, I, 259.

vision was made in the constitution of 1867–1871 was largely arbitrary. That is to say, except for the quotas of Prussia and Bavaria, it was perpetuated from the constitution of 1815, with no attempt to apportion voting power among the several states in exact relation to population, wealth, or importance. Upon any one of these bases Prussia must have been given an absolute majority, rather than a scant third. In 1867 the population of Prussia was four-fifths of that of the North German Confederation; in 1871, two-thirds of that of the Empire. The arrangement by which Prussia intrusted to the minor states a total of forty-one votes, while she retained for herself only seventeen, was intended by Bismarck as a means of convincing those states that they stood in no danger of Prussian domination. At the same time, an absolute control over the amending of the Imperial constitution, arising from the rule already explained,[1] safeguarded essential Prussian interests.

Organization and Procedure. — Each state is authorized, although not required, to send to the Bundesrath a number of delegates identical with the number of votes to which it is entitled. The full quota of members is therefore sixty-one. Legally, and to a large extent practically, the status of the delegate is that, not of a senator, but of a diplomat; and the Emperor is required to extend to the members of the body the " customary diplomatic protection." Delegates are usually officials (frequently ministers) of the states which they represent. By custom, they were formerly appointed afresh for each session, but the body has for years been in session almost continuously; so that new appointments are made whenever the state government desires. Members may be recalled or replaced at any time. The purely federal character of the Bundesrath is further emphasized by two principal facts. The delegates speak and act and vote, not at their own discretion, but under specific instructions of the governing authorities by whom they are accredited. Only rarely do their instructions allow them any considerable measure of independence. Strictly, the Bundesrath is not a deliberative assembly at all; although, unlike the former Diet, it is something more than a meeting of ambassadors of the states. In the second place, the votes cast are the votes, not of the individual members, but of the

[1] See p. 448.

states, and they are cast in indivisible blocks by the delegations of the states, regardless of the number of members in attendance. Thus, Bavaria is entitled to six votes. Whatever the individual opinions of the six Bavarian delegates, the six Bavarian votes are cast solidly upon any question that may arise. It is not necessary that six delegates actually participate in the decision; indeed, the decision, if the matter is an important one, is likely to be dictated by the home government and not formulated by the delegates at all. A single delegate may cast the entire quota of votes to which his state is entitled. The twenty votes controlled by Prussia are therefore always cast in a block, from which it follows that the Prussian will usually prevails in the chamber. On several occasions the smaller states have been able to combine in sufficient numbers to defeat a project upon which Prussia was bent, but such an action is exceptional.

The Bundesrath may be convened by the Emperor, which in effect means by the Chancellor, at any time. Practically, as has been said, it is in session continuously. The Chancellor presides, except when he designates some other member to act in his stead. Every member of the confederation, *i.e.*, every state, has a right to make motions and bring in measures. The Emperor, as such, is debarred from introducing proposals. But as king of Prussia he may bring forward any project through the medium of the Prussian delegation; and in actual practice it has not always been deemed necessary to resort to this subterfuge. The body invariably sits behind closed doors; and although ordinarily upon the conclusion of a sitting a statement regarding the proceedings is given to the press, the members may decide to withhold such information altogether. With a few exceptions, a simple majority of the sixty-one votes is sufficient for the adoption of a measure. In the event of a tie, the Prussian delegation has the deciding voice. The principal limitations upon decisions by simple majority are: (1) any proposal to amend the constitution may be rejected by as few as fourteen votes, whence, as has been explained, it arises that Prussia has an absolute veto on amendments; and (2) when there is a division upon proposed legislation relating to military affairs, the navy, the tariff, and various consumption taxes, the vote of Prussia prevails if it is cast in favor of maintaining the *status quo*. The work of the Bundesrath consists largely in the preparation of measures for the consideration of the Reichstag, and a considerable share of its labor is performed in committees. Of permanent committees there are now twelve — eight provided for in the constitution and four existing by virtue of standing orders. The committees required by the constitution are those on the army and fortifications; marine; customs and taxes; commerce and trade; railroads, posts, and telegraphs; judicial affairs; accounts; and foreign relations. Committees are made up for a year at a time. Under certain limitations they are chosen by the Bundesrath itself, by secret ballot; except that the Emperor appoints the members of the committee on the marine and all but one of the members of the committee on the army and fortifications. Strictly, however, the Bundesrath merely decides by ballot the states which shall be represented on each committee, leaving to the states themselves the right to name their representatives. All permanent committees consist of seven members, save that on the marine, which has five; and each includes representatives of at least five states. Prussia holds all chairmanships, save that of the committee on foreign affairs, which belongs to Bavaria.

Functions and Powers. — By reason of the pivotal position which the Bundesrath occupies in the German constitutional system the functions of the body are fundamental and its powers comprehensive. Its work is in the main legislative and fiscal, but also in part executive and judicial. The constitution stipulates that the legislative power of the Empire shall be exercised by the Bundesrath and the Reichstag, and that a majority of the votes of both bodies shall be necessary and sufficient for the enactment of a law. The right of initiating legislation is expressly conferred upon the Reichstag, but in practice it is exercised almost exclusively by the Bundesrath. Even finance bills regularly originate in the superior body. Under normal procedure, bills are prepared, discussed, and voted in the Bundesrath, submitted to the Reichstag for consideration and acceptance, and returned for further scrutiny by the Bundesrath before their promulgation by the Emperor. In any case the final approval of a measure must take place in the Bundesrath. Speaking strictly, it is the Bundesrath that makes law, with merely the assent of the Reichstag.

The Bundesrath's executive functions represent a curious admixture, but the sum total is considerable. In the first place, the body possesses supplementary administrative powers. The constitution requires it to take action upon "the general administrative provisions and arrangements necessary for the execution of the Imperial laws, so far as no other provision is made by law," as well as upon "the defects which may be discovered in the execution of the Imperial laws." This function is performed through the issuing of ordinances so devised as not to contravene the constitution, existing law, or the proper prerogatives of any constituted authority, Imperial or state. In the second place, certain powers vested in the Emperor may be exercised only with the Bundesrath's consent. Most important of these are: (1) the declaration of war, save in the event of an attack upon the territory or coasts of the Empire; (2) the concluding of treaties, in so far as they relate to matters falling within the range of Imperial legislation; and (3) the carrying out of an "execution" against a delinquent state. Finally certain relations are maintained with the Reichstag which involve the exercise of authority that is essentially executive. With the assent of the Emperor, the Bundesrath may dissolve the popular chamber; and every member of the Bundesrath has a right to appear in the Reichstag and to be heard there at any time upon his own request, somewhat after the manner of a minister in a parliamentary government. It should be observed, however, that the members of the Bundesrath are authorized to appear in the Reichstag, not for the purpose of advocating a measure which the Bundesrath has enacted, or would be willing to enact, but simply to voice the interests or demands of their own states. Large functions in connection with public finance, likewise, are vested in the body. It prepares the annual budget, audits the accounts which the Empire carries with the states, and maintains important supervisory relations with the Imperial Bank, the Imperial Debt Commission, and other fiscal agencies. Lastly, it participates in the power of appointment; for although that power, as such, is vested in the Emperor, officials of some kinds, *e.g.*, judges of the Imperial Court, are actually chosen by the Bundesrath, and in many other instances the body preserves an acknowledged right to approve appointments made.

In its judicial capacity the Bundesrath sits as a supreme court

THE IMPERIAL GERMAN GOVERNMENT

of appeal, to which cases may be carried from the tribunals of a state when it can be shown that justice is not to be had in those tribunals. It serves also as a court of last resort for the settlement of disputes between the Imperial government and a state; or between two states, when the point at issue is not a matter of private law and when a definite request for action is made by one of the parties. Finally, in disputes relating to constitutional questions in states whose constitution does not designate an authority for the settlement of such differences, the Bundesrath is required, at the request of one of the parties, to effect an amicable adjustment; or, if this proves impossible, to see to it that the issue is settled by Imperial law.

Such an aggregate of powers makes the Bundesrath easily the dominating element in the Imperial government, second, in law at all events, not even to the Emperor himself. Defenders of the German system have long been accustomed to argue that, since the body is largely composed of ministers and other officials of the various states, it is the most experienced and efficient legislative chamber in the world; and they insist that it has not been reactionary or unduly conservative. There is, however, no disguising the fact that the members are appointed by monarchs or aristocratic senates, that they are the spokesmen of these non-popular authorities and are in all respects controlled by them, and that the body is the bulwark of the forces that have always been opposed to change. An absolute condition of the establishment of democratic government in the country is the abolition of the Bundesrath, or a complete transformation of it in both composition and powers.

IV. THE REICHSTAG

In contrast with the Bundesrath, which is organized on a purely federal basis, the Reichstag is broadly national. It represents, not the states, nor yet the people of the states, but the people of the Empire as a whole. From what has been said concerning the predominance of autocracy and bureaucracy in the German system it follows that there is no room in that system for a parliamentary chamber of the nature of the British House of Commons or of the French Chamber of Deputies. None the less, restricted as are its functions, the Reichstag is one of the world's most interesting legislative bodies; and, being the one democratic element known to the Imperial constitution, it has peculiar importance as the basis upon which the defeated Empire's new and more popular scheme of government will have to be built.

Composition: Electoral System. — Under provision of the constitution, members of the Reichstag are chosen for a term of five years, by direct and secret ballot, at an election which takes place on a given day throughout the entire Empire. The number of seats, fixed by the constitution of 1871 at 382, was, by law of June 25, 1873, providing for the election of fifteen members from Alsace-Lorraine, increased to 397; and it has since stood unchanged. The electoral " circles," or districts, each of which returns one member, were laid out originally in such a manner as to contain 100,000 inhabitants each, and also in such a way that no district should embrace portions of two or more states. Prussia was allotted 235 members, Bavaria 48, Saxony 23, and other states smaller numbers, eleven having only one member apiece. The Election Law of May 31, 1869, provided that arrangements for redistributions of seats in accordance with changes of population should be made by future laws. But no such legislation was ever enacted, and there has been no reapportionment since 1871. The development of Germany as a great industrial and commercial nation has fallen mainly within this period, resulting in enormous shifts of population from one part of the country to another, and especially from rural localities to the towns. The result is the grossest inequality of electoral constituencies to be found anywhere in the world. In the rural province of East Prussia, shortly before the Great War, the average number of voters in a district was 121,000; in Berlin it was 345,000. Twelve of the most populous districts represented in the Reichstag contained 1,950,000 voters; twelve of the least populous, 170,000. The district of Schaumburg-Lippe had but 9891. There had long been urgent demand for a reapportionment. But the Imperial authorities firmly held out against it, urging with all the force they could that representation ought to be by *interests*, rather than by mere numbers, and that the existing distribution was, measured in this way, entirely satisfactory. The real reason for this obstructionist attitude is not difficult to discover: any change would mean a doubling or tripling of members returned by urban constituencies, with the effect of greatly increasing the already fast growing quota of Socialist and other radical members.

The suffrage, however, is fairly democratic. Male citizens twenty-five years of age and upwards, and duly registered, are entitled to vote in the district in which they reside; the only classes disqualified being persons under guardianship, bankrupts, beneficiaries of public charity, persons suffering judicial deprivation of certain of their rights as citizens, and persons in active service in the army and navy. There is no plural voting. Any qualified voter who has been a citizen of any one of the states for one year may be elected. Electoral procedure is regulated by the Election Law of 1869, amended in minor particulars at subsequent dates, and extended in 1871 and 1873 to the southern states and to Alsace-Lorraine respectively. Elections are held uniformly throughout the Empire on a day fixed by Imperial ordinance. In the event of a dissolution before the end of the five-year term an election is required to take place within a period of sixty days, and a new Reichstag must be convened not less than ninety days after the dissolution. Each constituency is divided into districts, and in each district the lists of qualified voters have to be made up and deposited for public inspection at least four weeks before the election. Secrecy of the ballot is specially safeguarded by regulations enacted in 1903. Each voter, upon appearing at the polls, is furnished with an envelope and a white voting-paper bearing an official stamp. In a compartment arranged for the purpose in the polling room he marks his ballot and incloses it in the envelope. As he leaves the room he hands the envelope to the presiding officer or deposits it in a voting urn. The election board consists of this presiding officer, his deputy, a secretary, and three to six assistants, all of whom are unpaid. Polling continues from 10 A.M. to 7 P.M., after which the board counts the votes; and the results, together with all the ballots and other documents, are sent to the election commissioners of the constituency, who are appointed by the local administrative authorities. For election on the first ballot an absolute majority of the votes cast in the district is required. If no candidate obtains such a majority, a second balloting (*Stichwahl*) follows a fortnight later, when a choice is made, not as in France among all candidates who care to remain in or to enter the race, but between the two who upon the first occasion polled the largest number of votes. In the rare event of a tie, decision is by lot. On account of the division of the voters in most constituencies among several parties, many second ballotings are required. In 1907 the number was 158; in 1912, 191. In forty per cent of the cases the candidate originally receiving a plurality finally fails to be elected; and the system usually works out to the advantage of the conservative and moderate parties, and hence to the disadvantage of the Socialists.

Organization and Procedure. — The constitution provides that the Reichstag shall meet at least once each year, and that it shall never be in session when the Bundesrath is not; otherwise the Imperial authorities are free to convoke sessions at will. The summons is issued by the Emperor, and sessions are opened by him, in person or by proxy, with much ceremony. He may prorogue the body for a period of thirty days without its consent, and with the assent of the Bundesrath he may also dissolve it. Attendance at the meetings has always been scant. An Alsatian deputy who took his seat in 1898 says that ordinarily at that time barely sixty of the members, or less than one-sixth, would be found in their places;[1] many appeared at Berlin only at times of unusual political stress. One explanation, no doubt, has been the assembly's powerlessness. But another is the meager compensation allowed. Bismarck opposed remuneration of any sort, and the Imperial constitution originally provided that members should, as such, "draw no salary or compensation." They were to be allowed to travel free on the railroads between their residences and Berlin; but that was all. And when the Socialist organizations began raising funds for the support of Socialist members, the Imperial Court of Appeal ruled that such action was illegal. Early in the present century, however, attendance became so slender that it was often difficult or impossible to raise a quorum, and in 1906 Chancellor von Bülow grudgingly agreed to meet the situation by providing for salaries to be paid out of the Imperial treasury. The salary provided — 3000 marks ($750) a year — was, however, only one-tenth of the amount paid our senators and representatives, and it has had only a moderate effect in the desired direction.

[1] Wetterlé, *Behind the Scenes in the Reichstag*, 38.

The Reichstag regulates its own procedure and discipline, and elects its own officers, consisting of a president, two vice-presidents, and eight secretaries. Under standing orders adopted in 1876, the president and the vice-presidents are chosen at the opening of the first session following a general election for a temporary term of four weeks, and upon the expiration of this period an election takes place for the remainder of the session. At the opening of each succeeding session an election of these officials for the session takes place at once. The secretaries are chosen at the beginning of each session for the entire session. All of these officers are regularly elected from the party coalition which at the time commands a majority. In 1912 the Socialists succeeded for the first time in capturing a vice-presidency. At the opening of a session the entire membership is divided by lot into seven *Abteilungen*, or bureaus, as nearly equal as it is possible to make them. The bureaus of the French Chamber of Deputies are made up anew once a month, and those of the Italian once in two months, but those of the Reichstag are maintained unchanged throughout a session, unless upon motion of as many as fifty members the body decides upon a fresh distribution. The functions of the bureaus are, as in other continental countries, mainly the validation of credentials of members of the chamber and the selection of members of committees. The Reichstag has but one standing committee — that on elections. All others are made up, as occasion requires, by the appointment by ballot of an equal number of members by each of the seven bureaus; although, in point of fact, the preparation of committee lists falls largely to the party leaders of the chamber. The function of committees is to give preliminary consideration to measures, and to report them, and evidence relating to them, to the chamber. Bills are not, however, in all cases referred to committees.

The hall in which the Reichstag meets is semi-circular, and the members are seated in the manner customary in continental legislatures, with the conservative elements on the right and the radical groups on the left of the presiding officer. Front benches, at both left and right, are reserved for members of the Bundesrath; for all these, including of course the Chancellor, have a right to appear and speak, although technically only as delegates of their particular governments. Debaters address the chamber from the platform in front of the president's chair or from their seats as they choose; and they speak whenever they can secure the recognition of the presiding official, not, as in France, in the hard and fast order indicated by a previously prepared written list. Like the Speaker of the House of Commons, the president of the Reichstag is supposed to be a strictly non-partisan moderator. A fixed tradition of the office is that during debate the chair shall alternately recognize the supporters and the opponents of the measure under consideration. As a general rule, closure of debate may be ordered upon the motion of thirty members.

Unlike the sittings of the Bundesrath, which always take place behind closed doors, those of the Reichstag are, by constitutional provision, public. Under the standing orders, however, the body may go into secret session, on motion of the president, or of ten members. Publicity is further assured by the constitutional stipulation that "no one shall be held responsible for truthful reports of the proceedings of the public sessions of the Reichstag."

Powers and Actual Character. — Enough has been said above about the Bundesrath to make it clear that that body is no ordinary senate or upper chamber. Indeed it is no upper chamber at all; for the Imperial government is not so organized as to provide for a bicameral parliament of the British or the French type. Rather, the Empire has essentially a unicameral parliament, consisting of the Reichstag — this parliament, however, working under the leadership and check of a semi-legislative, semi-judicial body, the Bundesrath, which has absolutely no counterpart in any other European country. On the face of things, the Reichstag is a body with extensive authority; the legislative power of the Empire is expressly vested by the constitution in the Reichstag and the Bundesrath, and a majority vote in both assemblages is necessary for the enactment of laws, for the adoption of constitutional amendments, and for the ratification of every treaty touching matters "within the domain of Imperial legislation." In point of fact, however, the functions of the chamber are purely subordinate, and its influence upon the conduct of public affairs is almost negligible.

The reasons are not far to seek. In the first place, partly by law and partly by custom, the initiative in legislation lies with the Bundesrath. A chief duty of that body, under the terms of the constitution, is indeed to prepare measures for the consideration of the popular chamber. Resolutions may originate in the Reichstag, and, after being passed there, go to the Bundesrath for examination. But few important proposals actually start in this way, and even the great pieces of finance legislation are formulated in the federal chamber. The Reichstag can hold up legislation, or even the budget, while it debates and criticizes the Bundesrath's bill or the policies of the Government. But if its obstructiveness is carried too far, there are clubs that can be swung over its head, the most generally effective being the threat of dissolution. The power of dissolution has been exercised several times since 1871 with the main, or sole, purpose of putting an end to opposition. And it is to be observed, of course, that the power is wielded in Germany without a shred of the ministerial responsibility which is its necessary complement in England and France. In the second place, the Reichstag is wholly without means of calling the executive authorities to account. As has been emphasized, neither the Chancellor nor the ministers recognize any responsibility to the popular chamber for their acts. The standing orders solemnly provide for interpellation. But the right is utterly hollow. There are no ministerial officers to whom an interpellation can be directly addressed except the Chancellor, and he usually shows his contempt for the whole proceeding by absenting himself on the days set apart for the purpose. In 1911 Chancellor von Bethmann-Hollweg agreed to a change of the rules so as to permit a vote of approbation or censure to follow an interpellatory debate. The radicals thought they had scored a victory; but they soon discovered that no matter how the vote went, nothing whatever happened. "Put me in a minority, if it so please you," the Chancellor continued to say; "I shall remain all the same at my post as long as I retain the confidence of my sovereign." [1]

Such dumb-show of governmental activity could hardly have gone on for decades without affecting the proceedings, and even the personnel, of the body in undesirable ways. The effect upon the conduct of business has been to crush out honest and fruitful initiative and wholesome effort to promote the public welfare, and to substitute either an attitude of discouragement and apathy or

[1] Wetterlé, *Behind the Scenes in the Reichstag*, 182.

a disposition to grovel and barter for favors, according to the moral fiber of the individual or the group. A few leaders, the spokesmen of their parties, do all the work; the mass of the members vote to order, often without even studying the bills. The reports of committees are short, dry analyses, usually actually written by Government officials and merely signed by the elected chairmen. "Above all," once said a cynical, but shrewd and experienced, Clerical member to a newcomer to whom he had taken a fancy, "attach no importance to the noisy declarations and tragic gestures of speakers on the first reading of a bill. All the work of the Reichstag is done behind the scenes. Our party leaders are augurs who have learned to look at each other in public assembly without laughing; but, surrounded by the mystery of their private counsels, they are hand and glove together. I know it because I am one of them. Everything is compromise with us. We set up a noisy opposition only to obtain privileges. . . . All [the leaders] are in continuous relations with the Wilhelmstrasse, which knows their ambitions and how to play with them skillfully. People abroad believe that we possess a national representation. But we have only a handful of operetta conspirators, whom an enlightened stage-manager directs as he thinks fit. With us, such big words as ministerial responsibility, liberty, and democracy have no meaning."[1] There is a certain amount of exaggeration in this, yet it lays bare an aspect of German parliamentary life which explains many otherwise inexplicable acts of servility on the part of the Reichstag under the aggressive, imperialistic régime of William II. It is generally agreed, too, that the level of education and ability of the members has of late been lower than in the early days of the Empire. Writers of German extraction have sought to explain the decline by saying that after the great national problem of unification was solved "the detail work of legislation with all its petty struggles began," parties lost their national character and became the representatives of special economic and social classes, and men of statesmanlike qualities and high ideals turned away in disgust, leaving the seats in the Reichstag to average politicians.[2] Another explanation given is that the increase of the Socialist quota has meant the influx of

---

[1] Wetterlé, *Behind the Scenes in the Reichstag*, 84–85.
[2] Krüger, *Government and Politics of the German Empire*, 59–60.

large numbers of members of limited education and narrow vision. These views are, to a degree, plausible. Yet the citizen of a democratic country cannot repress the feeling that the fundamental difficulty lies in the rigid restrictions which have long since reduced a promising parliamentary assemblage to a mere "debating society," a great legislative chamber to a "Hall of Echoes."

V. LAW AND JUSTICE

The Codes of Law. — On the subject of administration of justice the Imperial constitution of 1871 contained but a single clause, which vested in the Empire power of "general legislation concerning the law of obligations, criminal law, commercial law and commercial paper, and judicial procedure." An amendment adopted in 1873 modified the clause to read, "general legislation as to the whole domain of civil and criminal law and of judicial procedure." Each of the federated states has always had, and still has, its own judicial system, and justice is administered almost exclusively in courts that belong to the states. These courts, however, have been declared to be also courts of the Empire; and, to the end that they may be systematized, and that conditions of justice may be made uniform throughout the land, the federal government has not hesitated to avail itself of the regulative powers conferred in 1871 and amplified in 1873. In the first place, the past generation has witnessed a unification of German law worthy of comparison with the systematization of the law of France, accomplished through the *Code Napoléon*.[1] In 1871 the Empire contained more than two score districts each of which possessed a distinct body of civil and criminal law; and, to add to the confusion, the boundaries of these districts, although at one time coincident with the limits of the various political divisions of the country, were no longer so. The case of Prussia was typical. In 1871 the older Prussian provinces were living under a Prussian code promulgated in 1794; the Rhenish provinces held to the *Code Napoléon;* in the Pomeranian districts there were large survivals of Swedish law; while the territories acquired after the war of 1866 had each its indigenous legal system. Two German states only in 1871 possessed a fairly uniform body

[1] See p. 382.

of law. Baden had adopted a German version of the *Code Napoléon*, and Saxony, in 1865, had put in operation a code of her own devising. At no period of German history had there been either effective lawmaking or legal codification which was applicable to the whole of the territory contained within the Empire.

German legal reform since 1871 has consisted principally in the formation and adoption of successive codes, each of which has aimed at essential completeness within a given branch of law. The task had been begun, indeed, before 1871. As early as 1861 the states had agreed upon a code relating to trade and banking, and this code had been readopted, in 1869, by the North German Confederation. In 1869 a code of criminal law had been worked out for the Confederation, and in 1870 a code relating to manufactures and labor. Upon the establishment of the Empire, in 1871, a commission was created to draw up regulations for civil procedure and for criminal procedure, and also a plan for the reorganization of the courts. Beginning with a scheme of civil procedure, published in December, 1872, the commission brought in an elaborate project upon each of the three subjects. The code of civil procedure, by which many important reforms were introduced in the interest of publicity and speed, was well received. That relating to criminal procedure, proposing as it did to abolish throughout the Empire trial by jury, was, however, vigorously opposed, and the upshot was that all three reports were referred to a new commission, by which the original projects relating to criminal procedure and to the organization of the courts were completely remodeled. In the end the revised projects were adopted. October 1, 1879, a group of fundamental laws went into effect under which the administration of justice throughout the Empire has been controlled to the present day. The most important of these was the *Gerichtsverfassungsgesetz*, or Law of Judicial Organization, enacted January 27, 1877; the *Civilprozessordnung*, or Code of Civil Procedure, of January 30, 1877; and the *Strafprozessordnung*, or Code of Criminal Procedure, of February 1, 1877. It remained only to effect a codification of the civil law. A committee set up for this purpose completed its work in 1887, and the draft which it submitted was placed for revision in the hands of a new commission which reported in 1895. In an amended form the Civil Code was approved by the Reichs-

THE IMPERIAL GERMAN GOVERNMENT 481

tag, August 18, 1896; and it was put in operation January 1, 1900. Excluding matters pertaining to land tenure (which are left to be regulated by the states), the Code deals not only with all of the usual subjects of civil law, but also with subjects arising from the contact of private law and public law.

The Courts. — These and other unifying measures brought it about that throughout the Empire justice is administered in tribunals whose officials are appointed by the local governments, and which render decisions in their name, but whose organization, powers, and rules of procedure are regulated minutely by federal law. The hierarchy of tribunals provided for in the Law of Judicial Organization comprises courts of four grades. At the bottom are the *Amtsgerichte*, of which there are approximately two thousand in the Empire. These are courts of first instance, consisting ordinarily of but a single judge. In civil cases their jurisdiction extends to the sum of six hundred marks; in criminal, to matters involving a fine of not more than six hundred marks or imprisonment of not over three months. In criminal cases the judge sits with two *Schöffen*, or jurors, selected by lot from the jury lists. Besides litigious business the *Amtsgerichte* have charge of the registration of land titles, the drawing up of wills, guardianship, and other local interests.

Next above the *Amtsgerichte* are the 173 district courts, or *Landgerichte*, each composed of a president and a variable number of associate judges. Each *Landgericht* is divided into a civil and a criminal chamber. There may, indeed, be other chambers, as for example a *Kammer für Handelssachen*, or chamber for commercial cases. The president presides over a full bench; a director over each chamber. The *Landgericht* exercises a revisory jurisdiction over judgments of the *Amtsgericht*, and possesses a more extended original jurisdiction in both civil and criminal matters. The criminal chamber, consisting of five judges (of whom four are necessary to convict), is competent, for example, to try cases of felony punishable with imprisonment for a term not exceeding five years. For the trial of many sorts of criminal cases there are special *Schwurgerichte*, or jury courts, which sit under the presidency of three judges of the *Landgericht*. A jury consists of twelve members, of whom eight are necessary to convict. Still above the *Landgerichte* are the *Oberlandesgerichte*, of which there are twenty-nine in the Empire, each consisting of seven judges. The *Oberlandesgerichte* are largely courts of appellate jurisdiction. Each is divided into a civil and a criminal senate. There is a president of the full court and a similar official for each senate.

At the apex of the system stands the *Reichsgericht* (created by law of October 1, 1879), which, apart from certain administrative, military, and consular courts, is the only German tribunal of an exclusively Imperial, or federal, character. It exercises original jurisdiction in cases involving treason against the Empire and hears appeals from the consular courts and from the state courts on questions of Imperial law. Its members, ninety-two in number, are appointed by the Emperor for life, on nomination of the Bundesrath, and they are organized in six civil and four criminal senates. Sittings are held at Leipzig, in the kingdom of Saxony.

All judges in the courts of the states are appointed by the sovereigns of the respective states. The Imperial law prescribes minimum qualifications based on professional study and experience, the state being left free to impose any additional qualifications that it may desire. All judges are appointed for life, and all receive salaries which may not be reduced during their tenure; and there are important guarantees against arbitrary transfer from one position to another, as well as other practices that might diminish the judge's impartiality and independence.

SELECTED REFERENCES

J. E. Barker, *Modern Germany* (5th and rev. ed., London, 1915); J. E. Barker, *The Foundations of Germany* (London, 1916); W. H. Dawson, *The Evolution of Modern Germany* (London and New York, 1908); W. H. Dawson, *Municipal Life and Government in Germany* (2d ed., London, 1916); R. H. Fife, *The German Empire between Two Wars* (New York, 1916); G. S. Fullerton, *Germany of To-day* (Indianapolis, 1915); A. Guilland, *Modern Germany and Her Historians* (London, 1915); B. E. Howard, *The German Empire* (New York, 1906); F. C. Howe, *Socialized Germany* (New York, 1915); F. K. Krüger, *Government and Politics of the German Empire* (Yonkers, 1915); G. H. Perris, *Germany and the German Emperor* (London, 1912); Charles Tower, *Germany of To-day* (London, 1913); T. B. Veblen, *Imperial Germany and the Industrial Revolution* (New York, 1915).

CHAPTER XXIV

THE GOVERNMENT OF PRUSSIA

Prussian Preponderance in the Empire. — Germany on the eve of the World War was a federal empire composed of twenty-five states, besides an Imperial territory which had certain attributes of statehood, Alsace-Lorraine. Twenty-two of the states were monarchies, three were aristocratic republics. Unquestionably the most striking feature of the Empire's political organization and life was the dominance exercised by one of the states, Prussia, over all the others, and therefore over the affairs of the Empire itself. This dominance flowed from a variety of circumstances. First, there was the historical fact that Prussia was the organizer of German unity and the creator of the Empire. Second, Prussia physically overshadowed the sister states. Her area in 1914 was 134,616 square miles; that of the remainder of the Empire was 74,164 square miles. Her population in 1911 was 40,163,333; that of the remainder of the Empire was 24,740,090. Third, Prussia enjoyed, as has been pointed out, peculiar political rights under the Imperial constitution. Her king was *ipso facto* Emperor; the chairman of every standing committee in the Bundesrath, except that on foreign affairs, was a Prussian; all changes in the army, navy, or the system of taxation must have Prussia's assent; her seventeen votes in the Bundesrath were sufficient to defeat any constitutional amendment. Fourth, on the basis of interstate agreement, Prussia had substantial control of the armed forces of twenty-one of the states, together with an undefined power of inspection over the others. Finally, Prussia had in the Hohenzollern dynasty a ruling family of exceptional energy and ambition, and the Prussian people were somewhat more easily led along paths of aggression in both German and international politics than were their Bavarian or Württemberger neighbors.

The result of all this was that Prussia rapidly advanced after 1871 from mere leadership to almost unlimited control. She became, for all practical purposes, Germany. As a recent writer remarks, "The Fatherland was not formed by the absorption of Prussia into Germany, but by the absorption of Germany into Prussia; the part swallowed the whole."[1] Any attempt to understand the political condition of the German Empire and the rôle which Germany has of late played in world affairs therefore presupposes some knowledge of Prussian governmental organization, methods, and spirit. It will be the function of this and the succeeding chapter to supply information on these points.

The Constitution. — The written constitution under which the government of Prussia is carried on is a product of the revolutionary movements of 1848. It first took form as a rescript promulgated December 5, 1848, by King Frederick William IV, with a view to averting scenes of violence in Berlin such as the year had witnessed in Paris, Vienna, and other capitals. The king had promised not only that a constitution should at last be given the long-misgoverned country, but that the instrument should be "agreed upon with an assembly of the nation's representatives freely chosen and invested with full powers." This pledge hastily given at a time when revolution seemed imminent, proved embarrassing when the danger had somewhat subsided. But crafty ministers suggested a way out of the difficulty: the king might draw up a constitution to his taste, promulgate it, put it into operation, and allow the first *Landtag* elected under it merely to agree, if it could, upon a legislative revision. This is the plan that was followed. The constitution was proclaimed, elections were held, and early in 1849 the chambers took up the problem of revision. The result was disagreement and, in the end, the dissolution of the lower house. Along with the original instrument had been issued an electoral law introducing voting by secret ballot and conferring equal suffrage upon all male citizens. But the king now recalled this law and substituted for it another which not only abolished voting by ballot but made elections indirect, and, worse still, divided the voters into three classes whose electoral power was

[1] Schapiro, *Modern and Contemporary European History*, 280.

to be determined entirely by property qualifications or by official and professional status. In other words, he introduced the peculiar and grossly undemocratic three-class system which was already in use in some Prussian municipalities, and which has survived, in both national and city elections, to the present day.

When elections were held, in the summer of 1849, in accordance with this system, the democrats refused to participate. The upshot was that the new chambers, convened August 7, 1849, proved tractable enough, and the text of the constitution, after being discussed and revised article by article, was finally given formal approval. On the last day of January, 1850, the instrument was duly proclaimed at Charlottenburg. During the ensuing decade Austria, Russia, and other reactionary powers tried several times to influence the king to rescind the concession which he had made. He refused, however, to do so; and, with certain modifications, the constitution of 1850 remains the fundamental law of the Prussian kingdom to-day.

In form, the instrument is modeled upon the Belgian constitution of 1830. Provisions concerning the powers of the crown, the competence of the chambers, and the functions of the ministers are reproduced almost literally from the older document. None the less, the two rest upon widely differing bases. The Belgian fundamental law begins with the assertion that "all powers emanate from the nation." That of Prussia voices no such sentiment, and the governmental system for which it provides has as its corner stone the thoroughgoing supremacy of the crown. The liberals of the mid-century period were by no means satisfied with it; and, seventy-eight years after, it stands out among the great constitutional documents of the European world so conspicuous by reason of its disregard of fundamental democratic principle as to justify completely both the attacks made upon it by reformers in Prussia and the demand of an outraged world that it be brought into line with modern political development. It provides for the responsibility of ministers, without establishing means whereby that responsibility can be enforced. There is maintained under it the most antiquated and undemocratic electoral system in Europe. And, as is pointed out by Lowell, even where, on paper, it appears to be liberal, it is much less so than its text would lead one to suppose.[1] It contains, for example, a bill of rights, which alone comprises no fewer than forty of the one hundred eleven permanent articles of the instrument. In this section it guarantees the personal liberty of the subject, the security of property, the inviolability of personal correspondence, immunity from domiciliary visitation, freedom of the press, toleration of religious sects, liberty of migration, and the right of association and public meeting. But there is an almost total lack of machinery for giving effect to the provisions. Guarantees of what would seem the most fundamental rights, as those of public assemblage and of liberty of teaching, are reduced in practice to empty phrases.

The process of constitutional amendment is easy. With the approval of the king, an amendment may at any time be adopted by a simple majority of the two legislative chambers, with only the special requirement that an amendment, unlike a statute, must be voted upon twice, with an interval of three weeks between the two votes. During the first ten years of its existence the constitution was amended not fewer than ten times. Of later amendments there have been six, but none of more recent date than 1888. The Prussian system of amendment by simple legislative process was incorporated, in 1867, in the fundamental law of the North German Confederation (except that in the Bundesrath a two-thirds vote was required); and in 1871 it was perpetuated, in principle, although not in detail, in the constitution of the Empire.

The King and the Ministers. — The crown is hereditary in the male line of the house of Hohenzollern, following the principle of primogeniture.[2] Certain sections of the constitution are devoted to an enumeration of the royal powers; but it has never been regarded that the king is restricted to the powers there mentioned, and his sum total of authority is exceeded by that of no other European monarch. He is absolute commander of the army; he is head of the Church; all appointments to offices of state are made by him immediately or under his authority; the upper legislative chamber is recruited almost wholly

---

[1] *Governments and Parties in Continental Europe*, I, 286.
[2] The system of government here described is that which existed prior to the political upheaval following the armistice of November 11, 1918.

by royal nomination; and all measures, before they become law, require the king's assent, although his control of the upper chamber is such that no measure of which he disapproves is ever enacted by that body, so that there is never an occasion for the exercise of the formal veto. In the words of a celebrated German jurist, the king possesses "the whole and undivided power of the state in all its plenitude. It would, therefore, be contrary to the nature of the monarchical constitutional law of Germany to enumerate all individual powers of the king. . . . His sovereign right embraces, on the contrary, all branches of the government. Everything which is decided or carried out in the state takes place in the name of the king. He is the personified power of the state."[1] Except in so far as the competence of the sovereign is expressly limited or regulated by the constitution, it is to be regarded as absolute.

It has been pointed out that the German Emperor, as such, has no "civil list." He has no need of one, for the reason that in the capacity of king of Prussia he is entitled to one of the largest civil lists known to European governments. Since the increase provided for by law of February 20, 1889, the *Krondotations Rente*, as it appears in the annual Prussian budget, aggregates seventeen million marks; besides which the king enjoys the revenues from a vast amount of private property, comprising castles, forests, and estates in various parts of the realm. There are also certain special funds whose income is available for the needs of the royal family.

The organization of the executive — the creation of ministerial portfolios, the appointment of ministers, and the determination of departmental functions — rests absolutely with the king, save, of course, for the necessity of procuring from the Landtag, or parliament, the requisite appropriations. Beginning in the early nineteenth century with five, the number of ministries was gradually increased until since 1878 there have been nine, as follows: foreign affairs; interior; ecclesiastical, educational, and sanitary affairs; commerce and industry; finance; war; justice; public works; and agriculture, public domains, and forests. Each ministry rests upon an essentially independent basis, and there has been little attempt to reduce the group to

---

[1] Schulze, *Preussisches Staatsrecht*, I, 158.

the uniformity or symmetry of organization that characterizes the ministries of France, Italy and other continental monarchies. Departmental heads, as well as subordinates, are appointed with reference solely to their administrative capacity, not, as in parliamentary governments, in consideration of their politics or of their status in the existing political situation. They need not be, and usually are not, members of either of the legislative chambers. For it is essential to observe that the ministers are responsible only to the sovereign, which means that the parliamentary system, in the proper sense, does not exist. The constitution, it is true, prescribes that every act of the king shall be countersigned by a minister, who thereby assumes responsibility for it. But there is no machinery by which this nominal responsibility can be made, in practice, to mean anything. Ministers do not retire by reason of an adverse vote in the Landtag; and, although upon vote of either legislative chamber, they may be prosecuted for treason, bribery, or violation of the constitution, no penalties are prescribed in the event of conviction; so that the provision is of no practical effect. Every minister has the right to appear on the floor of either chamber, and to be heard at any time when no member of the house is actually speaking. In the exercise of this privilege the minister is the immediate spokesman of the crown, a fact which is apt to be apparent from the tenor of his utterances.

The Landtag: House of Lords. — Legislative authority is shared by the king with a national assembly, the Landtag, composed of two chambers, of which the upper is known as the *Herrenhaus*, or House of Lords, and the lower as the *Abgeordnetenhaus*, or House of Representatives. Under the original provisions of the constitution, the House of Lords was composed of (1) adult princes of the royal family; (2) heads of Prussian houses derived directly from the earlier Empire; (3) heads of families designated by royal ordinance, with regard for rights of primogeniture and lineal descent; (4) 90 members chosen by the principal taxpayers of the kingdom; and (5) 30 members elected by the municipal councils of the larger towns. Under law of May 7, 1853, this arrangement was, however, superseded by another which practically eliminated the elective elements. Since that time the body has been made up as follows: (1)

princes of the royal family who are of age; (2) scions of the Hohenzollern-Hechingen, Hohenzollern-Sigmaringen, and sixteen other once sovereign families of Prussia; (3) heads of the territorial nobility created by the king, and numbering some fifty members; (4) a number of life peers, chosen by the king from among wealthy landowners, great manufacturers, and men of renown; (5) eight titled noblemen appointed by the king on the nomination of the resident landowners of the eight older provinces of the kingdom; (6) representatives of the universities, of religious bodies, and of towns of over 50,000 inhabitants, presented by these various organizations respectively, but appointed ultimately by the king; and (7) an indefinite number of members, chosen by the king for life on any ground whatsoever, and under no restriction except that peers must have attained the age of thirty years.

The composition of the chamber is thus extremely complex. There are members *ex-officio*, members by royal appointment, members by hereditary right. But the appointing power of the crown is so extensive that the body is at all times practically the creature of royalty. Its membership is recruited almost exclusively from the stanchly conservative landowning aristocracy, so that in attitude and policy it is apt to be in no degree representative of the mass of the nation, at least of the industrial classes. As a rule, although not invariably, it is ready to support the measures of the crown unhesitatingly. In any event, through exercise of the unrestricted power of creating peers, the crown is in a position at all times to control its acts. The number of members varies, but is ordinarily about 300.

The Landtag : House of Representatives and Electoral System. — The *Abgeordnetenhaus*, or House of Representatives, consists of 443 members — 362 for the old kingdom, 80 added in 1867 to represent the provinces then acquired, and one added in 1876 to represent Lauenburg. Representatives are elected for a five-year term, and every Prussian is eligible who has completed his thirtieth year, who has paid national taxes for as much as three years, and whose civil rights have not been impaired by judicial sentence. At first glance, the suffrage seems fairly liberal. Every male citizen twenty-five years of age and upwards who is on the voters' lists of his *Gemeinde*, or commune, is entitled to vote at parliamentary elections. More closely viewed, however, the system is liberal only in that few males beyond the age of twenty-five are without the suffrage. In its actual workings it is the most undemocratic in Europe. From a brief description its shortcomings will be apparent. Representatives are chosen in electoral districts, each of which returns from one to three members — as a rule, two. But there has been no general redistribution of seats since 1860 (although some changes were made in 1906), and in many districts, especially in the urban centers whose growth has fallen largely within the past fifty years, the quota of representatives is grossly disproportioned to population. Until 1906 the entire city of Berlin returned but nine members, and its quota now is only twelve. The situation in this respect is fully as bad as in the Reichstag. In the next place, the enfranchised inhabitants of the district do not vote for a representative directly, nor do their votes have equal weight. The manner of election is, in brief, this : (1) each circle, or district, is divided into a number of *Urwahlbezirke*, or sub-districts ; (2) in each *Urwahlbezirk* one *Wahlman*, or elector, is allotted to every 250 inhabitants ; (3) for the choosing of these *Wahlmänner* the voters of the sub-district are divided into three classes, arranged in such a fashion that the first class will be composed of the payers of direct taxes, beginning with the largest contributors, who collectively pay one-third of the tax quota of the sub-district, the second class will include the payers next in importance who as a group pay the second third, and the last class will comprise the remainder ; (4) each of these classes chooses, by absolute majority, one-third of the electors to which the *Urwahlbezirk* is entitled; finally (5) all the electors thus chosen in the various *Urwahlbezirke* of the district come together as an electoral college and choose, by absolute majority, a representative to sit in the *Abgeordnetenhaus* at Berlin.

This unique system was devised as a compromise between thoroughgoing democracy based on universal suffrage and a government exclusively by the landholding aristocracy. The three-class arrangement originated in the Rhine Province where, by the local government code of 1845, it was put in operation in the elections of the municipalities. In the constitution of 1850 it was adopted for use in the national elections, and in subsequent years it was extended to municipal elections in practically all parts of the kingdom, so that it came to be a characteristic and almost universal Prussian institution. It need hardly be pointed out that the scheme throws the bulk of political power, whether in municipality or in nation, into the hands of the men of wealth. In not fewer than 2214 *Urwahlbezirke*, some years ago, a third of the direct taxes was paid by a single individual, who therefore comprised alone the first electoral class; and in 1703 others the first class consisted of but two persons. In most cases the number of the least considerable taxpayers who in the aggregate pay the last third of the tax quota is relatively very large. Taking the kingdom as a whole, it was estimated in 1907 that approximately three per cent of the electorate belonged to the first class, about 9.5 per cent to the second, and the remaining 87.5 per cent to the third. The operation of the system, combined with the failure to redistribute seats, gives an enormous advantage to the conservative and agrarian interests and almost completely deprives the Socialists and other popular elements of representation. At the elections of 1903 the Socialists attempted for the first time in an organized way to win seats in the Landtag. Under the system which has been described, a total of 324,157 Conservative votes sufficed to elect 143 representatives, but 314,149 Social Democratic votes did not secure the return of a single member. In the Imperial elections of the same year, conducted under a scheme of equal suffrage, the popular party sent to the Reichstag eighty members. At the Prussian elections of 1908 a Social Democratic vote which formed approximately twenty-four per cent of the total popular vote yielded but seven members in a total of 443.

The Movement for Electoral Reform. — For more than a generation there has been ceaseless agitation for electoral reform. In 1883, and again in 1886, the lower chamber debated, but rejected, a project for the substitution of the secret ballot for the existing *viva voce* method of voting. In 1883 the Social Democratic party announced the purpose of its members to abstain from voting until the inequalities arising from " the most wretched of all electoral systems " should have been removed. Gradually there was worked out a program of reform to which Socialists, Liberals, and progressives of various schools gave adherence, wholly or in part, comprising four principal demands: (1) direct elections; (2) equal weight for votes; (3) secret ballot, and (4) redistribution of seats. To this day these have been the objects chiefly sought by the reform elements.

In 1906 a bill raising the number of representatives from 433 to 443 and making provision for a slight redistribution of seats was carried, but a Radical amendment providing for direct and universal suffrage and the secret ballot was vigorously opposed by the Government and failed of adoption. In January, 1908, the country was stirred by socialist demonstrations in behalf of equal manhood suffrage. Prince von Bülow, while admitting that the existing system was defective, opposed the introduction in Prussia of the electoral arrangements of the Empire, alleging that it would not be compatible with the interests of the state, and contending that sound reform of the franchise must secure the preponderance of the middle class, and therefore must aim at the establishment of an equitable gradation in the weight of the various classes of votes. It was added that the Government would consider whether this object might best be attained by basing the franchise entirely upon the amount of taxes paid by the voter, or by taking into account age, educational attainments, or other qualifications. When the Radicals introduced a resolution declaring for equal manhood suffrage the Clericals and the Poles supported it, but the Conservatives and National Liberals of all shades stood by the Government, and the resolution was overwhelmingly rejected. The elections of June, 1908, at which, as has been pointed out, seven Social Democratic members were returned, demonstrated that even under existing electoral arrangements dissatisfaction could find some expression. The National Liberals and the Free Conservatives, who had been outspoken in opposition to the extension of the suffrage, lost, respectively, twelve and four seats. When, however, the Radical resolution reappeared it was again thrown out.

Popular demonstrations in Berlin and in other important towns at length brought the Government to the conviction that it was not wise to persist too long in its inflexible attitude. In a speech from the throne, January 11, 1910, the King announced the early introduction of a measure for electoral reform, and a month later it became the unwelcome duty of the new Chancellor, von

Bethmann-Hollweg, to lay the Government's project before the chambers. It was instantly evident, not only that the proposal had been prepared under bureaucratic direction, but that the real purpose of the Government was to carry through the Landtag an electoral bill designed to appease the reformers without abandoning the essential features of the existing system. The project provided, in brief: (1) that the tripartite system should be retained, although the quota of taxes admitting to the first class should be reduced to a uniform level of five thousand marks (no weight being given to payment beyond that amount), and voters of specified degrees of education, or occupying certain official positions, or having served a stipulated number of years in the army or navy, should be assigned to the higher classes, with but incidental regard to their tax contributions; (2) that *viva voce* voting should be retained; (3) that the choice of electors should be by districts rather than by *Urwahlbezirke;* and (4) that direct voting should be substituted for indirect. There was no mention of redistribution, and the secret ballot was withheld. The rearrangement of classes did not touch the fundamental difficulty; indeed, the only demand of the reformers that was really met was that for direct elections. In his speech in defense of the measure the Chancellor frankly admitted that the Government was irrevocably opposed to a suffrage system based on democratic principles.

The scheme was ridiculed by the liberal elements. In protest against the nonchalance with which the door had been shut in their faces the working classes in Berlin and elsewhere entered upon a fresh series of demonstrations which embarrassed the Government for several weeks. In the Landtag the Conservative and Free Conservative parties, forming the Government majority, stood solidly for the bill, in the conviction that if there must be change at all those changes which the bill proposed would be less objectionable than those which were being urged by the radicals. The Center wavered, while the National Liberals, the Poles, the Social Democrats, and the Progressive People's party stood firmly in opposition. On February 13 the bill was referred in the lower house to a committee, which reported it so amended as to provide for the secret ballot but not for direct elections. On March 16, by a vote of 283 to 168, the measure in this amended form was passed by the chamber, all parties except the Conservatives and the Center voting against it. On April 29 the bill was passed in the upper chamber, by a vote of 140 to 94, in the form in which it had originally been introduced. All efforts on the part of the Government to bring the lower house to an acceptance of the original measure proved fruitless, and the upshot was that the project was withdrawn from the chambers. The overhauling of the antiquated electoral system, both national and municipal, remained at the outbreak of the Great War a live issue; but agreement upon a definite project of reform seemed remote. The problem was enormously complicated by the traditions of aristocratic, landed privilege which permeate the inmost parts of the Prussian political system. In respect to redistribution, too, a fundamental obstacle lay in the consideration that such a step on the part of Prussia would almost of necessity involve a similar one on the part of the Empire. In both instances the insuperable objection, from the point of view of the Government, arose from the vast acquisition of political power which would accrue from such a reform to the Socialists and to other radical parties.

Actual Character of the Landtag. — The maximum life of a Landtag is five years. The lower chamber may, however, be dissolved at any time by arbitrary act of the crown, and there have been instances of the dissolution of a newly elected chamber on account of its objectionable political character, before it had been convened for so much as a single sitting. Each house elects its own officers, and regulates its own order of business, and proceedings are normally open to the public. At the opening of a session the House of Lords is divided into five *Abteilungen*, or sections, and the House of Representatives into seven. In the lower house the division is made by lot; in the upper, by the president. In both instances it is made once for an entire session, not monthly as in France, or bi-monthly as in Italy. The function of the *Abteilungen* is to appoint committee members, and, in the lower house, to examine election returns with a view to final validation by the chamber itself. Each house has eight standing committees, and special committees are created as need arises.

The Landtag is, of course, a national legislature. The rights of independent deliberation which it exercises, however, are so scant as to be almost negligible. In theory each chamber has full power to initiate legislation; in practice, almost all bills are introduced by the Government, and the chambers content themselves with discussion and proposing amendments. It sometimes happens that, as in the case of the Electoral Reform Bill of 1910, the lower house so emasculates a measure as to compel the Government to withdraw it. But, speaking broadly, it may be said that Prussian legislation is projected and formulated by the crown and the ministers and merely ratified by the Landtag. There is still a question as to whether the stipulation that all laws require the assent of the two houses covers, under every circumstance, the appropriation of money. In practice, appropriations are regularly voted in the chambers, and in fact it is required that the budget and all fiscal measures shall be presented first to the lower house, and shall be accepted or rejected as a whole by the upper. But during the years 1863–1867 the Government, under Bismarck's leadership, asserted and exercised the power of collecting and expending the revenues of the state on the basis of standing laws, thus entirely suspending the legislative appropriating power; and the question has never been finally settled by Prussian jurists as to whether such a thing might not again be done.

On the side of administration, also, the powers of the Landtag are merely nominal. Each chamber has a right to present memorials to the king; to refer to the ministers documents addressed to it, and to demand explanations concerning complaints made therein; and to appoint commissions for the investigation of subjects for its own information. The right of interpellation is expressly recognized. But, as has been pointed out, the ministers are not responsible to the legislative chambers, and neither they nor the king himself can be compelled to give heed, unless they so desire, to legislative protests, demands, or censure. Where a parliamentary system does not exist, the influence of the legislative branch upon matters of administration is likely to be confined to the simple assertion of opinion.

Local Government: Origins and Principles. — In most of their essential features, the machinery of local administration and the connections between the central and local authorities in

Prussia to-day date from the reforms of the Stein-Hardenberg ministries in the early years of the nineteenth century. By the memorable Municipal Edict (*Städt-Ordnung*) of November 19, 1808, Stein set up a complete municipal system, with burgomasters, executive boards, and town councils (all elective), and swept away the oligarchy of the guilds, broadened the franchise, and conferred upon the towns almost complete independence, even in the matter of taxation. An edict of 1831 revived the power of the central authorities to supervise local taxation and introduced a number of other changes; but, on the whole, the municipal system of the present day is based upon the edict of Stein. More immediately, it rests upon an act of 1853, applied originally only to the six eastern provinces of the kingdom, but eventually extended to the others. It was under this last-mentioned decree that the three-class electoral system as applied to local elections was gradually spread over the country. Neither Stein nor Hardenberg touched the country communes, but the extension, during the Napoleonic occupation, of the French communal system into all the Prussian territories west of the Elbe prepared the way for the essentially uniform system which was established by the Westphalian and Rhineland Edicts of 1841 and 1845. Edicts of 1807 and 1811 abolished the aristocratic basis of the ancient circles (*Kreise*), and after 1815 the circle as a unit of local government next above the commune was extended to all the conquered or reconquered territories. The revival of the old provincial organization was begun also in 1815, when the kingdom was divided into ten provinces; and in the same year were established twenty-six government districts (*Regierungsbezirke*), two or three within each province, each under the control of one of the government boards (*Regierungen*) whose creation was begun in 1808.

Soon after the founding of the Empire, Bismarck turned his attention to a reorganization of local government; and while his reforms were designed, of course, only for Prussia, they were copied to such an extent in other German states that the Empire was brought to a substantially common basis. The Chancellor was no believer in democracy. But he thought that, in the interest both of economy and of stability, the local administrative authorities should be made to include not only a paid, expert bureaucracy, but a considerable element of unpaid lay or non-official persons, drawn principally from the large landowners and taxpayers. The obstacles to be overcome, arising from public indifference, the opposition of the existing bureaucracy, the apprehensions of the conservatives, and sectional differences and antipathies, were enormous; but by proceeding slowly and in a conciliatory spirit the Government was able eventually to carry out its plans. The first enactments, for the circles in 1872 and for the provinces in 1875, were applied only to those provinces which had formed the old monarchy, but during the next ten years similar measures were extended to the remainder of the kingdom, and, finally, after the dismissal of Bismarck, the task was rounded out by a great *Landgemeinde-Ordnung* issued for the seven eastern provinces in 1891. This series of enactments gave the administrative methods and machinery of the kingdom almost precisely the character they have to-day.

Although the system is still one of the most complicated in Europe, it is infinitely simpler than it once was, and the bureaucratic forces in it, if still predominant, have been brought under restraint. The principles underlying it have been summarized by an English writer as follows: " The first is the careful distinction drawn between those internal affairs in which the central government is thought to be directly concerned, and those which are held to be primarily of only local interest. The former group includes, besides the army, the state taxes and domains, ecclesiastical affairs, police (in the wide Prussian meaning of the term), and the supervision of local authorities; whilst roads, poor relief, and a number of miscellaneous matters are left to the localities. These two groups are kept carefully separate, even when they are intrusted to the same authority. Secondly, the work of the central government is " deconcentrated," that is, the country is divided into districts (which may or may not be coincident with the areas of local self-government), in each of which there is a delegation of the central authority, doing its work, and thereby lessening the pressure upon the departmental offices in Berlin. Something like this deconcentration is found in the educational organization of France, and also in the office of the prefect, but it is far more elaborate, and the machinery much more complex, in Prussia.

2 K

Thirdly the comparative independence of the executive from the deliberative authority, and the predominance of the officials, which characterize the central government of Prussia, repeat themselves throughout the whole of local government. And, finally, in all except the largest of the Prussian areas of local self-government, the executive agents of the locality, elected by it, are also the representatives of the central government; as such they are members of the bureaucracy and controlled by it, and in consequence they naturally look to the center for guidance and direction in regard to local affairs. Therefore, whilst it would be inaccurate to say that local self-government, as understood in England, does not exist in Prussia, it is true that self-government there is weak, that it is not so much the exercise of the will of the locality within limits prescribed (for the protection of the whole community) by the central power, as the exercise of the will of the latter by the locality. In fact, the bureaucracy rules; and it is fortunate for Prussia that hitherto the bureaucracy has remained intelligent and respective of new ideas."[1] At the same time it is to be observed that, while the professional, lifelong holders of office continue to preponderate as in no other important country of western Europe, the class of non-professionals is large and increasing. As a rule, the first class is salaried, the second is not; the non-professionals being simply citizens who, moved by considerations of a civic and social nature, give their services without prospect of pecuniary reward. The principle of the system is, as Ashley characterizes it, that of government by experts, checked by lay criticism and the power of the purse, and effectively controlled by the central authorities.

Local Government: Province. — Aside from the cities, which have their special forms of government, the administrative units of Prussia, in the order of their magnitude, are: (1) the *Provinz*, or province; (2) the *Regierungsbezirk*, or district; (3) the *Kreis*, or circle; (4) the *Amtsbezirk*, or court jurisdiction; and (5) the *Gemeinde*, or commune. Of these, three — the first, third, and fifth — are spheres both of the central administration and of local self-government; two — the second and fourth — exist for administrative purposes only. Of provinces there are

[1] Ashley, *Local and Central Government*, 130–132.

twelve: East Prussia, West Prussia, Brandenburg, Pomerania, Silesia, Posen, Westphalia, Saxony, Hanover, the Rhine Province, Schleswig-Holstein, and Hesse-Nassau. Unlike the French and Italian departments, these Prussian provinces are historical areas, of widely varying extent and, in some instances, of not even wholly continuous territory. Thus Hanover is, geographically, the kingdom once united with the crown of Great Britain; Schleswig-Holstein comprises the territories wrested from Denmark in 1864; Saxony is the country taken from the kingdom of Saxony at the close of the Napoleonic wars; and Posen represents Prussia's acquisitions from the Polish partitions of the eighteenth century.

In the organization of the province there is a complete separation of functions relating to the affairs of the kingdom (*Staatsgeschäfte*) from those relating only to matters of a local nature. In the circle, as will appear, the two sets of functions are discharged by the same body of officials; in the district, the functions performed are wholly of a national, rather than a local, character. But in the province there are not merely two sets of functions but two entirely separate groups of officials. For the administration of affairs of national interest, such as police, education, and religion, the authorities within the province are (1) the *Oberpräsident*, or chief president, appointed by the king to represent the central government in the management of all such matters as concern the entire province or reach beyond the jurisdiction of a single *Regierungsbezirk* administration, and (2) the *Provinzialrath*, a provincial council consisting of, besides the *Oberpräsident* or his representative as presiding officer, one professional member appointed for an indefinite tenure by the Minister of the Interior at Berlin and five ordinary citizen members elected, usually for a term of six years, by the provincial *Ausschuss*, or committee. The *Oberpräsident* is the immediate agent of the ministry, as is the prefect in France, although he is a more dignified and important functionary than his French counterpart. None the less, by virtue of the fact that most of the *Oberpräsident's* acts are valid only after having received the assent of a body the majority of whose members are chosen within the province, his authority is not quite absolute.

By the side of this official group stands another, quite independent of it, for the control of affairs of purely local concern. Its organs comprise: (1) the *Provinzialausschuss*, or provincial committee, consisting of from seven to fourteen members elected for six years by the provincial Landtag, not necessarily, but almost invariably, from its own membership; (2) a *Landeshauptmann* or *Landesdirektor*, a salaried executive official elected by the Landtag for six or twelve years and confirmed by the crown; and (3) the *Provinziallandtag*, or provincial assembly. The *Landeshauptmann* is the executive, the *Provinzialausschuss* the consultative, organ of local self-administration; the *Provinziallandtag* is the provincial legislature. Members of the Landtag are elected for six years (one-half retiring every three years) by the diets of the circles, and they are, as a rule, local administrative officials of the circles, large landowners, and other well-to-do persons. Meetings are called by the crown at least every two years. The Landtag's functions include the supervision of charities, highways, and industry; the voting of local taxes and the apportionment of them among the circles; the enactment of local laws; the custody of provincial property; the election of the *Landeshauptmann* and the members of the provincial committee; and the giving of advice on provincial matters at the request of the central government. The Landtag is in practice less independent, however, than this enumeration of powers might seem to imply. All of its legislation requires the assent of the king; most of its fiscal arrangements must be submitted to one or more of the ministers; and the body itself may be dissolved at any time by the crown.

Local Government: Minor Areas. — Each province is divided into *Regierungsbezirke*, or districts, of which there are now thirty-six. Unlike the province, the district exists for purposes of general administration only. It therefore has no organs of self-government. Its *Regierung*, or "administration," consists of a body of professional, salaried officials, appointed by the crown and having at its head the *Regierungspräsident*, who is, on the whole, the most important official in the Prussian local service. The subjects that fall within the jurisdiction of the *Regierung*, including taxation, education, religion, forests, etc., are very comprehensive, and the work of administration is carried on chiefly through "colleges," or boards. For the management of police and the supervision of local bodies there exists a *Bezirksausschuss*, or district committee, composed of the *Regierungspräsident*, two other persons appointed by the crown, and four members elected by the *Provinzialausschuss* for six years. A very important function of this body since 1883 is that of sitting, under the presidency of one of its members appointed for his judicial qualifications, as the administrative court of the district.

In the *Kreis*, or circle, as in the province, there are two sharply distinguished sets of governmental functions, the general and the local; but for the administration of both there is a single hierarchy of officials. The number of circles in the kingdom is about 490, with populations varying from 20,000 to 80,000. Each includes all towns lying within it which have a population of less than 25,000. A town of over 25,000 is likely to be created, by ministerial order, a circle within itself, in which case the functions of government are exercised by the municipal authorities. The essential organs of government within the *Landkreise*, or country circles, are three: the *Landrath*, the *Kreisausschuss*, and the *Kreistag*. The *Landrath* is appointed for life by the crown, frequently on nomination by the *Kreistag*, or diet. He superintends all administrative affairs, general and local, within the circle; fulfills the functions of chief of police; presides over the *Kreisausschuss* and *Kreistag;* and, in general, occupies within the circle the place occupied within the province by the *Oberpräsident*. Associated with him, and organized under his presidency, is the *Kreisausschuss*, or circle committee, composed of six unofficial members elected by the *Kreistag* for six years. In addition to its consultative functions, the *Kreisausschuss* sits as an administrative court of lowest grade.

The *Kreistag* is the legislative body of the circle. Its members, numbering at least twenty-five, are elected for a term of six years by three *Verbände*, or colleges, the first being made up of the cities, the second of the large rural taxpayers, the third of a complicated group of rural interests in which the smaller taxpayers and delegates of the communal assemblies preponderate. The *Kreistag* is a body of substantial importance. It chooses, directly or indirectly, all the elective officials of the circle, of the district, and of the province; it creates local officers and regulates their functions; it enacts legislation of a local nature;

and it votes the taxes required for both its own and the provincial administration.

The smallest of Prussian governmental units is the *Gemeinde*, or commune.[1] Of communes there are two distinct types, the rural (*Landgemeinde*) and the urban (*Stadtgemeinde*). The governments of the rural communes (some 36,000 in number) are so varied that any general description of them is impossible. They rest largely upon local custom, although reduced at some points to a reasonable uniformity under regulating statutes such as were enacted for the communes of eight of the twelve provinces in the *Landgemeinde-Ordnung* of 1891. There is invariably an elective *Schulze*, or chief magistrate. He is assisted ordinarily by from two to six aldermen (*Schöffen*) or councilors. And there is generally a governing body (*Gemeindevertretung*), composed of elected representatives, when there are as many as forty qualified electors, — otherwise the people acting in the capacity of a primary assembly (*Gemeindeversammlung*), — for the decision of matters relating to local schools, churches, highways, and similar interests. It is to be observed, however, that most of the rural communes are so small that they have neither the financial resources nor the administrative ability to maintain a government of much virility. Such action as is taken within them is taken almost invariably with the approval of, and under the guidance of, the authorities of the circle, principally the *Landrath*.

In their governmental arrangements the urban communes are more uniform than the rural ones. The usual authorities comprise (1) the *Stadtrath*, an executive body consisting of a burgomaster and a number of assistants, elected for six, nine, or twelve years, or even for life, and (2) the *Stadtverordnete*, or municipal council, chosen for from three to six years, as a rule by an electorate identical with that which returns the members of the lower branch of the Prussian Landtag.

[1] The *Amtsbezirk* is essentially a judicial district. In the eastern provinces it is utilized also for purposes of police administration.

SELECTED REFERENCES

A. L. Lowell, *Governments and Parties in Continental Europe* (Boston, 1896); J. S. Shapiro, *Modern and Contemporary European History* (Boston, 1918); W. B. Munro, *Government of European Cities* (New York, 1914); H. G. James, *Principles of Prussian Administration* (New York, 1913); F. J. Goodnow, *Comparative Administrative Law* (New York, 1903); H. Tuttle, *History of Prussia* (Boston, 1884-1896); E. Lavisse, *General View of the Political History of Europe* (New York, 1891); C. Seignobos, *A Political History of Europe* (New York, 1900); C. H. Maurice, *The Revolutionary Movement of Europe of 1848-9 in Italy, Austria-Hungary and Germany* (New York, 1887); T. H. Dyer, *A History of Modern Europe* (London, 1901); R. B. Mowatt, *Select Treaties and Documents to Illustrate the Development of Modern European State Systems* (Oxford, 1916); C. MacCauley, *The Hohenzollern Dynasty* (Tokyo, 1916); J. A. R. Marriott, *The Evolution of Prussia* (Oxford, 1915); E. B. Cromer, *Political and Literary Essays* (London, 1916); F. J. Adkins, *The War, Its Origins and Warnings* (London, 1915); N. H. Loring, *Prussia, Its Position and Destiny* (New York, 1887); R. G. Usher, *Pan-Germanism* (Boston, 1913).

CHAPTER XXV

CROSS CURRENTS IN GERMAN POLITICS

I. THE BULWARKS OF AUTOCRACY

The Survival of Absolutism. — For a generation before the World War Germany was a paradox among nations. Her population had risen since 1870 from forty millions to sixty-seven millions; her advance in industry and trade, and her growth of wealth, had been phenomenal; she had outdistanced most, if not all, of the world in the application of science to manufacturing and agriculture; she had been the pioneer in most forms of social legislation; her scholarship was, in many fields, unsurpassed; her achievements in music, art, and literature commanded the world's admiration. But alongside these evidences of enlightenment and progress stood one of the most hopelessly antiquated governmental systems on earth. Not that the forms of liberalism were altogether lacking. "Whoever," says a former American ambassador to Germany, "will take in hand the constitution of the German Empire and read it merely as a document will be surprised, if not already familiar with its contents, at the façade of liberalism that presents itself. . . . Ninety-nine one-hundredths of the Imperial constitution could be transcribed into the constitution of the most democratic federal state without serious criticism." [1] Nor yet was there any lack of orderliness and efficiency in public administration. Not even the Roman government in its best days, nor the British government of later times, executed law, controlled finance, managed the armed forces, and held the respect of its subjects with greater success. Enough has been said in preceding chapters, however, to make it plain that while

[1] Hill, "Impressions of the Kaiser," *Harper's Monthly Magazine*, May, 1918, 791–792.

the German people may have had orderly, efficient, and even " scientific " government, this government was not of their own making, and was not under their control. Autocracy was the price they paid for their economic and social advantages; and, as will be pointed out presently, when the war came on in 1914 there were accumulating evidences that they had begun to regard the price as too great.

What is the explanation of this remarkable survival of autocracy and paternalism in a country of much general enlightenment, and in an age of rapidly spreading democracy? A full answer would demand many chapters of intricate political and social history. Enough has already been told, however, to reveal two or three main facts in the situation, especially (1) that for a decade or more preceding and including the revolutionary years 1848–1849 Germany wavered between the old autocracy and the new liberalism, (2) that, because of their lack of unity, experience, and practical sense the liberal elements lost their great chance, and (3) that the work of national unification and constitution-framing accordingly fell to the ultra-conservative forces, *i.e.*, the Prussian government, and especially Bismarck, who had the organization, the political skill, and withal, the military force, requisite for the carrying out of the work on lines favorable to its own interest. Once securely established, the system was maintained against all assaults (until the most recent days), by a dynasty of divine-right monarchs, governing under the ægis of a peculiarly reactionary Prussian political philosophy, supported by a powerful landed aristocracy, equipped with the best trained army in the world, buttressed by an imposing and apparently invincible *Kultur*, and grounded upon an ingrained habit of popular obedience.

The Hohenzollern Dynasty. — This leads to a somewhat closer scrutiny of the great bulwarks of German autocracy in the pre-war period. They have, indeed, already been named: the Prussian hegemony; the Hohenzollern dynasty; the " Junkers," or landed proprietors; the army; the somewhat ill-defined but none the less potent body of ideals and practices known as *Kultur;* and popular submissiveness and inertia. Of the preponderance of Prussia, as a state, in the German federation of the past fifty years enough has been said. In characterizing the several bulwarks of autocracy, however, we shall still be speaking of Prussia; for " Prussianism " has been in all generations the one great source of German illiberality of thought and action.

The first of these bulwarks is the Hohenzollern dynasty. The Hohenzollerns began, at least as early as the tenth century, as petty counts governing from a castle on the hill of Zollern near the present northern boundary of Switzerland. Their importance as a ruling family dates from the early fifteenth century, when the Emperor invested them with the electorate of Brandenburg, lying along the Oder River and including the future site of Berlin. A hundred years later they accepted Lutheranism and with its aid began building up leadership in the Protestant north. Another hundred years, and they gained by cleverly arranged marriage alliances the duchy of Cleves, carrying their power to the Rhine, and also the then almost purely Slavic duchy of East Prussia, carrying it eastward to the Russian border. In the seventeenth century the ruling prince was known simply as an " elector." But in 1701 Frederick III, son of the " Great Elector," was authorized by his Imperial overlord to take the title of " king." The title was first borne in Prussia alone; and hence *Prussia*, rather than Brandenburg, became the official name of the entire dominion. Most of the successive rulers — particularly Frederick William, the Great Elector (1640–1688), King Frederick William I (1713–1740), and King Frederick II, or Frederick " the Great " (1740–1786) — were masterful, crafty, autocratic monarchs, and during their long and eventful reigns the power of the dynasty steadily grew, by conquests, annexations, alliances, and diplomatic strokes. The rulers were of an iron race, and were not troubled with scruples in dealing with either friends or enemies. They reigned by " divine right," had nothing but contempt for ideas of popular sovereignty, and made the army the center and defense of their political system.

In the Napoleonic period Prussia fell on evil days; and for half a century afterwards its kings, while true Hohenzollerns in their claims to divine right and their exaltation of the army, were cast in an inferior mold. Even William I, the first wearer of the new Imperial crown, was completely overshadowed by

Bismarck. At his death, in 1888, Prussia (and therefore all Germany) came to the parting of the political ways. The heir to the throne was Frederick III, surnamed " the Noble," a man of known liberal views; and while he had declared to Bismarck three years earlier that he had no intention of setting up a parliamentary system of government,[1] it was widely believed then, and is commonly supposed now, that he was an admirer of the English system of government, and that if he had lived, the Imperial constitution would have been interpreted in a liberal spirit, ministers would have been selected with a view to harmony with majorities in the Reichstag, the king would have become rather an adviser than an actual executive, and the whole tendency would have been toward political freedom and responsibility. But Frederick was already stricken with fatal disease at his accession, and he reigned exactly ninety-nine days. His death brought to the throne the " young man," as Bismarck somewhat contemptuously called him, William II.

William II and the Prussian Doctrine of Monarchy. — The triumphs over Austria and France, the return of the victorious armies, the coronation of his grandfather, the exhilaration of a unified and exalted Germany, the new prestige of Prussia, the intoxicating successes of diplomat and soldier, had left indelible impressions upon the youthful prince's mind; and if any one wondered what the new ruler's principles and policies would be, all doubts were soon cleared away. All the characteristics and the traditions of the Hohenzollerns found place in William II's make-up, — some of them multiplied many fold. He believed implicitly in his own divine right to rule. " Remember," he said in an early proclamation to the army, " that the German people are the chosen of God. On me, as German Emperor, the spirit of God has descended. I am His weapon, His sword, and His vicegerent." As late as 1910 he declared in a public address that his " grandfather in his own right placed the crown upon his head, insisting once again that it was bestowed upon him by the grace of God alone, and not by parliaments or by the will of the people. . . . I too consider myself a chosen instrument of Heaven, and I shall go my way without regard to the views and opinions of the day." He frankly avowed his

[1] *Reflections and Reminiscences*, II, 304–305.

claim to absolute control of public affairs. " There is but one master in the country," he declared in 1891; " it is I, and I will bear no other." He held the constitutions of both Prussia and the Empire sacred, because they allowed free play for autocracy. " I am of the opinion," he said at his accession, " that our constitution establishes a just and useful partition of public powers in the life of the State; and for that reason also, and not only because of my oath, I will observe and defend it." He regarded education as the handmaid of his autocratic government. Of the elementary school teacher and the university professor alike he said: " According to his rights and duties, he is, n the first place, a state official. In this position, he should do what is demanded of him. He should teach the young and prepare them for resisting all revolutionary aims." " I want soldiers," he said angrily, when complaining that the schools made their pupils near-sighted.

The doctrine of divine right lost its influence in England with the final downfall of the Stuarts, in France at the time of the Revolution, in Belgium at the establishment of national independence, in Italy during the unification. In Germany, and especially in Prussia, it has lived on. The monarchs have continually reasserted it; and no organized portion of the people except the Social Democrats has developed a political philosophy that is opposed to it. The attitude of the political theorists and the constitutional jurists has not been clear. They have not, of late, given the doctrine direct support. Yet they, or most of them, enunciate views which lead to the same general result. The apotheosis of political power which one finds in their treatises raises the acts of the monarch, as one writer has put it, " above the plane within which considerations of ordinary morality apply, and ascribes to the political entity a welfare and a purpose other than and distinct from, and in some cases not even related to, the welfare of the individuals who are subject to its authority." [1]

The Army. — Of cardinal importance was, of course, the Emperor's attitude toward the army, whose sure support has for generations been one of autocracy's mightiest assets. " The

[1] Willoughby, "The Prussian Theory of Monarchy," *Amer. Polit. Sci. Review*, XI, 625.

absolute and indestructible fidelity of the army," runs the Kaiser's rescript addressed to the soldiery on the day of his accession, " is the heritage transmitted from father to son, from generation to generation. . . . We are inseparably united. . . . We are made for each other, I and the army, and we shall remain closely attached whether God gives us peace or storm." Addressing a body of recruits in 1891, he declared: " You are now my soldiers; you have given yourselves to me body and soul. There is now but one enemy for you, and that is my enemy." Paraphrasing, on another occasion, the famous saying of Bismarck, he asserted: " The soldier and the army, not parliamentary majorities, have welded together the German Empire — my confidence is placed in the army." From these and many other expressions that could be quoted, it is evident that William II looked upon the army as a dynastic possession, and as a personal tool wherewith to uphold the existing order of things and carry out the royal purposes. It was the army, as one writer has put it, that "could enable him to read into the Imperial constitution the full meaning of the Hohenzollern traditions, and make the whole realm what his ancestors had made Prussia, a patrimonial estate to be transmitted by him to future generations of his House." [1] The various devices by which the entire German military establishment was brought under Prussian control, and accordingly under the absolute direction of the Kaiser, have been explained elsewhere.[2] " The question by which to decide the essential character of a state," says a German scholar, is, " Whom does the army obey? " To 1918, this question in Germany could be answered in only one way. The Reichstag had practically no authority over it; the states had largely surrendered their control; the Kaiser alone dominated; even the army budget was voted, not annually, as in England, France, and the United States, where the military is under the full control of the civil power, but for five-year periods.

The " Junkers." — Another bulwark of autocratic government was the landed aristocracy of eastern and northeastern Prussia. German agrarian development has been regional rather than national; that is to say, the ownership and use of

---

[1] Hill, *ibid.*, 793.   [2] See pp. 460–461.

land took a different trend in each of three main sections of the country. The southwest (including Bavaria, Baden, Württemberg, and Rhenish Prussia) became, like France, a land of small holdings, and until now has been the only part of the Empire in which it was possible to discover peasant political influence of any importance. The northwest (including Westphalia, Lower Saxony, and parts of Hanover) developed a system of medium-to-large holdings, yet with many peasant proprietorships. From Brandenburg eastward, however, — and especially in the Prussian provinces of East Prussia, West Prussia, Posen, and Pomerania, — the land was long ago gathered almost entirely into great estates, and most of the people are landless, wage-earning agricultural laborers. The larger part of German agricultural land is not contained in the great estates of the north and east, and the national policy which is most profitable for the owners of these estates is not necessarily advantageous for the country's agricultural interests as a whole. Still less is it necessarily advantageous for the people generally. For forty years, however, the ultra-conservative, privileged, haughty, and oppressive landed aristocracy of Prussia held a rod of iron over the industrial classes, and over the government itself. When Chancellor Caprivi reduced the protective duties on imports of grain these landed magnates demanded and obtained his dismissal; and in 1902 they brought about a restoration of such duties on foodstuffs as would keep prices of their own products at a high level. For decades these Agrarians, or "Junkers," have supplied practically all the officers of the army and navy, and have almost monopolized the civil offices as well. If Prussia has ruled Germany, the Junkers have ruled Prussia, and through it the Empire itself. They have been a main prop of the Hohenzollern dynasty and of its autocratic, irresponsible system of government.

Kultur. — Yet another foundation stone of German autocracy has been the concept and influence of *Kultur*. This term, although constantly recurring in the discussions of the past four years, practically defies definition. The English word "culture" is too narrow to be considered an equivalent, the word "civilization" is somewhat too broad. The term includes not only learning in the ordinary sense, but attitude, spirit, temperament, ambition, achievement, purpose. The concepts involved in it have important political bearings for several reasons. In the first place, *Kultur* is state-made. It is, in the German view, the highest product of the schools and the universities, all of which are completely controlled by the state. In the second place, it is inextricably linked to militarism. The union of culture and militarism has long been the very bedrock of German education. Furthermore, it is not personal, but national. The nation creates and propagates it, and all the people share in it. " They have all had it at the same school. And it is all the same brand of culture, because no other is taught. It is the culture with which the Government wishes its citizens to be equipped. That is why all Germans tend not only to know the same facts, . . . but to have a similar outlook on life and similar opinions about Goethe, Shakespeare, and the German Navy. Culture, like military service, is a part of the state machinery." [1] Being a national rather than a mere personal possession, *Kultur* is deliberately handed on by the state from generation to generation, completely ready for use in whatever manner the state shall desire and direct. It is an integral body of ideas and attitudes, which goes steadily forward in lines of entire unity and self-consistency.

Finally, it maintains itself, under the guidance of the state, by ceaseless struggle. As German scholars and statesmen have looked into the future they saw nothing but conflict — perpetual conflict between rival national " cultures," each seeking to crush out its competitors. No amalgamation, no real amity, no compromise even, is possible. " In the struggle between nationalities," writes Prince von Bülow, " one nation is the hammer and the other is the anvil; one is the victor and the other the vanquished. It is a law of life and development in history that when two national civilizations meet they fight for supremacy." [2] And the thought is that they fight not alone with the pen but with the sword. Every culture considers itself superior; only force can settle the issue. " A Luther and a Goethe may be the puppets pitted in a contest of culture against Maeterlinck and Victor Hugo. But it is Krupp and Zeppelin and the War-Lord that pull the strings."

[1] Zimmern, *Nationality and Government*, 7. [2] *Imperial Germany*, 245.

Kultur as the Germans have developed it thus becomes a mighty bulwark of autocracy. It owes its origin and character to absolutist state control; it is systematically employed to promote the unity of the nation and to stimulate pride in and loyalty to the omnipotent state; it is at once the cause and the chief support of a policy of domination and aggression toward other nations. Its peculiar effectiveness is derived largely from the people's ingrained habit of obedience, bred, in part, of centuries of experience when security depended absolutely upon the consecration of the vassal to his lord, and when the economic ties of serfdom bound the peasants almost irrevocably to their masters — bred also, in part, of Bismarckian doctrine and practice, and again, in part, of the patriotism and pride that laid hold upon the German mind in the great era of unification and expansion.

II. POLITICAL PARTIES AND PARTY PROGRAMS

The Party Situation: General Aspects. — A final condition which has contributed, negatively yet powerfully, to the perpetuation of the autocratic régime is the inability of the liberal and discontented forces to come together in support of a plan of reform. "It will be recalled," says a recent writer, "that in England the first triumph of democracy came as a result of a combination of the middle and working classes, who forced through the reform bill of 1832; in France a similar combination succeeded in the revolution of 1830. History has proved that it takes two classes out of power to cope successfully with one class in power. In Germany the working classes have continually refused to combine with the middle classes against the intrenched aristocracy, on the ground that the middle classes would reap the benefit, as in England in 1832 and in France in 1830. Although the middle classes are opposed to the autocratic régime, they have consistently refused to combine with the workingmen to overthrow it, because they fear that the latter, who are largely Socialists, might endeavor to establish a socialistic republic, as was attempted in France in 1848 and in the Commune of 1871. Its opponents being thus divided, the autocratic system, supported by the landed aristocracy, or Junkers, has been able to maintain itself without serious difficulty."[1]

This leads us to a brief inquiry into the history and nature of political parties and party groups in the Empire. The first fact that stands out is that while political life is in many respects intense, parties as such have been of less *governmental* importance than in England, France, or Italy. The reason is obvious. In the countries mentioned public policy is controlled by the people, — and by the people organized in parties; government, as has been pointed out, is government *by party*. In Germany the people have not controlled. For purposes of propaganda or self-protection they group themselves in parties; but these parties do not, as such, formulate and carry out public policy.[2] Government is above party, not by party. Certain party groups lend the Emperor their fairly consistent support, but it is not they as such that map out policy, execute it, and bear responsibility for it. The true functions of party can be developed only under a popular form of government. A second fact is that Germany has no bi-party system, but rather a multiplicity of parties and party groups, so that, as in France and Italy, no one party is ever able to command a majority in the Reichstag. There is no cabinet system of government, and the tenure of the Chancellor and ministers is in no wise directly dependent upon the maintenance of any particular party majority in the chamber. Practically, of course, the Government must have sufficient support there to insure the enactment of its budgets and of its legislative proposals. To be effective and trustworthy, this support must be organized, and hence, in practice there is always a recognized " government majority." Party division, however, is carried so far that this majority must at all times be composed of two or three groups, more or less precariously united in a *bloc*. Thus Bismarck at one time governed with the combined aid of the Conservatives, Free Conservatives, and National Liberals, and von Bülow worked first with a " Blue-Black " (Conservative-Center) *bloc*, and later with a similar affiliation of Conservatives and Liberals.

[1] Schapiro, *Modern and Contemporary European History*, 283.
[2] It must be remembered that political conditions are here described as they were prior to the close of the Great War.

A third fact is that German parties are exceptionally "particularistic"; that is, they are not broadly national, drawing support from all parts of the country and from all classes of people, but are constituted, rather, on lines of race, section, and class. There are several minor practices in the newer portions of Prussia, and of the Empire, which are preëminently of this nature. Thus the Guelfs exist to make protest against the absorption of the kingdom of Hanover into Prussia in 1866; the Danes demand the cession of Danish-speaking Schleswig to Denmark; the Poles comprise the Slavic voters of the provinces of West Prussia, Posen, and Silesia, who have continued to send to the Reichstag representatives to protest against the Polish annexations to the kingdom and against the ruthless attempts to Germanize the subject people; the Alsatians similarly protest against the incorporation of Alsace-Lorraine into the Empire, and demand complete autonomy, so long as separation cannot be obtained, for its population. The Anti-Semites comprise a group formed, in 1879, on a somewhat different basis, with a view to curbing Jewish influence in politics and finance. But the greater parties are also far less coextensive with national boundaries, and far less representative of all elements of society, than are the parties of England, France or the United States. Only one, the Social Democratic party, can lay claim to substantial strength throughout the entire Empire; and even it is, in the first place, a *class* party, to which few people besides workingmen belong, and in the second place, a party whose support is drawn almost wholly from the cities.

Party Development: the Older Groups. — The party situation of recent years has come about as a result of the gradual disintegration of two great political groups which included most of the people of Prussia when Bismarck entered upon his ministry; and to this day the parties of the Empire and of the Prussian kingdom have been for all practical purposes identical. The two original Prussian groups were the Conservatives and the *Fortschritt*, or Progressives. From the revolution of 1848 to the war with Austria in 1866 the former, which was preëminently the party of the clergy and of the landed aristocracy of the northern and eastern parts of the kingdom, completely dominated the government and the army. Following the triumph over

Austria, however, Conservative power declined, and there set in the long process of party dissolution and realignment by which German political life was brought to the confused condition in which it was found at the opening of the Great War. To begin with, each of the two original parties broke into two distinct groups. From the Conservatives sprang the *Frei Conservativen*, or Free Conservatives; from the *Fortschritt*, the *National-Liberal-Partei*, or National Liberals. In the one case the new group drew off the more advanced elements of the old one; in the other, the more moderate; so that, in the order of radicalism, the parties of the decade following 1866 were the Conservatives, the Free Conservatives, the National Liberals, and the new *Fortschritt*, or Radicals. Among these four groups Bismarck was able to win for his policy of German unification the support of the two most moderate, that is to say, the second and third. The Conservatives clung to the particularistic régime of earlier days, and the genius of "blood and iron" broke definitely with them in 1866. The Free Conservatives included at the outset simply those elements of the original Conservative party who were willing to follow Bismarck.

Similarly among the Progressives there was division upon the attitude to be taken toward the Bismarckian program. The more radical wing of the party, *i.e.*, that which maintained the name and the policies of the original *Fortschritt*, refused to abandon its opposition to militarism and monarchism, opposed the constitution of 1867 for its illiberality, and withheld from Bismarck's government all substantial support. The larger portion of the party members, however, were willing to subordinate for a time to Bismarck's nationalizing projects the contest which the united *Fortschritt* had long been waging in behalf of constitutionalism. The party of no compromise was strongest in Berlin and the towns of East Prussia. It was almost exclusively Prussian. The National Liberals, on the contrary, early became an essentially German, rather than simply a Prussian, party. Even before 1871 they formed, in point both of numbers and of power, the preponderating party in both Prussia and the Confederation as a whole; and after 1871, when the Nationalists of the southern states cast in their lot with the National Liberals, the party's predominance was assured. Upon the National

Liberals as the party of unity and uniformity Bismarck relied absolutely for support in the upbuilding of the Empire. It was only in 1878, after the party had lost control of the Reichstag, in consequence of the reaction against Liberalism which flowed from the great religious contest known as the Kulturkampf, that the Chancellor was in a position to throw off the not infrequently galling bonds of the Liberal alliance.

Party Development: the Newer Groups. — Meanwhile the field occupied by the various parties that have been named was cut into by a number of newly organized parties and groups. Most important among these were the Clericals, or Center, and the Social Democrats. The origins of the Center may be traced to a project formulated in December, 1870, to found a new party, a party which should be essentially Catholic, and which should have for its purpose the defense of society against radicalism, of the states against the central government, and of the schools against secularization. The party, gaining strength first in the Rhenish and Polish provinces of Prussia and in Bavaria, was able in 1871 to win a total of sixty seats in the Reichstag. Employed by the Catholic clergy during the ensuing decade to maintain the cause of the papacy against the machinations of Bismarck, the party early struck root deeply; and on account of the absolute identification in the public mind of its interests with the interests of the Catholic Church, insuring its preponderance in the states of the south, and also by reason of the fact that it has always been more successful than any of its older rivals in maintaining compactness of organization, it became, and long remained, the strongest numerically of political groups within the Reichstag.

The Social Democratic party was founded in 1869 under the leadership of Wilhelm Liebknecht and August Bebel. In 1863 there had been organized at Leipzig, under the inspiration of the eloquent Marxist Ferdinand Lassalle, a Universal German Workingman's Association. The two bodies were for a time keen rivals, but at a congress held at Gotha, in May, 1875, they (together with a number of other socialistic societies) were merged in one organization, which has continued to this day to be known as the Social Democratic party. The development of socialism in the Empire between 1870 and 1880 was phenomenal. At the parliamentary elections of 1871 the Social Democratic vote was 124,655 (three per cent of the total) and two Social Democrats were returned to the Reichstag. In 1874 the popular vote was 351,952, and nine members were elected; in 1877 it was 493,288, and twelve candidates were successful. The Emperor William I and his Chancellor, Bismarck, as indeed the governing and well-to-do classes generally, viewed the progress of the movement with frankly avowed apprehension. Most of the great projects of the Imperial government were opposed by the Social Democrats, and the members of the party were charged with being enemies of the entire existing order, and even of civilization itself. Two attempts in 1878 upon the life of the Emperor, made by men who were socialists, but disavowed by the socialists as a body, afforded the authorities an opportunity to enter upon a campaign of socialist repression, and from 1878 to 1890 stringent anti-socialist legislation was on the statute-books and was systematically enforced. At the same time that effort was being made to stamp out socialist propaganda a remarkable series of social reforms was undertaken with the purpose not only of promoting the public well-being, but of cutting the ground from under the socialists' feet, or, as some one has observed, of " curing the Empire of socialism by inoculation." The most important steps taken in this direction were the introduction of sickness insurance in 1883, of accident insurance in 1884, and of old-age and invalidity insurance in 1889.

For a time the government's measures seemed to accomplish their purpose, and the official press loudly proclaimed that socialism in Germany was extinct. In reality, however, the cult thrived on persecution. In the hour of Bismarck's apparent triumph the socialist propaganda was being pushed covertly in every corner of the Empire. A party organ known as the *Social Democrat* was published in Switzerland, and thousands of copies found their way every week across the border and were passed from hand to hand among earnest readers and converts. A compact organization was maintained, a treasury was established and kept well filled, and with reason the Social Democrats declare to-day that in no small measure they owe their excellent organization to the Bismarckian era of repression. At the elections of 1878 the party cast only 437,158 votes, but in 1884 its vote was

549,990 (9.7 per cent of the whole) and the contingent of representatives returned to the Reichstag numbered twenty-four. In 1890 the socialist vote attained the enormous total of 1,427,298 (19.7 per cent of the whole), and the number of representatives was increased to thirty-five. Repression was manifestly a failure, and in 1890 the Reichstag, with the sanction of the new emperor, William II, wisely declined to renew the proscriptive statute. Thereafter development went on even more rapidly. In 1893 the popular vote was 1,876,738, and the quota of elected representatives was forty-four; in 1896 the vote was slightly over two millions, and the quota was fifty-seven; in 1903 the vote went beyond three millions (twenty-four per cent of the total, and larger than that of any other single party), and the quota was increased to seventy-nine.

Parties on the Eve of the War. — Without pursuing farther the intricate subject of party history, something may be said concerning the composition and character of parties in recent years, and especially of the great organization which goes under the name of the Social Democracy. The major parties are five in number; Conservative, Center, National Liberal, Radical, and Socialist. As has been explained, the Conservative party finds its leadership and main strength among the great landholders of eastern and northeastern Prussia; its popular support comes chiefly from agricultural wage-earners of these same sections and from public employees, including the railway operatives. The gravest abuse in connection with the conduct of campaigns and elections has been the pressure which the government brought upon the enormous official population to vote Conservative, or, in districts where there was no Conservative candidate, Centrist. This pressure was applied through the local bureaucratic organs, principally the *Landrath* of the *Kreis*, who usually was a youthful official of noble origin, related to some important landed family, and a rigid Conservative. It has been estimated that of late official influence controlled a million votes at every national election. Numerically small, the Conservative party has steadily maintained its position as the most important of all; for it has stood closest to the Prussian government, and has furnished the men who made the Imperial government what it was. Founded on the doctrine of authority as opposed to liberty, dedicated to the defense of the prerogatives of the king-emperor and the privileges of the nobility, it has resolutely resisted every proposal for reform in the political system. It has favored a high protective tariff on agricultural products, a larger navy, increased expenditure on the army, colonial expansion; and for years an influential " Pan-German " element urged many of the measures for German aggrandizement abroad. Opposition to Bismarck's policy of unification disappeared when the advantages of Imperial tariff legislation began to be clearly perceived.

The Center is the party of Catholicism. Founded upon an essentially religious basis, it has always contained both aristocratic and popular elements, and has been perhaps more representative of all classes of people in the Empire than any other party. Its leaders are largely drawn from the Catholic nobility of Silesia and Bavaria, and it finds its chief support among the Catholic peasants of Bavaria and the Catholic workingmen of the Rhine provinces. Geographically, its strength lies principally, therefore, in the south and southwest. The party has no clear-cut program. Its original purpose was largely attained when Bismarck was led to abandon his conflict with the Catholic Church; although the party is ever alert to defend Catholic interests, from whatever direction menaced. It has actively combated socialism, and with a view to winning the laboring classes from that creed has, like the Catholic *Action Libérale* in France, put a good deal of stress on social reforms. Its liberalism, however, is guarded; and while the name which it bears, Center, denotes a middle position between the conservative Right and the radical Left, the party has commonly acted with the Conservatives, partly because of its own innate conservative tendency, partly because the interests of its membership are also to a considerable extent agricultural. An able French observer has said of the party that " it appears to-day much more in the light of a group of clever opportunists, who show a rare genius for defending the temporal interests of Catholicism, rather than a really idealistic party which is systematically endeavoring to find a solution of the great international, political, and social problems of the moment." [1]

[1] Lichtenberger, *Germany and its Evolution in Modern Times*, 185.

Just as Conservatism forms the party of the nobility and of agriculture, the Center the party of the Catholic Church, and Socialism the party of the industrial masses, National Liberalism forms the party of the middle classes, and especially of the industrial leaders and managers. The party finds its strength therefore principally in the industrial districts of the center and west. Historically, it is the party of political reform; and of late it has put much emphasis on the abolition of three-class voting, the reapportionment of seats in the Reichstag, the restriction of clerical influence in education and government, and the suppression of government interference with the free exercise of the suffrage by Imperial and state employees. However, the party has given its best effort to the defense of its economic interests, and in this connection it particularly demands the revision of the tariff downwards on agricultural products, although not, of course, on manufactured goods. It has also supported armaments, colonial expansion, and a vigorous, if not indeed aggressive, foreign policy; and the lords of industry who lead the party bitterly resent the monopoly of civil offices and of command in the army and navy which the landed aristocrats of the Conservative groups enjoy.

The Radicals, or Progressives, are also a middle-class, and largely industrial, party. Except on one matter, they differ from the National Liberals rather in degree than in principle. That matter is the tariff. They would have the Empire abolish all protective duties — in other words, adopt the tariff policy of her great industrial rival, England. Like the National Liberals, they advocate reapportionment of seats, equal voting, and the suppression of clericalism; and they go farther by demanding a complete parliamentary system of government, and also the subordination of the military to the civil power. The party is not the tool of the great German industries in any such degree as is the National Liberal organization; yet it is not a party of the masses in the sense in which that phrase can be applied to the Social Democracy.

The Social Democrats. — Nominally revolutionary, the German Social Democracy comprises in fact a very orderly organization whose economic-political tenets are at many points so rational that they command wide support among people who do not bear the party name. For a generation the party has been growing steadily more practical in its demands and more opportunist in its tactics. Instead of opposing reforms undertaken on the basis of existing institutions, as it once did, in the hope of bringing about the establishment of a socialistic state by one grand *coup*, it labors for such reforms as are considered attainable and contents itself with recurring only occasionally and incidentally to its ultimate ideal. The party is the only one in Germany which has a complete and durable organization, on the English and American plan. The supreme governing authority is a congress composed of six delegates from each electoral district of the Empire, the Socialist members of the Reichstag, and the members of the party's executive committee. This congress meets annually to regulate the organization of the party, to discuss party policies, and to take action upon questions submitted by the party members.

Nominally, the principles of the party are those of Marx, and its platform is the " Erfurt program " of 1891, looking to the abolition of class government and of classes themselves, the termination of every kind of exploitation of labor and oppression of men, the destruction of capitalism, and the establishment of an economic régime under which the production and distribution of goods shall be controlled entirely by the state. The Radical Socialists, *i.e.*, the old-line members of the party, cling to these time-honored articles of faith. But the mass of the younger element of the party, ably led by Edward Bernstein — the " Revisionists," as they call themselves — consider that the Marxist doctrines are in many respects erroneous, and they have been insisting that the Erfurt program should be overhauled and brought into accord with the practical and positive spirit of the party to-day. Except Bebel and Kautsky, every socialist leader of note in Germany in 1914 was identified with the revisionist movement. The political significance of this situation arises from the fact that the " new socialists," long before the war, stood ready to coöperate systematically with progressive elements of whatsoever name or antecedents. Already the socialists of Baden, Württemberg, and Bavaria had voted for the local state budgets and had participated in court functions, and upon numerous occasions they had worked hand in hand, not only at elections but in the Reichstag and in diets and councils, with the National Liberals and the Radicals. For the future of sane liberalism in Germany this trend of the party in the direction of coöperative and constructive effort is auspicious. At the annual congress held at Chemnitz in September, 1912, the issue of revisionism was debated at length and with much feeling, but an open breach was averted and Bebel was again elected party president.

It was shown upon this occasion that the dues-paying membership of the party numbered about nine hundred thousand. This number represented only a fraction of the party's actual popular strength; for at the Reichstag elections of that year (the last that have been held) Socialist candidates polled 4,238,919 votes, or thirty-two per cent of the total, and the party quota of seats rose to 110, or more than one-fourth of the entire number. The popular votes and the quotas of seats of the other leading parties at this time were: Center, 2,012,990 votes, 90 seats; National Liberals, 1,671,297 votes, 45 seats; Radicals, 1,556,549 votes, 42 seats; Conservatives, 1,500,000 votes, 57 seats. When the new Reichstag was convened it was by dexterous "log-rolling" on the part of the Conservative-Clerical *bloc* that the election of Bebel himself to the presidency of the chamber was averted. As it was, a Socialist was chosen first vice-president. The enormous popular vote rolled up by the Socialists is to be accounted for not alone by the fact that the party had become the recognized channel for the expression of working-class discontent, but also by the fact that great numbers of men of the middle class voted with it as the most effective way of protesting against autocracy and militarism.

III. THE MOVEMENT FOR POLITICAL REFORM

Agitation Prior to 1914. — From what has been said it is manifest that the German governmental system has in these past decades by no means escaped criticism at the hands of the German people. The liberalism of 1848, which looked toward manhood suffrage and a parliamentary system of government, never wholly died out. On the contrary, the Socialists and other radicals continuously attacked the Prussian three-class system and, after 1871, the irresponsible position of the Imperial Chancellor and of the Emperor himself. As has been pointed out, the moderate parties have of late demanded equal voting, reapportionment, and ministerial responsibility; and in their Erfurt program the Social Democrats call for a long and remarkable list of political reforms: universal, equal, and direct suffrage by ballot in all elections for all subjects of the Empire over twenty years of age, without distinction of sex; proportional representation; biennial elections to the Reichstag; an annual vote of taxes; direct legislation by the people through the use of the initiative and the referendum; decision of questions of peace and war by the Reichstag; and "self-government by the people in Empire, state, province, and commune."

Since 1900 discussion in all parties has centered mainly around two proposed reforms: the establishment of real (instead of merely nominal) ministerial responsibility to the Reichstag, and the abolition of the Prussian three-class system. The first question was brought unexpectedly to the fore in the autumn of 1908 by the famous *Daily Telegraph* incident. At a moment when the international situation was exceptionally tense over the Casablanca episode there appeared in the London *Daily Telegraph* an account of an interview in which the Emperor declared that while the prevailing sentiment among large sections of the middle and lower classes of his own people was not friendly to England, the German government was well disposed and had actually befriended that country during the South African war. The interview was a masterpiece of indiscretion, and it aroused a storm of disapprobation in Germany such as the Emperor had never before encountered. "A stranger," relates the American ambassador of the time, "might easily have inferred from the tide of public feeling that swept over the Empire that William II was about to be deposed. The serious journals were loud in their protests. The comic papers were remorseless in their caricatures. One would have supposed that there was no law in Germany against *lèse majesté*."[1] At the Wilhelmstrasse it was revealed that the manuscript of the interview had been submitted before publication to the Chancellor, but had been returned to its author unread. For this

[1] Hill, "Impressions of the Kaiser," *Harper's Monthly Mag.*, CXXXVII, 384.

negligence Prince von Bülow was duly apologetic. When, however, the Emperor refused to accept his resignation the minister did not refrain from throwing the final burden on his master by pledging that while he remained Chancellor such personal interference in the conduct of foreign affairs should not be allowed to occur again. "The perception," the Chancellor declared in the Reichstag, "that the publication of these conversations in England has not had the effect the Kaiser wished, and in our own country has caused profound agitation and painful regret, will . . . lead the Kaiser for the future, in private conversation also, to maintain the reserve that is equally indispensable in the interest of a uniform policy and for the authority of the Crown. If it were not so, I could not, nor could my successor, bear the responsibility." Following this announcement, the *Official Gazette* stated that "His Majesty, while unaffected by public criticism which he regards as exaggerated, considers his most honorable Imperial task to consist in securing the stability of the policy of the Empire while adhering to the principle of constitutional responsibility. The Kaiser accordingly indorses the statements of the Imperial Chancellor in the Reichstag, and assures Prince von Bülow of his continued confidence." Chastened by the protests of his long-suffering people, the lordly monarch thus promised to mend his ways, when a less conciliatory policy might have produced revolution. The popular victory — if such it be considered — was, however, hollow. The Reichstag gained no new power; "constitutional responsibility" continued to mean responsibility to the Emperor only; the Chancellor was still to be merely the Emperor's "other self"; the régime of personal diplomacy was not ended, and the issues of war and peace still lay absolutely in the hands of the ill-balanced, irresponsible head of the Prussianized Empire.

The issue was kept alive by a prolonged controversy between the Chancellor and the Reichstag over financial reform. Von Bülow proposed to meet recurring deficits by a new inheritance tax, arranged to fall mainly on the landed and capitalist classes. Rather than approve the plan, the Conservatives deserted their newly acquired allies, the National Liberals, and resumed working relations with the Center; and the revived Blue-Black *bloc* thwarted the reform. The resignation of the Chancellor followed; but, as has been pointed out elsewhere, the act involved no recognition of responsibility to the Reichstag. Von Bülow retired partly because he was unwilling to go on without the tax upon which he had set his heart, but also partly, and perhaps mainly, because he felt that his relations with the Emperor could never again be what they had been before the *Daily Telegraph* affair. During the fiscal controversy the principle of ministerial responsibility was strongly asserted on the floor of the Reichstag. But the new Chancellor, von Bethmann-Hollweg, promptly and fully repudiated it. " A Chancellor dependent only upon the Emperor and the king of Prussia," he declared, " is the necessary counterpoise to the freest of electoral laws, devised by Bismarck on the supposition that the Bundesrath and the Imperial Chancellor would maintain their independence."

In 1913 the question was brought to the front again by the Zabern incident. During a street disturbance in the Alsatian garrison town of Zabern a swaggering lieutenant slashed an unoffending crippled cobbler with his sword. The affair brought the civil and military authorities of Alsace-Lorraine into conflict and aroused indignation among non-militaristic people throughout the Empire. In the Reichstag the Socialists and Radicals, who were in the majority, bitterly assailed the Government; and when the Chancellor announced that the action of the troops would be upheld, they carried a vote of " no confidence " by the heavy majority of 293 to 54. The only result was that the Emperor agreed to order the removal of the offending regiment from Zabern. In a stormy sitting the Reichstag demanded the Chancellor's resignation. But that official declined to recognize that he was in any way responsible to the Reichstag, and coolly declared that he would remain in office as long as the Emperor wished to retain him. A resolution withholding approval of the budget until the resignation should be submitted was narrowly lost; and the matter ended in the usual Government victory.

The movement for reform of the antiquated Prussian electoral system has been described elsewhere,[1] and hence calls for no

[1] See p. 491.

comment here, except to point out that all important proposals on the subject that got before the Landtag up to 1910 were private members' resolutions, foredoomed to failure, and that the Government bill of 1910 was obviously drawn in the hope that it would be defeated, but also in the confidence that, if passed, it would not seriously weaken the citadel of aristocracy and reactionism. The parties that wanted real reform opposed it because it did not go far enough; the conservative elements opposed it because it went too far. Under these circumstances, the end was inevitable.

Discussion of Reform during the War. — Notwithstanding these and many more reverses, Germany seemed in 1914 to be slowly advancing toward a moderate political reconstruction. Then came the war, whose political effect could not be foretold, beyond the probability that if a decisive victory were quickly attained the autocratic, militaristic forces would become yet more solidly intrenched, while a prolonged and indecisive contest, and especially a German defeat, would give liberalism a chance to express itself as perhaps never before. Events worked out substantially on these lines. The first effect of the conflict was to stabilize the government. Criticism and complaint suddenly ceased, and, to the astonishment of many observers, the Social Democrats, with some notable exceptions, voted for the early war budgets and in other ways lent much-needed support. In 1915 some restlessness appeared, and at the beginning of 1916 Chancellor von Bethmann-Hollweg deemed it advisable to appease popular sentiment by promising electoral reform for Prussia, although it was not to be carried out until after the war.

Speaking broadly, both the Prussian and Imperial governments went along until 1917 with little change of personnel and character. Then, however, the scene began to shift rapidly. War-weariness had laid hold of the masses, and both peace propaganda and agitation for government reform got beyond control. Two events, chiefly, crystallized the popular opposition — the Russian revolution and the entrance of the war by the United States. On the day before the Tsar of Russia abdicated (March 15, 1917) Chancellor von Bethmann-Hollweg was constrained to renew in the Landtag the promise of electoral reform, and was obliged to hear from the tribune the prediction of a Socialist member that " a republic was a coming inevitable development in Germany." Two weeks later he said in the Reichstag that the promised reform must not be undertaken while millions of men were in the trenches. But this did not deter the chamber from creating (by a vote of 227 to 33) a special committee of twenty-eight members to consider constitutional reforms, as related not only to the Prussian electoral system but to reapportionment and ministerial responsibility in the Empire; and so stormy became the discussion that the Reichstag was prorogued for a month. In a rescript of April 7 the Emperor himself admitted the necessity of constitutional changes, but insisted that they must await the restoration of peace.

In the early summer of 1917 an acute political crisis arose. On July 6 the Center leader, Erzberger, delivered a sensational speech in the Reichstag main committee, attacking the Pan-German and anti-democratic groups and throwing the weight of his party on the side of the Social Democrats and Radicals in favor of " peace without annexations " and democratic constitutional reform. Confronted by a hostile *bloc*, the Government was now forced to make some move that would at least seem to be a concession to the reform elements. A new pledge of Prussian electoral reform, to be carried out before the next elections, proved insufficient, and three days later Chancellor von Bethmann-Hollweg resigned, the scapegoat of a Government which was trying to stem the tide of public disapproval without in any way departing from his policy. The new Chancellor, Dr. Georg Michaelis, was an inconspicuous bureaucrat, and obviously a puppet in the hands of the military leaders. His first utterances in the Reichstag were anxiously awaited. But they were evasive; and the year passed with much further discussion, but without definite progress. In October, Michaelis was succeeded in the chancellorship by Count von Hertling, a Bavarian (the first of German chancellors who was not a Prussian); but, while the new official's choice was at first regarded as a concession to liberalism, no real reason for such a supposition subsequently appeared. During the winter of 1917–1918 strikes were organized in Prussia as protests against the dilatory tactics of the Government in dealing with electoral reform; but they were suppressed without result. In the spring of 1918 the movement seemed to go backwards rather than forwards. Inspired with fresh arrogance by the humiliation of Russia in the Brest-Litovsk treaty and by the success of the new "drive" on the western front, the Prussian reactionaries repudiated the Emperor's pledges and carried, in the lower branch of the Landtag, by a substantial majority, a bill substituting an elaborate six-class electoral scheme for the promised plan of equal suffrage.

Political Changes in the Hour of Defeat. — The last chapter in the history of the reform movement, prior to the collapse of the Central Powers and the signing of the German armistice, November 11, 1918, is the most curious of all. The tide of battle was now running strongly in favor of the Entente nations; German statesmen instinctively felt the end to be near; and the central feature of the constitutional discussion became the earnest, even frantic, effort of the Imperial authorities to convince the world, and especially President Wilson, that reforms were under way which would make the German government thoroughly representative of the people, if indeed it had not already acquired that character. The primary object, of course, was to persuade the American Executive that the urgent correspondence concerning peace which was about to begin was with a Government entirely different from that with which he had declared himself unwilling to treat. In early September Chancellor von Hertling made a sensational speech before the ultra-conservative constitution committee of the Prussian House of Lords, ardently advocating electoral reform and in effect declaring that the survival of the Hohenzollern dynasty was at stake. At the end of the month he was himself superseded in the chancellorship by Prince Maximilian of Baden, whose appointment was expected to have considerable effect, because of his reputation for somewhat liberal opinions. The simultaneous appointment of two Socialists to ministerial posts was also not without purpose. On September 30 the Emperor issued a proclamation in which he professed a desire that the German people should "coöperate more effectively than hitherto in deciding the fate of the Fatherland." On October 2 the world was informed that the Prussian upper chamber had passed the franchise bill, so amended as to provide for direct and equal suffrage. Various announcements were made looking to a system of ministerial responsibility to the Reichstag. And finally, the Bundesrath voted a constitutional amendment depriving the Emperor of the power to declare war without the consent of both Bundesrath and Reichstag, "except in the case where the Imperial territory has already been invaded or its coasts attacked."

Thus Germany, sore beset by Marshal Foch's armies without and by incipient revolution within, sought to purge itself in the eyes of the world. How sincere were the expressions and the actions of the aristocrats and militarists will probably never be fully known. For the steps that led to the complete acknowledgment of defeat and to the cessation of hostilities were accompanied by a political collapse which threatened to drag down to ruin old and new governmental machinery alike. The declaration of Prince Maximilian in the Reichstag, just before the surrender, that the changes of the preceding month had "put full control in the hands of the people" must be accepted with much reservation. The task was not so simple; and much that had been done bore the appearance rather of dumb-show than of real reform. At all events, the chapter was merely opened rather than closed. For as these pages go to print, William II and the former Crown Prince, having renounced their Imperial rights, are cowering in the shelter of a Dutch château; a dozen lesser German monarchs have abdicated their thrones; republics have been set up in Bavaria, Baden, and Saxony; a Socialist, who was once a saddle-maker, has assumed the chancellorship; workmen's and soldiers' councils have taken over control of cities and of industries; and a movement is under way to convert the whole Empire into a republic. The pillars of absolutism seem to be overthrown, and aristocratic privilege to lie in the dust. Only time can tell what order of things will rise out of the ruins.

SELECTED REFERENCES

A. L. Lowell, *Governments and Parties in Continental Europe* (New York, 1896), II, Chap. vii; F. K. Krüger, *Government and Politics of the German Empire* (Yonkers, 1915), Chap. xvii; H. Lichtenberger, *Germany and its Evolution in Modern Times* (New York, 1913), Bk. II, Chap. v; H. Perris,

Germany and the German Emperor (New York, 1912), Chaps. viii, xi; A. E. Zimmern, *Nationality and Government* (New York, 1918), Chaps. i, xiv; J. H. Rose, *Nationality in Modern History* (New York, 1916), Chap. vii; J. S. Schapiro, *Modern and Contemporary European History* (Boston, 1918), Chap. xii; F. A. Ogg, *Economic Development of Modern Europe* (New York, 1917), Chap. xxii; S. P. Orth, *Socialism and Democracy in Europe* (New York, 1913), Chaps. vii–viii; R. Hunter, *Socialists at Work* (New York, 1908), Chaps. i, viii; W. W. Willoughby, "The Prussian Theory of Monarchy," *Amer. Polit. Sci. Review*, Nov., 1917; ibid., *Prussian Political Philosophy* (New York, 1918); J. Dewey, *German Philosophy and Politics* (New York, 1915); H. W. C. Davis, *The Political Thought of Heinrich von Treitschke* (London, 1914); E. A. B. Hodgetts, *The House of Hohenzollern* (New York, 1911); S. Shaw, *William of Germany* (New York, 1913); W. von Schierbrand [ed.], *The Kaiser's Speeches* (New York, 1903); F. W. Wile, *Men around the Kaiser* (Philadelphia, 1913); E. Wetterlé, *Behind the Scenes in the Reichstag* (New York, 1918); B. von Bülow, *Imperial Germany*, trans. by M. Lewenz (New York, 1914); R. H. Fife, *The German Empire between Two Wars* (New York, 1916); E. B. Bax, *German Culture, Past and Present* (London, 1915); K. L. Krause, *What is the German Nation Dying For?* (New York, 1918); W. H. Dawson, *What is Wrong with Germany?* (New York, 1915); G. S. Fullerton, *Germany To-day* (New York, 1915); J. W. Gerard, *My Four Years in Germany* (New York, 1917).

CHAPTER XXVI

AUSTRIA-HUNGARY AND ITS GOVERNMENT

The Rise of Habsburg Dominion. — In the throne room of the Hofburg at Vienna, the most ancient and picturesque of royal residences in Europe, the eye meets, here and there, embossed or in intricately intertwined gilt lettering, the mystic dictum of the Habsburgs — A E I O U. The symbol was adopted by King Frederick III in 1443, and stands for the proud prophecy, *Austria erit in orbe ultima* — " Austria will last forever." [1] In these later days the motto seems an idle boast; for while there will still be some sort of an Austria after Europe is remade, the Empire bids fair to have been shorn of most of its territory, population, prestige, and power. Nevertheless, the remarkable thing about the Habsburg dominion is not that it has fallen in pieces under our very eyes, but that it has managed to last so long in reasonable vigor — in other words, that the Hofburg prediction has come so near being fulfilled. Probably no great political creation ever survived for four hundred years on a foundation so insecure.

The key to Austrian government and politics, as well as the explanation for the impending break-up, is supplied by the racial complexity of the country's population, and by the resulting conflicts of uncongenial and irreconcilable peoples. Prior to the Great War the ramshackle dominion of the aged Francis Joseph included one-sixteenth of the area, and one-eighth of the population, of all Europe. It formed one of the six so-called great European powers. It had been brought up to this magnitude, however, not by a natural expansion and amalgamation such as produced the modern English, French, and American nations, but by chance inheritances, ruthless conquests, unscrupulous diplomacy, and other means which took no cognizance of the

[1] Schierbrand, *Austria-Hungary: the Polyglot Empire*, 26.

traditions and wishes of the peoples affected. To the last it remained a dominion created by force and by craft, and upheld by terrorism and intrigue. It would be futile to attempt to tell here the whole story of the growth of the Habsburg power. A few main facts will afford sufficient background for a description of recent governmental and political conditions.

The original *Osterreich* (eastern "empire," or "dominion"), *i.e.*, Austria, was a mark, or border county, lying along the south bank of the Danube, east of the Enns, and founded by Charlemagne (771-814) as a bulwark of the Frankish kingdom against the Slavs. In the twelfth century the mark was raised to a duchy, and in 1276 it passed by conquest into the hands of Rudolph of Habsburg, who three years earlier had gained, by election, the throne of the Holy Roman Empire. Hitherto, Rudolph and his ancestors had lorded it over only a petty district of some two hundred square miles. But now the family fortunes began to rise. Territories were lost on the west to the Swiss cantons, but eastward and southward there were steady accessions. In 1453 the duchy was raised to the rank of an archduchy, and four years later, when the Austrian branch of the ruling dynasty became extinct, the Styrian branch came in, bringing with them not only Styria itself but Carinthia, Carniola, the Tyrol, and the important city of Trieste. The greatest acquisitions, however, were Hungary and Bohemia. The former, after alternately falling under and out of Habsburg control for upwards of a century, was definitely brought into a personal union with Austria in 1526. The latter, after also being held temporarily once or twice by right of inheritance, was, in the same year, induced by fear of a Turkish subjugation to enter into what purported to be a free federation and to elect the Austrian archduke king. Promises of autonomy were freely given the new lands, but were promptly broken. To the amazement of the Bohemians, the new common sovereign — the Archduke Ferdinand, later Emperor Ferdinand I — proclaimed the Bohemian crown hereditary in the Habsburg family, and for a hundred years the country was ruled with little regard for the interests and wishes of its people. An uprising in 1618 had no effect save to precipitate the great civil and international conflict known as the Thirty Years' War and to bring upon Bohemia itself fresh disaster.

For two more centuries the country lay under the heel of the Habsburg oppressor, " a land of desolation, her peasants serfs, her native nobility destroyed and expropriated, her rights and prerogatives denied and disregarded." The experience of Hungary was similar. The Hungarians, who have ever been noted for their love of independence, clung desperately to their nationality, and even kept up the forms of an elected kingship. At intervals they, or some of them, threw off the Austrian yoke completely. But after the close of the seventeenth century the union was unbroken, and in 1687 the Hungarian crown was officially declared hereditary in the Habsburg family. Notwithstanding repeated oaths to preserve the Hungarian constitution intact, even the " enlightened despots," Maria Theresa (1740–1780) and her son, Joseph II (1780–1790), curtailed the privileges of the subject nation as much as they dared.

The Polyglot Empire. — Set in the midst of a whirlpool of races, the old Austrian duchy became, by centuries of conquest and expansion, the polyglot dominion which has been a chief danger-spot of Europe throughout our own times. On the eve of the Great War, the scepter of the Emperor-King extended over at least twenty different races or fragments of races, falling into four main groups: German, Slavic, Magyar, and Latin. The original Austria was, of course, German; and to this day the wealthiest and best educated elements in the Empire are German.[1] The Germans have also been the ruling element, and they have always proceeded on the assumption that the Empire is, or at all events is to be made, a German country. In 1910, however, the Germans, numbering twelve millions, comprised only a little more than twenty-five per cent of the population. They occupied almost solidly the older portions of Austria proper (Upper Austria, Salsburg, Vorarlberg, etc.), formed a strong minority in Bohemia, and were found in considerable colonies in Hungary. More than forty-seven per cent of the aggregate population was Slavic, the number being twenty-four and one-fourth millions. One great group of Slavs lived mainly in the north; another in the south. In the north were (1) the eight

---

[1] This chapter must deal with the Dual Monarchy as it was in the summer of 1918, before the changes which set in in the more recent period of military collapse, territorial disintegration, and political upheaval.

and one-half million Czechoslovaks, in Bohemia, Moravia, Austrian Silesia, and northern Hungary; (2) the five million Poles, in northwestern Galicia and in Silesia; and (3) the four million Ruthenians, in eastern Galicia and in Bukowina. In the south were (1) the one and one-fourth million Slovenes, in Carniola, Görz, Gradisca, and Istria, and (2) the five and one-half million Serbo-Croats, in Croatia, Slavonia, Bosnia, and Dalmatia. The ten million Magyars were the Hungarians proper, descendants of the conquering Turanian hosts that at the close of the ninth century swept down into the lowlands of the Theiss and middle Danube and drove a permanent wedge into what otherwise would have been solidly Slavic soil. Encircled and outnumbered by Slavs, the Magyar kept his weaker neighbors under his heel for a thousand years, even after he had himself sacrificed his independence to German power as represented in the Habsburg government. The principal peoples of Latin stock were (1) the seven hundred and fifty thousand Italians and Ladini, in Tyrol, Görz, Gradisca, Dalmatia, and Trieste, and (2) the three and one-fourth million Rumans (Rumanians), in Transylvania and Bukowina. It must not be supposed that each of these racial elements occupies an altogether compact or contiguous territory. In many great regions, as Bohemia and Moravia, two or more peoples are inextricably intermingled; and there are numerous "enclaves," *i.e.*, districts inhabited by one race, while the whole surrounding country is inhabited by another.

In this remarkable heterogeneity of race lay, obviously, a vast political problem. Two courses were open to the Habsburgs: (1) to accept the situation as it was, permit the several peoples to retain their autonomy, and be content with an imperial state which should be a federation, with Austria proper as only one of the leading members, or (2) to deny local autonomy, thrust Austrian rule upon a mass of powerless "subjects," centralize and Germanize without mercy. Unfortunately the latter course was chosen; and, century after century, the Vienna authorities strove to force the many discordant peoples into one huge mass, devoid of all individual traits. Ancient constitutions were overthrown; autonomous governments were curbed or suppressed; education was restricted and kept under close surveillance; the press was regulated, in some cases almost to the point of extinction; the use of non-Germanic languages in official circles, or even in the schools, was prohibited; nationalist aspirations were frowned upon, nationalist demands denied, and nationalist uprisings ruthlessly suppressed.

It is hardly necessary to say that the results aimed at were not attained. Racial groups refused to be broken up and racial interests to be forgotten. On the contrary, the greater peoples — Czechs, Poles, Magyars, and others — clung to their ancient rights and lost no opportunity to strike a blow in their defense. Even such "submerged" elements as the Rumans and the Italians stood out as distinct and unyielding in 1914 as three hundred years earlier. It goes without saying that this complexity of population has given color to all Austrian history. It has been the controlling factor in party alignments, in legislation, in local administration, and in the discussion of political reform. More than anything else, it brought about the peculiarly vexatious and indefensible Austro-Hungarian system of government by, and in the interest of, privileged minorities.

The Dual Monarchy: Constitutional Basis. — All of the peoples and territories that have been mentioned are gathered in one or the other of two great political divisions, the Empire of Austria and the Kingdom of Hungary; and it will meet our present purpose to take some account of, first, the nature of the union existing between these two lands, and, second, the systems of government hitherto operating in each. "If," says an American writer, "France has been a laboratory for political experiments, Austria-Hungary is a museum of political curiosities, but it contains nothing so extraordinary as the relation between Austria and Hungary themselves."[1] At the opening of the nineteenth century Hungary was governed nominally under her ancient constitution, as a land united with Austria only through the crown. But in point of fact the autocratic system which lay like a blanket upon the Austrian territories proper extended to Hungary as well; and throughout the long period of political stagnation covered by the ministry of the reactionary Metternich (1809–1848) the diet was rarely summoned, the Viennese monarch did not even take the trouble to be separately crowned at Budapest as the constitution enjoined, and the privi-

[1] Lowell, *Governments and Parties in Continental Europe*, I, 177.

leges of the people were ruthlessly trampled under foot. After 1840 a vigorous Liberal party arose, whose program eventually came to comprise autonomy for the country, a responsible ministry, fuller representation in the diet, and control by the diet of all public expenditures. But the great uprising prompted by the revolutions of 1848 failed, and in the reaction the country lost every vestige of its constitutional system, its diet, its local self-government, and much of its territory. Such lands as remained were cut into five districts, to be administered separately, largely by German officials, from Vienna. So far as possible, all traces of the historic Hungarian nationality were obliterated.

The decade following the suppression of the revolutions was, in both Austria and Hungary, a period of political torpor. Embarrassed by financial difficulties and harassed by the ill-concealed hostility of the oppressed nationalities, the Vienna government struggled desperately to maintain the *status quo* as against the many forces that would have overthrown it. For a time the effort was successful, but toward the close of the period a swift decline of Imperial prestige, caused mainly by ill-chosen policy during the Crimean war and by the loss of Lombardy in 1859, compelled the adoption of a more conciliatory policy. In 1860 new powers were bestowed on the provincial diets, and the Hungarian political system, swept away in 1849, was restored. In 1861 a fresh " patent " made provision for a united parliament, to be composed of deputies elected by the provincial diets, to sit at Vienna, and to exercise substantial powers of legislation and finance. The subject nationalities, however, were not satisfied, and least of all the Magyars, whose " minimum program " was full autonomy. Not a common parliament, but a national parliament with ample powers, was what was wanted. Determined to press their advantage, the Magyars refused to send deputies to the Vienna assemblage; whereupon their own lately restored diet was dissolved and the country was put practically in a state of siege.

For four years the deadlock continued. As time went by, however, it became clear that Austria would have to surrender, and at last the Emperor was brought to the point where he was willing, by a fresh recognition of Hungarian nationality, to supply the indispensable condition of reconciliation. In June, 1865, he paid a visit to the Hungarian capital, where he was received with unexpected enthusiasm, and in September the patent of 1861 — which, indeed, the Hungarians had refused to allow to be put into execution — was suspended. Negotiations were then set on foot looking toward a fresh trial of constitutionalism. Proceedings were interrupted, in 1866, by the Austro-Prussian war, but in the following year they were pushed to a conclusion. In anticipation of the international outbreak which came in June, 1866, the Magyar leader, Deák, had reworked a program of conciliation drawn up in the spring of 1865, holding it in readiness to be used as a basis of negotiation in the event of an Austrian triumph, and as an ultimatum in the event of an Austrian defeat. The Austrians, as it proved, were swiftly and decisively defeated, and by this development the Hungarians, as Deák had hoped would be the case, were given a highly advantageous position. Humiliated by her expulsion from a confederation which she had been accustomed to dominate, Austria, after the Peace of Prague (August 20, 1866), was no longer in a position to defy the wishes of the disaffected subject state. On the contrary, the necessity of consolidating her resources was never greater.

On July 3 occurred the disaster at Sadowa. Twelve days later the Emperor summoned Deák to Vienna and put to him squarely the question, What does Hungary want? On July 17 he gave provisional assent to the main features of the Deák *projet* and named Count Julius Andrassy premier of the first responsible ministry in modern Hungarian history. The working out of the details of the settlement fell chiefly to two men — Deák, representing the Hungarian Liberals, and Baron Beust, formerly chief minister of the king of Saxony, but in 1866 brought to Vienna and made Austrian chancellor and minister-president. After prolonged negotiation a *projet*, differing from the original one of Deák in few respects save that the unity of the monarchy was more carefully safeguarded, was made ready to be acted upon by the parliaments of the two states. On February 17, 1867, the Andrassy ministry was formed at Budapest, and on May 29, by a vote of 209 to 89, the terms of the *Ausgleich* (Compromise) were given formal approval by the Diet. At Vienna the Reichsrath would have been disposed to reject the arrangement but for the fact that Beust held out as an inducement the reëstablishment of the constitutional system in Austria set up in 1848. The upshot was that the Reichsrath added some features by which the *projet* was still farther liberalized, and at the same time made provision for the rehabilitation of the Imperial patent of 1861. During the summer two deputations of fifteen members each, representing the respective parliaments, drew up a plan of financial adjustment between the two states; and by acts of December 21-24 final approval was given on both sides to the whole body of agreements. Already, on June 8, in the great cathedral at Buda, Francis Joseph had been crowned Apostolic King of Hungary, and the separate royal succession under the terms of the Pragmatic Sanction of 1713, after eighteen years of suspension, had been definitely resumed.

The Dual Monarchy : the Joint Government. — The underlying principle of the *Ausgleich* is dualism, rather than either absolute unity or subjection of an inferior to a superior state. Under the name Austria-Hungary was set up, indeed, a novel type of state consisting of an empire and a kingdom, each of which, retaining its identity unimpaired, stands in law upon a plane of complete equality with the other. Each has its own constitution, its own parliament, its own ministry, its own administration, its own courts, its own official language. Yet the two have but one sovereign and one flag, and within certain large and important fields the governmental machinery and public policy of the two are maintained in common. The laws which form the basis of the arrangement are the product of international compact. They provide no mode of amendment, and hence can be changed only in the manner in which they were adopted, *i.e.*, by international agreement, supplemented by reciprocal parliamentary enactment.

Of common organs of government there are three : (1) the monarch ; (2) the ministries of Foreign Affairs, War, and Finance ; and (3) the " Delegations." The functions and prerogatives of the monarch are threefold, *i.e.*, those which he possesses as emperor of Austria, those which belong to him as king of Hungary, and those vested in him as head of the Austro-Hungarian union. In theory, and largely in practice, the three sets of relationships are clearly distinguished. All, however, must be combined in the same individual ; there is but one law of succession. But

there is a coronation at Vienna and another at Budapest; the
royal title reads, " Emperor of Austria, King of Bohemia, etc.,
and Apostolic King of Hungary "; and the relations of the sovereign with each of the two governments are most of the time conducted precisely as if the other of the two were non-existent. In
the capacity of dual sovereign the monarch's principal functions
are the command of the army and navy, the appointment of heads
of the joint ministries, the promulgation of ordinances applying
to the states in common, and the exercise of a power of veto upon
measures passed by the dual legislative body.

By the Compromise of 1867 the three departments of administration which most obviously require concentration and uniformity were reorganized upon a joint basis. The first is the ministry of Foreign Affairs. Neither Austria nor Hungary, as such,
maintains diplomatic intercourse with other powers. Under the
direction of the Foreign Minister (known, until 1871, as the
Imperial Chancellor) all dealings with foreign governments are
carried on through a diplomatic and consular service representing
the monarchy as a whole. The second ministry is that of War.
After 1867 military and naval administration continued, however, to be a prolific source of misunderstanding between the two
states. The *Ausgleich* vested supreme command of the army and
navy in the joint monarch. Yet the armed establishments of the
states are maintained under separate, even if approximately identical, laws; and each is placed under the immediate supervision
of a separate minister of national defense. Each country has
had its own arrangements for the raising of the yearly contingent
of recruits. It is only after the quotas have been raised that
the dual monarch can exercise his power of appointing officers
and regulating the organization of the forces. The authority
of the joint war minister is confined largely to matters of secondary importance, such as equipment and the commissariat.
Only a close understanding between the ministries at Vienna and
Budapest can be depended upon, in the last analysis, to avert
an utter breakdown of the entire military establishment.

The third common ministry is Finance. Each of the two states
maintains an independent finance ministry and carries its own
budget, because, within certain limitations, the administration
of fiscal matters is left to the states in their separate capacities;

but questions of joint expenditure, the preparation of the joint budget, and the examination of accounts are committed to a common ministry at Vienna. The powers of the joint minister of finance are, in point of fact, limited. Like the other joint ministers, he cannot be a member of either the Austrian or the Hungarian cabinet, nor may he have access to the separate parliaments. His function is essentially that of a cashier, being largely confined to receiving the contributions made by the two states to the common expenses and handing them over to the several departments. Common expenditures are met, as far as possible, from the joint revenues, especially the customs, and common outlays in excess of these revenues are borne by the states in a proportion fixed at decennial intervals by the Reichsrath and the Hungarian Parliament. Other joint interests of an economic nature — trade, customs, the debt, and railway policy — are likewise readjusted at ten-year intervals. In respect to contributions, the arrangement originally hit upon was that all common deficits should be made up by quotas proportioned to the tax returns of the two countries, namely, Austria 70 per cent and Hungary 30 per cent. The periodic overhauling of the economic relationships of the two states has been productive of frequent and disastrous controversy. The task was accomplished successfully in 1878, and again in 1887. But the readjustment due in 1897 had the curious fortune to be delayed until the year in which another readjustment was due, *i.e.*, 1907. At that date the Hungarian quota was raised to 36.4 per cent.

All legislative power of the Reichsrath and of the Hungarian Parliament, in so far as it relates to the joint affairs of the states, is exercised by two " delegations," one representing each of the two parliaments. The Austrian Delegation consists of sixty members, twenty of whom are chosen by the upper chamber from its own members, and the other forty of whom are elected by the lower chamber in such manner that the deputies from each province designate a number of delegates allotted to them by law. The Hungarian Delegation consists likewise of sixty members, twenty elected by and from the upper, forty by and from the lower, chamber, with the further requirement that there shall be included four of the Croatian members of the Chamber of Deputies and one of the Croatians in the Chamber of Magnates.

All members of both Delegations are elected annually and may be reëlected. The bodies must be convened by the Emperor-King at least once a year. Every device is employed to lay emphasis upon the absolute equality of the two Delegations, and of the states they represent, even to the extent of having the sessions held alternately in Vienna and Budapest. The two bodies meet in separate chambers, each under a president whom it elects, and the proposals of the Government are laid before them by the joint ministry. In the Austrian Delegation all proceedings are in the German language; in the Hungarian, in Magyar; and all communications between the two are couched in both tongues. In the event of a failure to agree after a third exchange of communications all of the Delegates may be brought together in joint session, but only to vote, not to debate. The powers of the Delegations are limited. They in no case extend beyond the common affairs of the two states; and they comprise little more than the voting of supplies asked by the Government and a certain supervision of the common administrative machinery. Of legislative power, in the proper sense, the two bodies have virtually none. Practically all law in the dual monarchy takes the form of statutes enacted concurrently by the separate parliaments of Austria and Hungary. The system is not ideal. It involves delay, confusion, and an excess of partisan wrangling. Probably upon no other basis, however, would even the semblance of an Austro-Hungarian union be possible. The arrangement has operated somewhat to the advantage of Hungary, because the Hungarian Delegation, being homogeneous, votes as a unit, whereas the Austrian is composed of mutually hostile racial and political groups.

The Austrian Constitution: Emperor and Ministers. — The fundamental law of the Austrian Empire,[1] in so far as it has been reduced to writing, exists in the form of a series of diplomas, patents, and statutes covering, in all, a period of some two hundred years. Of these instruments the most important are:

[1] It should be emphasized that the phrase "Austrian Empire," properly used, denotes Austria alone. Hungary is no part of the Empire. Throughout this chapter effort is made to avoid inaccuracy of expression by referring to Austria-Hungary as the "dual monarchy," or simply as "the monarchy." The nomenclature of the Austro-Hungarian union is cumbersome, but therein it merely reflects the character of the union itself.

(1) the Pragmatic Sanction of the Emperor Charles VI, promulgated originally April 19, 1713, and in final form in 1724, which regulates the succession to the throne; (2) the Pragmatic Patent of the Emperor Francis II August 1, 1804, which confers upon the sovereign the Imperial title; (3) the diploma of the Emperor Francis Joseph, October 20, 1860, which introduced the principle of constitutional government; (4) the patent of Francis Joseph, February 26, 1861, which regulated in detail the nature of this government; and (5) a series of five fundamental laws (*Staatsgrundgesetze*) dated December 21, 1867, comprising a revision and extension of the patent of 1861. In a narrower sense, indeed, the constitution may be said to consist of these five last-mentioned documents, all of which were sanctioned by the crown as a part of the same general settlement that produced the *Ausgleich*. Of them, one is essentially a bill of rights; a second is concerned with Imperial representation; a third provides for the establishment of the Reichsgericht, or Imperial court; a fourth covers the subject of the judiciary; and a fifth deals with the exercise of administrative and executive powers. All parts of the written constitution are subject to amendment at the hands of the Imperial Parliament, or Reichsrath, by a two-thirds vote in both houses. Since 1873 several amendments have been adopted, the most important being those of 1896 and 1907 concerning the election of representatives.

All natives of the lands represented in the Reichsrath have a common Austrian citizenship; and, as has been stated, one of the five fundamental laws of 1867 is devoted to citizens' rights. All citizens, it is declared, are equal before the law. Public office is open equally to all. Freedom of passage of persons and property, within the territory of the state, is guaranteed, as is both liberty of person and inviolability of property. Every one is declared free to choose his occupation and to prepare himself for it in such place and manner as he may desire. The right of petition is recognized; likewise, under legal regulation, that of assemblage and of the formation of associations. Freedom of speech and of the press, under legal regulation, and liberty of religion and of conscience are guaranteed to all. Science and its teaching is declared free. One has but to recall the repression of individual liberty and initiative which prevailed in the era of

Metternich to understand why, when the Austrian state was being liberalized under the constitution of 1867, it should have been deemed desirable to put into the fundamental law these and other guarantees of personal right and privilege. It must be added, however, that in practice these well-sounding pledges have not always been observed, especially when questions arose involving the personal immunities of citizens of Slavic or other non-German race.

The sovereign authority of the Empire is vested in the Emperor, and the fundamental law frankly declares him "sacred, inviolable, and irresponsible." Duties are assigned to the ministers, and privileges are granted to the legislative bodies; but all powers not expressly bestowed elsewhere remain with the Emperor as supreme head of the state. These Imperial powers are, it is true, exercised largely through ministers who are declared responsible for the constitutionality and legality of governmental acts performed within their respective spheres, and nominally, the parliamentary system prevails, as in Great Britain, France, and Italy. Actually, however, cabinet government operates in a very halting fashion, and the ministers stand in much closer relation to the Emperor than to the chambers. There are two principal reasons for this. One is the multiplicity of parties and party groups, which, in Austria as in France and Italy, interferes with the smooth operation of parliamentarism. A second more serious but closely related reason is the enormous number of racial divisions and the prevalence of deadlocks and obstructionism incidental to ceaseless racial controversy. There are not only Clericals, Liberals, Radicals, Agrarians, and Social Democrats, but *German* Clericals, *Czech* Clericals, *Slovene* Clericals, *Italian* Clericals, and so on, in ramifications of racial-political division which become inextricable. At the elections of 1911 the 516 seats in the popular chamber were sought by some three thousand candidates, representing not fewer than fifty-one parties and factions, and second ballotings, made necessary by lack of majorities at the first ballotings, were held in almost two-thirds of the constituencies. Obviously, in a situation such as this no party group can be sufficiently powerful to govern alone, and no party alignment can long be kept intact. The consequence is that the Imperial authorities can easily play off one element against another and secure their own way, and that, in practice, the responsibility of the ministers to the chambers amounts to little.

The Reichsrath. — The Reichsrath, or Parliament, consists of two houses, the upper being known as the Herrenhaus, or House of Lords, the lower as the Abgeordnetenhaus, or House of Representatives. The Herrenhaus contains a variable number of members, part of whom sit by *ex officio* right, part by hereditary right, and part by special Imperial appointment. Since 1907 the power of the Emperor to create life peers has been limited by the requirement that the number of such peers in the chamber shall never fall below 150 nor rise above 170. The total membership is, as a rule, about 270. None of the members are elected, even indirectly; and the body is one of the most aristocratic and reactionary to be found in Europe. The lower house, as organized in 1867, was made up of 203 representatives, apportioned among the several provinces and chosen by the provincial diets. The system worked poorly, and a law of 1868 authorized the voters of a province to elect the stipulated quota of representatives in the event that the diet failed to do so. Still there was difficulty, arising largely from the racial rivalries in the provinces, and by an amendment of 1873 the right of election was vested directly in the people. The number of members was at the same time increased to 353, though without modifying the proportion of representatives of the various provinces. Further amendment, in 1896, brought up the membership to 425, where it remained, until 1907, when it was raised to the present figure, 516. Originally no limit was fixed for the period of service of parliamentary representatives. The life of a Reichsrath, and consequently the tenure of the individual deputy, was terminated only by a dissolution. By amendment of 1873, however, members are now elected for a term of six years. They receive a stipend of 20 crowns (about $4.00) for each day's attendance, with an allowance for traveling expenses.

The fundamental law prescribes that the Reichsrath shall be convened annually, " during the winter months when possible." The Emperor appoints the president and vice-president of the Herrenhaus; the Abgeordnetenhaus elects its own officers.

As a rule, sessions are open to the public. Bills may be introduced either by the minister in behalf of the Government or by private members; but the Emperor and his representatives so dominate the entire governmental system that private members' bills rarely become law. Measures pass by majority vote; but no act is valid unless at the time of its passage there are present in the lower house as many as 100 members, and in the upper house as many as 40. A curious provision is that if, on a question of appropriation or of the size of a military contingent, no agreement can be reached between the two houses, the smallest figure approved by either house shall be regarded as voted. By decree of the Emperor the Reichsrath may be adjourned at any time, or the lower chamber dissolved. Ministers and chiefs of the central administration are entitled to take part in the deliberations of both houses, and to present their proposals personally or through representatives. Each house may, indeed, require a minister's attendance. According to the fundamental law of 1867, the Reichsrath's powers extend to all matters relating to the rights, obligations, and interests of the provinces represented in the chambers, in so far as these matters are not required to be handled conjointly with the proper representatives of the Hungarian portion of the monarchy. The Reichsrath examines and ratifies or rejects commercial treaties, and likewise political treaties which place a fiscal burden on the Empire or any portion of it, impose obligations upon individual citizens, or involve any change of territorial status. It makes provision for the military and naval establishments. It enacts the budget and approves all taxes and duties. It regulates the monetary system, banking, trade, and communication. It legislates on citizenship, public health, individual rights, education, criminal justice and police administration, the duties and interrelations of the provinces, and a wide variety of other things. It exercises the right of legalizing or annulling Imperial ordinances which, under urgent circumstances, may be promulgated by the Emperor with provisional force of law when the chambers are not in session. Such ordinances may not introduce any alteration in the fundamental law, impose any lasting burden upon the treasury, or alienate territory. They must be issued, if issued at all, under the signature of all of the ministers, and they lose their legal force if the Government does not lay them before the lower chamber within the first four weeks of its next ensuing session, or if either of the two houses refuses its assent thereto. Each of the houses may interpellate the ministers upon all matters within the scope of their powers, may investigate the administrative acts of the Government, may demand information from the ministers concerning petitions presented to the houses, may appoint commissions, to which the ministers must give all necessary information, and may give expression to its views in the form of addresses or resolutions. Any minister may be impeached by either house. On paper, the Reichsrath seems to be a fully-equipped parliamentary assemblage, insuring substantial popular control of governmental policy. In point of fact, however, it is aristocratic in temper, sharply divided on racial and party lines, alternately desultory and tempestuous in its proceedings, and altogether a fit tool of the Habsburg monarchs in the attainment of their arbitrary, dynastic policies.

The Electoral System. — With the introduction of constitutional government, and of an elective parliamentary body, in 1867 a problem of peculiar and growing difficulty was found in the suffrage. There were three main complicating factors: first, the conflicting claims of the several provinces among which parliamentary representatives were to be distributed; second, the ambitions of the different racial elements for parliamentary power; and, third, the utter lack of experience and of traditions on the part of the Austrian peoples in the matter of democratic government. When, in 1873, the right of electing deputies was withdrawn from the provincial diets it was conferred, without the establishment of a new electorate, upon those elements of the provincial populations which had been accustomed to take part in the election of the local diets. These were four in number: (1) the great landowners, comprising those who paid a certain land tax, varying in the several provinces from 50 to 250 florins ($20 to $100), and including women and corporations; (2) the cities, in which the franchise was extended to all males of twenty-four who paid a direct tax of ten gulden annually; (3) chambers of commerce and of industry; and (4) rural communes, in which the qualifications for voting were the same as in the cities. To each of these curiæ, or classes, the law of 1873 assigned a number of parliamentary representatives, to be elected thereafter in each province directly by the voters of the respective classes, rather than indirectly through the diets. The number of voters in each class and the relative importance of the individual voter varied enormously. In 1890, in the class of landowners there was one deputy to every 63 voters; in the chambers of commerce, one to every 27; in the cities, one to every 2918; and in the rural districts, one to every 11,600.

The system was, of course, grossly undemocratic. During the ministry of Count Taaffe (1879-1893) there was strong demand for a new electoral law, and in 1893, the premier brought forward a reform measure which, had it been enacted, would have transferred the bulk of political power to the working classes. The bill did not provide for the general, equal, and direct suffrage which the radicals wanted, and by which the number of voters would have been increased from 1,700,000 to 5,500,000. But it did contemplate the increase of the electorate to approximately 4,000,000. This it proposed to accomplish by abolishing all property qualifications of voters in the cities and rural communes and by extending the voting privilege to all adult males who were able to read and write and also had resided in their electoral district a minimum of six months. To avoid the danger of an excess of democracy Taaffe planned to retain intact the curiæ of landed proprietors and chambers of commerce, so that it would still be true that 5402 large landholders would be represented in the lower house by 85 deputies, the chambers of commerce by 22, and the remainder of the nation — some 24,000,000 people — by 246. There never was any real chance of the measure's adoption. The conservatives opposed it because they thought it would open the floodgates for socialism; the socialists condemned it, on account of its half-way character, as " an insult to the working classes." Anticipating defeat, Taaffe resigned, before it came to a vote.

For a time, no further effort was made. In 1896 the ministry of Count Badeni carried a measure which indeed established the general suffrage that was demanded, although for the election, not of the 353 representatives already composing the lower chamber, but merely of a body of 72 new representatives

to be added to the existing membership. In the choice of these
72 additional members every male citizen twenty-four years of
age who had resided in his district as long as six months prior
to an election was to be entitled to participate; but elections
were to be direct only in those districts in which indirect voting
had been abolished by provincial legislation. Votes were to be
cast, as a rule, by ballot, although under some circumstances
orally. All preëxisting classes of voters were left intact, and
to them was simply added a fifth. The aggregate number of
electors in the Empire was raised to 5,333,000. Of the number,
however, the 1,732,000 comprised in the original four curiæ were
still to elect 353 of the 425 members of the chamber. Although,
therefore, the voting privilege was now conferred for the first
time upon millions of small taxpayers and non-taxpayers, the
nation had by no means attained a fair and democratic electoral
system.

Throughout the ensuing decade agitation for electoral reform
was kept up steadily, but not until 1905 did the situation become
favorable for further action. Convinced that the establishment
of universal and direct suffrage would stimulate loyalty to the
dynasty, and at the same time put an end to the obstructionist
tactics of the irreconcilable groups in the lower chamber, the
Emperor authorized the prime minister to pledge the Government
to the immediate introduction of a bill upon the subject;
and early in 1906 the promise was fulfilled. The outlook for
the measure was for a time not promising, and ministries rose
and fell rapidly, while the debates continued. But the bill passed
both houses before the close of 1906, and received the royal assent,
January 26, 1907. In form an amendment of the fundamental
law of 1867 concerning Imperial Representation, the act
deserves to be ranked with the Italian electoral law of 1912 and
the British Representation of the People Act of 1918 as one of
the three or four great electoral measures of the twentieth century.
It, in the first place, increased the membership of the
lower chamber from 425 to 516, and made a new distribution of
seats among the racial elements, and also among the several
provinces. But the great thing that it did was to abolish the
class system of voting in national elections and to establish in its
stead a plan of equal and direct manhood suffrage. With un-

important exceptions, every male subject twenty-four years of age and upwards, and resident in his commune for one year, was endowed with the suffrage. Voting was to be in all cases by secret ballot, and it was stipulated that, when so ordered by provincial diet, voting should be obligatory, under penalty of fine, as in Belgium. In the provinces of Lower Austria, Upper Austria, Silesia, Salsburg, Moravia, and Vorarlberg every elector is required by provincial regulation to appear at every parliamentary election in his district, and to present his ballot, the penalty for neglect (unless explained to the satisfaction of the proper magistrate) being a fine ranging from one to fifty crowns. In the Herrenhaus where there was strong opposition to the principle of manhood suffrage, effort was made to introduce in the act of 1907 a provision conferring a second vote upon all voters above the age of thirty-five. The Emperor and ministry urged, however, that the injection of such a change would wreck the measure; and when the lower chamber tacitly pledged itself to enact a law designed to prevent the " swamping " of the peers by Imperial appointment at the behest of a parliamentary majority, the plural voting project was abandoned. All representatives except those of Galicia are selected from single-member districts. An absolute majority of all votes cast is necessary for a choice. In default of such a majority, there is a second ballot between the two candidates who at the first test received the largest number of votes.

The Government of Hungary. — By reason of both its antiquity and its adaptability to varying conditions, the constitution of the kingdom of Hungary deserves to be considered one of the most remarkable instruments of its kind. Like the fundamental law of England, it is embodied in a maze of ancient statutes and customs, and it is the creation of a people possessed of a considerable genius for politics and government. Its documentary history goes back at least to the Golden Bull of Andrew II, promulgated in 1222; although that instrument, like the contemporary Great Charter in England, comprised only a confirmation of national liberties that were already old. Under Habsburg domination, from the early sixteenth century onwards, the political system and the long-established laws of the Hungarian kingdom were repeatedly guaranteed. Much of the time they were, in practice, disregarded; but the Hungarian nationalist vigor invested them with unlimited power of survival, and even during the reactionary second quarter of the nineteenth century they were merely held in suspense. In large part, the constitution in operation to-day took form in a series of measures enacted by the Hungarian parliament during the uprising of 1848. Thirty-one laws, in all, were at that time passed, revising the organization of the legislative chambers; widening the suffrage, creating a responsible cabinet, abolishing feudal survivals, and in general modernizing the institutions of the kingdom. The broad lines which remained were those marked out in the ancient constitutional order; the new measures supplemented, revised, and imparted definite form to preexisting laws, customs, and jealously guarded rights. Not all of these inherited constitutional elements, however, were included in the new statutes; and to this day it is true in Hungary, as in Great Britain, that a considerable portion of the constitution has never been put into written form. The *Ausgleich* gave final guarantee to the laws, autonomy, and territorial integrity of Hungary and its subordinate countries; and throughout all of the unsettlement and conflict which the ensuing half-century brought in the Austro-Hungarian world the constitution of the kingdom stood firm against every shock.

As has been explained, the king attains his position *ipso jure*, by reason of being emperor of Austria, and he is crowned monarch of Hungary at Budapest in a special ceremony in which is used the crown sent by Pope Sylvester II to King Stephen upwards of a thousand years ago. As in Austria, the powers of the sovereign are exercised largely through the ministry. The Hungarian laws contain special safeguards against royal despotism, and this fact, together with the almost continuous absence of the monarch from the kingdom, would tend to promote true parliamentary government. Other conditions, however, — the multiplicity of party groups and the stormy character of parliamentary proceedings, — enable the ministers to evade, in large part, the responsibility which they are supposed to bear, with the result that the cabinet system works to hardly better advantage than in Austria. Ministers have seats in Parliament and are entitled to be heard in either chamber.

Parliament consists of two houses — a Chamber of Magnates and a Chamber of Deputies. The former is descended from the ancient aristocratic "Table of Magnates," and has a membership of about four hundred, made up on the several principles of heredity, royal appointment, *ex officio* qualification, and indirect election, but with the hereditary element predominant. The Chamber of Deputies consists of 453 members (413 from Hungary proper and 40 from the subordinate kingdoms of Croatia, Slavonia, and Dalmatia), elected under the terms of an elaborate statute passed in 1874. Qualifications for the exercise of the suffrage are based on age, property, taxation, profession, official position, and ancestral privileges. Nominally liberal, they are, in actual operation, notoriously illiberal. The prescribed age for an elector is twenty years, indeed, as compared with twenty-four in Austria; but the qualifications based upon property-holding are the most rigorous in Europe. These qualifications — too complicated to be enumerated here — vary according as they arise from capital, industry, occupation, or property-holding. With slight restrictions, the right to vote is enjoyed without regard to property or income, by members of the Hungarian Academy of Sciences, professors, notaries public, engineers, surgeons, druggists, graduates of agricultural schools, foresters, clergymen, chaplains, and teachers. On the other hand, state officials, soldiers in active service, customs employees, and the police have no vote; servants, apprenticed workingmen, and agricultural laborers are carefully excluded; and there are the usual disqualifications for crime, bankruptcy, guardianship, and deprivation by judicial process. In an aggregate population of approximately 20,000,000 in 1914 there were not more than 1,100,000 electors.

The explanation of this state of affairs is to be found in the racial character of Hungary's population. Like Austria, Hungary contains a *mélange* of races and nationalities. The original Hungarians are the Magyars, and the Magyar element has always sought to preserve, as against the Slav and German elements, an absolute superiority of social, economic, and political power. The Magyars occupy almost exclusively the more desirable portion of the country, *i.e.*, the great central plain intersected by the Danube and the Theiss, where they preponderate heavily in as many as nineteen counties. Clustered around them, and in more or less immediate touch with kindred peoples beyond the borders, are the somewhat scattered Germans and the densely grouped Slavs — the Slovaks in the mountains of the north, the Ruthenes on the slopes of the Carpathians, the Serbs on the southeast, and the Croats on the southwest. When the census of 1910 was taken the total population of Hungary (including Croatia-Slavonia) was 20,500,000. Of this number 10,000,000 were Magyars; 8,500,000 were Slavs (including Rumanians); and 2,000,000 were Germans. The Magyars thus composed almost exactly one-half of the population. The fundamental fault of the Hungarian electoral system is that it has been shaped, and is deliberately maintained, in the interest of the Magyars alone. Even in Hungary proper the electorate in 1906 comprised but 24.4 per cent of the male population over twenty years of age; and, despite the disqualifications that have been mentioned, one-fourth of the men who voted were officials or employees of the state. For decades, and especially after the Austrian electoral reform of 1907, there was agitation among the Slavic populations for a suffrage law that would overthrow the Magyar monopoly of parliamentary power, or at all events assure to the non-Magyar peoples something like a proportionate share of political influence. The Magyar ministries went so far at times as to bring in bills on the subject. These measures — notably one of 1908 — were, however, avowedly drawn in such a manner as not " to compromise the Magyar character of the Hungarian state "; all were artfully shaped to give the appearance of manhood suffrage while yet withholding the substance; after bitter popular and parliamentary conflicts all were either defeated or withdrawn. The electoral system is further antiquated in that voting is public and oral. Prior to 1899 the elections were tempestuous, and frequently scandalous; but a law of that year bettered conditions somewhat.

General Aspects of the Austro-Hungarian Political Situation. — " Fully recognizing, free of compulsion," ran a proclamation of the youthful Emperor, Francis Joseph, at his accession in 1848, " the need and high value of free institutions adapted to the times, we confidently enter the path which is to lead us to a glorious transformation and rejuvenation of the whole monarchy. Our homeland will rise anew, resting on the broad basis of equal justice for all citizens before the law, as well as equal sharing of all representatives in legislation." Unhappily this roseate forecast was never realized. Grudgingly, and by slow stages, a system of constitutional government was built up during the next fifty years, but not a system insuring " equal rights and opportunities for all peoples " or " equal justice for all citizens." To 1914 Austrian (and also Hungarian) political liberty was a form rather than a reality. The members of the lower branch of Parliament were elected by the people; but Parliament itself had little ultimate control over national affairs. The cabinet system was nominally in vogue; but the ministers were chosen by the Emperor, not to map out and execute a program supported by a parliamentary majority speaking for the nation, but to undertake to range enough members of Parliament on the Government's side to carry out a policy whose author was the monarch himself. The country was cursed with a costly, cumbersome, inquisitorial, and generally inefficient bureaucracy. Civil rights were often invaded, and semi-official terrorism kept thousands of men from taking the part in political affairs which the laws supposedly opened to them.

The whole mechanism of government turned on questions of race. In Austria and Hungary alike the object was to maintain the dominance of a minority over a majority; the principle of action was *Divide et impera*. To an extent, the *Ausgleich* of 1867 marked an abandonment of the old plan of unbending centralization, of the Metternichian subordination of all the lands and peoples to a single government at Vienna. But only *one* of the hitherto subordinated lands, *i.e.*, Hungary, received a new status; and the whole arrangement was based on the absolute dominance of, not a single people, it is true, but of two nominally coequal peoples, the Germans in Austria and the Magyars in Hungary. Since 1867 the rigid maintenance of this dominance has been the cardinal feature of the Dual Monarchy's political life. It is one of the curious turns of history that the Magyars, after suffering sorely for centuries under the old Austrian system of centralization, adopted the system themselves the moment they gained the power to manage their own internal affairs. They forthwith undertook to denationalize the great masses of

Slavs and the considerable numbers of Germans living within their borders; and, as has been pointed out, they have contrived to this day to preserve a complete monopoly of political power. In doing so they have heaped up a heritage of Slavic hatred which will one day bring them grief. The German dominance in Austria has been maintained with greater difficulty. The German elements are less united than are the Magyars in the sister state, and they are less advantageously situated geographically. But the numerically preponderant Slavic and Latin peoples have been played off one against another with a cleverness of which only Viennese statesmen are capable, and the essential result has been generally attained.

Count Taaffe, who held the premiership through fourteen barren years, had a saying to the effect that the Dual Monarchy would continue to live from hand to mouth. That is the only fashion in which the ramshackle monarchy has ever lived. Long before the clash of arms in 1914, however, it was becoming apparent that matters could not thus go on forever. The forces of disruption were growing too strong. The Archduke Francis Ferdinand (heir-apparent to the Austrian and Hungarian thrones), whose murder at Serajevo touched the match to the powder, had a plan for the reorganization of the lands of the monarchy in three great divisions instead of two, a new one being created with a view to unification and autonomy for the South Slavs at present under Austrian dominion. Each great division — Austria, Hungary, and the South Slav state — was to be independent of the others, save in respect to foreign relations, the army and navy, and a few other necessary matters. And the Czechs of Bohemia and Moravia were to be reconciled by a rather limited autonomy, such as already existed in Galicia.

The plan was interesting, and far more liberal than Austrian official circles had ever been willing (or, indeed, were willing in 1914) to consider. But its adoption could not have solved the main problem. Hungary, *i.e.*, the Magyar people, was strongly opposed to it; many subject nationalities in both Austria and Hungary — the Ruthenians, the Slovaks, the Rumanians, the Italians — would have derived no benefit from it; there was no guarantee that government in the three dominions would be any more democratic and enlightened than it was in the several territories under the existing régime. One cannot escape the conclusion that — short of utter dissolution, involving the rise of fully independent Magyar, Czecho-Slovak, Ruthenian, and South Slav states — no final solution was possible, save perchance the reorganization of the monarchy upon a purely federal basis, similar to the organization of Germany under the Empire, but with very much smaller powers in the central government. Opportunity to try the latter expedient in favorable times of peace was lost; the involuntary adoption of the first was decreed by a disastrous war.

SELECTED REFERENCES

A. L. Lowell, *Governments and Parties in Continental Europe* (Boston, 1896), II, Chaps. viii-x; *Cambridge Modern History* (London, 1902-1910), XI, Chaps. vi-vii, XII, Chap. vii; J. S. Schapiro, *Modern and Contemporary European History* (Boston, 1918), Chap. xvi; G. Drage, *Austria-Hungary* (London, 1909); W. von Schierbrand, *Austria-Hungary, the Polyglot Empire* (New York, 1917); A. R. Colquhoun, *The Whirlpool of Europe* (New York, 1907); H. W. Steed, *The Hapsburg Monarchy* (2d ed., London, 1914); H. Rumbold, *Francis Joseph and His Times* (London, 1909); R. W. Seton Watson, *Corruption and Reform in Hungary: a Study of Electoral Practice* (London, 1911); ibid., *The Southern Slav Question and the Hapsburg Monarchy* (London, 1911); ibid., *German, Slav, and Magyar* (London, 1916); C. M. Knatchbull-Hugessen, *The Political Evolution of the Hungarian Nation*, 2 vols. (London, 1908); J. Andrassy, *Development of Hungarian Constitutional Liberty* (London, 1908); P. Alden [ed.], *Hungary of Today* (London, 1910); W. F. Dodd, *Modern Constitutions* (Chicago, 1909), I, 71-122, for texts of the fundamental laws.

PART IV. THE WAR AND POLITICAL RECONSTRUCTION

CHAPTER XXVII

AMERICAN WAR AIMS IN RELATION TO GOVERNMENT

By virtue of a recognized principle almost as old as the Constitution itself, the President of the United States is the authorized spokesman of our country in dealing with all foreign powers. Thomas Jefferson, the first Secretary of State, writing to a representative of the French government, informed him that the President was "the only channel of communication between this country and foreign nations," and that "it is from him alone that foreign nations or their agents are to learn what is or has been the will of the nation, and whatever he communicates as such, they have a right and are bound to consider as the expression of the nation." Accordingly it is fitting and proper that in seeking for the war aims of the United States we should turn to the official utterances of President Wilson. Other aims and other purposes may lie in the minds of individual citizens or groups of citizens, but there is no other source of authority on this point so widely accepted or so profoundly approved.

National Self-Defense. — In his address to Congress on April 2, 1917, calling for a declaration of war on Germany, President Wilson made it clear and presented the facts to prove that our country was not challenging another nation pursuing its own way in accordance with the rights of nations, but was in very truth taking up arms to repel acts of violence and wrong already being committed against the United States.

"Vessels of every kind," he said, "whatever their flag, their character, their cargo, their destination, their errand, have been ruthlessly sent to the bottom without warning and without thought of help or mercy for those on board, the vessels of friendly neutrals along with those of belligerents. Even hospital ships and ships carrying relief to the sorely bereaved and stricken people of Belgium, though the latter were provided with safe conduct through the proscribed areas by the German Government itself and were distinguished by unmistakable marks of identity, have been sunk with the same reckless lack of compassion or of principle. . . . One of the things that has served to convince us that the Prussian autocracy was not and could never be our friend is that from the very outset of the present war it has filled our unsuspecting communities and even our offices of government with spies and set criminal intrigues everywhere afoot against our national unity of counsel, our peace within and without, our industries and our commerce. Indeed it is now evident that its spies were here even before the war began; and it is unhappily not a matter of conjecture but a fact proved in our courts of justice that the intrigues which have more than once come perilously near to disturbing the peace and dislocating the industries of the country have been carried on at the instigation, with the support, and even under the personal direction of official agents of the Imperial Government accredited to the Government of the United States. Even in checking these things and trying to extirpate them we have sought to put the most generous interpretation possible upon them because we knew that their source lay, not in any hostile feeling or purpose of the German people towards us (who were, no doubt, as ignorant of them as we ourselves were), but only in the selfish designs of a government that did what it pleased and told its people nothing. But they have played their part in serving to convince us at last that that government entertains no real friendship for us and means to act against our peace and security at its convenience. That it means to stir up enemies against us at our very doors the intercepted note to the German Minister at Mexico City is eloquent evidence. We are accepting this challenge of hostile purpose because we know that in such a government following such methods we can never have a friend."

To this thought President Wilson returned again and again, lest with the progress of time the people might forget the extraordinary circumstances amid which the conflict began. In his Flag Day address of June 14, 1917, he said:

"It is plain enough how we were forced into the war. The extraordinary insults and aggressions of the Imperial German Government left us no self-respecting choice but to take up arms in defense of our rights as a free people and of our honour as a sovereign government. The military masters of Germany denied us the right to be neutral. They filled our unsuspecting communities with vicious spies and conspirators and sought to corrupt the opinion of our people in their own behalf. When they found that they could not do that, their agents diligently spread sedition amongst us and sought to draw our own citizens from their allegiance, — and some of those agents were men connected with the official Embassy of the German Government itself here in our own capital. They sought by violence to destroy our industries and arrest our commerce. They tried to incite Mexico to take up arms against us and to draw Japan into a hostile alliance with her, — and that, not by indirection, but by direct suggestion from the Foreign Office in Berlin. They impudently denied us the use of the high seas and repeatedly executed their threat that they would send to their death any of our people who ventured to approach the coasts of Europe. And many of our own people were corrupted. Men began to look upon their own neighbours with suspicion and to wonder in their hot resentment and surprise whether there was any community in which hostile intrigue did not lurk. What great nation in such circumstances would not have taken up arms? Much as we had desired peace, it was denied us, and not of our own choice."

America Has No Selfish Aims in the War. — In inviting Congress to consider the reasons why arms should be taken up against the Imperial German Government, on April 2, 1917, President Wilson announced to all the world that the United States sought no material gains from the war — no new territories, no forcibly won markets for American trade, no compensations in money for wrongs done — but rather to overthrow militarism and imperialism, making way for peace and democratic governments throughout the earth. " We are glad . . . ," he said, " to fight thus for the ultimate peace of the world and for the liberation of its peoples, the German peoples included: for the rights of nations great and small and the privilege of men everywhere to choose their way of life and of obedience. The world must be made safe for democracy. Its peace must be planted upon the tested foundations of political liberty. We have no selfish ends to serve. We desire no conquest, no dominion. We seek no indemnities for ourselves, no material compensation for the sacrifices we shall freely make. We are but one of the champions of the rights of mankind. We shall be satisfied when those rights have been made as secure as the faith and the freedom of nations can make them."

International Law and Right Must be Sustained. — Under long accepted principles of international law, battleships of countries engaged in war could not destroy a merchant vessel even of any enemy power (to say nothing of merchant vessels of neutrals) without first providing for the safety of passengers and crew. American citizens thus had a right to travel with security not only on American merchant ships, but also on those of the warring countries of Europe. Even if established law had not forbidden the wanton killing of non-combatants, the dictates of humanity would have prevented such outrageous conduct. This was emphasized by President Wilson in his note to the German Imperial Government after the sinking of the *Lusitania*, in 1915; and in laying before Congress the just causes of war, he again referred to it:

"International law had its origin in the attempt to set up some law which would be respected and observed upon the seas, where no nation had right of dominion and where lay the free highways of the world. By painful stage after stage has that law been built up, with meager enough results, indeed, after all was accomplished that could be accomplished, but always with a clear view, at least, of what the heart and conscience of mankind demanded. This minimum of right the German Government has swept aside under the plea of retaliation and necessity and because it had no weapons which it could use at sea except these which it is impossible to employ as it is employing them without throwing to the winds all scruples of humanity or of respect for the understandings that were supposed to underlie the intercourse of the world. I am not now thinking of the loss of property involved, immense and serious as that is, but only of the wanton and wholesale destruction of the lives of noncombatants, men, women, and children, engaged in pursuits which have always, even in the darkest periods of modern history, been deemed innocent and legitimate. Property can be paid for; the lives of peaceful and innocent people can not be. The present German submarine warfare against commerce is a warfare against mankind.

"It is a war against all nations. American ships have been sunk, American lives taken, in ways which it has stirred us very deeply to learn of, but the ships and people of other neutral and friendly nations have been sunk and overwhelmed in the waters in the same way. There has been no discrimination. The challenge is to all mankind. Each nation must decide for itself how it will meet it. The choice we make for ourselves must be made with a moderation of counsel and a temperateness of judgment befitting our character and our motives as a nation. We must put excited feeling away. Our motive will not be revenge or the victorious assertion of the physical might of the nation, but only the vindication of right, of human right, of which we are only a single champion."

The Rights of Nations and the Freedom of Peoples to be Respected. — Nothing has been more marked in the course of European history during the nineteenth and twentieth centuries than the struggle of all nationalities for self-government and the full control of their own destinies. Nothing has been more thoroughly repudiated among the friends of mankind and the liberal thinkers of the world than the subjugation of civilized peoples by alien conquerors. Everywhere submerged and oppressed nationalities lifted up their voices against attempts to stamp out their languages, customs, literatures, and instruments of autonomous government. President Wilson early in the War heeded this call of small nations for help, and in his message to Russia, on May 26, 1917, he said:

"We are fighting for the liberty, the self-government, and the undictated development of all peoples, and every feature of the settlement that concludes this war must be conceived and executed for that purpose. Wrongs must first be righted, and then adequate safeguards must be created to prevent their being committed again. We ought not to consider remedies merely because they have a pleasing and sonorous sound. Practical questions can be settled only by practical means. Phrases will not accomplish the result. Effective readjustments will; and whatever readjustments are necessary must be made.

"But they must follow a principle, and that principle is plain. *No people must be forced under sovereignty under which it does not wish to live. No territory must change hands except for the purpose of securing those who inhabit it a fair chance of life and liberty. No indemnities must be insisted on except those that constitute payments for manifest wrongs done. No readjustments of power must be made except such as will tend to secure the future peace of the world and the future welfare and happiness of its peoples.*

"And then the free peoples of the world must draw together in some common covenant, some genuine and practical coöperation that will in effect combine their force to secure peace and justice in the dealings of nations with one another. The brotherhood of mankind must no longer be a fair but empty phrase; it must be given a structure of force and reality. The nations must realize their common life and effect a workable partnership to secure that life against the aggressions of autocratic and self-pleasing power."

War for a Lasting Peace — the League of Nations. — From the Declaration of Independence down to the Great War, the United States had taken pride in its freedom from huge standing armies, the dominance of military cliques, the enticements of conquest and brazen war glories. On every public holiday orators had rehearsed with pride how the great armies had melted away at the end of the Civil War, how America had returned quickly to the ways of peace and industry, and how naturally the high military powers of the President and the generals had been subjected completely to civilian control. Nothing was farther removed from the genius of America than the German military system and the German ideal of war for the sake of war, war for conquest, war for glory, war for the benefit of ruling classes. For a long time before 1917 there had been growing up in America a movement for international conciliation and good and wise people had labored for an agreement among nations making resort to arms for the settlement of international disputes extremely difficult if not impossible. The one power of the earth that stood out most vigorously against the steadily growing demand for a union of the nations against war was Germany under her imperial and military masters bent upon designs of conquest and subjugation.

Far-seeing men had known that before a concert of nations could be effected the sword of the German military masters would have to be broken either by a revolution of the people or on the field of battle. In the economy of Providence the latter way was chosen. This was in President Wilson's mind when he said in his address to Congress on April 2, 1917: "We are accepting this challenge of hostile purpose because we know that in such a government, following such methods, we can never have a friend; and that in the presence of its organized power, always lying in wait to accomplish we know not what purpose, there can be no assured security for the democratic governments of the world. We are now about to accept gauge of battle with this natural foe to liberty and shall, if necessary, spend the whole force of the nation to check and nullify its pretensions and its power."

It was in reality in response to a war against war that the American people so quickly rallied to the call to lay aside the ways of peace and embark upon the trying and costly enterprise of beating German militarism on the field of battle, thus throwing down imperialism to make way for the union of nations against war. "A steadfast concert for peace," said President Wilson to Congress on April 2, 1917, "can never be maintained except by a partnership of democratic nations. No autocratic government could be trusted to keep faith within it or observe its covenants. It must be a league of honour, a partnership of opinion. Intrigue would eat its vitals away; the plottings of inner circles who could plan what they would and render account to no one would be a corruption seated at its very heart. Only free peoples can hold their purpose and their honour steady to a common end and prefer the interests of mankind to any narrow interest of their own."

The last and culminating of the fourteen points in President Wilson's program of peace laid before Congress in his message of January 8, 1918, was: "A general association of nations must be formed, under specific covenants, for the purpose of affording mutual guarantees of political independence and territorial integrity to great and small states alike." Again in his speech at the Tomb of Washington, July 4, 1918, President Wilson placed among the four summary aims of America in the war: " The establishment of an organization of peace which shall make it certain that the combined power of free nations will check every invasion of right and serve to make peace and justice the more secure by affording a definite tribunal of opinion to which all must submit and by which every international readjustment that cannot be amicably agreed upon by the peoples directly concerned shall be sanctioned."

With the passage of time it seems that the President's vision of a concert for the world peace became clearer and the urgency of the plan as a part of the final settlement loomed larger on his horizon. When victory was at last in sight and all doubt as to the complete and early triumph over German militarism was removed, namely, on September 27, 1918, President Wilson, in opening the campaign for the Fourth Liberty loan, said: " If it be in deed and in truth the common object of the governments associated against Germany and of the nations whom they govern, as I believe it to be, to achieve by the coming settlement a secure and lasting peace, it will be necessary that all who sit down at the peace table shall come ready and willing to pay the price, the only price, that will procure it; and ready and willing, also, to create in some virile fashion the only instrumentality by which it can be made certain that the agreements of the peace will be honoured and fulfilled.

"That price is impartial justice in every item of the settlement, no matter whose interest is crossed; and not only impartial justice but also the satisfaction of the several peoples whose fortunes are dealt with. That indispensable instrumentality is a League of Nations formed under covenants that will be efficacious. Without such an instrumentality, by which the peace of the world can be guaranteed, peace will rest in part upon the word of outlaws and only upon that word. For Germany will have to redeem her character, not by what happens at the peace but by what follows.

" And, as I see it, the constitution of that League of Nations and the clear definition of its objects must be a part, in a sense the most essential part, of the peace settlement itself. It cannot be formed now. If formed now, it would be merely a new alliance confined to the nations associated against a common enemy. It is not likely that it could be formed after the settlement. It is necessary to guarantee the peace; and the peace cannot be guaranteed as an afterthought. The reason, to speak in plain terms again, why it must be guaranteed is that there will be parties to the peace whose promises have proved untrustworthy, and means must be found in connection with the peace settlement itself to remove that source of insecurity."

The End of Secret Diplomacy. — " This war," said President Wilson to Congress, on April 2, 1917, " was determined upon as wars used to be determined upon in the old, unhappy days when peoples were nowhere consulted by their rulers and wars were provoked and waged in the interest of dynasties or of little groups of ambitious men who were accustomed to use their fellowmen as pawns and tools. . . . Cunningly contrived plans of deception or aggression, carried out, it may be, from generation to generation, can be worked out and kept from light only within the privacy of courts or behind the carefully guarded confidences of a narrow and privileged class. They are happily impossible where public opinion commands and insists upon full information concerning all the nation's affairs."

The solution for the problem presented by secret diplomacy, President Wilson found in open diplomacy. First among the fourteen points in his program of peace laid before Congress on January 8, 1918, was: "Open covenants of peace, openly arrived at; after which there shall be no private international understandings of any kind, but diplomacy shall proceed always frankly and in the public view."

A Just and Generous Peace as the Preliminary to a Lasting Peace. — On every occasion the President of the United States has warned his countrymen against a peace of hatred, revenge, and vindictive punishment sowing the seeds of bitterness and making way for a renewal of war at an early date. This he pointed out at the very beginning of the war, saying to Congress on April 2, 1917: " We have no quarrel with the German people. We have no feeling towards them but one of sympathy and friendship. It was not upon their impulse that their government acted in entering this war. It was not with their previous knowledge or approval."

In thus distinguishing between the German people and the German Imperial Government, President Wilson did not mean that the former could continue to accept the rule of their masters, and at the same time escape all responsibility for the war, finding at the war's end a hearty admission to the councils of the nations. On the contrary, on December 4, 1917, he said, in his address to Congress: "The worst that can happen to the detriment of the German people is this, that if they should still, after the war is over, continue to be obliged to live under ambitious and intriguing masters interested to disturb the peace of the world — men or classes of men whom the other peoples of the world could not trust — it might be impossible to admit them to the partnership of nations which must henceforth guarantee the world's peace. That partnership must be a partnership of peoples, not a mere partnership of governments. It might be impossible, also, in such untoward circumstances, to admit Germany to the free economic intercourse which must inevitably spring out of the other partnerships of a real peace. But there would be no aggression in that; and such a situation, inevitable because of distrust, would in the very nature of things sooner or later cure itself, by processes which would assuredly set in."

Summaries of America's War Aims. — On three different occasions President Wilson summarized briefly the war aims of the United States. The first of these was when he laid down the famous "fourteen points" in his address to Congress on January 8, 1918, as follows:

"I. — Open covenants of peace, openly arrived at; after which there shall be no private international understandings of any kind, but diplomacy shall proceed always frankly and in the public view.

"II. — Absolute freedom of navigation upon the seas, outside territorial waters, alike in peace and in war, except as the seas may be closed in whole or in part by international action for the enforcement of international covenants.[1]

"III. — The removal, so far as possible, of all economic barriers and the establishment of an equality of trade conditions

[1] Right to further interpretation of this point was reserved by the Allies in the note to Germany relative to an armistice, November 5, 1918.

among all the nations consenting to the peace and associating themselves for its maintenance.[1]

" IV. — Adequate guarantees given and taken that national armaments will be reduced to the lowest point consistent with domestic safety.

" V. — A free, open-minded, and absolutely impartial adjustment of all colonial claims, based upon a strict observance of the principle that in determining all such questions of sovereignty the interests of the populations concerned must have equal weight with the equitable claims of the Government whose title is to be determined.

" VI. — The evacuation of all Russian territory and such a settlement of all questions affecting Russia as will secure the best and freest coöperation of the other nations of the world in obtaining for her an unhampered and unembarrassed opportunity for the independent determination of her own political development and national policy, and assure her of a sincere welcome into the society of free nations under institutions of her own choosing; and, more than a welcome, assistance also of every kind that she may need and may herself desire. The treatment accorded Russia by her sister nations in the months to come will be the acid test of their good-will, of their comprehension of her needs as distinguished from their own interests, and of their intelligent and unselfish sympathy.

" VII. — Belgium, the whole world will agree, must be evacuated and restored, without any attempt to limit the sovereignty which she enjoys in common with all other free nations. No other single act will serve as this will serve to restore confidence among the nations in the laws which they have themselves set

---

[1] In a letter (October, 1918) to Senator Simmons, of North Carolina, President Wilson explained the third point as follows: "I, of course, meant to suggest no restriction upon the free determination by any nation of its own economic policy, but only that, whatever tariff any nation might deem necessary for its own economic service, be that tariff high or low, it should apply equally to all foreign nations; in other words, that there should be no discriminations against some nations that did not apply to others. This leaves every nation free to determine for itself its own internal policies and limits only its right to compound these policies of hostile discriminations between one nation and another. Weapons of economic discipline and punishment should be left to the joint action of all nations for the purpose of punishing those who will not submit to a general programme of justice and equality."

and determined for the government of their relations with one another. Without this healing act the whole structure and validity of international law is forever impaired.

"VIII.—All French territory should be freed and the invaded portions restored, and the wrong done to France by Prussia in 1871 in the matter of Alsace-Lorraine, which has unsettled the peace of the world for nearly fifty years, should be righted, in order that peace may once more be made secure in the interest of all.

"IX.—A readjustment of the frontiers of Italy should be effected along clearly recognizable lines of nationality.

"X.—The peoples of Austria-Hungary, whose place among the nations we wish to see safeguarded and assured, should be accorded the freest opportunity of autonomous development.[1]

"XI.—Rumania, Serbia, and Montenegro should be evacuated; occupied territories restored; Serbia accorded free and secure access to the sea; and the relations of the several Balkan States to one another determined by friendly counsel along historically established lines of allegiance and nationality; and international guarantees of the political and economic independence and territorial integrity of the several Balkan States should be entered into.

"XII.—The Turkish portions of the present Ottoman Empire should be assured a secure sovereignty, but the other nationalities which are now under Turkish rule should be assured an undoubted security of life and an absolutely unmolested opportunity of autonomous development, and the Dardanelles should be permanently opened as a free passage to the ships and commerce of all nations under international guarantees.

[1] The tenth point was modified by President Wilson in his note to Austria, October 19, 1918, as follows: "Since that sentence was written and uttered to the Congress of the United States, the Government of the United States has recognized that a state of belligerency exists between the Czechoslovaks and the German and Austro-Hungarian Empires and that the Czechoslovak National Council is a de facto belligerent Government clothed with proper authority to direct the military and political affairs of the Czechoslovaks. It has also recognized in the fullest manner the justice of the nationalistic aspirations of the Jugoslavs for freedom. The President is, therefore, no longer at liberty to accept the mere 'autonomy' of these peoples as a basis of peace, but is obliged to insist that they, and not he, shall be the judges of what action on the part of the Austro-Hungarian Government will satisfy their aspirations and their conception of their rights and destiny as members of the family of nations."

"XIII. — An independent Polish State should be erected which should include the territories inhabited by indisputably Polish populations, which should be assured a free and secure access to the sea, and whose political and economic independence and territorial integrity should be guaranteed by international covenant.

"XIV. — A general association of nations must be formed under specific covenants for the purpose of affording mutual guarantees of political independence and territorial integrity to great and small States alike."

The second epitome of American war aims was made by the President in his address at the Tomb of Washington, July 4, 1918:

"There can be but one issue. The settlement must be final. There can be no compromise. No halfway decision would be tolerable. No halfway decision is conceivable. These are the ends for which the associated peoples of the world are fighting and which must be conceded them before there can be peace:

"1. The destruction of every arbitrary power anywhere that can separately, secretly, and of its single choice disturb the peace of the world; or, if it cannot be presently destroyed, at the least its reduction to virtual impotence.

"2. The settlement of every question, whether of territory, of sovereignty, of economic arrangement, or of political relationship, upon the basis of the free acceptance of that settlement by the people immediately concerned, and not upon the basis of the material interest or advantage of any other nation or people which may desire a different settlement for the sake of its own exterior influence or mastery.

"3. The consent of all nations to be governed in their conduct toward each other by the same principles of honour and of respect for the common law of civilized society that govern the individual citizens of all modern States in their relations with one another; to the end that all promises and covenants may be sacredly observed, no private plots or conspiracies hatched, no selfish injuries wrought with impunity, and a mutual trust established upon the handsome foundation of a mutual respect for right.

"4. The establishment of an organization of peace which shall make it certain that the combined power of free nations will check every invasion of right and serve to make peace and justice the more secure by affording a definite tribunal of opinion to which all must submit and by which every international readjustment that cannot be amicably agreed upon by the peoples directly concerned shall be sanctioned.

"These great objects cannot be put into a single sentence. What we seek is the reign of law, based upon the consent of the governed and sustained by the organized opinion of mankind."

The third and last summary, perhaps the most vivid and striking of all, President Wilson laid before the world in his New York address of September 27, 1918, opening the campaign for the Fourth Liberty loan:

"First, the impartial justice meted out must involve no discrimination between those to whom we wish to be just and those to whom we do not wish to be just. It must be a justice that plays no favourites and knows no standard but the equal rights of the several peoples concerned;

"Second, no special or separate interest of any single nation or any group of nations can be made the basis of any part of the settlement, which is not consistent with the common interest of all;

"Third, there can be no leagues or alliances or special covenants and understandings within the general and common family of the League of Nations;

"Fourth, and more specifically, there can be no special, selfish economic combinations within the League and no employment of any form of economic boycott or exclusion except as the power of economic penalty by exclusion from the markets of the world may be vested in the League of Nations itself as a means of discipline and control;

"Fifth, all international agreements and treaties of every kind must be made known in their entirety to the rest of the world;

"Special alliances and economic rivalries and hostilities have been the prolific source in the modern world of the plans and passions that produce war. It would be an insincere as well as an insecure peace that did not exclude them in definite and binding terms."

War and American Domestic Policies. — President Wilson's domestic policies in relation to war may be briefly summed up under four heads : (1) The support of the war as far as equitably possible by taxation falling upon the present generation ;[1] (2) the conditions of labor not to be made more onerous by the war and the instrumentalities by which the conditions of labor are improved not to be blocked or checked ;[2] (3) just prices must be paid, but patriotic business men should not seek riches while soldiers are shedding their blood upon the field of battle for their country ;[3] (4) the mob spirit of lawless persecution or open violence to be suppressed and the ancient processes of justice to be respected.[4]

Conclusion. — No one can bring under review these remarkable declarations of principles without seeing at once how profoundly the course of historical development and international rivalry is to be affected by them. They represent not merely the views of one man, the spokesman of a great nation; they voice the slowly maturing opinion of the masses of the people everywhere in the earth. It is not to be expected that they will be universally accepted or lived up to by all nations in spirit as well as letter; but for the first time revolutionary concepts of national life and government and international relations are woven by high authority into the very warp and woof of the world's thinking. Currents of opinion once obscure are thus given high sanction, and afforded the impetus of official authority. These principles will undoubtedly be differently interpreted from age to age as were the doctrines of the Declaration of Independence and the axioms of the Declaration of the Rights of Man; contradictions and obscurities will appear; and baffled mankind may turn now and then away from them; but those who have the faith will believe that a real change has come in the long course of history and that the years 1917–1918, as surely as the age of the American and French Revolutions, will mark the opening of a new epoch in the rise of government by the people and in the growth of a concert among the nations.

---

[1] Address to Congress, April 2, 1917.
[2] Address to the American Federation of Labor, November 2, 1917.
[3] Appeal to Business Men, July 11, 1917; and to the People, April 16, 1917.
[4] Address to the American Federation of Labor, November 2, 1917.

SELECTED REFERENCES

J. B. Scott, *Diplomatic Correspondence between the United States and Germany* (New York, 1918); ibid., *A Survey of International Relations between the United States and Germany* (New York, 1918); ibid., *President Wilson's Foreign Policy* (New York, 1918); R. C. Minor, *A Republic of Nations* (New York, 1918); D. S. Jordan, *Democracy and World Relations* (Yonkers, N. Y., 1918); Stoddard and Frank, *Stakes of the War* (New York, 1918); Davis, Anderson, and Tyler, *The Roots of the War* (New York, 1918); Charles Seymour, *The Diplomatic Background of the War* (New Haven, 1918); A. M. Low, *Woodrow Wilson* (Boston, 1918); H. H. Powers, *The Great Peace* (New York, 1918); H. M. Kallen and R. S. Rounds, *The League of Nations* (Boston, 1918); Ordway Tead, *The People's Part in Peace* (New York, 1918).

CHAPTER XXVIII

THE PROBLEM OF INTERNATIONAL GOVERNMENT

Nationalism and the Balance of Power. — For four hundred years the dominant principle of European political organization has been nationalism. The term is one which does not lend itself to easy definition. It obviously denotes an arrangement under which men are grouped for purposes of government and a common economic life in *nations*. But difficulty arises when one undertakes to say precisely what a " nation " is. It is not the same thing as a race; the Slavs are a race, but not a nation. It is not the same thing as a state; Austria-Hungary hitherto has been a state, but not a nation. Present purposes, however, will be fully met by a definition given by a recent English writer, as follows: a nation is " a body of people who feel themselves to be naturally linked together by certain affinities which are so strong and real for them that they can live happily together, are dissatisfied when disunited, and cannot tolerate subjection to peoples who do not share these ties." [1]

In the Middle Ages the principle of nationalism was weak. The two dominating institutions, the Holy Roman Empire and the Christian Church, were grounded upon the idea of world-unity, and only very slowly did society disintegrate into distinct, self-conscious, and rival national bodies. The process was helped on by the Renaissance, whose whole political influence was cast on the side of individualism and independence. It was furthered also by the Protestant Revolt, which rent the seamless garment of the Universal Church and deprived Europe as a whole of the last surviving political expression of its unity. Throughout the seventeenth and eighteenth centuries the sense of national separatism continued to grow, notably in England, France, Prussia, and Russia; and in the nineteenth century the

[1] Muir, *Nationalism and Internationalism*, 38.

desire for autonomy and self-subsistence became a universal passion. Between 1820 and 1878 the nationalist spirit, indeed, remade the map of central Europe. It created united Italy; working on different lines, it erected the German Empire; it gave Belgium her independence; it set up a cluster of free states in the Balkans — Serbia, Greece, Montenegro, Bulgaria, Rumania. So deeply did the idea strike root that among great numbers of people — although not, as a rule, in the governing classes — it has of late been simply taken for granted that every nation, just because it is a nation, has an inherent right to be united and to be free. The country in which the principle won smallest triumphs was Austria-Hungary; and it was entirely in keeping with the general trend that the struggle of the Habsburgs against its further advance should furnish the immediate occasion of war in 1914.

Nationalism has thus laid firm hold upon the European world, and for a hundred years has swept opposition powerfully before it. It will, and should, win many new triumphs as a result of the recent war. But its progress has not been without disadvantages, some of them very grave, and its critics have by no means been confined to reactionary governments desirous of keeping an iron hand upon subject peoples. It has tended to a narrowing of views and of ideals, to an intolerance of everything that is " alien," and to an emphasis upon unity which easily becomes a glorification of mere uniformity. The main count in the indictment against it, however, is that it accentuates rivalries and animosities, and breeds wars. Every state (whether or not, properly speaking, a nationality), becomes self-conscious and, so far as possible, self-contained. It seeks to play a rôle commensurate with what it conceives to be its true worth and strength. It reaches out for markets and for new territory. It grows distrustful of its neighbors and seeks to circumvent them. It builds up alliances, and arms itself to the teeth. It expects war, and not infrequently gets it. For three decades before the Great War the whole international system of Europe rested on a doctrine of balance of power, which kept the continent an armed camp; the war itself was the logical outcome of the kind of peace that preceded it. Over against the Triple Alliance was set the Triple Entente; when Germany laid down a super-dreadnought, England felt constrained to lay down two; when Germany strengthened her army, France did likewise; every great power watched events with hawk-like keenness to detect moves against itself; the smaller states followed in the wake of the larger ones; so delicately adjusted was the balance that every advance of one people seemed tantamount to a reversal for another; there was no international organization which had the strength or the prestige requisite to allay fears, inspire confidence, and guarantee justice. The world in 1914 was living under a régime not far removed from international anarchy.

The International Idea to 1815. — Up to a certain point, the reorganization of the world on the principle of nationalism was not only inevitable but desirable. A world-state had ceased to be even theoretically possible, and the only thing to do was to recognize that men would, and must, group together in nations in accordance with their interests and sympathies. The dangers inherent in a nationalistic policy when carried to its logical conclusion were, however, from the outset apparent. And hence we find, beginning hundreds of years ago, a remarkable series of efforts and of proposals looking to the counterbalancing of the nationalistic system by a scheme of internationalism which would restore, on an entirely different basis but with somewhat the same result, the unity and harmony presumably lost with the disappearance of medieval cosmopolitanism. Two phases, only, of this earlier internationalism can be noted here. One is the development of international law; the other is the discussion of plans of world federation.

There has been a certain amount of international law in all ages; whenever and wherever independent states are thrown into contact practical necessity obliges them to work out rules under which to carry on their dealings one with another; and, for reasons of convenience, such rules tend to be adopted by the whole community of civilized states at the given period. It was not by accident that the great body of international law which formed one of humanity's choicest possessions at the outbreak of the World War began to take shape in the sixteenth and seventeenth centuries. That was the period in which the new national separatism became completely triumphant, a time when the horrors of warfare and the faithlessness and brutality of states roused men to the need of some clear enunciation of restrictions under which governments should agree to act. Two or three feeble attempts in this direction were made late in the sixteenth century; but the work of the great Dutch scholar and jurist Grotius, *De Jure Belli et Pacis*, published — amid the savagery of the Thirty Years' War — at Paris in 1625, marked such an immense advance upon anything that had yet been done, and attained so quickly an authoritative position, that it has been justly asserted that modern international law " sprang fully-developed from the brain of Grotius." [1] The system thus originated was amplified and strengthened in succeeding centuries by the writings of masterful jurists like Pufendorf, Bynkershoek, and Vattel (all of them, significantly, citizens of small and helpless states); and, notwithstanding that these scholars obviously were endowed with no legislative authority, the legal fabric which they built up won general acceptance by the governments and the courts of all enlightened nations. Furthermore, to the rules which the writers drew from the old Roman law, from feudal and commercial usage, and from treaties, the public authorities themselves added much, by specific international agreements or in other ways.

By tempering the asperities of the nationalistic régime, international law served a highly useful purpose. It, however, did not wholly meet the situation. It was difficult to modify and expand; it provoked constant differences of interpretation; there was no authority outside of the states themselves to enforce it; and it did not prevent frequent war. Hence, publicists and scholars looked constantly for something better — for some sort of international organization that should have the will and the power to preserve peace and to see that essential justice, as between nations, was done. Before the close of the seventeenth century the Duke of Sully, chief minister of Henry IV of France, drew up a *Grand Design* for a " Christian republic " composed of fifteen autonomous European states, pledged to make war only upon the Turks; [2] and in 1693 William Penn published a trenchant *Essay towards the Present and Future Peace of Europe*,

---

[1] Muir, *Nationalism and Internationalism*, 147.
[2] The plan was not made public until after Henry's death, in 1610.

in which he suggested a general European diet whose decisions should be enforced upon a recalcitrant state by joint action of all the other states represented. Another notable plan was put forward at the close of the War of the Spanish Succession by Charles de St. Pierre, a priest who acted as secretary to the French plenipotentiary at the Congress of Utrecht (1713). Under this plan there was to be a perpetual alliance of European rulers and a diet in which disputes should be settled; and the diet was to have full power to levy taxes, make laws, and enforce its decisions by arms. Throughout the eighteenth century this project, while generally considered impracticable, was widely discussed. Both Voltaire and Rousseau wrote essays approving it.

The closing years of the century were prolific of "peace" literature. In England, Jeremy Bentham advocated a league of states, with a legislature and courts of justice, although the enforcement of decisions was to be left to public opinion; and Adam Smith propounded principles whose tendency would have been to transform Europe into a group of friendly, economic units. In France the *Économistes* lent their influence to the same sort of doctrine, and in Germany both Lessing and Kant made noteworthy contribution. In his tract, *Zum ewigen Frieden* ("Towards Lasting Peace"), published in 1795, the great Königsberg philosopher outlined a league of perpetual peace, to be composed exclusively of republican states, and to be fully equipped with powers of enforcement and with both judicial and administrative machinery.

The International Idea in the Earlier Nineteenth Century. — The first head of a great state to propose an organization of nations to maintain peace was Alexander I of Russia; for although Napoleon is reported to have drawn up a plan for a "European Association," no knowledge of it reached the world until after Waterloo, and it is not unlikely that it was really an afterthought designed to aid in building up a Napoleonic legend of liberalism and benevolence. Alexander came to the throne in 1801 as a liberal and a lover of peace, and to him it fell to become the motive power of the remarkable attempt to create a federation of Europe which forms the main interest of the decade 1815–1825. As early as 1804 he submitted to the younger Pitt a somewhat vague plan for a league of nations, to be carried into effect as soon as Napoleon should have been overthrown. Pitt's reply was cautious, and ten years of war and of tangled diplomacy rolled by before opportunity came to attempt the desired reconstruction. At the Congress of Vienna (1814-1815) the Tsar steadily used his influence for a plan of federation, and he was duped by clever statesmen into thinking that his hopes were about to be realized. In point of fact, the Congress — from which, as its secretary, von Gentz, tells us, men expected " an all-embracing reform of the political system of Europe, securities for peace, in short, the return of the Golden Age " — utterly failed to approach and execute its great task in a statesmanlike spirit. The princes and diplomats haggled over territories, parceled out privileges, traded off dynastic claims, and never rose to a higher level of statecraft than that involved in setting off self-interest against self-interest. From the meeting came, as von Gentz further says, " no act of a higher nature, no great measure for public order or for the general good, which might compensate humanity for its long sufferings or pacify it for the future."

It is true that after the Congress had completed its work two new international affiliations came upon the scene. The first was the Holy Alliance, signed by all the states of Europe except Great Britain, Turkey, and the Papal State, and proclaimed November 26, 1815. Its author was the Tsar who, with characteristic simple-mindedness, seems to have expected much from it. From the outset it was entirely useless, a mere piece of " sublime mysticism and nonsense "; and it would be difficult to discover that it had any influence whatever on the course of affairs. The second affiliation was of a different sort. It was the so-called " Concert of Europe," sponsored by Castlereagh and Metternich, and officially based on a treaty signed by Great Britain, Austria, Prussia, and Russia on the same day on which the last three of these states gave their adherence to the Holy Alliance. The avowed objects of this Quadruple Alliance were the enforcement of the late treaty with France, joint action in the event that France should again disturb the peace, and the consolidation of the " intimate tie which unites the four sovereigns for the happiness of the world." Meetings were to be held from time to time for the general discussion of European affairs; and at the first such gathering, at Aix-la-Chapelle in 1818, France, now deemed worthy of trust, was admitted to the charmed circle. At this same congress the Powers solemnly asserted their purpose never " to depart, either among themselves, or in their relations with other states, from the strictest observation of the principles of the law of nations; principles which, in their application to a state of permanent peace, can alone effectually guarantee the independence of each government and the stability of the general association." A league of nations to preserve peace seemed an accomplished fact.

The " Concert " and the New Balance of Power. — Without question, much of the credit for giving Europe a longer period of continuous peace after 1815 than she had enjoyed since the fifteenth century belongs to the Concert. None the less, the arrangement finally proved a failure, and for four main reasons: (1) the combination was one of princes, largely for dynastic purposes; (2) its activities were quickly diverted to the suppression of liberalism in central and southern Europe, so that a league of princes to preserve peace became a league of despots to make combined resistance against the democratic impulse; (3) it took no account of the national aspirations of subject peoples; and (4) no provision was made for alteration of the agreements on which the system rested. Persuaded that France was no longer a menace, and disgusted by the reactionary trend of the alliance, Great Britain soon withdrew; and the formal basis of the affiliation gradually dissolved, although under the leadership of Metternich the continental states continued to act in substantial coöperation until the great revolutions of the mid-century period. The Concert gave up all pretense of being a real federation; but the leading nations, especially those that inclined to " legitimacy," managed to act fairly well together.

In the third quarter of the century came a series of wars — the Crimean war, the wars of Italian liberation, the wars of Prussia against Denmark, Austria, and France, and the Russo-Turkish war — that not only reconstructed the map of Europe but put an entirely different face on the international situation. The Concert continued in existence (although with rapidly diminishing harmony) in connection with affairs in the Near East until the Congress of Berlin in 1878. Thereafter it disappeared completely, and in its stead arose a new régime of an entirely different nature. The great Powers could no longer even pretend to act together; general congresses for the settlement of international affairs became fewer, and finally ceased. Once more the ruling principle became, as in the eighteenth century, the Balance of Power. On the one hand, Germany and Austria-Hungary and Italy drew together in a Triple Alliance; on the other, France and Russia entered into a Dual Alliance, which in 1904–1907 became a Triple Entente through the adhesion of Great Britain. These alignments were formed under no urgent necessity, in times of no peculiar unsettlement or stress. They were not emergency measures, to be abandoned when the need disappeared. On the contrary, they were built up slowly and deliberately, and were intended to be permanent.

The effect was the very negation of everything that internationalism implies. The Concert was a weak instrumentality of international concord. But it at least had the merit of seeking to hold all the great nations in one group, so that all might discuss and decide and act together. The Balance of Power assumed that unity of international action was impossible or undesirable, and deliberately substituted a system under which one great group of powers was set squarely over against another. Formerly, a dispute between two states was the signal for a general European congress, which became for the time a crude sort of international tribunal; now, a dispute was the occasion for separate consultation by the two mutually distrustful groups, with a probability also of feverish military preparations. " The Balance of Power was directly responsible for turning Europe into a collection of armed camps. With two huge opposing alliances, rivalry in military forces and armaments was inevitable. Neither alliance, though formed for defensive purposes, could afford to allow the states of the opposing alliance to be better prepared than were the states of its league. Any improvement in military equipment, any increase in the number of forces, was at once met by corresponding measures in other states. . . . Europe bristled with guns and well-drilled armies, all avowedly for defense, but all ready for instant war. Such a situation in itself constituted an ever-present peril."[1] For twenty years, jealous-eyed alliances, competitive armaments, hot contests for territories and for markets, increasing racial hostilities, seemed to many observers to mean only one thing, namely, that Europe was rushing straight in the direction of a new, and a greater, cataclysm.

The Peace Movement, 1899-1914. — Heroic effort was made to stave off the catastrophe; and for some time it seemed that the closer economic interrelations of peoples, together with growing community of thought and action on political, educational, philanthropic, religious, and scientific lines, and a general development of "international-mindedness," would make great wars among the civilized nations forever impossible. These favoring conditions were reënforced, especially in the opening decade of the twentieth century, by positive effort of five main kinds: (1) propaganda designed to create public sentiment opposed to war, (2) great international conferences or congresses, for the codification and expansion of international law, (3) proposals for the reduction of armaments, (4) more general resort to international arbitration, and (5) the creation of special machinery of international government.

An English Peace Society was organized as early as 1816, and an American Peace Society, composed of local and state societies, made its appearance in 1828. On the continent, peace societies were founded at Geneva in 1828 and Paris in 1841. Thereafter organizations of the kind multiplied, until in 1914 there were about 160, with many branches and a membership running into millions. International peace congresses grew in frequency, and in 1891 permanent headquarters of the world-wide movement were established at Berne. In the early years of the present century wealthy men of various countries provided large sums for "associations" and "foundations" to investigate and urge forward the interests of peace. Lectureships were established; meetings were held; scholarly books were published; the earth was flooded with popular literature. A public sentiment seemed to be developing which, reënforced by other conditions that have been mentioned, would make wars among leading states practically an impossibility.

[1] Holt and Chilton, *European History, 1862-1914,* 289.

A second line of attack was through great congresses or conventions assembled to deal with subjects of international law. The illustrations that will at once suggest themselves are the Pan-American conferences of 1906 and 1910, and the Hague peace conferences of 1899 and 1907. The Hague conferences were convoked by Tsar Nicholas II of Russia, and had as their object an attempt to restate and impart new sanction to many portions of international law, and especially to arrive at understandings relative to the limitation of armaments and of expenditure upon armaments. The first meeting was attended by representatives of twenty-six states, the second by representatives of forty-four. Much was accomplished in the direction of humanizing the rules of warfare and creating machinery for international adjudication, although on the limitation of armaments no conclusions could be reached. Various proposals on this last-mentioned subject came also from other quarters, notably from the British government in 1912 and 1913; but, owing mainly to the unfavorable attitude of Germany, no results were obtained.

The chief mode of actual progress was the extension of the principle of international arbitration. This principle was by no means unknown in ancient and medieval times, but with the development of the nationalistic, balance-of-power system of the seventeenth and eighteenth centuries it almost wholly dropped out of use. Gradually, in the nineteenth century, it was revived. Between 1820 and 1840 there were eight international arbitrations; between 1840 and 1860, thirty; between 1860 and 1880, forty; between 1880 and 1900, ninety; from 1900 to the outbreak of the Great War there were not fewer than 200. Practically all of the leading powers have been parties to these agreements, but leadership has been assumed by Great Britain, France, and the United States. In a number of cases, *e.g.*, the Alabama Claims question between Great Britain and the United States and the Dogger Bank question between Great Britain and Russia, the disputes settled were of an extremely difficult and dangerous character, such as in earlier times might easily have led to war.

In this connection it is to be observed, finally, that before 1914 the nations had found it possible to set up certain formal machinery for the adjustment of their differences. The first Hague conference created a tribunal to adjudicate disputes, thereby giving the world for the first time a standing international court of law. The Hague Court is, speaking strictly, a panel or list of judges (each signatory nation appointing from one to four) from which actual courts can be formed, by agreement of the nations concerned, to hear cases as they arise. The first cause argued before one of these tribunals was carried there by the United States; and of the twelve decided up to 1912, five involved disputes to which this country was a party. A less imposing, but significant, tribunal of a similar nature is the Central American Court of Justice, set up by the five Central American states at Cartago in 1908. The second Hague conference, furthermore, made provision for two important tribunals which were never actually established. The first was a permanent Court of Arbitral Justice, of fifteen members, designed to supplement and improve the panel system in use in the existing Permanent Court of Arbitration; and the second was an International Prize Court, of fifteen members, to hear appeals from decisions of national prize courts arising out of maritime warfare.

The Need of International Government. — There are really only three possible bases on which international relations may be made to rest. The first is world-dominance by one incomparably superior state. This was the arrangement that prevailed in the days of Roman greatness; and it was fundamentally to prevent its being revived in German hands that the recent World War was waged. The second basis is the balance of power, involving the grouping of states in two or more mutually jealous and hostile leagues. This plan, as we have seen, was tried in earlier modern days and again after 1878, both times with disastrous results. The third basis is world-federation, involving the coöperative action of at least the more powerful states, working in a single group. This was the character of the Concert which held sway, with a certain amount of vigor and success, from 1815 to 1878. This Concert, as has been pointed out, was in many respects faulty. It was dynastic, reactionary, and oppressive. None the less, it pointed the way to a better organization of international affairs than had yet been known; and if it had not been superseded, forty years ago, by the principle of the balance of power, the world might have been spared the recent great catastrophe.

Standing at the close of the vastest international struggle in history, and confronted with colossal tasks of political and social reconstruction, men are fast coming to certain fundamental convictions about the future world order. One of them is that the nations must not be allowed to fall apart again, and, for purposes either of aggrandizement or of protection, to enter fresh leagues grounded in suspicion and hate. A second conviction is that peace and justice are hereafter to be assured only through the revival of the principle (although not the form or spirit) of the early nineteenth-century Concert. And a third conviction is that this new international affiliation must be no mere league with functions limited to discussion and admonition, but must be, rather, a close and durable federation, endowed with powers of punishment and compulsion, and equipped with actual machinery of legislation, administration, and justice; in short, it must be a *government*. It is recognized, of course, that this program bristles with difficulties. How many, and what, states shall be admitted to the new partnership? More specifically, shall Germany be admitted? What subjects shall lie within the federation's field of action? How far shall the federation be authorized to go in regulating matters that touch the domestic affairs of the several states? How can a state enter the league without impairing its sovereignty, and can (and ought) a state to be expected to suffer such impairment? Shall the league bind itself to take joint action against a recalcitrant member, or shall it trust to the state's own sense of moral obligation, backed up by the public opinion of the civilized world? What shall be done with armaments? What with tariffs and other economic policies of a divisive nature? For the United States there is the further question of what is to become of her historic policy of isolation.

All of these are weighty problems. And yet they are hardly more difficult than were the problems that confronted the founders of our own American national government a century and a quarter ago. Even within the international field there are leagues and unions that testify forcefully to the possibilities of the federal principle. The so-called British Empire is in reality a great league of self-governing states. In a different way, the Pan-American Union, working through its periodic conferences and its administrative board at Washington, impresses the same lesson.

The Proposed League of Nations. — International government obviously requires some kind of league of nations, bound together under the terms of a written compact and prepared to act in harmony to accomplish certain purposes. Since 1914 proposals for such a league have been offered by statesmen, by scholars, and by societies in practically every important country. It is impossible to survey all of these plans here. Rather it must suffice to present the salient features of a scheme which was worked out in our own country, and which, in its essentials, has won wide acceptance both here and abroad. This is the plan sponsored by a well-known organization, the League to Enforce Peace (of which ex-President Taft is executive head), and promulgated at a large and representative voluntary gathering at Philadelphia in June, 1915. The platform of this society, embracing the cardinal features of the plan, calls for a league of nations which the United States shall join, and contains the following definite proposals:

First: All justiciable questions arising between the signatory powers, not settled by negotiation, shall, subject to the limitations of treaties, be submitted to a judicial tribunal for hearing and judgment, both upon the merits and upon any issue as to its jurisdiction of the question.

Second: All other questions arising between the signatories, and not settled by negotiation, shall be submitted to a council of conciliation for hearing, consideration, and recommendation.

Third: The signatory powers shall jointly use forthwith both their economic and military forces against any one of their number that goes to war, or commits acts of hostility, against another of the signatories before any question arising shall be submitted as provided in the foregoing.

Fourth: Conferences between the signatory powers shall be held from time to time to formulate and codify rules of international law, which, unless some signatory shall signify its dissent within a stated period, shall thereafter govern in the decisions of the Judicial Tribunal mentioned in Article One.

The argument in favor of the sort of organization here outlined may be paraphrased from a statement prepared by the chairman of the League's executive committee, President Lowell of Harvard University, as follows.[1] The nations of the world to-day find themselves in the position of frontier settlements in America half a century ago, before orderly government was set up. They are, in the main, well disposed. But in the absence of an authority that can enforce order, they feel obliged to look out for their own security by arming themselves against possible insult or attack. A society, however, in which everybody carries arms and stands ready for an instant engagement is certain to be troubled with much unnecessary violence. Quarrels are easily provoked, belligerent actions are precipitate. In the frontier community this situation was met by the organization of vigilance committees having the support of all good citizens; and in time these temporary agencies were replaced by the policeman and the sheriff with the *posse comitatus*. These authorities maintained order because they were given the power and the means to meet violence with force, and because they had the bulk of the community behind them.

The nations, however, while suffering from precisely the same disorders incident to excessive individualism and belligerency, have not as yet created any common police authority. They have met the situation, in a degree, by the building up and acceptance of international law, and by cultivation of the habit of submitting disputes to arbitration. But, as recent events have shown, international law is a restraint only in so far as nations choose to be bound by it; and there is no power, beyond a somewhat ethereal public sentiment, to compel a state to submit its controversies to arbitration or other processes of peaceful settlement. The league of nations proposed in the above platform is put forward to meet this need. It is freely admitted that there are " differences in the conception of justice and right, divergencies in civilization, so profound that people will fight over them, and face even the prospect of disaster in war rather than submit," and hence it is recognized that attempts to abolish all war are futile. But it is felt that a much larger proportion than at present of the disputes that arise among states could be settled in a peaceful manner if an organization existed which could compel every member to submit its justiciable

[1] "A League to Enforce Peace," *World Peace Foundation, Pamphlet Series*, **V**, No. v, pt. 1.

disputes (*i.e.*, those that can be settled strictly on the basis of international law) to a tribunal and its non-justiciable disputes to a council of conciliation, in full knowledge that if it fails to do this it will bring down upon itself both the economic and the military resistance of the remaining members of the league.

Fundamental Conditions of the League. — On matters of detail there is room for much difference of opinion; they will have to be carefully worked out by experts in international law and diplomacy. But there are certain main features of the plan upon which there is already substantial agreement. The first is that the members of the league, while as a matter of course retaining their essentially separate and independent character, must be prepared to accept certain limitations upon their sovereignty. There are widely differing conceptions of the term "sovereignty," and the matter of definition cannot be entered into here. But if the absolutist view be taken, *i.e.*, that an independent state is entirely self-contained and free of all restriction, a league of nations cannot be more than a rope of sand unless the members renounce, to some extent, their individual sovereignty and bind themselves to act in a given situation, not under their own will, but under the collective will of the league. This is a phase of the matter that troubles many people. But unless the point is conceded there is no use of pursuing the project farther. A second requisite is that the map of Europe, and of the world, shall be remade so as to satisfy great and legitimate nationalist aspirations before the plan goes into effect. The league must rest upon a *status quo* which is maintained not simply, as was the Concert after 1815, because it is a legal fact and its disturbance would be inconvenient to the rulers, but because it is inherently equitable.[1] The territorial and political readjustments which the war has made necessary will undoubtedly go far toward meeting this requirement.

A third essential is that, at the beginning at all events, membership in the league shall be confined to a few of the greater nations. It is true that most proposals hitherto made contemplate a league formed of all nations that care to enter. But this plan presents insuperable difficulties. While all independent states, large and small, are juristically equal, they are, in strength and

[1] Zimmern, *Nationality and Government*, 28.

influence, very unequal. If, therefore, in the words of a recent writer, " representation in international bodies — legislative, judicial, and executive — were equal, it would involve a certain subjection of the great powers to the will of the small states to which they would not willingly submit. If, on the other hand, representation were proportioned to wealth, population, extent of territory, or any other similar standard, the smaller states would feel that they were in danger of being subordinated by their more powerful neighbors."[1] In particular, difficulty would arise from the pride of nations of intermediate strength and influence, who would be prone to claim as their right the weight attached to the first-class powers. The membership of the league ought, therefore, to be restricted at the outset to nations, five or six in number, that could fairly be given equal representation. It might later be expanded if experience showed that the change could safely be made.

Closely related to this matter is the further essential condition that the league be composed exclusively of democratic states, therein differing completely, of course, from the old Concert. It must be a league of *free* nations, of nations whose policy is under popular control, and whose great object in international as in domestic affairs is justice and concord. The first members should be the five great states that have borne the larger part of the burden of the late war against autocracy — Great Britain, France, Italy, Japan, and the United States. Germany might eventually be admitted; but not until she is wholly purged of autocratic and militaristic domination and has completely abandoned the unholy doctrine of might. She must be put on probation until such a time as she shall have proved, to the satisfaction of the league itself, her right to communion with free nations.

Still another necessity is that the league be endowed with real power; if it is to be a league of peace, it is also to be a league to *enforce* peace. Many reformers hesitate at this. Bentham did so a century and a quarter ago; William J. Bryan and his school have done so in our own day. But the people of the frontier did not wait for a gradual disappearance of shooting affrays through the raising of ethical standards. Even their

[1] Hill, *The Rebuilding of Europe*, 185–186.

descendants of the third and fourth generations have never been able to dispense with the policeman and the *posse comitatus*. Conference, discussion, arbitration, moral appeal — all are good. But they do not wholly meet the situation in which the peoples of the earth now find themselves. There must be somewhere an agency with power to compel respect for law and obedience to it. How far this right of compulsion is to be carried is still a question. The League to Enforce Peace proposes that it shall extend to the punishment of any member that refuses to submit its controversies to the proper agency of adjudication, without obligating the league to enforce the decision of the tribunal or the award of the council of conciliation. This is a minimum. The League acknowledges that the power of compulsion might some day be made to include the right to force nations not only to arbitrate their differences but to accept the findings of the arbitral body; and many persons feel that this should be a feature of the system from the first.

Finally, the league must have machinery through which to accomplish its ends. The platform of the League to Enforce Peace contemplates at least three important agencies: (1) a Court of Arbitration (either that already created at the Hague or one freshly constituted) to hear justiciable cases; (2) a Council of Inquiry and Conciliation, to consider non-justiciable disputes; and (3) a conference of the signatory powers, to be convened from time to time to " formulate and codify rules of international law." Other schemes have been suggested, but none is better than this. Many vital questions of detail would, of course, have to be worked out, whatever general plan were adopted.

America and the League of Nations. — One fact looms above all others, namely, if a league of nations is to become a reality it must be brought into existence as a part of the general international settlement immediately following the war. The great free nations are now in exceptionally sympathetic relation. Under the stress of conflict they have fast acquired the habit of working together for great ends. Furthermore, the statesmen of most countries are on record in favor of the new organization. In England, Mr. Asquith, while yet premier, declared that he looked forward to the league as coming " immediately within the range, and presently within the grasp, of European statesmanship." Viscount Grey, former foreign minister, has declared that the conditions that once made such an organization impracticable have disappeared. The premier, Mr. Lloyd George, and the foreign minister, Mr. Balfour, have pledged their unreserved support. In its Memorandum on War Aims, approved by a special conference December 28, 1917, the Labor party declared a "supernational authority, or league of nations," a necessary part of the coming peace. And a long list of leaders in the nation's thought and life have subscribed to the plan and are working diligently to promote its realization. The statesmen of France have had less to say. The government has taken no stand upon the question, and the press has voiced a feeling, which is undoubtedly widely prevalent, that the nation should not enter any international combination in which Germany or anything German has a place. However, there is little likelihood that Germany would be included in any league at the outset; and it is probable that by the time when her admission would become a practical question the righteous wrath of the French people would have been somewhat assuaged. Individual statesmen and publicists of Italy and Japan, and of Germany herself, have spoken out strongly for the league.

What of the United States? Ten years ago the suggestion that she should become a partner in a permanent and force-employing confederation of nations would have aroused only mild interest, and would have met almost universal dissent, among her statesmen and people. The war has totally changed this situation, and to-day strong sentiment exists, in both official and non-official circles, in favor of a league of which this country shall be an active member. This sentiment has found organized expression chiefly through the League to Enforce Peace, already mentioned. It has found its most authoritative expression through President Wilson, who on sundry occasions has indicated his adherence to the plan. In his celebrated address to Congress, January 8, 1918, in which American war aims were for the first time officially enumerated in some detail, the President named as one of his "fourteen points" the formation of a general association of nations "under specific covenants for the purpose of affording mutual guarantees of political independence and territorial integrity to great and small states alike." In an address delivered in the Metropolitan Opera House, New York, September 27, 1918, he raised the question whether "the assertion of right" after the war should be "haphazard and by casual alliance," or whether there should be "a common concert to oblige the observance of common rights"; and in reply he declared unequivocally for a league of nations which should be "a part, and in a sense the most essential part, of the peace settlement itself." Further essentials, as he conceived them, were stated as follows: "There can be no leagues or alliances or special covenants and understandings within the general and common family of the League of Nations; . . . and more specifically, there can be no special, selfish economic combinations within the league and no employment of any form of economic boycott or exclusion except as the power of economic penalty by exclusion from the markets of the world may be vested in the League of Nations itself as a means of discipline and control."

Entrance into a League of Nations would mean for the United States a complete abandonment of her traditional policy of isolation. To such a course strong objection is certain to be raised. But there are two cardinal facts to be observed. The first is that already during the war the country has abandoned the policy of isolation and has acted in practical alliance with the nations fighting the Central Powers. It is true that the other Powers were always alluded to officially as "associates in war," or "co-belligerents," rather than as "allies." But this was merely a matter of punctilious terminology. The United States not only was really an ally of the other nations; she took the initiative in making the general alliance stronger through a united command and in numerous other ways. In the second place, even if the country had not already abandoned her isolation, the conditions obtaining in the modern world would sooner or later have compelled her to do so. Isolation was a natural, wise, and almost inevitable policy when the Atlantic was a great gulf between the Old World and the New. But in these days, when cables flash news instantly from one continent to another, when goods cross to England or France in a week, when the trade and the very life of each nation depend on materials derived from other nations, when the United States is grown large and rich and strong, isolation is no longer possible. The world has become one great body, and neither the United States nor any other nation can live to itself or refuse to bear its share in the common tasks of civilization. Far from meaning the entrance of the country into an " entangling alliance " of the kind which Washington wisely warned against, and whose probable consequence would be to involve us in war, accession to the League of Nations means, for the moment, insurance against war, and, for the future, a step toward coöperative world organization, and therefore toward an enduring world peace.

SELECTED REFERENCES

C. D. Hazen, *Europe since 1815* (New York, 1910), Chap. xxxii; C. J. H. Hayes, *Political and Social History of Europe* (New York, 1916), II, Chap. xxx; J. H. Rose, *Nationality in Modern History* (New York, 1916), Chaps. ix–x; P. M. Brown, *International Realities* (New York, 1917), Chaps. i–v; D. J. Hill, *The Rebuilding of Europe* (New York, 1917), Chap. vi; ibid., *World Organization as Affected by the Nature of the Modern State* (New York, 1911); J. S. Bassett, *The Lost Fruits of Waterloo* (New York, 1918); J. A. Hobson, *Towards International Government* (New York, 1915); R. Muir, *Nationalism and Internationalism* (Boston, 1917); R. Goldsmith, *A League to Enforce Peace* (New York, 1917); T. Marburg, *A League of Nations*, 2 vols. (New York, 1918); L. S. Woolf, *International Government* (New York, 1916); H. G. Wells, *In the Fourth Year* (New York, 1918); A. H. Fried, *The Restoration of Europe* (New York, 1916); W. Lippmann, *The Stakes of Diplomacy* (New York, 1915); O. Tead, *The People's Part in Peace* (New York, 1918); H. N. Brailsford, *A League of Nations* (London, 1917); N. M. Butler, *The International Mind, an Argument for the Judicial Settlement of International Disputes* (New York, 1912); E. B. Krehbiel, *Nationalism, War, and Society* (New York, 1916); G. H. Perris, *Short History of War and Peace* (New York, 1911); W. A. Phillips, *The Confederation of Europe* (London, 1914); P. S. Reinsch, *Public International Unions, Their Work and Organization* (Boston, 1911); W. I. Hull, *The Two Hague Conferences and Their Contributions to International Law* (Boston, 1908); J. B. Scott, *The Hague Peace Conferences of 1899 and 1908*, 2 vols. (Baltimore, 1909); **J. H. Latané,** *From Isolation to Leadership* (New York, 1918).

INDEX

Abgeordnetenhaus, Prussian House of Representatives, 488, 489–490.
Absolutism, contest between parliamentary government and, in England, 171–180; survival of, in Germany, 504–505; overthrow of German, 529.
Action Libérale, French political party, 361–362.
Administrative Boards in English system of government, 206–207.
Admiralty, officials of the, in England, 205.
Aëronautics, National Advisory Committee for, in United States, 159.
Agencies for war administration, federal, in United States, 158–161.
Agriculture, United States Department of, 117.
Aid to dependents of enlisted men, in United States, 163.
Aircraft Board, the, in United States, 159.
Alaska, representation of, in House of Representatives, 64 n.; administration of government in, 127.
Albany, N. Y., date of municipal charter of, 22; intercolonial conference at, in 1754, 23–24.
Alien Property Custodian, United States, 161.
Aliens, registration of, in United States, 162.
Ambassadors, appointment of, by President of United States, 102.
Amendment of French constitution, 332–333.
Amendments to American Constitution, effect of, on power of states, 41–42.
America. *See* United States.
American citizenship, privileges and duties of, 128–144.
American Republics, International Bureau of, 118.
American Revolution, two aspects of, 24; union of colonies forced by, 24–26.
Amsterdam, International Socialist Congress at (1904), 368.
Amtsbezirk, Prussian judicial district, 502 n.
Amtsgerichte, courts of first instance in German Empire, 481.

Annapolis Convention of 1786, 33–34.
Anne, Queen, reign of, 182, 186.
Appointment, powers of, of President of United States, 98–100; of federal employees by Civil Service Commission, 121–122.
Appropriation Act, in Parliament, 266.
Arbitration, extension of principle of international, by peace conferences, 581.
Army, question of obedience by, in democratic government, 11; power of President of United States in regard to, 100–101; importance of the German, to Emperor William II, 508–509.
Arrondissement, French electoral department, 349, 398, 399; officers of the, 401.
Articles of Confederation, formation of, by second Continental Congress, 28–29; failure of, 30–32; the great and radical vice of, 32; movement for revision, resulting in national constitutional convention of 1787, 32–35; the Constitution contrasted with, 36–39.
Asquith, Herbert, opposition of, to woman's suffrage, 231; causes of conversion of, to suffrage for women, 234; quoted on a coming league of nations, 588–589.
Australia, account of Commonwealth of, 312–314.
Austria, declaration of war against, by United States, 147; early rivalry of Prussia and, 442–443; Prussian victory over, in 1866, 444; rise of Habsburg dominion, 531–533; character of polyglot empire of Austria-Hungary, 533–535; nature of union between Hungary and, 535–541; constitution of, 541–543; distinction made between Austrian Empire and Austria-Hungary, 541 n.; the Emperor and the ministers, 543–544; the Reichsrath, 544–546; electoral system, 546–549; government of Hungary, 549–552; general aspects of Austro-Hungarian political situation, 552–555.
Autocratic ideal of government, the, 2–3; application of, in Germany, 12–14; the bulwarks of autocracy in German Empire, 504–512.

594 INDEX

Baden, alliance of, with Prussia, 444; becomes a member of German Empire, 449; rights reserved by, 454; votes of, in Bundesrath, 466; code of law in, 480.
Bahama Islands, government of, 315.
Balance of power, doctrine of, 573–574; Concert of Europe superseded by, 579; detrimental effect of, on international principle, 579–580.
Ballot Act of 1872, in England, 184, 236.
Basutoland, character as a crown colony, 315.
Bavaria, steps leading to incorporation of, in German Empire, 444, 447, 449; rights reserved by, 454; votes of, in Bundesrath, 466; number of members in Reichstag, 472.
Bebel, August, a founder of Social Democratic party, 516.
Belgium, proportional representation in, 354, 430–434; creation of, as a nation, 421; constitution of, 421–423; governmental system of, 424–426; the suffrage in, 426–430.
Bermuda, government of, 315.
Bill of Rights, the English, 4; provisions of, 179–180.
Bills, course of, in American Congress, 84–85; in British Parliament, 263–267.
Bismarck, Otto von, leadership secured for Prussian autocracy by, 443; the "blood and iron" policy of, 443; constitution of North German Confederation drafted by, 444–445; part taken by, in establishing German Empire, 446; reorganization of local government of Prussia by, 496–497.
Boards, United States federal, in war time, 158–161; administrative, in English system of government, 206–207.
Bohemia, incorporation of, in Habsburg dominion, 532–533.
Borough franchises in England in early 19th century, 223.
Borough government in England, 394–396.
Bourbon government in France, 325–326.
Briand, Aristide, French socialist leader, 369.
Bribery in elections, punishment of, in England, 237.
British Empire, character of, 304–307; the self-governing dominions, 307–308; Dominion of Canada, 308–311; Commonwealth of Australia, 312–314; the Union of South Africa, 314–315; crown colonies, 315–316; protectorates, 316–317; the Empire of India, 317–320; problem of imperial reorganization, 320–323; promised readjustment of constitutional relations of British government, 323. See England.
Bryan, W. J., pacifist school of, 587.
Budget, in House of Commons, 267–268.
Bundesrath, peculiar character of, as a feature of a modern government, 465–466; origins and composition of, 466–467; organization of and procedure in, 467–469; functions and powers of, 469–471.

"Cabal" of Charles II, the, 184.
Cabinet, of President of United States, 114–116; rise of the, in English constitutional system, 184–186; development of rule that members must be in sympathy with dominant party in House of Commons, 186–187; composition of British, 208–209; discussion of British, 210–217; the imperial war cabinet (1916–18), 217–219, 322–323; how increased power of, affects Parliament in legislation and in administration, 260–263; absence of a, from German system of government, 465.
California, use of the recall in, 137, 138.
Campaign, Presidential, in United States, 90–91.
Campbell-Bannerman, leader of Liberal party in England, 277.
Canada, Dominion of, form and character of government of, 308–311.
Canton, unit of local government in France, 401.
Capital Issues Committee, in United States, 161.
Casimir-Perier, President of France, 333.
Cassation, Court of, in France, 386.
Censorship Board, in United States, 160.
Central American Court of Justice, 582.
Ceylon, government of, 315.
Chamber of Deputies, in France, 349–352; the Italian, 409.
Chamberlain, Joseph, founder of National Liberal Federation, 281; new tariff system advocated by, 291–292.
Chancellor, German, functions of, 461–463.
Chancery court in England, 379–380.
Charles I of England, 176.
Charles II of England, 178.
Chinese, exclusion of, from American citizenship, 130.
Church, the Christian, grounded on idea of world-unity, 572.
Cities, initiative and referendum in American, 135.

INDEX

Citizenship, privileges and duties of American, 128–144.
Civil list, the, in England, 197; of King of Prussia, 487.
Civil proceedings in English legal system, 378–381.
Civil service, in United States, 118–119; in English government, 207–208.
Civil Service Commission, United States, 118.
Civil Service Law, passage of, 119; operation of, 120–121; appointment and removal of federal employees under, 121–123.
Closure, in House of Commons, 269.
Coalition cabinet in English government, succeeded by war cabinet, 217–219.
Codes of law, French, 381–383; in German Empire, 451, 479–481.
Colonial origins of American system of government, 15–17.
Commerce, powers of Congress regarding, 72–74; United States Department of, 117.
Commissions, principal federal, in United States, 118; creation of new, in war time, 158–161.
Committee on Public Information, United States, 160–161.
Committee system in Congress, 81–82.
Commons. *See* House of Commons.
Commonwealth, period of, in England, 176–178.
Commune, local governmental division in France, 401–404; the true focus of local life, 404.
Commune of Paris (1871), 328.
Concert of Europe, formation of the, 577–578; credit due, and reasons for failure of, 578; wherein proposed League of Nations differs from, 587.
Congress of United States, legislative power vested in, under articles of Constitution, 56; membership and powers of, and methods of conducting business by, 62–85; relations between President and, 103–107; duties of departmental heads prescribed by, 111.
Connecticut, colonial governor of, 18–19; colonial legislature in, 19.
Conservative party, in England, successor to Tories, 275; characteristics of, 276–277; history of, since 1874, 277–279; present-day principles and policies of, 282; main strongholds of, 283.
Constitution, development of English, 181–188; meaning of, in England, 189–190; component elements of English, 190–192; power of Parliament to alter, 193–194; of France, 325–332; of Italy, 406–408; of Belgium, 421–423; of German Empire, 447–449; of Prussia, 484–486; of Austria, 541–543; of Hungary, 549–550.
Constitution of United States, origins of the, 16; meeting of convention of 1787 which formulated, 34–35; drafting of, 35–36; provisions of, contrasted with Articles of Confederation, 36–39; ratification of, by the states, 39–40; scope of, as applied to states of Union, 41–48; supremacy of the, 54–55; provisions of, for election of President and Vice-President, 91; personal and property rights of citizens under, 138–142.
Constitutional government, England's lead in solving problem of, 165.
Constitutions of states of United States, 51–53.
Continental Congress, the first, 26–27; the second, 27–28.
Convention, national, for nomination of President, 86–90.
Convention system for nominating candidates for House of Representatives, 65–66.
Copyrights, Congressional control of, 73; international, 73.
Corrupt and Illegal Practices Act of 1883, in England, 184, 237.
Council of State, French administrative tribunal, 387–388.
Counties, in England, 390.
County council, in England, 390–391.
County government, in middle colonies in pre-Revolutionary America, 23; in Virginia, 23.
Courts, the federal, under American Constitution, 58–61; power of Congress over, 75; English, 373–388; French, 384–388; in German Empire, 481–482.
Crimes, powers of Congress in regard to, 74–75; definition of new, in United States, during war, 162–163.
Criminal justice in England, 375–378.
Cromwell, Oliver, Protector of England, 177–178.
Crown colonies of British Empire, 315–316.
Cuba, proportional representation in, 354 n.

Daily Telegraph incident, 523.
Dartmouth College case, 45.
Deák, Magyar leader, 537.
Declaration of Independence, the, 1; Jefferson quoted concerning, 1–2.
Declaration of the Rights of Man, issuance of, in France, 6.

Defense, national, powers of Congress regarding, 72.
Delaware, colonial governor of, 19.
Democratic ideal, the, 1-2; practical application of, in England, France, and United States, 3-12.
Denmark, proportional representation in, 354.
Department, French governmental division, 397-398.
Departments, federal, in United States, 110-111; heads of, 111-114; President's Cabinet composed of heads of, 114-116; list of, with chief officers, subdivisions, and agencies embraced by, 116-117.
Diplomacy, secret and open, 564.
Diplomatic positions, powers of President and of Congress concerning, 101-102.
Disraeli, Benjamin, chief of Conservative party, 276.
Divine right theory, 2-3; held by Stuart dynasty in England, 174; end of, in England, with adoption of Bill of Rights, 180; held by Bourbon kings in France, 325; Bismarck a believer in, 443; held by Hohenzollern dynasty, 506; Emperor William II's statement of, 507-508; has lived on in Germany only, 508.
Dominions of British Empire, 307-308.

Education Act of 1902 in England, 391.
Education, popular, in United States, France, and England, 10.
Egypt, position of, as a British protectorate, 316-317.
Electoral procedure in France, 350-352.
Electoral system, operation of, in choice of President of United States, 86-94.
Emergency Fleet Corporation, United States, 158-159.
Eminent domain, power of, held by federal government in United States, 142.
Employees' Compensation Commission, United States, 118.
Employees, United States federal, examinations for, 120-121; appointment and removal of, 121-123; political rights and duties of, 123-125.
Employment Service, in United States, 160.
England, practical application of ideal of self-government in, 3-5; control of the army in, 11; leadership in Parliament vested in Prime Minister, 82-83; rise of free government in, 165 ff.; political importance of, 165-166; early political development of, 166-167; granting of Great Charter, 167-168; rise and growth in power of Parliament, 168-171; contest between absolutism and parliamentary government, 171-180; development of constitution in 18th and 19th centuries, 181-188; nature and sources of constitution, 189-190; component elements of constitution, 190-192; power of Parliament to alter constitution, 193-194; position of King, as to privileges, powers, real authority and service, 196-200; the ministers and the administrative machinery, 203-219; Parliament and the growth of democracy, 220-246; Parliament at work, 247-271; party system in, 272-275; party history and organization, 275-281; party composition, 281-283; recent party issues, 283-285; tariff and taxation, 291-293; the land and rural employment questions, 293-294; trade-unionism and socialism, 294-296; legal and judicial system, 373 ff.; character and form of the law, 373-375; criminal justice and its agencies, 375-378; civil proceedings, 378-381; local government, 388-396; attitude of, toward plan for League to Enforce Peace, 588-589. *See also* Great Britain.
Espionage Act of 1917, 139, 156-158.
Executive agreements, power of President of United States to make, 102.
Executive departments, power of Congress over, 75.
Express service, government control of in United States, 156.
Extradition laws, in United States, 54.

Fabian Society, the, 296.
Fallières, Armand, President of France, 333.
Farm Loan Board, Federal, in United States, 118.
Faure, Félix, President of France, 333.
Federal courts of United States, 58-61.
Federal employees in United States, political rights and duties of, 123-125.
Federalist, The, 40.
Federal Reserve Board, United States, 118.
Federal system in United States government, 41-61.
Filibustering, practice of, 69-70; derivation of term, 80 n.
Finance Act, in Parliament, 266.
Finland, proportional representation in, 354.
Food Administration, in United States, 159.
Food conservation in United States, 162.
Food and fuel control law in United States during war against Germany, 152-153.

INDEX

597

Foreign relations, powers of Congress in regard to, 74; responsibility of President of United States concerning, 101–102.
Fourteen points, President Wilson's, 565–569.
France, practical application of ideal of self-government in, 5–7; extreme democracy of government of, 7–8; origins of constitution of, 325–329; circumstances of formation of constitution, 329–330; general features of constitution, 330–332; amendment of constitution, 332–333; the office of President, 333–337; the ministry, 337–345; composition of parliament, 346–356; sessions and organization of parliament, and powers and procedure, 356–359; political parties since 1871, 359–372; legal and judicial systems of, 381 ff.; the codes of law, 381–383; appointment and tenure of judges, 383–384; ordinary courts, 384–386; administrative law and administrative tribunals, 386–388; local government, 397–404.
Francis Joseph I, Emperor of Austria-Hungary, 531, 538, 542, 552.
Frankfort, Peace of (1871), 328.
Frederick II, "the Great," of Prussia, 506.
Frederick III of Prussia, 507.
Freedom of speech of American citizens, 139.

George III of England, 182–183.
German Empire, autocratic ideal of government in, 2–3; application of autocratic principle in, 12–14; declaration of war against, by United States, 147; political heritage of, 436–438; autocracy vs. liberalism in, from 1815 to 1848, 438–440; the liberal failure of 1848, 440–442; leadership taken by Prussian autocracy, 442–444; the North German Confederation, 444–445; establishment of Empire, 445–447; constitution of, 447–449; states which compose, 449; federal character of Empire, 449–450; division of powers between Empire and states, 450–453; the privileged states, 453–454; status and powers of Emperor, 456–461; the Chancellor and the ministers, 461–465; the Bundesrath, 465–471; the Reichstag, 471–479; law and justice, 479–482; reasons for Prussian preponderance, 483–484; position of Emperor as King of Prussia, 486–487; the survival of absolutism in, 504–505; importance of the army, 508–509; political parties and their programs, 512–522; history of movement for political reform, 522–529;

present conditions and outlook in, 529; aims of America in war against, 556–570; question of admittance of, to League of Nations, 587, 589.
Gerrymander, the, 64.
Gettysburg Address, Lincoln's, 8–9.
Gibraltar, character as a crown colony, 315.
Gladstone, W. E., praise of American Constitution by, 16; chief of English Liberal party, 276.
Government Printing Office, United States, 118.
Governor, the colonial, in pre-Revolutionary America, 17–19.
Great Britain, creation of, by union of Scotland with England, 187; union of Ireland with, 187–188. *See* England.
Great Charter, granting of the, 167–168.
Grévy, Jules, President of France, 333.
Grotius, *De Jure Belli et Pacis* of, 575.
Guam, government of, 127 n.
Guesde, Jules, French socialist leader, 366, 367, 368–369.
Guillotine, in House of Commons, 269–270.

Habsburg dominion, rise of, 531–533.
Hague Court, 582.
Hague peace conferences, 581–582.
Hamilton, Alexander, faults and vices found in Articles of Confederation by, 32, 38; instrumental in drafting of national Constitution, 33–34; writings by, in favor of ratification of Constitution, 40.
Hanoverian dynasty in England, 182–183; adoption of name "Windsor dynasty for," 196 n.
Hawaii, representation of, in House of Representatives, 64 n; administration of government in, 127.
Henderson, Arthur, exponent of aims of English Labor party, 299.
Herrenhaus, Prussian House of Lords, 488.
Hesse, votes of, in Bundesrath, 466.
Hohenzollerns, rule of the, in Prussia and in Germany, 13; account of the, 505–507.
Holy Alliance, signing of the, 577.
Holy Roman Empire, 437; ending of, 438; grounded upon idea of world-unity, 572.
Home Rule movement, Irish, 188; secession from Liberal party caused by, in 1886, 277; momentousness of, in 1914, 279; account of, 285–290.
House of Commons, British, growth of ascendancy of, over House of Lords, 183–184; composition of, 221–222; problem of electoral reform in early 19th century, 222–224; problem of redistribution of seats, 224–225; Reform Act of 1832, 225–

226; Representation of the People Acts of 1867 and 1884, 226-228; questions of manhood suffrage, plural voting, and redistribution (1885-1918), 228-230; question of woman's suffrage (1885-1918), 230-231; Representation of the People Act of 1918, 231-235; elections to, 235-236; regulation of electoral expenses, 236-237; account of work of, 247 ff.; hall in which sessions are held, 248-249; officers of, 250-252; committees of, 252-254; privileges of members, 255-256; payment of members, 256-257; procedure in, 263-268; rules of, 268-269; closure and the guillotine, 269-270; votes and divisions, 270-271.

House of Commons, Canadian, 310.

House of Lords, British, composition of, 237-238; long-standing breach between the nation and, 238-239; reform proposals up to 1909, 239-241; antecedents of Parliament Act of 1911, 241-243; passage of Parliament Act and effects, 243-244; question of further reform, 245-246; account of work of, 247 ff.; hall in which sessions are held, 248-249; organization of, 254-255; privileges of members, 255-256; rules of procedure in, 271; reform of, 284; control of, over criminal and civil tribunals in Great Britain, 380-381.

House of Lords, Austrian, 544.

House of Lords, Prussian, 488-489.

House of Representatives, American, membership of, 62-65; comparison of Senate and, 70-71; party organization in, 77-78; rules of, 79-81; committees of, 81-82; leadership in, 82-83; transaction of legislative business in, 83-85.

House of Representatives, Australian, 313.

House of Representatives, Austrian, 544.

House of Representatives, Belgian, 425-426.

House of Representatives, of Prussian Landtag, 489-491.

Humble Petition and Advice, the, constitution of England under Cromwell, 177.

Hungary, union of, with Austria, 532, 533; nature of union, 535-541; constitution and government of, 549-552. *See also* Austria.

Illinois, Public Opinion System in, 134.

Impeachment, powers of Congress in regard to, 76-77.

Independent Labor party in England, 296.

India, government of, 317-320.

Indiana, the referendum in, 134-135.

Initiative and referendum in United States, 132-137.

Instrument of Government, earliest of written constitutions, 177.

Insurance of United States soldiers and sailors during European war, 150.

Interior Department of United States, 117.

International government, the problem of, 572 ff.; nationalism and the balance of power, 572-574; growth of the international idea, 574-578; Concert of Europe and the new balance of power, 578-580; peace propaganda and movements from 1899 to 1914, 580-582; need of international government, 582-584; present-day solution found in a league of nations for enforcement of peace, 584-588.

Interpellation, in France, 343.

Interstate commerce, powers of states relative to, 43.

Interstate Commerce Commission, United States, 118.

Ireland, early political history of, 187-188; union of, with Great Britain, 188.

Irish Home Rule, history of question, 285-290.

Irish Nationalist party, 281.

Isolation, abandonment of policy of, by United States, 590-591.

Italy, political organization of, 405 ff.; unification of, 405-406; constitution of, 406-408; governmental system of, 408-409; electoral arrangements in, 409-412; strained relations between Quirinal and Vatican, 412-414; political parties in, 414-416; growth of socialism in, 416-420.

Jamaica, government of, 315.

James II of England, 178-179.

Japan, proportional representation in, 354 n.

Japanese, exclusion of, from American citizenship, 130.

Jaurès, French socialist leader, 366-367.

Jefferson, Thomas, quoted concerning the democratic ideal, 1-2; views of, on term of office of President, 96; quoted on President's veto power, 107-108.

Judiciary, supremacy of the, in American federal system, 57-58; power of Congress over federal, 75; English, 373-382; French, 383-384; in German Empire, 481-482.

Junkers, account of landed Prussian aristocracy called, 509-510.

Justice, Department of, of United States, 117.

Kant, Immanuel, contribution of, to 18th century peace literature, 576.

Kiel, acquisition of, by Prussia, 444.

INDEX

King of England, privileges of, 196-197; reason for survival of monarchy, 200-202.
King's Bench, Court of, in England, 379-380.
Kultur, significance and scope of term, 510-511; a bulwark of autocracy, 512.

Labor, United States Department of, 117.
Labor party in England, growth of, 275; reason for, 281-282; composition and character of, 296-298; program of, as set forth by Arthur Henderson, 298-303; plan of a league of nations advocated by, 589.
Landgerichte, German district courts, 481.
Land question in England, 293-294.
Landtag, the Prussian, 488-491; actual character of, 494-495.
Lane, Franklin K., quoted on war legislation and socialism, 146-147.
Law, English, 373-375; French, 381-388; in German Empire, 479-481.
Law lords in British upper chamber, 238.
League of Nations, President Wilson quoted on a, 561-564; main features of plan for, 584-588; the time now ripe for, 588-589.
League to Enforce Peace, the, 584-586; fundamental conditions of, 586-588; America and the, 589-591.
Legislatures, colonial, in America, 19-22.
Leo XIII, Pope, decrees of, 414.
Liberal party in England, successor to Whigs, 275; characteristics of, 276-277; history of, since 1874, 277-279; present-day principles and policies of, 282; main strongholds of, 283; cause of free trade championed by, 292.
Liberal Unionist party in England, 277.
Liberty loans in United States, 150-151.
Liebknecht, Wilhelm, one of founders of Social Democratic party, 516.
Lincoln, Abraham, American ideal of self-government expressed by, 8-9.
List system of balloting, 431-433.
Local government, in colonial America, 22-23; in England, 388-396; in France, 397-404; in Prussia, 495-502.
Log-rolling, practice called, 79.
Lord High Chancellorship in England, 205-206.
Lords. *See* House of Lords.
Los Angeles, use of recall in, 137, 138.
Loubet, Émile, President of France, 333.
Lusitania message of President Wilson, 559-560.

MacMahon, Marshal, elected President of French Republic, 329.
Magna Carta, granting of, 167-168.

Magyars, the, 534, 551-552.
Malta, government of, 315.
Maryland, colonial governor of, 19.
Massachusetts, colonial government in, 18; colonial legislature in, 19-21; resolution passed in, concerning advisability of calling a national assembly (1785), 33.
Mayor, office of, in England, 395; in France, 403-404.
Merit system, in America, 119; in England, 207.
Military census, United States, 161.
Military instruction in schools in United States, 162.
Military service, obligations of American citizens in regard to, 142.
Militia laws, state, 161-162.
Mill, John Stuart, woman's suffrage amendment advocated by, 230.
Ministry, in England, composition and organization of, 203-204; Treasury, Admiralty, and Lord High Chancellorship, 204-206; responsibility of, 212-213; overthrowing of, 213-214; in French system of government, 337-345; in Italy, 408; in German Empire, 463-465; in Prussia, 487-488; in Austria, 543-544.
Model Parliament of 1295, 169.
Monetary system, limitations on powers of state governments relative to, 43-44; regulation of, by Congress, 74.
Money bills in Parliament, procedure in case of, 265-267.
Montesquieu, doctrine of separation of powers originated by, 55-56.
Municipal government, initiative and referendum in America, 135.
Municipal institutions in colonial America, 22-23.

Nationalism, the principle of, 572-573; advantages and drawbacks of, 573-574.
National Liberal Federation in England, 280.
National Union of Conservative and Constitutional Associations, in England, 280.
Naturalization, admittance to American citizenship by, 129-130.
Navy, power of President of United States in regard to, 100-101.
Navy Department of United States, chief officers, subdivisions, and agencies embraced by, 117.
Nebraska, initiative and referendum in, 134.
New England Confederation of 1643, 23.
New York, date of municipal charter of, 22; congress of colonies at, in 1765, 24.
North America Act, British, of 1867, 309.

North German Confederation, formation of, 444-445.

Oberlandesgerichte, German courts of appellate jurisdiction, 481-482.
Oklahoma, initiative and referendum in, 133, 134.
Opportunism, policy of, in France, 367-368.
Oregon, initiative and referendum in, 133-134; the recall in, 137; proportional representation in, 354 n.
Overman act, the, 110-111.

Pan-American conferences, 581.
Parish, the, in England, 392-393.
Parliament, the British, 5; rise of, 168; growth of, in power, 170-171; position of, under the Tudor monarchs, 172-174; power of, to alter the constitution, 193-194; importance of, 220-221; the House of Commons, 221-235; elections to, 235-236; the House of Lords, 237-246; meetings, organization, and privileges of members, 247-257; physical surroundings, 248-250; functions and powers of, 258; loss of power to cabinet and to electorate, 259-260; the cabinet and, in legislation and in administration, 260-263; procedure in, 263-271; party organization in, 279-280. *See also* House of Commons *and* House of Lords.
Parliament Act of 1911, 241-244, 278.
Parliamentary system, in Canada, 310; in Australia, 313; in France, 340-359; in Italy, 408-409; in Belgium, 425-426; in Austria, 544-546; in Hungary, 551.
Parnell, C. S., leader of Irish Home Rule movement, 286.
Parties, in France since 1871, 359-372; in Italy, 414-420; in German Empire, 512-522; in Austria-Hungary, 543.
Party, beginnings of system in England, 186-187; importance and uses of, 272-273; government by, in England, 273-274; the two-party organization, 274-275; history of English, to 1874, 275-277; history since 1874, 277-279; national and local organization, 279-281; recent party issues, 283-285.
Party organization, in American Congress, 77-78.
Patents, Congressional control of, 73.
Peace movement of 1899-1914, 580-582.
Pennsylvania, colonial governor of, 19; colonial legislature in, 19; county government in colonial, 23.
Pensions, question of, for civil service employees in United States, 125.

Personal rights of American citizens, 138-141.
Philadelphia, date of municipal charter of, 22.
Philippine Islands, representation of, in House of Representatives, 64 n.; stages in government of, 127.
Pius IX, Pope, hostility of, to Italian government, 413-414.
Plural voting, problem of, in England, 229-230; under Act of 1918, 233; in Belgium, 428-429.
Poincaré, Raymond, President of France, 333.
Police power of states of United States, 48.
Political parties. *See* Parties.
Political rights of federal employees, 123-125.
Poor relief in England, 393.
Pope, relations between king of Italy and, 412-414.
Porto Rico, representation of, in House of Representatives, 64 n.; administration of government in, 127.
Postal system, federal control of, in United States, 73-74.
Post-Office Department of United States, chief officers, subdivisions, and agencies embraced by, 117.
Poyning's Law of 1494, 187.
Prefects of departments in France, 399-400.
Prefectural council in France, 388.
President of France, 7; election, qualifications, and privileges of, 333-335; executive and legislative powers of, 335-337; relations of the ministry to, 337-338.
President of United States, executive power vested in, 56; action of, on legislative bills, 85; nomination and election of, 86-94; inauguration of, 94-95; qualifications of, 95-96; order of succession to office, 95 n.; salary of, 95 n.; as a political leader and as head of national administration, 96-98; power of appointment and removal, 98-100; war powers of, 100-101; power concerning foreign affairs, 101-102; power of pardon, 102-103; relations between Congress and, 103-107; veto power of, 107-109; power in regard to creation of federal offices and agencies, 110-111; relation between heads of departments and, 111-112; the Cabinet, 114-116.
Prime minister, appointment of, in England, 209-210; the guiding force within the ministry, 215-216.
Priorities Board, United States, 158.
Privy Council in English government, 208 n.
Proclamations, issuing of, by Tudor monarchs in England, 173.
Property rights of American citizens, 141-142.

INDEX

Proportional representation, spread of idea of, in Europe, 354; in Belgium, 430-434.
Proportional Representation League in France, 354.
Protectorate, period of the, in England, 177-178.
Protectorates of British Empire, 316-317.
Provinz, administrative unit of Prussian local government, 498-500.
Prussia, practically an absolute monarchy, 12-13; iron rule of Hohenzollerns in, 13; leadership among German states assumed by, 442-444; the preponderating power in German Empire, 453-454, 483; votes of, in Bundesrath, 466; number of members in Reichstag, 472; account of government of, 483 ff.; reasons for preponderance of, 483-484; constitution of, 484-486; the king and the ministers, 486-488; the Landtag, 488-491; movement for electoral reform, 491-494; actual character of Landtag, 494-495; origins and principles of local government, 495-498; account of rise of Hohenzollerns in, 505-506; the army, 508-509; the Junkers, 509-510.
Public Opinion System in Illinois, 134.

Quadruple Alliance of 1815, 577-578.
Qualifications of President of United States, 95-96.
Quarter sessions, courts of, in England, 377.
Quirinal and Vatican, relations between, 412-414.
Quorum, in Congress, 69.

Radical party, in England, in early 19th century, 276.
Railroads, government control of, in United States, 154-156.
Recall, the, in American government, 137-138.
Red Cross, American National, 161.
Redistribution of seats, problem of, in electoral reform in England, 224-225.
Redistribution of Seats Act of 1885, 184, 228.
Reed, Thomas B., as Speaker of House of Representatives, 83.
Referendum, the popular, in United States, 132-137; of legislative questions to the electorate, in England, 260, 285.
Reform Bill of 1832 in England, 4-5, 184, 225-226.
Regierungsbezirke, districts of Prussian provinces, 500.
Reichsgericht, federal court of German Empire, 482.
Reichsrath of Austria, 544-546.

Reichstag, special interest of, as a legislative body, 471-472; composition of, and election to, 472-474; organization of and procedure in, 474-476; powers and actual character of, 476-479.
Religious freedom, in United States, 139; in House of Commons, 221.
Removal, powers of, of President of United States, 98-100; of federal employees by Civil Service Commission, 122-123.
Representation of the People Acts of 1867 and 1884, 184, 226-228; of 1918, 231-235.
Reserve Board, United States Federal, 118.
Revenue laws in United States for support of war, 152.
Revolution of 1688 in England, 179-180.
Rhode Island, colonial government of, 18-19.
Rights of Man, Declaration of, in France, 6.
Roosevelt, Theodore, woman's suffrage approved by, 9; as party leader while President, 105; use of veto power by, 109; extension of merit system in civil service by, 120.
Rousseau, J. J., influence of, on self-government in France, 6.
Royal governors in colonial America, 17-18.
Rural employment question in England, 293-294.

Sadi-Carnot, F., President of France, 333.
Sadowa, defeat of Austria at, 444, 537.
Saxony, votes of, in Bundesrath, 466; number of members in Reichstag, 472; code of law in, 480.
Schwurgerichte, German jury courts, 481.
Scotland, union of, with England, 187.
Scrutin d'arrondissement, 349; discussion of, 352-353.
Scrutin de liste, 350, 352-353.
Secretaries of State in English system of government, 206.
Secret diplomacy, President Wilson quoted on, 564.
Selective draft law of May, 1917, in United States, 147-150.
Self-defense as one of America's war aims, 556-558.
Self-government, the democratic ideal, 1-2; practical application of ideal of, in England, France, and United States, 3-11; the forms of, 11-12.
Seligman, E. R. A., quoted on taxation during European war, 152.
Senate, the American, 66-68; comparison of House of Representatives and, 70-71; party organization in, 77-78; committees of, 81-82; organization of, 84; action of,

on bills, 85; power of, concerning foreign affairs, 101–102.
Senate, Canadian, 310; Australian, 313; French, 347–349; Italian, 408–409.
Separation of powers, doctrine of, in American federal system, 55–57.
Septennial Act of 1716, 183.
Shays's Rebellion, 31.
Sherman, John, quoted on relation between President and departmental heads, 111–112.
Shipbuilding in United States during war against Germany, 153–154.
Shipping, government control of coastwise, in United States, 154–156.
Shipping Board, United States, 118.
Slavs, the, 534; location and numbers of, 552.
Small Holdings and Allotments Act of 1907, 293.
Smith, Thomas, doctrine of, 173–174.
Social Democratic party in Germany, 516–518, 520–522.
Socialism, distinction between war legislation and, 146–147; in England, 294–296; in France, 365–367; Jaurès and the plea for opportunism, 367–368; the *Parti Socialist Unifié*, 368–370; general aspects of French, in recent years, 370–372; in Italy, 416–418; in Belgium, 430, 433; in Germany, 516–518, 520–522.
South Africa, Union of, 314–315.
Speaker's Conference of British Parliament, 232.
Speech from the Throne, prepared by cabinet, 198, 216.
Spoils system, in United States, 119.
State Department of United States, chief officers, subdivisions, and agencies embraced by, 116.
State governments, formation of, in America, 29–30.
States, position of, in the American federal system, 41–50; admission of new, 50–51; constitutions of, 51–53; interstate relations, 53–54; apportionment of members of House of Representatives among, 63–64.
Straits Settlements, government of, 315.
Stuart dynasty, period of, in England, 174–176; restoration of, 178–179.
Succession to office of President of United States, 95 n.
Suffrage, right of, in United States, 130–132; in England in early 19th century, 223; in England from 1885 to 1918, 228–230; in Italy, 409–412; in Belgium, 426–434; in German Empire, 473; in Prussia, 489–494; in Austria, 546–549; in Hungary, 551.

Supreme Court of United States, judicial power vested in, under articles of Constitution, 56; position of, in American federal system, 57–58; jurisdiction of, 61.
Sweden, proportional representation in, 354.

Taft, W. H., as party leader while President, 105.
Tariff Commission, United States, 118.
Tariff question in England, 291–293.
Tariff Reform League in England, 292.
Tasmania, proportional representation in, 354 n.
Taxation, by states of United States, 42–43; powers of Congress regarding, 71–72; provisions concerning federal government's power of, 141–142; in United States during war against Germany, 152; questions concerning, in England, 291–293.
Telephone and telegraph systems, government control of, 156.
Territories, American, administration of, 75, 126–127.
Thiers, Adolphe, Chief of the Executive Power in France, 327, 328; given title of President of French Republic, 328; succeeded in authority by MacMahon, 328–329.
Third term doctrine, meaning of, 95–96.
Thirty Years' War, 532.
Tories in England, principles represented by, 186; succeeded by the Conservatives, 275.
Town, the, as unit of local administration in colonial New England, 22; combination of county and, in local government of middle colonies, 23.
Trade Commission, Federal, in United States, 118.
Trade-unionism, in England, 294–295; in France, 366.
Treason, trial and punishment of American citizens for, 140.
Treasury, officials of the, in England, 204–205.
Treasury Department of United States, control of Congress over, 97, 106–107; chief officers, subdivisions, and agencies embraced by, 116.
Treaties, powers of President and of Congress concerning, 101–102.
Trenton, date of municipal charter of, 22.
Tudors, period of the, in England, 171–172; Parliament under the, 172–174.

Unification of Italy, 405–406.
Unified Socialist Party in France, 368–370.

INDEX

Unionist, significance of party name, in English politics, 277; tariff reform a plank in platform of party, 292.
United States, practical application of ideal of self-government in, 8–12; control of and provision for army and navy in, 11–12; stages in development of system of government, 15–40; the federal system, 41–61; the national administration, 110–127; privileges and duties of citizenship, 128–144; government in war time, 145–164; war aims of, in relation to government, 556–570; domestic policies of, as related to war, 570; significance of entrance of, into League to Enforce Peace, 589–591; abandonment of policy of isolation by, 590–591.
Unit rule, application of, in Democratic national conventions in United States, 89.
University franchise in England, 233.
Urban areas of local government in England, 393–396.

Vatican, antagonistic attitude of, toward government of Italy, 412–414.
Veto power of American President, 85, 107–109.
Vice-President of United States, presiding officer of Senate, 69.
Victoria, Queen, effect of reign of, 183; decisive influence wielded by, as monarch, 200.
Virginia, county government in colonial, 23.
Virgin Islands, government of, 127.
Viviani, Réné, French socialist leader, 369.
Vocational Education, United States Board for, 160.

Walpole, Robert, ministry of, 183–184; first to act as prime minister in modern sense, 215.
War cabinet in England (1916–1918), 217–219, 322.
War Department of United States, chief officers, subdivisions, and agencies embraced by, 116.

War Finance Corporation, United States, 161.
War Industries Board, United States, 158.
War Labor Board, 159.
War Labor Policies Board, 160.
War powers of President of United States, 100–101.
War risk insurance, 145; Bureau of, 160.
Washington, George, attitude of, regarding third term for President, 95–96.
Whigs, principles represented by, 186; succeeded by the Liberals, 275.
Whips, party, in Parliament, 280.
William I, German Emperor, 446, 448.
William II, German Emperor, autocratic theory of government set forth by, 2–3, 507–508; accession of, 507; attitude toward the army, 508–509.
William III of England, accession of, 179; inclinations of, as a ruler, 182; development of the cabinet under, 185.
Wilson, Woodrow, passage of national women's suffrage amendment urged by, 9–10; as party leader, 105; quoted on purpose of democracy, 143–144; war aims of United States as expressed in utterances of, 556–570; the "fourteen points," 565–569; adherence of, to plan for a League to Enforce Peace, 589–590.
Windsor dynasty, substitution of term, for Hanoverian dynasty, 196 n.
Woman's Social and Political Union, in England, 231.
Woman's suffrage, question of, in England (1885–1918), 5, 230–231; causes which brought about, 234; question of lowering age qualification next to be agitated, 285.
Women, progress in enfranchisement of, in United States, 9.
Württemberg, proportional representation in, 354; alliance between Prussia and, 444; incorporated in German Empire, 447; reserved rights of, 454; votes of, in Bundesrath, 466.

Zabern incident, 525.
Zollverein, formation of, as a means of securing economic unity among German states, 439.

Printed in the United States of America.

WORKS OF PROFESSOR FREDERICK A. OGG

The Governments of Europe

Cloth, 8vo, $3.00

"He has prepared excellent studies of the Constitutions of England, France, Italy, Austria, Switzerland, Scandinavia, the Low Countries, and the Iberian States. And he has put them together conveniently. This useful work has been done most competently, and students will be most grateful for the facilities for study. . . . The compilation is timely, and authoritative, and up-to-date." — *New York Times.*

"A very painstaking, comprehensive, and useful compendium. . . . The treatment follows three general lines: a comparative study of political institutions; a summary of historical origins; and a brief, impartial exposition of political parties and of the institutions of local administration. . . . Its thoroughness and scope make it a very useful addition to the ever lengthening list of works on political history and political institutions." — *The American Review of Reviews.*

Economic Development of Modern Europe

Cloth, 8vo, $2.50

"In a book which is a masterly example of condensation without sacrifice of interest, the reader is led through the 'antecedents of nineteenth century growth' to the 'agriculture, industry and trade since 1815,' and then the history of population and labor and of socialism and social insurance during the time is taken up. Of special interest in connection with the present war is the chapter on the economic reconstruction of Russia, and from the standpoint of our own internal policy the fourth part of the work, dealing with socialistic aspiration and legislation, deserves thorough reading." — *The Chicago Evening Post.*

"He has produced a volume of exceptional information, valuable for standard and permanent reference, and timely for the use of all who would refresh or increase their knowledge of the economic condition of Europe just before and at the outbreak of the war, and of the processes through which that condition was attained; and who, upon the basis of that knowledge would consider intelligently the economical reorganization of the world which must take place after the war." — *New York Tribune.*

THE MACMILLAN COMPANY
Publishers   64-66 Fifth Avenue   **New York**

WORKS OF PROFESSOR CHARLES H. BEARD

American Government and Politics

New and Revised Edition, cloth, 8vo, index, $2.25

A work designed primarily for college students, but of considerable interest to the general reader. Full attention has been paid to topics that have been forced into public attention by the political conditions of the present time. A special feature is the page references made to the author's " Readings in American Government and Politics."

In this revised edition the author has recorded the leading changes of the last four years, with special emphasis on local tendencies and general principles.

" The great merit of the work is its absence of dogmatism. It gives exactly what it pretends to give, a clear, scholarly review, first of the history of our political system and secondly of its practical operation. . . . The book can be highly recommended." — *The Nation.*

" The citizen who gives it a careful reading will arise from it a better citizen. . . . It is, in brief, a truly notable book, and one that was long needed." — *Baltimore Sun.*

Readings in American Government and Politics

New and Revised Edition, cloth, crown 8vo, $2.00

A collection of interesting material illustrative of the different periods in the history of the United States, prepared for those students who desire to study source writings.

The author has brought the work abreast of current questions by adding extracts from the party platform of 1912 and selections illustrating presidential preference primaries, changes in the procedure of the House of Representatives, the recall of judicial decisions. The Constitution, with the latest amendments, has been included.

" The volume will be useful as a textbook and convenient for reference by those who wish to have an intelligent conception of our political life and history." — *Education.*

" The book affords a very valuable adjunct to the work of instruction in American history and political science." — *The Dial.*

" The work is well planned and well executed." — *The Nation.*

THE MACMILLAN COMPANY
Publishers　　64-66 Fifth Avenue　　**New York**

The Government of European Cities
By WILLIAM BENNETT MUNRO
Professor of Government in Harvard University.

Cloth, 8vo, $2.00

"The book gives a detailed account of the way in which municipal government is formed and carried on in France, Germany, and England. The style is clear, straightforward, and unpretentious, and the treatment is steadily confined to the subject in hand without any attempt to point a moral or aid a cause. The writing, while succinct, is copious in detail, and only administrative experts in the countries respectively considered could check off all the statements made; but the work itself affords intrinsic evidence of its painstaking accuracy."

— *The Nation.*

"On the whole the most comprehensive, accurate, painstaking, and thorough work which has been done in the English language on the subjects which are treated. The objectiveness of the treatment and the copious references to the sources of his information give what Dr. Munro has done an authoritativeness as to descriptive details which no other book on the subject possesses."

— FRANK J. GOODNOW in *Political Science Quarterly.*

"The work as a whole reflects the greatest credit upon the author. For thoroughness, fairness, scope, and breadth of treatment it leaves nothing to be desired. It is conceived in the scientific spirit, and aims to present facts accurately and to indicate their possible bearings; but it betrays no partisan spirit, and is not given to preaching or the furtherance of a cause. It will rank as a standard work, embodying the best scholarship of our day." — *New York Tribune.*

"A sound contribution to the study of local government."
— *Local Government Review* (London).

THE MACMILLAN COMPANY
Publishers   64-66 Fifth Avenue   New York

The Government of American Cities
By WILLIAM BENNETT MUNRO
Professor of Government in Harvard University.

Cloth, 8vo, $2.00

"The various topics are discussed with more thoroughness than in any other work covering the whole of this field; and the presentation throughout bears the stamp of the scientific observer. The author's scientific discussion is not cumbered with statistics or technical terms; but is presented with the clear and dignified diction of the modern Harvard school of English." — *National Municipal Review.*

"The treatment is wholly satisfactory. There is no erudite theorizing, no philosophical padding, but a practical statement, lucid, direct, simple and candid, of the machinery at present employed in conducting the affairs of the municipality." — *American Political Science Review.*

Principles and Methods of Municipal Administration
By WILLIAM BENNETT MUNRO

Cloth, 8vo, $2.25

"The most important of recent books upon that prolific subject, the city, is Professor William B. Munro's 'Principles and Methods of Municipal Administration,' a volume whose 'readability' is scantily suggested by its title. . . . The result is a volume which, if less encyclopedic than some others, is alone in supplying an informed, reasoned, and attractive record of what our cities are doing, the machinery by which they are performing it, their success and failure — in a word, in showing us where we are." — *The Nation.*

"From city planning to municipal finance he covers his subject, and the various subdivisions of his subject, in a lucid, direct, simple and candid manner, employing a clear and dignified diction as pleasing in itself as the scientific accuracy and balance which characterize the work." — *Philadelphia Evening Ledger.*

THE MACMILLAN COMPANY
Publishers   64-66 Fifth Avenue   New York